SOCIAL PROBLEMS

SOCIAL PROBLEMS

5th EDITION

JAMES WILLIAM COLEMAN
California Polytechnic State University

DONALD R. CRESSEY
Late, University of
California Santa Barbara

HarperCollinsCollegePublishers

Acquisitions Editor: Alan McClare
Developmental Editor: Randee Falk
Project Editor: Lauren G. Shafer
Design Supervisor: Paul Agresti
Cover Design: Paul Agresti
Cover Illustration: Jean Dubuffett, *Ideoplasme*, October 1984
acrylic on canvas-backed paper, 39 ½ × 26 ½ inches
Photograph by Bill Jacobson
Courtesy The Pace Gallery
© 1992 ARS, New York/ADAGP, Paris
Photo Researcher: Mira Schachne
Production Manager/Assistant: Willie Lane/Sunaina Sehwani
Compositor: Waldman Graphics, Inc.
Printer and Binder: R. R. Donnelley & Sons Company
Cover Printer: The Lehigh Press, Inc.

Social Problems, Fifth Edition

Library of Congress Cataloging-in-Publication Data

Coleman, James William, 1947-
    Social problems / James William Coleman, Donald R. Cressey.—5th ed.
        p.   cm.
    Includes bibliographical references and index.
    ISBN 0-06-500144-3
    1. Sociology.   2. Social problems.   3. Social institutions.
4. United States—Social conditions—1980-   5. United States—Social policy—1980-   I. Cressey,
Donald R. (Donald Ray), 1919-
II. Title.
HM51.C593   1993
361.1—dc20   92-24775
                                                                                                          CIP

93 94 95 9 8 7 6 5 4 3

BRIEF CONTENTS

CONTENTS

Chapter 8 · Health and Illness   195

Chapter 9 · The Old and the Young   231

Chapter 10 · Women and Men   253

PART THREE
CONFORMITY AND DEVIANCE 277

PART FOUR
PROBLEMS OF A CHANGING WORLD 363

PREFACE

Through earlier editions of this text, the late Donald Cressey and I wrote *Social Problems* with one principal goal in mind: to communicate to students. In this fifth edition, my objective remains the same—to familiarize students with the most important problems of their times and to stimulate them to think in a critical, scientific way. I try to challenge the half-truths and pat answers that are so often repeated about our social problems and get students to actively participate in a dialogue about these issues rather than merely stand back and observe.

Instructors familiar with the fourth edition will notice that I have continued the special features that helped make this book so successful—the broad coverage, the strongly worded debates, the clear and informative graphics, and the consistent theoretical organization that includes a section on theoretical perspectives in each chapter.

Because the fourth edition was the most extensive rewrite of the text since its inception, I originally thought that the fifth edition would require only a minor revision and updating. But in a rapidly changing world, that proved not to be the case, and the fifth edition includes major changes. My review of the last edition convinced me that we needed to strengthen the coverage of Third World problems and to do a better job of placing North American social problems in their global context. The result was an entirely new chapter (14): "The Global Divide: Problems of the Third World." But the inclusion of this new chapter created a serious concern about the length of the book, so I combined the separate chapters on crime and delinquency and personal violence, which contained a considerable amount of overlapping material. The resulting new chapter (13), "Crime and Violence," is better focused and more effective in its treatment of this crucial problem than the two chapters it replaces. In doing this work, it became clear that two issues covered in separate chapters in the last edition—the problems of physical health and mental health—could also benefit from a more integrated presentation. The result is a new chapter (8), "Health and Illness." Several improvements were also made to the overall format of the book. Where needed, the debate boxes are now preceded by a short paragraph explaining the issue to be discussed. Key terms are defined at the end of each chapter and not just in the Glossary at the back, and there is a brief description of each of the books listed in the Further Readings sections at the end of each chapter. In addition, all the chapters have been revised and updated to keep them fresh and relevant. The new material added during this process includes the following:

Chapter 1 *Sociology and Social Problems*   Exchange theory is now included among the social psychological perspectives.

Chapter 2 *Problems of the Economy*   The chapter begins with a new section, "Understanding the Economy," includes a new discussion of the problems caused by computers in the workplace, and presents some current responses to problems of the economy.

Chapter 3 *Problems of Government*   This chapter now discusses the problems created by the lopsided advantage incumbent officeholders often hold over their challengers and also includes a new debate on government funding for election campaigns.

Chapter 4 *Problems of Education*   New discussions address the academic achievement of American students and the Headstart program, and two new sections discuss ways to improve schools: "Requiring More Work" and Restructuring the Schools."

Chapter 5 *Problems of the Family*   This chapter includes a new discussion of the effects of divorce and separation on children, and a new section on "Helping Parents."

Chapter 6 *The Poor*   This chapter has been reorganized, and includes new sections on "The Rich and Poor: A Widening Gap" and "The Life of Poverty" along with extensive new material on the underclass.

Chapter 7 *The Ethnic Minorities*   This chapter has been heavily reorganized and expanded. A new section discusses the "Problems and Prospects" of each of the major minority groups, supplementing the institutional approach of the section on "Institutional Inequality." A new analysis of the causes of the problems of ethnic minorities is presented in "Explaining Ethnic Inequality," and the chapter features a new debate: "Are Affirmative-Action Programs Fair?"

Chapter 8 *Health and Illness*   This chapter, completely redone, presents the latest issues in health care, and includes mental health along with other health problems.

Chapter 9 *The Old and the Young*   This chapter now includes expanded coverage of the problems of the young and some new responses to the problems of aging.

Chapter 10 *Women and Men*   The discussion of sexual harassment and of the responses to the problems of gender inequality have both been expanded, and there is new coverage of the men's movement.

Chapter 11 *Sexual Behavior*   This chapter features expanded coverage of AIDS and child molestation, and there is a new discussion of the best ways to respond to the problems of sexual behavior.

Chapter 12 *Drug Use*   New material on the "War on Drugs" and its effectiveness has been included, along with a new section on the Dutch approach to the drug problem.

Chapter 13 *Crime and Violence*   This chapter has been completely revised to accommodate all the material on crime and violence in the same chapter.

Chapter 14 *The Global Divide: Problems of the Third World*   This entirely new chapter looks at the origins and implications of global inequality and sets the stage for the chapters that follow. The debate discusses whether the industrialized nations are taking advantage of the Third World.

Chapter 15 *Urbanization*   This chapter has a new introduction, a new section on the "Decline of the Central City," and a new discussion of the "Crisis on the

Farm.'' It also presents current social psychological perspectives on urban problems.

Chapter 16 *Population*   There is a new treatment of the "Responses to the Problems of Population," in this chapter and the "Sociological Perspectives" have been revised.

Chapter 17 *The Environment*   This chapter offers a more extensive discussion of atmospheric pollution, and presents new material on the damage done by the Chernobyl reactor accident that the former Soviet government concealed from the public. It also includes a new debate: "Are We Headed For an Environmental Disaster?''

Chapter 18 *Warfare and International Conflict*   This chapter has undergone a general reorganization, and includes new material on the collapse of the Soviet Union, the end of the cold war, terrorism, and the Persian Gulf War. There is also a new discussion of arms control, and a new section on "The Prospects for Peace.''

Space permits the mention of only a few of the many people who contributed to this edition. First and foremost are the hundreds of students who have given invaluable suggestions over the years. I would also like to thank the following professors who served as academic reviewers for this edition: Warner Bloomberg, San Diego State University; Mary Cain, Our Lady of the Lake University; Harry Gold, Oakland University; Billy Gunter, University of South Florida; Julia Hall, Pennsylvania State University; Robert Miller, Baker University; Anthony Orum, University of Illinois— Chicago; John Pease, University of Maryland; Scott Pimley, University of Southern Mississippi; Judy Plummer, Arkansas Technical University; David Prok, Baldwin-Wallace College; and Philo Washburn, Purdue University.

The insightful suggestions of these reviewers were of great assistance, as were those made by the professors who used earlier editions of *Social Problems* and kindly volunteered their comments. The work of Alan McClare, Lauren Shafer, and the other members of the HarperCollins team who have labored on this project over the years is also greatly appreciated.

James William Coleman

SOCIAL PROBLEMS

chapter 1

Sociology and Social Problems

- What is a social problem?
- What part do social movements play in creating social problems?
- What are the sociological perspectives used to analyze social problems?

- What techniques do sociologists use to study social problems?
- How can we evaluate the claims made about social problems?

War, poverty, discrimination, violence, overpopulation, pollution—the list of our social problems is depressingly long, so long that many people throw their hands up in despair. Though a picture of a starving Asian baby or the sight of a homeless old woman may stir our concern, most of us quietly decide that there is nothing we can do to help. But is this true? Can we do nothing? The sociological study of social problems is founded on the belief that something can indeed be done if we first make the effort to systematically study our problems and then act on our understanding.

Politicians and community officials spend much of their careers trying to solve social problems that include everything from double parking to nuclear war. Voters select the candidates who claim to have the best solutions, but the average citizen's ideas about many social problems are distorted or confused. While the serious study of social problems can clear up much of this confusion and misunderstanding, beginning students often have the uncomfortable feeling that the more they read, the less they understand. There are so many conflicting viewpoints. One group sees a social problem one way and another group with conflicting interests sees it another way. Even the results of objective, scientific research may appear to be contradictory.

Sociology is a framework for sorting out all these facts, ideas, and beliefs. It provides the perspective and the tools we need to make sense of our social problems. Use of the sociological perspective helps reduce confusion in the minds of those who wish to participate intelligently in public discussions of these important issues. With this perspective we can develop programs to deal with our problems and evaluate their results once they have been put into effect. This is not to say, of course, that all sociologists agree on the exact causes of our social problems or their solutions. But fortunately such disagreements can result in a richer understanding for the student who is willing to examine all sides of the issues involved.

WHAT IS A SOCIAL PROBLEM?

Most people define a **social problem** as a condition that is harmful to society. But the matter is not so simple, for the meanings of such everyday terms as *harm* and *society* are far from clear. Conditions that some people see as social problems harm some segments of society but are beneficial to others. Consider air pollution. On the one hand, an automobile manufacturer might argue that government regulation of free enterprise is a social problem because laws requiring antipollution devices on cars raise costs, decrease gasoline mileage, and stimulate inflation. On the other hand, residents of a city with heavy air pollution might argue that the government's failure to outlaw noxious automobile emissions is a social problem because the smog created by automobiles harms their health and well-being. One person's social problem is another person's solution. Clearly, most people define social problems as something that harms or seems to harm their own interests.

A more precise sociological definition holds that *a social problem exists when there is a sizable difference between the ideals of a society and its actual achievements.*[1] Social problems are created by the failure to close the gap between the way people want things to be and the way things really are. According to this definition, racial discrimination is a social problem because although we believe that everyone should receive fair and equal treatment, some groups are still denied equal access to education, employment, and housing. Before this definition can be applied, someone must first examine the ideals and values of society and then decide whether these goals are being achieved. Sociologists and other experts thus decide what is or is not a problem, because they are the ones with the skills necessary for measuring the desires and achievements of society.

Critics of this approach point out that no contemporary society has a single, unified set of values and ideals. Instead, there are many conflicting and contradictory beliefs. Thus, sociologists must decide which ideals and values will serve as standards for judging whether a certain condition is a social problem. Critics charge that sociologists select those ideals and values on the basis of their personal opinions and prejudices, not objective analysis.

The most widely accepted sociological definition holds that *a social problem exists when a significant number of people believe that a certain condition is in fact a problem.*[2] Here "the public"—not a sociologist—decides what is or is not a social problem. The sociologist's job is to determine which problems concern a substantial number of people. Thus, in this view pollution did not become a social problem until environmental activists and news reports attracted the public's attention to conditions that had actually existed for some time.

The advantage of this definition is that it does not require a value judgment by sociologists who try to decide what conditions are social problems. Such decisions are made by "the public." However, a serious shortcoming of this approach is that the public often is uninformed or misguided and does not clearly understand its problems. If thousands of people were being poisoned by radiation leaking from a nuclear power plant but didn't know it, wouldn't radiation pollution still be a social problem?

All the topics discussed in the chapters that follow qualify as social problems according to both sociological definitions. Each problem involves conditions that conflict with strongly held ideals and values, and all are considered social problems by significant groups of people. The goal of every chapter is to discuss the problem fairly and objectively. However, it is important to understand that even selecting the problems requires a value judgment, whether by social scientists or by concerned citizens, and honest disagreements about the nature and importance of the various issues competing for public attention cannot be avoided.

SOCIAL PROBLEMS AND SOCIAL MOVEMENTS

The social issues that concern the public change from time to time, and an examination of the results of the numerous surveys of public opinion reveals some interesting trends. War and peace and various economic issues have consistently ranked high on the public's list of social concerns. Interest in other problems seems to move in cycles. Thus, concern over taxes, foreign policy, drugs, and lack of religion and morality is high in some years and low in others. Still other social problems are like fads, attracting a great deal of interest for a few years before dropping from public attention.[3]

Social movements create public awareness about social problems and push the government to take action to resolve them.

These changes have many different causes: shifts in ideals and values, the solution of an old problem, the creation of new ones. But the most important forces affecting changes in public opinion are **social movements** that focus attention on a certain social problem. For example, none of the polls in the 1930s and 1940s showed civil rights or race relations to be significant problems, even though racial discrimination was widespread and openly practiced. It was not until the civil rights movement began in the late 1950s that the polls began to reflect an interest in this problem. The civil rights issue would probably have remained buried if a powerful social movement had not developed.

Such movements begin when a large number of people start complaining about something they feel is a social problem. This group may be composed of people who believe they have been victimized, such as black victims of racial discrimination or female victims of sexual discrimination. Or it may be made up of concerned outsiders, such as opponents of alcohol use or those favoring the death penalty. As people with a common interest in an issue begin to talk with one another and express their feelings about the problem, leaders step forward to lead the developing movement.[4] Martin Luther King, Jr., was such a leader for the civil rights movement, as Ralph Nader has been for the consumer movement.

The leader's first job is to mold separate groups of dissatisfied people into an organized political movement. The success of the movement depends on publicity, for it is only through publicity that the general public can be made aware of the problem and encouraged to do something about it. In other words, it is through publicity that the problem of a particular group becomes a social problem.

Three factors help a social movement gain public support and favorable action by government. The most important is the political power of the movement and its supporters. If the movement's supporters are numerous, highly organized, wealthy, or in key positions of power, it is more likely to be successful.

A second factor is the strength of the movement's appeal to the people's values and prejudices. A movement to protect children from sexual abuse by adults is much more likely to gain widespread support than an effort to protect the civil liberties of child molesters.

The strength of the opposition to a movement is a third element determining its success or failure. Money is always limited, and the advocates of various social programs must compete with one another for funds. For example, few people object to the proposition that our children deserve a better education. However, a variety of opponents quickly emerge when someone suggests raising taxes to pay for improving the schools. Opposition to social movements also comes from people whose special interests are threatened by the goals of the movement. Thus, a proposal to raise the minimum wage for farm workers is bound to be opposed by agricultural businesses.

A principal goal of many social movements is to create awareness of a social problem and then mobilize government action to resolve it. But even when a movement achieves these objectives, government action may be ineffective. Governments all over the world have created huge bureaucracies to deal with poverty (departments of welfare), health care (medicare and medicaid), pollution (the Environmental Protection Agency), and crime (police, courts, and prisons). But like all bureaucracies, these agencies are clumsy and slow-moving, and are often more concerned with their own survival than with the problems they are designed to solve. After all, if narcotics enforcement agencies stopped all drug abuse, if police departments prevented all crime, or if mental hospitals quickly cured all disturbed people, the employees of these agencies would soon be out of work. Occasionally, it appears that the agencies set up to deal with a particular social problem are not actually expected to solve it. Politicians have been known to approve funds for a social program just to silence troublesome protesters, creating new agencies with impressive titles but no real power.

THE SOCIOLOGICAL APPROACH: BASIC IDEAS

In their attempt to study society scientifically, sociologists have often borrowed standards and methods developed in the physical and biological sciences. But they have found that human behavior is more complex and more difficult to understand than the topics studied by physicists, chemists, and biologists. Despite these handicaps, sociologists have developed a body of knowledge, theories, and methods that guides their research and forms the heart of sociology. Like other sciences, sociology has its own terms to describe what it studies, often words taken from everyday language. But because precision is necessary, sociologists give special meanings to common terms such as *role*, *group*, and *culture*.

Roles   In the theater or the movies, a role is the part a particular person plays in the show. Sociologists use the term in much the same way except that the role is played in real-life social situations. A **role** is usually defined as the set of behaviors and expectations associated with a particular social position (often known as a **status**). All roles—daughter, son, student, automobile driver, and countless others—offer certain rights and duties to the player. A student, for example, has the right to attend classes, to use the school's facilities, and to be graded fairly; the student also has the duty to read the texts, complete assigned work, and behave in an orderly manner. However, the way actual people carry out their roles often differs enormously from such idealized expectations.

Everyone plays many roles. A woman may be a wife, mother, sister, worker, consumer, student, and criminal—all at the same time. Some people experience **role conflict** because what is expected of them in one role clashes with what is expected in another. For instance, the roles of student and employee may each require large amounts of time and energy; the individual who attempts to fulfill both is likely to experience considerable role conflict.

Roles are one of the basic building blocks of our social world, and every society has countless positions with roles attached. Roles are interwoven in complex ways, so that it is often impossible to understand a particular role apart from the social network in which it is embedded. How, for example, can the role of wife be defined without reference to the roles of husband, daughter, son, mother, and father? This interdependence stems from the fact that the rights of one position—wife, for example—are interlaced with the duties of other positions—husband, daughter, son. Each of us is judged by our performance as we carry out our roles, and the negligent mother, the abusive father, the incompetent professor, and the disruptive student who fail to meet role expectations are judged harshly.

Norms A **norm** is a social rule that tells us what behavior is acceptable in a certain situation and what is not. Every human group, be it a small circle of friends or an entire society, generates norms that govern its members' conduct. Individuals who violate norms are often labeled **deviants** and given some kind of formal or informal punishment. A person who violates the norm against taking the lives of others may be tried and formally punished with a prison term, whereas a person who violates the trust of his or her friends is informally punished by ridicule or exclusion from the group. But like roles, the norms of various groups may conflict. Thus, some people are placed in the uncomfortable position of being forced to violate the norms of one group to which they belong in order to meet the norms of another.

Groups In the sociological sense, a **group** is not just a gathering of people in the same place at the same time. Instead, it consists of a number of individuals who have organized and recurrent relationships with one another. Within the group, members quickly identify the roles and norms that govern their behavior and relationships. Groups have boundaries, and most group members share some common purpose or goal, even if it is only to enjoy one another's company.

To take a simple example, there is a great difference between students who sit quietly in a college library reading their sociology books and a similar number of students who have formed a study group. The group has norms. All members are expected to come prepared to discuss and criticize what they have read and to be helpful rather than competitive. No member is to waste time discussing the weather or last week's football game. In time, the group develops specialized roles such as "the brain," "the joker," and "the plodder." A few students may even make their contribution to the group by looking intelligent and dignified while saying little or

In the socialization process, children learn to play the roles expected of them from their interaction with other people.

nothing. The group thus has a division of labor whereby various individuals help achieve the group's goal, each in his or her own particular way.

Socialization **Socialization** is the process by which individuals learn the appropriate ways of behaving in their culture. Put another way, it is the process of becoming human. Roles, norms, customs, values, how to speak, even how to think—all these are learned in the process of socialization. Almost everything humans think or do is influenced by what they have learned from those around them.

Our basic socialization occurs in the early years of life. The rare child who has been hidden away from contact with the world in a closet or attic has limited speech and appears to be mentally defective. But socialization is not confined to the childhood years; it continues throughout our lives. As we enter new social groups, we begin a new process of socialization and begin acquiring new attitudes, perspectives, and behavior patterns.

Institutions Social **institutions** are relatively stable patterns of behavior centered on the performance of important social tasks. All societies have institutions for producing children and giving them guidance and support (family), relating to the supernatural (religion), producing and distributing food and other goods and services (economics), training its people (education), and making and enforcing rules (politics). Social institutions thus are organized around one or more of the necessities of social life. But sometimes the norms of one institution conflict with those of another, as when the norms of an economic institution that stresses free competition and accumulation of individual wealth clash with the norms of a family institution that stresses cooperation, mutual care, and sharing.

Social Classes A **social class** is a category of people with similar shares of the things that are valued in a society. They have common life chances—a similar chance to get an education, to get health care, to obtain material possessions, to gain a position in life, and so on. This concept of social class is one of the most important and most useful in all sociology. Virtually all the problems examined in the next seventeen chapters of this book—from crime to the population explosion—are profoundly influenced by the class structure in which they are embedded. Many nineteenth-century thinkers including Karl Marx and his followers defined social class solely in economic terms.[5] Today most sociologists use a broader definition taken from the work of the German sociologist Max Weber.[6] According to Weber, the valuables a society distributes include social status and power as well as money. **Status** rests on a claim to social prestige, inherited from one's family or derived from occupation and life style. **Power** is the ability to make others do something whether they want to or not. Power is often associated with politics, though it may have other sources as well. In order to assess the class positions of individuals and groups, we must therefore know their social and political standing as well as their income.

Sociologists use several different schemes to describe the class system in capitalist societies, but the most common divides these societies into four different classes (see Figure 1.1). The **upper class** is composed of individuals with great wealth, who often

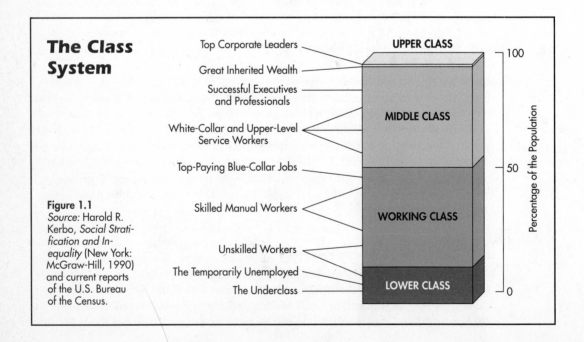

The Class System

Top Corporate Leaders
Great Inherited Wealth
Successful Executives and Professionals
White-Collar and Upper-Level Service Workers
Top-Paying Blue-Collar Jobs
Skilled Manual Workers
Unskilled Workers
The Temporarily Unemployed
The Underclass

UPPER CLASS
MIDDLE CLASS
WORKING CLASS
LOWER CLASS

Percentage of the Population — 100 — 50 — 0

Figure 1.1
Source: Harold R. Kerbo, *Social Stratification and Inequality* (New York: McGraw-Hill, 1990) and current reports of the U.S. Bureau of the Census.

hold key positions of corporate power as well. Next comes the **middle class**, made up of an upper segment of highly paid professionals and successful executives and entrepreneurs, and a much larger group of middle-level managers and white-collar (nonmanual) workers. The **working class** is about the same size as the middle class, but its members are mainly blue-collar (manual) workers and lower-level service workers. Although the best paid blue-collar workers earn more money than many white-collar employees, on the average, members of the working class make far less than their middle-class counterparts. At the bottom of the social hierarchy is the **lower class**, whose members live in conditions of poverty or very close to them. This class can be further divided between an upper segment composed of the working poor and the short-term unemployed, and an **underclass** who usually have few prospects for a permanent job and are heavily dependent on the welfare system (see Chapter 6).

There is a popular belief that most Americans are middle class, perhaps because the majority of the people we see on television and in the movies are from that class. But the truth of the matter is much different. Of every 100 people in the United States, only 1 is from the upper class, 15 to 20 are from the lower class, and the remainder are more or less evenly divided between the working class and the middle class.[7]

Culture In everyday speech *culture* refers to the refinements of civilization, such as art, music, and literature. But to sociologists **culture** is the way of life of the people in a certain geographic area, and particularly the ideas, beliefs, values, patterns of thought, and symbols that make it possible. A culture provides individuals a way of understanding the world and making it meaningful. A **subculture** has its own ideas and beliefs yet is influenced by the larger culture. It is thus a culture within a culture. In industrialized nations it is accurate to speak of a working-class subculture, a youth subculture, a criminal subculture, and so on, despite the fact that working-class people, youths, and criminals all share the same overall culture.

Society Although culture and society cannot be separated in real life, sociologists sometimes distinguish between the two so that each can be studied more easily. In such studies, **society** refers to a group of people in a particular geographic area who share common institutions and traditions, while the physical and mental products of those people are known as their culture. All societies have an overall **social structure**, which is simply an organized pattern of behavior and social relationships. They also have many more focused social structures such as a particular pattern of family life, social class, and government.

SOCIOLOGICAL PERSPECTIVES ON SOCIAL PROBLEMS

Over the years sociologists have developed and refined several broad theoretical perspectives to account for the many different kinds of phenomena they study. These perspectives help us understand social problems by drawing our attention to important social forces that are often neglected by the media and the politicians when they discuss these issues. But all these theories do not serve the same purpose. **Macro theories** try to make sense of the behavior of large groups of people and the workings of entire societies; **micro theories** are concerned primarily with the behavior of individuals and small groups.

The **functionalist perspective** and **conflict perspective** are the two most widely used types of macro theories. (See Table 1.1 for a summary of some of the key differences between these theories.) The micro theories are known as **social psychological perspectives** because they focus on the psychological effects of social groups and the social effects of individual behavior. We will consider four of the most important social psychological theories: **biosocial**, **personality**, **behavioral**, and **interactionist theories** (see Table 1.2). The supporters of the various theoretical perspectives often disagree with one another, but none of the theories can be said to be "right" or "wrong," although some theories are more effective than others in analyzing a particular social problem. Of course, more than one theory can be applied to the same problem, and, in most cases, the greatest understanding comes from combining the insights gained from different theoretical perspectives.

The Functionalist Perspective   Functionalism has been one of the most influential schools of social thought of recent times. Starting with the work of the French sociologist Émile Durkheim, functionalist theory was refined by Talcott Parsons, Robert K. Merton, and many others.[8] Functionalists see society as a well-organized system in which most members agree on common norms and values. Roles, groups, and institutions

TABLE 1.1 Theories of Society (Macro Level)

Basic Issues	The Functionalist Perspective	The Conflict Perspective
What holds society together?	Agreement on basic norms and values	Power, authority, and coercion
What is the basic nature of modern society?	A balance among various institutions, each performing different functions necessary to the survival of society	A competitive struggle for dominance among various social groups
Is society normally static or dynamic?	Static—when significant changes occur, a healthy society quickly readjusts and returns to a stable equilibrium	Dynamic—society is in a continual state of flux as it adjusts to the shifting balance of power among its competing groups
What is the major cause of social problems?	Social disorganization caused by rapid social change	The exploitation and oppression of some groups by others

fit together into a unified whole. People do what is necessary to maintain a stable society because they accept its rules and recognize its importance in their lives.

According to functionalist theory, the various parts of society are in delicate balance, and a change in one part affects the others. Each part has a **function** in maintaining the balanced order. For instance, the function of the economic institution is to provide the food, shelter, and clothing that people need in order to survive, while the function of the educational institution is to train individuals in the skills needed to keep society operating.

But societies, like machines and biological organisms, do not always work the way they are supposed to work. Things get out of whack. Changes introduced to correct a particular imbalance may produce other imbalances, even when things are going well. When an action interferes with the effort to carry out essential social tasks, it is said to be **dysfunctional**. For example, educators may train too many people for certain jobs. Those who cannot find jobs in their special line of work may become resentful, rebelling against the system that they feel has treated them unfairly. Thus, ''overeducation'' may be said to be a dysfunction of modern education.

Some of the functions and dysfunctions of an organization are *manifest*—that is, obvious to everyone. A manifest function of police departments, for example, is to keep crime rates low. Other functions and dysfunctions are *latent*—hidden and unintended. A latent function of police departments is to serve as a symbol of the importance of law and order. Sociologists who study social problems have placed particular emphasis on exposing **latent dysfunctions** that are unknown to the general public. For instance, sociologists who have studied police departments note that these agencies burden the people they arrest with stigmatizing labels (''criminal,'' ''delinquent,'' ''outlaw,'' ''hoodlum,'' and so on), and those who have been labeled may actually commit more crimes than if they had been left alone. Thus, in trying to stop crime, criminal-justice agencies may unintentionally contribute to its increase (see Chapter 13).

According to functionalists, social problems arise when society or some part of it becomes disorganized. This **social disorganization** involves a breakdown of social structure, so that its various parts no longer work together and norms lose their influence on particular groups or individuals. Functionalists see many causes of social disorganization. Norms may be violated because of inadequate socialization, or society may fail to control the aggression produced in its members. A society's relationship to its environment may be disrupted, so that it no longer has sufficient food, oil, building materials, or other resources. However, in modern industrial societies, one cause of social disorganization underlies all the others—namely, rapid social change. According to most functionalists, society responds well to change only if it occurs slowly.

Social disorganization is particularly severe in the modern era because more change has occurred in less time than in any other period of human history. Basic institutions have undergone drastic changes, with technology advancing so rapidly that other parts of the culture have failed to keep pace. This **cultural lag** between technological changes and our adaptation to them is one of the major sources of social disorganization. For instance, when knowledge about nutrition, public health, and medical technology began spreading through the world in the nineteenth century, many lives, especially those of the newly born, were saved. Yet traditional attitudes toward the family have not changed fast enough to adjust to the fact that more children survive to adulthood. The result has been a worldwide population explosion.

Although functionalism has been a standard theoretical approach to social problems for many years, it has a growing number of critics. Despite its claims of objectivity, many sociologists see functionalism as a politically conservative philosophy that automatically assumes that society is good as it is and should be preserved without major changes. Functionalism blames social problems on individual deviance or temporary social disorganization while seeming to ignore the basic injustices of society. The critics of functionalism claim that it is often impossible to say whether or not a particular social phenomenon is functional for society as a whole, because such phenomena usually have different impacts on different groups. For example, a law that forbids sleeping in the lobbies of public buildings would benefit wealthy people who may be disturbed by such behavior but hurt the homeless who have nowhere else to go. The critics charge that too often what the functionalists really mean when they say something is functional is that it works to the benefit of the privileged classes.

The Conflict Perspective   The conflict perspective is the major alternative to the functionalist approach to the study of social problems.[9] This perspective is based on a different set of assumptions about the nature of society and comes to different conclusions about the causes of its problems. As the name implies, conflict theory sees society as a struggle for power among various social groups. Conflict is believed to be inevitable and in many cases actually beneficial to society. For instance, many needed social changes arose from such conflicts as the French Revolution and the American War between the States.

The conflict perspective can most easily be understood by contrasting it with functionalist theory. Functionalists assume that society is held together by the agreement of its members on a common set of values, attitudes, and norms. For example, they say that most people obey the law because they believe it is fair and just. In contrast, conflict theorists insist that social order is maintained by authority backed by the use of force. One or more groups hold legal power, and use it to make others obey their will. To this way of thinking, most people obey the law because they are afraid of being arrested, jailed, or even killed if they do not obey. Another important difference between functionalism and the conflict perspective may be seen in their assumptions about social change. Functionalists tend to view society in relatively static terms, asserting that too much change is disruptive and that society has a natural tendency to regain its balance whenever it is disturbed. But conflict theorists see society in more dynamic terms. Because people are constantly struggling with one another to gain power, change is inevitable. One individual or group is bound to gain the upper hand, only to be defeated in a later struggle.

Neither the conflict perspective nor the functionalist perspective can be said to be a single unified theory. Rather, each consists of a number of related theories that share many common elements. The conflict perspective not only contains a large number of sociological theories but also encompasses a wide range of political views as well.

At least partially because of these political differences, different conflict theorists tend to focus on different kinds of conflict. Some are primarily concerned with **value**

conflict, which arises from the differences in attitudes and beliefs among different social groups; others focus on **class conflict**, rooted in differences in power, wealth, and prestige; and still others emphasize conflicts based on gender or ethnic differences. There is, however, no reason why a conflict theorist must focus on only one of these and ignore the others. Different social problems involve different conflicts, and it is important to be sensitive to them all.

Sociologists who emphasize value conflict strongly disagree with the common functionalist assumption that most people in a society share the same set of norms and values. They point out that modern societies are composed of many different groups with different attitudes, values, and norms that are bound to create conflict. For instance, consider the abortion issue. Many conservative Christians believe that the human fetus, at any stage of its development, is a complete, living human being and that aborting a pregnancy is a form of murder. Feminists and others who support the right to a legal abortion hold that an unborn child is not yet a human being because it is unable to survive outside the womb. They assert that if the state forbids a woman to obtain an operation that she desires, it is violating her right to control her own life. Conflict theorists say that the clash between these two groups is a result of conflicting values and does not reflect social disorganization.

But all conflicts do not stem from disagreement over values and their interpretation. Some conflicts arise in part *because* people share the same values. If two groups of people place a high value on wealth and power and only one group has access to them, conflict is likely to result. Many sociologists believe that conflict over wealth, power, and status is the basic cause of most social problems. Although the competing groups may be based on various characteristics such as ethnicity, race, or gender, conflict sociologists have traditionally focused most heavily on class differences.

One of the first theorists to see class conflict as the underlying cause of social problems was Karl Marx, who lived in the nineteenth century. For Marx, the position

The conflict perspective holds that the unequal distribution of wealth, power, and prestige is one of the most basic causes of social problems in contemporary society.

a person holds in the system of production determined his or her class position. In a capitalist society a person may be in one of two different positions. Some people own capital and capital-producing property (for example, factory owners, landlords, and merchants) and are therefore members of the **bourgeoisie**. Other people work for wages as producers of capital (for example, factory workers, miners, and laborers of all kinds). Marx called this class the **proletariat**. Marx asserted that these two classes have directly opposing economic interests because the wealth of the bourgeoisie is based on exploitation of the proletariat. He thought that the workers (proletariat) would develop an increasing awareness of their exploitation by the bourgeoisie and that that awareness, combined with growing political organization, would eventually result in violent class conflict. A revolution won by workers over their masters would, Marx contended, lead to a classless society. Private property and inheritance would be abolished; steeply graduated income taxes would be introduced; education and training would be free; and production would be organized for use, not profit.[10]

Marx's ideas have had an enormous influence in the twentieth century. However, not everyone who sees class conflict as a cause of social problems is a Marxist. All sociologists recognize that modern industrial society has a class system and that the classes have competing interests that generate conflict. But most sociologists do not believe that a classless society is possible under present conditions, or that a violent social revolution is inevitable. Many social scientists who use the class conflict approach believe that society can best be changed through gradual reforms rather than violent revolution.

Just as functionalism has been criticized for being too conservative, the conflict perspective has been criticized for being too radical. Critics say that conflict theorists overemphasize the role of conflict, arguing that if there were as much of it as these theorists claim, society would have collapsed long ago. Functionalists do not agree that the maintenance of a capitalist society benefits only the bourgeoisie. Finally, many conflict theorists, particularly Marxists, are criticized for judging capitalist society too harshly. Critics argue that the classless utopia that Marx envisioned is impossible to achieve and that capitalist societies generally do a good job of dealing with their social problems.

Functionalism and conflict theory are the two principal macro-level approaches to social problems. While some sociologists claim that one or the other is the only valid approach, most use whatever theory seems to work best for the problem at hand. The use of both functional and conflict approaches often sheds more light on a problem than either approach used alone. For instance, crime can usefully be studied as a product of social disorganization, of class conflict between the poor and the other classes, and of value conflict between those who accept the law and those who don't. Obviously, all of these perspectives are useful if we are to understand social problems.

The Social Psychological Perspective   Social psychological theories operate on a level different from that of the functionalist and conflict theories. Social psychology is concerned with the behavior of single individuals and small groups, and their relationships with one another and with the larger society. Socialization and the part that group interactions play in the individual's psychological development are a central concern of social psychology. A second major concern is to explain why some indi-

	TABLE 1.2 **Social Psychological Theories (Micro Level)**			
Basic Issues	**Biosocial Theories**	**Personality Theories**	**Behaviorist Theories**	**Interactionist Theories**
What is the most fruitful area for research?	The physical human organism and its hereditary makeup	Individual personality	Behavior	Social interaction
What is the principal source of human behavior?	Human biology	Individual personality	Reinforcements from the environment (human and physical)	Interaction with people and groups through symbols and shared meaning
What is the major cause of social problems?	Innate human characteristics; biological defects in certain individuals	Personality disorders, maladaptive personality traits	Reinforcement of inappropriate behavior	Social support of deviant or dysfunctional behavior

viduals conform to the norms and expectations of their groups while others become deviant. Most contemporary explanations of crime, mental illness, and gender role behavior are based on the findings of social psychologists.

Even social problems that seem to stem from social disorganization or class conflict have a social psychological side to them. Therefore, micro social psychological theories supplement the macro theories. However, the supporters of various social psychological theories are often at odds with one another. Of the many micro theories, the ones most commonly applied to the study of social problems include biosocial theories, personality theories, behavioral theories, and interactionist theories.

Biosocial Theories Scholars have long tried to explain social behavior by pointing to the biological traits of the human species. At one time such explanations were extremely influential in economics, political science, psychology, and sociology. A host of different behaviors were said to be instinctual. Warfare was seen as stemming from an "aggressive instinct," cooperation from a "social instinct," capitalism from an "acquisitive instinct," and so on. As the list of such "instincts" grew, critics began to charge that these theories had little factual support and added nothing to an understanding of human behavior. They argued that even if there were, for instance, an instinct for aggression, this biological fact would help very little in the understanding of the complex economic, political, religious, and social conflicts that lead to wars. Most scientists eventually lost confidence in instinct theory and turned instead to explaining human behavior in terms of social and cultural conditions. "To explain a social fact," Émile Durkheim said, "seek other social facts." However, many social scientists believe that the pendulum has now swung too far in the other direction, and biosocial theories of human behavior have begun to receive new attention.

Some of the new biosocial theories seem to imply that virtually all human behavior is inherited. It is argued that even such values as altruism (unselfishness), which appear to be entirely cultural, have actually been built into our genetic structure in the process of evolution.[11] After studying the incredible diversity of behavior in human societies, few anthropologists or sociologists can accept the idea that most human behavior is directly determined by genetics. Most contemporary biosocial theorists therefore emphasize the importance of the interaction between biological predispositions and the social environment. For example, many criminologists who argue that there is a hereditary predisposition toward crime see the problem as being as much with society as with genetics. They argue that people with low intelligence, which they hold to be a biological characteristic, are rejected by teachers and more competent students because they do poorly in school. As a result, they are more likely to become rebellious and antisocial (see Chapter 13). Whether we accept this argument or not, there is little doubt that the structure of the human body and its biological needs have enormous influence on both individual and social behavior. After all, the most basic task of any society is to provide for the biological needs of its members. Imagine how different human society would be if we reproduced without sexual intercourse, as some plants do, or if human beings matured into adults in a few weeks, as some animals do.

Although no single, broad biological theory is accepted by all social scientists, dozens of different theories are relevant to specific social problems. Although some are very convincing, others are based on little more than myth and prejudice. Sociologists have traditionally avoided biological explanations of social problems, in part because the social policy implications of these theories are often very pessimistic. If a social problem is believed to be biologically caused, policymakers have little incentive to try to solve it because they obviously have little chance of changing human biology. For example, if people live in poverty only because they are biologically inferior (a proposition that virtually no contemporary social scientist would support), there is little chance that policymakers could do much to eliminate poverty. Even more disturbing is the blatant racism of some biosocial theories. In the past, many reputable scientists believed that blacks and members of other minorities were poor because they were racially inferior. But the obvious errors in this theory should not be taken as evidence that all biosocial theories are in error. On the contrary, many sociologists believe that the biosocial perspective will make an increasingly important contribution to the understanding of human behavior in the years ahead.

Personality Theories *Personality* is one of the most widely used words in psychology. It refers to the stable characteristics and traits that distinguish one person from another and that account for differences in individual social behavior. For example, criminals are said to break the law because they have "sociopathic personalities" (impulsive, unstable, and immature). Racial prejudice is said to stem from an "authoritarian personality" (rigid, insecure, with repressed feelings of guilt and hostility).

Although there are many different personality theories, the one developed by Sigmund Freud has been the most influential.[12] Freud divided the personality into three parts. The most basic is the **id**—the instinctual drives, particularly sex, which are said to motivate all human behavior. The second part of the personality to develop is the **ego**—the individual's conscious, reality-oriented experience. The **superego**—the individual's conscience or sense of morality—is the last to develop. Freudians assume that these three parts of the personality are balanced in normal people and that personality disorders arise either from disturbances in one part or from an imbalance among the different parts. Freudians also place much importance on the unconscious mental life that is presumed to go on without the individual's awareness.

Freud's theory has been attacked because of its overemphasis on the sex drive, its neglect and misunderstanding of females, and its departure from standard scientific procedure. As a result, few sociologists or psychologists today apply Freud's theory in its original form. However, many psychologists have used Freud's ideas as a basis for new theories that try to avoid these faults. Still other psychologists have developed entirely different perspectives on the nature and origins of personality. But because most theories of personality rely upon subjective reports in which people try to describe how they think and feel, they are often subject to criticism for an alleged vagueness and lack of supporting factual evidence.

Behavioral Theories Some social psychologists are convinced that it is a waste of time to try to figure out what is going on inside people's heads. They argue that because the psychological traits that are said to determine behavior cannot be observed, such efforts ultimately reflect the subjective judgments of the theorist. Because these social psychologists confine their studies exclusively to observable behavior, this theoretical perspective, founded by J. B. Watson and developed by B. F. Skinner, is known as **behaviorism**.[13]

Behavior, from this perspective, depends on the **reinforcements** the actor receives from its performance. If an individual is rewarded (one type of reinforcement) for a certain behavior in a certain situation, he or she is likely to repeat the behavior when the situation recurs. If punishment is given, the behavior is less likely to be repeated. For instance, if parents respond to their daughter's temper tantrum with concern and attention, she is likely to repeat that behavior the next time she wants attention. But if the girl's tantrum is ignored, she will use a different means to attract attention. Thus, behavioral theory explains human action primarily in terms of the individual's environment. Of course, the process of learning is not nearly as simple as this illustration implies; behaviorists have developed an elaborate set of principles about the many kinds of reinforcements that encourage or discourage the learning of specific behaviors.

Critics of behavioral theory object to its exclusion of mental processes and the subjective outlooks of individuals, arguing that it is impossible to understand human behavior without understanding the way people think and feel and the structure of their personalities. They agree that it is difficult to study personality directly but assert that this is hardly enough reason to conclude that personality has no influence on human behavior.

A related school of thought known as **exchange theory** attempts to account for the social aspects of human behavior by combining behaviorist principles with insights drawn from classical economics. Exchange theorists, such as George Homans and Peter Blau, still see rewards and punishments as the basic motivation of human behavior, but they focus on the way our desire to be rewarded by other people shapes our relationships. For example, exchange theorists hold that there is a kind of balance in most relationships in which both sides receive roughly equal rewards from the other. If some participants feel they are giving too much or receiving too little, they are likely to be dissatisfied and seek out more equitable arrangements. If, however, there is a large imbalance in power between the participants, the weaker ones may well be forced to accept fewer rewards and more punishments than the more powerful ones. Critics claim that this approach ignores the role of irrational impulses, emotion, and habit, and reduces the complexities of human behavior to a simple calculation of what maximizes pleasure and minimizes pain.

Interactionist Theories Interactionists also see human behavior as a product of learning. But to the interactionist it is not a simple set of rewards and punishments that guides our behavior but the ideas, values, and beliefs that we learn. To understand individuals' behavior, interactionists seek to look at the world from their eyes, and see how they define themselves and their environment. This **definition of the situation** is learned in interaction with other people and is the foundation upon which we base our behavior. For example, a gang member who sees the police as the tools of repression will respond to an officer's calls for help very differently from a banker who sees the police as the defenders of law and order. But our interactions with others teach us far more than how to define a particular social situation or even how to define the world in general. It is from these interactions that we develop our basic concept of who we are, and such understanding, in turn, tells us what to expect from other people and how to act in a particular social context. Thus, the world has no inherent meaning to the interactionist. Meaning is created by people as they struggle to define themselves and the world around them, and that meaning is what determines their behavior.

The work of the American philosopher George Herbert Mead was the original force behind the interactionist theory.[14] Mead argued that the ability to communicate in symbols (principally words and combinations of words) is the key feature that distinguishes humans from other animals. Individuals develop the ability to think and to use symbols in the process of socialization. Young children blindly imitate the behavior of their parents, but eventually they learn to "take the role of the other," pretending to be "Mommy" or "Daddy." From such role-taking, children learn to understand the relationships among different roles and to see themselves as they imagine others see them. According to Mead, the key to a child's psychological development is the creation of a **self-concept**—the relatively stable mental image we all have of who and what we are. This self-concept is created out of the responses a child receives from the important people in his or her life. For example, if a girl's parents constantly tell her how smart she is, she is likely to formulate a concept of herself as an intelligent person. This concept of self is not a fixed unchanging structure, however. If later in life her teachers and friends begin to treat her as if she isn't really very bright, her self-concept is likely to change. The concept of self is one of the most important in social psychology, for our self-concept influences almost every aspect of individual behavior. Another important influence on behavior, according to Mead, is the **generalized other**, the idea we form of what kind of behavior people expect of us—in other words, our conscience.

After Mead's death, in 1931, his ideas continued to gain stature among sociologists and social psychologists. Those who adhered most closely to Mead's original ideas became known as symbolic interactionists.[15] They have been very active in the study of social problems and have contributed a great deal to our understanding of critical social issues. For example, differential-association theory, an important explanation of delinquency and crime, is a direct offshoot of Mead's theories, as is the labeling theory of mental illness and the cultural-learning theory of drug use (see Chapters 12, 13, and 14). Despite his enormous influence, Mead has many critics. As with Freudian theory, the most common criticism of interactionist theory is that it is vague and difficult to substantiate.

DOING SOCIOLOGICAL RESEARCH

The theoretical perspectives discussed so far serve as a guide and a point of reference for the student of social problems. Theories are of little value, however, unless they deal with facts, and in the study of social problems, people often disagree about what "the facts" really are. Many sociologists long for the simplicity of other sciences such as physics, because it is much easier to study the movement of inanimate objects than to predict or explain human behavior. Because their task is so difficult, sociologists give a great deal of attention to the study of **methodology**—that is, how to do research. Volumes have been written on this subject, yet no one can say that any particular technique is better than all the others. The decision about which research techniques to use must be based on the nature of the problem being studied and the skills and resources of the researcher. Among many possible alternatives, the four most common sources of sociological data are public records and statistics, case studies, surveys, and experiments.

Public Records and Statistics Governments and organizations like the United Nations and the World Bank publish a wealth of statistics and information. A look through the references in this book will reveal numerous citations to data from the Bureau of the Census, the Bureau of Justice Statistics, the Department of Labor, and similar organizations, for such information is vital to the efforts of sociologists to understand today's social problems. One of the oldest and most reliable sources of statistics is the U.S. census, which is taken every ten years. The goal of the census is to count every person in the United States and determine such characteristics as their age, gender, and employment status. This is obviously a massive undertaking, and so many organizations also take surveys that question only a sample of the total population. There are periodic government surveys of selected groups such as the elderly or the unemployed, as well as general surveys designed to measure, for example, the number of people who have been the victims of crime. Another important source of data is the bureaucracies that register births, marriages, divorces, and deaths; and the official records of government agencies, such as the federal budget and the *Congressional Record*.

Despite their importance to the sociologist, such statistics still have serious shortcomings. Almost every researcher has had the experience of spending long hours looking through official publications searching for a particular figure that is nowhere to be found. You might, for example, be interested in comparing the income and educational levels of Chinese Americans and Filipino Americans, only to find that the Department of the Census lists only whites, blacks, Hispanics, and "others." More serious is the problem of bias and distortion. It has, for example, long been known that many black males from the underclass vanish from census reports in their early years of adulthood only to reappear in middle age. Government statistics may also be biased by political considerations. Such things as the rates of poverty, unemployment, and crime are often hot social issues, and many sociologists have charged that the standards and procedures for calculating those figures are slanted for political reasons.

The Case Study A detailed examination of specific individuals, groups, and situations is known as a **case study**. There are many different sources of information for such investigations, including the official records just discussed, histories, biographies, and newspaper reports. **Personal interviews** and **participant observation** are two of the most direct ways of conducting a case study.

Suppose you were interested in studying juvenile delinquency. You might locate a gang of delinquent boys and interview them, asking each boy why he became involved in the gang, what he does with the other gang members, what his plans for the future are, and so on. You would then study the replies, put them together in some meaningful way, and draw your conclusions. On the other hand, in a participant observation study you would actually take part in gang activities. You might disguise yourself and work your way into the gang as a regular member, or you might tell the boys your purpose and ask their permission to watch their activities. One problem with the interview technique is that we can never be sure the subjects are telling the truth, even if they think they are. Although the participant observation technique avoids this problem, it is difficult and sometimes even dangerous to study people in this way, for they often resent the intrusion of nosy outsiders. Another problem is that the presence of a sociologist may make the people being studied change their behavior.

When compared with other research methods, the case study has the advantage of allowing researchers to come into close contact with the object of their study. Interviews and direct observation can provide rich insights that cannot be obtained from statistics. But the case study method has its limitations, especially when the cases selected for study are not typical. For instance, a researcher might unknowingly select a group of delinquents who are strongly opposed to drug use, while all the other gang members in the same area are heavy drug users. Another common criticism of the case study method is that it relies too heavily on the ability and insights of the person doing the study. Although this problem is common to all research methods, it is especially troublesome in case studies because all the "facts" that are disclosed for examination are filtered by the researcher.

The Survey   Rather than concentrating on an in-depth study of a few cases, the **survey** asks more limited questions of a much larger number of people. Because it is seldom possible to question everyone concerned with a certain social problem, a **sample** is used. For instance, suppose you were interested in the relationship between age and attitudes toward the abortion issue. You might select an appropriate city for your study and randomly select a sample of 100 names from the city directory. If the sample is properly drawn, it will be representative of all the people in the city. Each person in the sample would then be interviewed to determine his or her age and attitude toward abortion. You would then analyze the responses statistically to determine the relationship between these two variables.

The survey is an invaluable tool for measuring the attitudes and behaviors of large numbers of people. The Gallup poll is a good example of how the survey method can be used effectively. However, because this method reports answers to a limited number of fixed questions, it is not as effective as the case study approach in developing new ideas and insights. Another problem is that people do not always answer the questions honestly, particularly if the survey deals with sensitive issues such as sexual behavior or crime. A third difficulty is that surveys are expensive and time-

The survey, in which a sample of people are asked a series of questions about their opinions or behavior, is one of the most common methods of sociological research.

consuming to conduct. But when conducted properly, a survey ensures that the people studied are not misleading exceptions, and case studies seldom provide this assurance.

The Experiment In social science, as in the physical and biological sciences, the **experiment** provides an opportunity for the most carefully controlled type of research. Although there are many types of experimental designs, experimenters usually divide their subjects into an experimental group and a control group. Then the experimental group is manipulated in some way the other group is not. By comparing the two groups at the end of the experiment, researchers try to discover the effects of what was done to the experimental group. To illustrate, suppose you were interested in the effects of violent programs on television viewers. You might select two groups of people and show one, the experimental group, a number of violent television programs and the other, the control group, nonviolent programs. You would then test the two groups to see whether the violent programs caused any increase in violent behavior or attitudes.

A major problem arises because most experimental studies of human behavior must be conducted in laboratory settings. Watching violent television programs in a laboratory is likely to have different effects from watching the same programs at home because the conditions in the two settings differ so greatly. True "social experiments," in which a social change is introduced into real-life settings to determine its effect on a social problem, are very rare because control is difficult in such conditions and few social scientists have the authority or the money to carry out such research. Another problem with experimental research is that the subjects may be inadvertently harmed by the experimental manipulations, and many potentially valuable experiments cannot be done for ethical reasons.

INTERPRETING CLAIMS
ABOUT SOCIAL PROBLEMS

Even those of us who never do research on social problems sooner or later will have to interpret claims about them. Politicians, journalists, and sociologists, as well as an assortment of cranks and oddballs, constantly bombard the public with opinions and "facts" about these problems. Each citizen must decide whether to believe or disregard these assertions. Many of the claims are patently false, but some are presented with impressive-sounding arguments. Reasonable skepticism is an important scientific tool. It should be practiced by anyone who is interested in knowing how social problems arise, persist, and change.

Some people find it easy to believe almost anything they see in print, and even accept the exaggerated claims of television commercials and newspaper advertisements. The ability to speak well may be taken as a sign that the speaker is trustworthy and honest. The belief that those who lie in public are usually sued or even put in jail adds to the credibility of public speakers. But there are many ways of telling lies without risking trouble with the law. One technique is to lie about groups rather than individuals. While a speaker could not say that John Jones is a narcotics addict without some proof, the speaker could say that college students or musicians are addicts.

Another technique is to imply guilt by association. A speaker might charge that Judge Mary Jones is "frequently seen in the company of thugs, degenerates, and narcotics addicts." Consider the difference between these two statements:

> Mary Jones, the Communist party, and student revolutionaries agree that there are great injustices in the American economic system.

> Mary Jones, the National Council of Churches, and Supreme Court judges agree that there are great injustices in the American economic system.

Another way of conveying a misleading impression is to quote out of context. This sort of misrepresentation has been brought to the level of a fine art by the merchandisers of paperback books. For example, a reviewer in *The New York Times* might say something like this: "This book is somewhat interesting, but certainly not one of the greatest books of the decade." And it might end up being quoted like this: "Interesting . . . one of the greatest books of the decade.—*The New York Times*."

It is essential to read claims about social problems and their solutions carefully. Wild propaganda and intentional distortions usually are self-revealing. However, most people who are concerned about social issues do not intentionally lie or distort the truth. They may merely be vague, using phrases such as "many people believe" and "it is widely thought" because their knowledge is incomplete. But people also tend to unconsciously distort their perceptions to fit their own biases, and misleading statements are hardest to detect when the speaker is sincere. There are a number of standards that can be used to measure the validity of a statement, but none of them is foolproof.

The Author One of the best places to begin evaluating an article or speech is with the author. What are his or her qualifications? Why should the speaker or writer know anything more about the problem than the audience? Titles and academic degrees in themselves do not mean very much unless they have some clear relation to the problem under consideration. For instance, a professor of physics might be qualified to talk about nuclear power, but her opinion about the influence of international politics on our oil supplies could well be of little value. A professor of sociology might be well qualified to comment on the causes of crime but know little or nothing about how police departments should be organized. An impressive title does not always guarantee authority or expertise.

It is also helpful, when possible, to know an author's biases. They will often become clear if one looks at the author's other work. For example, suppose that an economist who has always supported the social security system publishes a study concluding that the system has been a failure. These findings should be given more weight than the same conclusions published by a longtime opponent of social security. The same is true of articles published by people with special interests. An article concluding that criminals have been mistreated by the police is more persuasive if it is written by a police officer than if it is written by a burglar.

The Support Scientific research projects are expensive. If authors say their assertions are based on research, it is important to know who paid for the research and what, if anything, its supporters stand to gain from its conclusions. Few organizations, including federal agencies, will fund a study that is likely to arrive at conclusions harmful to their interests. It is not very surprising to find a study funded by an oil company that asserts that oil drilling will produce little environmental damage, or to find a study funded by a tobacco company that says that smoking cigarettes is as safe as playing badminton. However, a study funded by an oil company that concludes that oil drilling will cause serious damage to the environment merits attention.

The Distribution Where an article is published or a speech is given can be another important guide to the reliability of the statements made. One can usually assume that articles published in recognized professional journals such as the *American Journal of Sociology* or *Social Problems* meet some minimal professional standards. But an article on race relations published in a newspaper affiliated with the Ku Klux Klan, an article on minimum wages published in a trade union weekly, or a speech on gun control before the National Rifle Association is likely to contain few surprises.

The Content There are no firm rules for judging which conclusions are reasonable and which are not. Some research papers are so technical that only an expert can judge their value. But most books, magazine articles, and speeches about social problems are not directed at expert audiences; so readers and listeners need no special qualifications when they make a judgment about the accuracy of what is said. Asking the following questions is a good way to begin when judging the value of an article or speech.

Does the Article or Speech Make Sense? It is important to get involved with what is being said rather than just passively accepting it. Are the author's arguments logical? If a person says that drug addiction is widespread because enemy agents are trying to weaken the country by enslaving its youth, ask yourself whether it is reasonable to claim that such methods could be used in secret. It is also logical to ask why those who are being enslaved by drugs are the least powerful people in the population. Do the author's conclusions seem to follow from the evidence presented? There is good reason to reject an argument that, for example, asserts that college students who smoke marijuana do so because of poverty. Subtler gaps in logic can also be detected by the attentive listener.

Why Does the Writer or Speaker Use a Particular Style? A book or speech need not be boring to be accurate. Nevertheless, there is a difference between a calm, thoughtful analysis and demagoguery. Skillful speakers who give emotion-packed examples of human suffering may only be trying to get an audience's attention, or they may use such examples to cloud the issue. Most articles, speeches, and books necessarily contain some vague claims or assertions. One should always ask whether the vagueness is necessary because some facts are unknown or because the author is trying to obscure the subject or conceal information. Conversely, a collection of numbers and statistics does not guarantee that conclusions are valid. An old saying holds that figures don't lie but liars figure.

Do an Author's Claims Fit In with What Others Say About the Subject? The truth of a proposition is not decided by democratic vote. Majorities can be wrong and minorities right. Even an individual who strays far from what most people—including experts—accept as true is not necessarily wrong. In scientific work especially, a successful experiment by a lone researcher can challenge truths that have long been accepted. But if an author's claims differ greatly from those of others who know something about the subject, there is reason to be skeptical. The question to be asked is whether the author presents enough evidence to justify rejection of the old ideas and the accepted beliefs.

SUMMARY

There are two major sociological definitions of the term *social problem*. One says that social problems are created by gaps between a society's ideals and actual conditions in that society. The other defines a social problem as a condition that a significant number of people consider to be a problem.

The public's perceptions of social problems change from time to time. The major forces influencing these changes are social movements that try to bring about social change. These movements usually begin when people who share a common problem communicate with each other and commit themselves to finding a solution. If the supporters of a social movement are powerful, or if they can appeal to popular values and prejudices, the movement has a good chance of success. If the opponents of the social movement have more influence, the desired action is less likely to be taken. But even if the government takes official action, the agencies that are supposed to deal with the problem may do little or nothing to change it.

Over the years sociologists have developed a body of knowledge, theories, and methods that aid in the study of social problems. Eight basic sociologic terms essential to the understanding of the sociological approach are *roles, norms, groups, socialization, institutions, classes, culture,* and *society*.

Sociologists approach the study of social problems from different theoretical perspectives. The two major approaches dealing with large groups and entire societies are the functionalist perspective and the conflict perspective. Functionalists see a society as a delicate balance among its basic components. Every society has a set of needs that must be fulfilled if it is to survive, and all the components of a society have functions that they perform to meet these needs. But they may also have dysfunctions or harmful consequences for society. Social problems occur when a society becomes so disorganized that its basic functions cannot be performed as well as they should be. Conflict theorists see social order as a set of power relationships. Coercion, not shared values and beliefs, is the cement that holds a society together. Some conflict theorists emphasize conflicts between people whose values are incompatible; others emphasize conflicts between people from different classes, ethnic groups, or genders. But they agree that the oppression of one group by another is a basic cause of our social problems.

Social psychological theories focus on individuals and small groups rather than on entire societies. Biosocial theories emphasize the role of heredity in human behavior. Personality theories focus on the traits that an individual develops in early socialization. Behavioral theories discount internal mental processes and are concerned only with observable behavior and the ways in which it is learned. Interactionist theories note the important effects of social interaction on behavior.

Theory is an important guide, but it becomes effective only when applied to facts. Social scientists use four principal methods to gather data to test theories and uncover the facts. Public records and statistics provide social scientists with a rich source of data so that they do not have to collect it themselves. The case study is a detailed examination of specific individuals, groups, or situations. Surveys put questions to cross sections of the population. Experiments usually try to duplicate the social world in a laboratory so that the various factors being studied can be carefully controlled.

Even those who never do research on social problems should be able to interpret and judge the claims of others. There are at least four commonsense methods for evaluating speeches, books, and articles about social problems: (1) Check the qualifications and biases of the author. (2) Check the biases of the people who pay the bills of the speaker or author. (3) Check the publishers of magazine articles and the special interests of the audience listening to a speech. (4) Check the content of the speech or article and the logic of the arguments the author uses to support a point.

KEY TERMS

All words appearing in **bold type** *in the chapter are also defined in the glossary at the end of this book.*

case study   A detailed examination of specific individuals, groups, or situations. It may involve such techniques as personal interviews or participant observation.

conflict perspective   A broad sociological approach that sees the conflict between different groups as a basic sociological process, and holds that the principal source of social problems is the exploitation and oppression of one group by another.

experiment   A research technique in which the behavior of individuals or groups is studied by manipulating one or more variables to which they are exposed.

functionalist perspective   A broad sociological approach that sees society as a delicate balance of parts, each with its own functions and dysfunctions, and holds that most social problems result from the disorganization of society.

social psychological perspectives   A large group of theories—including the biosocial, personality, behaviorist, and interactionist theories—that attempt to explain the effects of individuals and social groups on each other.

sociology   The scientific study of society and social behavior.

survey   A research technique in which a group of people are asked about their attitudes and/or activities in personal interviews or by means of questionnaires.

FURTHER READINGS

C. Wright Mills, *The Sociological Imagination* (New York: Oxford University Press, 1959). A classic statement of the value of the sociological approach in dealing with the social problems of everyday life.

Anthony Giddens, *Introduction to Sociology* (New York: W. W. Norton, 1991). A full-length introduction to sociology by one of today's leading theorists.

Theodore Caplow, *American Social Trends* (San Diego: Harcourt Brace Jovanovich, 1991). An insightful analysis of the current trends in American society.

Malcolm Spector and John I. Kitsuse, *Constructing Social Problems* (Hawthorne, N.Y.: Aldine de Gruyter, 1987). An interesting look at the sociology of social problems that focuses on the way particular conditions come to be labeled as social problems.

Jonathan H. Turner, *The Structure of Sociological Theory*, 5th ed. (Chicago: Dorset Press, 1991). One of the best general texts on social theory.

Earl Babbie, *The Practice of Social Research*, 6th ed. (Belmont, Calif.: Wadsworth, 1992). A good introduction to the techniques and goals of sociological research.

PART ONE

Troubled Institutions

chapter 2

Problems of the Economy

- What is the "world economy"?
- Who controls corporations?
- Is the "work ethic" dead?
- Why has the economy stagnated?
- What can the government do to solve our economic problems?

What has happened to the American dream? People seem to be losing their faith in the promise of unbounded opportunity and success for anyone who is willing to work hard enough to achieve it. Stores are flooded with foreign products that are not only cheaper but often of better quality than domestic goods. Inflated real estate prices have put the cost of owning a home beyond the grasp of millions of young Americans. The manufacturing jobs that offered good pay and good benefits in exchange for an honest day's work are disappearing, leaving many workers with no other options than to flip hamburgers or sweep floors. And through all this, those at the top seem to get an ever-larger share of the economic pie, while the desperation of those at the bottom only gets worse.

Of course, the American dream has always been just that—a dream. In the past, women and minorities were excluded from the dream, and countless others tried and failed to win the promised success. Moreover, despite some recent setbacks, the standard of living is still much higher today than could have been imagined 100 years ago, and the Great Depression certainly brought greater economic hardship than any we know today. Still, such facts are little consolation to people who have come to expect the seemingly endless prosperity that followed World War II. Until recently, American society has depended on its growing affluence to provide the wherewithal to deal with its other social problems. Now the economy is undergoing fundamental changes that are calling that assumption of ever-greater prosperity into question, and American society is facing one of the most difficult adjustments in its history.

UNDERSTANDING THE ECONOMIC SYSTEM

The world is a vast and confusing place, and most people are familiar with only a small part of it. When economic problems crop up, people seek explanations by looking at familiar events close to home. Although some problems can be understood in terms of a single nation or even a single city, today's economic woes are world problems. No one can understand the causes of inflation, unemployment, or economic stagnation by looking only at a single nation in isolation from the **world economy**.

But although all nations are part of the world economy, all countries do not play the same part in it. The principal dividing line in the modern world is between the wealthy industrialized nations and the poor agricultural nations of the **Third World**. Although most of the world's products are manufactured in the industrialized nations, more than three-fourths of the world's population is in the Third World.[1] Most Third World people make their living from agriculture and the export of raw materials. Although there is a growing industrial economy in many Third World nations, their industries pay low wages and are often owned and operated by foreigners. In contrast to the poverty of the Third World, the industrialized nations have accumulated huge reserves of wealth, not just in terms of money but also in the things it can buy: highways, buildings, factories, power plants, public facilities, and, of course, an educated populace and a well-trained work force. In between these two extremes are the most prosperous nations of the Third World, such as Thailand and South Korea, that have a higher standard of living and are more industrialized than other Third

World countries but are still far behind such nations as the United States and Japan (see Chapter 14 for a discussion of the problems of the Third World).

All this may sound as if the fully industrialized nations have few economic problems, but that is hardly the case. To understand those problems, we must examine their basic economic system: capitalism. It is generally recognized that the United States, Canada, Japan, and the other wealthy industrialized nations have capitalist economies. But exactly what does this mean? Although it is difficult to define **capitalism** precisely, capitalist economic systems display three essential characteristics. First, there is private property. Second, a market controls the production and distribution of valuable commodities. Third, privately owned businesses compete with one another in the free market, each aiming to make the greatest possible profit. The classic statement of the principles of free-market capitalism was set forth in Adam Smith's book *The Wealth of Nations*, first published in 1776.[2] Smith argued that individuals will work harder and produce more if allowed to work for personal profit. Private greed will be transformed into public good through the workings of a free market regulated only by supply and demand. The profit motive will drive manufacturers to supply goods that the public demands, and competition will ensure that the goods are reasonably priced. The market will regulate itself in the most efficient possible way—as though guided by an "invisible hand"—if the government does not interfere with the free play of economic forces.

Although some economists and politicians still fervently believe in the principles set forth in Smith's writings, it is clear that no real economic system operates the way Smith said it should and no nation has completely "free" markets. Smith himself realized that businesses can reap large profits by restricting free competition and raising prices: "People of the same trade seldom meet together, even for merriment and diversion, but the conversation ends in a conspiracy against the public, or in some contrivance to raise prices."[3] Since those words were written, major corporations have grown to a colossal size that Smith could hardly have imagined, and, as a result, such conspiracies have become a far greater problem. But markets are now restricted in many other ways as well. The untrammeled competition advocated by free-market economists created a whole new class of fabulously wealthy industrialists, but it also led to grinding poverty for those who were less able to compete. As a result, workers joined together into unions to demand better treatment, and governments around the world created welfare programs to help the most disadvantaged. Government became more deeply involved in economic affairs in other ways too. Laws were passed to forbid **monopolies** and other anticompetitive practices by business and to regulate markets in which completely free competition is not desirable, such as water, electric power, and health care. Finally, most governments now seek to give their own nation's businesses whatever advantages they can in world trade, while attempting to limit the success of foreign companies in their markets. In order to understand the way our economy operates, we must therefore go beyond economic theory and look at the actual role of four major economic players—the corporations, government, small business, and the workers.

The Corporations If the world's largest organizations, including governments, were listed in order of size, half would be corporations. Such giants as Masushita, Phillips, and

Exxon have assets worth billions of dollars. As we have seen, antitrust laws prohibit a single corporate giant from monopolizing an entire industry. But corporations can get around these laws by expanding into related fields and buying out suppliers and distributors.

Another distinctive characteristic of today's major corporations is their **market control**. The markets for many important products and services, ranging from automobiles and gasoline to aspirin and broadcasting, are dominated by just three or four enormous firms—an arrangement known as an **oligopoly**. About 60 percent of all the goods and services produced in the United States (not counting those produced by the government) are made in industries dominated by such oligopolies. And even in these restricted markets there is usually one giant that is larger and stronger than any other. For instance, General Motors produces more cars than all other American car manufacturers combined. The largest corporation in an industry often becomes the **price leader**. It sets the prices for the merchandise it sells, and other corporations set theirs at the same level, ignoring the principles of supply and demand envisioned by Adam Smith and his followers. Major businesses also communicate and cooperate through **interlocking directorates**. Although it is illegal for a member of the board of directors of one large firm to sit on the board of a competing firm, it is not illegal for directors of competing firms to be on the board of a third firm in a different industry. Accordingly, powerful individuals sit on the boards of directors of several corporations, exchanging ideas and plans with other corporate leaders. Some leading businesses are also linked together as **corporate interest groups** based on common family holdings or controlled by the same large banks. The enormous power of the major banks comes not only from their ability to provide (or withhold) loans and other essential financial services but also from the management of pension funds and trust accounts that own huge blocks of corporate stock.[4] Obviously, corporations that are controlled by the same financial interests are more likely to cooperate than to compete.

Although competition among domestic firms has declined, recent years have seen the arrival of strong new foreign competitors. In the automobile industry, for example, mergers and bankruptcies have left only three significant American automobile manufacturers. Because they tend to make similar products that sell for similar prices, their strongest competition often comes from Japanese firms like Toyota or Honda or from cars produced in low-wage countries, such as the Korean Hyundai.

Who Runs the Corporations? The modern corporation is a vast financial network. The relationships between a given corporation and its competitors, banks, subcontractors and suppliers, stockholders, directors and managers, workers, unions, and various local and national governments are extremely complex and may change without warning. Researchers who try to determine who, or what, controls this network rarely have the cooperation of corporations. Because they must rely on secondhand data on this politically charged issue, their conclusions are often contradictory.

Supporters of the system claim that corporations are democratic institutions owned by many different people, and they point to the fact that almost 50 million citizens own stock in American corporations.[5] However, critics note that although many people own some stock, most stock is owned by a small group of wealthy

Because the same individuals serve on the boards of directors of many different firms, most large corporations are said to have interlocking directorates. *This system creates channels of communication among major corporations and encourages them to cooperate to promote their common interests.*

individuals. It is estimated that the wealthiest one-half of 1 percent of the American people own about half of all privately held stock.[6] Institutional stockholders such as banks, insurance companies, and investment firms also hold major blocks of stock. In fact, most of the public trading on the New York Stock Exchange is conducted for institutional stockholders, not private individuals. Although the stock in these financial institutions is held by individual investors, the directors nevertheless have considerable influence on the affairs of the corporations whose stock their company owns. Moreover, banks and other financial institutions exercise great influence over corporate decision making through their power to grant or reject loans to finance corporate projects.[7]

Most economists agree that there is a significant separation between ownership and control in most corporations. Because there are so many stockholders, most of them simply vote for or against the current management and have little influence on individual corporate decisions. The technical complexity of modern business is so great that many stockholders do not even understand the key issues facing management. Economist John Kenneth Galbraith calls the group of managers who make the important decisions the "corporate technostructure." He points out that most national and international corporations are no longer run by a single powerful person like Andrew Carnegie or John D. Rockefeller. Decisions are made by anonymous executives and managers who spend their entire careers gaining the technical skills and knowledge needed to manage a modern corporation. However, corporate managers must still serve the primary interest of their stockholders—making profits—or risk losing their jobs. David R. James and Michael Soref, for example, found that declining profits were the single major reason that corporate presidents lost their jobs, regardless of whether the firm was owned by a large number of stockholders or by a single individual.[8]

Corporate managers do not make their decisions simply on the basis of their knowledge and skills, however. High-level corporate managers are a distinct social class, and they act to promote their own self-interest. In the last decade, top executives have increased their own pay almost four times faster than their workers' pay and three times faster than profits of their corporations.[9] If young managers are to get to the top, they must have more than just technical skills, ability, and drive. They must also accept the ideology and worldview of the corporate elite and support its interests. As C. Wright Mills put it, "in personal manner and political view, in social ways and business style, [the new manager] must be like those who are already in, and upon whose judgements his own success rests."[10]

The Multinationals In recent years most large corporations have expanded across national boundaries, setting up a complex web of sales, manufacturing, distribution, and financial operations. Although these firms are usually based in a single country and run by people of that nationality, they are often transnational in organization and perspective. The international executive is, as Jonathan Schell notes, "not dependent on the labor, capital or technical knowledge of any particular country. He can pick and choose from anywhere in the world . . . [H]e is not an 'American' businessman or a 'Japanese' businessman. He belongs to no country."[11] Furthermore, those who invest in corporations are developing the same transnational orientation. In 1991, about 14 percent of the stocks and bonds sold in the United States were for foreign companies, and that figure is projected to reach 25 percent by 1995.[12]

The growth of these powerful multinational corporations has generated tremendous controversy. Some people see their rise as the first step toward world unity. They are convinced that by linking the economies of the world's nations, the multinationals are laying the foundations for a global government that will usher in a new era of peace and prosperity. But the critics of the multinationals see them as international bandits who exploit small countries and play large ones against one another.

The expansion of multinational corporations among the industrialized countries has created problems of international control and regulation. Canadians are, for example, extremely concerned about the economic power of American multinationals, which hold 80 percent of all foreign investments in Canada.[13] Even though the Canadian government has made repeated efforts to promote economic independence, more of Canada's economy is in foreign hands than is true of any other industrialized nation. For instance, despite the creation of Petro-Canada, a government-owned petroleum company, foreigners still control about 60 percent of the Canadian gas and oil industry.[14] Many Canadians have come to see this foreign economic domination as a grave threat to their national independence.

Multinational corporations do business all over the world, and their expansion into weak and impoverished nations often brings with it the fear of foreign domination.

Even the United States is beginning to worry about the growing influence of foreign capital. Foreigners have direct investments of over $230 billion in the United States, and some estimate that they control as much as 40 percent of the pharmaceutical industry, 25 percent of the kitchen appliance industry, and 20 percent of the tobacco industry.[15]

But the worst abuses of the multinational corporations have resulted from their expansion into the poor Third World countries of Africa, Asia, and Latin America. Although the multinationals bring advanced technology and encourage some types of economic development, the "host" nations must pay a heavy price. Foreign corporations with heavy investments wield tremendous political power, and too often the critical economic decisions are made by foreign corporate executives who have little concern for the welfare of the local people.

In addition to the problem of foreign political domination, there are strong grounds for questioning how much economic benefit poor nations actually reap from foreign investments. Numerous statistical comparisons of nations that depend on their own resources for economic development with those that encourage foreign investment indicate that such investments do produce immediate economic benefits. However, once the initial investment is made and the multinationals begin taking home their profits, the economies of the nations with large foreign investments begin to falter.[16] Thus, in the long run, more self-reliant nations have greater economic growth.

Corporate Crimes   The business world is sometimes described as a lawless jungle where profits rule and where those who let ethics stand in their way are considered fools. Although this is certainly an exaggeration, there is ample evidence that the crime rate is high in the business world.

Everyone has had the experience of buying an article of clothing or an appliance that seemed to fall apart after the slightest use. Although the manufacture and sale of such merchandise is not a violation of the law, making false claims for a product is a type of **fraud**. There are countless examples in industries ranging from cosmetics to automobiles. But the most costly fraud of all times was probably the savings and loan scandal that came to light in the 1980s. The collapse of the savings and loan industry is ultimately expected to cost as much as $500 billion, most of it to be paid by the taxpayers. Although estimates vary about what percentage of those staggering losses was caused by corporate crime, some kind of fraud was probably involved in the majority of bank failures.[17] Some fraudulent claims endanger the health or even the life of the consumer. The major pharmaceutical companies have, for example, frequently been caught making fraudulent claims about their products or concealing information to cover up their hazards. Two well-known examples are the painkiller known as Oraflex, which is thought to have killed 49 people and injured almost a thousand more, and the Dalkon Shield contraceptive, which is believed to have killed at least 17 women and caused about 200,000 injuries.[18]

Price fixing (collusion by several companies to cut competition and set uniformly high prices) is another common corporate crime. A survey of the heads of the 1,000 largest manufacturing corporations asked whether "many" corporations engaged in price fixing. Among those heading the 500 largest corporations, a surprising 47 percent agreed that price fixing is a common practice. An overwhelming 70 percent of the heads of the remaining 500 corporations also agreed.[19] It is quite possible that violations of the laws against price fixing cost consumers more than any other crime.

Many companies also use illegal practices to drive their competitors out of business. One technique is for a big company to sell certain products at a loss in order to bankrupt a small competitor. The loss is recovered and profits increased by selling products at much higher prices after the competition has been eliminated. Another technique is for a giant corporation to buy out producers of key raw materials and cut off supplies to its smaller competitors. As in many corporate crimes, the damage extends far beyond the immediate victims to the general public, who in one way or another foot the bill.

The Government   Although many conservatives argue that the government should avoid all interference in the economy and allow the free market to regulate itself, the governments of all industrialized nations are deeply involved in directing their economies. Actually, governments play two key economic roles in contemporary capitalist societies. First, government is a major employer, providing jobs and paychecks for millions of people who do everything from sweeping streets to flying jet bombers. Second, government regulates the economic activities of the private sector. Some regulation is done directly through the legal system—for example, when the courts decide civil suits involving private business or when the government brings legal action for the violation of antitrust laws. But government has many other means to direct a country's economic activities.

Government officials can influence the economy by manipulating the amount of money in circulation and the interest rates on loans. By increasing the money supply and lowering interest rates, the government can give a boost to the economy—but at the risk of increasing inflation. Restricting the money supply and raising interest rates help reduce inflation but are likely to dampen economic growth and increase unemployment. Tax policies also have a tremendous impact on the economy, influencing the general rate of economic growth, providing special benefits, or creating certain problems in specific industries. Whatever techniques it uses, the average citizen now expects the government to do everything possible to ensure economic prosperity. When the economy is in decline, the government is blamed and politicians have a difficult time getting reelected. Conversely, a prosperous economy is a great asset to officeholders.

One of the most common myths is the idea that big business and big government are bitter rivals competing for economic power. In fact, government and business cooperate more often than they compete. As John Kenneth Galbraith put it, "The industrial system, in fact, is inextricably associated with the state. In notable respects the mature corporation is an arm of the state. And the state, in important matters, is an instrument of the industrial system."[20] Of course, this does not mean that corporation executives wouldn't prefer lower taxes and less government control, or that government officials wouldn't like the corporations to show more concern for the welfare of citizens. Businesspeople are sometimes antagonistic toward government, but they nevertheless look to the government when they are in economic trouble. In most capitalist countries, the government's economic strategy has been to encourage general prosperity by ensuring the profitability of the big corporations.

Government regulatory agencies such as the Federal Trade Commission and the Food and Drug Administration have come under strong attack in recent years. Consumer groups charge that although these agencies were set up to protect the public interest, they often end up helping the industries they regulate rather than the public: "The regulatory agencies have become the natural allies of the industries they are supposed to regulate. They conceive their primary task to be to protect insiders from new competition—in many cases, from any competition.[21] One problem is that the directors of these agencies often come from the industries they are supposed to regulate and return to those same industries when they leave the government. In such circumstances the regulators are unlikely to sacrifice their future by offending powerful corporate executives. But even when the officials try to do their job, the power of the corporation is so great that these small, underfunded government agencies are too weak to get the job done.

Business groups often make the opposite criticism, charging that government regulation damages the economy by requiring a mountain of costly and time-consuming paperwork and placing unnecessary restrictions on their activities. As a result of these criticisms, the last decade has seen a trend toward the deregulation of some important industries. Unfortunately, the results of deregulation have often been disappointing.

Deregulation of the airline industry, for example, produced not only a drop in ticket prices but also a decline in the safety and quality of service. Moreover, it touched off a wave of mergers and buyouts that have reduced competition and have once again led to higher prices. Deregulation of the savings and loan industry had even more serious consequences. Many managers pursued speculative high-risk investments or fraudulent schemes to enrich themselves at their company's expense, and the result, as we have seen, was virtual collapse of the savings and loan industry.

Small Business Although overshadowed by the huge bureaucracies of the corporations and the government, small business still plays a key role in the economy. Numerically, small business has always been in the majority. And with the current limitations in the growth of government employment and the decline in many traditional manufacturing industries, small business has played an increasing role in creating new jobs for the growing work force. Employment in big business, in contrast, has shown little growth in recent years. As *Forbes* magazine put it, large corporations "do not appear to be efficient engines of job creation."[22]

But those who do find jobs in small businesses quickly discover that working conditions are very different from those in the government or corporations. The main attraction of small business is the independence it offers to its many owner-operators. But most new businesses go bankrupt in their first year or two, and many of the entrepreneurs who succeed work long hours for a modest return. The employees of many small businesses share their boss's economic insecurity but without the com-

Although small businesses are an increasingly important source of new jobs, they lack the political power and the financial resources of the big corporations.

pensation of greater independence. In comparison with corporate workers, the employees of small businesses are less unionized and receive lower pay and fewer fringe benefits.

Although small business and corporations are often lumped together as part of the private sector, there are fundamental differences between the two. The large corporations are able to restrict competition among themselves and thus safeguard their profitability. Small businesses generally face a host of competitors in a very real struggle for survival. Another important difference is political. The corporations wield enormous political power and as a result can obtain many benefits and special favors from the government. Because small business is much less influential, small businesses pay higher taxes, receive fewer government benefits, and cannot expect a government bailout when they run into financial trouble. For that reason, some economists refer to the corporations as the monopoly sector of the economy and small business as the competitive sector.

Perched between the corporate giants and the legions of "mom and pop" businesses are the medium-sized firms that are at the center of much economic innovation and technological development. Unlike small companies, these firms have the size and economic resources necessary to get the job done. But compared with the giant corporations, medium-sized firms have less cumbersome bureaucracies and are more subject to the competitive pressures of the marketplace. Because medium-sized firms are not large enough to dominate their principal markets, they face the same choice as small businesses: be efficient and competitive, or go under.

The Workers Not only are workers the heart of the economic system, but their work is often a central focus of their lives. People's self-concepts—their ideas of who and what they are—are profoundly affected by their occupations and their place in the occupational hierarchy. Our occupation brings us into contact with specific social worlds and specific groups of people. If we consider, for example, the differences between the social world of a police officer and that of a ballet dancer, it becomes obvious how deeply people are influenced by their work.

The Work Force Both the types of jobs and the kinds of people who work at them have changed radically in this century. Two significant trends are apparent in the job market. First, farm workers, owners, and managers—once the largest job category— have steadily declined. They now make up only 2.8 percent of the work force in the United States.[23] Mechanization and technology have enabled a handful of workers to feed millions, so fewer people are needed on the farm. Second, because of the increasing competition from foreign products and automation, there has been a shift of workers away from manufacturing and other **blue-collar** occupations and into **white-collar** and service occupations. Ninety-one percent of the new jobs created since the recession of 1982 have been in the service sector, while millions of blue-collar jobs in basic manufacturing industries have been lost.[24]

These changes have brought great hardship to many people in the working class. Although a service job may sound more attractive than working in a factory, the reality is often quite different. Most service work is just as dull, menial, and repetitive as most factory work, but on the average the pay is only 70 percent as high. The result has been a growing income gap between the working class and more highly trained managers and professionals (see Chapter 6) and the deterioration of entire towns that depend on failing manufacturing concerns.

There have also been major changes in the role of women in the work force. For one thing, unprecedented numbers of married women have been taking jobs outside the home. In 1900, only 1 out of 20 married women participated in the work force; today more than half of all married women hold jobs.[25] Another major trend has been the entrance of women into occupations that used to be reserved almost entirely for men. (See Chapter 10 for a full discussion of these trends.)

Although the problem of **unemployment** is often overlooked, it should be remembered that those who are out of work are still part of the work force. During the 1980s, they averaged over 7 percent of all workers.[26] Although unemployment insurance may help for a time, the percentage of unemployed workers who actually receive checks has steadily declined for the last decade as eligibility standards were increased and the length of benefits reduced. Moreover, official unemployment statistics do not count discouraged workers who have given up looking for jobs and those who are victims of **underemployment**—that is, those who take part-time jobs when they want full-time work. If those two groups were added in, the unemployment figure would almost double. There are currently about 21 million Americans who work part time, and almost a third of them want full-time work.[27] On the average, part-time workers earn less than 60 percent as much per hour as full-time workers, and most of them receive no medical or retirement benefits.[28]

Worker Alienation The mechanization of the workplace during the industrial revolution led to a progressive dehumanization of workers. Although the hours may not be as long as they were a century ago, many of today's factory workers still find their jobs tedious and trivial and see themselves as little more than cogs in a machine. These feelings are so common that they have been given a name: the "blue-collar blues." David J. Charrington's survey of worker attitudes found that "feeling pride and craftmanship in your work" was one of the most highly desired characteristics in a job.[29] Yet technology is rapidly eliminating skilled craftspeople and replacing them with complex computer-controlled machinery. The people displaced from such jobs often drift into low-skilled service industries. But even those who are retrained to repair such equipment often lose the old sense of pride that came from being directly responsible for producing a high-quality product.

A number of programs have been created to help blue-collar workers gain greater satisfaction on the job. Some corporations, for example, give a group of workers responsibility for assembling a finished product rather than give each individual responsibility for only one small part of it. Other companies encourage workers to rotate from one job to another in order to vary their tasks. Some managers allow employees to set up their own working procedures and schedule their own hours. Allowing workers to participate in management decisions that affect their jobs has also proven to reduce alienation. However, conflict theorists argue that worker alienation will not be reduced significantly until workers receive a greater share of the profits of the companies using their labor.

Ironically, just as the corporations are discovering the problem of worker aliena-tion among the shrinking blue-collar labor force, the computer revolution is creating the same problem among the rapidly growing number of clerical workers. Computers were supposed to liberate office workers from the drudgery of performing the same tasks again and again, but so far that hasn't been the result. As in the early days of factory automation, computers have been used to break down jobs into smaller and simpler tasks. The use of computers has also tended to isolate workers from other employees, and, at the same time, new technology has increased employers' ability to scrutinize the actions of their workers. For example, workers who deal with the public on the phone often find that computer-generated reports show how many calls they answer and how long they spend with each customer, while supervisors randomly audit the calls that exceed a given length. Moreover, the repetitive move-ments required by some computerized equipment, such as the cash registers that read "zebra-striped" codes, have caused a sevenfold increase in "repetitive-strain ill-nesses," such as strained wrists, since 1981.[30]

Death on the Job Boredom and alienation are not the only problems workers have to face on the job. Working for the wrong company or in the wrong industry can have fatal consequences. The National Safety Council estimates that 14,000 people are killed in industrial accidents every year, and most of those deaths are preventable. Data from Wisconsin indicate that 45 percent of the industrial deaths in that state result from violations of the state safety code, and the safety codes themselves often fail to provide adequate protection for workers. In addition to the thousands of work-ers who die as a direct result of accidents, a much larger number die more slowly from the effects of occupationally caused diseases. The U.S. government estimates that there are 100,000 such deaths a year, but that figure is only an educated guess. Many workers who die from occupational diseases never know the source of their condition. Besides this huge death toll, at least 2.2 million workers a year are injured in occupational accidents, and many more are probably made ill by the work they do.[31]

It is clear that some employers simply do not care about the deaths and injuries they cause their workers. New procedures are constantly being developed by indus-try, but few employers take time to test them adequately before bringing them into the workplace. There are now over half a million chemicals used in industry, but only a few thousand have been thoroughly tested to see if they are dangerous. And even when tests do show a chemical to be hazardous, some firms try to keep the results secret. For example, when an Italian scientist discovered that vinyl chloride (a popular plastic) causes a rare form of cancer that had been found among vinyl chloride work-ers, the Manufacturing Chemists Association joined with the European firm that spon-sored the research in a coordinated effort to keep the findings secret. Confidential memos indicate that the manufacturers of asbestos followed the same policy, and intentionally concealed the dangers of asbestos exposure from their workers. The ultimate death toll among these men and women is expected to be well over 200,000.[32] Nonetheless, there are signs of improvement. A growing concern about industrial safety, combined with the decline in the number of workers in the most dangerous occupations, has reduced the rate of job fatalities by a third in the last 20 years.[33]

The Labor Unions The early period of industrialization created misery among workers. Entire families labored in mines and factories. Industrialists paid the barest subsistence wages, claiming that workers were lazy and would stop working if they were better paid. Working conditions were terrible, and deaths from occupational accidents were rampant. Workdays were long, often 14 hours or more, and holidays were few and far between. Conditions were so bad that Karl Marx proclaimed that the workers would soon destroy capitalism in a violent revolution. But the workers did not respond with revolution. They responded with unionization.

The early labor unions faced bitter struggles with employers and the government, which supported the employers' interests. In many places unions were outlawed and organizers jailed; even when unionization became legal, organizers found themselves harassed at every turn. But the unions gradually gained official recognition and acceptance, and, as they won power, the conditions of the average worker improved. The unions eventually became a major economic and political force that was often critical to the success of politicians and business enterprises alike.

Yet despite the successes of the past, unions are in a serious decline. In 1970, almost 30 percent of those who worked for American business were in a union. Today that figure is only 12 percent, and, if current trends continue, it is expected to fall to as little as 5 percent by the year 2000.[34] And with dwindling membership has come

---

The threat of a strike has been the unions' most effective weapon in their struggle for better pay and working conditions. In today's anti-union climate, however, the number of successful strikes is far lower than it was in the past.

timidity and ineffectiveness. The average number of strikes a year has dropped to only one-fifth of what it was in earlier decades, and the wage settlements unions win are also far smaller than in the past.[35] Indeed, 17 percent of the strikes between 1985 and 1989 resulted in the permanent replacement of the strikers with nonunion labor.[36]

What caused this erosion of union membership and union power? Since union membership is highest in manufacturing and blue-collar jobs, a significant part of the decline in union membership resulted from a decrease in the importance of those occupations. Unions are now directing more efforts toward organizing government workers and white-collar employees, but resistance remains strong. Today's unions face other serious problems as well. On one side are the increasingly sophisticated industrial robots that threaten more and more union jobs; on the other are the masses of the world's poor who will eagerly work for a fraction of union wages. Ironically, increasing output through automation is one of the few ways workers in high-wage countries like the United States and Canada can continue to compete with low-wage workers in the Third World. Thus, the unions are often faced with the choice of losing jobs to automation or to foreign labor. To make matters worse for the unions, the conservative political trend has led to increasing government hostility toward the labor movement.

THE ECONOMIC CRISIS

North America has always been seen as the land of opportunity—a magnet that has attracted millions of immigrants over the years. Although times have not always been good, North Americans enjoyed a period of unprecedented prosperity after World War II, and it seemed for a time that the abundance would keep on growing forever. Many came to believe that each generation would inevitably be better off than its predecessor. But the 1970s saw a sharp reversal of those rosy economic trends, and today serious questions are being raised about the validity of the old assumptions and ideals.

Measuring economic trends is, however, no easy task. Comparisons between single years are misleading because all capitalist economies go through a **business cycle**: alternating periods of "boom" and "bust" in which the economy swings from growth and prosperity to stagnation and recession. During the downturns in the cycle, unemployment generally goes up while real wages (after controlling for inflation) stagnate or go down, and during the upswings these trends are reversed. **Inflation** is usually lower in the downward part of the cycle and higher during the upswing.

What is important, then, is not what happens in any particular year but the long-term trends. Such an analysis does not produce very optimistic conclusions. Inflation was significantly higher in the 1980s than it was in the 1950s and 1960s (although the oil crisis made the 1970s the worst of all). And decade by decade, the unemployment rate has only gone up. As noted earlier, the average unemployment rate in the 1980s was over 7 percent, and that was higher than the annual rate in all but two of the years between 1950 and 1979.[37] Real wages—perhaps the most significant indicator of economic well-being—have declined over 10 percent since their peak in

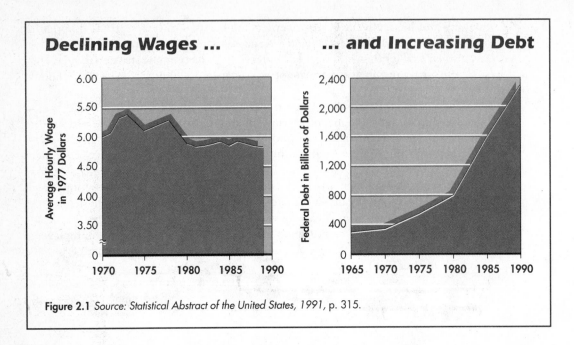

Figure 2.1 *Source: Statistical Abstract of the United States, 1991,* p. 315.

1973, and for young males the drop has been almost twice that much (see Figure 2.1).[38]

The 1980s also saw another important trend that bodes ill for the future—a huge increase in debt. In its first three years alone, the Reagan administration ran up more government debt than all its predecessors combined, and the mountain of red ink has continued to grow since then. Today, about one in every four dollars the federal government takes in (excluding social security) must be used to pay the interest on the national debt.[39] To finance this debt, the United States has had to borrow huge amounts of money abroad. Traditionally a creditor nation, the United States became a net debtor in 1985, and today it has larger debts than any other nation in the world. But this explosion of debt was not confined to the government. A wave of buyouts and takeovers led to huge increases in corporate debt during the 1980s. And consumers, struggling to keep their standard of living growing, almost tripled their debt to a staggering $3.4 trillion in 1990.[40] As a result, the number of bankruptcies (personal and business) also nearly tripled during the last ten years.[41] Obviously, we cannot go on borrowing from the future forever. Sooner or later these debts must be paid off, and when that happens, it is bound to put more downward pressure on our standard of living.

The Causes To solve these economic problems, we must understand their causes, and the first place to look is the changing world economy. At the end of World War II, all the major industrialized nations except for the United States and Canada lay in ruins. Because the factories of North America emerged from the war undamaged, their products were sometimes the only ones available. As Europe and Japan began to recover from the war, they were hungry consumers of North American goods. The United States became the world's dominant economic power, and the American dollar was virtually an international currency. But that era is over. Europe and Japan now have vigorous industries of their own that compete with American firms in the world market.

But all the new competition does not come from foreign companies. As we have seen, the big American corporations have become truly international organizations with little allegiance to the interests of their home country. Because the United States was the most prosperous country in the world during the postwar period, its workers received the highest wages. But the availability of cheap labor in the poor nations led large American corporations to shift many of their manufacturing operations to other countries, thus increasing unemployment in the United States.

The increase in world competition was an inevitable result of the recovery from the devastation of World War II. But many American industries have failed to keep up with that foreign competition. For example, the American markets for radios, stereos, videocassette recorders, and cameras are now dominated by Japanese firms. Many other domestic industries, such as shoe manufacturing, survive only because they are protected from foreign competition by tariffs (taxes on imports) or by import quotas.

Why aren't American products more competitive? The high wages paid to workers and managers is certainly one factor. But Americans have enjoyed a higher standard of living than most of the rest of the world for generations; moreover, the cost of labor in some European countries is now actually higher than in the United States. (U.S. managers, however, continue to earn much more than their European and Japanese counterparts.) The key to maintaining a high standard of living and competitiveness in the world market lies in high productivity. If workers make more products per hour, they can be paid higher wages without increasing the price of the products they make. The shift to a service-based economy makes it harder to measure productivity accurately, but it is generally agreed that although the American work force remains among the most productive in the world, many other nations have been improving their productivity considerably faster.

The most obvious cause of this faltering productivity is the fact that the United States continued to use some aging and inefficient factories built well before World War II. In contrast, West Germany and Japan were forced to rebuild their factories virtually from scratch after the war. The war alone is not, however, a sufficient explanation. After all, American businesses could have built new factories, since the United States was the world's strongest financial power during most of the postwar period. As compared with its principal competitors, the United States has reinvested a significantly lower percentage of its national income in new plants and equipment. On the average, Japan invests twice the proportion of its national economy in new plants and equipment as the United States does, and West Germany about 50 percent more.[42]

Much the same picture comes from a look at another major key to a healthy economy: investment in research and development. Expressed as a percentage of the gross national product, private corporations spend about 25 percent more on civilian research and development in Germany and about 50 percent more in Japan.[43] Government outlays for research and development are also important, but here America's problem is slightly different. The U.S. government spends over 65 percent of its research budget on military projects, while in Japan that figure is less than 5 percent.[44] Moreover, federal spending for other things that produce long-term improvements in productivity, such as highways, dams, and education, has been slashed since 1980. The federal investment in building projects has dropped 34 percent (as a percentage of the national income), and its investment in education has declined 27 percent.[45]

There are many reasons why the United States has failed to reinvest enough money to keep its industries leaders in the world market. Part of the problem is psychological. Americans became complacent about their technological edge and decided to enjoy the fruits of their labor instead of investing for the future. The oligopolistic control of key manufacturing industries is another crucial factor. When the major corporations in an industry work together to control the market for their products, they have less incentive to make big new investments in plants or equipment because their profits are already assured. The huge overseas investments made by American companies in the last few decades are also important because the flow of money out of the country has reduced the pool of capital available for domestic investment.

The economic domination of the large corporations has hurt reinvestment in another way: when large firms decide to use some of their profits to move into a new industry, they generally buy out an existing firm rather than build a new factory. Thus, money that would otherwise have been used for basic investments ends up being paid out to the stockholders of the firms that are being bought out. The desire to expand into a new business is not the only, or even the most harmful, motivation for corporate acquisitions. In the 1980s, an increasing number of wealthy "corporate raiders" were buying up corporations with borrowed money, and leaving them with such heavy debt that the firms were later forced into bankruptcy.

One of the biggest drains of investment comes from the heavy military burden carried by the United States. The enormous cost of the American defense establishment siphons off billions of dollars that might otherwise be used for more economically productive ventures. Although some nations, such as North Korea and Israel, spend a greater percentage of their income on the military, it is no coincidence that America's strongest economic competitors carry a far lighter military burden (see Figure 2.2).

One final factor in our current economic problems must be mentioned: the environment. Much of the reason North Americans traditionally enjoyed a higher standard of living than the rest of the world was the vast stores of natural resources that were easily put into use—productive farmlands, timber, coal, iron, and petroleum, to name just a few. But North Americans were foolish and shortsighted in their exploitation of these natural treasures. The environment was seen as an endless horn of plenty, whole forests were razed, farmlands overworked, and petroleum reserves pumped dry. Moreover, the dizzying growth in population has meant that the resources that remain must serve the needs of more and more people every year (see Chapter 17).

The Consequences These facts and figures may seem distant and abstract, but they reflect fundamental economic changes that are transforming the way we live. Despite these

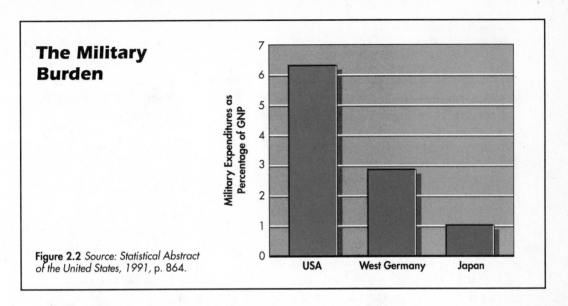

The Military Burden

Military Expenditures as Percentage of GNP

USA West Germany Japan

Figure 2.2 *Source: Statistical Abstract of the United States, 1991, p. 864.*

economic difficulties, Americans have managed to keep their standard of living grow-ing. From 1970 to 1989, average household income increased about 3.5 percent after controlling for inflation,[46] but this figure was achieved only because more and more married women have gone to work outside the home (see Chapter 5). In other words, declining real wages have meant that more people have to work to earn the same or a slightly higher standard of living. One obvious consequence of this trend is a sharp drop in leisure time and a high level of personal stress. According to the Harris poll, the amount of leisure time enjoyed by the average American has decreased 32 percent since 1973.[47] Almost 60 percent of Americans report that they experience "high stress" at least once or twice a week, and 30 percent say they live with high stress every day.[48] This growing burden has probably been an important contributor to the declining birthrate, as couples have less time for children and the demands they inevitably make.

Another major consequence of these economic changes is an increasing gap be-tween the "haves" and the "have-nots." The old saying about the rich getting richer and the poor getting poorer was not true for most of the postwar years until the 1970s. But according to a study by the Congressional Budget Office, the portion of the national income earned by the bottom half of the population dropped 9 percent from 1977 to 1988; during that same period, the top 1 percent's portion of the national income increased by a huge 46 percent.[49] These changes hit particularly hard at young people at the beginning of their careers, whose wages have undergone the sharpest decline of any population group. Runaway inflation in the price of a family home (a 1,200 percent increase since 1960) has locked many younger people out of the housing market and provided windfall profits to their elders who purchased a home when prices were low.[50]

RESPONDING TO THE ECONOMIC CRISIS

A staggering number of proposals for dealing with the economic crisis have been advanced. Most of them can be grouped into two broad categories. The first category contains ideas about ways to improve the economy and reverse the economic stagnation just described. The second category includes proposals for adjusting to the new economic environment and improving the quality of life regardless of the ups and downs of the economy. Advocates of the first kind of proposals often claim that their theories can restore the vigorous economic growth of the past, whereas advocates of the other approach are more likely to feel that those days are gone forever. Despite such disagreements, both kinds of responses will be needed if this critical problem is to be brought under control.

Rebuilding the Economy Some strategies to revitalize the economy cut across ideological lines. For example, the proposals to raise tariff barriers to protect U.S. industries from foreign competition have supporters and opponents from throughout the political spectrum (see the Debate in this chapter). But in general, the political right and left propose very different strategies to rebuild the economy. Conservatives generally want to cut back on the size of government in order to free more money for private investment and to reduce sharply the government's role in regulating the economy to avoid the inefficiency they feel regulation produces. Thus, many conservatives advocate a sharp across-the-board cut in taxes. Supporters of *supply-side economics*— so named because it focuses on increasing the supply of goods, unlike the more traditional approach, which seeks to increase demand—argue that such tax cuts would create so much economic growth that they would make up for the lower tax rates. More traditional conservatives feel that deep reductions in spending will be needed to bring the federal budget back into balance. And both groups of conservatives agree that tax cuts will stimulate investment by putting more money into the hands of the wealthy than they are likely to spend. The economic benefits that those investments produce are supposed to "trickle down" to the average citizen. Critics argue that such policies are unfair, because they benefit the rich far more than the poor. The also note that tax breaks for the wealthy are often spent on luxuries or invested in things like gold and antiques and therefore produce few benefits for anyone but the rich. Supply-siders have come under especially severe attack in recent years, because the tax cuts of the Reagan era did not produce the additional revenue they promised but only a huge increase in the national debt. Critics also charge that the conservatives' push to cut back on government regulation has created serious economic problems and was the direct cause of the savings and loan crisis.

The principal alternative to the conservative program calls for much greater *economic planning* on the part of the government. Advocates of economic planning point out that the governments of America's successful economic competitors—Germany, Sweden, and Japan—are much more deeply involved in planning and directing the economies of their nations than is the U.S. government. In these countries, government, private industry, and labor unions work much more closely together. Proponents of this approach argue that the government must develop a comprehensive

D E B A T E

Should We Increase Tariff Barriers to Protect Our Industry from Foreign Competition?

Countless suggestions have been made to solve our economic crisis. One proposal is to enact new import taxes that will make foreign products more expensive. It is hoped that such legislation would encourage consumers to buy more domestic products and thus create more American jobs.

YES Our basic industries are in the midst of an unprecedented economic crisis. The stores are flooded with cheap imports, the rates of industrial unemployment and bankruptcies are soaring out of control, and large parts of the industrial Midwest are turning into a "rust bowl" reminiscent of the "dust bowl" of the Great Depression. Something must be done or we will soon be facing an economic collapse.

The cause of all these problems is not difficult to find. It is unfair competition from corporations that pay virtual starvation wages in poor countries around the world. How can North American workers ever compete with workers who are eager to accept jobs that pay only a few dollars a week? Some claim we can compete by increasing our productivity. Such an increase may help, but it can never solve the fundamental problem. For one thing, increased productivity means using fewer workers to produce more goods, and that obviously will do nothing to help unemployment. More important, we must realize that the world is now an integrated community, and technological advances that used to give our workers a big advantage in productivity spread quickly to factories in other parts of the world.

The only solution to this growing crisis is to put up stronger barriers to foreign imports. Critics claim such a program would spur other countries to raise their trade barriers and touch off a devastating trade war. Such fears are not groundless, but

NO It is always tempting to pursue easy solutions to complex problems. Our economic difficulties have many causes, but they cannot be cured by the quick fix of protectionism. It seems simple enough to say that the best way to help firms losing sales and jobs to foreign competition is to keep foreign products out of the country. But the matter is much more complex than that. History has shown that when one country raises its trade barriers, other nations respond by raising theirs, which in turn spurs more retaliation. If the spiral is not checked, the ultimate result is a trade war like the one that contributed so much to the Great Depression. We dare not be fooled into thinking that a depression as severe as the one in the 1930s can never happen again. It can, and a new wave of protectionism is likely to set it off.

But even if protectionist policies do not start another depression, they are likely to have other harmful consequences. The absence of cheap foreign goods will lead to an increase in prices that will make us long for the double-digit inflation of the 1970s, and some goods we do not produce at home will not be available at any price. Without foreign competition the pace of technological innovation will slacken, our industries will become less and less efficient, and the quality of our products will decline. But the most devastating consequences will be to the poorest people of the world. Without the North American market, many foreign companies would fail, and the a carefully thought out program that retaliated only against nations that consistently sell far more products to us than they buy could avoid this problem. For example, if we reduced our trade deficit with Japan from $40 or $50 billion a year to $10 billion, how could the Japanese retaliate without hurting themselves still further? Another objection to raising trade barriers is that it will hurt American consumers by increasing the cost of the goods that are available. But what is the use of low-priced goods if we have no jobs to earn money to pay for them? The ultimate choice is simple: either our workers must learn to live on wages comparable to those paid in India and Hong Kong, or we must protect them from foreign competition. Surely we must choose the second alternative.

already staggering levels of unemployment in the Third World would become unmanageable. The ultimate result would be starvation and massive political unrest.

The proposals to raise our trade barriers are not really intended to help the economy as a whole. Rather, they are designed to benefit a small group of workers in failing heavy industries who are so overpaid that they have simply priced themselves out of the world market. The majority of our people would be better off without trade protectionism. The best way to solve our economic problems is to make our industry slimmer and more efficient so that it can compete on the world market, not to let it rot behind artificial trade barriers.

---

economic plan that identifies areas of economic strength and weakness and outlines a coherent series of programs to improve the economic environment.

Although advocates of economic planning have not agreed on a set of specific programs, many suggestions have been made. One proposal is to create a federal bank or finance corporation to provide special low-interest loans to high-growth industries and to assist older industries to become more competitive. Another is to reduce American military spending to the same level as our main economic competitors and redirect the savings into more productive programs. For example, supporters of economic planning recommend that much more money and effort be spent on education so that the schools can teach the growing population of poor and immigrant children the skills needed in a high-tech economy. Another pressing need, according to supporters of economic planning, is to create better systems of mass transit and to rebuild our decaying highways and railroads.

In addition to the call for greater economic planning, many progressives advocate new programs to encourage *economic democracy*. Past experience has shown that employees have a more cooperative attitude, accept necessary cuts in wages, and work harder when they are their own bosses. It therefore seems logical that the government assist workers to take over the ownership of financially troubled firms, help workers start new cooperative enterprises, and pass legislation to force financially healthy employers to give workers more power to control their economic destiny. Many supporters of economic democracy feel that forceful action must also be taken to loosen the big corporations' domination of the economy. They advocate much tougher enforcement of antitrust laws, legislation to require major corporations to place publicly elected representatives on their boards of directors, and the nation-alization of corporations that restrict free competition or repeatedly act against the public interest.

Critics of the government's role in the economy point to the damage done by some government programs in the past. They argue that, as in the communist countries, deep government involvement in the economy results in waste and inefficiency. Supporters of economic planning say that the conditions here are completely different and that we should seek a healthy balance that avoids both the anarchy and exploitation that comes from unregulated capitalism and the oppressive centralized control of the communist system.

There are also many ways private firms can improve their own operations. American management has recently come under strong criticism from such unexpected sources as the *Harvard Business Review* and *Business Week*. These critics are charging that American managers are too concerned with short-term profits and paying big dividends to their stockholders and that such attitudes are harmful to the long-term interests of their companies. The critics also charge that far too many American managers are accountants and lawyers who don't understand their firm's products and how they are made. To deal with this problem, it is often proposed that American managers adopt some of the techniques of their successful foreign competitors. More specifically, it is suggested that managers be rewarded for actions that contribute to the long-term, not the short-term, interests of their company and that more engineers and scientists be promoted to top management positions. Many experts also recommend that American managers learn from the Japanese approach to labor, which has worked so successfully in the last several decades. One component of this success has been greater worker involvement in the decision-making process, which not only fosters a greater commitment to the organization but also takes advantage of the workers' intimate knowledge of the day-to-day problems that arise on the job. But greater commitment by workers to their company requires the employer to show greater commitment to its workers by avoiding layoffs and making a genuine effort to improve their welfare.

Adjusting to Economic Change Because of increasing international competition and dwindling natural resources, many social scientists are convinced that there is nothing we can do that will create new economic growth comparable to that of the 1950s and 1960s, and that we must therefore take measures to adjust to slower growth and longer periods of recession.

Because most nations depend on economic growth to create enough new jobs for their expanding work force, economic stagnation threatens millions of people with permanent joblessness or underemployment. Moreover, the programs to improve productivity may actually make unemployment worse. When an employer buys more efficient machines to increase the workers' productivity, fewer people are needed on the assembly line and surplus workers are laid off.

Western European nations have responded to this problem with large-scale programs of job retraining. The idea is to train unskilled workers for new occupations, as well as to retrain skilled workers who have lost jobs in declining industries. Such a program is clearly needed in the United States. However, even if all unemployed workers were retrained, there would still not be enough jobs to go around. Either workers must put in fewer hours to spread the work around, or new jobs must be created. One response to this problem is the call for government to create jobs for those who are unable to find any other work. Critics charge that such "make-work" programs are wasteful and inefficient, but it is difficult to see how they could be more wasteful than unemployment itself. Nonetheless, it is important that new job programs be effectively managed and targeted to meet pressing social needs, such as highways and railroads, mass transit, and hydroelectric and solar energy plants. If these goals are met, such a program could provide a major boost for the economy.

More and more people are coming to believe that the economy should be made as diversified and as self-sufficient as possible. For example, it is about two decades since the first "energy crisis," yet the United States is still so dependent on foreign oil that a new crisis in the Middle East could have the same or even worse consequences. To reduce this danger, communities could be given more help to develop local hydroelectric and solar resources and to conserve energy with better insulation and effective systems of mass transit. By the same token, no one can predict how well any product will sell in the ever-changing world market. But a domestic program to stimulate the construction of new low-cost housing would not only improve the quality of life for the residents of the new homes but would stimulate an industry that is largely immune to foreign competition.

Finally, it is important to remember that the quality of life is not measured solely by the economist's computations of average income or the standard of living. The quality of life can be improved regardless of the economic climate. Numerous suggestions for such improvements are discussed in this book, including proposals to clean up the environment, make the workplace safer, reduce crime, improve the lives of the elderly and poor, and upgrade the educational system so that people can better understand the complexities of the world around them. Of course, all these things are expensive. But if only a small fraction of the money wasted on extravagant consumption were redirected to these ends, we could significantly improve the quality of our daily lives.

SOCIOLOGICAL PERSPECTIVES ON PROBLEMS OF THE ECONOMY

Shrinking wages, foreign competition, the hardships of unemployment, and similar difficulties seem to be matters for technically trained economists. Indeed, some economists devote their lives to the study and solution of these problems. But sociologists feel that a "dollars and cents" approach cannot, by itself, yield genuine understanding of our economic difficulties. To the sociologist, economic ills can be understood only in their social context. It makes no more sense to study economic problems apart from their social background than it does to try to solve social problems without understanding their economic basis. Sociologists use the three perspectives discussed in Chapter 1 to analyze economic problems and their relationship to society as a whole.

The Functionalist Perspective   Functionalists see the economic system as a machine that produces and distributes the commodities a society needs. If the system functions efficiently to give the society what it wants, there are few economic problems. But sometimes the machine balks or strains. One part may run faster or slower than others, throwing the whole system out of balance. For example, distribution may not keep up with production, or we may produce too many goods of one kind and not enough of another. Such maladjustments may correct themselves (free enterprise) or may be corrected by officials (government intervention). Economic crises occur when the whole machine becomes disorganized and coordination throughout the system falters.

Functionalists blame contemporary economic problems on rapid changes that have thrown the traditional system out of balance. It took hundreds of years for Western society to develop and perfect an economic system based on open competition among private individuals in a free market. But as the system became larger and more complex, its problems multiplied. As we have seen, huge corporations sprang up and gained control of many vital markets; the government stepped in to regulate the economy; and powerful unions began to control the labor market. Thus, these new cogs destabilized the old machinery. And as we were struggling to bring the system back into balance, major shifts were occurring in the world economy that greatly increased the competitive pressures on North American business. Under these conditions, many of the old economic ideas no longer worked as they had in the past, and dysfunctional economic decisions followed. The breathtaking pace of economic change made it impossible to resolve old economic problems before new ones arose.

Most functionalists shy away from radical, far-reaching proposals for solving economic problems, principally because they know that change brings problems as well as solutions. Disruptive change in an unbalanced system makes a new balance even more difficult to achieve. Functionalists favor specific, limited curves for specific, limited problems, such as education and training for the unemployed and better law enforcement to deter corporate crime. The basic goal of the functionalist is to reduce the disorganization in economic institutions and to improve the coordination between them and other social institutions. Only when this goal has been reached will the economic system function smoothly and efficiently.

The Conflict Perspective   Conflict theorists take a very different view of the economic system. Unlike functionalists, they do not consider society a unified whole based on a consensus about norms and values. Consequently, they do not say that the economic system performs either well or badly for the entire society; rather, they believe that it benefits certain groups at the expense of others, and that who benefits, and to what degree, changes from time to time.

From the conflict perspective, society is composed of many different groups, each trying to advance its economic interests at the expense of the others. Most economic problems arise because one group—or a coalition of groups—seizes economic power and acts in ways that advance its own interests at the expense of the rest of society. Thus, conflict theorists say that recent changes in the economic system reflect competition among different groups. Each works for its own selfish interests, as Adam Smith said they should. But conflict theorists do not, like Smith, assert that this competition brings advantages to everyone. They say it benefits only the most powerful competitive groups. Conflict theorists charge that ever since businesspeople and industrialists seized power from the landed nobility, they have busily enlarged their power and their affluence at the expense of everyone else.

According to the conflict perspective, the underlying cause of most economic problems is the exploitation of workers by their employers and other members of powerful elites. If these problems are to be solved, the workers must somehow gain enough control to make the elites give up their advantages and create a more just economic order. The first step, according to Marxists, is for oppressed workers to develop "class consciousness," a sense of unity based on the realization that they are being exploited. Then the workers must organize themselves for political action and achieve change either through peaceful conflicts—elections, protests, and strikes—or, if need be, through violent conflicts. Conflict theorists see the widening gap between the income of the haves and the have-nots as a direct result of the decline in the power of the unions and the failure of political organizations to represent the interests of working men and women. They feel that these trends must be reversed if most people are ever going to see their economic conditions improve.

Social Psychological Perspectives Because social psychologists are concerned mainly with individuals, they rarely address large-scale economic problems. Instead, they are more interested in the impact of the economic system on an individual's psychological makeup, attitudes, and behavior patterns. They also examine the impact of these ways of behaving on the larger economic system. Social psychologists have found, for example, that unemployment has devastating psychological consequences for many workers. Feelings of boredom, uselessness, and despair are common, and some frustrated workers suffer much more serious difficulties. Studies show that the rates of such stress-related problems as high blood pressure, alcoholism, mental disorder, and suicide are significantly higher among the unemployed. Unemployed workers are also more likely to lash out at those around them. An increase in the unemployment rate increases the rate of child abuse and other family violence.[51]

But the psychological damage caused by the economic system is not limited to the unemployed. Our competitive economy encourages a strong achievement motivation that often leads to dissatisfaction and anxiety. When a large percentage of a population is oriented toward individual competition, the culture they share is likely to show many forms of innovation and creativity. But this system also promotes insecurity, anxiety, and hostility. Social psychologists have observed, however, that these burdens are not equally shared by everyone in a society. On the average, the unskilled and downwardly mobile have far more social and psychological problems than other people. They are more likely to be hostile and aggressive and to suffer from low self-esteem and bouts of intense anxiety.

Effective solutions to the psychological problems created by our economic system are not easy to find. One possibility would be to deemphasize the values of competition and achievement and to emphasize instead cooperation and mutual support. But despite the fact that a noncompetitive orientation has long been stressed in family and religious institutions, its application to society at large meets with strong resistance. This opposition seems to be based on fear that reducing competitiveness will destroy initiative and creativity. Perhaps this is why more emphasis is placed on the clinical treatment of psychological disorders than on changing the economic and social conditions that produce them. But many social psychologists continue to argue that reducing economic insecurity, even in a competitive society, would improve the mental health of our entire population.

SUMMARY

Change has come so rapidly to our economic system that many people have difficulty seeing things as they really are. One common mistake is to look at the American economy as though it were an independent, self-contained system and to overlook its dependence on the web of international relationships that make up the world economy. A second is the belief that the American economy is an open, free-market system much like the one described by Adam Smith; in reality, the growth of giant corporations, labor unions, and big government has wrought fundamental changes in the way the economy operates.

The corporation is a major force in the modern economic system. Some corporations have grown so large that they control dozens of different companies in many countries. Although the government no longer permits most markets to be controlled by a monopoly (one corporation), many industries are controlled by an oligopoly (a few large corporations). However, in recent years the entrance of new foreign firms into domestic markets has reintroduced competition into some oligopolistic industries.

There is considerable debate over who runs the corporations. Some people see stockholders as the owners and controllers, while others argue that power rests with corporate managers, who have the special technical skills needed to make decisions that will increase profits. Most sociologists hold that high-level corporate decision makers represent the interests of a small elite. Others suggest that the decision makers represent a wide variety of conflicting interests.

Most large corporations are multinationals; that is, they have offices and facilities in different nations around the world. These big multinationals are tied in to the world market, and often have little allegiance to the interests of their home country. Some think the multinationals are laying the foundation for a new era of world peace and cooperation, but others see them as exploiters of poor and powerless people.

In the United States, government, like corporations, has come to play a key role in the economic system. The government is not only a major employer but also is deeply involved in managing the economy.

Workers are at the heart of any industrial economy. Recent years have seen a sharp decline in the number of workers in the old manufacturing industries, but white-collar and service jobs have been on the increase. Women, especially married women, have been entering the work force in increasing numbers, and unemployment and underemployment remain a significant problem.

The United States is faced with a crisis posed by the stagnation of its economy. Numerous explanations for this stagnation have been offered, including increased competition in the world economy, faltering American productivity, and less abundant natural resources. In a growing number of families, these changes have forced both husbands and wives to take jobs outside the home, and there is a significant widening of the income gap between the rich and the poor. Many proposals have been made for dealing with this crisis, most of which focus on either rebuilding and improving the economy or adapting to the changing economic realities of our times.

KEY TERMS

business cycle The ups and downs that characterize the economies of all capitalist nations.

capitalism An economic system characterized by private property, profit orientation, and a competitive market for goods and labor.

inflation An increase in the average price of the goods consumers buy.

monopoly A market controlled by a single firm.

underemployment The situation of workers who want permanent, full-time work but can find only part-time or temporary work.

unemployment The situation of workers who want to work but cannot find a job.

world economy The system of international economic relationships in which all countries participate.

FURTHER READINGS

Kendall W. Stiles and Tsuneo Akaha, *International Political Economy: A Reader* (New York: HarperCollins, 1991). An excellent collection of articles that examine many of the key issues affecting the modern world economy.

Beth Mintz and Michael Schwartz, *The Power Structure of American Business* (Chicago: University of Chicago Press, 1985). A careful analysis of the power structure of the United States that emphasizes the dominating role of banks and other financial institutions.

Lester Thurow, *The Zero-Sum Solution* (New York: Simon & Schuster, 1986). Proposals by a well-known economist of some possible solutions to our economic problems.

David Bensman and Roberta Lynch, *Rusted Dreams: Hard Times in a Steel Community* (New York: McGraw-Hill, 1987). An analysis of what happened in a Chicago neighborhood when its major employer closed its doors.

Kitty Calavita and Henry N. Pontell, "Other People's Money Revisited: Collective Embezzlement in the Savings and Loan and Insurance Industry," *Social Problems* 38 (1991): 94–111. An insightful analysis of the role of criminal fraud in the savings and loan crisis.

chapter 3

Problems of Government

- Why do we have so much bureaucracy?
- Do special-interest groups serve a useful purpose?
- Is there a power elite?
- What are the threats to our civil liberties?
- How can government be made more democratic?

The essence of politics is **power**—the power to determine what is a criminal act and what is not, the power to start or avoid wars, the power to collect vast sums of money and spend them on everything from ballpoint pens to nuclear bombs. Those who wield political power regulate thousands of aspects of our daily lives, from issuing birth certificates to demanding burial licenses. Clearly, political institutions are of crucial importance to modern society; when the government stumbles, it's everybody's problem.

A government may fail its citizens in countless ways, but the central concern of any democratic government is democracy itself: the need to reflect fairly the will of the people. Despite centuries of developmental changes and reforms, true democracy is still a long way off. Democratic governments are subjected to fierce pressures from powerful groups seeking special privileges at the public's expense, and the people themselves sometimes give up their democratic rights and responsibilities. In times of war or severe economic depression, people sometimes seem willing to give almost unlimited power to leaders who promise to set things right.

Government is also crucial in providing solutions to social problems. Even such personal problems as divorce, mental disorder, and drug addiction have their political side. In modern societies such problems are often given to the government to handle, usually by passing new laws or spending tax dollars in ways that are expected to help. As government has grown in size and influence, it has become the principal institution for dealing with social problems. It is hard to imagine effective solutions to such diverse issues as crime, poverty, environmental pollution, or urban decay without political action. Yet the government's efforts to cope with such pressing problems are often disorganized, underfunded, and ineffective.

THE GROWTH OF GOVERNMENT

Governments throughout the world have been growing rapidly since the beginning of this century. For example, in 1940, federal spending equaled about 10 percent of the goods and services produced in the United States; by 1988, it equaled about one-fourth.[1] In 1929, the year of the great stock market crash, there were a little more than 3 million government employees in the United States; today there are almost 19 million. Of course, the country's population was also increasing, but the percentage of all those employed by the government still rose from 6.5 to 15.1 percent. The charge that there has been runaway growth in the size of the government in recent years is false, however. There has actually been a significant decline in the percentage of the labor force employed by the government since 1980, when it totaled 16.4 percent; and the share of our national income that goes to taxes has also gone down since then.[2]

The influence of government on the daily lives of its citizens has grown along with its size. In past centuries most centralized governments were distant and ineffective. Important decisions were made locally and were based on custom and tradition. Today governments are much stronger and less tightly bound by traditional restraints. But most of this growth in size and influence has been a response to changes in other social institutions. As the family became smaller and less stable, the government had to assume some of the functions that the family once performed, such as educating children and caring for the elderly. Similarly, industrialization has produced economic instability that has proven too great for private firms to manage. Even in the United States, with its deep suspicion of centralized authority, conditions became so bad during the Great Depression that the government was forced to get more involved in the economy.

The Nature of Bureaucracy   The first thing that most of us think of when someone mentions **bureaucracy** is the huge labyrinth of federal offices and bureaus. Although the federal government of the United States is one of the largest bureaucracies that have ever existed, from a sociological standpoint most private corporations are just as bureaucratic. In fact, one researcher concluded that over 90 percent of all American workers are employed in some kind of bureaucratic organization.[3] What then is a bureaucracy? Max Weber, a founder of modern sociology and one of the first to study bureaucratic organizations, concluded that they have five defining characteristics:

1. A clear-cut *division of labor*. Each office has its own task to perform, and workers are specialists.
2. A *hierarchy of authority*. Each worker is part of a ranked order in which superiors supervise and direct their subordinates.
3. A set of *formal rules* that guide the workers and supervisors and the operations of the organization as a whole.
4. *Impersonal enforcement of rules.* Officials treat all people impersonally, applying the rules to specific cases without feelings for or against the individuals involved.
5. *Job security.* Employment in a bureaucracy is based on technical qualifications; the employee who does his or her duty is protected against arbitrary dismissal. Promotion is decided on according to objective standards and rules.[4]

Of course, this is only a theoretical model—no real organization can meet all these criteria perfectly. Many of the studies since Weber's time have therefore focused on bureaucracy's other face: the informal procedures and routines that develop among individual employees. It is common, for example, for the responsibilities of an incompetent official to be taken over by lower-status employees, or for employees to swap some of their duties unofficially. Sometimes rules are so awkward that employees must develop ways of circumventing them if they are to get the job done. In fact, when employees want to protest their working conditions without actually going on strike, they sometimes "work to the rule." That is, they follow every rule to the letter and do nothing not specified by the rules; and as a result, productivity inevitably plummets.

Although everyone complains about bureaucratic waste, Weber and many other sociologists see bureaucracies as the most effective form of large-scale social organization. Although some bureaucracies are inefficient, the other options are even worse. The principal alternative to bureaucracy is an organization based on personal loyalty and allegiance without formal rules. Such an organization can work extremely well as long as the person at the top is fair and effective, but eventually the complete reliance on the whims and personal preferences of a single individual usually gets the organization into trouble. Moreover, when that person dies or steps down, these

Both public and private bureaucracies have grown rapidly in the last century, and complaints about their dehumanizing effects are voiced by many people.

organizations are thrown into a crisis, while in a bureaucracy one official is easily replaced by another. As Weber put it, bureaucratic organization "is, from a purely technical point of view, capable of attaining the highest degree of efficiency. . . . It is superior to any other form in precision, in stability, in the stringency of its discipline, and in its reliability."[5]

The Problems of Bureaucracy The strength of a bureaucracy can also be its weakness, however. The formal rules that permit a government agency to function smoothly can also drown it in a sea of red tape. No system of rules is perfect, and when unusual cases occur, it may be necessary to bend the rules to meet the organization's goals. But meeting these goals is not the only concern of most employees of bureaucratic organizations. Holding on to their jobs is often a more important aim, and because they can be fired for breaking rules, the tendency is to play it safe. Employees try to give at least the appearance of following all the rules, regardless of the consequences for the organization. For example, a welfare worker may know that a family is needy and deserves government assistance but is ineligible because of some technicality. An employee who is afraid to violate the rules "passes the buck" by sending the applicant to another office. At the next office the applicant may be referred to someone else, and so on through the bureaucratic maze while the family goes hungry.

Such **displacement of goals** is extremely common in bureaucracies both in the government and in private industry.[6] Even Max Weber was concerned about the depersonalizing effects of bureaucratization. He came to fear that the unending drive for bureaucratic efficiency would imprison people in an "iron cage" of reason, with little room for human emotions.

The problems of depersonalization and goal displacement are produced by the structural demands of bureaucratic operation, but other common problems come from the activities of individual employees or the way the organization as a whole is run. Foremost among these is the favoritism and corruption that plagues so many government agencies around the world. A second common problem is the inefficiency and waste that often result from the failure of the legislature or executive to provide clear goals and to closely supervise the operation of public bureaucracies. Finally, bureaucracies often become a powerful political force in themselves, lobbying for programs and policies that may not be in the public interest.[7]

WHO RUNS THE GOVERNMENT?

Many governments claim to be democratic, but few actually are. Even the claims of such countries as Britain, the United States, and Canada that "the people" hold the political power are open to question. Does power really reside in the people, or is it in the hands of special-interest groups or an exclusive "power elite?" There is no simple answer. An enormous number of factors influence important government decisions—including court rulings and administrative decisions as well as actual lawmaking. Exactly how these decisions are made, or by whom, has been the subject of much research, but the results are open to conflicting interpretations.

The Citizens   In an ideal democracy, political power is shared by all citizens. But today's nation-states are too large for direct participation by everyone, making elected representatives a special power group in and of themselves. This is not to say that elected representatives never express the interests of the majority of their constituents. Majority rule is certainly possible, but there are sizable obstacles in its way.

One of the major problems of any democracy is the apathy of its citizens. The number of Americans who vote has never been high, and it has declined significantly in recent years. The percentage of eligible citizens who vote in presidential elections dropped from 63 percent in 1960 to 50 percent in 1988, and the turnout is even lower when only congressional or local offices are at stake. In the 1990 congressional elections, only 36 percent of those eligible actually voted.[8] Other forms of political participation, such as working in a political campaign or taking part in a political rally, are even less common than voting.

It is not necessary for all the citizens in a democracy to participate if those who do are representative of those who do not. But this is not the case. Studies of citizen participation reveal a strange paradox. Those who most need the government's help are least likely to take part in the political process. People with higher incomes and better education are much more likely to be active politically, while minorities and the poor are less likely to get involved.[9] Thus, it seems that wealth and education

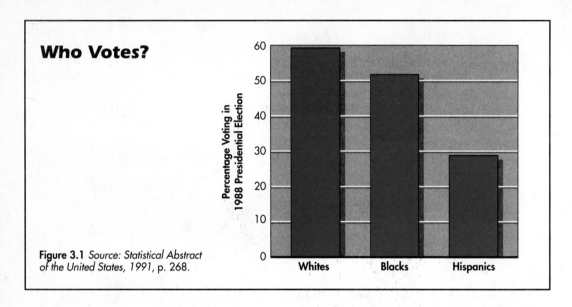

Who Votes?

Percentage Voting in 1988 Presidential Election

Whites   Blacks   Hispanics

Figure 3.1 *Source: Statistical Abstract of the United States, 1991, p. 268.*

create the interest and the resources necessary for political participation (see Figure 3.1). There are, however, some signs of hope. Years of effort by black leaders to register voters have succeeded in reducing the voting gap in recent years.

But even citizens who are interested in politics often find it difficult to decide where a particular politician stands on the issues. For one thing, politicians often try to conceal their opinions about controversial matters. In addition, the voters seldom get a chance to talk directly with candidates, relying instead on the mass media for their information. Effective campaigners try to project a positive image in their advertising and television speeches, which often have little to do with the issues. Advertising agencies sell candidates like soaps and deodorants. In a 30-second television commercial there is little time for serious consideration of political issues. Moreover, candidates of minor political parties and those without strong financial backing have little access to the media and are thus frozen out of the arena of serious political debate.

Another source of voter apathy is distrust of the government and a feeling of powerlessness. Many people do not think their votes or opinions count for much against the powerful special-interest groups and the huge number of other voters. A single vote, the argument goes, is almost never decisive in even the closest elections.

Special-Interest Groups   Legislators and other government officials are strongly influenced by **special-interest groups** that have a particular stake in specific legislation. Physicians, realtors, small businesses, big businesses, labor unions, and numerous others are all special-interest groups. Many such groups are concerned about the laws and policies that affect their economic well-being. Other people form organizations because of their feelings about a certain issue. Examples include antiabortion groups, civil liberties groups, and patriotic groups. The influence of these groups depends to a large extent on their size, their degree of organization, and the money at their disposal. Big business is the most powerful of all interest groups because it has command of more of those resources.

Lobbying various legislative bodies is the principal activity of most special-interest groups. The lobbyists' principal aim is to convince lawmakers to pass the kind of legislation they desire. One of their most effective tools is information. Because individual legislators are seldom well informed on all the bills they must consider, and because legislative bodies lack the funds to make independent investigations of all the issues before them, the facts and figures supplied by lobbyists can often sway lawmakers' votes. Lobbyists also try to influence legislation by cultivating the friendship of individual legislators. Many well-heeled Washington lobbyists are notorious for their lavish parties and their ingratiating manner. Moreover, a lobbyist's promise of political support from a powerful special interest often determines an elected official's decision. Threats by a special interest can be effective too. Opposition by a powerful labor union or an important corporation has resulted in the defeat of many politicians.

Money is one of the special-interest groups' main resources. Political campaigns are becoming more and more expensive, and the special interests are supplying the money. The price tag of the presidential campaign has increased from under $20 million in 1960 to over $200 million in 1988, and that amount was spent after a primary campaign costing another $200 million.[10] In 1990, the *average* senator's reelection campaign cost almost $4 million, which means that senators need to raise at least $12,000 every week of their six-year term to finance their next campaign (see Figure 3.2).[11] Most of the money comes from powerful special interests. One of the

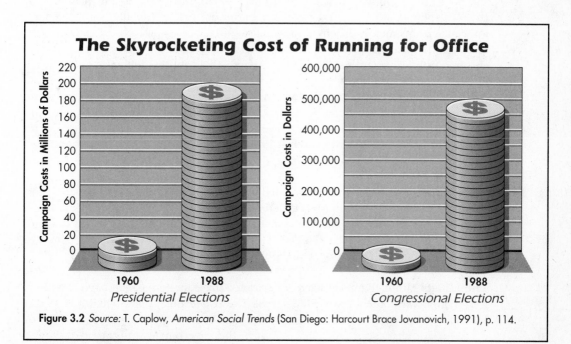

Figure 3.2 *Source:* T. Caplow, *American Social Trends* (San Diego: Harcourt Brace Jovanovich, 1991), p. 114.

main sources of funding is the political action committees (PACs) set up to represent various special-interest groups. And, of course, many of the individual contributions come from people with a particular interest in a specific policy or program. For example, it has become common for a group of executives who work for a corporation seeking some political favor to send in large "personal" contributions at the same time—a practice that has come to be known as "bundling."[12]

Politicians inevitably claim that such contributions are merely a sign of support from those who favor their policies and have no influence on their votes, but few outside observers find such statements very convincing. It is too simplistic to say that most politicians overtly sell favors and influence for campaign contributions (although periodic corruption scandals show that it certainly does occur), but those millions of dollars often exert a dominating influence on the political process.

In theory, the ability of special interests to hire lobbyists and give campaign contributions that help elect sympathetic politicans wouldn't make much difference as long as supporters on both sides of important issues had roughly the same amount of money to spend. But that is clearly not the case. In the year and a half from the start of 1985 to June of 1986, PACs representing corporate interests gave over three and a half times more money to politicians than the PAC representing labor.[13] Even more unequal was the battle between corporate polluters and the environmentalists. In 1983 and 1984, environmental groups gave $275,000 to members of the House, while the chemical industry alone gave $4.5 million in an effort to head off tougher environmental restrictions. This same disparity is reflected in the contributions to political parties. In 1985–1986, the Republican party's three main campaign committees raised $252 million, while the Democrats raised only $61 million.[14] Obviously, the poor and the underprivileged will never be able to spend as much money to advance their political interests as the wealthy do, just as broadly based "general interest" groups such as the environmentalists and the consumer advocates are unable to match the financial power of the big corporations whose policies they oppose.

Some political scientists argue that, despite their abuses, lobbyists and special-interest groups are important to a political democracy. Like political parties, they provide a channel of communication between citizens and their government. Moreover, reasonable political compromises can come out of the conflict between competing interest groups. But the poor, the uneducated, and the deprived lack the resources to create an effective interest group and are therefore denied the right to participate in this key political arena.

Is There a Power Elite?   One of the most heated debates in the social sciences concerns the existence of what C. Wright Mills called a power elite—a small unified ruling class. Supporters of the idea that the United States and other capitalist nations are ruled by a small upper class are called **elitists**. Those who believe that political decisions are made by changing coalitions of many political forces are called **pluralists**.

The Elitists Although radicals have long argued that America is dominated by a small group of powerful men, it was Mills's book *The Power Elite*, published in the 1950s, that started the current debate. According to Mills, the power elite is a coalition of people in the highest ranks of the economy, the government, and the military who together form a unified and self-conscious social class:

There is no longer, on the one hand, an economy and, on the other hand, a political world, containing a military establishment unimportant to politics and to money-making. There is a political economy numerously linked with military order and decision. This triangle of power is now a structural fact, and it is the key to any understanding of the higher circles in America today. For as each of these domains has coincided with the others, as decisions in each have become broader, the leading men of each—the high military, the corporation executive, the political directorate—have tended to come together to form the power elite of America.[15]

According to Mills, one of the major sources of the unity of the power elite is its members' common social background. They tend to come from upper-class and upper-middle-class white families living in urban areas. They attend the same Ivy League colleges and, by and large, share the same attitudes toward the world and their position in it. In addition, the social networks that they represent are closely interconnected, with many common interests. Finally, although the power elite does not represent some great conspiracy, its members meet both socially and professionally and often coordinate their activities.

Below the power elite Mills saw two other levels of power in American society. At the bottom of the heap are the great masses of people—unorganized, ill informed, and virtually powerless. Between these masses and the elite are the "middle levels" of power, where some true competition between interest groups still exists. Mills saw the U.S. Congress as part of these middle levels of power. Although Congress decides some minor issues, the power elite ensures that no serious challenge to its control is tolerated in the political arena.

More recent writings of the elitist school accept Mills's conclusion that power is concentrated in the hands of the few but question his inclusion of the military leadership in the power elite. Although they recognize the importance of the military, they are convinced that the most critical decisions, even in the field of international relations, are made by an economic-political elite. This elite is not, however, an equal partnership between top corporate and top government officials. The lion's share of the power is held by those in key positions of corporate power, for they not only greatly outnumber powerful government officials but possess far more wealth, and their careers are not dependent on the uncertainties of the electoral process.[16]

The Pluralists Pluralists believe that democratic societies are indeed democratic. Although they recognize that there is a large apolitical mass with little power, they argue that critical political decisions are not made by a single "power elite" but are decided in a contest among many competing groups. David Riesman, a pluralist writing at about the same time as Mills, arrived at some very different conclusions. He called interest groups "veto groups" because he thought their main objective was merely to block policies that might threaten their interests.[17] Where Mills saw common interests among powerful groups, Riesman saw divergence; where Mills saw growing concentration of power, Riesman saw growing dispersion of power.

Current pluralist thought runs along the lines taken by Riesman. However, his idea that interest groups are concerned mainly with stopping unacceptable proposals is no longer widely accepted. Arnold M. Rose, a sociologist who was also a state legislator, pointed out the obvious fact that interest groups take action on their own behalf. From Rose's perspective, the pluralist:

conceives of society as consisting of many elites, each relatively small numerically, and operating in different spheres of life. . . . While it is true that there are inert masses of undifferentiated individuals without access to each other (except in the most trivial respects) and therefore without influence, the bulk of the population consists not of the mass but of integrated groups and publics, stratified with varying degrees of power.[18]

The debate between the elitists and the pluralists is not likely to be resolved quickly. As G. William Domhoff has pointed out, "These disagreements often reflect differences in style, temperament and degree of satisfaction with the status quo as well as more intellectual differences concerning the structure and distribution of political power."[19] Indeed, both sides seem to agree on more than they are willing to admit. Most elitists will grant that conflicting interest groups play a political role at some level of power, and most pluralists will grant that a disproportionate share of the power is held by elites. The real question is a factual one: How unified or competitive are the elites?

THE MILITARY

The military poses a dilemma for democratic societies. It is essential but at the same time extremely dangerous. With its traditions of command, authority, and unquestioning obedience, the military often responds when disorganization and confusion paralyze a democratic government. The list of struggling democracies that have been taken over by their military is a long one, particularly in the less developed nations of Asia, Africa, and Latin America. Developed countries with long democratic traditions—such as Great Britain, Canada, the United States, and Switzerland—are in little danger of a direct military takeover because civilian control of the military is well established. But even these nations face the danger of growing too dependent on the military, both politically and economically.

Because a military force is necessary for defense, the critical question is not whether or not to have one but how much of the national budget should be spent for this purpose. Different nations answer this question in different ways. The United States spends a high percentage of its income on its military, while Japan and Germany, with similar economic and political systems, spend comparatively little.

One point is clear, however. Although military spending can give a temporary boost to a lagging economy, serious long-range damage results. Most military products have no practical use unless there is a war: you can't eat them, wear them, or live in them. Moreover, military research and development takes scientific talent away from more productive civilian research. As was noted in Chapter 2, the military burden borne by the American economy is an important part of the reason the United States has grown less competitive with such nations as Germany and Japan.

The prolonged struggle of World War II, closely followed by the cold war with the Soviet Union and the Korean and Vietnam conflicts, left the United States with an enormous military establishment. At the peak of the Vietnam war, the United States had over 3.5 million men and women in the armed forces. The current *peacetime* figure remains over 2 million.[20] Workers in defense industries and civilian employees of the Air Force, Army, and Navy swell the number of defense personnel to over

5 million, not counting those who depend indirectly on military spending. The military budget was about $288 billion in 1991.[21] And when the costs of veterans' benefits and of military expenditures in other budgets are added in, almost one-third of all federal funds go to the military, making it the single largest customer of American business.[22]

There have, moreover, been repeated charges that the Department of Defense is riddled with waste and corruption. In 1982, the General Accounting Office concluded that there was a 91 percent chance of a major cost overrun (53 percent or more) on the average military contract, and that fraud and waste cost the Department of Defense at least $15 billion a year.[23] In an effort to respond to such criticism, the Department of Defense started to use more fixed-price contracts that did not allow such massive overruns. But the defense contractors, unused to such budgetary restrictions, still ran up excessive costs, and many of them faced a financial crisis as a result. During the 1980s, the United States spent more than $2 trillion on a massive military buildup. Pointing to such programs as the A-12 attack plane, which cost the government over $3 billion and was then canceled, and the Sergeant York anti-aircraft gun that cost almost $2 billion before it was canceled, the critics have charged that the nation got very little for its money.[24] Defenders of military spending point with pride to the American success in the war with Iraq in 1991. But the critics remain unconvinced. They argue that the defeat of a backward Third World country with less than one-tenth the population of the United States was hardly a real test of the strength of the American military and the international coalition that supported it.

Given the enormous size and economic strength of the American military, it is not surprising that many observers have expressed concern about its influence in a democratic society. One of the most unexpected warnings came from President Dwight D. Eisenhower, a career Army officer. In his farewell address, President Eisenhower warned against the influence of the "military-industrial complex" and the growing interdependence between the military and giant corporations. Such companies as General Dynamics, Lockheed, and Rockwell International are not owned by the military, but their profits come largely from military contracts. Hundreds of other companies also sell a substantial percentage of their product to the military, with the result that corporations and the armed forces have many interests in common. The military has its own lobbyists, who wield tremendous influence in Washington. They are assisted by lobbyists for organized labor, which sees military spending as an important source of jobs, and by lobbyists for corporations, which see military spending as good business. Even if there were no military lobbyists, senators and representatives from states with high concentrations of military bases or defense industries would still be vigorous supporters of military appropriations. Although all this does not add up to military control of the American government, the military-industrial complex obviously has enormous influence and power.

With the collapse of the Soviet Union and the end of the Cold War, it is obvious that scarce government resources may now be shifted to deal with our domestic problems. But the strength of the military-industrial complex and the fact that the American economy has grown so dependent on military spending will make this an extremely difficult task. Special interests continue to fight tenaciously to protect almost every military program. Once cuts are made, the government must help former

An enormous amount of money was poured into the military build-up of the 1980s. With the end of the cold war, a difficult economic adjustment must be made to smaller military budgets.

defense contractors and military employees make the transition to civilian work or the nation will face a dire economic shock.

FREEDOM OR OPPRESSION?

Of all the dilemmas confronting democratic government, none is more important than the issue of how to protect personal freedom while still maintaining social order. The fear that the government wants to control every aspect of our lives and strip us of our basic human rights is shared by people in many walks of life. The nightmare that could come from a fusion of technology and totalitarianism, depicted in such books as George Orwell's *1984* and Aldous Huxley's *Brave New World*, has haunted the Western world for decades.

Lists of human rights usually include freedom of speech, assembly, and movement, and the right to privacy, autonomy, and political expression. But the ideas embodied in these noble generalizations are difficult to apply in practice. The expression of one person's rights may interfere with the rights of another, and there is always someone to claim that "the common good" or "the general welfare" requires the suppression of individual freedom.

The list of systematic violations of individual liberties is tragically long, even in democratic countries. One famous example was the anticommunist "witch hunts" that took place in the United States in the 1950s. The hysterical search for communist subversives led to the blacklisting and professional ruin of many people whose only offense was belonging to the wrong political organization or holding an unpopular opinion. A more recent example comes from Canada, another country with a long democratic tradition. When two prominent Canadians were kidnapped in 1970 by members of a group seeking independence for the province of Quebec, the national government invoked the War Measures Act, thereby suspending civil liberties. Membership in or support for the group responsible for the kidnapping was forbidden and about 490 "separatist sympathizers" were rounded up and jailed. Of these, 435 were eventually released without ever being charged with a crime. Polls indicated that the Canadian people clearly approved the use of the War Measures Act, just as the American people approved of the anticommunist crusades.[25]

Watergate, one of the biggest political scandals in American history, involved a different sort of violation of civil liberties. President Nixon's White House was not riding a wave of popular fear and resentment but rather was working behind a cloak of official secrecy to harass and silence its political opponents. Among other crimes, the Watergate scandal involved burglaries of the offices of political groups, including the Democratic party, and the use of illegal wiretaps, listening devices, tax audits, and false rumors against those on the "enemies list" put together by the White House. Once the scandal began to come to light, administration officials perjured themselves, paid bribes, and destroyed evidence in order to obstruct the investigation.[26]

Similar tactics were used by several presidential administrations to try to undercut the civil rights movement and crush the opposition to the Vietnam war. Evidence that came to light years later shows that the FBI and other government agencies used a variety of illegal surveillance techniques, including wiretaps and burglaries, to gather information. More serious, they engaged in a direct campaign of political harassment and repression. Phony letters were sent to the friends and families of political activists accusing them of everything from embezzlement to cheating on their spouses, false stories were planted in the media, police were urged to arrest activists for minor charges, utilities were encouraged to shut off their services, and some activists were attacked and even killed by those acting under government sponsorship. Such illegal activities tapered off after the end of the war and the collapse of the militant organizations the government had targeted. But the bits and pieces of information that occasionally leak out to the public indicate that the government's surveillance and harassment of American citizens who support unpopular causes still continues.[27]

Many private corporations now pose their own threat to civil liberties. For one thing, many companies are using a host of new techniques to peer into the private lives of their employees. This trend began with the use of the polygraph machine (lie detector) to screen job applicants and ferret out employee theft. In 1988, when a new law banned most involuntary polygraph tests,[28] the corporations jumped on a new bandwagon—drug testing. A 1991 study by the American Management Association found that 63 percent of the companies surveyed had some kind of drug-testing program.[29] Another invasion of workers' privacy comes from employers' attempts to avoid the rising costs of health benefits. Not only do some companies refuse to hire smokers (who have more health problems than nonsmokers), but current employees have actually been fired for off-the-job smoking. There is also increasing job discrim-

The growing sophistication of computer technology has made it possible to store and retrieve detailed records of citizens' private lives. The creation of a centralized data bank for all personal records poses an obvious threat to individual liberties.

ination against the overweight (who are presumed to have more health problems) and homosexuals (who are seen as possible victims of the AIDS virus).

People of all political persuasions are becoming concerned about the threat that the use of technology may pose to civil liberties. The federal government maintains a staggering number of files of information about its citizens. At latest count, there were over 3.5 billion of these files, an average of 15 files on each American.[30] They range from files on "subversives" and criminals kept by investigative agencies such as the FBI, the CIA, and military intelligence agencies to the files in the massive record-keeping systems of the Internal Revenue Service and the Social Security Administration. The Department of Justice alone keeps lists of persons involved in civil disturbances, members of criminal syndicates, narcotics addicts, criminal defendants, individuals wanted by the police, passers of forged checks, and aliens. Clearly, government agencies need many of these files if they are to do their work efficiently. But is such efficiency dangerous? The prospect that all these files might be centralized frightens civil libertarians. It is now possible to establish a system that could, at the punching of a single identification number, reveal all the significant events in an individual's entire life. The power available to the controller of such a system would be immense.

The Privacy Act of 1974 was supposed to prevent the indiscriminate sharing of files between government agencies, but it has failed to do the job. A loophole that exempts routine sharing "compatible" with the purpose for which the information was collected has been used to justify virtually any kind of exchange of information. An additional concern is the fact that some of the information in government and private data files is false or misleading. People have lost their jobs, or been unable to find new ones, because false information was included in one of their files. The Freedom of Information Act was intended to solve this problem and prevent government agencies from covering up their mistakes by giving everyone more access to the information the government collects about itself and its citizens. But the bureaucracy has proven ingenious in developing ways to obstruct the public's access to information. In 1990 alone, the federal government created 6.8 million new secrets, which were therefore exempt from the Freedom of Information Act.[31] But even if all the information in the government's files were accurate, the prospects of a hapless man or woman being haunted by a single mistake for the rest of his or her life is not a pleasant one. Clearly, the totalitarian nightmares of such authors as Orwell and Huxley are now technologically possible. The problem facing all free people is to prevent them from coming true.

BURDENS AND BENEFITS

More than any other social institution, the government is concerned with social justice. In theory, at least, it is supposed to right social wrongs through the legal codes—such as the prohibition of discrimination against women and minorities—and by creating programs to help the disadvantaged and the deprived. In addition, the government has numerous other programs intended to help more privileged groups. But none of this comes free; someone must bear the cost of these programs. The continuing battle over who is to receive the benefits of government action and who is to pay for them is a central feature of modern politics.

Taxation is one of the most difficult issues our political leaders must face. The voters constantly demand more and more government services, yet they don't want more taxes to pay for them. There is, of course, nothing new about this dilemma. But it has grown worse in recent years as the economic decline that started in the 1970s has made it increasingly difficult for many people to maintain their standard of living. In 1978, California's famous Proposition 13 slashed property taxes, which were being pushed up by skyrocketing real estate values, and touched off a nationwide "tax revolt." Yet while taxpayers were demanding lower taxes, neither the cost of running the government nor the demand for its services was going down.

The federal government took the easy way out. In 1981, federal income taxes were substantially reduced, but instead of cutting away at the programs the voters wanted, the government simply borrowed the extra money and ran an ever-larger budget deficit. Although the long-term economic consequences are likely to be grave, for a time this approach allowed us to have our cake and eat it too. But the problems at the state and local level have been much more severe. At the same time that state and local governments were facing increasing pressure to reduce taxes, the federal government was cutting the financial assistance it used to provide. Because it is much more difficult for them to run big deficits year after year, many state and local governments have experienced repeated financial crises.

Despite all the political rhetoric, no major industrialized nation in the world has a lower overall tax rate than the United States.[32] In France, taxes total 48 percent of the gross national product; in Britain, it is 39 percent; in Canada, 38 percent; but in the United States, it is less than a third (see Figure 3.3).[33] Of course, along with lower taxes goes a much lower level of social services. The United States is, for example, the only industrialized nation without some kind of national health care program for all its citizens.

Along with the issue of how high taxes should be is the critical question of who is to bear the tax burden. In recent years, there has been a significant shift from the wealthy to the poor and the middle class. In 1966, the richest 1 percent of the American population paid about 40 percent of its income in taxes (local, state, and federal). Ten years later, that figure had dropped to 29 percent, and by 1989 it was less than 27 percent. In contrast, the tax burden of the bottom 20 percent of the population increased by one-sixth during the 1980s.[34]

In addition to shifting the tax burden away from the wealthy, the U.S. government has also made significant changes in its priorities. In the last decade, military spending increased by 46 percent (after controlling for inflation), while social programs for such programs as housing and child nutrition were slashed. Another big loser were the programs designed to make long-term investments for the future. From 1980 to 1990, the percentage of the gross national product the federal government invested in public infrastructure, such as highways and mass transportation, declined by 34 percent, and spending for education fell by 27 percent.[35]

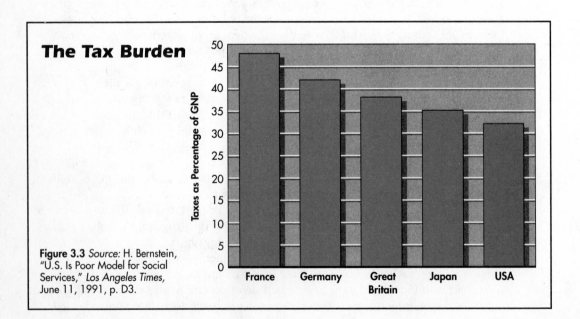

The Tax Burden

Figure 3.3 *Source:* H. Bernstein, "U.S. Is Poor Model for Social Services," *Los Angeles Times,* June 11, 1991, p. D3.

RESPONDING TO PROBLEMS OF GOVERNMENT

Practically all social problems are in part governmental problems. But *the* problem of government is the problem of democracy itself: creating and maintaining political systems that are truly a government "of the people, by the people, and for the people." In recent years there have been three principal responses to the challenge of getting people involved in the affairs of their own government.

Being More Democratic Democracy is not just a system of government; it is a process of constant struggle to protect and expand the power of the people. The current system is clearly far from the democratic ideals we espouse. The political deck is stacked in favor of those with great wealth and against those who would challenge incumbent officeholders. In the 1990 elections, a year in which the polls showed a deep discontent with the direction of government, 96 percent of incumbents who ran for the House of Representatives won, as did 100 percent of the incumbent senators. One of the most important reasons for this corruption of democracy is the current system of campaign financing. For example, in 1990 there were over 400 seats in the House up for election. Yet only 23 of the challengers were able to spend *half* as much as the incumbents, and the two richest incumbents spent more than all the challengers combined.[36] The obvious reason for this enormous imbalance is that those in office are in a far better position to offer political rewards to big contributors than are the challengers. Political action committees, for example, contribute seven times more to incumbents than to challengers.[37]

The current laws that regulate campaign financing look good on paper, but do virtually nothing to limit the ability of the wealthy to use their money to frustrate the will of the majority. The law limits direct contributions to a candidate's election committee, but the wealthy can still spend all the money they want to help a candidate as long as they do so as individuals, or give the money to PACs that support their views. Presidential candidates are eligible for federal funds if they agree to a fixed spending limit, but there are no spending limits or federal financial assistance for other federal candidates. And even in presidential elections, individuals and PACs are once again allowed to spend an unlimited amount to support a candidate so long as they do so independently of the candidate's election committee.

The plain fact is that the current system forces politicians to sell the powers of their office to the highest bidders and creates grossly unequal contests between candidates running for the same office. The best solution to this problem is to provide federal financing in all campaigns for national office, not just in presidential elections. This law would have to be written so that third-party candidates would be eligible for government financing along with Republicans and Democrats. But if properly drawn, such a law would eliminate the problems of campaign financing that make the current system so undemocratic. Another proposal, intended to counteract the slick professional television commercials that tell so little about the real political issues, is to provide free media time for all candidates to discuss their views in depth. Finally, some people advocate the use of a system of proportional representation

DEBATE

Should the Government Finance Our Election Campaigns?

Countless political commentators have complained about the corrupting influence of politicians' constant need to collect money for their election campaigns. The most far-reaching proposal for change would have the government, instead of private contributors, provide most or all of the money necessary for an election campaign.

YES Imagine you are an American senator, and you need to raise $12,000 *a week* to pay for your next election campaign; without that money you will probably lose your job. Now imagine that the only place you can get that kind of money is from the special-interest groups and lobbyists who want your votes when their issues come before the Senate. Don't you think you would listen more carefully to contributors who gave you tens of thousands of dollars than to an average citizen who disagreed with them but couldn't give any money?

The current system of campaign finance is based on a kind of legal bribery in which the rich and the well-financed special-interest groups give millions of dollars to politicians in order to buy political influence. Of course, in some cases supporters on both sides of an important issue have equal amounts of money to spend and would therefore balance each other out, and in other cases a courageous politician might take a risk and go against the powerful special interests. But the fact remains that huge campaign contributions buy political influence, and as a result we do not get a government of the people but a government of the highest bidders.

There are many proposals to correct this shameful state of affairs, but the only way to really do the job is to completely end the politicians' dependence on gifts from contributors in order to finance their campaigns. And that means that the government must provide serious candidates with the money

NO Our current system of government has served us well over the years, and we shouldn't change it now. What other nation has been more prosperous, more stable, and more democratic than the United States? Why fix what isn't broken?

Although the critics are always making wild claims that our political leaders sell the powers of their office in exchange for campaign contributions, there isn't a shred of evidence that this is a common practice. Popular politicians can easily raise the money they need to run their campaigns no matter how they vote on the issues that affect big campaign contributors, and unpopular politicians are not going to be re-elected anyway. Besides, it is clearly against the law to sell your vote in exchange for campaign contributions or anything else, and only very foolish politicians would take the risk of going to jail just to get a few more dollars for their campaign fund. The fact that several well-known political leaders have been convicted on bribery charges in recent years shows that the enforcement effort really works.

Placing limits on private campaign contributions may seem to be a democratic step, but it is actually just the opposite. How can a free nation tell its citizens that they cannot spend or give away their own money in order to support a cause in which they believe? Moreover, government financing of election campaigns will only lead to new and serious problems. You can be sure that any legislation to create such a system they need to run for office. Critics claim that public financing would be a big burden on the taxpayers, but that assertion is just a smokescreen erected by politicians and special interests who have profited from the current system. Actually, the amount of money needed is a minute sum compared with the overall federal budget. If we really believe in the principles of democracy, then we must end the corrupt influence of wealthy campaign contributors once and for all.

would be written to favor incumbents and the candidates of the two major parties, and that everyone else would be hurt. But even if that problem could be avoided, these proposals raise other troubling questions. What right do we have to take money from taxpayers to support the campaign of a politician with whom they disagree? Why should any taxpayers be burdened with what are really politicians' business expenses? Our current political system is working well the way it is, and these so-called reforms would only make things worse.

rather than the winner-take-all system now used in the United States, so that political minorities would have a more significant role in the governmental process.

Limiting Government Secrecy   There are good reasons for government secrets. National governments must keep military and sometimes economic information from potential enemies. Local governments must not let speculators know that a certain piece of land is about to be purchased for public use. But the "secret" stamp used for these purposes can also be used to cover up official mistakes and incompetence and, worse yet, crimes and violations of civil liberties. The cold light of publicity can do a great deal to restrain overzealous government officials, and that is the reason the Constitution prohibited Congress from making any law that abridges the freedom of the press. In effect, the press was given the duty of uncovering government secrets.

Making sure government bureaucrats inform the public about their behavior is not easy. In 1966 the Freedom of Information Act became law. This act requires U.S. government agencies to hand over any information they have about an individual citizen if that person requests it. However, many government bureaucracies responded to requests with months of stalling, and some charged fees for the information they furnished. Other agencies protect information they do not want the public to see by classifying it as secret. In response, Congress added tough new amendments to the bill, establishing a deadline for responding to requests for information, limiting the fees that could be charged, and providing for judicial review of classified material. This legislation gave the public much greater access to government records, but the bureaucracies continue to put up a determined resistance.

Moreover, other legislation has expanded government secrecy. In 1982, the Intelligence Identities Act was enacted, providing jail sentences for Americans who reveal the names of undercover agents working for the government, even if those agents are involved in criminal violations of civil liberties. President Ronald Reagan also sharply reduced restrictions on CIA operations, for the first time allowing that agency to conduct covert operations within the United States and to infiltrate domestic political organizations. And the FBI later admitted that it was investigating such organizations as the National Council of Churches, the United Automobile Workers, and the National Education Association because they opposed administration policy in Central America.[38] Such developments show that stronger laws are still needed to limit government secrecy and protect the right of free political expression.

Getting Politically Involved Despite the range of complex political problems facing modern democracies, one response can help resolve them all: increased involvement of ordinary citizens in the process of government. But while that sounds simple enough, there are enormous obstacles to be overcome. Some sociologists argue that in politics, as in sports, the media have transformed the average citizen into a passive spectator rather than an active participant. Although there is some truth in such assertions, political apathy has many other causes as well. The sheer increase in total population has meant that each elected official represents more and more people and, as a result, is less responsive to any single individual. The growing anonymity of the modern metropolis has broken down the sense of social responsibility and shared community so essential to the political life of traditional small-town America. And, as we have seen, the political deck is stacked against the average citizen, who has little influence compared with the powerful and the privileged.

There is, however, reason for optimism. It is easy to idealize the political life of small-town America, but in many important respects the United States is far more democratic than in its early days. In the early days of the republic, only white males who owned property could vote. But step by step, the poor, minorities, and finally women were let into the political process, even if they still do not enjoy equal representation. Today's society presents daunting obstacles to individual citizens who want to influence government, but history has shown us that those individuals can have an important impact when they band together in political organizations to press for change.

SOCIOLOGICAL PERSPECTIVES ON PROBLEMS OF GOVERNMENT

Practically everyone agrees that the government has serious shortcomings. Indeed, pointing out these weaknesses has become a career for some public figures. Yet there is considerable disagreement over exactly what the problems are. Conservatives are usually concerned about government inefficiency and waste, maintenance of military preparedness, and what they consider excessive interference with the economy. Liberals and progressives are more concerned about violations of civil liberties, protection of minority rights, erosion of the democratic process, and the government's effectiveness in dealing with society's other problems. An examination of the different sociological perspectives helps clarify the situation by pointing out the ways these diverse problems are linked to wider social forces.

The Functionalist Perspective The government performs at least five basic functions that are essential to modern society. First, government enforces society's norms when other methods of social control fail. This responsibility is usually carried out by the police and the other parts of the criminal-justice system, but other government agencies occasionally serve these ends as well. Second, government maintains order by acting as the final arbiter of disputes arising between individuals and groups in the thousands of lawsuits settled by the courts every year. Third, government is responsible for the overall planning and direction of society and the coordination of other social institutions. Fourth, government must deal with the social needs that are left unmet by other social institutions, for example, maintaining roads and caring for homeless children. Finally, government is responsible for handling international relations and, if necessary, warfare.

According to functionalists, the rapid social changes of the past century have made it very difficult for many governments to perform these functions effectively. Government has accepted more and more responsibilities but has been ill prepared for its new tasks. Many governments are saddled with old-fashioned systems of organization that were adequate in the eighteenth and nineteenth centuries but are ineffectual today. Government officials often fail to understand their duties, or they pursue their own interests rather than the public's. High offices are given out to reward the supporters of victorious candidates, and bribery and corruption are everyday occurrences. Another problem is created by technological changes that take place so rapidly that government officials are unable to control their applications. As a result of all this, government fails to function effectively.

Functionalists suggest that steps be taken to reduce this disorganization by reshaping the government. The tasks of government bureaucracies should be spelled out in detail, and each bureau should be rationally organized to achieve them. The decision-making machinery should be revamped to remove the awkward traditional structures that impede efficiency. For example, the U.S. Congress should reform its committee system so that more effective laws can be enacted. Tougher laws that reduce unnecessary secrecy and protect civil liberties should also be passed. Finally, functionalists recommend that law enforcement agencies launch a more vigorous effort to root out bribery and corruption.

The Conflict Perspective Conflict theorists see the government as a source of tremendous political power that is used to advance the interests of those who control it. Government works to repress conflict rather than to resolve it. That is, the groups in control of the government (the upper class) use their power to smother their opposition. Vagrancy laws, for example, have been used to force the poor to work in dangerous, low-paying jobs. Tax laws with loopholes that benefit the rich are another example of the expression of class interests through legislation. When value conflicts produce tension, opposing groups often go to the government asking for favorable legislation. For instance, those who believe homosexuality, drug use, or abortion to be immoral often seek to outlaw such behavior. When successful, such efforts result in the use of the power of the state to oppress those who think or act in unpopular ways.

According to the conflict perspective, control of government is a prize that is won through political conflict. Once a group gains such control, it uses the power of the government to maintain its position, and thus the group becomes difficult to dislodge. The law and its administration become tools of the power elite and are used to exploit the masses. The solution to this problem is to give a stronger voice to the "common" man and woman. Such measures as providing government financing for political campaigns, restricting lobbying, and requiring full disclosure of all government deliberations and proceedings are steps in this direction. But conflict theorists believe that greater economic equality is also necessary to achieve a true democracy. The key to a more equal distribution of both wealth and power is greater political activism and organization by those who are not being represented in government. The government will change only when those groups gain enough power to force it to change.

Social Psychological Perspectives Social psychologists focus on relationships between political systems and individual personality. Some suggest that the character of a nation's people affects its political system; others assert that political systems affect personality just as economic systems do. The citizens of some nations seem to accept their leaders with almost unquestioning obedience, while other cultures breed rebellious individualists who are suspicious of all higher authority. One of the most famous psychological studies of fascism concluded that many of the followers of totalitarian leaders have "authoritarian personalities."[39] Such persons are said to be rigid, extremely conformist, and uncomfortable with ambiguity and uncertainty. As a result, this type of individual favors strong leadership that provides order and conformity at the expense of individual liberty. It could well be, however, that fascism generates authoritarian personalities rather than the reverse.

Another concern of social psychologists is **political socialization**: the ways in which people learn their political values and perspectives, whether authoritarian or

Children usually pick up their parents' political values and attitudes at an early age, in a process known as political socialization.

democratic. Children learn most of their political attitudes from their parents and early in life develop attachments to such symbols as the flag, patriotic slogans, and well-known public figures. As they grow older, their views are affected by their peer groups, teachers, and others. A democratic society can do little to change the home environment of its children without threatening basic civil liberties. However, schools can teach children to respect the rights of others, to understand how governments actually operate, and to work for the equality of all people. Another important aspect of political socialization is the ideas we learn about political activity itself. Is it the duty of every citizen or a waste of time? And once again, the schools and the media can help encourage positive political attitudes.

SUMMARY

Governments and their bureaucracies have expanded rapidly in the last century. Although both public and private bureaucracies are often criticized, they are still more efficient than other forms of organization. However, today's huge government bureaucracies are not without problems. Employees sometimes become more concerned with protecting and enhancing their jobs than with the real goals of the organization. And for the same reason, they resist attempts to reduce the size of their organization, even if some of its functions could be performed more efficiently elsewhere.

Social scientists have spent much effort trying to determine who really controls democratic governments. Theoretically, the power of the vote should give control to the people. But citizens are often apathetic, and they can be misled as well. The richest and most well-educated citizens are most active in expressing their opinions to government officials. Special-interest groups wield tremendous power through their lobbying activities, by giving large sums of money to candidates they like, and by using their influence to defeat those who oppose them. Some social scientists, known as elitists, believe that the government is controlled by a small, unified power elite. Others, the pluralists, see many different groups competing for power and are not convinced that a single ruling class exists.

The military poses a basic dilemma in a democratic society. Its traditions of unquestioning obedience and authoritarianism can be a real threat to democratic institutions, yet its power seems essential to national survival.

Protection of civil liberties is a critical task in every democracy. There are many recent examples of governments violating individual rights and interfering with democratic processes. The use of modern technology to collect, store, and retrieve information about individual citizens is a growing threat to civil liberties.

Local, state, and national governments have been caught in a financial dilemma caused by a revolt of taxpayers demanding lower taxes, combined with a continued insistence on a high level of government services. Since 1980 there has also been a shift in federal priorities from social services to military spending.

Many responses to these problems have been proposed, including federal financing of election campaigns, limiting government secrecy, and maximizing political participation by citizens.

Functionalists see the problems of government as signs of failure; the political institution has failed to work correctly and must be adjusted so that it runs smoothly again. Conflict theorists are more likely to feel that the political system creates social problems because it was intentionally designed to favor the elite and special interests rather than the poor. If political problems are to be resolved, this dominance must be ended. Social psychologists note that there is a relationship between political systems and personality, and they have found that people's political behavior is learned, just as other behavior is learned.

KEY TERMS

bureaucracy A social organization with a division of labor and a hierarchy of authority governed by a set of formal rules that are impersonally enforced.

elitist One who believes that industrial nations are ruled by a small elite class.

pluralist One who believes that decisions in industrialized nations are made by a democratic process involving changing coalitions among many different interest groups.

power The ability to force other people to do something whether they want to or not.

special-interest group A group of people who have a stake in a particular area of public policy.

FURTHER READINGS

Michael Parenti, *Democracy for the Few*, 5th ed. (New York: St. Martin's Press, 1988). An analysis of the American political system from an elitist perspective.

Robert Dahl, *Dilemmas of Pluralist Democracy* (New Haven, Conn.: Yale University Press, 1982). An analysis of the American political system by an influential pluralist.

G. William Domhoff, *Who Rules America Now? A View for the 80s* (Englewood Cliffs, N.J.: Prentice-Hall, 1983). An updating of his earlier book, *Who Rules America?*, by today's leading elitism theorist.

C. Wright Mills, *The Power Elite* (New York: Oxford University Press, 1956). The classic work that gave rise to contemporary elite theory.

Anthony M. Orum, *Introduction to Political Sociology: The Social Anatomy of the Body Politic*, 3rd ed. (Englewood Cliffs, N.J.: Prentice-Hall, 1989). A general text analyzing our political system from a sociological perspective.

chapter 4

Problems of Education

- Why is an educated population so important to modern societies?
- Does our educational system favor middle-class children?
- Do our schools do a good job of educating minority students?
- What is the cause of declining scores on student achievement tests?
- How can we improve our educational system?

We place tremendous faith in education. We expect it to provide a guiding light for the young and to pass on the democratic traditions of our society. Education is seen as a path out of the slums for new immigrants and out of poverty for the sons and daughters of the disadvantaged. But it is also essential for the "good life" and professional careers so highly valued by the middle class. As technology becomes more sophisticated, even our hopes for our economic future are coming to rest on the quality of our educational system and the graduates it produces.

But while our goals and aspirations continue to grow, our educational institutions seem to be mired in one crisis after another. On the one hand, the poor and minorities are charging that the educational system has shut them out, and they are demanding their share of the educational dream. At the same time, the middle class, which has long been the backbone of the educational system, is beginning to have doubts about how well it is serving their needs. Several national reports have issued stinging attacks on the quality of American education, and the glut of young men and women seeking a career in education has turned into a serious shortage of high-quality teachers.

The picture is not really so bleak, however, for North Americans are still among the most educated and best-informed people in the world. The educational system is

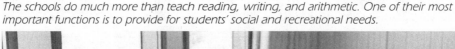

The schools do much more than teach reading, writing, and arithmetic. One of their most important functions is to provide for students' social and recreational needs.

a "failure" only because the goals we set for it are so high. The history of our educational institutions is one of continual expansion, and our population has become more and more highly educated over the years.

In small traditional societies, education takes place in the home and in children's informal day-to-day association with adults. Training for the few specialized occupations that exist is the responsibility of those who hold the jobs, usually members of the same family. Customs and traditions are passed along from one generation to the next without the assistance of schools or professional teachers. In more complex societies, specialized organizations for the transmission of knowledge developed. In the beginning, these schools were mostly for the training of priests and other religious officials, but secular education soon followed. Until the nineteenth century, education was reserved for aristocrats and a few of their important servants. The masses had little need to read or write, and some aristocrats saw any attempt to develop these skills in the lower classes as a threat to their power. It was only a little more than 200 years ago that the governor of the colony of Virginia condemned all popular education: "Thank God there are no free schools or printing; . . . for learning has brought disobedience and heresy into the world, and printing has divulged them. . . . God keep us from both."[1]

It was not until the end of the eighteenth century, when democratic revolutions took place in America and France, that the idea of education for the common people began to catch on. Education for the lower classes became more important as the masses began to share in important governmental decisions and religious groups emphasized the need for everyone to be able to read the Bible. Yet progress toward equality has been slow, and the children of the wealthy continue to receive more and better education than the children of the poor.

A high school education is now the rule, not the exception. In 1890 only 7 percent of children of high school age in the United States were in school; today more than ten times that percentage actually graduate.[2] Because of this growth, education has become a big business. Virtually every American receives some formal education, and most people spend a good portion of their lives in school. There are now about 1.6 million primary school teachers and 1.1 million secondary school teachers in the United States. Another 350,000 people teach at the college and university level, making the total number of teachers around 3 million.[3]

EQUAL EDUCATIONAL OPPORTUNITY FOR ALL?

In the past, the keys to economic success usually involved such things as the ownership of good farmland or the canny skills of the small businessman. As formal education and professional training have gained in importance, so has the issue of educational equity. Many have charged that our educational system fails to provide equal opportunity for all, and, as a result, the poor, immigrants, and minorities have far less chance of "making it" than they did in the days of the frontier. To understand this significant issue, we will first examine the role social class plays in a student's academic success, and then look at how good a job the educational system does of meeting the needs of minority students.

Social Class and Achievement Grade-school teachers and university professors alike can easily see that the daughters and sons of affluent parents do better in school than the children of the poor. In fact, numerous studies have found social class to be the single most effective predictor of achievement in school. As Robert James Parelius and Ann Parker Parelius put it:

> Whether we look at scores on standardized ability or achievement tests, classroom grades, participation in academic rather than vocational high school programs, involvement in extracurricular activities, number of years of schooling completed or enrollment in or completion of college and professional school, children from more socioeconomically advantaged homes outperform their less affluent peers.[4]

There are two principal explanations for this difference. One focuses on the advantages higher-status children have because they come from home environments in which books, a large vocabulary, and an emphasis on achievement are common. The other notes that the schools themselves are often organized in ways that ignore the educational needs of the poor.

Family Background Lower-class children live in a very different world from middle-class children. The homes of the poor tend to have fewer books, newspapers, and magazines, and the parents have less education. People with low incomes are less likely to read for entertainment; thus, children in low-income homes are less likely to be encouraged to learn that vital skill. Lower-class families are also larger and are more often headed by only one adult. Children in such families often receive less parental contact, guidance, and educational encouragement. Another factor is health: poor children are more likely to be undernourished than their middle-class counterparts, and they are sick more days a year.[5] And unhealthy children simply do not learn as well as healthy ones.

More positively, the academic success of children from affluent homes stems from the value their parents place on education. A number of surveys have shown that children from wealthy families want more education than children from poorer backgrounds.[6] Some of this difference results from the fact that middle-class homes place a higher value on education and long-range planning. But some of it also reflects a realistic adjustment by poor children to the fact that they have less chance of getting a good education.

Children who speak only Spanish or some other language foreign to the schools are obviously handicapped. But language differences also have an important impact on the educational achievements of the various social classes in the *same* ethnic group. Standard English is more commonly spoken by African Americans with middle-class backgrounds, while those from the lower class are more likely to speak "Black English" dialects. Because schoolwork is done in standard English, the lower-class children are at a disadvantage. Similar language differences are found among whites. People from the lower class tend to use short, simple sentences, while middle-class people use longer, more complex sentences containing more abstract concepts and a larger vocabulary. These differences give middle-class students a big head start in their schoolwork and also make it easier for them to understand their teachers.

The Schools In addition to the obstacles in the home environment of many lower-class students, the school system itself favors the education of middle- and upper-class students. This fact is obvious, first of all, in the way schools are financed. Even a brief examination of the American system of school finance reveals glaring inequities both in how taxes are levied and in how they are spent. Wealthy tax districts spend much more money on their students' education than do poorer communities.

There are great differences among the various states in the importance placed on education and in each state's ability to pay for it. For example, Alaska spends more than two and a half times as much money per pupil as Utah.[7] But the differences between local school districts within the same state can be even greater. Because property taxes are a major source of school funding, districts with expensive homes and other valuable real estate often receive much more revenue than poor districts. In Illinois, for example, the poorest districts spend about $2,100 per student while the richest spend over $12,000.[8] Moreover, such inequities occur even though the rich school districts often have a lower tax rate than the poor ones. In 1990, property owners in the Edgewood School District in San Antonio, Texas, had to pay $1 in taxes for every $100 of the assessed value of their property. In some of the oil-rich districts in Texas, tax rates were as low as eight cents and yet they still raised more money for their schools.[9]

Defenders of the present system of financing may point to studies that conclude that the amount of money spent per student has little direct effect on educational achievement.[10] And there is little doubt that a badly run school can spend a great deal of money and still achieve poor results. But such findings hardly justify the practice of making the disadvantaged pay higher property taxes than the rich while their children languish in understaffed and underfunded schools.

There have been some serious efforts to correct this inequitable system through the courts. By 1990, ten state supreme courts had ruled their state's system of school finance unconstitutional and had required basic reforms, and court cases were pending in more than a dozen other states.[11] But because the U.S. Supreme Court has refused to get involved in this issue, the process of reform is a hit-or-miss affair. Eight state courts have upheld their system of school finance and no challenge has yet been made in many others.[12] Moreover, such cases do nothing to rectify the great imbalance in school funding among different states.

Family finances also have an important effect on educational achievement. Despite the fact that public education itself is free, children from poor families simply cannot afford as much education as those from more well-to-do backgrounds. Students from poor homes are more likely to drop out of school and go to work. At the college and university level, the costs of tuition, books, and transportation put extra pressure on poor students. Many highly qualified lower-class students must attend local community colleges, which emphasize technical careers, because they cannot afford a university education. Less qualified upper- and middle-class students may go to expensive private universities to prepare for professional careers. Moreover, the financial pressure on college students has gotten substantially worse in recent years. Even after adjusting for inflation, the cost of a college education has more than doubled since the 1960s, and the last decade has also seen large cuts in the financial aid available to college students.

Of course, colleges and universities are not the only educational institutions that charge their students. In 1990, a little less than 12 percent of American children attended private schools.[13] The quality, the cost, and the philosophical orientation of these schools varies enormously. The most prestigious of them are the so-called prep schools, which offer a much higher level of education than most public schools, but only to the children of families who can afford to pay the price (or the gifted few who receive scholarships). Thus, the finest primary and secondary schools are largely closed to poor, working-class, and even most middle-class children.

But even less prestigious and less affluent private schools have a major advantage over the public schools. It is far easier for them to kick out the troublemakers and the low achievers and thereby isolate their students from disruptive influences. But the public schools must try to meet the needs of all the young people in their community, even if they are having social or academic problems.

Because children from upper-class families generally receive a better secondary education, they have easier access to the elite universities that lead students to top positions in government and the corporations. Moreover, some less qualified students from upper-class families are able to attend elite universities because of admission programs that favor the children of alumni and the children of big contributors to the university's fund-raising campaigns.

Aside from the differences in the quality of the schools, achievement is also affected by the expectations of the teachers for their students. There is considerable evidence that teachers expect less from lower-class students, in terms of both academic achievement and behavior, than they expect from others. Students respond to such expectations by underachieving and misbehaving. The expectation of low achievement thus acts as a self-fulfilling prophecy: students become what they are expected to become.[14] Robert Rosenthal and Lenore Jacobson performed an interesting experiment to demonstrate this fact.[15] Experimenters gave a standard IQ test to pupils in 18 classrooms in a neighborhood elementary school. However, teachers were told that the instrument was the "Harvard Test of Inflected Acquisition" (which does not exist). Next, the experimenters arbitrarily selected 20 percent of the students' names and told their teachers that the test showed that these students would make remarkable progress in the coming year. When the students were retested eight months later, those who had been singled out as intellectual bloomers showed a significantly greater increase in IQ than the others. Rosenthal and Jacobson concluded that the increase was the result of the higher expectations of the teachers and the communication of these expectations to the students. Many similar studies have since been made, with mixed results. Most of them supported Rosenthal and Jacobson's findings, but some did not, and it is not yet clear under exactly what conditions teachers' expectations are most likely to become a self-fulfilling prophecy.[16] One thing we do know is that lower-class and minority students are the ones most likely to be harmed by this process, for they are the ones for whom teachers hold the lowest expectations. For example, when D. G. Harvey and G. T. Slatin gave teachers pictures of students and asked them to evaluate their chances for success in school, the teachers reported the highest expectations for white students who looked to be from middle- and upper-class backgrounds.[17]

The chances are, however, that lower-class students will not be in the same high school classes as middle-class students even if they attend the same school. Most high school students are placed in one of several different "tracks" or "ability groups." The "most promising" are put into college preparatory courses, while others go into vocational or "basic" classes. There is considerable evidence that lower-class students are more likely to be placed in the vocational or basic track.[18] Tracking is supposed to be based on such criteria as academic record, performance on standardized tests, and the students' own feelings about college, but there is little doubt that the schools themselves have lower expectations for students from the lower classes. And even when there is no bias, a serious problem remains. Once students have been placed in a lower track, they will be exposed to less challenging material, and teachers will have lower expectations of them. Because they are isolated from college-bound students, even the best students in the lower tracks are less likely to want to go to college. Karl Alexander, Martha Cook, and Edward L. Dill found that students in a college preparatory track were 30 percent more likely to plan to go on beyond high school than equally motivated and able students in nonacademic tracks.[19]

Minority Education   The history of the American educational system's treatment of minorities has not been a bright one (see Chapter 7). Black Americans have been the victims of particularly harsh treatment. During the era of slavery they were seldom given any education at all. As recently as 35 years ago, blacks in the South attended segregated schools that were clearly inferior to those attended by whites. A landmark Supreme Court decision in 1954 recognized the fact that segregated schools were inherently unequal and declared them unconstitutional. In the turmoil that followed, intentional legal segregation was ended, but unlike **de jure** (legal) **segregation**, **de facto** (actual) **segregation** has been resistant to change. Although blacks and whites were assigned to the schools nearest their homes regardless of race, most schools remained segregated because most neighborhoods were segregated.

To deal with this problem, the Court ruled that school districts must aim for racial balance in their schools, even it it became necessary to bus students long distances. Intense opposition from whites made school busing an inflammatory racial issue for two decades, but public interest in this controversy has been declining in recent years. Polls show that a large majority of Americans support integrated schools, and, as the furor at the start of busing programs died down, parents and students often came to accept them. Moreover, migration to the suburbs has left too few white children in many big cities to create truly integrated schools. For example, when suit was first brought to force desegregation of the Los Angeles city schools in 1963, about 55 percent of the students were white; but by 1988 they made up only 17 percent of the pupils in the L.A. schools.[20]

The debate over school integration has generated a great deal of concern about the effects of integration on students. The Coleman report, published in 1966, found that the quality of schools attended by blacks and by whites was similar when measured by such factors as physical facilities, curriculum, and the qualifications of teachers.[21] The greatest influence on achievement was found to be the students' class background. Middle-class students did much better than students from the lower class. However, Coleman found that disadvantaged students did better when they were in the same classes with middle-class students. He concluded, logically enough, that integration would improve the performance of lower-class black children if they were integrated with middle-class white students. The effects of desegregation on academic performance have been the subject of dozens of studies since the Coleman report was first published. These studies vary widely in methodology and overall quality and have reached many contradictory conclusions. Rita E. Mahard and Robert L. Crain reviewed 93 different studies on this topic, and after they had eliminated investigations based on poorly designed research, an analysis of the others led them to some interesting conclusions. Desegregation did indeed improve the academic performance of black students, but mainly in the primary grades, not junior high or high school. Moreover, there seems to be an optimum ratio of white students to black students, which varied in the different studies from three to one to nine to one. Finally, the most successful approach to desegregation was the so-called metropolitan plan that integrated inner-city and suburban schools.[22]

In addition to the academic benefits, school integration may help reduce racism and create understanding among the nation's many diverse ethnic groups. But unless school administrators modify some of their traditional policies, minorities may be resegregated into different classes within an integrated school. For example, academic tracking often results in predominantly white college preparatory classes and predominantly black vocational classes. Well-intentioned bilingual and compensatory education programs may also result in the removal of minority students from regular classrooms for a large part of the day.[23] Thus, to realize the full benefits of an integrated education, it is necessary to do more than just integrate the schools. Administrators, teachers, and concerned parents must work to create an integrated and supportive environment within individual schools as well.

How well are minority groups doing in today's educational system? The answer is a complex one. Some Asian groups have done extremely well and now have a higher level of education than European Americans. The gap between Americans of European and African descent has also narrowed considerably in the last 30 years. Today, the average white has 12.7 years of schooling and the average black 12.4.[24] Just as important, the academic performance of the African Americans who are in school has shown significant improvement. For example, in 1971, 18 percent of black 17-year-olds who were in school ranked at the "basic (lowest) level" in the reading tests given by the National Assessment of Educational Progress, but by 1988 less than 3 percent were in this category.[25] Yet despite substantial improvements at the high school level, the percentage of African Americans who go on to college declined from 22.6 percent in 1976 to 21.1 percent in 1988.[26] The reasons for this decrease are mainly economic—the rising cost of a college education combined with a decrease in financial aid and a drop in the real income of African American families.

The educational achievement of Hispanics remains below that of African Americans. In 1989, the average Hispanic had about 12.0 years of school, and the percentage of Hispanics who dropped out before completing high school has actually been increasing.[27] (See Figure 4.1.) There are two main reasons for this situation. The first is language. Many Hispanics come into English-speaking schools with little knowledge of that language, and many others are less proficient in English than their classmates

**Fewer Minorities
Finish High School**

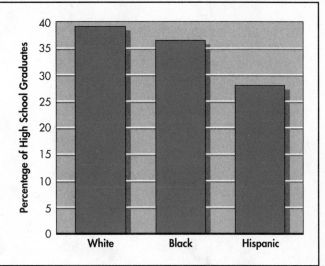

Figure 4.1 *Source: Statistical Abstract of the United States, 1991, pp. 38, 40.*

who grew up speaking it. The second is immigration. There has been a heavy influx of new immigrants from Latin America, and they frequently come from low-income groups that have received an inadequate education in their own country.

AUTHORITY AND REBELLION

Our leaders are fond of talking about the need to teach children democratic principles and the ability to think for themselves. But most schools are large bureaucracies that demand obedience to a rigid set of rules over which the students, and even most teachers, have little influence. Our schools have been compared to factories in which workers (teachers) turn raw materials (students) into finished products (educated citizens) under the strict supervision of the management (school administration); they have even been likened to prisons, with principals as wardens and teachers as guards. Although such comparisons can easily be taken too far, it is hard to see most schools as places that encourage creativity or individual initiative.

In one sense, the bureaucratic structure of our school system both reflects and requires authoritarianism. Students are required by law to go to school, where they are compelled to spend large amounts of time in classrooms and where truancy is considered a form of delinquency. All bureaucracies require strict rules and regulations if they are to coordinate the activities of large numbers of people. School life would quickly degenerate into chaos without such rules. However, some observers believe that the schools carry the emphasis on authority and obedience to harmful extremes. They argue that many schools are experiencing a problem common to bureaucracies—a displacement of goals (see Chapter 3). In this case, there has been a shift from education to the maintenance of order and authority as the primary goal of the schools. Many conflict theorists charge that there is thus a **hidden curriculum**

The problem of maintaining order is a particularly serious one in poor inner-city schools. In this photograph, a school official is using a metal detector to check students for weapons.

in our schools: that along with reading, writing, and arithmetic, our students are taught conformism and obedience to authority. Those who do not learn this lesson are doomed to failure in the educational bureaucracy, no matter how academically talented they may be.

While some criticize the authoritarianism of the schools, others condemn what they see as chaos in the classroom. The Gallup poll has repeatedly shown that the public believes "lack of discipline" to be the biggest problem in the schools today. To most people this lack of discipline conjures up images of lazy or disrespectful students refusing to do their work. But there have been frequent reports of far more serious problems: drug dealing, students carrying weapons, and assaults and rapes directed against students and even teachers. These stories, combined with an increase in the number of reported incidents of school violence, have led many to believe that a new crime wave has swept our junior and senior high schools. However, such statistics are notoriously unreliable (see Chapter 13), and most criminologists would probably agree with Joan Newman and Graeme Newman, who concluded that "although we are faced with the disturbing statistics on current school violence, the evidence available to us suggests that this phenomenon is not much more serious today than it was in previous centuries. . . . Our general conclusion is, then, that a 'crisis of discipline' has always existed in schools."[28] Such conclusions are, unfortu-

19th-Century Social Problems

Miss Mary Jeffrey, a teacher in one of the schools of Centerville, was badly beaten by one of her pupils, a 14 year old girl. The teacher, for some offense committed by the girl's brother, proceeded to punish him, when the sister interfered and struck the teacher in the face. The teacher, in attempting to avoid the blow, dodged, throwing back her head, with the result that her hair caught on a hook in a hat rack and held her. While in this position, the girl rained blow after blow on the face of the defenseless teacher who was not a match for a strong, husky country girl. . . . She had just been pounded into unconsciousness when people attracted by the teacher's screams ran in and released her.

June 1, 1899

These selections, which appear throughout the text, are from the *Badger State Banner*, a newspaper published in Black River Falls, Wisconsin.

nately, of little solace to teachers who must spend more time controlling their students than teaching them, or to the students who fall victim to campus violence.

THE QUALITY OF EDUCATION

The controversy about the quality of our educational system has jumped out of the specialized journals and into the center of the political stage. Several prestigious national commissions have been highly critical of our schools, and there is a growing fear that American students are falling behind their counterparts in other countries. Such attention is certainly long overdue. But before we can go very far to make the schools more effective, we must first decide what they are supposed to do. Teach students to do well on standardized tests of academic achievement? Teach the skills of critical, independent thinking? Essay writing? Higher mathematics? Public citizenship? Or do we focus on students' social needs, such as preventing delinquency and drug abuse? In this section we will discuss some of the main issues in the debate about the quality of our educational system. But because the parties to this debate do not agree about the underlying goals of our educational system, they tend to see these problems very differently.

Declining Achievement? It is estimated that 3 million Americans cannot read or write at all. Moreover, almost ten times that number are "functionally illiterate"—that is, their skills in reading, writing, and math are so poor that they cannot perform many of the basic tasks necessary to daily life in an industrial society. The demand for a more educated work force has made the problem of illiteracy an increasingly serious

DEBATE

Is the Quality of Public Education Deteriorating?

YES The decay of public education is obvious to anyone who cares to look. The cheap, run-down buildings that house so many public schools are the most visible signs of trouble, but inside those walls lie much greater problems. Year after year, our schools have been given more responsibility to solve social problems. We now expect our schools to combat racism, stop drug abuse, prevent unwed pregnancies, help the handicapped, and reduce delinquency. But at the same time, we are cutting away at already inadequate school budgets instead of providing the additional money necessary to deal with the demands of our technological age. Teachers are paid less than cocktail waitresses, and positions in math, science, and engineering go begging. Our schools often lack basic supplies, much less the expensive computer systems that are necessary if students are to learn the skills contemporary society demands.

Not only are our schools failing to meet the technological challenges of the 1990s, considerable evidence shows that they are not even teaching the basics of reading, writing, and arithmetic very well. Many of our classrooms exhibit a kind of educational paralysis. Students are unruly, attendance is sporadic, the use of drugs and alcohol is common, and an atmosphere of violence prevails. Too many teachers have given up on discipline, and too many administrators allow students to dodge academic classes and take trivial electives instead. The private schools aggravate these already serious problems by skimming off the wealthiest and most motivated students. Not only does this situation tend to lower classroom standards even further, but it deprives the public schools of the support of the parents

NO Determining the quality of public education is not like weighing a cabbage. There are enormous disagreements about the ends that a good education ought to achieve and few effective ways to measure how well those ends are met. It is easy to point to the decline in standardized test scores as proof that our educators are not doing a good job. But the realities are much more complex. The fact is that the explosive growth of electronic communications and the ever-increasing number of children living in single-parent homes have changed students in a fundamental way. If our students are given less family support and less exposure to the written word, how can we expect them to earn higher marks than their predecessors? Moreover, there is reason to doubt the validity of standardized tests as a measure of educational achievement. At best, these tests, which ask students to fill in hundreds of little bubbles, measure only the narrowest of educational skills. What about the appreciation of good literature and music, the knowledge of world affairs, the ability to communicate verbally, and the countless other skills that sound education should impart?

The growing emphasis on equipping our students to deal with the social problems they will encounter in the real world makes today's education more relevant and more valuable for the average student than it ever was in the past. Aren't students better off gaining the knowledge that helps them prevent an unwanted pregnancy and an early marriage than learning calculus? Our schools are reaching out to meet the emotional and social needs of a generation that lacks the family support that was assumed by traditional education. All in all, who would be most effective in pushing demands for reform. The tragic fact is that a growing number of students are emerging from high schools illiterate and uneducated.

our educational system is doing a better job of meeting the needs of students; those needs have simply changed.

one. Yet although more than one out of every four high school students in the United States and Canada drops out before graduation, the long-range trends have actually been toward a rise in the number of years the average person spends in school and a decline in illiteracy.[29]

Despite the fact that people are getting more years of education, there is a growing concern that educational achievement is declining among secondary school students. One of the most worrisome statistics has been the poor performance of American students on standardized tests of academic achievement. For example, scores on the Scholastic Aptitude Test—the most widely used college administration test for high school students—have declined significantly since their peak in the mid-1960s (see Figure 4.2). The National Commission on Excellence in Education summarized the problem in these words: "For the first time in the history of our country, the educational skills of one generation will not surpass, will not equal, will not even approach, those of their parents."[30]

There are three common explanations for the decline in student test scores. The first holds the schools responsible. The second blames the drop on changes in students' social environment, and the third attacks the tests themselves, arguing that test scores don't accurately reflect how much students are actually learning. Critics of the validity of these tests point out that some (but not all) of the decline in average scores

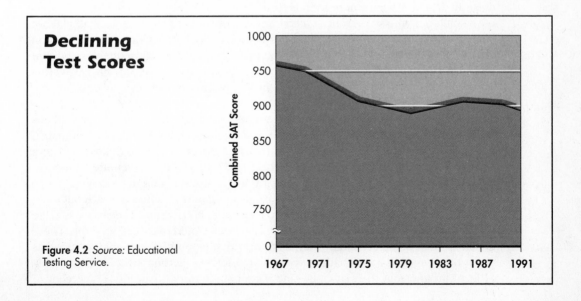

Declining Test Scores

Figure 4.2 *Source:* Educational Testing Service.

can be attributed to the increasing number of poor and minority students who are taking college entrance tests. The critics also raise a more fundamental issue; such tests, they assert, focus on only a single type of educational skill and should not be used to make an overall evaluation of educational achievement. The other side generally agrees that these tests do not measure all aspects of educational achievement, but they argue that the tests are a valid indicator of important educational skills. And they point out that in addition to doing more poorly than past generations, American students fare badly on international comparisons. For example, in an international test of the math skills of twelfth graders, the United States ranked fourteenth among the 15 nations tested—behind poverty-stricken Hungary and just ahead of Thailand.[31]

Those who blame the schools for the decline in test scores attribute much of it to a downslide in academic standards. In response to the protests of the 1960s, many schools reduced the number of required courses and gave students more freedom in course selection. As a result, enrollments in basic academic courses fell. A report to the National Commission on Excellence in Education found that since 1969, the amount of time spent on academic courses has dropped from 70 to 62 percent of all class time, while the time spent on such courses as driver education has increased from 8 to 13 percent. It seems reasonable to expect that achivement scores will decline if students do not take courses designed to teach basic skills. It can also be expected that scores will fall even more if the content of basic courses is watered down. A 1988 survey found that only 38 percent of twelfth graders do an hour or more of homework a night.[32] Such softening of standards has often been covered up by the practice of **grade inflation**: assigning grades of A or B to students who have barely learned to read and write.

But whatever the shortcomings of the schools, experts agree that students' home environment has an enormous influence on how well they master their studies. And there are good reasons to believe that the environment of today's students is less conducive to educational achievement than it was in the past. For example, the average high school senior now spends three hours a day watching television.[33] Obviously, children who sit in front of television sets instead of playing basketball will not become good basketball players. Just as obviously, children who watch television instead of reading books will not become good readers and, consequently, will not learn to write very well either. Some also blame dependence on electronic calculators for the decline in math scores, although there is at present little evidence to support such a conclusion.

Teachers often complain that their students have been growing more rebellious and less interested in their studies. But it is difficult to determine if such comments reflect a real change in students or just an idealization of the "good old days." There is, however, one good reason to believe that these complaints are accurate—the huge increase in percentage of families in which there is only one parent or in which both parents work outside the home. These changes in family structure often reduce the amount of time and energy parents have to give their children, and it seems reasonable to assume that some students' behavior at school would suffer as a result. These structural changes in the family may also mean that parents are not able to spend as much time assisting their children with their studies or getting involved in the educational programs of their schools. One recent study found that only 17 percent of the parents surveyed said they had taken the time to talk with their children's teachers to discuss their children's performance.[34]

RESPONDING TO PROBLEMS OF EDUCATION

The problems of education are economic and political problems as well. Some proposals for change call for modification of the entire structure of our society, including the institution of education. But educational problems are also bureaucratic problems, and other proposals for change call for improved efficiency in the existing school system and its teaching methods. Some of these suggestions have already been implemented in private schools, with varying degrees of success. The proposals to upgrade the educational system fall into two broad categories: recommendations for providing more equal educational opportunities for all citizens and suggestions for improving the quality of education.

Toward Equal Educational Opportunity Almost everyone agrees with the idea that there should be equal educational opportunity for all. But as we have already noted, there is widespread disagreement about what this means and how it can be achieved. Integration of students from different ethnic backgrounds into the same schools is often proposed as a solution to educational inequality. A second approach is to set up special **compensatory education** programs to help disadvantaged students. A third widely accepted idea is to remedy educational inequality by spending an equal amount of money on each student's education.

Effective Integration For years the American government, particularly the judicial branch, has been trying to achieve racial and ethnic integration in the schools. Despite many advances, this goal has still not been achieved. Following court-ordered integration, unofficial resegregation often occurred as whites moved to the suburbs or enrolled their children in private schools. It has been suggested that resegregation should be reduced by merging suburban school districts with inner-city school districts and then busing children within each district. One difficulty with this proposal is distance. Some suburban communities are so far from the city centers that students would have to spend a large part of their school day on a bus. Another difficulty is prejudice. The proposal does nothing to discourage white parents from putting their children in private schools, and in fact might encourage them to do so.

As an alternative, some have proposed voluntary desegregation plans that give students the right to attend any school they wish, provided that it does not have a higher percentage of students of their ethnic group than their neighborhood school. A related proposal is to create **magnet schools** with unique educational programs that can attract students from all ethnic groups. The goal of these plans is to reduce "white flight" while still allowing minority and lower-class students to attend integrated middle-class schools if they wish. Critics of such plans argue that they are not likely to reduce segregation significantly because most students choose to attend their neighborhood school.

Another possibility would be to encourage the integration of residential areas so that neighborhood schools would automatically be integrated. In many ways this is the most appealing solution, for it would provide the broadest possible opportunity for development of interracial friendships and cooperation. However, daunting obstacles stand in the way of any effort to create truly integrated communities. For one thing, a long history of prejudice and suspicion makes many Americans prefer to live in neighborhoods in which the residents have similar economic and ethnic backgrounds. Moreover, the poor and minorities simply cannot afford to live in affluent neighborhoods with the best schools. One possible solution is to create more subsidized housing for low-income families in wealthy neighborhoods, and tax incentives for affluent families to refurbish older homes and move back into lower-income neighborhoods. But specific proposals to encourage such actions usually run into intense opposition from wealthy home owners who fear that low-cost housing will decrease their property values, or from the residents of low-income neighborhoods who fear they will be displaced by more prosperous newcomers.

Compensatory Education Another way to boost the educational achievement of the poor and minorities is to provide them with special programs and assistance. The most popular and widely known compensatory program of this kind is Project Head Start, which gives preschool instruction to disadvantaged children. At first the results of the project seemed quite promising, but follow-up studies found that most of the early gains made by those in the program faded away by the time the children reached the second or third grade.[35] A related program under Title I of the Elementary and Secondary Education Act provides federal money to give extra help to disadvantaged students who are already in school. Over 5 million elementary school students are aided under this program, and its supporters credit it with much of the reduction in the gap between the achievement scores of black and white students that has occurred in recent years. But critics point to studies showing that the benefits of elementary school programs do not carry over into high school.[36]

The research on both Head Start and Title I programs thus reaches much the same conclusion: these programs significantly improve the performance of the underprivileged students who are enrolled, but after they finish the program, the benefits tend to diminish.[37] The solution to this problem is obvious: don't stop the programs after only a few years. Disadvantaged students should continue to receive extra help as long as they need it, which in many cases would probably be until their final years of high school. The difficulty with this proposal is, of course, money. Today, despite the growing popularity of Head Start, only 48 percent of the eligible students participate in the program for even a single year, and the funding per student has declined by over 15 percent since 1981.[38] It would certainly take a lot more money to provide help for all the students in all grades who need it. But such an investment in the future would pay enormous dividends in terms of a healthier, more competitive economy, lower rates of crime and welfare dependency, and, most important, a more just society.

A variety of educational-opportunity programs have also been established on the college level. Generally, these programs make special provisions for the admission of disadvantaged and minority students who do not meet standard admissions require-

Compensatory education programs, such as the Head Start class shown in this photograph, are one of the best hopes for improving the educational achievement of disadvantaged students.

ments. They also provide tutoring and assistance to help these students stay in school. Although these programs have their critics, they have become an accepted part of most colleges and universities. The greatest conflicts have arisen over special admissions programs for graduate and professional schools. Competition for places in these schools is intense, and white students complain that they are the victims of reverse discrimination, because some whites are rejected in favor of less qualified minority students. Supporters of special admissions programs argue that minorities have already been subjected to a great deal of discrimination and that **affirmative action** programs merely attempt to compensate for some small part of it (see Chapter 7).

Reforming School Finance As was pointed out earlier, schools in rich districts often receive much more money per student than do schools in poor districts. Although this problem could be dealt with by reforming the system of school finance in individual states, such an approach cannot do anything to rectify the huge inequalities among states. The only solution to that dilemma is a much greater federal role in funding the schools. For example, if the federal government paid for all primary and secondary education, it could provide equitable funding for all schools. There is, however, a strong tradition of local control of the schools in the United States, and many people fear that national financing would mean federal control that would be unresponsive to the needs of local communities.

Although such concerns are certainly well grounded, there appear to be few alternatives to increased federal aid to education, even if it stops far short of complete financial support. When economic distress causes troubled school districts and financially strapped states to cut back on education, the result may be a vicious cycle, in which poorer education creates a less competent work force that, in turn, causes more economic problems. Federal money is needed to break this cycle. There is, moreover, another important reason for the federal government to get more involved: it is the only level of government that has the resources to significantly increase the overall funding for our educational system. Although critics of proposals to increase spending for education point out that the amount of money spent per child actually rose during the 1980s (largely as a result of declining student enrollments), America's commitment to education still ranks far behind most other industrialized nations. When the 15 major industrialized countries are ranked in terms of the percentage of national income they devote to primary and secondary education, only Australia ranks lower. In Sweden, the figure is 7 percent; in Canada, 4.7 percent; and in the United States, only 4.1 percent.[39]

Improving the Schools   The original Coleman report created a furor when it was first published in 1966, because it found that none of the measures of school quality it used—funding, teacher qualifications, or physical facilities—had much effect on the educational achievement of the students. These results were widely interpreted to mean that "schools don't make any difference." Subsequent research has shown that those results were largely a product of the extremely narrow questions the researchers asked and were highly misleading. For instance, Michael Rutter's 1979 study of London high schools found that they had a critical impact on student achievement. Not surprisingly, the best schools were those that maintained high standards, required more homework, and had clear and well-enforced standards of discipline yet still created a comfortable, supportive atmosphere for students.[40] Coleman himself later acknowledged that schools do make a substantial difference. In a comparison of private and public schools published in 1982, Coleman and his colleagues wrote that "the indication is that more extensive academic demands are made in the private schools, leading to more advanced courses, and thus to higher achievement."[41] In addition to the idea of requiring more work, reformers also propose reorganizing the school system and hiring better teachers.

Requiring More Work The most obvious way to improve academic performance is to raise the schools' requirements and make students work harder. In the 1960s, the schools were heavily criticized for their bureaucratic rigidity, and the curriculum was loosened to allow more individual choice. Now, with the increasing concern about scholastic achievement, these electives are being replaced with tougher requirements for more academic courses. A related suggestion that has yet to be implemented in most schools is to increase the amount of homework so that students must meet higher standards in the courses they do take. A criticism commonly heard from minority leaders is that tougher requirements force disadvantaged students out of the schools and into the streets. The efforts to make our schools more rigorous must therefore be accompanied by the kinds of compensatory educational programs discussed in the last section. Otherwise, the result is likely to be lower, not higher, academic performance among some groups.

While programs to increase academic standards and require more homework win at least verbal support from teachers and school administrators, another fundamental change, which these groups often oppose, needs to be made. The fact is that the United States has one of the shortest school years of any industrialized nation, and things are not much better in Canada (see Figure 4.3). The average student in the United States goes to school about 180 days a year, while in Japan schools are in session for around 240 days and in West Germany about 230 days. Moreover, the average school day is only six hours in North America, while eight-hour days are common in other nations.[42] It is unrealistic to expect American students to compete with their counterparts abroad who have over 30 percent more school days a year. The recommendation of the National Commission on Excellence in Education that the average school day be increased to seven hours and the school year be increased to between 200 and 220 days has largely been ignored, but it is hard to see how North American students can remain competitive without this kind of reform.

Restructuring the Schools The last decade has been a time of ferment in our educational system, and there are literally dozens of proposals for restructuring our schools. One of the most popular among conservatives is the **voucher system**. Under most versions of this plan, automatic support for existing public schools would be withdrawn and parents would be given a voucher that could be "spent" at any school, public or private. Advocates of the voucher system claim it would stimulate competition among the schools and force schools and teachers to provide top-quality edu-

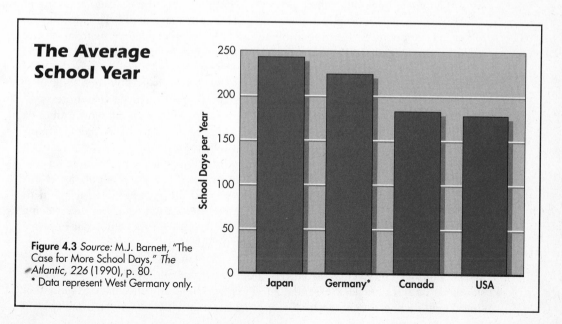

The Average School Year

School Days per Year

Japan   Germany*   Canada   USA

Figure 4.3 *Source:* M.J. Barnett, "The Case for More School Days," *The Atlantic, 226* (1990), p. 80.
* Data represent West Germany only.

cation or go out of business. Critics of these proposals, who include many of the nation's leading educators, say that such changes would create educational chaos as tens of thousands of independent schools sprang up, with enormous differences in quality, curriculum, and objectives. California's Superintendent of Public Instruction described the voucher proposals as "dangerous claptrap" that would produce the same disastrous results as the deregulation of the savings and loan industry, and Wisconsin's superintendent likened this approach to "nuking" the public school system.[43]

A less radical proposal is to open the enrollment of public schools so that students can attend any school they want. The idea is that such a program would cause a mass exodus from the weak schools and force them to improve in order to get their students back. Left unanswered are the questions of how the good schools could physically accommodate all the students who would want to come and what would happen to the teachers and facilities at the weaker schools. The school district in Richmond, California, recently tried this approach, converting its 47 campuses into specialty schools, each with its own distinctive focus, and allowing parents to choose among them. Although it was nationally touted as a creative response to the crisis of our schools, only three years after the start of the program the Richmond district is teetering on the edge of bankruptcy, with its expenditures running more than 25 percent higher than income.[44] However, critics disagree about whether the Richmond district's difficulties are the fault of bad management or of the reform program itself.

The Chicago school district, often called one of the worst in the nation, has attempted to solve its problems by a sweeping decentralization program that gives control of local schools to boards elected in each neighborhood. The initial implementation of the program resulted in a great deal of confusion, but it is too early to say if the long-term results will be positive. Whether or not the Chicago experiment works, many educators support more "school-based management." The idea here is to cut out the countless bureaucratic rules and requirements that come from central school administrators and give the decision-making power directly to principals and teachers at the local schools. But to be successful, such a policy must make the local schools accountable for the results of the program, as measured by such indicators as their dropout rates or student performance on standardized achievement tests.

A proposal for educational reform that has been tried throughout North America calls for the public schools to get "back to basics." According to this concept, schools should create a more rigorous curriculum that focuses on the basic skills of reading, writing, and mathematics, and both teacher and student performance should be continually evaluated by standardized tests. But despite the increasing popularity of this approach, troubling questions remain. As more and more importance is given to standardized tests, teachers have been accused of "teaching to the test": sacrificing the broader goals of education and focusing exclusively on the skills that improve test scores. Moreover, many educators reject the idea that successful education involves nothing more than teaching students to excel at basic skills. Is it better, they ask, to produce creative, well-adjusted children or neurotic overachievers who ace standardized tests but lack essential social skills? Obviously the matter is not that simple, but there are many alternative approaches that hold out a much broader ideal for education. The famous Summerhill "free" school, for example, encourages open expression and democratic principles among its students and allows them to focus their studies on whatever subjects interest them the most,[45] and the rapidly growing Waldorf schools give as much importance to art and personal development as to basic academic skills.[46]

Better Teachers In the long run, there is nothing more important to the schools than the quality and dedication of their teachers. Recruiting and keeping the best possible faculty is therefore a vital task facing our schools. The most obvious way to achieve that goal is to recognize that there is less prestige in being an elementary or secondary teacher than there was in the past, and then to offer a substantial increase in pay to attract and retain high-quality professionals. One proposal already implemented in many school districts provides additional merit pay for superior teachers. A related approach is to create master-teacher programs in which a school's best teachers are given extra pay to provide counseling and assistance to other teachers.

Money, however, is not the only problem. Teachers also complain about the frustrations of working within a bureaucracy that is often more concerned about the smooth functioning of its schools than about education. Other sources of discontent are excessive paperwork, and the conflict between the demand that they be class-

Great improvements in computer-assisted education have been made in recent years, but to take full advantage of these advances, schools must have better trained teachers and more equipment.

room police officers and the need to be educators. It is no surprise, then, that teachers suffer such a high burnout rate. Fewer than one in five new teachers is still in the profession after ten years.[47]

But streamlining the bureaucracy and increasing pay will not guarantee that enough top-quality teachers will be recruited. Success will depend largely on society's attitude toward education. As Tom Hayden, chair of the California Assembly's Subcommittee on Higher Education, put it:

> The desire to teach is fostered in a social climate that supports the personal mission of helping others grow, of creating and sharing knowledge and pursuing a higher quality of life. Such values are not promoted in a climate of self-serving shortsightedness that lures people toward the quick fix, the fast buck, and the easy answer. Until a new emphasis on public service and social responsibility arises to balance narrow self-interest, the teaching crisis will remain difficult to resolve.[48]

SOCIOLOGICAL PERSPECTIVES ON PROBLEMS OF EDUCATION

The Functionalist Perspective Functionalists see education as a basic institution that must meet a growing list of social needs. Originally, the two principal functions of education were to teach students a body of skills and knowledge, and then to grade them on how well they had mastered their studies. Education also became an important channel for social mobility for talented students from disadvantaged backgrounds. As industrial societies became more diverse and education became virtually universal, the schools took on an increasingly important role in transmitting values and attitudes as well as skills. They also assumed the important **latent** (hidden) **function** of reducing unemployment by keeping many young people out of the labor market. Finally, as the traditional family unit became more unstable, educational institutions were asked to take up some of the slack by launching programs to prevent delinquent behavior and to help deal with students' social and psychological needs.

Many functionalists believe that our schools have been given so many conflicting tasks they are unable to do any of them very well, and as a result their efforts to achieve one goal often conflict with the other goals they have taken on. For example, the time spent on drug education or "teen skills" can detract from the schools' academic programs, and the attempts to modify the curriculum to prevent disadvantaged students from getting discouraged may lower the achievement of more gifted students. Functionalists also complain that many schools have become disorganized because of poor management and the lack of sufficient concern on the part of parents and the community.

All functionalists do not agree on how to make the schools more effective. Many advocate the elimination of a number of new programs that have been introduced in recent years. Although such changes might well improve fundamental education, they are also likely to disrupt the efforts to deal with other pressing social problems. Proposals for employing more effective teaching methods are also compatible with the functionalist perspective. But most functionalists argue that such reforms can work only if they are accompanied by a reorganization of the schools. For example, teachers must be rewarded for good teaching, rather than for being efficient bureaucrats or for the length of time they have spent on the job. Finally, many functionalists advocate better planning and coordination with other social institutions in order to reduce the problem of unemployment and underemployment among the educated. But such a program must be combined with an effort to reduce the instability of our economic institutions, since it is impossible to train students to meet the needs of an economy that is in a state of rapid and unpredictable flux.

The Conflict Perspective   Conflict theorists are not convinced that providing equal educational opportunity and upward mobility for the poor have ever been goals of our educational system. Rather, they argue that the schools are organized to do the opposite: to keep members of subordinate groups in their place and prevent them from competing with members of more privileged classes. They point to the fact that free public education for all children is a relatively new idea and that even today many poor children must drop out of school to help support their families. Moreover, expensive private schools provide a superior education for children from the upper classes, whereas the public schools that serve the poor are underfunded, understaffed, and growing worse. Conflict theorists also argue that the old system of officially segregated education and the current system of de facto segregation serve to keep blacks and other oppressed minorities at the bottom of the social heap. Their general conclusion is that the social and cultural biases in the educational system are not accidents but rather are reflections of a social system that favors the powerful.

Conflict theorists also see the schools as powerful agents of socialization that can be used as a tool for one group to exercise its cultural dominance over another. For example, feminists point out that schools perpetuate sexist attitudes by showing boys and girls in stereotyped gender roles, and encouraging girls to be the "cheerleaders" while the boys are the achievers. (See Chapter 10 for a further discussion of sexism in education.) Another striking example of socialization comes from the educational system's treatment of minorities. Until relatively recently, young Native Americans were likely to be taught that their ancestors were bloodthirsty savages, and African Americans often read in history textbooks that their forebears were happy-go-lucky "darkies" who actually enjoyed being slaves.

From the conflict perspective, the best and perhaps the only way to change these conditions is for the poor and cultural and ethnic minorities to organize themselves and reshape the educational system so that it provides everyone with equal opportunity but does not indoctrinate students in the cultural values and beliefs of any particular group. All children must be given the same quality of education that is now available in private schools; cash subsidies must be provided for poor students who would otherwise be forced to drop out of school; and special programs must be set up to provide extra help for children whose parents have a weak educational background. Nevertheless, most conflict theorists probably agree with Christopher Jencks, who concluded that the educational system can do little to reduce inequality without changes in the broader society. Even if there were complete educational equality and everyone were given a college education, social and economic disparities would remain. Such changes would not produce more interesting, highly paid professional jobs or reduce the number of menial, low-paying ones. Thus, educational and social change must be carried out together.

Social Psychological Perspectives Social psychologists are concerned with how schoolchildren learn. They also study the impact of the educational system on students' psychological development. Many have commented on the possibility that the authoritarianism so common in our schools impedes learning and encourages undemocratic behavior in later life. Moreover, schools create serious psychological problems for students who for one reason or another do not fit into the educational system. The heavy emphasis on competition and the consequent fear of failure are disturbing to those students who are already anxious and insecure. Students who do not do well in school are often troubled by feelings of depression and inadequacy, and the failure to live up to the academic expectations of parents and teachers is a major contributor to teenage suicide. Summerhill and other free-school experiments are attempts to improve the socialization process and, thus, to deal with these problems.

Other social psychologists, however, are not convinced that the social relationships in most traditional schools are harmful. They note that rational discipline may benefit children by exposing them to the rules and regulations that they will be expected to follow after they leave school. Moreover, some behaviorists have charged that children in more open schools are reinforced for behavior that is unacceptable outside the school. These social psychologists do not necessarily favor the programs of traditional schools, however. Some children need a great deal of discipline and an emphasis on obedience to authority, but social relationships of this kind impede the ability of other children to learn and to function effectively. Thus, it seems logical to provide the greatest possible range of educational alternatives so that the needs of each student can be met.

SUMMARY

Schools, colleges, and universities were originally reserved for the elite. Today, however, education has become a big business, employing millions of teachers and administrators.

Children from the lower classes generally do not do as well in school as children from the middle and upper classes. Poor children usually come to school with a variety of economic and cultural handicaps, and the school system discriminates against these children in a number of ways as well. Racial and ethnic discrimination in the American educational system goes back to the days of slavery. Since the Supreme Court's decision outlawing school segregation (1954), most legal (de jure) discrimination has been abolished. However, de facto (actual) segregation arising from segregated housing patterns is still widespread.

Schools are always struggling to deal with the twin problems of authority and rebellion. If schools lack discipline, students run wild and education suffers. But if discipline is too strict, students learn antidemocratic values and attitudes, and the likelihood of rebellion and delinquency is increased.

There has been a growing concern about the quality of our educational system because of the decline in high school students' scores on standardized achievement tests. Some critics argue that those tests are not a good measure of educational quality, others claim that the problem lies in the changing family environment of today's students, while still others hold the schools themselves responsible.

Many proposals for creating more equal education have been offered. These include programs to achieve more effective integration, programs to give special assistance to poor and minority students, and reforms in school finance. Suggestions for improving the educational process itself include raising academic standards and requiring more homework, lengthening the school year, restructuring the schools to give teachers and local administrators more power, and making education a more attractive career so that the schools can hire better teachers.

Functionalists argue that the educational system is not running smoothly and that solving the problems of education is mostly a matter of reorganizing schools so that they will operate more efficiently. Conflict theorists are prone to look behind the stated goals of the educational system and argue that economic and political elites have an interest in achieving other, unstated goals that favor those in positions of power. Social psychologists are concerned about the harmful effects the educational system may have on individual students and about the best ways to correct these problems.

KEY TERMS

compensatory education   A program designed to help make up for the educational difficulties disadvantaged students experience.

de facto segregation   A system in which different ethnic or racial groups are in fact separated from each other even though the law does not require it.

de jure segregation   A system in which the law requires the separation of different ethnic or racial groups.

grade inflation   The practice of assigning increasingly higher grades to work of the same quality.

hidden curriculum   The attitudes and beliefs that students must learn in order to succeed in school, such as obedience to authority, that are not part of the formal curriculum.

voucher system   A program in which the government gives students a voucher that may be used to pay for their education at any school they or their parents choose.

FURTHER READINGS

Robert James Parelius and Ann Parker Parelius, *The Sociology of Education*, 2nd ed. (Englewood Cliffs, N.J.: Prentice-Hall, 1987). A good general text examining our educational system from a sociological perspective.

Jeannie Oakes, *Multiplying Inequalities* (Santa Monica, Calif.: Rand Corporation, 1990). A report on the way schools promote social inequality.

Helen Lefkowitz Horowitz, *Campus Life* (Chicago: University of Chicago Press, 1987). An interesting historical look at the subculture of college undergraduates and how it has changed.

Christine H. Rossell and Willis D. Hawley, eds., *The Consequences of School Desegregation* (Philadelphia: Temple University Press, 1983). A collection of essays that provide a comprehensive look at what we know about the effects of school desegregation.

Merry White, *The Japanese Educational Challenge: A Commitment to Children* (New York: Free Press, 1987). An examination of the educational system in the nation that has been the twentieth century's biggest economic success story.

chapter 5

Problems of the Family

- How is the modern family changing?
- Is divorce a social problem?
- What are the causes of family violence?
- Are children victims of their parents' problems?
- How can the family be strengthened?

The family is found in one form or another in every known society. Yet observers dating back as far as ancient Greece have bemoaned its "decay," complaining of everything from youthful rebelliousness to a breakdown of traditional moral values. But these age-old complaints have taken on new meaning in the industrial era. Traditional beliefs about the family, from the assumption of male dominance to the restriction of sexual relations to the married couple, are being challenged. The divorce rate has soared, and an increasing number of women are having children without ever having been married at all.

Some take all this as a sign of the impending collapse of our family system, but such arguments ignore the many strengths of today's families. The family is certainly changing, but it shows no signs of disappearing. Almost everyone eventually marries, and most people who divorce marry again. And it is not at all clear that families in the past were any happier than they are today. In fact, the opposite may be true. In traditional family systems, marriage partners were pressured to maintain even bitterly unhappy marriages that would be quickly dissolved today. The fact that the divorce rate was lower a hundred years ago than it is today hardly means that families then were healthier or happier. Although the erosion of traditional family structure has caused problems for many people, it has also given many others the opportunity to create a new family network that is better suited to the needs and desires of our times.

THE NATURE OF THE FAMILY

A **family** is usually defined as a group of people related by marriage, ancestry, or adoption who live together in a common household. Although the family is universal to all human societies, its structure and traditions vary enormously from one place to another. For example, some societies permit only one husband and wife, while others allow many more. Anthropologist George P. Murdock's classic study of 565 societies found that about one-fourth followed the pattern of **monogamy** (only one husband and one wife at a time), whereas over 70 percent allowed **polygyny** (more than one wife). Murdock also found 4 societies in which a woman is allowed more than one husband.[1] Another useful classification divides families into two types: nuclear and extended. The **nuclear family** consists of a married couple and their children. Although there are often close ties between the members of the nuclear family and the other relatives of the husband and wife, nuclear families are independent, self-controlled units. When two people marry, the couple and their children become a separate family unit, usually living apart from the families in which the wife and husband were reared. The nuclear family is the dominant pattern in all the world's industrialized nations.

Although the nuclear family is the norm in our culture, anthropologists have found that the **extended family**, which includes a much wider range of relatives than the nuclear family, is the ideal in most agricultural societies around the world. At the time of marriage, the wife usually becomes a member of the husband's family, which consists of his grandparents, their sons and their wives, and their grandchildren. There are also a substantial number of societies in which the husband joins his wife's family. In a few societies, the grandparents are excluded and the extended family is based on the tie between brothers and sisters of the same generation.[2]

The contemporary nuclear family typically consists of only a married couple and their children.

Life in an extended family is very different from the life most of us know in the nuclear family. For one spouse at least, marriage does not represent a sharp break with the past, as it does in our culture. That spouse continues to live with his or her parents, as before. Although the adjustment is more difficult for the spouse who must move into a new family, husband and wife both remain under the authority of the older generation. They have little chance of controlling their own lives unless they outlive their siblings and take over the responsibility for the entire family.

In an extended family, everyone is expected to marry and have children, and those who do not are often seen as failures. The needs of the family are considered more important than those of its individual members, and people are expected to stay in their marriage no matter how bad it becomes. The father is usually the absolute head of the family, and he exercises great authority over his wife and children. The woman's place is in the home, and she is often denied the right to control her own property or to participate in society as an independent person. On the other hand, each family member receives far more support and protection from the family unit. For example, many more adults are involved in the rearing of the children, so if something happens to one of the parents, there is always someone else to take over.[3]

The industrial revolution transformed family life as the large extended family deteriorated under the impact of changing economic conditions. Because most production took place outside the home, the economic base of the family weakened, forcing younger members to leave home to find employment.

Because the emerging nuclear family was smaller and less stable than the extended family, the development of the industrial economy spurred other institutions to take over part of the tasks that used to be the exclusive responsibility of the family. In the past, the family was the primary unit of economic production, but in industrialized nations corporate farms and factories have assumed most of that responsibility. The schools play an increasing role in the socialization of the young, just as government welfare programs are helping the family support the young and the old. The extended family also was once the primary agency of social control. In many agricultural societies the victims of a crime first looked to the family of the offender to make restitution before they attempted to complain to outside agencies (if such agencies even existed). Today, police, courts, and schools have a significant role in controlling the young, while the criminal-justice system has almost completely taken over responsibility for the control of adult behavior.[4]

Because many of the family's functions are now carried out by other social institutions, it is much easier to live without family support. Marriage has become a matter of individual choice. Couples marry out of the desire for companionship and personal happiness, not because of duty to their families or economic necessity. **Romantic love** has taken on tremendous importance as the process of mate selection has focused on finding a compatible person and "falling in love." Love is considered a kind of magic potion that can overcome almost any problem. In sharp contrast, traditional societies see romantic love as a frivolous basis for marriage and a threat to the smooth operation of the family system. And in one sense it is, for our emphasis on love and personal happiness leads to the belief that unhappy marriages should be dissolved. When we say that two people have "fallen in love," we imply that the matter is beyond their control, a bit like fate. It follows that they can also fall out of love.

THE MODERN FAMILY

Although modern industrial societies have already gone through the wrenching change from the extended to the nuclear family system, that does not mean that we have reached a new plateau of stability. The pattern of family life continues to show the same restless change that seems to characterize all facets of industrial society. The most significant trends are the ongoing decline in the size of the family, the shifting relationships between husbands and wives, and the continued importance of the family in the daily lives of most people.

Growing Smaller Year by year, generation by generation, the American family has been getting smaller. In 1790 the average American household had almost six persons; today it contains less than three.[5] One important reason for this trend is that people are staying single longer than they did in the past, so there are now more one-person households. (See Figure 5.1.) Between 1970 and 1987, the average age at marriage increased by about three years, and the statistics also indicate that people are waiting longer after a divorce before they remarry. Industrial society's ever-increasing demand for education and training is certainly one reason more marriages are delayed, but there are other important factors as well. Greater acceptance of premarital sex makes

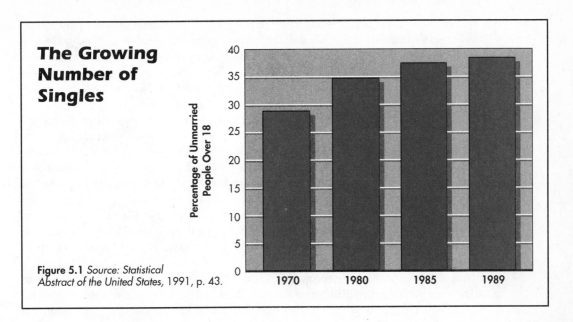

The Growing Number of Singles

Percentage of Unmarried People Over 18

40
35
30
25
20
15
10
5
0

1970   1980   1985   1989

Figure 5.1 *Source: Statistical Abstract of the United States,* 1991, p. 43.

the single life more attractive, and the public's attitude toward singles has undergone a remarkable change. The nineteenth-century stereotypes of the lonely bachelor and the neglected spinster have been replaced by the new stereotype of affluent, carefree singles who often elicit envy instead of pity among their married friends. The high disposable income of some singles has made them the focus of a new consumer industry that includes everything from singles-only apartment buildings to packaged singles vacations. These changes, along with a significant increase in the population of young adults, led to a 50 percent rise in the number of single people during the 1970s and another 24 percent increase in the 1980s.[6] But these figures should not be misinterpreted. The vast majority of Americans eventually get married (over 90 percent); they are simply choosing to remain single for a somewhat longer part of their lives.

Another reason families are shrinking is that they are having fewer children. We will examine the reasons for this more thoroughly in Chapter 16, but there is little doubt that they are closely linked to the process of industrialization. Technology has helped to bring down the death rate, so that it is no longer necessary to have many children to ensure that a few survive. And although children were an economic asset in a traditional agricultural society, they are often a financial burden in the industrial world.

Finally, there has been a significant growth in the number of single-parent families. In 1970, single-parent families made up less than 13 percent of all American families, but today that figure is over 23 percent; and those families contain about a quarter of all American children.[7] The causes of this increase are easy to find. As we shall see in the next section, the percentage of single-parent families headed by widows has declined, but there has been a sharp increase in the number of families headed by women who have been divorced or have never married.

Changing Roles Our ideas about what role the wife and the husband should play in the family are undergoing a profound change. The traditional ideal of the breadwinning husband who makes the decisions and rules the family and his stay-at-home wife who raises the children and does the housework is being challenged by a new vision of marital equality. In the egalitarian marriage, husband and wife are considered equal partners. They make important decisions together, and they share the work necessary to keep the family going. Both husband and wife often work outside the home, but the key is that the tasks of child care, housework, and breadwinning are fairly distributed so that the two partners shoulder an equal share of the burden. As recently as 1974, a majority of both men and woman surveyed by the Harris poll considered "a traditional marriage" best, "with the husband assuming responsibility for providing for the family and the wife running the home and taking care of the children." But little more than a decade later, in 1985, a majority of women (57% to 37%) and men (50% to 43%) were convinced that a better marriage is one "where the husband and wife share responsibilities more—both work, share the housekeeping and the child responsibilities."[8]

But although more and more people claim to believe in marital equality, we are still a long way from realizing those ideals. Most wives still assume the primary responsibility for the "women's work" of child care and housekeeping, and most men continue to see their role as the primary breadwinner. The great importance that our society attaches to financial success, the relatively low status given to child rearing, and the cultural traditions of male dominance often mean that the husband has a disproportionate share in the decision-making power.

One area where there has been the most obvious change is in the economic role of the wife. In 1938, a national survey found that three-fourths of all Americans disapproved of a woman working if her husband could support her. But 40 years later, another survey found a complete reversal of public opinion: three-fourths of those surveyed approved of wives holding a job.[9] And the statistics show that behavior has changed along with the attitudes. In 1989, 57.8 percent of all married women were employed outside the home, as were 65.8 percent of married women with children.[10] Since less than one-third of all families have only a single male breadwinner, the typical American family is now a **dual-earner family**. It should be noted, however, that males continue to carry greater responsibilities as "breadwinners," both because they usually earn higher wages than their wives (see Chapter 10) and because a much greater proportion of working wives are employed in part-time jobs than their husbands.

Continued Importance Critics of contemporary society often see a rising tide of narcissism washing away the sense of commitment and self-sacrifice necessary to maintain a healthy family. In this view, we have become so obsessed with our personal satisfactions that we have no time left for anyone else. Public opinion polls offer no support for this dismal view of modern life, however. The American public consistently rates a good family life as their single most important goal—more important than good health, self-respect, or personal happiness. Moreover, the public sees no contradiction between personal happiness and the demands of family living. When the Harris poll asked Americans who is happiest, 65 percent said married people and only 18 percent said single people.[11]

D E B A T E

Are Dual-Earner Families Harmful to Children?

YES The wrenching changes of industrialization gravely weakened the family. Just two parents are now expected to perform all the duties that had been carried out by a whole team of relatives working together. Moreover, most of these new responsibilities were placed on the mother. It is ridiculous to argue that the children do not suffer if the mother works outside the home, in addition to performing all her other duties. There are only so many hours in the day, and the working mother simply cannot do as much for her children. The father may be able to assume a few of her tasks, but he is likely to be just as busy and overworked as she.

Children in families with two wage earners return from school to an empty home or, worse, simply run wild on the streets until their parents come home from work. Even those who are in day-care are little better off. Most day-care facilities are private businesses, and the children's emotional needs take a backseat to the demand for profit. Even the best day-care centers cannot provide the love and attention we expect from a child's parents.

Children in dual-earner families also suffer from an increase in conflict between the parents. The demands of trying to manage two careers and perform the many duties of child rearing place continual pressure on both partners. The result is more fights and more hostility. Tired, overworked parents lose their tempers more quickly with their children and each other. Some even come to resent the burdens their children place on them. But whatever the parents' attitude toward their children, their sons and daughters are bound to be affected by the rise in tension in the home.

There are some families in which both parents must work just to keep everyone

NO There is no scientific evidence to show that children are harmed when both their parents work. On the contrary, there is good reason to believe that they actually benefit. The most obvious advantage is the extra income that enables children to have things they otherwise would be denied. A higher standard of living does not simply mean more toys, hamburgers, and sweaters. It means music lessons, travel, special tutoring, a computer, or perhaps even a private school with superior academic standards.

Contrary to the charges of traditionalists, working mothers are often more satisfied with their lives than are those who stay at home. As a result, they do a better job of parenting. Certainly the working mother provides a much more positive role model for her children. And daughters and sons both benefit from the fact that fathers generally assume more responsibilities of parenting in dual-earner families. Finally, an independent income gives the mother more power in the dual-earner family; the children are therefore more likely to believe in the value of equality because their families are in fact more egalitarian.

Critics charge that professional day care harms children, but the evidence indicates that children benefit enormously, if the parents select good quality care. Children in day-care centers are exposed to new ideas and playmates, and, as a result, they have a more enriched background and usually do better in school.

Although critics of dual-earner families make a lot of charges, they haven't proven any of them. The real reason for their objections is that these families violate their prejudiced notion that a woman's place is in the home. In modern society, the woman's place is anywhere she chooses to be.

fed. In most cases, however, it is sheer greed that sends both parents off to work, for our people are already among the richest in the world. Children are more important than money, and their needs must come first.

Dual-earner families promote greater human freedom and more equality and therefore benefit both children and adults.

Thus, there is no reason to believe that we see the family as any less important than in the past. If anything, we demand more from it. The expectation of love and emotional gratification from one's spouse is probably higher than it has ever been, and the increasing impersonality of modern society has made the family the only island of warm personal relationships that many people have. There is, moreover, evidence that most people are happy with their married life. A 1976 survey found that 80 percent of married Americans described their marriages as "very happy" or "above average,"[12] and a more recent Harris poll found that 85 percent of married people said that they would remarry their spouse if they had it to do all over again.[13]

Most early studies of the nuclear family pictured it as an independent unit relatively isolated from other kin.[14] But other researchers argue that modern kinship networks are much stronger than was first believed.[15] Most nuclear families are certainly enmeshed in a significant web of relationships with other relatives. Substantial amounts of financial aid flow from one generation to another, usually from parents to young married couples and later from middle-aged couples to aging parents. Members of kinship networks also provide one another with important services, ranging from

Most nuclear families still maintain close ties to grandparents even though they do not usually live in the same home.

babysitting to emotional and financial support in times of personal distress. There are also extensive social and recreational contacts between the members of many kinship networks. It is true, however, that kinship ties are much narrower in modern society than they were in the past. The primary bonds are with parents, siblings, and children, and other kinship ties are usually much less important.[16]

FAMILY PROBLEMS

The modern family is in much better shape than is commonly believed, but it is still plagued by a host of problems we are still struggling to solve. In this section we will examine five of today's most important family issues: divorce, births outside of marriage, violence, child rearing, and the inequalities of family life.

Divorce This century has seen a dramatic increase in divorce rates. In 1920 there was one divorce for every seven marriages in the United States; 50 years later the rate had climbed to one divorce for every three marriages. There is now almost one divorce for every two marriages, making the divorce rate in the United States nearly twice as high as in Canada and clearly one of the highest in the world.[17] However, the divorce rate peaked in 1985 and has declined slightly since then.[18] But at this time it is unclear whether this is a temporary pause or if the years of steady increase are over.

Who Gets Divorced? In the nineteenth century, divorce was mainly for the wealthy. Great Britain and many American states required a special government act for each divorce, and the poor lacked the influence and money necessary for such decrees. Now divorce is most common among the poor, and the divorce rate declines as education and income increase.

19th-Century Social Problems

John and Leo Koelbel, well-to-do farmers residing in the town of Newton, had a hearing in Manitowoc in the county court before Judge Anderson, having been cited there on the charge of contempt for failing to comply with an order of the court commanding them to pay 60 cents a week each for the support of their aged parents. . . . The 2 sons have positively refused to give a single cent toward the support of their father and mother. The court ordered them both to be committed to the county jail until they saw fit to comply with the order. . . .

June 11, 1900

These selections, which appear throughout the text, are from the *Badger State Banner*, a newspaper published in Black River Falls, Wisconsin.

One cause of the higher divorce rate among the poor is the special economic problems they experience. As an old saying puts it, "When poverty comes in the door, love goes out the window." It is possible, too, that divorce is less frequent among the wealthy because dissolution of marriage requires complex arrangements for distributing wealth and income among family members. Also, the availability of travel, entertainment, and servants helps the wealthy adjust more easily to married life.

Age is an important factor in marital instability. A teenage marriage is almost three times more likely to end in divorce than a marriage of partners over 30.[19] The divorce rate also varies significantly among different ethnic groups. Black females are about 20 percent more likely to be divorced than white females, and the difference for males is larger: about 40 percent.[20]

Most divorces occur fairly soon after marriage. About 5 percent of all divorces occur within the first year of marriage, and the second and third years of marriage are the most likely time for a divorce.[21] Considering the length of time it takes to get divorced in many states, this means that many couples begin divorce proceedings shortly after their wedding.

Why the Upward Trend? The increase in divorce has caused considerable alarm among those who consider it a sign of personal failure or moral decay. Sociologically, the increase is most clearly related to the decline of the extended family. The partners in today's marriages receive considerably less support from relatives than their great-grandparents did. Thus, when trouble arises, they have fewer resources on which to draw. At the same time, unhappy couples are now under much less pressure from their families to stay together and avoid divorce. Even if parents want a married couple to stay together, they seldom have the economic power to enforce their wishes.

The shift from the extended family system to the nuclear family has made it easier to see the goal of marriage as nothing more than the personal satisfaction of the two partners. The romanticism on which courtship is now based leads many young people to expect marriage to be a state of perpetual happiness and conflict-free bliss. When they start quarreling about money matters, about how much time they should spend with each other, about recreational or intellectual interests, or about who is supposed to sweep the floor and carry out the garbage, they imagine that love has flown out the window and that they can no longer continue their relationship.

Changes in the role women play in our society have also made divorce a more practical economic alternative than it was in past years. More and more women are working outside the home, making them less dependent on their husbands and, thus, less likely to stay married to a man they have grown to dislike. Attitudes toward divorce have changed too. Only 50 years ago divorce was seen as an immoral act, an affront to "decent" people. The divorced woman was stigmatized as a "grass widow" and her virtue exposed to public question. Public sentiment was so strongly against divorce that it was forbidden in some countries, and many others made it extremely difficult. Today divorce carries less stigma, and the consensus seems to be that it is better to separate than to continue in an unhappy marriage. And as attitudes have changed, so have the laws. In 1969, California became the first state to pass a "no-fault" divorce law, and its example has been followed by other states. Instead of having to go through the painful process of proving that one partner did not fulfill the conditions of the marriage contract, the "no-fault" law allows for divorce by mutual agreement, substantially reducing the legal costs of a divorce.

Is Divorce a Social Problem? There is no doubt that a divorce is often the only satisfactory solution to an impossible family situation. Nevertheless, divorce continues to be seen as a sign of failure—an admission by the marriage partners that they lack the ability, trust, or stamina to continue an intimate relationship. Many of the problems confronting divorced people stem from such attitudes, and because the parties to a divorce often share them, they feel guilty and ashamed about the breakup of their marriage. Despite the high frequency of divorce, we have not developed effective means for helping newly divorced people make the transition to a different life style. When a spouse dies, relatives rally around the widow or widower to provide emotional and financial support. There are also a variety of rituals, such as the funeral service, to help ease the pain of transition. Yet the divorced person, who experiences many of the same problems, seldom receives the same kind of support.

But whatever social support a couple may receive, divorce is bound to cause personal suffering. The termination of an intimate relationship and the accompanying feelings of anger and failure make divorce a painful experience, even if there are no serious clashes. From a social viewpoint, the major cost of divorce is the division of families with children into smaller and therefore weaker units. Because of the occupational discrimination against women, a family consisting of a mother and children is likely to have a lower income than a two-parent family. And single parents, regardless of their sex, have great difficulty handling both the role of breadwinner and the role of parent.

The greatest concern about divorce centers on the children. The parents chose to have their divorce, and, it is hoped, have the maturity and judgment to deal with it. The children are clearly another matter. Studies of the children of divorce show high levels of fear, grief, sadness, and anger at what has happened to them.[22] Although most children eventually learn to adjust to their new situation, a divorce can have lasting effects. Children whose parents are divorced have higher rates of school absenteeism and delinquency and are themselves more likely to become divorced when they grow up.[23] But all this does not mean that children are better off if conflict-ridden marriages are kept together. A recent study of more than 20,000 children by a research team headed by Andrew Cherlin concluded that children whose parents were divorced did indeed suffer significantly more behavioral and psychological problems than other children. However, many of their difficulties actually started long before their parents' divorce, as tensions and conflicts built up within the family.[24] Another study of 1,400 children found that the effects of persistent conflicts in the home were just as harmful as the breakup of a marriage.[25] However, these findings apply only to families with very serious problems. As Cherlin put it, "Among families wracked by intense conflict, violence, and substance abuse, many children would be better off if their parents split up. But in the average divorce . . . I'm not at all convinced that [the] children are better off."[26]

Births Outside of Marriage Like divorce, the number of childbirths by single women has shown a remarkable increase in recent years. The percentage of babies born to single women more than doubled in the last two decades, and now represents about 25

19th-Century Social Problems

Lena Watson of Black River Falls gave birth to an illegitimate child and choked it to death.

October 9, 1890

percent of all births. But such general statistics obscure some important differences between ethnic groups. Almost 64 percent of black babies are born to single women, whereas that figure is about 34 percent for Hispanics and 18 percent for whites.[27]

The reasons for the high birthrate among single African American women are a matter of heated debate. When a widely publicized report by Daniel Moynihan first called attention to this issue in 1965, it was denounced as a racist attack on black Americans. But there is now a growing concern with this problem in the black community itself. Although the causes are not entirely clear, several factors stand out. First and foremost, blacks are much more likely to be poor than whites, and the illegitimacy rate is much higher among poor people from all ethnic groups. Second, the prejudice and discrimination that have been aimed at blacks for so many years have hit particularly hard at black males from poor homes. As William Julius Wilson has shown, a deteriorating labor market for young black males has produced a significant decline in the number of desirable marriage partners for black women.[28] A third factor is the devastating effects slavery had on the black family (see Chapter 7).[29]

It is, however, easy to exaggerate the differences between blacks and whites. The birthrates of unmarried women are growing rapidly among all ethnic groups; blacks were merely the first ones to feel the effects of this trend. In fact, since 1960 the birthrate has increased almost twice as fast among single white women as among single black women.[30]

The overall increase in the birthrate of single women is ultimately a result of the same social forces that broke down the extended family. Among the more immediate causes, the rise in sexual activity among teenagers combined with the failure to use appropriate contraceptive techniques stands out as the major contributor (see Chapter 11). Although American teenagers have about the same level of sexual activity as European teenagers, they are less likely to use birth control, and consequently their illegitimacy rate is far higher. Another important factor is the growing unwillingness of young couples to marry simply because the woman becomes pregnant. Studies of births in past centuries, when illegitimacy rates were low, show that about 20 to 25 percent of all weddings occurred after the conception of a child.[31] Today the "shotgun wedding" (in which a pregnant woman's father threatens the young man if he does not marry the virgin he has "spoiled") has gone out of style. The children of unwed mothers are still often condemned, but the stigma has decreased over the years.

The social position of an unmarried woman with a child in today's society is not very different from her divorced counterpart. However, she is more likely to suffer from such problems as feelings of embarrassment and guilt, the belief that she has been deserted by the father of the child, and the lack of emotional support she needs during the difficult months of pregnancy. But the greatest problem of unmarried mothers comes from the fact that most of them are not ready for the responsibilities of parenthood. The vast majority of single mothers are under 25 when they give birth, and about a third of all such births are to teenagers.[32]

These births are seldom planned, and the arrival of an unexpected and often unwanted child may have wrenching consequences for the young mother. Teenagers who become pregnant are more likely to drop out of school and either work at lower-paying jobs or be unemployed than their peers. Their children have a higher rate of infant mortality and more serious health problems than those of others. Three of every four children born to unmarried women live in poverty.[33]

Violence Beatings, slashings, stabbings, burnings, and chokings are common events in many families. Mildred Daley Pagelow estimates that about 12 million wives are beaten by their husbands and that somewhere between 1 and 2 million children are abused every year in the United States.[34] Family violence ranges in severity from the spanking of a troublesome child (which, though usually socially acceptable, is still a form of violence) to cold-blooded murder. Until quite recently, much family violence remained hidden behind closed doors. Even now, law enforcement agencies seldom get the cooperation they need to prosecute wife beaters and child abusers.

Violence Between Husband and Wife The relationship between husbands and wives is one of the strongest bonds in our society. It is deep, passionate, and often violent. The exact amount of husband-wife violence is difficult to determine, but it is one of the most common of all forms of violence. More calls to the police involve family disturbances than all other forms of violent behavior combined. In one of the most comprehensive studies of family violence to date, Murray A. Straus, Richard J. Gelles, and Suzanne K. Steinmetz found that about a quarter of the husbands and wives they interviewed admitted that there had been violence between them at some time in their marriage. But the researchers suspect that their study may have underestimated the rate of husband-wife violence. They estimate that it actually occurs in some form in about one of every two marriages.[35]

In many societies, such as those in the Middle East, husbands have traditionally had the legal right to physically punish wives who refuse to accept male authority. Although this practice is no longer approved of in Western culture, it still occurs. However, as women gain financial and social equality, they also gain greater power in the home, making it easier for them to demand an end to the violence or to leave abusive husbands. Straus, Gelles, and Steinmetz found that families that make their decisions democratically have lower rates of both child abuse and husband-wife violence than families in which one member dominates the other.[36]

The effort of husbands to dominate their wives is, however, only one of many causes of family violence. Recent surveys show that a surprising number of violent incidents are actually begun by the wife, not the husband.[37] There is a great deal of evidence that there is a "cycle of violence" that is passed down from one generation to the next. Children raised in violent homes learn that violence is a way to deal with frustration and anger and are therefore much more likely to be violent themselves.[38] (See Chapter 13 for a more complete discussion of the causes of violence.)

Child Abuse No one really knows how many children are abused by their parents each year. For one thing, there is no clear line between "acceptable" punishment and child abuse. The vast majority of parents spank their children at some time or other. These parents are certainly not child abusers. Yet severe and repeated spankings can be just as cruel as other forms of violence. According to one estimate, 14 percent of all children are severely beaten by their parents each year.[39] Straus, Gelles, and Steinmetz found that 8 percent of the married couples with children they questioned admitted having kicked, bitten, or punched their children, and 4 percent admitted having "beaten up" their children.[40]

Although such figures are shocking, we probably do not abuse our children as much as our ancestors did. Traditionally, severe physical punishment was considered essential to the learning process. Many parents believed that "if you spare the rod, you spoil the child." In colonial America a statute even provided for the execution of sons who were "stubborn and rebellious" and failed to follow parental authority. There is, however, no record of such an execution actually taking place.[41] A comparison of the rates of child abuse in a survey first done in 1975 and repeated in 1985 found a 47 percent decrease in that ten-year period.[42] Although some of that difference may reflect a greater reluctance to admit having abused a child, it seems that the recent attention given to this problem is paying off.

David G. Gil's study of officially reported child-abuse cases provides some interesting insights into the type of child who is most likely to be mistreated.[43] Contrary to popular opinion, children of all ages, up to their senior year in high school, are abused. Abused children are much more likely to come from broken homes, and less than half of the abused children in Gil's sample were living with their natural father. Children from large families are also more likely to be abused. Gil found that the usual indicators of social class—income, occupational prestige, and education—are all negatively related to child abuse. In other words, the lower the parents' social and economic status, the more they tended to hurt their children. The children in Gil's sample were more likely to be abused by their mothers than by their fathers, in part because the fathers were not present in many homes. Many of Gil's findings, such as those concerning the sex and class differences in child abuse, were confirmed by the Straus, Gelles, and Steinmetz survey.

There are many explanations of child abuse. Psychologists tend to picture child abusers as people who are mentally ill or at least have severe emotional problems. The typical child abuser is described as impulsive, immature, and depressed, with little control over his or her emotions. Social workers are inclined to see environmental stress as the most important cause of child abuse. They note that an unwanted pregnancy, desertion by the husband, or unemployment and poverty put special pressures on a parent that may result in child abuse. Social psychologists have found evidence that most child abusers learned that behavior when they were abused during their own childhood (see Chapter 13). That is, they themselves were beaten when they were young, and they in turn beat their own children.

Many sociologists argue that child abuse occurs so frequently in America because the physical punishment of children is condoned and even encouraged. They call for laws that would make it a crime to inflict physical punishment on children, as has already been done in Sweden. But it is important to remember that child abuse can be psychological as well as physical. Countless parents cause severe emotional damage to their children without ever being physically violent.

Child Rearing Raising children to replace family members who grow old and die is the most critical function of the family. The vitality and even the survival of a society depends on how effectively the family does this job. Thus, every society is only about 20 years from extinction, for if a society fails to socialize its children for that length of time, it will cease to exist. Of course, this is very unlikely to happen. But it is clear that there are many dysfunctional families in which the relationship between parents and children is disturbed, and even "healthy" families often fail to socialize their children effectively.

Child rearing has never been an easy task, but it is particularly difficult today. Our nuclear family system gives parents almost exclusive responsibility for the support and upbringing of children, and they receive far less assistance from other relatives than parents did in the past. If one of the parents is unable to perform his or her duties, the family is almost automatically plunged into crisis, since there are usually no other relatives in the household to help out. There is, moreover, a growing feeling among parents that our society has turned its back on their children. In 1986, pollster

Child rearing has always been one of the most important and difficult tasks of the family.

Louis Harris found that 74 percent of all adults believed that the problems our children face are getting worse, and that 63 percent believed that too little effort had been made to solve them. In Harris's words: "For nearly a generation now, there has been a gradual but steady decline in the attention that society has paid to children."[44]

The growing number of **single-parent families** has made many of the problems of child rearing even more difficult (see Figure 5.2). The percentage of children living with only one parent has more than doubled since 1970, and about one-quarter of all American children now live in single-parent homes.[45] Financially, most single-parent families are always on thin ice, for the majority of them are headed by women, and women on the average earn far less money than men. To make matters worse, they usually have to pay for child care service out of their meager earnings. Child support payments may help, but only about 60 percent of single mothers have been awarded support payments from the father of their child, and in one out of four cases he fails to make those payments.[46] As a result of these factors, the *majority* of the children in single-parent families now live in poverty.

But the problem of poverty is not confined to single-parent families. Today, one out of every four American children under the age of 6 lives in poverty, and one out of eight children goes to bed hungry at night. To make matters worse, the federal government has, in the words of one researcher, "abandoned children." In the 1980s and early 1990s, spending on programs for the elderly increased 52 percent, while spending on children dropped 4 percent. School lunch programs have been cut back, health care has become more difficult for poor families to get, and welfare benefits for mothers with dependent children have been reduced.[47]

Another common child-rearing problem in single-parent families is the lack of parental supervision and guidance. As noted earlier, single parents often do not have time to meet all the demands of both their breadwinning and their child-rearing roles.

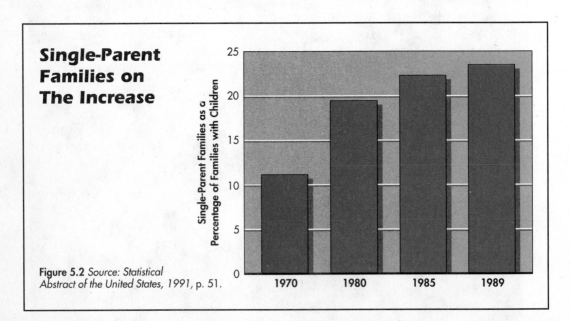

Single-Parent Families on The Increase

Single-Parent Families as a Percentage of Families with Children

Figure 5.2 *Source: Statistical Abstract of the United States, 1991, p. 51.*

After reviewing 50 different studies, L. Edward Wells and Joseph H. Rankin concluded that children from single-parent families are about 10 to 15 percent more likely to become delinquent than children from two-parent families.[48] The relationship between discipline and delinquency is not, however, a simple one. Studies show that parental discipline can promote delinquency when it is too strict as well as when it is too lax.[49]

A great deal of concern has also been expressed about the children of dual-earner families. But although working mothers often bear extra burdens, the fear that maternal employment somehow harms children apparently is unfounded. Having reviewed all the available research on this subject, Thomas C. Taveggia and Ellen M. Thomas concluded that "there are no substantial differences between the children of working and nonworking mothers" in terms of the characteristics tested, such as intelligence, personal development, school achievement, and social adjustment.[50]

Dual-earner families do have some special difficulties in raising their children, however. The biggest problem reported by working mothers, whether single or married, is the lack of accessible high-quality child care. A Harris poll found that 42 percent of nonworking mothers said that they would look for work if there were more day-care centers where they live.[51] Because of this shortage, only about 10 percent of dual-earner families with children are currently sending them to day-care centers. Twenty-five percent of those families leave their children with relatives, and 29 percent arrange their work so that one or the other parent is home with the children. But at least 13 percent provide no adult supervision during a substantial part of the day.[52]

The big increase in the number of marriages between people who already have children has created another set of problems. If these **blended families** are formed when the children are still young the difficulties they encounter will probably be minor, but the older the children are the greater the problems are likely to be. If both partners bring children of their own into the family, conflicts and competition between them is almost inevitable. And whether or not the partners both have children, they often report difficulties disciplining the children of their spouse—a problem that tends to be particularly severe if the children have already entered the rebellious years of adolescence.

A different sort of problem arises from the growth of the mass media and the expansion of formal education, which have greatly reduced the control parents had over what their children learn. Some of the greatest concerns are about the effects of profit-oriented television programming. It is estimated that by the time the average American child graduates from high school, he or she will have spent 15,000 hours watching television, compared with only 11,000 hours spent in the classroom. During that time the youngster will have seen about 18,000 fictional murders and watched over 650,000 commercials. Research shows, moreover, that children who watch a lot of television see the world as a more dangerous and frightening place than children who watch little television.[53]

One of the clearest indicators of the difficulties modern families are having with child rearing comes from the increasing number of **runaways**. The General Accounting Office of the United States estimates that about one million young people run away from home every year. Although four out of five return within a few days, the rest are likely to suffer serious hardships. Both males and females turn to crimes such as prostitution and shoplifting to support themselves. Because they are often on the streets and vulnerable, they are also victims of sexual abuse, and their rates of alcoholism and drug addiction are extremely high. In some cases, however, the label of "runaway" that is applied to these young people is quite misleading. A substantial number are actually **pushouts** who are forced to fend for themselves because their families no longer want them.[54]

Work and Family Inequality   Our ideas about the proper role of wives and husbands have, as we have seen, been undergoing some remarkable changes, and this redefinition of traditional roles has placed considerable stress on the modern family. In the past, each partner in a marriage generally had a clear-cut idea of what to expect from the other. But today a bride and groom can no longer assume that their conceptions of their respective roles coincide, and considerable compromise is required to resolve such differences. More women are working outside the home and demanding an equal share of the decision-making power within the family. Some husbands, socialized to see women as subordinates, consider these demands a threat to their masculinity, particularly if their wives have more success in their careers than they do. But even when both partners accept the ideal of sexual equality, career conflict can still arise. For example, one partner may be offered an important promotion that requires a move that would be disastrous to the career of the other, or because a child is sick, one parent may have to miss a critical assignment at work.

The dramatic increase in the number of wage-earning women often leads us to forget about the other essential type of family labor: housework. Although many people assume that fewer children and modern home appliances have greatly reduced the total amount of housework, that has not proven to be true. New expectations for sparkling dishes and dust-free tabletops have raised the standards that homemakers strive to meet. Some technological "advances" have in fact created more rather than less work. The classic example is the automobile, which produced a new category of household work (chauffeuring) that slowly demanded more and more time. As the car became increasingly common, door-to-door peddlers, home delivery by retail stores, and house calls by physicians were sharply curtailed, and automobile-based surburbanization placed schools and jobs farther away from home. These changes transformed the car from a convenience to a costly necessity.[55] Many of the other "labor-saving" devices women went to work to buy actually saved less time than was required to earn the money to pay for them. Despite the dreams of science-fiction writers that technology would create a society in which most of us would not have to work at all, the Harris poll found that the amount of leisure time available to the average American has actually declined 32 percent since 1973.[56]

The growing shortage of leisure time makes the division of labor in the family a particularly important issue. In general, men usually work more hours outside the home and perform automobile and home repairs and other heavy household tasks. Women tend to work fewer hours outside the home but generally do most of the work that needs to be done around the house, including child care, cooking, cleaning, and laundry. How fairly are the family burdens divided? Research shows that when the husband is the only wage earner, the wife works about the same number of hours in the house as he does on the job. But since he also does some work at home, the husband puts in more total hours of work than does his wife. In dual-earner families, however, a sharp increase in the wife's duties reverses this relationship. Although the husbands of working wives generally do a little more around the house and more services are purchased from outsiders, the total number of hours the wife must work is greatly increased.[57] Working mothers are especially likely to report feeling heavily burdened by their wide-ranging responsibilities.[58]

RESPONDING TO PROBLEMS OF THE FAMILY

In one sense there are as many responses to family problems as there are families. Because each family is unique, its members respond to their problems in unique ways. In another sense, however, family problems are institutional, and therefore affect us all. Despite its weaknesses, the nuclear-family system is very much in tune with the economic and social institutions of modern industrial society. For this reason, most reformers have chosen to direct their efforts toward strengthening the nuclear family rather than trying to reestablish the larger family units typical of the extended-family system.

Better Preparation   One way of strengthening the nuclear family is to see that people are better prepared for marriage. Perhaps the easiest way to achieve this goal is simply to discourage early marriage, so that partners are older and more mature when they do marry. Census Bureau figures show that the average age of couples at the time of their first marriage has gradually increased during the last three decades. From 1970 to 1987 the average age at first marriage jumped from 20.6 years to 23.6 years for women, and from 22.5 years to 25.3 years for men.[59] Publicizing the difficulties of early marriage might encourage this trend and stop some young couples from marrying, but it is far from certain that such a campaign would be effective.

Another approach is to prepare the young for marriage through educational programs in high schools and colleges. Although such programs encourage realistic expectations about married life and teach techniques for dealing with marital problems, most of them have not been notably successful. Regrettably, a few hours of classroom instruction are not likely to change long-held attitudes and expectations about marriage.

Fortunately, all educational efforts do not have to change deep-seated attitudes in order to be successful. One of the most serious family problems is unwanted pregnancy among teenage girls. More effective sex education programs in the schools could go a long way toward reducing this crisis. But to be effective, such educational programs must be combined with a well-publicized effort to provide unrestricted access to birth control devices for teenagers who need them (see Chapter 11). However, many people advocate restricting rather than expanding the availability of birth control information and devices for teenagers. Attempts are also being made to restrict the availability of abortions to teenagers and mature women alike. Since about 45 percent of all teenage pregnancies end in abortion, the complete elimination of abortion in the United States could be expected to nearly double the birthrate among teenagers.[60] (See the debate in Chapter 8 for arguments for and against the prohibition of abortion.)

An increasing number of young couples are living together before deciding on marriage. Some people feel that this practice promotes stronger marriages, while others believe that it promotes weaker ones, but the effects of this trend are still unclear. A four-year study by M. D. Newcomb and R. R. Bentler found no differences in marital satisfaction or divorce rates between couples who "cohabited" before marriage and those who did not,[61] and J. Jacques and K. J. Chason found no differences in the way couples described their marriages when they compared couples who had cohabited with those who had not.[62]

Reducing Family Conflicts   Ideally, the family is a cooperative, trouble-free unit that shelters its members from the stresses of the outside world. But real families seldom, if ever, achieve this ideal. Periodic episodes of tension and conflict are the rule, not the exception. Indeed, open disagreements and even arguments are an excellent way of resolving the differences that inevitably develop between family members. Families that avoid conflict by avoiding unpleasant subjects or conflict-laden situations are weaker, not stronger, for it. As feelings of resentment build up, such families are likely to break up or deteriorate into an "empty shell," where family members carry out the obligations of their roles but without mutual love, affection, or understanding. Thus, an open and honest airing of disagreements is an excellent way to manage family conflict and keep it within acceptable bounds.

Often, however, differences become so great that they cannot be resolved within the family unit. Friends and relatives can sometimes be helpful, but there has been a significant increase in the number of people seeking professional counseling for marital problems. When there are fundamental conflicts between personalities, attitudes, or life styles, even the best professional counseling may prove futile. Such counseling is most helpful for couples with specific, limited problems. For example, the sex therapy pioneered by the famous Masters and Johnson research team has been helpful to many couples because it deals with specific problems, such as impotence or frigidity, that respond to straightforward treatment.[63] A growing number of counseling programs are also being established to deal with family violence. A number of these programs have apparently achieved significant reductions in violence among their clients, but sufficient scientific evidence has not yet been collected to make a final judgment on their effectiveness.

Many conflicts are rooted in the way family roles are defined by our society. Traditional family patterns have subordinated women and deprived them of the power to control their own destinies. As a result, some women feel frustrated and angry about their position in the family, while traditional role expectations blind their husbands to the problem. Moreover, the traditional division of labor in the family may require both men and women to do work for which they are poorly suited. Some families clearly would be much better off if the husband stayed home to care for the children while the wife worked. It therefore seems likely that the nuclear family system will be strengthened by the continuing growth of the new pattern of marriage based on sexual equality. In such families the division of labor is based on the skills and abilities of each partner rather than on their gender, and decision-making power

Today, more couples are sharing child-rearing responsibilities by allowing each member to perform the tasks he or she does best—regardless of sexual stereotypes.

is equally shared. Although many families already function in this manner, traditional standards lead some people to brand any deviation from the customary patterns as wrong and unnatural, and the entire family system is weakened by this attitude. Public opinion polls show that the ideal of sexual equality is gaining increasing acceptance, although there is still a significant group who believe in the traditional standards. In 1970, 63 percent of Americans said they would have less respect for a man who stayed home with his children, but by 1985 that figure had dropped to 25 percent.[64]

Helping Parents Americans have always looked at the family as something private and personal that is none of the government's business. Perhaps for that reason, the United States lags far behind the European nations, and even its Canadian neighbor, in providing basic services for parents and their children. But the changes that have transformed the family—the breakup of the extended family, the huge increase in mothers who work outside the home, and the explosive growth in single-parent families—have created serious new problems that demand government attention.

The kinds of birth control programs discussed in Chapter 11 could significantly reduce the number of single teenage mothers, if such efforts won vigorous government backing. But whatever measures we take, the number of single-parent families is likely to keep increasing for the immediate future, and much more needs to be done to deal with their special problems. Women head most single-parent families, and an effective program to eliminate sexual discrimination in the workplace would go a long way toward reducing the acute financial problems experienced by many of these families. But to reach all needy families, the government must also increase its direct welfare benefits to poor families, whether headed by one or two parents (see Chapter 6).

A step that would benefit a wide range of families is the creation of a network of government-supported preschool and day-care programs. In countries like France, Belgium, Italy, and Denmark, the vast majority of children are already in some kind of state-funded preschool program.[65] Not only could such broadly based programs provide a financial lifesaver for low-income families, but increased government supervision could help ensure that the highest possible standards are met for the care of children from all economic backgrounds—thus going a long way to relieve the nagging fear so many parents have about what is happening to their children while they are away at work. Nonetheless, opposition to such a plan has been strong. Critics argue that government agencies are poor substitutes for parents and point to the bureaucratic indifference and coldness that are typical of many orphanages, institutions for delinquents, and schools. They fear that day-care centers will harm children by depriving them of parental love. Advocates of day-care centers respond that children in such facilities still have ample contact with their parents and that properly run day-care centers enrich children's lives rather than deprive them. Alison Clarke-Stewart's study of children in average or above-average day-care centers found no evidence of harm done to the children. In fact, the day-care children were more advanced in cognitive and social skills than children who stayed home.[66]

Another way the government can help deal with the realities of today's family is to enact legislation guaranteeing a "family leave," so parents can take time off to deal with the demands of a newborn baby and still be assured that they will have a job when they are ready to return to work. Mothers are already provided 16 weeks of paid leave in France, and 14 weeks in Germany.[67] Yet a 1991 bill to grant American parents 12 weeks of *unpaid* leave was vetoed by President George Bush because he felt it would be too expensive for business. A recent survey in four states that already have such laws nonetheless found that only 9 percent of businesses reported that the law caused them any hardship.[68]

Sixty-seven countries around the world, including Canada and all of northern and Western Europe, provide some kind of child or family allowances to help parents with their heavy financial burdens. In most countries, all families are given a monthly cash payment based on the number of children they have. Typically, the amount is between 5 and 10 percent of the average wage, but it is higher in some countries.[69] Although wealthy families would end up paying this money back in taxes, the family allowance can be a significant aid to middle- and lower-class parents.

SOCIOLOGICAL PERSPECTIVES ON PROBLEMS OF THE FAMILY

Concern for the "decaying" family is nothing new. Because the family is such a basic social institution, it has always been the center of great social concern. But the rapid change that the family has undergone since the industrial revolution has created new and difficult problems for sociologists to study and has led to considerable debate among the proponents of the different sociological theories.

The Functionalist Perspective Functional analyses of human society have led many sociologists to conclude that the family is *the* most basic social institution. Not only is it found in one form or another in all societies, but no other institution is responsible for performing as many important tasks. Most of us begin and end our lives in the family context, and we are seldom far from its influence during the years in between.

Most social scientists agree that the family's most vital function is to provide replacements for those members who have died or are disabled. Such replacement has four aspects. First, the family *provides for reproduction* by creating a stable mating relationship that supports the mother during her pregnancy and the children during the critical early months of life. Second, the family *socializes the young*. It is in the family that the child learns how to think, talk, and follow the customs, behavior, and values of his or her society. The family is, therefore, an important agency of social control. Third, the family *provides support and protection* for its children. The family must satisfy a wide range of emotional needs as well as physical needs for food and shelter. Fourth, the family is a primary *mechanism of status ascription*. Each child is given a social status on the basis of the family into which he or she is born. Thus, children of the wealthy are automatically upper class, while children of low-income families are assigned to the bottom rungs of the social ladder. The family also performs significant functions for adults. As a primary group of great importance, it provides emotional support and reinforcement and physical care in times of illness and old age. The family also transfers wealth from parents to young children and, later, from older children to aging parents.

Functionalists see family problems as stemming from the disorganization caused by industrialization. The extended family is compatible with the traditional cultures in which it is found but ill suited to the modern industrial world. Industrialization broke up the extended family and forced changes in the nuclear family system. The resultant disorganization and the structural weaknesses of the nuclear family have made it increasingly difficult for the family to perform its functions efficiently. Nor did change cease with the industrial revolution. The increase in the number of women in the work force and the ideal of sexual equality are bringing about another realignment of family structure. From the functionalist perspective, the present family system is in trouble because it has not had enough time to adapt to these ceaseless social and economic changes.

Functionalists agree that the prosperity and even the survival of contemporary society depend on the strength of its family system. However, functional analysis does not lead to any single proposal for improvement. One possibility would be for other agencies—such as day-care centers and schools—to assume more of the family's functions, permitting the family to handle its remaining functions more effectively. Another approach is to promote trial marriages as a test of compatibility and easier divorce for marriages that fail. However, many functionalists fear that such proposals would contribute to the erosion of the traditional family and the vital functions it performs. These functionalists therefore recommend a return to the values associated with the traditional nuclear family, such as a stronger prohibition of divorce and greater restrictions on sexual behavior.

The Conflict Perspective Many conflicts of values and attitudes affect the modern family. Traditionalists place great emphasis on the value of a stable family environment for child rearing and thus reject the idea of divorce; modernists see personal happiness as the most important goal of family life and believe that a child will suffer more from an unhappy home than from a broken one. Traditionalists are convinced that sexual relations should be restricted to one's spouse; modernists advocate greater sexual freedom. Modernists condemn traditional attitudes toward women as exploitive and unjust, and they support full sexual equality. Traditionalists, in contrast, are likely to believe that male dominance is based on innate differences between the sexes and that any other sort of family relationship is unnatural. Traditionalists condemn the increase in families in which both parents work as a threat to the welfare of children. Modernists see the increasing financial power of women as a positive development that may help create more egalitarian families and a more just society.

When conflict theorists look beneath these conflicts in values, they see a fundamental struggle between male dominance and female liberation. Friedrich Engels long ago wrote that the oppression of women in the family was the original form of human exploitation. Present-day conflict theorists still argue that the family is organized for the benefit of the husband at the expense of his wife. The husband has more authority, prestige, and independence, while the wife must carry out the subordinate role. It would, of course, be wrong to assume that these statements apply to all families. There are certainly egalitarian families and families in which the wife plays the dominant role, but conflict theorists hold that these are the exceptions, not the rule.

Conflict theorists are also concerned about the effects class conflict has on the family. The poor have significantly higher rates of divorce, illegitimacy, and overall family instability than do other classes, and conflict theorists attribute these conditions to exploitation of the poor by the upper classes. For instance, many men cannot get decent jobs because the financial pressures of a life of poverty and the low quality of local public schools prevented them from learning basic reading, writing, and mathematical skills. Because these men cannot provide their families with the standard of living our society has led everyone to expect, they come to see themselves as failures. This sense of failure may in turn lead to a host of other problems, including the breakup of the family, alcoholism, and violence against other family members.

In the eyes of most conflict theorists, the solution to family problems will come only from greater equality, both within the family and in society as a whole. They recommend that the government undertake a vigorous program to eliminate occupational discrimination against women and minorities, and make a serious effort to reduce unemployment and the overall levels of economic inequality in our society (see Chapters 2, 6, 7, and 10 for more details). They also support proposals for a nationwide system of federally funded day-care centers for children and shelter houses for the victims of physical abuse. Finally, they advocate a concerted effort to combat sexism in all sectors of our society, including education, business, and the media, to free women from exploitation by men.

Social Psychological Perspectives Most social psychologists have focused on the family's role in the socialization of children. Social psychological research has linked faulty socialization to problems ranging from mental disorder to juvenile delinquency.

Clearly, some families socialize their children to play conformist roles, whereas other families encourage children to behave in ways that others consider indecent and even illegal. But most problems with the process of socialization in the family come from neglect and indifference or, in more extreme cases, from the hostility and even violence parents direct at their children. Personality theorists have long held that traumatic events in early family life can cause lifelong psychological problems that can be corrected only with years of intensive psychotherapy. And interactionists point out that the kind of responses we receive from our family during early socialization, whether positive or negative, are critical in forming the self-concept that guides our behavior.

For adults, the nuclear family's most critical social psychological role is to provide emotional support and comfort. The family is the only shelter many people have from the relentless demands of modern civilization—the one place where an individual can develop a sense of stability and belonging—and for that reason dissension and conflict within the family can have devastating psychological consequences for all its members.

Social psychologists point to several possible ways to create the kind of stable, emotionally supportive families that do an effective job of socializing their children and providing security and comfort for all their members. The ideal of romantic love is given so much importance in our culture that young people approach marriage expecting more of each other than either can possibly give. Too often they end up bitter and disappointed when their romantic fantasies fail to come true. More realistic expectations, encouraged by schools and the mass media, may be one way of solving the problem. Another approach is to build more supportive families with a wider network of kin and friends to share the emotional burdens of family life. Such family structures might also do a better job of socializing children. Because more adults would be involved in the socialization of each child, the harmful effects of an incompetent or abusive parent could be neutralized more easily.

SUMMARY

The institution of the family is found in all societies, but in many different forms. The two main types of family are the *nuclear family* and the *extended family*. The nuclear family consists of a married couple and their children. The extended family usually includes several generations of parents, grandparents, and children and is typical of agricultural societies. The demands of modern industrial society place tremendous pressure on these large, cumbersome family units. As industrialization has transformed one country after another, the nuclear family has largely replaced the extended family. The traditional extended family had the sole responsibility for many different tasks, but in modern society the family's role is supplemented by specialized government agencies such as schools and juvenile courts.

The modern family has continued to change even after the breakup of the extended family, and three trends are particularly important. First, declining birthrates, the increase in single-parent families, and the tendency to stay single longer have led to a steady decline in the size of the average household. Second, the sharp increase in the number of women working outside the home and the growing popularity of the ideals of sexual equality have led to major changes in the roles that husbands and wives play in many contemporary families. Third, despite generations of rapid change, most of us continue to see the family as one of the most important and satisfying facets of our daily lives.

Of all family problems, the rising divorce rate has generated the most public concern. Many problems are associated with divorce, including personal stress, family instability, and increased difficulty in child rearing. But it is not at all clear that divorce is worse than the alternative of continuing an unhappy marriage. The number of births to single mothers has increased in recent years. The unmarried mother who keeps her child has many of the problems experienced by other single-parent families, but because so many of these mothers are teenagers, they are generally less prepared for the changes a baby brings into their lives.

Although there are no dependable statistics, it appears that violence between husband and wife is a common way of settling disputes and leads to a substantial number of injuries and homicides every year. Another form of family violence, child abuse, is even more dangerous because the victims are too young to take action to protect themselves. Many explanations of child abuse have been advanced, including emotional disturbances in the parents and the transmission of child abuse from one generation to the next through learning.

Because the modern nuclear family often has little support from its kinship network, child rearing can be difficult. The single-parent family is likely to have the most serious economic and behavior problems because only one adult must carry all the burdens that are customarily divided between two people.

Another source of strain in the modern family is the changing expectations about the behavior of husbands and wives. Because increasing numbers of women have gone to work outside the home, and because there are now a variety of alternatives to traditional sex roles, the expectations of husband and wife may conflict. One particularly common problem is that the burdens of housework are not fairly reallocated to take into account the time working women must put in on the job.

Many proposals have been made for resolving problems in the family. One approach would strengthen the existing nuclear family system through education, marriage counseling, and a reduction in unwanted births among teenage girls. Sexual equality and greater fairness within the marriage are also frequent suggestions. Many proposals have been made to help parents with the difficult task of child rearing, including legislation to guarantee paid family leave when a child is born and the creation of a nationwide system of government-sponsored day care.

Sociologists of the functionalist school are convinced that problems of the family are symptoms of the social disorganization caused by rapid social change. Industrialization broke up the extended family but has not produced a strong nuclear family system to replace it. Conflict theorists note the many conflicting values and beliefs about modern family life and point to them as a major source of tensions. They also stress the notion that many problems, from divorce to family violence, arise because society allows the powerful to make profits at the expense of the weak and encourages the exploitation of women by their husbands. Social psychologists are concerned about the ineffectiveness of the nuclear family as a socializing agency. They hope to encourage the development of stable families that will provide continuity in children's lives and, at the same time, more security and emotional support for all family members.

KEY TERMS

dual-earner family   A family in which both the husband and the wife are wage earners.

extended family   A family in which other relatives besides a single set of parents and children live together in the same home.

monogamy   A marriage in which there is only one woman and one man.

nuclear family   A married couple and their children.

pushout   A child who is driven out of his or her family.

romantic love   The passionate affection toward another that is considered to be the ideal basis for marriage in Western culture

single-parent family   A family with one parent and one or more children.

FURTHER READINGS

Randall Collins, *Sociology of Marriage and the Family: Gender, Love, and Property*, 2nd ed. (Chicago: Nelson-Hall, 1988). A good general examination of the sociology of the family.

Arlene S. Skolnick and Jerome H. Skolnick, *Family in Transition*, 5th ed. (Boston: Little, Brown, 1986). A collection of articles focusing on the major issues confronting today's families.

L. Edward Wells and Joseph H. Rankin, "Families and Delinquency: A Meta-analysis of the Impact of Broken Homes," *Social Problems* 38 (Feb. 1991): 71-93. A comprehensive examination of the research concerning the impact of single-parent families on delinquency.

Murray A. Straus and Richard J. Gelles, eds., *Physical Violence in American Families* (New Brunswick, N.J.: Transactions Publishers, 1990). A collection of papers on family violence edited by two leading specialists in the field.

Philip Blumstein and Pepper Schwartz, *American Couples: Money, Work and Sex* (New York: William Morrow, 1983). An examination of the lives of American couples based on the results of an eight-year survey of over 6,000 heterosexual and homosexual couples.

PART TWO

The Problems of Inequality

chapter 6

The Poor

- Who are the poor?
- Why is the gap between the rich and the poor growing wider?
- What is the underclass?
- Are the poor to blame for their poverty?
- Is the welfare system fair?

The modern industrial economy has produced fantastic wealth. Middle-class Americans have luxuries that were undreamed of in past centuries, and the world we see in television shows, movies, and books is one of affluence and comfort. But there is an underside to our material well-being—the millions of faceless people who do not share in the abundance. Poverty is a basic characteristic of our industrial society; it is the other side of affluence.

The poor in North America do not look like the starving millions in famine zones of the Third World, but their misery is just as real. In fact, poverty can be more difficult in a rich country than in a poor one. There is no shame in poverty in India because most people are poor; but in North America, poor people are constantly confronted by the wealth they are denied.

Although the poor are a minority in every sense of the word, they are a sizable one. According to official government estimates there are over 30 million poor people in the United States, which means that around 13 percent of all Americans are considered to be poor.[1] Such figures should, however, be viewed with a skeptical eye, for, as we will see, there is considerable debate about how to determine whether someone is poor. But whatever measure is used, the problem is an enormous one.

Despite the appearance of widespread affluence, North America has some of the worst slums in the industrial world. Poor nutrition, nagging hunger, shabby clothing, and a crowded room or two in a deteriorating old building are all that many families can hope for. Moreover, Americans' attitudes toward the poor appear remarkably callous when compared with those of people in many European countries.

THE RICH AND THE POOR: A WIDENING GAP

When television commentators and politicians talk about the problem of poverty, they seldom have much to say about those at the other end of the economic ladder. But wealth and poverty are two sides of the same coin. The deprivation of some creates abundance for others. To understand the problem of poverty, it must therefore be seen in the context of the social and economic inequality between those at the top and those at the bottom of society.

All the data show that there is an enormous gap between the haves and the have-nots and that it has been growing wider for more than a decade. There are two general ways of determining how great this gap actually is. One approach attempts to measure differences in income, and the other focuses on wealth. Although these two yardsticks are related, there are important differences between them. **Income** refers to the amount of money a person makes in a given year. **Wealth** is the value of a person's total assets: real estate and personal property, stocks, bonds, cash, and so forth.

The distribution of income in the United States is extremely unequal. In 1989, the richest 5 percent of American families received 18 percent of the nation's income—more than three times more than the share of the poorest 20 percent of American families (4.6 percent).[2] These differences become even clearer when we look at actual dollar figures. According to *Business Week* magazine, the *average pay* for a chief executive of an American corporation in 1990 was $1,952,806, while the 5 million people earning the minimum wage made only $7,670 if they worked full time for the entire year.[3]

Wealth and poverty are two sides of the same coin. The more equally income is distributed, the less there is of both.

Examining the distribution of wealth is more difficult. For one thing, it is not always clear how much a particular asset, such as a famous painting or a mansion, is actually worth, and those with great wealth often conceal many of their assets from the scrutiny of outsiders. The U.S. Bureau of the Census does not even attempt to publish yearly reports of wealth, as it does for the distribution of income. The last comprehensive study, which was sponsored by the Joint Economic Committee of Congress, was for 1983. It concluded that a small group of "super rich" families (about one-half of 1 percent of the population) controlled over a quarter of all the wealth in the United States, while the 60 percent of the population at the other end of the economic scale were left with only 6.8 percent of all assets. A comparison with the income figures for that year shows that wealth is even more highly concentrated in the hands of the few than income. For example, the poorest 20 percent of the population earned 4.7 percent of the income, but they had only −0.4 percent of the wealth.[4] That is, their debts actually exceeded their assets.

Why is wealth so much more unequally distributed than income? There appear to be two principal reasons. First, lower-income people usually have to spend everything they make just to get by and are therefore unable to build up savings accounts or investments. Second, wealth tends to be passed on from one generation to another. Poor people usually have poor parents and receive no inheritance. Wealthy people, on the other hand, usually have wealthy parents and are much more likely to come into a substantial estate. For example, a recent study found that children whose parents left legacies of $1 million to $2.5 million already had incomes that were double the national average.[5]

Although many Americans see their country as the land of opportunity and equality, international comparisons do not bear out this view. There is certainly far more economic inequality in the nations of the Third World than in any of the developed countries (see Chapter 14). But the research indicates that the United States has the biggest gap between the rich and poor of any industrialized nation, while Canada is in the middle of the pack and the Scandinavian countries and Japan have the least inequality.[6] In 1990, for example, the average pay for chief executives in the United States was 85 times higher than for workers, while in Japan the boss received only 17 times more money than a typical worker.[7] The infant mortality rate—a common indicator of the amount of poverty in a nation—is also substantially higher in the United States than in Japan, Canada, and most Western European nations.[8]

The old saying that "the rich get richer and the poor get poorer" has not always proven to be true, but since the late 1970s there has clearly been a significant widening of the gap between the haves and the have-nots. A study by the Congressional Budget Office found that between 1977 and 1988 the bottom half's share of all income decreased by 9 percent, while the share of the top 1 percent increased a startling 45 percent.[9] A study by *Business Week* magazine showed that the pay of chief executives increased four times faster between 1980 and 1990 than the pay of average workers.[10] In fact, after controlling for inflation, workers' real wages actually declined since the early 1980s (see Figure 6.1).[11]

Many complex forces contribute to the growing inequality of American society, but four stand out as particularly important. First, the economy has stagnated in recent years, so that the poor can no longer benefit from steady improvement in the overall standard of living. A second factor, of even greater importance, is foreign economic competition. Increasing industrial development in Third World countries has placed the North American worker in direct competition with workers who receive far lower wages. The result has been a decline in real (after-inflation) wages for the average

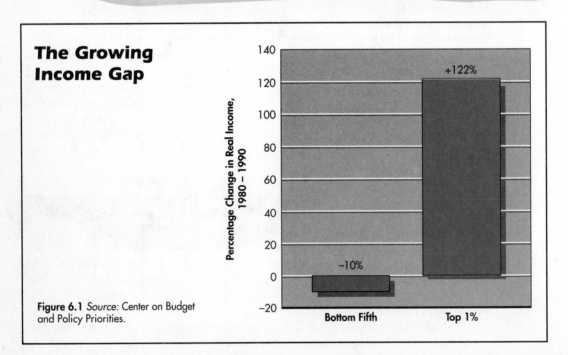

The Growing Income Gap

Percentage Change in Real Income, 1980 – 1990

+122% (Top 1%)

−10% (Bottom Fifth)

Figure 6.1 *Source:* Center on Budget and Policy Priorities.

American worker. However, those low-paid Third World workers are not competing with engineers, scientists, or other highly skilled professionals, and their incomes have continued to increase. And of course, the managers and stockholders of multi-national corporations actually benefit from the profits made possible by lower labor costs. A third factor has been the use of technology to reduce or eliminate well-paying jobs for skilled laborers, as well as the corresponding increase in low-paying service jobs. The fourth cause of the growing inequality in American society is a political one. Since 1981, taxes on the rich have been substantially reduced, while government programs that benefit the poor and the working classes have been cut to help make up the loss in revenue (see Chapter 3).

MEASURING POVERTY

Even though everyone has a general idea of what *poverty* is, it is a difficult term to define precisely. Certainly, poor people lack some of the goods and services that others enjoy. They may have insufficient food, shelter, clothing, or entertainment, but how much is "insufficient?" Are people poor if they have no means of private transportation, no bicycle, no car, only one car?

Poverty is usually defined in one of two ways: absolute or relative. The **absolute approach** divides the poor from the nonpoor by using some fixed standard, usually the lack of money to purchase a minimum amount of food, shelter, and clothing. The **relative approach** holds that people are poor if they have significantly less income and wealth than the average person in their society. Supporters of the relative approach argue that what is really important is not the fact that the poor have a low standard of living but that they are psychologically and sociologically excluded from the mainstream of society. But despite the appeal of such arguments, the absolute approach is far more widely used both by government agencies and social scientists—perhaps because what most concerns the public is not the **relative deprivation** of the poor but their lack of what are seen as basic necessities.

Every year the U.S. government publishes a "poverty line" for families of different sizes. If a family's income falls below the line, they are officially considered to be poor. The poverty line was originally based on studies showing that the average low-income family spent about a third of its budget on food. The Department of Agriculture's Economy Food Budget was then multiplied by 3 to calculate the poverty line. Beginning at $3,000 in 1964, the poverty line for a family of four had reached $11,662 by 1989.[12]

Although such numbers make the poverty line sound precise and objective, it is actually a rather arbitrary figure. A different approach to these computations could easily lead to a very different figure, and there is considerable debate about whether the poverty line is too high or too low. Some conservatives feel that it is too high (thus overestimating the amount of poverty), because welfare benefits that are not given in cash, such as food stamps and medicaid, are not counted as income. Advocates for the poor counter that the original calculation that a poor family spends a third of its income on food didn't include such benefits either (although it is true that benefits are higher now than they were in 1964). Furthermore, they point out that the Department of Agriculture itself admits that the Economy Food Budget was intended only as a temporary or emergency budget and is not adequate to meet long-term nutritional needs. In 1969 the government stopped adjusting the poverty line on the basis of the rising cost of food and used a measure of overall inflation instead. But since then the cost of necessities, especially housing, has gone up much faster than the Consumer Price Index as a whole, and, as a result, families living at the poverty line are unable to buy as much of the things they need as they did in the past. Significantly, when a recent Gallop poll asked a sample of Americans to estimate an appropriate poverty line for a family of four, it was 24 percent higher than the official poverty line.[13]

Who Are the Poor?   One of the major reasons for trying to define who is poor and who is not is to discover which segments of our society experience the greatest poverty. Single-parent families, for example, have a much higher than average poverty rate, and their growing numbers have had a major impact on the problem of poverty. From 1970 to 1989, the percentage of all households with children headed by a single woman (that is, the vast majority of all single-parent families) doubled, from 10 to 20 percent, and single mothers with children are now the fastest growing segment of the poverty population. In fact, about two-thirds of all families below the poverty line are now headed by single women and the poverty rate of such families is almost two and one-half times the rate for the total population (see Chapter 5 for more details).[14]

As a result of this trend and the higher birthrates among the poor, children under 18 are almost 50 percent more likely to be poor than is the average American (see Figure 6.2).[15] But while poverty has been rising among the young, the social security program has helped bring it down among the elderly, and their poverty rate is now lower than the national average.[16]

Contrary to popular stereotypes, most poor people in the United States are white, not black. U.S. census figures indicate that about two-thirds of all poor people are white. However, the *percentage* of whites below the poverty line is considerably lower than it is for most minorities. For example, in 1989 about 10 percent of all whites were poor, compared with over 30 percent of all African Americans.[17] Income figures show the same disparity—$19,329 for the average black family and $33,914 for the average white.[18] (See Chapter 7 for an explanation of these differences.)

When we think of the poor, it is the crowded urban ghettos that often come most quickly to mind, but the percentage of people below the poverty line is almost as high in rural areas.[19] The majority of poor people do live in cities, but that is simply because our population is so highly urbanized. The suburbs have the lowest poverty rate—less than half that of the central cities or rural areas[20]—but as our original suburbs have aged they too have developed growing pockets of poverty (see Chapter 15).

The Trends in Poverty   Another important use for statistics on poverty is to point out the changes in the poverty population. Poverty declined sharply in the 1960s: from over 22 percent of the total population at the start of the decade, to around 11 percent in the early 1970s. The two main reasons for this improvement were the economic prosperity of the times and a strong government commitment to what was known as the War on Poverty. But as both economic prosperity and the government's com-

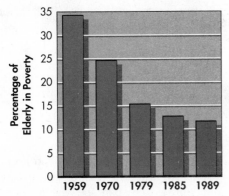

Poverty Declines Among the Elderly ...

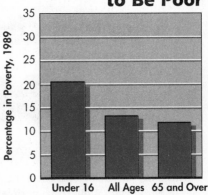

... and the Young Are Now More Likely to Be Poor

Figure 6.2 *Source: Statistical Abstract of the United States, 1985, p. 456; Statistical Abstract of the United States, 1991, p. 463.*

mitment to reduce poverty faded, the improvements stopped and poverty began to grow. It reached a peak of over 15 percent in 1984 and then leveled out in the 13 to 14 percent range. As we have seen, there is little agreement about where to draw the poverty line, so the statistics giving the exact percentage of the population living in poverty are not very meaningful. But if the same standards are consistently applied, then they ought to measure the trends in poverty accurately. For example, when Christopher Jencks reanalyzed the poverty statistics using a different measure of inflation and adding in government benefits not included in the official measure, he still found the same trends even though his results showed a lower overall level of poverty (about 2 percentage points below the official figure).[21]

Although the studies show that there is less poverty now than there was 30 years ago, they also show that the problems associated with poverty have gotten far worse in recent years. Between 1975 and 1988, the percentage of poor people who lived in extreme poverty (defined as those with incomes less than half the poverty line) increased by one-third.[22] And because the majority of poor children now live with only one parent, they must often rely on that one person to meet an enormous range of psychological and economic needs.

THE LIFE OF POVERTY

Being poor in an affluent nation has profound psychological and sociological consequences. In our materialistic society, people are judged as much by what they have as what they are. Because the children of poverty lack so many of the things everyone is "supposed" to have, they often feel there is something wrong with them or their families. Poor people of all ages are constantly confronted by things they desire but have little chance to own.

But the poor are deprived of more than just material possessions. In contrast to the rich and even the middle classes, those brought up in poverty often appear to speak crudely with heavy accents and a limited vocabulary. They have less education, are less informed about the world, and are less likely to vote. Significant numbers of poor people cannot even read or write and so are cut off from much of mainstream culture. Under these conditions, poor people can hardly avoid feelings of inadequacy, frustration, and anger. Some bottle up those feelings, contributing to such psycho-somatic illnesses as high blood pressure and ulcers. In others, the hostility and anger is expressed in violent crime. The rates of murder, assault, and rape are all much higher among poor people than the rest of the population (see Chapter 13).

Economic uncertainty is also part of being poor. Even poor people who are lucky enough to have a permanent job ordinarily work in low-paying, dead-end positions that are the first to be cut in bad times. Others can find only temporary work or are unemployed. Welfare sometimes helps out, but, as we shall see, the benefits are meager and the bureaucracy demeaning. To make this insecurity worse, the poor have far higher rates of family instability than others. The poor marry younger and have the highest rates of divorce, separation, family violence, and childbirth by single women. This pattern of inequality even carries over into matters of life and death. Poor people are far more likely to fall victim to murders and assaults. And although we hear a great deal about medical miracles such as organ transplants, most of these "miracles" are reserved for those with good health insurance. As a rule, the poor receive second-rate health care, a deficient diet, and inadequate shelter. Consequently, they catch more contagious diseases and have higher rates of infant mortality and a shorter life span.

While these generalizations apply to all the poor to one degree or another, it is important to recognize that people who live in poverty are as diverse as those in any other class. While some are so desperately poor they starve or freeze to death, for others poverty is just a short-term condition that is soon overcome. Among the many groups of poor people, three require special attention: the homeless, the underclass, and the working poor.

The Homeless We have all seen them—the bag ladies who push around everything they own in a rusty shopping cart, the disheveled men sleeping on park benches or over heating grates to keep warm, an entire family living in an abandoned car. Lack of protection from the elements is the most obvious hardship they face: in the summer they swelter, and in the winter some freeze to death. But even getting enough food to eat is a continual concern for many of the homeless. Because they are almost always on the streets, they are easy targets for criminals and thugs. And aside from a few overworked charity and social-work agencies, the homeless confront a society that seems indifferent to their plight. The police, to whom most of us turn for protection, see the homeless as a nuisance who must be moved out or arrested when their numbers become too great.

No one is really very sure how many Americans are homeless on any given day. The Census Bureau counted 228,621 homeless people in its 1990 survey. But that figure has been repeatedly criticized as a gross underestimate, and even the Census Bureau itself says it never set out to count every homeless person.[23] The Urban Institute estimates that there are about 600,000 homeless, the Department of Health and Human Services says 2 million, and advocates for the homeless put the figure at about 3 million or more.[24] The one thing about which virtually everyone agrees is that the number of homeless men and women has grown substantially in recent years.

There are several reasons why homelessness appears to have risen even in years when poverty has not. The most popular explanation is that the deinstitutionalization movement, which sharply reduced the population of mental hospitals, has left many severely disturbed patients to wander the streets (see Chapter 8). Although there is little doubt that this policy has been a major contributor to the ranks of the homeless, it is not the only factor. Articles in national magazines such as *Time*, *Newsweek*, and *People* have claimed that the majority of the homeless are mentally disturbed, but several scientific studies have put the figure much lower than 50 percent. Most research suggests that somewhere around a third of the homeless have mental problems.[25] A study of homeless adults in Texas concluded that "the most common face on the street is not that of the psychiatrically-impaired individual, but one caught in a cycle of low-paying, dead-end jobs that fail to provide the means to get off and stay off the streets."[26] Another cause of the increase in homelessness is the indifference of the federal government. During the Reagan administration, the amount of money spent on subsidized housing programs was cut by 75 percent.[27] Moreover, large increases in the cost of rental housing have simply priced many poor people out of the market. Over a million flophouse rooms have been torn down since 1970, and the average cost of rental housing has grown twice as fast as the average income of renters.[28]

The number of homeless women and men has increased sharply in recent years. This photograph shows a homeless man, who spends his nights walking the streets or riding buses, being interviewed by a researcher.

The Underclass Originally coined by sociologist Gunnar Myrdal in the early 1960s, the concept of the **underclass** was picked up in series of articles published in the *New Yorker* magazine in 1981, and from there it jumped into the daily vocabulary of educated Americans. But like most such terms, it is defined differently by different people. Common to most of these definitions is the idea that the underclass comprises the bottom of the poverty class and the implication that its members are excluded from the economic and cultural mainstream of our society.[29] The disagreements arise over the standards that define who is in the underclass and over how large a group they are. The broadest standard holds that the underclass consists of those who are trapped in long-term poverty. By that definition, the underclass would include somewhere between 40 and 60 percent of all poor people.[30] Another approach defines the underclass as the "poorest of the poor"—that is, those who have the lowest income. Estimates of the proportion of the poverty class who are "acutely poor" range from 30 to 45 percent.[31] Finally, the most restrictive standard would include only those who live in neighborhoods that are overwhelmingly poor. Rough estimates based on the data from census tracts (which don't follow the boundaries of actual neighborhoods) place that number at a little under 10 percent of the poor.[32] But despite its usefulness, some sociologists have become uncomfortable with the whole concept of the underclass, because of the sensationalistic way many journalists use the term. Herbert J. Gans, for example, writes that it is an "increasingly pejorative term that seems to be becoming the newest buzzword for the *undeserving* poor."[33]

However the term is defined, the underclass is, in the words of William Julius Wilson, "the heart of the problem of poverty."[34] Members of the underclass are much more likely to have been raised in poverty than the population of poor people as a whole. They are also far more likely to come from ethnic minorities, especially if we define the underclass as those living in overwhelmingly poor neighborhoods. By that definition, 65 percent of the underclass are black and 22 percent Hispanic.[35] Members of the underclass tend to come from single-parent families with a poor educational background and a history of welfare dependency. A substantial proportion of the people in the underclass can't read or write and lack other basic job skills. As a result of these factors, they are trapped in a self-perpetuating cycle of poverty that is extremely hard to break. The frustration and hopelessness of life in the underclass extracts a heavy toll. Compared with other Americans, members of the underclass have significantly higher rates of mental disorder, alcoholism, drug abuse, and suicide, and they are far more likely to fall victim to murder and other violent crimes.

The Working Poor Many people assume that the solution to the problem of poverty is simply to find jobs for the poor. But statistics from the Bureau of the Census show that almost one in ten poor people works full time the year round, and 40 percent work at least part time. Furthermore, the working poor are one of the fastest growing groups in the poverty population. Since 1978, the number of full-time workers living in poverty has risen almost twice as fast as the overall poverty population.[36]

How can so many people hold full-time or nearly full-time jobs and still be poor? The answer is simple. A person working full time for minimum wage does not make enough to keep a family out of poverty. In 1990, for example, someone working all year at minimum wage would earn $7,670—barely enough to keep a single person out of poverty, and far less than the $9,890 needed to keep a family with only one child above the poverty line.[37] To make matters worse, such low-wage jobs have been the fastest growing segment of the labor market in recent years (see Chapter 2).

Despite laboring long hours for little pay, the working poor do have some important advantages over other poor people. Psychologically, they have the self-respect that comes from knowing that they are working and contributing to society. They also have far better prospects of eventually moving out of poverty. But unfortunately, a great many poor people do not really have the option of working, even if they could find a job. About a third are below the age of 15, and another substantial group are elderly or in bad health. Even the welfare mothers who bear the brunt of so much criticism cannot realistically be expected to take a minimum wage job without continued public assistance, since the cost of medical and child care alone would eat up most of their take-home pay.

UNDERSTANDING THE WELFARE SYSTEM

Before we examine the general causes of poverty, we must first take a look at the welfare system, which has become so much a part of the phenomenon of poverty in the twentieth century. And the first step toward understanding the welfare system is to understand the public's attitude toward the poor.

Attitudes Toward the Poor The rejection of the old European class system and the availability of a vast new land to conquer helped create a tremendous faith in the value of hard work and competition among North Americans. To this way of thinking, each individual is responsible for his or her own economic destiny. Many people believe that even in a period of economic depression and high unemployment, anyone who works hard enough can be successful. It is also generally held that "there is always room at the top" for capable and hardworking people, no matter how humble their origins.

Despite its attractiveness, this belief in individual responsibility has a negative side. If the rich are personally responsible for their success, it follows that the poor are to blame for their failure. "Poor folks have poor ways," the old saying goes. Joe R. Feagin has summarized the principal points in this "ideology of individualism" as follows:

1. Each individual should work hard and strive to succeed in competition with others.
2. Those who work hard should be rewarded with success (seen as wealth, property, prestige, and power).
3. Because of widespread and equal opportunity, those who work hard will in fact be rewarded with success.
4. Economic failure is an individual's own fault and reveals lack of effort and other character defects.[38]

Surveys show that this ideology is still a potent force in American life. When asked about the causes of poverty, most people respond with individualistic explanations that blame the poor themselves, rather than with structural explanations that hold society responsible or with fatalistic explanations that blame such things as bad luck

19th-Century Social Problems

Within 5 miles of Milton Junction and in a thickly settled part of Rock County, Mrs. Ira Ames starved and froze to death. The case was reported to the authorities at Janesville and it was found that the father had spent most of his time fishing while his wife and 7 children were in a rickety shanty without fuel or food. The youngest child died a week ago and was buried under the snow by the father in a soap box.

March 16, 1893

These selections, which appear throughout the text, are from the *Badger State Banner*, a newspaper published in Black River Falls, Wisconsin.

or illness. In one survey, for example, 58 percent of the respondents said that lack of thrift and proper money management is a significant cause of poverty, and 55 percent said that lack of effort by the poor is a very important cause of poverty.[39]

The History of the Welfare System The ideology of individualism has had an enormous impact on the response to poverty in the United States. Those receiving government assistance are stigmatized even when they are recognized as "legitimately poor" or "truly needy." Frances Fox Piven and Richard A. Cloward argue that the growth of the modern welfare system resulted more from an attempt to silence the political discontent of the poor than from a desire to improve their living conditions, and their findings have been supported by several more recent studies.[40]

The origins of today's welfare system are to be found in the Great Depression of the 1930s, when unemployment rose dramatically and armies of the newly impoverished demanded assistance: "Groups of men out of work congregated at local relief agencies, cornered and harassed administrators, and took over offices until their demands were met."[41] Despite such determined protests, reforms were made grudgingly. Poor relief was still largely a local matter, but cities and counties proved unable to shoulder the financial burden. The federal government began to give small direct payments to the unemployed, but it soon shifted to work relief programs, which were more in tune with the ideology of individualism. With the coming of President Franklin D. Roosevelt's New Deal, a host of new government agencies were created to create work for unemployed Americans. But public opposition to these and other welfare programs remained strong through the Depression, and one of the few New Deal programs that survives is social security, which is seen more as an insurance than a welfare program.

The 1950s brought only modest increases in welfare support for the poor, but a "welfare explosion" occurred in the 1960s. From December 1960 to February 1969, Aid to Families with Dependent Children (AFDC), which is the main welfare program designed to give financial aid to poor mothers, increased by 107 percent.[42] Daniel

Patrick Moynihan laid the blame for this increase on the deteriorating black family and on the general increase in female-headed families.[43] Piven and Cloward disagree, maintaining that family deterioration made only a minor contribution to the growing welfare rolls and that the real cause was increased activism among the poor, who began to demand greater social support.

The 1960s also saw the launch of President Johnson's War on Poverty. Such programs as the Job Corps, the Neighborhood Youth Corps, VISTA, Head Start, and family planning clinics were launched to help the poor improve their lot. Many of these programs missed their mark because they were inefficiently organized or because they were aimed primarily at young urban males and neglected females, the rural poor, and the elderly. Yet despite all its faults, most researchers agree that the War on Poverty did help bring about a significant reduction in poverty in the United States.

The 1970s did not bring any new initiatives against poverty comparable to those introduced in the 1960s, but progress continued to be made for most of that decade. There was, however, a sharp reaction against welfare programs for the poor in the early 1980s, spearheaded by the Reagan administration. Between 1981 and 1985, a period of unprecedented growth in the number of single-parent families, federal welfare spending dropped by 19 percent, about 400,000 families were cut from AFDC rolls, food stamp recipients were reduced by about 1 million people, and 3 million children were cut from school lunch programs.[44] Since then some of these programs, such as food stamps, have bounced back, and others, such as WIC (which provides food for children and pregnant women) have actually grown.[45] But several of the most important programs, including unemployment insurance, disability, and Aid to Families with Dependent Children, have continued to decline. For example, in 1972, 63 percent of single women with children received AFDC, but that figure has dropped steadily since then and by 1988 only 45 percent of single mothers collected AFDC.[46]

The Structure of the Welfare System America's current welfare system is a confusing hodgepodge of overlapping programs and agencies. Funding comes from various mixtures of federal, state, and local governments, depending on the program. Benefits also vary widely from one state to another and even from one city to the next. At the federal level, AFDC, which gives a monthly check to families who would otherwise be unable to provide for their children, is the largest of the programs that give direct cash grants to poor people. The other large cash program is SSI (supplemental security income), which gives financial assistance to poor people who are blind, disabled, or elderly. The federal government also has a variety of "noncash" programs that provide goods or services instead of money. The food stamp program gives recipients coupons that can be exchanged only for food, and medicaid helps pay its recipients' health care bills. (Medicaid is only for poor people; medicare is a more generous program for everyone over age 65.) Housing assistance is provided through rent subsidies and public housing projects that offer low rents to those poor enough to qualify. The states make a financial contribution to some of these programs, and state and local governments also supplement federal programs with short-term emergency aid and other benefits.

Canada has many programs similar to those in the United States, but, like most European countries, it tends to be more generous with the poor. Canada also relies more heavily on "noncategorical" programs—social programs for which everyone is eligible. For example, all Canadians receive government-financed health care and all parents get a small family allowance (a government payment to parents). This approach to welfare eliminates the costly red tape necessary to determine who is eligible for welfare payments. And because people are not excluded from these programs on the grounds that they earn too much money, work is encouraged rather than discouraged. However, Canadian welfare programs often suffer from the same lack of coordination among federal, provincial, and municipal governments that plagues American programs.

The Myths and Realities of Welfare   Many Americans have a distorted picture of the welfare system. They believe that the welfare rolls are full of able-bodied loafers and mothers who have children just to get a government handout, that people stay on welfare for their entire lives without ever working, and that the benefits provide a comfortable standard of living for those who qualify.

In reality, welfare benefits are meager and getting worse. Among the 15 major industrialized nations, the United States is third from the bottom in the percentage of its national income it spends on welfare programs and it is the only country without some form of guaranteed income plan for families or a comprehensive national health system. In 1987, there were only three states in which the combined total of AFDC and food stamps would keep a family above the poverty line.[47] After adjusting for inflation, the average value of welfare payments has declined by more than a third in the last 20 years.[48]

Even though benefits are often small, many poor people get nothing at all. Only about half the Americans whose income is below the poverty line receive some kind of welfare payment. Noncash programs are more widely available, but still fall far short of the need. In 1990, the food stamp program (which is much bigger than any other noncash program) provided assistance to only 68 percent of poor Americans.[49]

AFDC is clearly the most controversial welfare program in the United States. Perhaps this is because it was created with the intention of assisting children whose fathers had died or been disabled, but only a small percentage of AFDC recipients still fit that description; or perhaps it is simply hostility toward members of ethnic minorities (who are somewhat more likely to receive AFDC payments). There are, however, some more reasonable criticisms. One of the biggest problems is that AFDC tends to discourage welfare mothers from getting a job, because the money they earn is simply deducted from their welfare check and they also run the risk of losing their medicaid benefits if they earn too much. Another common criticism is that AFDC encourages the breakup of families by denying them assistance if an unemployed man is in the home. A third concern is that the program helps perpetuate the "cycle of poverty," because children who grow up in welfare families may fail to learn the basic work habits and attitudes necessary for success in the job market.

EXPLANATIONS OF POVERTY

The economic base of some societies is so fragile that hunger is a daily reality for most people. Such extreme scarcity of food, clothing, and shelter clearly does not characterize modern industrial societies or even most traditional ones. The poverty problem in these societies is one of distributing wealth rather than one of producing it. From a global viewpoint the fact that some nations are poor while others are rich can also be seen as a problem in the distribution of wealth (see Chapter 14). There are many explanations of economic inequality, but most fall into three overlapping categories: those explanations based on an analysis of economic structures, those based on an analysis of the culture of the poor, and those based on an analysis of political relationships among power groups.

Economic Explanations Much poverty can be traced directly to simple economic causes: low wages and too few jobs for those at the bottom of the social hierarchy. In technological societies like Canada and the United States, people without education and skills find it hard to get any kind of employment, and those who find work are likely to be employed in low-paying jobs. We have already seen that even a full-time job at the minimum wage isn't enough to keep a family out of poverty, and there are a growing number of people who are forced to take part-time or temporary jobs because they cannot find full-time work.

Although the unemployment rate goes up and down with the changes in the business cycle (see Chapter 2), the underlying trend in the last three decades has clearly been toward increased unemployment. For example, the peak unemployment rate during each recession has grown steadily higher over the years. But the official unemployment rate is not a very good measure of joblessness, since it doesn't count those who have given up looking for work. When those discouraged workers are added in, the picture gets far worse, for their numbers have grown even more rapidly than the unemployed. For instance, Jencks's analysis of joblessness among men in their prime earning years (which includes both the officially unemployed and the discouraged workers) shows three recent peaks: in 1961, at around 8 percent; in 1975, at around 11 percent; and in 1983, at around 14 percent.[50]

In addition to the overall national problem, many areas have a particularly high unemployment rate because of local conditions—for example, the Appalachian coal region of Kentucky and West Virginia. Early in this century thousands of workers left their homes and farms to take jobs in the Appalachian coal mines. Soon the coal industry dominated the area, and it became almost impossible to find a job that was not dependent on coal mining. The mines, however, were owned and controlled by outside corporations. After World War II the mines were automated, the work force plummeted, and there were no new jobs for those who became unemployed. A similar problem can be found in areas that depended on heavy industries that are no longer competitive in the world economy, and especially in the slums of the central cities, where a variety of forces combine to create an unhealthy economic climate. The low average income in these areas makes it tough going for businesses that depend on local residents for their customers. A high crime rate, the lack of local services, and a significant measure of fear and racism, keep the wealthy away and discourage outside investment. At the same time, inadequate transportation and the long commuting distances to prosperous areas make it difficult for residents of inner-city slums to find work in other neighborhoods. A recent study by James E. Rosenbaum and Susan J. Popkin, for example, found that poor women assigned to public housing in middle-class suburbs were much more likely to find a job than those given housing in the central city.[51]

But even finding a job may not solve a poor person's economic woes. In 1990, there were over 4 million full-time workers below the poverty line, and the situation is getting worse all the time. The reason is that the wages of American workers have been dropping for over a decade. The average hourly wage of workers in the United States has declined from a high of $5.38 in 1973 to only $4.80 in 1989 (to control for inflation, these wage figures are expressed in dollars valued at the 1977 level).[52]

To add to the other problems, the poor often get less for their hard-earned dollars than other consumers do. Slum dwellers, for example, may pay more rent for a run-down apartment than people living in a small town pay for a house with a garden. More generally, because the poor are not mobile, it is difficult for them to shop around for sales and special values. They are obliged to patronize local merchants, who usually charge higher prices than those in affluent areas. When unexpected expenses occur, the poor must borrow money; but because they are not considered good credit risks, it may be impossible for them to get bank loans at standard interest rates. Instead, they must go to loan companies, which charge much higher interest rates, or to loan sharks, who charge exorbitant illegal rates. Many stores in slum areas actively solicit sales on credit because the interest charges are more profitable than the sale itself. If the customer cannot meet the installment payments, the merchandise is repossessed and sold to another poor customer.[53]

Cultural Explanations There are clear cultural differences between the social classes in all modern societies, and some scientists see these differences as a major cause of poverty. The foremost advocate of this position has been Oscar Lewis, who argued that some poor people share a distinct **culture of poverty**.[54] Lewis did not ignore the

---

Supporters of the culture of poverty theory believe that the children of the poor learn attitudes and values that trap them in a life of poverty.

economic basis of poverty; his thesis was simply that a separate subculture has developed among the poor as a reaction to economic deprivation and exclusion from the mainstream of society. Once a culture of poverty has taken hold, it is passed down from generation to generation. Children who grow up in poverty acquire values and attitudes that make it very difficult for them to escape their condition.

In the culture of poverty the nuclear family is female centered, with the mother performing the basic tasks that keep the family going. The father, if he is present, makes only a slight contribution. Children have sexual relations and marry at an early age. The family unit is weak and unstable, and there is little community organization beyond the family. Psychologically, those who live in the culture of poverty have weak ego structures and little self-control. Although Lewis did not use the term, most people living in the culture of poverty would clearly be part of the underclass.

Lewis studied a number of societies and concluded that the culture of poverty is international. It develops in societies with capitalist economies, persistently high unemployment rates, low wages, and an emphasis on accumulation of wealth and property. However, Lewis found a number of societies that have a considerable amount of poverty but no *culture* of poverty. India and Cuba, for example, have no culture of poverty because the poor are not degraded or isolated. But even in the United States, most poor people do not live in the culture of poverty. Because of the influence of the mass media and the relatively low level of illiteracy, Lewis estimated that only 20 percent of the poor live in a culture of poverty.[55]

Most social scientists agree that poor people are more likely to have some of the characteristics described by Lewis, but there is much skepticism about claims that they have any special personality type or that they value work less than other groups. Some of Lewis's critics are not even so sure that a distinct life style is passed from one generation to the next. Rather, it is argued by "situationalists" that each generation of the poor exhibits the same life style because each generation experiences the same conditions: poor housing, crowding, deprivation, and isolation. Charles A. Valentine, for example, argued that the conditions Lewis described are imposed on the poor from the outside rather than being generated by a culture of poverty.[56] But most sociologists accept the notion that some poor people are members of a self-perpetuating underclass, and it follows that those individuals need special government assistance if they are ever to escape from a life of poverty.

Political Explanations   Poverty is as much a political problem as a problem of economics and culture. This is evident from the fact that industrialized nations that are less wealthy than the United States have been more successful in reducing the gap between the haves and the have-nots. A high degree of inequality persists in the United States because most Americans have little concern about the conditions of the poor, and those who do care are not politically organized. Politicians win votes by promising to eliminate crime and high taxes, but few votes are won by promising to eliminate poverty. The ideology of individualism has convinced most Americans that the world is full of opportunities and that the poor deserve to be poor because they are too lazy or incompetent to seize those opportunities. As long as the poor are seen to be responsible for their poverty, political action to change the conditions that cause poverty is unlikely.

Poverty, as Herbert Gans has pointed out, is valuable to the wealthy, and many powerful groups do not want it eliminated.[57] First, it ensures that society's dirty work gets done, for without poverty few people would be willing to do the low-paying, unpleasant, and dangerous jobs. Second, the low wages the poor receive for their work subsidize the wealthy by keeping the prices of goods and services low, and profits high. Third, poverty creates jobs for the many people who service the poor (such as welfare workers) or try to control them (such as police officers and prison guards). Fourth, the poor provide merchants with last-ditch profits by buying goods that otherwise would be thrown away: stale bread, tainted meat, out-of-style clothing, used furniture, and unsafe appliances. Fifth, the poor guarantee the status of the people above them in the social hierarchy. The poor provide a group that "respectable" people can brand as deviants—examples of what happens to those who break social rules. Thus, the contribution of poverty to the comfort of the middle and upper classes creates powerful opposition to any program that is likely to reduce it significantly.

RESPONDING TO PROBLEMS OF POVERTY

No one knows whether it is possible to create a classless industrial society in which all people are economically equal. Certainly no such society exists today. It does, however, seem possible to eliminate poverty in an absolute sense, even if some people remain richer than others. Many societies have, in fact, made much greater progress toward alleviating the hardships of those at the bottom than the United States has. Some of the approaches to reducing poverty are discussed in this section.

Reducing Unemployment Reducing unemployment is a continuing concern of governments around the world. The easiest approach is to stimulate the national economy by cutting taxes and interest rates, or by increasing the amount of money the government spends. The problem with this kind of "quick fix" is that it drives up inflation and the national debt, and if carried on too long may actually cause economic harm. Long-term improvements in the economy will require the kind of basic structural changes described in Chapter 2. Unfortunately, reforms that aim to increase the rate of savings and investment, improve the educational system, and provide better government planning often have little political appeal because they are expensive and seldom produce results quickly enough to influence the next election. Some critics even charge that an overall improvement in the economy wouldn't help poor people very much, because most of them lack even basic job skills. But the available research does not support such claims. Richard B. Freeman, for example, found that the labor shortage caused by Boston's economic boom in the middle 1980s helped slash the unemployment rate of poor young men and increased their average wages as well.[58]

Job retraining is an approach to reducing unemployment that is used widely in European countries. The idea is a simple one: teach unemployed workers skills that are in demand so that they can find new jobs. While this approach is reasonable in this age of rapidly changing technology, it has basic limitations. For one thing, many of the hard-core unemployed can barely read and write and thus are unable to learn the high-tech skills that are in demand. These people need financial support for re-medial education, not job training. But there is a more fundamental problem: if the millions of unemployed workers were taught the latest skills, there would still not be enough jobs to go around unless there was a fundamental improvement in the overall economy.

For that reason, many governments have attacked unemployment by creating new government jobs. It is often suggested that government work programs should be greatly expanded to permit the government to give a job to anyone who is unable to find one in the private sector. Making government an "employer of last resort" could virtually end unemployment. Critics have repeatedly charged that such programs are wasteful and inefficient, and the funding for job programs of all types has been greatly reduced in the last few years. But despite such criticisms and cutbacks, there is little doubt that a well-run government job program would be much less costly to society in the long run than the lives and productive energy wasted by unemployment.

Workfare or Welfare? One of the most popular proposals for changing our welfare system is the notion of making employment or job training mandatory for mothers who receive AFDC. The goal of these so-called **workfare** programs is to get mothers off the welfare rolls by training them and placing them in jobs, thus improving the lives of the poor and saving tax dollars at the same time. With this goal in mind, the federal Work Incentive Program, which encourages welfare mothers to find employment, has been significantly expanded, and many states have developed similar programs of their own. But such programs face serious obstacles. The first one is money, since, at least at the beginning, an effective program will cost considerably more money to set up and run than it saves. The second difficulty is finding and paying for enough good day care to handle the participants' children while they are in training or at work. The third problem is that most current proposals are based on unrealistic expectations for success. In the past, even the most successful of these programs still failed to place about a third of the participants in a job, and typically those who do find work still do not make enough money to get off welfare.[59] A final drawback is that this approach is too negative. Although welfare mothers are threatened with the loss of their benefits if they do not participate in these employment programs, those benefits are still cut back or eliminated when they start earning money, so they receive few positive rewards for holding down a job. Despite these difficulties, a well-designed employment program for welfare mothers could be a very positive step, but only if it avoids the kind of punitive approach based on unfair stereotypes of welfare mothers as loafers living high at the taxpayers' expense.

Extending Public Assistance America's welfare system has many bureaucratic snags. Programs are administered by a patchwork of federal, state, and local agencies. A tremendous amount of time and money that might be used to help poor people is spent on determining who is eligible for assistance. Such administrative waste would be drastically reduced if certain welfare services were provided to all citizens, not just to those who can demonstrate special needs. As mentioned earlier, Canada has taken this approach, providing all citizens with medical care, a small retirement pension, and a family allowance for each dependent child. Most European countries have

D E B A T E

Should the Government Provide Free Housing for the Homeless?

Many cities and towns provide temporary shelters for the homeless, but there are many more homeless people on the streets than the shelters can accommodate. Some people, therefore, propose that federal funds be provided to guarantee every homeless person a place to sleep if he or she wants one.

YES A new wave of homeless men, women, and children is flooding the nation, and we must do something more than just pick up the bodies when they freeze to death. Some people say that we should rely on churches and other private charities to handle the problem. But although such an approach may have worked in a nation of small, tightly knit farming communities, it is hopelessly inadequate in a complex urban society. The charities themselves openly admit that they do not have the money or the resources to solve this problem.

The government is the one organization that can provide adequate housing for our most needy citizens. The only question is whether or not these people deserve to be helped, and the answer is a resounding yes. More fortunate people often look down their noses at the homeless and blame them for their own misery. But no one chooses to be born in the underclass, to have a mental disorder, or to fall victim to the disease of alcoholism. And even the most zealous ideologue would have a difficult time finding a reason to blame homeless children for their plight. The real reason so many wealthy people oppose aid to the homeless is simple greed. They would rather see these unfortunates die on the streets than pay another $25 a year in taxes. But surely we are a more generous and public-spirited people than that. Our values and our traditions demand that we take

NO As soon as we hear about a new social problem, the first thing some people want to do is rush in and start throwing money at it. But a gigantic new government program to house the homeless would inevitably prove as wasteful and ineffective as other welfare programs have been. For one thing, the government is so inefficient and hamstrung by political pressures that most of the money is likely to be wasted before it ever gets to the homeless. And even if enough free housing were created to put a roof over their heads, that would do nothing to solve the underlying problems that made them homeless in the first place. The alcoholics and the mentally disturbed would simply be suffering from the same conditions indoors rather than on the streets.

A free housing program for the homeless would be a financial monster. It would grow bigger year by year, and eventually we would be forced to abandon it. We might begin by providing housing only to those who are now homeless, but what about the poor people who are working at low-paying jobs and still paying rent? They would soon walk away from their old apartments so that they too could become "homeless" and claim a free place to live.

The solution to the problem of the homeless is for individual citizens to give more to the private charities that have already proven that they can do an efficient forceful action to solve this tragic problem, and it is time we stopped talking and got the job done.

job in dealing with the problem. Setting up another huge government bureaucracy would only make things worse, not better.

---

similar programs. The poor are not discouraged from working by the threat of a reduction in their welfare benefits when they start to earn some money. Welfare fraud and the time and money spent on detecting and apprehending chiselers are also greatly reduced.

Another approach to simplifying the complex maze of welfare programs is called the guaranteed annual income. A central feature of such a proposal is a negative income tax. The basic idea is simple: families earning less than a certain amount would receive a government grant, called a negative tax, from the Internal Revenue Service. Families with incomes above that amount would pay "positive" taxes, just as they do now. Most proposals provide some incentive to ensure that poor families with working members make more money than the nonworking poor. The main advantage of such a program is that it eliminates a lot of unnecessary bureaucracy and therefore reduces the cost of delivering welfare services.

In the 1960s, poor people won significant political and economic gains by organizing and working together for social change. But that spirit of political activism declined, and many of those gains have slipped away.

Organizing the Poor Reducing unemployment, extending public assistance, and guaranteeing a certain minimum income all have very high price tags. Americans give much lip service to the ideal of equality, but they appear unwilling to put the ideal into practice with financial support. As we have seen, sociological research shows that programs to help the poor are created only when the poor organize and demand a bigger piece of the economic pie. Amid the activism of the 1960s, a number of poor people's organizations sprang up to press such demands and were able to win support from more broadly based groups. As a result, the welfare system was improved and poverty decreased. If the government is once again to become concerned with the plight of the poor, new organizations and new coalitions will have to be formed to push for change.

SOCIOLOGICAL PERSPECTIVES ON PROBLEMS OF THE POOR

Poverty has not always been a social problem. Although concern for poor people has a long history, until quite recently poverty was considered an inevitable part of social life or the fault of the poor themselves—a lowly status deserved by the lazy and incompetent. But in the past six decades, poverty has increasingly come to be seen as an institutional matter rather than a personal one. The Great Depression of the 1930s, tragic though it was, made a significant contribution to social science. It helped people see that the conditions of poverty are determined by economic, political, and social processes that are beyond the control of individual citizens. Most social scientists now view poverty as a social problem rather than as a collection of personal problems, even though they still disagree about its causes and solutions.

The Functionalist Perspective Functionalists consider the extremes of poverty and wealth, common in many nations, to be a result of malfunctions in the economy. In many parts of the world, rapid industrialization has disrupted the economic system, leaving it disorganized and unable to perform many of its functions. At first, people who lack job skills are forced into menial work at low wages and then, with the coming of automation, find that they are not needed at all. Industrial products become outdated (horse carriages, steam engines, milk bottles), and unless rapid adjustments are made, workers lose their jobs. Training centers and apprenticeship programs may continue to produce graduates whose skills are no longer in demand. Discrimination, whether it is based on sex, age, race, or ethnic status, also wastes the talents of many capable people, and society is the loser.

Functionalists point out that the welfare system intended to solve the problem of poverty is just as disorganized as the economy. Administrators often show more concern for their own well-being than for that of their clients. Too often the poor go hungry because bureaucrats are afraid to help a deserving family that is technically ineligible for assistance. Legislative bodies establish programs without enough funds for efficient operations. Inadequate communication systems fail to inform the poor about benefits to which they are entitled. Job training and educational programs are not coordinated with the needs of agriculture, commerce, and industry.

The best way to deal with poverty, according to the functionalist perspective, is to reorganize the economic system so that it operates more efficiently. The poor who have been cast out and neglected must be reintegrated into the mainstream of economic life. Members of the underclass must be provided with training and jobs so that they can resume their roles as productive citizens. But they must also be given a new sense of hope based on the knowledge that the rest of society cares about them and is willing to help them overcome their poverty. Functionalists also recommend reforms to help stabilize the economic system so that it will not produce new poor people to replace those who have escaped from poverty.

In general, functionalists are much more concerned about absolute poverty than about relative poverty. They doubt that relative poverty (economic inequality) can or should be eliminated. Kingsley Davis and Wilbert E. Moore, for example, argued strongly that economic inequality is functional (that is, good for society).[60] Their main point is that the desire for more money motivates people to work hard to meet the standards of excellence that are required in many important jobs. Without inequality of reward, the most capable people would not be motivated to train for or perform the demanding jobs that are essential to the economic system. It should not be concluded, however, that functionalists are convinced that the social system should remain unchanged or that the amount of economic inequality should not be reduced. The functionalist conclusion is simply that *some* inequality is necessary for the maintenance of society as we know it.

The Conflict Perspective Conflict theorists start with the assumption that because there is such enormous wealth in industrialized nations, no one in such societies need be poor. Poverty exists because the middle and upper classes want it to exist. Conflict theorists argue that the working poor are exploited: they are paid low wages so that their employers can make fatter profits and lead more affluent lives. The unemployed are victims of the same system. Wealthy employers oppose programs to reduce unemployment because they do not want to pay the taxes to support them. They also oppose such programs because the fear of unemployment helps keep wages down and workers docile. Thus, conflict theorists argue that the economic system of capitalist countries operates to create and perpetuate a high degree of economic inequality.

Conflict theorists also note that wealthy and middle-class people are more likely than the poor to say that unemployment and poverty stem from a lack of effort rather than from social injustice or other circumstances beyond the control of the individual. This application of the ideology of individualism enables the wealthy to be charitable to the poor, giving some assistance freely while ignoring the economic and political foundations of poverty. Charity, including the government dole, blunts political protests and social unrest that might threaten the status quo. Moreover, some poor people come to accept the judgments passed on them by the rest of society and adjust their aspirations and their self-esteem downward.

Conflict theorists view these adjustments to poverty as a set of chains that must be broken. They believe that the poor should become politically aware and active, organizing themselves to reduce inequality by demanding strong government action.

In other words, political action is seen as the most effective response to inequality and, thus, to the problem of poverty. Most conflict theorists doubt that economic inequality can be significantly reduced without a concerted effort by poor people that gains at least some support from concerned members of the upper classes.

Social Psychological Perspectives Social psychologists study the effects of attitudes and beliefs on behavior, pointing out that poor people learn to behave like poor people. The values of those who live in the culture of poverty are passed on to their children, thus directing them into lives of poverty. Stated differently, socialization practices among the poor promote attitudes and behavior patterns that make upward social mobility difficult. For example, the children of the poor learn to seek immediate gratification. Unlike middle-class achievers, they are not inclined to defer small immediate rewards so that long-run goals, such as a college education, can be reached.

Interactionists emphasize the fact that the main reference group for poor people is in their poor neighbors. In many parts of the world, including some places in North America, a successful person is one who knows where the next meal is coming from, and a "big success" may be the assistant manager of a shoe store. People with such attitudes become trapped in their own poverty. More generally, interactionists point to cultural differences in the ways poor people and wealthy people define their worlds, and they note that even if new economic opportunities arise, these differences in definitions persist and function to keep the poor at the bottom of the social ladder.

Social psychologists also study the psychological effects of being poor in a wealthy society. The easy availability of television and other media of mass communication encourages the poor to compare themselves with more fortunate people. And when they do so, many come to believe that they are failures. Some attribute their failure to personal shortcomings rather than to social forces that are beyond their control. The outcome is likely to be a low sense of self-esteem, which may be combined with a variety of personal problems, ranging from drug addiction and mental disorders to delinquency and crime.

The social psychological perspective implies that poverty traps poor people psychologically as well as economically and socially. The trap can be sprung by eliminating absolute poverty (the lack of adequate food, shelter, and clothing) and by opening up more opportunities for the children of the poor, thus reducing overall inequality. Social psychologists also agree that the poor must be encouraged to redefine their social environment. Even if avenues for upward mobility are created, little change will occur as long as the poor are convinced that they can expect no better than a life of poverty. Many poor people will also have to be helped to change a self-image shaped by defeat and rejection before they will be able to take advantage of any new opportunities that are created.

SUMMARY

Whether economic inequality is measured by income distribution or by distribution of wealth, there are large gaps between the rich, the middle class, and the poor that have grown much wider in recent years. Significant differences also exist in the cultural perspectives and life styles of these different groups. In cities the poor are trapped in run-down, crime-ridden neighborhoods, while the affluent have a multitude of opportunities from which to choose. Psychologically, the poor have to cope with feelings of inadequacy and inferiority because they lack the money and goods that everyone is expected to have. The families of the poor are more unstable, and they have more health problems and a shorter life span.

There are two common ways to measure poverty. The relative approach holds that people are poor if they are significantly less well off than the average person in their society. The absolute approach, which is used by most government agencies, defines poverty as the lack of the essentials of life, such as sufficient food, shelter, and clothing. According to the official figures, the poverty rate decreased from over 20 percent in the early 1960s to a low of around 11 percent in the 1970s. Since then, the poverty rate has climbed to around 13 to 14 percent.

A look at the distribution of poverty shows that the young are more likely to be poor than the middle aged or the elderly, as are children from single-parent families and the members of ethnic minority groups. The poverty rate is highest in the inner city and in rural areas and lowest in the suburbs. There are many important differences among poor people. The working poor are those who hold down a job but still make too little to be above the poverty line. The underclass is composed of the long-term poor who are shut out of the mainstream of society. And at the very bottom of the social heap are the homeless, who seem to lack almost all the essentials of the life style expected in our society.

The ideology of individualism, which stresses personal responsibility and self-reliance, has fostered the belief that the poor are to blame for their own condition. From the beginning, the welfare system was established on the assumption that being poor was one's own fault. Today the welfare system in the United States includes a variety of overlapping programs and jurisdictions. Included are programs that make cash payments to families with dependent children (AFDC) as well as to the blind, the aged, and the disabled (SSI). Other programs distribute food stamps and assist with housing and medical costs. In Canada, the federal government has emphasized programs that provide welfare services to all citizens. Among these are government-financed health care, old-age pensions, and a small family allowance for each child.

There are many explanations of poverty. In some societies the economic base is so weak that many people must go hungry. In modern industrial societies poverty results from unemployment, low wages, and unequal distribution of wealth. The poor do not receive a proportionate share of the wealth, and they often pay more than wealthy people for the same goods and services. Another explanation for poverty is based on Oscar Lewis's idea that some nations develop a "culture of poverty," with its own distinctive characteristics. In addition, there are political reasons for the continued existence of poverty in North America. Poverty is valuable to the rich and the powerful. It ensures that dirty work gets done, that prices remain low, and that welfare workers have jobs.

There are many proposals for reducing poverty. First, unemployment could be reduced by stimulating the economy, providing job training, and increasing government employment. Second, welfare rolls might be reduced by helping AFDC mothers to get a job. Third, administrative waste could be cut if the welfare system were reformed by reducing programs with strict eligibility standards and replacing them with social programs for which everyone qualifies. Fourth, the poor should organize themselves to influence legislation and government policies.

Functionalists see extremes of poverty and wealth as resulting from breakdowns in social organization. Conflict theorists are convinced that poverty thrives because the wealthy and powerful benefit from it. Social psychologists note that the socialization of the poor develops attitudes and behavior patterns that make upward social mobility difficult.

KEY TERMS

absolute approach   A means of defining poverty based on the lack of basic necessities, such as food, shelter, and clothing.

culture of poverty   A theory that holds that there is a self-perpetuating subculture among some (but not all) poor people that helps trap them in poverty.

income   The amount of money a person earns or receives from other sources in a given year.

relative approach   A means of defining poverty based on the expectations and average standard of living in a particular society.

underclass   Those in the lower part of the poverty class, who are excluded from the economic and cultural mainstream of society.

wealth   A person's total economic assets (cash, real estate, stocks and bonds, etc.).

workfare   A welfare program that emphasizes job training and placement, especially for welfare mothers.

FURTHER READINGS

Harold R. Kerbo, *Social Stratification and Inequality: Class Conflict in Historical and Comparative Perspective*, 2nd ed. (New York: McGraw-Hill, 1991). An excellent text on social stratification that puts the problem of poverty into its larger context.

William Julius Wilson, *The Truly Disadvantaged: The Inner City, the Underclass, and Public Policy* (Chicago: University of Chicago Press, 1987). A penetrating look at the causes of the deteriorating conditions of the American underclass. Probably the most influential work on poverty of the last decade.

Christopher Jencks and Paul E. Peterson, eds., *The Urban Underclass* (Washington, D.C.: Brookings Institution, 1991). A first-rate collection of essays stimulated by Wilson's work on the underclass.

Barbara Ehrenreich, *Fear of Falling: The Inner Life of the Middle Class* (New York: HarperCollins, 1991). An insightful analysis of the middle class by one of America's most thoughtful social critics.

Jonathan Kozol, *Rachel and Her Children: Homeless Families in America* (New York: Crown, 1988). An analysis of homelessness in America, based on the author's direct contact with the problem.

chapter 7

The Ethnic Minorities

- What are the most common patterns of ethnic relations?
- What are the problems shared by ethnic minorities in North America?
- What are the special problems unique to each different minority group?
- Why do most minority groups have such a high poverty rate?
- What are the best ways to deal with the problem of ethnic inequality?

The violent face of ethnic relations—riots, beatings, and murders—is familiar to any-one who watches the evening news. From the Middle East to Yugoslavia, ethnic conflict is a burning issue. Virtually every nation with more than one ethnic group has had to deal with ethnic clashes. Some have managed to achieve long-term stability and harmony; others have been torn apart by violence and hatred. But most have just muddled through with alternating periods of conflict and cooperation.

The exploitation and oppression of one group by another are particularly ironic in democratic nations, which claim to cherish justice and equality. But the attempt to create real ethnic equality always meets stubborn resistance. The dominant group that controls the economic and political institutions seldom voluntarily agrees to share its power. And because the members of minority groups tend to be less skilled and less educated than members of the mainstream culture, they are often unable to unseat those at the top. Moreover, the fear of change causes people from all ethnic groups to hold fast to the way things are.

ETHNIC GROUPS

The members of an **ethnic group** share a common set of cultural characteristics, or at least a common national origin.[1] What sets an ethnic group apart is its sense of common identity and the belief that its members share a unique social and historical experience. The term **ethnic minority** is used in two different ways. Sometimes it simply refers to an ethnic group that has fewer members than those of the majority group in the society. But sociologists generally restrict the term to those groups that also suffer prejudice and discrimination at the hands of the majority.

Although a racial group is often an ethnic group as well, the two are not the same. A **race** is a group of people with a common set of physical characteristics, but the members of a race may or may not share the sense of unity and identity that holds an ethnic group together. The concept of "race" as it is used in everyday speech is more a social idea than a biological fact. Among the more than 5 billion people in the world, there is an incredible range of skin colors, body builds, hair types, and other physical features. Different cultures and even scientists who study racial types do not agree on a single classification system.[2] Thus, physical characteristics are bio-logical in origin, but the way they are classified and the meanings they are given are socially determined.

People from all ethnic groups tend to see their own culture as the best and most enlightened. This attitude is known as **ethnocentrism**.[3] Because values and behavior patterns differ from one culture to another, one's own culture naturally appears su-perior when judged by its own standards. Thus, ethnocentrism seems to be universal. All cultures show some prejudice against foreigners, who are commonly viewed as heathens, barbarians, or savages. **Racism** is usually defined as a belief in the superi-ority of one racial group to another that leads to prejudice and discrimination. The main difference between racism and ethnocentrism is that the former is concerned with the physical differences between people and the latter with their cultural dif-ferences. Although racism is common throughout the world, it is not as universal as ethnocentrism. In many societies, people who share a culture and a religion do not consider the racial differences between themselves important. But where racism does exist, it is often more vicious and divisive than ethnocentrism. Two chilling examples are Hitler's mass executions of European Jews and Gypsies, and the colonists' nearly successful attempt to wipe out the native population of North America.

Patterns of Ethnic Relations   The relationships between ethnic groups take a bewildering variety of forms. Even the relationships among ethnic groups in North America can be difficult to grasp. Sociologists have described three general patterns of ethnic relations that help us simplify this confusing picture. In some cases, known as **domination**, one group holds the power and the other groups are under its economic and political control. The instances in which different groups are more or less equal follow two patterns. In a system of **integration**, different ethnic groups go to the same schools, work in the same businesses, and live in the same neighborhoods. In **pluralism**, different ethnic groups are still equal, but they are more separate and distinct. Children are likely to go to a school that places emphasis on teaching the traditions of their group, families live in their own ethnic neighborhoods, and adults work in businesses run by other members of their ethnic group. But it is important to note that these are only general patterns and that conditions of domination, integration, and pluralism often occur together in the same society.

   When two ethnic groups come into close contact for the first time, ethnocentrism stimulates competition and conflict, and one group usually emerges as the winner. That group becomes dominant, holding most of the political and economic power and discriminating against the subordinate group. The domination of black slaves by white Americans is a typical example. Politically, the displaced Africans were powerless, sharing none of the rights of other Americans. They had no weapons or organizations with which to fight their oppressors. Their work produced riches for plantation owners, but their lowly condition was far beneath mere poverty. They

19th-Century Social Problems

The right of colored people to attend public places of amusement under the laws of Wisconsin is to be tested. Rachel and Clara Black are the nearly white and attractive daughters of a colored barber, Alfred Black. The young women visited the Century Roller Skating Rink at Oshkosh as spectators. The next day they received a note requesting them to discontinue their visits. They went again and were invited to leave, which they did. The reason assigned by the management of the rink is that it had established a rule not to let colored people frequent the place.

February 9, 1899

These selections, which appear throughout the text, are from the *Badger State Banner*, a newspaper published in Black River Falls, Wisconsin.

were isolated, rejected, and considered more animal than human. Although American slavery is an extreme case of ethnic domination, the pattern in other cases is the same.

In pluralistic systems, ethnic groups maintain a high degree of independence. The ethnic groups in a pluralist society identify with the larger society but control some of their own social and political affairs. Usually, this situation is possible because different ethnic groups live in different neighborhoods or different parts of the country and are therefore able to control their local schools, governments, and economic institutions. Although different groups in a pluralist system are roughly equal, in practice some inequality exists, so that deciding whether a relationship is one of domination or pluralism is a matter of judgment. For instance, French Canadians are usually considered part of a pluralistic system. Although they maintain a distinct identity and have a strong cultural tradition, there are some ways in which French Canadians are dominated by English-speaking Canadians. Anglo-Canadians (and Americans) control the Canadian economy, and the English and American cultural influence is very strong throughout Canada.

But pluralism, even when it is regionally based, may result in ethnic conflicts, as in Belgium, or in open warfare, as in Lebanon. In the extreme, separatist movements may divide the pluralist nation into two or more independent countries. This was the case in the division of India and Pakistan and of Pakistan and Bangladesh. A similar process is even possible in Canada, where some French Canadians want to divide the country into separate French- and English-speaking nations.

An integrated society, like a pluralistic one, strives for ethnic equality, but the interests of one ethnic group are not balanced against those of another. Rather, ethnic backgrounds are ignored, and, ideally, all individuals are treated alike.

In a truly integrated society all people attend the same local schools, go to the same houses of worship, and vote for political candidates on the basis of merit alone. Of course, complete integration never occurs in an actual society, any more than does completely equal pluralism. As long as people living together define themselves as members of different ethnic groups, some degree of prejudice and discrimination always remains. Most societies that encourage ethnic equality through integration have therefore enacted various laws that prohibit discrimination and try to help its victims.

Just as pluralism can lead to ethnic conflicts and the eventual partition of a society, integration may lead to the gradual reduction or elimination of distinctive ethnic characteristics. Groups that live in close contact, watch the same television shows, eat at the same fast-food stands, and even intermarry are bound to grow increasingly similar as time passes. Today, many North Americans with European backgrounds have given up their separate ethnic identities and simply see themselves as Americans. Even racial differences may begin to fade after years of intermarriage, as they have in Mexico.

A Melting Pot or a Salad Bowl?   So far we have been describing the kinds of relationships that exist between different ethnic groups. But aside from what *is*, people are naturally concerned about what *ought to be*. In North America, it was traditionally assumed that minority groups should take on the culture of the dominant group in a process known as **assimilation**. Because immigrants were expected to conform to the standards of Anglo-American culture, this ideal is often known as Anglo-conformity. To be accepted, the immigrant had to learn English, convert to Protestantism, and adopt Anglo-American values and ways of life. Blacks and Native Americans, as well as whites who refused to adopt Anglo-American ways, were condemned to be permanent outsiders. They were not "real Americans."

Although the pressure for conformity to Anglo-American standards continues to be an important force, it has weakened over the years. As more and more different ethnic groups came to North America, people began proposing ideals that were less one-sided. The most influential was the theory of the **melting pot**, which holds that the different immigrant groups that came to the United States have blended into a distinctively new culture. To this way of thinking, the assimilation of ethnic minorities is still a good thing but should be a two-sided process. Immigrants should be encouraged to adopt the culture of their new home, but the majority group should learn from the newcomers and change their cultural expectations accordingly. Critics of this view often complain that while the ideal of the melting pot may be fine, in actual practice it has been used as a justification for the continued demand for conformity to Anglo culture.

A third ideal, which is sometimes called the **salad bowl**, holds that North America works best as a diverse blend of "unmelted" subcultures. Although Mexicans, Jews, blacks, Chinese, Puerto Ricans, Koreans, Europeans, Indians, Cubans, and other groups all participate in many common elements of American culture, they are not all the same. These groups remain equally American, but each retains its own distinctive traditions. Advocates of the ideal of the salad bowl hold that melding together these diverse groups would not only destroy valuable ethnic traditions but would make the United States a far less interesting place in which to live. The critics argue that it is unrealistic to think that immigrants, who often come from poor Third World nations, can keep their traditional culture alive in the middle of an alien industrialized society. At best, they might hang on to a few of their traditional ways in segregated ethnic subcultures, but, the critics charge, the discrimination and conflict such a system breeds is far too high a price to pay.

ETHNIC MINORITIES IN NORTH AMERICA

Historical Background The Indians were the first Americans and for that reason they are often referred to as Native Americans. Contrary to popular stereotypes, not all Native Americans were nomadic warriors. Indeed, there were many different native cultures. Some Indians were wandering hunters, but many others lived in stable villages and grew their own food. In some areas, principally Mexico and South America, the Native Americans had highly advanced civilizations. American Indians spoke about 300 different languages in just the area north of what is now the Mexican border.[4]

Three major groups of European colonists settled in North America: French, British, and Spanish. In the beginning, European–Indian relations were generally peaceful, and a lively trade developed. But the influx of colonists disrupted this early system of pluralism. European peoples came to dominate the eastern tribes and then slowly moved westward, first driving the native peoples from their lands at gunpoint, then restricting them to isolated reserves, and finally requiring even reservation Indians to obey their law.

Conflict was not restricted to whites and Indians, for the European powers also were bitter enemies, fighting among themselves for power, money, and Indian lands. The British emerged as the victors, and the lands north of what is now the Mexican-American border have been dominated by English-speaking peoples ever since. The boundaries of the newly independent United States changed slowly, moving westward as Americans took over vast sections of land formerly held by Spain, France, and Mexico. This westward conquest meant, of course, that sizable European and non-European minorities were brought under the domination of the English-speaking majority.

The two new North American nations took very different approaches to the problems of their native minorities. Canadian treaties with Indians were usually honored, and the government attempted to minimize stealing, looting, and pillaging by the white settlers. In tragic contrast, the United States government repeatedly signed treaties with the Indians and then broke them as white settlers demanded more and more Indian lands.[5] The loss of their land, the disruption of their economy, and the spread of European diseases almost led to the annihilation of the Indian people in North America. In 1500, there were between 12 and 15 million Indians in North America (excluding Mexico), but by 1850 only about a quarter of a million survived.[6] After the resistance of the Native Americans was broken, they were subjected to cruel domination:

> Most Indian people were denied the vote, had to obtain passes to leave the reservation and were prohibited from practicing their own religions, sometimes by force. Children were dragooned off to boarding schools where they were severely punished if they were caught speaking their own language.[7]

The French minority in Canada and the Spanish minority in the United States took divergent paths after they fell under Anglo domination. French Canada had a substantial population at the time of the English conquest, and it has maintained itself as a self-perpetuating community with little new immigration. Quebec has become an island of French in an English-speaking sea. In contrast, the Spanish-speaking population in most of the areas taken from Spain and Mexico was quite small. With the advent of the transcontinental railroad and the California gold strikes, these people were soon overwhelmed by waves of English-speaking immigrants. However, later immigration from Mexico and other Latin American countries eventually led to significant increases in the Hispanic population in the United States.

In the first century following the American Declaration of Independence, most immigrants to the United States came from the Protestant countries of northern Europe. But from 1870 to 1920, immigrants increasingly arrived from the Catholic areas of Europe: Italy, Ireland, and eastern Europe, especially Poland. At first it was assumed that these immigrants would quickly assimilate into British Protestant culture; when they failed to do so, ethnic tensions and hostilities grew. In addition, nonwhite immigrants, principally from China and Japan, arrived on the West Coast to be greeted with even more prejudice and discrimination. A federal law passed in 1924 severely restricted immigration from southern Europe and stopped all immigration from Asia.

Unlike other immigrants, blacks were forced to come to North America against their will. Most were put to work as slaves on Southern plantations.

The history of the Africans in North America is unique because the immigrants from that continent arrived in chains. American slavery was concentrated in the Southern plantation regions, and slaveholders intentionally tried to extinguish African culture. The African family system was broken up, and fathers were routinely separated from their children. Slaves who shared common cultural roots were systematically separated and forbidden to speak their own language. They were even forced to abandon their native religions and to become Christians.

After slavery had been abolished, African Americans continued to be plagued by racism. Black political power blossomed briefly after the Civil War, but this fragile flower was soon plucked. African Americans were systematically murdered, terrorized, and subjugated. Terrorist organizations such as the Ku Klux Klan and the Knights of the White Camellia drove blacks back into their subordinate status. Slavery was replaced by a system of segregation that denied blacks full rights of citizenship and isolated them from the mainstream of American society.

The rigid segregation system in the Southern states and the more informal segregation practiced in the rest of the country thrived for 100 years. It was not until the 1950s and 1960s that the civil rights movement finally broke the back of legal segregation. With a new sense of political awareness, thousands of blacks and their white supporters, backed by Supreme Court decisions, organized, demonstrated, and demanded equal rights. Militant Hispanics, Asians, and Native Americans organized and began echoing demands for "black power" with calls for "brown power," "yellow power," and "red power." In Canada, the *Quebecois* (French Canadians) also began to assert their cultural identity, and some demanded a new nation separate from Canada.

One of the most important developments of the 1980s was the big surge in immigration. The United States legally admitted over 6 million new residents during that decade and granted amnesty to another 2.3 million illegal immigrants—more than double the figure for the previous decade. Although exact figures are hard to come by, there was probably an even greater surge in illegal than legal immigration. The Immigration Act of 1965, which eliminated the quota system that had favored European immigrants, helped produce another major change in migration patterns—in the past few decades, most new immigrants to the United States have been coming from the Third World. During the 1980s, there were about 637,000 legal immigrants from Europe, while 2,247,000 came from Asia and 1,673,000 from Latin America. As a result of this immigration and the differences in birthrates among ethnic groups, nearly one in every four Americans is now a member of a non-European ethnic minority.[8]

Institutional Inequality   To understand the problems ethnic minorities face today, the first thing most sociologists do is look at such questions as: ''What kind of jobs do they have?'' ''What is their average income?'' ''What is their educational background?'' The answers reveal a high degree of institutional inequality in North American society—in other words, members of most ethnic minorities are much more likely to be at the bottom than the top of our institutional hierarchies.

Education North American culture puts tremendous faith in education. Numerous studies have shown that people with more education are likely to have higher-paying and higher-status jobs (see Chapter 4). But blacks, Hispanics, and Native Americans receive significantly less education than others. In 1989, 78 percent of whites had finished high school, whereas only 65 percent of blacks and 51 percent of Hispanics had finished. Some Asian groups, such as the Japanese, are exceptions to this pattern and actually have a higher level of educational achievement than white Americans, but others, such as Laotians and Cambodians, are far below the American average.[9]

The sources of this educational inequality are rooted in domination. During the period of slavery, most black Americans received little schooling, and after emancipation they were put into separate schools, of decidedly inferior quality. The civil rights movement and the Supreme Court eventually ended legal segregation. But as was noted in Chapter 4, school segregation has continued, largely as a result of segregated housing patterns in cities. In response to this new problem, courts have ordered that schoolchildren be bused from one school to another to achieve racial balance. But a storm of protest and conflict has made the courts back away from this approach.

In many ways the history of Native American education is even more dismal than that of black education. Many of the early Indian schools were run by missionaries who were determined to ''civilize'' and Christianize the ''heathen savages.'' The government-run boarding schools that eventually replaced the missionary schools were no better:

> The young Indian, torn from his family, was shipped to the school where his hair was immediately cut and where he was given a military uniform and taught close order drill. One of the prime objectives of the system was to teach him the English language as rapidly as possible. He was given demerits for speaking in his native language. Since the incoming student could speak no other language, great personal tragedies resulted, leading to high suicide rates.[10]

Many young Indians returning from boarding school were adrift: they did not fit into the white world, yet they were no longer comfortable in the traditional world of their parents, either.

The cultural assumptions of the white middle class are built into today's schools, and that creates behavioral as well as learning problems for some minority students. For example, success in school depends largely on the student's ability to meet middle-class standards of discipline and self-control. Students from homes that allow free emotional expression and provide few controls on behavior are therefore at a disadvantage. In addition, textbooks and other course materials are often culturally biased. Imagine Native American children's reaction on reading that traitors in their ancestors' struggle to keep their land are to be called "friendly" Indians. Only recently have American textbooks acknowledged the contributions of ethnic minorities to U.S. society. Cultural biases are also institutionalized through language. Immigrant children are often required to do their schoolwork in English whether or not they are fluent in that language. Obviously, children who must struggle to learn mathematics, science, and history in a language they do not fully understand are less likely to get good grades or even to finish high school.

It should not be concluded, however, that the differences in educational achievement between most ethnic minorities and the dominant group stem entirely from the cultural biases built into the school system. For one thing, the children of the poor are under strong economic pressure to drop out of school, and ethnic minorities are more likely to be poor. Further, there are significant differences in the value placed on education and in the family structure of various ethnic groups, and these differences affect achievement. For instance, Japanese Americans and several other Asian groups who are noted for their cohesive family structure have been very successful in school despite the barriers of language and racial prejudice.

Employment Members of minority groups often have low-status and low-paying jobs. Whites are more than twice as likely as blacks or Hispanics to work as managers or professionals. Similar patterns are found in the distribution of income. In 1989, the average black family earned only about 57 percent as much as the average white family, down from a high of 61 percent in 1970. Hispanic families earned about 64 percent as much as white families, putting them ahead of blacks but substantially behind the average American. These figures are somewhat misleading, however, because Hispanics have larger families than do blacks. When we look at income per person instead of per family, Hispanics are actually slightly behind.[11] A look at the unemployment figures shows much the same story. In 1989, only 4.5 percent of white workers were unemployed, while that figure was 8 percent for Hispanics and 11.8 percent for blacks (see Figure 7.1).[12]

Much of this inequality can be explained by the educational differences already discussed. Because minorities have less education, they have fewer members who qualify for high-paying jobs. But education is not the whole story, for minority members receive less pay than whites with the same level of education. On the average, a black family headed by someone who has completed four years of high school has about the same income as a white family headed by someone with only eight years of education.[13] Because blacks are physically the most distinct ethnic group, they are

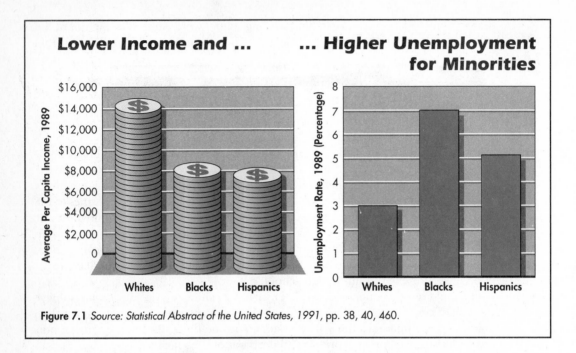

Figure 7.1 *Source: Statistical Abstract of the United States, 1991, pp. 38, 40, 460.*

most often the victims of job discrimination. Such racism is common in labor unions as well as in businesses and results in the exclusion of blacks from union apprentice-ship programs that pave the way to high-paying jobs.

A related problem arises from cultural discrimination. Despite the talk about equal opportunities for those with equal ability, many people are hired and promoted be-cause of their personal relationship with an employer or manager. And generally speaking, it is mutual understanding and a common background that promote such friendships. If the personnel manager and boss are white (which is likely to be the case), members of a minority group may be at a distinct disadvantage even if company policy prohibits job discrimination. A survey of 24 of America's largest corporations found that eight out of ten blacks and about half of the members of other ethnic minorities felt that women and minorities were excluded from informal networks and work groups in their company.[14]

Law and Justice Discrimination in the legal system has a long history. The U.S. Constitution did not explicitly mention race or slavery, but it nonetheless provided for the return of escaped slaves and held that a slave should be counted as two-thirds of a person for congressional apportionment and tax purposes. In 1857 the Supreme Court ruled that constitutional rights and privileges did not extend to blacks:

We think . . . that they [blacks] are not included, and were not intended to be included, under the word "citizen" in the Constitution, and can therefore claim none of the rights and privileges which that instrument provides for and secures to the citizens of the United States. On the contrary, they were at that time considered as a subordinate and inferior class of beings, who had been subjugated by the dominant race, and whether emancipated or not . . . . had no rights or privileges but such as those who held power and the government might choose to grant them.[15]

Even though such racist ideas are no longer part of the law, numerous studies have shown that blacks are more likely than whites to be arrested, indicted, convicted, and committed to an institution. A recent analysis of Justice Department data, for example, shows that the racial difference in incarceration rates is huge and getting bigger. Today, about 1 in every 4 young black men is either in prison or on probation or parole. In contrast, the same figure for white males is only a little more than 1 in every 20 and for Hispanics 1 in 10.[16]

Some criminologists say that these differences occur because blacks are more often involved in serious and repeated offenses than whites. And there is little doubt that the urban underclass has an extremely high crime rate and that its members are disproportionately drawn from the ranks of African Americans (see Chapter 13). But other social scientists hold racial prejudice to be more important. They argue that the expectations of police officers, prosecutors, and judges that African Americans are more likely to be criminals becomes a self-fulfilling prophecy. Because African Americans are expected to commit more crimes, they are watched more closely, and therefore they are arrested and prosecuted more often. But whether or not members of ethnic minorities are more likely to be arrested for their crimes, minority leaders are nearly unanimous in their complaints about excessive force and police brutality in their communities. The most infamous case of police brutality in recent times was that of Rodney King. A group of Los Angeles police officers were videotaped beating

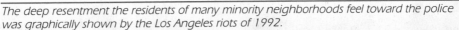

The deep resentment the residents of many minority neighborhoods feel toward the police was graphically shown by the Los Angeles riots of 1992.

Mr. King as he lay helplessly on the ground. In 1992, the officers were acquitted of the criminal charges against them by a jury without a single black member. Los Angeles's minority community saw this verdict as proof of the inequities of the justice system, and it touched off some of the bloodiest rioting in the history of urban America.

Problems and Prospects As we have seen, ethnic minorities in North America have many difficulties in common. But all ethnic groups also have their own unique problems and their own prospects for the future. In order to understand the ethnic mosaic of North American life, it is therefore necessary to examine each of its largest ethnic groups separately.

Native Americans Although they were the original residents of North America, the Indian peoples are now far outnumbered by other groups. The 1990 census of the United States counted only about 2 million Native Americans, which was less than 1 percent of the total population. But they nonetheless have a special status among the minorities of North America. While they share the economic problems experienced by most minority groups, no one else has signed legal treaties with the governments of the United States and Canada, and no other groups have the reservations (lands granted to Indian tribes by those treaties).[17]

Indians who live on those reservations have higher rates of poverty and unemployment and less education than other Indians. Moreover, many of the reservations

Native Americans who live on the reservations suffer from high rates of poverty and other social problems. This photo shows an Ute Indian being taken into custody by tribal police for an alcohol offense.

suffer from inadequate housing, poor health care, and a lack of public facilities. Figures from Canada indicate that the average Indian can expect to live eight years less than the national average, largely a result of the poverty and deprivation of those on the reservations. On the other hand, the reservations give native peoples more political autonomy than other minorities have. Elected tribal governments have a wide range of political and economic powers to regulate the affairs of their own people. And despite the fact that native peoples were given only the worst land in the most undesirable locations, many of these remote reservations have turned out to have considerable natural resources. One estimate holds that while native people own about 5 percent of the land in the United States, they have 10 percent of the known gas and oil reserves, a third of the strippable coal, and half of the uranium reserves.[18] This situation has led to large economic disparities among the tribes that have rich natural resources and those that do not, as well as some bitter disputes between tribes over the control of reservation lands. Many Indian tribes are also engaged in legal battles over lands they believe were given to them in treaties and then illegally taken away. If all the claims made by Canadian Indians are totaled up, they come to over half of the land mass of the entire nation.[19]

Despite the popular stereotype, most Native Americans now live in the cities, not on the reservations. While still falling considerably below the national average, these urban Indians are better off economically than those who remain behind, but at the price of growing separation from their traditional culture. Urban Indians are, for example, considerably less likely to speak a native language or practice a native religion than those who live on the reservations.[20]

Europeans The descendants of the European immigrants are, of course, the majority in North America. But within this large group there are many different ethnic traditions. Some writers divide the Europeans into two main groups: the WASPs (white Anglo-Saxon Protestants) and the "white ethnics," such as the Irish, Italians, Jews, and Polish. However, the term *white ethnic* is misleading, since WASPs are obviously as much an ethnic group as any other. Over the years, religion has become one of the primary focuses of ethnic identity among European Americans, and the distinctions between Protestants, Catholics, and Jews is often more important than those based on the country from which their ancestors came.

Recent years have seen two contradictory trends among these groups. On the one hand, many European Americans responded to the minority activism of the 1960s and 1970s with an increased interest in their own ethnic traditions and a renewed identification with their ancestral homeland. On the other hand, the differences between European groups have sharply declined as immigrants have assimilated into the mainstream of American culture. Richard D. Alba's research shows, for example, that successive generations of Italian Americans have fewer and fewer distinctive cultural characteristics that set them off from other European Americans and that they have grown increasingly likely to marry outside their group.[21] Stanley Lieberson and Mary C. Waters's research shows the same trends among other European ethnic groups as well.[22] Such data led Alba to conclude that these groups are in the "twilight of ethnicity." While it is unlikely that the identification with different European nationalities is going to disappear any time in the near future, this kind of ethnic identity has become a voluntary choice, and a growing number of people descended from those groups see themselves simply as Americans.

It is a mistake, however, to look at this merely as a process of assimilation that has left the dominant WASP group unaffected. Recent research by Andrew M. Greeley shows that Jews and Catholics now actually have higher educational achievement and income than white Protestants. Greeley found that the average income of Jews, and Italian, Irish, and Polish Catholics all exceeded the income of Presbyterians, who were the most affluent white Protestants.[23]

There is, however, one group of Europeans in North America that have not followed this pattern of assimilation. Whether it is their long history in this continent or the fact that they are heavily concentrated in the province of Quebec where they are the majority, not a minority, the French Canadians continue to maintain a very different linguistic and cultural tradition from Anglo-Canadians. In fact, separatist feelings run so high in Quebec that they have placed the survival of a unified Canada in doubt several times in the last two decades.

Africans According to the 1990 census, slightly more than 12 percent of all Americans are of African descent, making them the largest minority in the United States.[24] For that reason and because black Americans have always been singled out as the targets of special prejudice and discrimination, they have come to symbolize the problems all ethnic minorities face in the United States. But the black community itself is now deeply divided between a growing middle class and the increasingly desperate poor. Since 1950, the number of African Americans holding white-collar jobs has risen four times faster than their population as a whole, and the number of elected black officials has shown even larger gains.[25] African Americans became increasingly important in the entertainment business and came to dominate several highly paid professional sports. Real family income and educational achievement went up, while infant mortality went down.

Yet as more affluent African Americans left the ghettos for the suburbs, the conditions of the poor who remained behind deteriorated. Since the late 1970s, the percentage of blacks living in extreme poverty (defined as family income of less than 50 percent of the poverty line) grew from a third of all poor black people to almost half.[26] The rates of violent crime in the ghettos rose so alarmingly that the average life expectancy of black males actually decreased in the last decade (see Figure 7.2).[27] Another troubling trend is the continued decline of the two-parent family; over 60 percent of black children are now born to single women.[28]

The reasons for the crisis of the black underclass are not entirely clear, but William Julius Wilson argues that there are two major sources.[29] First, there has been a major shift in employment away from the lower-skilled jobs that many poor blacks depended on. Second, the exodus of more successful African Americans to the suburbs led to what Wilson terms "concentration effects." In other words, the concentration of poor urban blacks in homogeneous neighborhoods without a significant middle class intensified their social isolation and encouraged the decay of community institutions. In addition, many observers lay part of the blame on the cutbacks in welfare benefits and other social programs that have been made in the last decade and a half, and the indifference of more wealthy Americans to the plight of the urban poor.

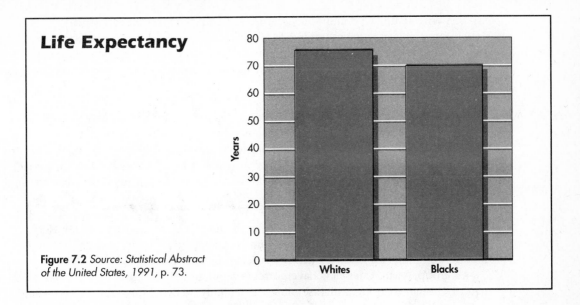

Figure 7.2 *Source: Statistical Abstract of the United States, 1991, p. 73.*

Hispanics Hispanics are the second largest American minority (about 9 percent), but because of the heavy flow of immigration and a high birthrate, they will probably come to outnumber African Americans in the near future. Many outsiders think of everyone who speaks Spanish as part of the same culture, but actually the Hispanics are a very diverse group. Well over half of the Hispanics in the United States are of Mexican origin. Most of them live in California, Texas, and the other states of the Southwest. The next largest group is made up of the Puerto Ricans, whose population is centered in New York City and the Northeast (and, of course, on the island of Puerto Rico, which is affiliated with the United States as a commonwealth but does not hold full status as a state). Cubans are the third largest Hispanic group, and they are most heavily concentrated in Florida. Because so many well-educated middle-class Cubans came to the United States to escape the Cuban revolution, Cubans are better off economically than other Hispanic groups in North America. On the other end of the economic scale are the Puerto Ricans. The poverty rate for Puerto Ricans is about 50 percent higher than for Mexican Americans, as is their percentage of single-parent families.[30]

The constant influx of newcomers who are often poorly educated and unfamiliar with the ways of American society creates some special problems for the Hispanic community. Because many of these immigrants come illegally, they are subject to exploitation by unscrupulous employers who violate minimum wage and safety laws, knowing that their workers dare not turn them in. The problems of overcrowding, poverty, and the lack of proper health care are also especially severe among new immigrants.

Spanish is the second most commonly spoken language in the United States. The large and rapidly growing Hispanic community has given rise to everything from Spanish-language newspapers and television networks to billboards and traffic signs. These changes have produced a concern among some non-Hispanics that the nation will be permanently divided into separate English-speaking and Spanish-speaking societies. But such fears are unfounded. While the Hispanics, like other immigrants, are certainly helping to reshape American culture, there is no evidence that they are any less interested in moving into the mainstream of American life than the immigrants who preceded them.

Asians Asians are the fastest-growing ethnic group in North America. The Asian population of the United States more than doubled between 1980 and 1990, and Asians now make up almost 3 percent of the total population.[31] But it is even more misleading to talk about Asian Americans as if they were a single cultural group than it is for Hispanics. At least Hispanics share a common language and some general similarities in cultural background. Today's Asian immigrants come from dozens of different countries that in many cases have little or nothing in common. A cross-section of recent Asian immigrants might, for example, include everything from a Hong Kong shipping tycoon seeking a more stable economic climate to a refugee from the isolated hill tribes of Southeast Asia or a poverty-stricken peasant from Bangladesh.

As a group, Asian Americans have gotten a reputation for being a kind of "model minority"—hardworking, well disciplined, and highly successful. While there is some truth in this image, such generalizations mislead as much as they inform. Studies do indeed show that Asians have a higher educational level, higher family income (although not necessarily a higher income per person), and lower rates of infant mortality than white Americans. Yet the largest Asian American groups tend to have a "bipolar" occupational structure. In other words, Asian workers tend to be clustered either in high-paying professional jobs or in low-paying service jobs, with fewer in the middle of the occupational hierarchy.[32] Such generalizations also ignore the plight of the many new Asian immigrants from poor countries who are trapped in poverty in an unfamiliar land.

Many fear that the stereotype of Asian Americans as workaholic superachievers is fanning the flames of racism and prejudice. Asian leaders complain that informal quotas are being used to restrict their admission to the most prestigious universities, that movies stereotype them in more blatant ways than any other minority, and that they often bear the brunt of the anger and frustration of workers who suffer from foreign economic competition. Certainly Japanese Americans have a special reason to fear such racism. Not only were they singled out for internment in concentration camps during World War II, but Japan's recent economic success has made them easy targets for those seeking a scapegoat for America's economic problems.

EXPLAINING ETHNIC INEQUALITY

The first job of the sociologist facing an important social problem is to describe it as precisely as possible. Although this is usually a lot harder than it sounds, our second task—explaining the causes of the problem—is harder still. In the last section we described the pervasive problem of ethnic inequality, and now it is necessary to examine its causes. There are far too many theories and hypotheses to discuss them all here, but we can explore three major factors that are the keys to solving this riddle: conflict and competition, prejudice and discrimination, and class.

Conflict and Competition If we go back far enough into the history of the relationship between different ethnic groups, we almost always find a period of open conflict as the groups compete for control of resources, power, and prestige. If the groups are roughly equal in strength, there will probably be some equitable solution to their differences. But if one group enjoys significant advantages over the other, the weaker group is likely to be stripped of its resources and forced into a position of subordination. For example, the European settlers who came to North America were far more technologically developed than the native peoples they encountered, and their military forces were far stronger as well. The immigrants used that superiority to take the Indians' land and force Native Americans into a subordinate role in the new European-style society they created.

Although the initial competition between ethnic groups often takes a military form, it is likely to become more peaceful over the years. The military advantage of one group is transformed into economic and political advantages. The stronger group seizes resources from the weaker and then passes that wealth down to their descendants. They also create political and economic systems that in one way or another favor members of their own group. As time goes by, people may forget the origins of this inequality and come to see it as the natural order of things. Of course, things do not always happen this way. There are many examples of ethnic conflicts that result in seemingly endless rounds of bloodshed and military strife, and others in

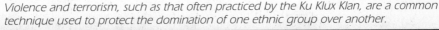

Violence and terrorism, such as that often practiced by the Ku Klux Klan, are a common technique used to protect the domination of one ethnic group over another.

which the groups ultimately come to some equitable solution or forget the ethnic differences that set them apart.

Prejudice and Discrimination   Prejudice and discrimination are closely associated, but they are not the same. **Prejudice** refers to attitudes; **discrimination** refers to actions. Gordon Allport used the following definition in his classic study, *The Nature of Prejudice*: "Ethnic prejudice is an antipathy based upon a faulty and inflexible generalization. It may be felt or expressed. It may be directed toward a group as a whole, or toward an individual because he is a member of that group."[33] Discrimination is the practice of favoring one person or penalizing another because of that individual's ethnic status. It usually surfaces when members of a dominant group deny equal treatment to a subordinate group, but even the oppressed may discriminate against others when they have the chance. Although prejudice and discrimination usually occur together, this is not always so.[34] Sometimes we are prejudiced toward a person but reject discrimination because of moral conviction or the fear of legal penalties. On the other hand, economic and social pressures may lead us to discriminate against someone without feeling any prejudice.

Like other types of human behavior, prejudice and discrimination are not easily accounted for. Many influences come together to create them, and their origins cannot be found entirely in individual psychology or oppressive social institutions. Rather, psychological and social processes blend together, like prejudice and discrimination themselves.

Psychological Theories Many psychologists believe that those with an **authoritarian personality** are the most likely to be prejudiced.[35] Such people are rigid and inflexible and have a low tolerance for uncertainty. They place a high value on conventional behavior and feel threatened when others don't follow their own standards. Indeed, their prejudices help reduce the threat they feel when confronted by unconventional behavior. By labeling others as "inferior," "immature," or "degenerate," the authoritarians avoid any need to question their own beliefs and attitudes. But the

19th-Century Social Problems

Some of the boys in this city have been indulging in a kind of sport of late which may soon prove to be something besides sport. They have been harassing the Chinese laundryman by tapping on his windows, throwing stones and sticks of wood against the side of the house, against the doors, and even through the windows. They have even gone so far as to open the door and throw in a dead cat. . . . We advise the boys to desist or some of them may soon be called to answer for their folly before the magistrate.

1894

notion that this personality type is responsible for prejudice and discrimination has come under severe attack. Critics charge that the characteristics that are said to make up an authoriarian personality are not a unified whole but are merely a number of undesirable traits gathered under a single label.

Another common psychological theory focuses on the use of minority groups as **scapegoats** for other people's problems—when people are frustrated and unhappy, minority groups can provide a safe target for their rage. The term originates with a Jewish tradition. On Yom Kippur a goat was set loose in the wilderness after the high priest had symbolically laid all the sins of the people on its head. Ironically, the Jews themselves often became scapegoats in Western history. When hundreds of thousands of people died in the plagues that swept through medieval Europe, rioters stormed into Jewish ghettos and burned them down, believing that Jews were some-how responsible for the epidemic. Six centuries later, when the Nazis set up their extermination camps, the Jews were still being blamed for the troubles of Europe.

Cultural Theories Although prejudice and discrimination are fueled by frustration and by certain personality traits, both are learned. South African whites do not need authoritarian personalities to have strong racial prejudice, because they learn such attitudes from their culture. Most prejudice is acquired early in the socialization process. Children often adopt their parents' prejudices as naturally as they adopt their parents' language, and discrimination follows prejudice as regularly as night follows day.

Some of the most common prejudices are taken from ethnic **stereotypes**—ideas that portray all the members of a group as having similar fixed, usually unfavorable, characteristics. The "happy-go-lucky Mexican," the "lazy Negro," and the "cunning Jew" reflect ethnic stereotypes that most of us have heard at one time or another.[36] In situations of ethnic conflict, "contrast conceptions" often develop. That is, people from two ethnic groups develop strong negative stereotypes about each other. For instance, while white racists in the United States perpetuate vicious antiblack stereotypes, black racists have developed their own stereotypes that depict all whites as greedy, selfish, and bent on subjugating the black race.

Although the prejudice expressed in ethnic stereotypes is usually obvious, it can also be quite subtle. For example, a white schoolboy living in an integrated neighborhood learns prejudice when he hears his mother explain that it is all right for him to sleep overnight at the home of a black friend because "that house is so clean you could eat right off the floor." An unspoken but potent prejudice is at the base of the mother's praise: blacks are crude and dirty, but this family is an exception.

Structural Theories Another important source of prejudice and discrimination can be found in the way a society structures its economic, political, and social activities. This form of bigotry is often termed **institutional discrimination**, because the inequality is built into the social structure and occurs whether or not the individuals working in that system are themselves prejudiced. For example, when Hispanic immigrants take civil service examinations, they are often at a severe disadvantage, because English is their second language and it is hard for them to do as well on a test written in English as those who grew up speaking that language.

There is ample evidence that the realities of economic competition lie beneath much prejudice and discrimination. If Jews, blacks, or members of other minority groups cannot get into elite colleges and professional schools, they obviously will not be able to compete with members of the dominant group in occupations requiring a high degree of training. In times of high unemployment, members of the dominant group can protect their jobs by making sure that minorities are the first to be fired and the last to be hired. It has long been noted that antiblack prejudice is highest among white working-class men who compete with blacks for low-paying unskilled jobs.

In other cases, the practice of discrimination is so firmly entrenched that subordinate groups have practically no chance to compete. Members of the dominant group are not necessarily aware of the exploitation, however, because their stereotypes of ethnic and racial inferiority justify their behavior. Those in subordinate groups, however, realize that they are being exploited, and their anger and resentment find expression in their own prejudices, and may ultimately lead to revolutionary violence.

Racism and prejudice can also play an important part in class conflict. Racial animosities between black and white workers in the United States have been used to divide and weaken the working class. Employers often intentionally encourage racial conflicts to keep workers from forming a united front in their demands for higher wages and better working conditions. In the early part of this century, when most unions excluded black workers, it was common for employers to bring in black strikebreakers to end union disputes. The unions eventually realized that all workers were being hurt by these racial divisions and began recruiting black members, although a good deal of more subtle racism still remains in some unions.

Class   In the late 1970s, the sociologist William Julius Wilson published an influential book, *The Declining Significance of Race*, in which he argued that racial prejudice and discrimination are no longer as important a cause of the problems of black America as they used to be.[37] The principal source of today's problems is, according to Wilson, the fact that blacks are trapped in a self-perpetuating cycle of poverty. Minority children are more likely to live lives of poverty because they are more likely to be born into poverty. Thus, the historical effects of the racism and discrimination that originally forced minorities into a subordinate position in the class system are seen to be more important than the discrimination they currently encounter. And just as the class system passes along the burdens of past discrimination to minority children, so are the benefits of past favoritism passed along to the descendants of the dominant groups.

The supporters of this theory can cite considerable evidence for their conclusion that class is now the key factor. Surveys show that racial and ethnic prejudice have been declining in recent years, and explicit laws have been passed against occupational discrimination. There is, as we noted, a vigorous and expanding black middle class that seems to have been able to overcome the barriers of racism. And there are a substantial number of whites in the underclass who seem every bit as disadvantaged as the minorities (see Chapter 6). But it is important to recognize that although progress has been made in the fight against prejudice and discrimination, it is still a powerful force in American life. The members of minority groups must still deal with major obstacles that whites do not have to face.

RESPONDING TO THE PROBLEMS OF ETHNIC MINORITIES

Although true equality remains a distant goal, the history of this century shows significant progress toward racial and ethnic justice. The elimination of the oppressive segregation system in the United States was a major step forward, as was the legislation officially outlawing discrimination in housing and employment. At least partially as a result, minorities have gained access to numerous high-level business and professional careers that used to be closed to them. Illiteracy rates among minorities have dropped, and their level of education has increased (see Chapter 4). Although racism and ethnic stereotypes remain, these prejudices are seldom publicly voiced by business and political leaders, as they once were. Public opinion surveys show that prejudice against minorities has significantly declined. In 1963, for example, 66 percent of the whites questioned by the Harris poll agreed that "blacks have less ambition than most other people," but by 1985 only 23 percent agreed.[38]

Disturbing signs over the last decade, however, indicate that hard economic times have led to a deterioration of ethnic relations and that a new crisis may be brewing. Whites have grown increasingly resentful of the affirmative action programs designed to help win equality for minorities, and a few politicians have used attacks on welfare recipients and street crime in thinly veiled attempts to make minorities the scapegoats for the nation's troubles. Yet the gap in income between blacks and Hispanics and those of European origin has actually grown wider, not narrower, in the last decade.[39] Factors including the loss of millions of manufacturing jobs in North America, the new influx of Third World immigrants, the exodus of middle-class blacks from the cities, and over a decade of government neglect have all contributed to ever-worsening conditions in the inner cities. This volatile mixture exploded in the Los Angeles riots of 1992, which took 58 lives and caused close to $1 billion in damage. Outside the ghettos, the number of hate crimes directed against one ethnic group or another has steadily increased; even our colleges and universities, which are supposed to teach us how to get along with each other, have been the scene of an increasing number of ugly racial incidents.[40]

Even those working to solve these serious problems—and there are many of them—often disagree about the ultimate goals of their efforts. Should we work toward a melting pot that merges us all into a single new group, or should the goal be to achieve true equality among a salad bowl of distinct ethnic groups? While this is a significant philosophical issue, it is important to remember that no matter which approach we prefer, the goal is the same—justice and fair treatment for all—and the proposals that follow all aim to achieve it.

Political Activism   Most of the government's actions to help minorities have come about only because of organized political pressure. The segregation system that denied those of African descent the rights enjoyed by other Americans was not declared unconstitu-

Political activism has proven to be the most effective tool for winning social justice for minority groups. Here, the late Dr. Martin Luther King, Jr., is shown leading a protest march in Boston. Such protests were part of the civil rights movement that brought an end to official racial segregation in the United States.

tional until almost a hundred years after the Civil War. Even then, a tremendous political effort was necessary to win the implementation of that decision. The civil rights movement—a coalition of activist blacks and liberal whites—used nonviolent demonstrations, marches, and sit-ins to demand an end to segregation. Despite their eventual success, many blacks became increasingly frustrated with their failure to win full equality. The black power movement came to reject integration as just another form of domination and demanded separation of the races, but on an equal basis. As the movement turned increasingly violent, it was repressed by force and most of its leaders were killed or jailed.

The spirit of minority activism, nonetheless, lives on. But the activists, many of whom now hold government offices, are generally working within "the system." Native American activists have been particularly successful in using legal actions to win back the rights granted in government treaties. They won the right to fish in Puget Sound and Lake Michigan and legal title to lands in North Dakota, Maine, and Rhode Island. In the last decade, Native peoples have also been among the most militant of all ethnic groups in directly confronting the political system. This militancy is perhaps best symbolized by the armed confrontation between Mohawk warriors and army troops near the small town of Oka, Quebec, in the early 1990s. Although this incident began as a conflict over an attempt to put a golf course on Native burial grounds, it soon escalated into a direct challenge to the authority of the government.

The success of black political activism can be seen in the growing representation of African Americans among the nation's officeholders. The number of blacks holding elected office was six times higher in 1990 than it was 20 years ago.[41] Yet despite such advances, an increasingly conservative political climate has meant that efforts of minority leaders have been largely devoted merely to protecting the victories won in the past.

Reforming the Educational System   Many people feel that the best way to compensate for the lingering effects of past discrimination and to help break the vicious cycle of poverty among minorities is through better education. In the early 1970s, the hottest issue in the entire field of education was whether to pursue that goal through integration, as the advocates of mandatory school busing proposed, or though pluralism, as was favored by supporters of neighborhood schools. Today the focus has shifted to finding the best ways to improve the academic performance of poor and minority children regardless of the makeup of their school's student body. Many different proposals have been made, and many experimental programs have been carried out. But the most promising approach is probably the most obvious one—provide extra tutoring and other special programs to help compensate for the barriers poverty and prejudice place in the way of a good education (see Chapter 4).

Another important issue concerns education's responsibility to help reduce prejudice and discrimination. Until the wave of minority activism in the 1950s and 1960s, textbooks and teaching materials often contained blatantly racist stereotypes or simply ignored ethnic minorities altogether. Great improvements have been made since then, but critics charge that our educational system still presents a "Eurocentric" view of the world. In other words, they charge that the curriculum and the general orientation of our schools and our universities still have a European slant and still largely ignore the perspectives of those from Africa, Latin America, and Asia. These critics therefore call for a new **multicultural education** to reflect the background and perspectives of all Americans. Such proposals have, nonetheless, met strenuous opposition from those who see them as a threat to the European cultural traditions. Another proposal calls for colleges and universities to require all students to take at least one class in ethnic studies in order to help them understand the perspectives, problems, and concerns of those from other groups.

Fair Employment   The idea that everyone deserves an equal opportunity to make a living has a great deal of popular support, but implementing this idea has been difficult. The civil rights movement succeeded in winning the passage of the Civil Rights Act of 1964, which forbids discrimination by unions, employment agencies, and businesses employing more than 25 workers. But the problems in enforcing such a law have been immense, for it is extremely difficult to prove why someone was not hired or promoted. The laws forbidding discrimination have now been supplemented by affirmative-action programs that require a positive effort to recruit and promote qualified minority-group members. Employers can no longer defend themselves by claiming that a decision not to hire a minority-group member was based on some criterion

D E B A T E

Are Affirmative-Action Programs Fair?

Affirmative-action programs are designed to encourage employers to hire and promote women and minorities if they are underrepresented in the work force. Under such programs, women and minorities would be selected ahead of equally qualified white males in order to compensate for past and present discrimination.

YES In a perfect world we wouldn't need affirmative action. Personnel decisions would be made on the basis of each individual's abilities and qualifications, without regard to ethnic group or gender. But we all know that things don't really work that way. Centuries-old prejudices will not simply vanish because the law tells everyone to stop discriminating. Even with current affirmative-action programs, women and minorities still get lower pay and have fewer chances for advancement than white males. Without the government's pressures to meet affirmative-action goals, the situation would be far worse. Affirmative action merely provides a small counterweight to a system that still treats women and minorities as second-class citizens.

Critics claim that laws prohibiting discrimination are all we need to ensure fair treatment for all. But unfortunately it is extremely hard to prove to a court that you were the victim of discrimination, for employers can always think of some excuse to explain their decision. All affirmative action does is to shift the burden of proof to the employers to show that they are not discriminating. After all, the employers are the ones with the money to hire lawyers to make their case in court.

Even if we could wave a magic wand and end all discrimination tomorrow, we would still need affirmative-action programs to compensate for the effects of past discrimination. Remember that Africans were brought to this land in chains. For generations they were brutalized, tortured, and

NO Two wrongs do not make a right. It was wrong to discriminate against women and minorities in the past, and it is wrong to discriminate against males with a European background today. Of course, supporters of affirmative action claim that such programs are not discriminating against white males but just correcting for past discrimination. But what else do you call it when an employer refuses to hire the most qualified candidate because of his race and gender? Racism is still racism even when the victims are white. Sexism is still sexism even when the victims are males.

Under current affirmative-action laws, the daughter of a black television star with a hundred million dollars in the bank would be given *preference* in employment over the son of a homeless alcoholic who happened to be white. How can you call that fair?

The supporters of affirmative action say that simply banning discrimination is not enough to bring about true justice in our society, but you cannot fight racism and sexism by means of a law that requires employers to discriminate on the basis of race and sex. There are many far better ways to correct social injustices—for example, the government could work to improve the terrible schools in the urban slums, provide job retraining for the unemployed, and create jobs. But, of course, such projects cost money, and it is far easier for politicians simply to pass a law requiring employers to give special preferences to the groups that are pressuring them to act. Programs even killed at the "master's" whim; their family structure was shattered and their culture destroyed. Women from all ethnic groups were themselves in a slavelike position. Traditionally, a woman was considered to be the property of her husband, whom she must "love, honor, and obey." She couldn't vote, she couldn't hold a responsible job, and her husband had complete control of all her property (if she was even allowed to have any). The effects of this kind of brutality and discrimination are passed on from one generation to the next. Their consequences will never go away unless we take affirmative action to correct them, and fairness demands that we do.

that seek to aid the poor and disadvantaged make this a stronger society by helping to bring those people (the majority of whom are minorities and women) into the mainstream of social life. Programs that give special privileges to someone only because of race or sex make this a weaker society by fostering a sense of injustice and feelings of hostility between members of different groups. Fairness demands that the law resolutely condemn all forms of discrimination, including that against white males. Affirmative-action laws are based on pure hypocrisy and must be repealed.

---

other than ethnic-group membership. They must prove that they are not discriminating. If the percentage of minority-group members in their employ is significant lower than the percentage in the work force, companies must accept a goal for minority employment and set up timetables stating when these goals are likely to be met.

These procedures have created a powerful "white backlash." Critics charge that the ratios are not goals but quotas and that affirmative-action programs really call for reverse discrimination (discrimination against white males). Resolution of this conflict will be extremely difficult. It is true that some minority-group members are given preferential treatment and that therefore some whites are discriminated against. But it is also true that minority-group members still face far more discrimination than whites do.

The Supreme Court has yet to resolve these difficult legal issues. In the 1978 *Bakke* decision the Court upheld the general principle of affirmative action but ruled that Alan Bakke (a white) had suffered illegal discrimination when he was denied admission to a medical school that reserved a fixed quota of its admissions for minority students. In 1984 the Court struck down layoff procedures that protected the jobs of blacks by requiring layoffs of whites with greater seniority. But in a series of rulings in 1986 and 1987, the Court upheld affirmative action in the workplace as a remedy for past discrimination by the same organization. More recently, the Court seems to have shifted again, placing new obstacles in the way of those seeking to sue employers for discriminatory practices. Thus, it is still not clear which kinds of affirmative-action programs are constitutional and which kinds are not. Because laws that merely prohibit employment discrimination against minority-group members do not seem to be enforceable, some form of affirmative-action procedures must be continued if equality of opportunity is to be achieved, but there is considerable disagreement about how to do so fairly. Public opinion polls show that even among whites, about two-thirds of the people support affirmative-action programs. However, there is strong opposition to any program that has fixed quotas of jobs reserved for a particular ethnic group.[42]

Economic Justice   No social problem stands alone. The dilemmas of ethnic relations are interwoven in complex ways with other social problems. Solutions to the problems discussed in other chapters in this book would also go a long way toward alleviating ethnic conflicts as well. Perhaps the foremost issue among them is the lack of economic equality. For example, a careful reader might have noticed the seeming contradiction between the fact that the economic gap between European Americans and the largest minority groups has been increasing at the same time that prejudice toward those groups has been declining. The reason is that regardless of ethnic group, the gap between rich people and poor people has grown significantly wider since 1980 (see Chapter 6). Thus, programs to reduce unemployment, retrain unskilled workers, provide good-quality health care, reduce poverty, and shift the tax burden to those best able to carry it are as essential to achieving ethnic justice as are the programs specifically attacking prejudice and discrimination.

SOCIOLOGICAL PERSPECTIVES ON PROBLEMS OF ETHNIC MINORITIES

Public concern about ethnic inequality waxes and wanes with the political climate. The interest in equality is particularly intense in times of change, when old patterns of ethnic relations are breaking up and there is conflict over future directions. In the United States, ethnic relations raised the most public concern during the Reconstruction period after the Civil War and during the era of the civil rights and black power movements that marked the end of the segregation system 100 years later. At both times ethnic inequality became a pressing social problem because an old system of ethnic relations was deteriorating and a new pattern was taking shape. But even in most stable periods, the problem of fairly managing ethnic relations in so diverse a society is never far below the surface.

The Functionalist Perspective   Functionalists believe that shared values and attitudes are the cement that holds a society together. The more disagreement there is over basic values, the more unstable and disorganized a society is likely to be. Although the various ethnic groups in North America have come to share many values over the years, significant differences remain, and these differences are an important source of conflict. North America lacks the unity, consensus, and organization that are essential to a harmonious society. Although the efforts of the largest ethnic groups to dominate others have become less and less successful, neither pluralism nor integration has replaced domination. Society is disorganized, unable to muster its people to work together for the common good.

From the functionalist perspective, ethnic discrimination is both a cause and an effect of contemporary social disorganization. The failure to give minorities full equality wastes valuable human resources and generates ethnic hostilities that reduce economic production and undermine political authority. These hostilities, in turn, contribute to prejudice and discrimination as different ethnic groups come to see one another as enemies.

To functionalists, the best response is to reduce discrimination by reorganizing social institutions. Unity is the objective, whether it is achieved through domination, pluralism, or integration. But integration is the ideal because an integrated society is likely to have the fewest conflicts. Functionalists ask for an attack on discrimination in housing, education, criminal justice, and elsewhere, arguing that an effective reform movement must increase support for "the system" among ethnic minorities while at the same time maintaining the allegiance of the majority.

The Conflict Perspective Conflict theorists see the history of ethnic relations in North America as one of conflict and oppression. European colonists fought with each other and with the Indians. Eventually English-speaking whites conquered most of the continent, but conflict did not end there. As new groups settled in the "promised land," some were assimilated. Those who refused to give up their ethnic identity were shunted into inferior positions: employees rather than employers, police officers rather than judges, farmhands rather than landowners, blue-collar workers rather than white-collar workers, and so on.

From the conflict perspective, the history of all ethnic relations is the history of a struggle for power. When one group is more powerful than others, a system of domination develops in which weaker groups are exploited for the political, social, and economic advantage of the dominant group. When power is more equally distributed, pluralism develops. But whether ethnic groups are in a relationship of domination or equality, there is no guarantee that the system will remain stable. Social change is primarily a process by which one group grows stronger at the expense of others. Those who have power want peace and stability; those who are out of power want conflict and change. Institutionalized discrimination is, thus, a technique for keeping the dominant group in power and protecting it from competition.

Conflict theorists assert that ethnic equality can be achieved only through struggle. A group that has improved its status is by definition a group that has seized some political and economic power. Conflict theorists argue that political change is often necessary to bring about economic change in such things as employment, education, housing, and health care. The key to increased power is organization for political action. Even a small ethnic group that is unified can wield much greater power than its numbers would suggest. In a democratic society, political change can be achieved by outvoting and outmaneuvering one's opponents according to the established rules of the game. Political change can also be achieved by attacking the established rules in demonstrations and protests that may threaten—or provoke—violence. Both techniques are being used in ethnic struggles in North America and around the world, and conflict theorists counsel those who would change the system to study the historical record of the successes and failures of such efforts.

Social Psychological Perspectives Social psychologists have put much effort into investigating the causes of prejudice and discrimination and their effects on individual victims. Interactionist theory, for instance, holds that individuals develop their concepts of personal identity from their interaction with the people around them. When members of a minority group are constantly treated as though they were inferior, they are bound to be affected. Some become convinced that they really are inferior, resulting in low self-esteem and feelings of inadequacy. They are also more likely to develop other personal problems, such as alcoholism and drug addiction. The rate of heroin and crack cocaine addiction among blacks and Hispanics is much higher than the national average, and alcoholism is an especially severe problem among Native Americans. Other minority-group members reject these ethnic stereotypes, forcefully asserting their own value and importance—behavior that occasionally results in trouble with the law. Still others try to avoid the effects of prejudice and discrimination by isolating themselves in segregated ethnic communities.

Proposals by social psychologists for reducing ethnic discrimination and prejudice fall into two broad categories. Those in the first category are based on the fact that whatever is learned can be unlearned. Included here are recommendations for more ethnic contact and communication and for direct attacks on ethnic stereotypes in the media and in schools. By showing people from different ethnic groups as they actually are, and not as stereotypes depict them, barriers to communication and understanding can be removed.

Proposals in the second category go to the root of the problem, recommending long-term changes that will reduce ethnic competition. More contacts and communication among ethnic groups will enable people to overcome their prejudices. But research shows that these contacts must be among ethnic groups of equal social status who are working together for a common goal rather than competing with one another for survival. In other words, social psychologists say that prejudice and discrimination will decrease as fear of economic competition decreases.

Unlike other social psychologists, biosocial theorists have concerned themselves with the effects of biological rather than social differences between ethnic groups. The visible physical differences between people from different ethnic backgrounds, for instance, make it easier to identify members of ethnic minorities, in turn making it easier to discriminate against them. A few biosocial theorists have even claimed that heredity is the cause of important differences in the behavior of different racial groups. For instance, some argue that blacks have lower intelligence than whites. Such claims have stirred up a storm of controversy, but the overwhelming majority of social psychologists hold that the hereditary differences between people from different racial backgrounds are very slight. Indeed, social psychologists point out that the practice of grouping people into common categories on the basis of such characteristics as skin color and type of hair is simply a cultural tradition, and one that has caused enormous social problems. The best solution to the "racial problem" is to abandon those traditional attitudes and adopt the more scientifically supportable view that all people are members of a single human race.

SUMMARY

Throughout history, tension and conflict have existed between ethnic groups who live in close contact with one another. People who share a sense of identity and togetherness tend to be ethnocentric, believing that their ways of doing things are better than those of other groups. Ethnocentrism becomes racism when it is based on the idea that people with certain physical traits are superior to others and deserve special privileges.

The relationship between ethnic groups usually follows one of three general patterns. Domination exists when one ethnic group holds the power and exploits another group or groups. When two or more ethnic groups have roughly equal power so that each controls its own affairs, a system of pluralism exists. Finally, when two or more ethnic groups blend together and share power, customs, and social institutions, the relationship is known as integration.

North American society has promoted several different ideals for ethnic relations. Originally, all other ethnic groups were expected to assimilate and conform to the Anglo-American cultural pattern. A second, more recent, ideal is that of the melting pot, which holds that different ethnic groups should merge together to form a single new culture. Finally, there is the ideal of the "salad bowl," which encourages ethnic groups to retain their cultural distinctiveness.

Historically, North America has seen the conquest and domination of the Indians, French, Spanish, and Mexicans by English-speaking peoples. Domination also characterized relations with African slaves and with most immigrant groups. But that domination has met increasing challenges. Some ethnic groups have won more equal status with the old dominant group, while the differences between other groups have slowly decreased as they have become more integrated. Nonetheless, our social structure still shows a high degree of inequality. Whether in education, jobs, or housing, the members of most minority groups still lag behind the national average. Each of the large ethnic groups—Native Americans, Europeans, Africans, Hispanics, and Asians—also has its own special characteristics and problems, and each contains several distinct subgroups.

There are several common explanations for the problem of ethnic inequality. The historical cause is the economic competition and military conflict between ethnic groups from which one group wins a dominant position and forces the others into a subordinate status. A second major factor is prejudice and discrimination, which, in turn, have psychological, cultural, and structural causes. Finally, there is the influence of class and the fact that a life of poverty or of privilege tends to be passed down from one generation to the next.

Many suggestions have been made to deal with the problems of ethnic relations. Greater political activism by members of minority groups and their supporters is often considered an important starting point for reform. Changes in the schools to include the perspectives of ethnic minorities is a common suggestion, as is a greater commitment to compensatory education programs designed to correct the damage done by poverty and discrimination. An end to bias in employment and promotion is another obvious need. Finally, many programs designed to help all poor people can also do a great deal to foster greater ethnic justice for everyone.

According to functionalists, North American society is disorganized and unable to muster its many ethnic groups to work in harmony for the common good. But conflict theorists see institutionalized discrimination as an intentional way of protecting the economic and political power of the dominant groups. The key to increasing the power of minority groups, in their view, is political activism. Social psychologists point out that prejudice and discrimination are learned and that both are associated with fear of competition. They recommend more ethnic contacts and a reduction of economic competition among ethnic groups.

KEY TERMS

discrimination An action that arbitrarily penalizes someone because of such characteristics as their ethnic group, religion, or gender.

domination A social system in which one ethnic group holds power and uses it to keep other groups in a subordinate position.

ethnic group Individuals who share a sense of togetherness and the conviction that they form a distinct group or "people."

integration A social system in which an individual's ethnic background is considered unimportant and those from different ethnic groups live in the same neighborhoods, attend the same schools, work in the same businesses, and so on.

melting pot The belief that the different ethnic groups in a nation should learn from each other and merge to create a single new culture.

pluralism A social system in which there are distinct and separate ethnic groups that nonetheless maintain equal social, economic, and political relationships.

prejudice A negative attitude toward a large category of people or an individual because the group or person belongs to that category.

race A group of people who are thought to have a common set of physical characteristics and a common ancestry.

salad bowl The belief that a society should encourage its different ethnic groups to maintain their distinctive cultural characteristics.

FURTHER READINGS

S. Dale McLemore, *Race and Ethnic Relations in America*, 3rd ed. (Boston: Allyn & Bacon, 1991). A comprehensive text on ethnic relations in the United States.

Richard D. Alba, ed., *Ethnicity and Race in the U.S.A.* (Englewood Cliffs, N.J.: Prentice-Hall, 1988). A good reader on ethnic issues.

William Julius Wilson, *The Declining Significance of Race: Blacks and Changing American Institutions*, 2nd ed. (Chicago: University of Chicago Press, 1980). The controversial book in which Wilson argues that class is now more important than racial prejudice as a cause of the disadvantaged economic position of African Americans.

Joan Moore and Harry Pachon, *Hispanics in the United States* (Englewood Cliffs, N.J.: Prentice-Hall, 1985). A good overview of the Hispanic population of the United States.

Malcolm X, *The Autobiography of Malcolm X* (New York: Grove Press, 1964). The autobiography of one of America's most influential black activists.

Ronald Takaki, *Strangers from a Different Shore* (Boston: Little, Brown, 1989). An excellent history of Asians in the United States.

Vine Deloria, Jr., ed., *American Indian Policy in the 20th Century* (Norman: University of Oklahoma Press, 1985). A collection of articles on the political situation of Native Americans.

chapter 8

Health and Illness

- What are the most frequent causes of our physical and mental disorders?
- Why is health care so costly?
- How does the American system of health care differ from the Canadian and British systems?

- What are the ethical dilemmas posed by modern medicine?
- How can our health care system be improved?

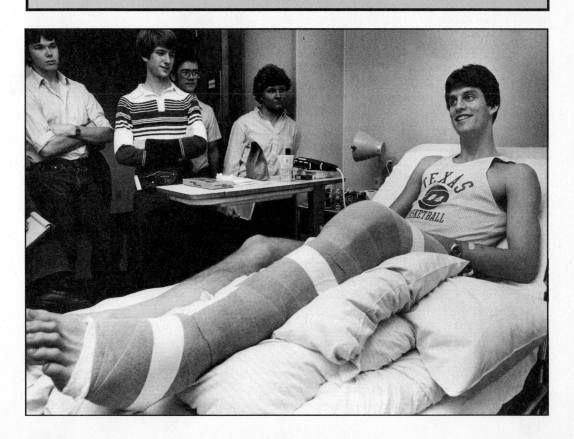

Good health, like good food and water, is easy to take for granted. It is not until our health is threatened that we realize how important it is. The pain and discomfort accompanying most serious physical illnesses are obvious. But the other costs of physical and mental health problems are often much greater. The nagging fear of death or permanent disability torments many sick people. Their inability to carry out their normal social roles may place a heavy burden on friends and relatives. Some families even shut themselves off from outsiders and make the sick person the focus of their daily lives. Too often, the result is a growing sense of guilt and estrangement that is harmful to everyone involved.

Illness and death are, of course, an unavoidable part of human life. But society still has a profound influence on our health. For one thing, society tells us when we are sick and when we are healthy. The visions that modern psychiatry interprets as a symptom of mental illness, for instance, may be seen as a special religious insight by some tribal people. The diarrhea and upset stomach that send us to the doctor are often accepted as a normal condition by people in poor countries. Social factors such as public sanitation and safety, diet, stress, environmental pollution, and occupational hazards play a profound role in determining how healthy we are. And when we do get sick, the availability, quality, and organization of health care help determine how quickly we recover, or whether we recover at all.

WHAT IS GOOD HEALTH?

To many people, good health means simply that they have no obvious illnesses or physical symptoms. But some people who are depressed, lack vitality, and say they are "not feeling well" cannot be shown to have any specific illness. For this reason, the World Health Organization defines **health** as "a state of complete physical, mental and social well-being and not merely the absence of disease and infirmity."[1] It is clear that health involves social and psychological conditions as well as biological ones. For example, some people who suffer from a variety of medical symptoms still maintain a positive mental outlook and a definition of themselves as basically healthy, while others who see themselves as seriously ill have literally created symptoms where no organic cause exists.

The way we define good health also varies among different nations and even different classes within the same nation. The tired, listless feeling associated with poor nutrition is considered normal by poor people in most parts of the world, but is seen as a sign of illness by the middle and upper classes. But even in poor countries, the standard of what constitutes good health has steadily increased. Overall, the world's population today is healthier and will live longer than those of any other generation in history. In the eighteenth century, the average life span in even the most prosperous nations was no more than 35 years. But dramatic declines in infant mortality and deaths from contagious diseases have helped extend the average life expectancy in the industrialized nations to more than 70 years.[2] And with this increase in life span has come a similar increase in our expectations for our physical health.

Although it is much harder to measure historical changes in mental health, the standards by which we judge it have certainly grown much higher, too. Only a century ago, conditions that would warrant serious medical concern today, such as depression or severe anxiety, were usually just ignored. Only those who were unable to carry on a normal life were considered to be mentally disordered. Thus, the difference between health and illness is a relative one that changes from time to time and place to place.

PHYSICAL ILLNESS

The great improvement in living conditions in the twentieth century is the main reason we live longer today than we did in the past. A rising standard of living and increased agricultural production have meant better food, shelter, and clothing for the average person. The construction of sewer and water purification systems have sharply reduced waterborne disease. Although sophisticated and expensive medical procedures such as open-heart surgery have added little to the average life span, some medical breakthroughs such as those that led to the development of antibiotics and immunizations against contagious disease, have also been extremely important.

But not all the changes that have transformed the twentieth-century world have been beneficial to our health. Stress, overindulgence, and environmental pollution can cripple and kill as effectively as typhoid or tuberculosis. Moreover, the ancient scourges of contagious disease and poverty are still the cause of a multitude of health problems.

Unhealthy Life Styles   Most North Americans are far less active than their ancestors were. Labor-saving devices ranging from the automobile to the electric toothbrush have reduced the amount of physical effort required for daily living, and automation has created an increasing number of "thinking jobs" that demand no harder work than picking up a pencil or making a phone call. Medical research shows that regular exercise is essential to good health. Not only do people who exercise regularly report that they feel better, but exercise has been shown to reduce the risk of heart disease—the leading cause of death in North America. A San Francisco study found that dock workers who did hard physical labor had fewer heart attacks than dock workers who did only light work. In their study of Boston men, Charles Rose and his associates found the amount of exercise a person does to be one of the best predictors of longevity.[3]

Diet is another aspect of life style that has a profound impact on health. Although there are many disagreements about what type of diet is most conducive to good health, there is a growing consensus among nutritionists about what is wrong with the way we eat. As the Surgeon General's Report on Nutrition and Health concluded in 1988, North Americans eat too many fatty foods such as red meat and not enough fruits, vegetables, and whole-grain products.[4] Our sugar consumption should be reduced and the fiber in our diet increased. But despite repeated warnings, North Americans' love of high-calorie food and our tendency to overeat have caused obesity to become a serious problem. Research shows that heart disease, high blood pressure, and diabetes are all associated with obesity.[5]

Despite heated denials from the tobacco industry, there is no longer any doubt that smoking is a serious health hazard. It has been linked to a long list of diseases, including lung cancer, emphysema, ulcers, and heart disorders. The Surgeon General's yearly reports on smoking state that, among other things, the death rate of smokers is 70 percent higher than that for nonsmokers of the same age, and the death rate for heavy smokers (two or more packs a day) is double that for nonsmokers. The reports have also noted that tobacco is a highly addictive drug comparable to cocaine or heroin.[6] New concerns are also being raised about the effects of the exposure to tobacco among nonsmokers. A recent report to the Environmental Protection Agency estimates that 53,000 Americans die from this "passive smoking" every year.[7] Ironically, at the same time that the U.S. government was issuing these warnings, it was paying millions of dollars in subsidies to help tobacco farmers grow their deadly crop.

While smoking is a personal choice, stress seems to be an almost unavoidable part of modern life. The initial symptoms of stress, such as irritability, insomnia, and a queasy stomach, are usually minor, and a certain amount of stress may even be necessary to good mental health. But high levels of stress over long periods of time can lead to serious health problems. One study found that two-thirds of all air traffic controllers in the United States have peptic ulcers, probably as a result of the demands of a job in which a mistake may mean death for hundreds of people.[8] Stress is also associated with heart disease. A study of lawyers, dentists, and physicians found a strong correlation between the amount of stress associated with their specialty and their rates of heart disease; thus, general-practice lawyers had less heart trouble than trial lawyers, who had less heart trouble than patent lawyers. But a study conducted by Columbia University found that such jobs as waitress and telephone operator, which place heavy demands on workers but give them little decision-making control, were the most highly correlated with heart and circulatory problems.[9]

Environmental Hazards The pollutants that industries dump into the environment are more than just an ugly nuisance; they are killers. Air pollution has been found to be related to deaths from bronchitis, heart disease, and emphysema as well as several types of cancer. A study recently released by the American Lung Association concluded that between 50,000 and 120,000 deaths a year are linked to the air pollution caused by trucks and cars.[10] The sharp rise in deaths from breast cancer, cancer of the white blood cells, and brain tumors over the last two decades has also led many researchers to suspect environmental causes (see Figure 8.1).[11] And there is little doubt that the depletion of the ozone layer caused by atmospheric pollution is a major factor in the increase in skin cancer (see Chapter 17). The contamination of water with poisonous wastes, such as lead and mercury, has already taken many lives, and the list of new dangers grows daily. American industry alone creates 3,000 new chemicals every year, and most of the hundreds of thousands of chemical compounds used by industry have never been thoroughly tested to find out how dangerous they are.

Not surprisingly, laborers who work directly with dangerous substances are at greatest risk. Steelworkers are 7.5 times more likely to die of cancer of the kidney and 10 times more likely to die of lung cancer than people in other occupations. But steelworkers are lucky compared with asbestos workers. Almost half of the 500,000 workers who were exposed to high doses of asbestos will die as a result: 100,000 are expected to die of lung cancer, 35,000 of asbestosis (another lung disease), and 35,000 of mesothelioma (an otherwise rare cancer of the linings of the lungs and

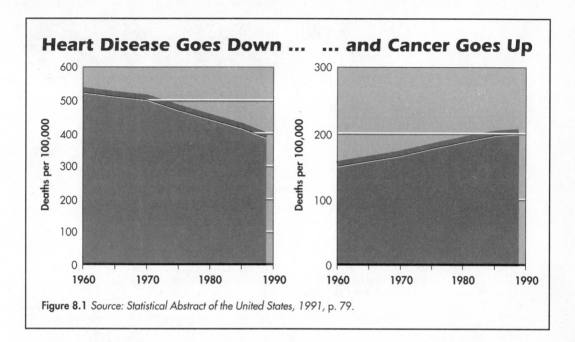

Figure 8.1 *Source: Statistical Abstract of the United States, 1991, p. 79.*

stomach).[12] Altogether, it is estimated that one in every four American workers is exposed to a serious health hazard on the job. About 5.5 million workers are injured or made ill, and about 75,000 workers die from "job-induced" causes every year.[13]

Contagious Disease Cancer and diseases of the heart and circulatory system are the most frequent causes of death in wealthy industrial societies. But such killers are seldom the causes of our daily health problems. Most common difficulties result from the relatively minor contagious diseases that are a seemingly inevitable part of daily life. A ten-year study of families in Cleveland, Ohio, found that common respiratory and intestinal diseases (colds, bronchitis, flu, and the like) accounted for 76 percent of all illnesses. The average person in this study had 5.6 respiratory and 1.5 intestinal diseases a year.[14]

Although these relatively minor ailments remain a continuing problem, great progress has been made against the death-dealing epidemics that once threatened humanity. Improvements in sanitation and water treatment have all but eliminated such waterborne diseases as cholera and typhoid from the industrialized nations and sharply reduced their incidence in some of the poor nations of the Third World. Vaccinations have had even greater success against other dread diseases such as polio and smallpox. For a while it seemed that we were on the way to eliminating many of the contagious diseases that had threatened the human race for countless centuries. But recently the tide has shifted in the other direction, and it is obvious that the battle against these killers is far from over.

Some of our current problems stem from overconfidence and neglect. Measles—a well-known disease most common in children—provides a good example. A vigo-

19th-Century Social Problems

Dr. H. B. Cole, health officer, reported to the council, as board of health, that the present year, according to the opinions of celebrated authorities, is to be a year of great danger as regards to epidemics, etc., and recommended that our citizens be required to use unusual care in the disposition of garbage and slops, and that all pig stys in the thickly settled portion of the city be declared nuisances, and that none be allowed except they maintain a floor and it be cleaned twice a week during the summer, that privies be thoroughly disinfected, and that slaughter houses be not permitted to run the blood on the ground and let the hogs create as much filth as before.

May 7, 1886

These selections, which appear throughout the text, are from the *Badger State Banner*, a newspaper published in Black River Falls, Wisconsin.

rous program of vaccination slashed the number of cases in the United States from over 400,000 in 1960 to fewer than 1,500 by 1983. But declining federal support led to a reduction in the percentage of children who had been vaccinated, and the total incidence of measles once again started to increase, reaching around 18,000 cases a year by the end of the 1980s.[15] There have also been "mini-epidemics" of some diseases among such vulnerable groups as the homeless and intravenous drug users. Although conditions in the Third World have improved, the struggle against contagious disease has never been as successful there as it has been in the industrialized nations. Half the world's people lack safe drinking water, and three-fourths have no sanitary facilities. Fewer than 40 percent of the children of the Third World have been vaccinated against measles, tetanus, whooping cough, diphtheria, or the other major childhood diseases, which take about 4 million young lives every year.[16]

Although the effects of this kind of neglect were predictable, the other blow to our efforts to control contagious disease came from an entirely unexpected source: the emergence of a deadly new virus. That virus, of course, is HIV (human immunodeficiency virus), which causes acquired immune deficiency syndrome (AIDS). Virtually unknown as recently as 1980, there were over 175,000 reported cases of AIDS in the United States and Canada by 1991.[17] The disease attacks the body's immune system, leaving it vulnerable to a host of other diseases. AIDS often lies dormant without symptoms for years, but once it becomes active, it is almost always fatal. Treatment can extend the life of the patient, but at present there is no known cure.

Fortunately, AIDS is not very easily transmitted from one person to another. Some direct exchange of body fluids is usually necessary. The most common forms of transmission in the industrialized nations are anal intercourse and needle sharing among intravenous drug users. About 70 percent of the victims of AIDS in the United States

Because the AIDS epidemic first began among groups that were unpopular with large segments of the public, its victims and their supporters have had to band together and demand greater public attention to the problem.

are homosexual men, and a quarter are intravenous drug users. Although no one is quite sure why, most AIDS cases in Third World countries are transmitted through heterosexual activities such as prostitution. While heterosexual transmission is less common in the industrialized nations, it is still a major threat. Like many other diseases, AIDS is most widespread among the poor and minorities. The rate of infection among Hispanics and African Americans is more than double the national average, and women and children from those groups are at least three times more likely to be infected than those from other groups.[18]

One of the most frightening things about the AIDS epidemic is the projections of how many people it will strike down. Federal health officials believe that as many as 1.5 million Americans have already been infected with the HIV virus, and, unless a cure is found, the vast majority of them can be expected to die from the disease. The human impact of such an occurrence would obviously be staggering. Moreover, the health care system is ill prepared to deal with the flood of desperately sick AIDS patients it is likely to receive.

Medical researchers are working around the clock to find a cure or at least an effective vaccine, but until they are successful, the only way to combat this epidemic is by changing our behavior. The two steps most likely to be effective are the use of condoms by all sexually active people who are not in a strictly monogamous relationship, and an end to needle sharing by intravenous drug users. But as serious as the AIDS epidemic is, it is important to keep it in perspective. Although AIDS is by far the most serious contagious disease in the industrialized nations, on a global scale it ranks far down the list. Worldwide, about 10 million people are believed to be infected with the AIDS virus, but about 200 million people have schistosomiasis (a parasite that can cause blindness), another 200 million are infected with hepatitis, and about 220 million more with malaria. In Africa alone, about 1 million children die of malaria every year.[19]

Poverty There is overwhelming evidence that poor people have more health problems than those who are better off. The effects of poverty are obvious in the overpopulated agricultural nations. Lack of clothing, housing, and food takes a frightening toll, epidemic disease is commonplace, and 10 to 20 million people simply starve to death every year (see Chapter 14). The infant mortality rate in such countries as India, Zaire, and Iran is about ten times higher than in the United States, even though the United States itself has the highest infant mortality rate of any industrialized nation.

The problems of the poor in the industrialized nations are less visible, but they are no less real. They include lower life expectancies, higher rates of infant death, and more contagious disease, heart ailments, arthritis, and high blood pressure. Black children are twice as likely as white children to die in their first year of life, and a number of studies show that the poor and members of the ethnic minorities are sick more days a year than are the wealthy. Black Americans are 32 percent more likely to die from cancer, 82 percent more likely to die from a stroke, and 132 percent more likely to die from diabetes. A black man in Harlem now has a shorter life expectancy than the impoverished citizens of Bangladesh. When asked about their health, poor people are about three times more likely to say that it is only fair or poor, or that they have some serious chronic illness.[20]

Poverty is the indirect cause of most of these problems. About 25 million Americans cannot afford to keep themselves adequately fed and are therefore particularly susceptible to illness and disease. Because their diet contains more cheap, fatty foods, poor people are more likely to be overweight. Lack of proper sanitation and protection from rain, snow, cold, and heat also takes its toll. Reports of rat bites in slum areas number in the thousands each year, and contaminated water is a hazard for many Native Americans. Moreover, daily life for the poor is stressful, as they struggle to pay their bills and buy groceries. As Leonard Syme and Lisa Berkman put it, the poor have "higher rates of schizophrenia, are more depressed, more unhappy, more worried, more anxious, and are less hopeful about the future."[21] Finally, as we will see, the poor receive inferior care when they get sick.

MENTAL DISORDERS

Psychologists estimate that over 5 million Americans suffer from some kind of acute psychological disorder and that over 20 percent of the population have mental problems that seriously interfere with their life.[22] Millions of people receive treatment for mental conditions every year. American men between the ages of 14 and 45 spend more time in the hospital for mental disorders than for any other cause, and only the delivery of a child accounts for more days in the hospital for women of this age.[23] Yet most people who have mental problems never get to a hospital or receive professional help of any other kind. Some turn to friends or to one of the dozens of new "pop psychology" books published every year. But many others simply ignore their problems and hope that somehow they will go away.

What Are Mental Disorders?   Few things are more frightening than the thought of "going crazy," but what does that expression really mean? Terms like *mental illness* or *insanity* may bring to mind images of a madman foaming at the mouth, struggling to break free of his straitjacket, or a disheveled woman babbling incoherently while she wanders the streets. But most mental disorders are neither bizarre nor dramatic; instead, they involve the common experiences of anxiety or depression with which we are all familiar.

Speaking generally, a person may be said to have a **mental disorder** if he or she is so disturbed that coping with routine, everyday life is difficult or impossible. But this definition—like most others—is vague. Exactly how does one determine whether individuals can or cannot cope with their everyday affairs? Or, for that matter, if their circumstances are "normal" or so difficult that most people would have trouble dealing with them? Although many social scientists have attempted to define *mental disorder* more precisely, none of the definitions has received universal acceptance.

In the past, mental disorders were commonly believed to be caused by demons and spirits. "Treatments" such as flogging, starving, prayers and chants, and dunking the sufferer in boiling water were used to drive the devils out. As the scientific approach to social problems gained strength, serious psychological disorders came to be seen as **mental illnesses** caused by the same natural forces as physical illnesses. Thus, the concepts and methods of modern medicine came to be used to diagnose and treat mental illness in the same fashion as, for instance, a sprained knee or the measles.[24]

The use of the "medical model" to explain and treat mental disorders was a great advance over the old superstitious beliefs, but some observers charge that it has outlived its usefulness. Thomas Szasz, a psychiatrist and harsh critic of the medical model, argues that the whole idea of mental illness is a myth used to make the values and opinions of the psychiatric establishment resemble scientific fact.[25] He believes that although everyone knows what it means to be physically healthy and there is general agreement among doctors about the causes and treatment of most physical illnesses, there is no similar agreement about the nature of mental health or the causes and treatment of mental illness.

A major alternative to the medical model holds that mental disorders represent problems of **personal maladjustment**. According to this perspective, mental disorders arise when someone is unable to deal effectively with his or her personal difficulties, and disturbed behavior is therefore seen to be caused by the same forces that govern other behavior. Therapists who use this approach do not look for symptoms of a specific disease but instead examine their patients' overall adjustment to their environment.

Supporters of the personal-maladjustment approach point to several advantages it has over the medical model. First, it does not consider individuals in isolation from their environment, as a physician would when treating a broken leg or a "mental

The difference between being labeled a prophet and being labeled mentally disturbed depends on the reaction of the audience. This photograph shows the victims of the mass suicide in Jonestown, Guyana. The followers of Jim Jones considered him a great religious leader, but others said his role in encouraging this carnage was the act of a deranged mind.

illness.'' Second, because abnormal behavior is seen to be produced by the same processes as normal behavior, this perspective discourages the assumption that mentally disturbed people are freaks or lunatics. Third, it accepts the fact that any diagnosis of mental problems is a highly uncertain affair and, therefore, that there are no specific cures for these conditions. But the personal-maladjustment approach also has its shortcomings. Although it does not ignore the individual's environment, it still assumes that the individual—not the social order—is responsible for psychological disturbance. But some problems stem from an unlivable environment rather than an individual's deficiencies. In some circumstances, the healthiest individuals may actually be the ones who are not well adjusted to their social environment.

The newest approach to mental disorders derives from the labeling theory, which will be discussed in Chapter 13. The idea here is that there are really no objective standards by which to judge someone's mental health. *Mental illness* is merely a label applied to those who break the tacit rules that govern our daily behavior without some socially acceptable reason.

Because the social-deviance approach places responsibility for mental disorders on the environment rather than on the individual, the stigma of mental illness is removed. Therapists are encouraged to deal with the patient's family and personal environment rather than assuming that the patient is suffering from a personal defect or disorder. However, this approach has been severely criticized by experts who hold more traditional ideas about mental health and mental illness. These experts point out that the labeling approach neglects the disturbed individuals themselves. Even if no one were labeled "mentally ill," they argue, disturbed people would still have problems. Further, labeling people "mentally ill" is the only way we can identify those who are in need of help.

The Distribution of Mental Disorders   Sociologists have long been interested in the way mental disorders are distributed throughout society, both because of the inherent importance of the issue and for the clues it might offer about the causes of psychological disturbance. Starting in the 1930s with the research of Robert E. L. Faris and H. Warren Dunham,[26] and followed by numerous others, including August B. Hollingshead and Frederick C. Redlich,[27] and Leo Strole and colleagues,[28] sociologists have been particularly interested in the relationship between social class and mental health. After reviewing 44 studies on this subject, Bruce P. Dohrenwend and Barbara Snell Dohrenwend concluded that "analysis of these studies shows that their most consistent result is an inverse relation between social class and reported rate of psychological disorder."[29] In other words, the less money someone has, the more likely he or she is to have a mental disorder. Many of these studies also show that even though mental disorder is more widespread among poor people, the poor are less likely to receive any treatment.

Many sociologists also expected to find higher rates of mental disorders in the cities than in rural areas, but it didn't turn out that way. For example, a study of the Hutterites—a religious group that lives in close-knit farming communities—concluded that their rate of severe mental disorder was roughly equal to the rate of hospitalization for mental disorders in New York State.[30] The most important difference was that the Hutterites usually cared for their disturbed people in their homes rather than in hospitals. A comparable study by Eleanor Leacock found a high rate of psychosis in some decaying rural areas and a low rate in some relatively well-off urban areas.[31] It therefore appears that the characteristics of an individual's immediate community has more to do with mental health than does the number of people who live in it.

Men and women are equally likely to receive treatment for a mental disorder, but there are some important differences. Men are more often hospitalized, while women more often receive outpatient care. The two sexes are similar in their rates of diagnosed schizophrenia, but women are twice as likely to be treated for depression. Men are commonly thought to be four or five times more likely to suffer from alcoholism. Marital status also has a bearing on the odds of being treated for a mental disorder. Married people have the lowest rates of treatment, while rates for those who have never married are considerably higher for men but only slightly higher for women.

However, among divorced, widowed, or separated people the rates are high for both sexes. Age is significant too: although the highest rate of treatment appears in the 18 to 44 age group, the elderly are much more likely to be treated for organic psychoses resulting from senility. But it is important to remember that although these statistics are the best source of data we have, the rates of *treatment* may not necessarily reflect the true rates of mental disorder in these groups.[32]

The Causes of Mental Disorder   Considering the amount of disagreement over the definition and classification of mental disorders, it is not surprising that there are repeated arguments about their causes as well. Although there are many different theories, they can be grouped in three general categories—those based on biology, on early childhood development, and on environment.

Biology Most psychologists and psychiatrists believe that there is an inherited predisposition to contract schizophrenia, the most common of the serious mental disorders. However, they disagree about the relative importance of inheritance versus environment. The bulk of the evidence for the importance of heredity comes from the study of twins. Franz Kallmann and B. Roth studied 17 pairs of identical twins (who have much greater genetic similarities than fraternal twins) and found that if one twin had schizophrenia, the other had the same problem 88.2 percent of the time.[33] However, the rate of concordance (if one has it, both have it) was only 22.9 percent for the 35 pairs of fraternal twins they studied. More recent studies have also concluded that close genetic relationships between twins are reflected in higher concordance rates. However, the differences found were not nearly as large as those reported by Kallmann and Roth. For instance, A. Hoffer and W. Polin found a concordance rate of 15.5 percent for identical twins and 4.4 percent for fraternal twins in a sample of almost 16,000 twins in the American armed forces.[34] Of course, the concordance rate among identical twins may result from the fact that the physical similarity of identical twins leads their family and friends to treat them alike. But other research shows a higher concordance rate among identical twins even when they have been raised apart.[35] Supporters of the biological theories also point to the effectiveness of various new drugs in combating the symptoms of some types of mental disorders. Although such evidence hardly proves that the disorders are biological in origin, it tends to suggest that they have some biological component. But the critics of the biological approach remain unconvinced. They have raised numerous questions about the validity of the procedures used in conducting the twin studies, and they point out that nearly 90 percent of diagnosed schizophrenics have no close relatives with the disorder. A recent Finnish study followed 271 children of schizophrenic mothers who were put up for adoption and found that none of the children who were placed in what they judged to be psychologically healthy homes became schizophrenic.[36]

Early Childhood Development One of the most popular theories among psychotherapists is that mental disorders are caused by disturbances in the individual's early psychological development in the family. For example, it is generally believed that parental love and affection are vital to the normal maturation of a child. Children who are rejected by their parents may display a variety of psychological problems, including anxiety, insecurity, low self-esteem, and hostility. Parental standards of discipline are also important for proper development. Harsh, rigid standards may produce either a hostile and rebellious child, or a passive, guilt-ridden one. Lack of discipline is thought to encourage antisocial and aggressive tendencies. Others feel that the children of overprotective parents develop "passive-dependent personalities."[37] Gregory Bateson and his associates attribute schizophrenia to the "double bind" some parents place on their children. For example, when a mother tells her son that "I love you" but flinches or pulls away every time he touches her, the child receives two contradictory messages at the same time. As a result, he may come to mistrust and misinterpret normal communications and eventually become seriously disoriented.[38]

Critics claim that this approach is too vague about the exact conditions that cause mental disorders. Almost every family has some conditions that developmental theorists consider conducive to psychological disorder, but most children do not develop mental problems. David Mechanic, among others, has criticized psychologists for their tendency to seize on a minor problem in an individual's life history as an explanation for mental disorder:

> . . . the usual variances in childrearing patterns appear to play a relatively small part in producing such profound difficulties. . . . The contexts which appear to breed pathology are those which are emotionally bizarre or deprived and in which the child experiences profound rejection, hostility, and other forms of social abuse. . . .[39]

Environment It is obvious that social environment plays a major role in determining whether or not someone develops a mental disorder, but there are several different theories about how this influence is expressed. Advocates of **learning theory** were among the first to reject the idea that hidden inner conflicts or biochemical processes cause mental disorders. Instead, they see such conditions merely as inappropriate behavior that has been learned, as other behaviors are learned. People who display such behaviors have simply been conditioned by the rewards and punishments in their environment to act in that manner. Critics of this approach assert that just because it is more difficult to investigate internal psychological and biochemical processes, we should not assume they have no impact on our behavior.

Stress theory is based on commonsense ideas about psychological problems that are widely accepted in our society. Simply put, the theory holds that each individual has a breaking point and that if stress builds up beyond this level, the individual will experience serious psychological problems. This theory is used by military psychiatrists to explain the symptoms of "battle fatigue." But it can also be used to account for the behavior of harried parents, pressured executives, or overworked students. Since sociologists have found that social stress is much greater among the poor than among the affluent, it is not surprising to find a higher rate of serious mental disorder in the lower classes.

The relationship between stress and mental disorder is, however, more complex than our simple illustrations suggest. A certain amount of stress is actually beneficial because it provides a challenge that motivates an individual to respond in new and creative ways. But too much stress over too long a period of time seems to exhaust individual resources. The problem is to determine how much stress is appropriate and how much is harmful. Individuals have different tolerance levels, so that something that constitutes a healthy challenge for one person may bring serious psychological consequences to another.

Advocates of the **labeling theory** argue that there is nothing inherently normal or abnormal in human behavior and that mental illness is just a label given to individuals who behave in ways that others do not like or accept. Few labeling theorists try to explain why people do things that cause them to be labeled as mentally ill. But they argue that once someone has been declared mentally ill, he or she experiences great pressure to act out that role. Their opportunities to play "normal" roles are increasingly reduced as friends shun them, prospective employers turn them away, and even their efforts to shed the label are taken as evidence of their instability. Because everyone behaves as though the labeled person is sick, he or she eventually comes to believe it and act that way. Indeed, the sick role, with its promise of escape from responsibilities and blame, may be an attractive one under some circumstances.[40]

Critics of labeling theory vigorously deny the idea that mental illness is just a social label and point to the labeling theorist's inability to explain why someone who is not unbalanced would act in ways that everyone knows will get them labeled as mentally ill. But whatever labeling theory's weaknesses in explaining the causes of mental disorder, there is increasing recognition that the labeling process does indeed have harmful effects on many mental patients. For example, a study by Bruce Link found that labeled mental patients ended up with lower incomes and lower occupational status than people with the same background and the same psychological symptoms who had not been labeled.[41]

HEALTH CARE IN THE UNITED STATES

The organization of America's health care system remains unique among the industrialized nations. In response to ever-rising costs and the demand that competent health care be available to everyone, the other industrialized countries have all adopted broadly based systems of government-supported health care. The United States, however, took a different course, creating a medical welfare system for the poor and the elderly but leaving the rest of the health care system in private hands.

How well does the American system work? Unfortunately, the evidence is not very encouraging. For one thing, the U.S. health care system is clearly the most expensive in the world (see Figure 8.2). Americans spend 171 percent more per person on health care than the British, 124 percent more than the Japanese, and 38 percent more than the Canadians. But despite the more than *$600 billion* spent on health care every year, the United States does rather poorly in a comparison of international health statistics. Although the United States is the world leader in many branches of medical research, it ranks only twelfth in life expectancy, twenty-first in the number of deaths among children under age 5 (nations with the lowest death rate are, of course, ranked highest), twenty-second in infant deaths, and twenty-fourth in the percentage of children born with a low birth weight.[42] It would be wrong to attribute all these differences to the health care system alone. Variations in life style, diet, and environment are also important. But there is no question that such things as infant

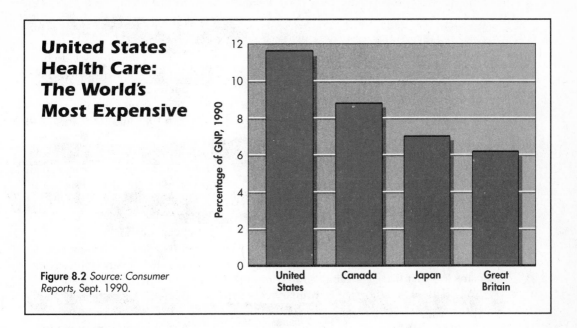

United States Health Care: The World's Most Expensive

Percentage of GNP, 1990

United States | Canada | Japan | Great Britain

Figure 8.2 *Source: Consumer Reports*, Sept. 1990.

mortality and the percentage of babies born underweight are heavily influenced by the quality of health care.

Structure In order to understand the complex and confusing system of health care in the United States, we must examine its three basic parts more closely. We will begin by looking at the physicians and the other health care professionals who work under them, then we will examine the hospitals and mental institutions, and finally the huge bureaucracies that pay most of the bills.

Doctors and Nurses Physicians command more respect and admiration than people in virtually any other profession, and, as is so often the case, high income accompanies high prestige. But there is nonetheless a growing discontent with their performance. Many patients now see themselves as "health care consumers," and complaints that physicians are more concerned about their income than about their patients are becoming increasingly common. As medical technology has grown more complex and the health care system more bureaucratic, the doctor-patient relationship has often been depersonalized. The old general practitioner who was a family adviser and friend has been replaced by an army of narrow specialists. As late as 1931, general practitioners outnumbered specialists by five to one. Today that ratio is reversed: only about 12 percent of American physicians practice general medicine.[43]

Over the last two decades, high salaries led physicians from all over the world to migrate to the United States, and domestic medical schools increased their enrollments. As a result, the number of physicians in the United States grew more than three times faster than the overall population.[44] In theory, competition among physicians ought to drive the price of medical services down. However, physicians appear to behave like monopolistic corporations, raising their fees so they can maintain or enhance their current income while treating fewer patients.[45]

Whether or not we have too many physicians, it is clear that the ones we do have are poorly distributed. For one thing, there is a shortage of general practitioners, internists, and pediatricians. Currently, there is only about one pediatrician for every 1,350 children in the United States, and the number of medical school graduates selecting internal medicine declined by 27 percent between 1985 and 1990. In a 1990 survey of internists by the American College of Physicians, less than 40 percent said they would pursue the same career again. Part of the problem is that internists make less money than most other medical specialists. In 1989, the average internist had an income of about $120,000, compared with $180,000 or more for anesthesiologists, obstetricians, and surgeons.[46] Another difficulty is the demand that internists and general practitioners be the "gatekeepers" of the health care system. Many cost-conscious insurance companies are now providing financial incentives for these primary care providers to hold down the services they give to patients and are requiring them to decide if patients should be allowed to see a specialist. Many of these physicians feel that these restraints compromise their ability to care for their patients.

While there is a shortage of primary care physicians, there are too many doctors in the prestigious and highly paid specialties such as surgery. Moreover, the surplus of surgeons has encouraged many unnecessary and potentially dangerous operations. A 1987 Rand Corporation study found extremely high rates of unneeded surgery for the three types of operations they studied. The most overused of these three procedures was the carotid endarterectomy, intended to reduce the risk of stroke. The Rand study concluded that only about one-third of the 100,000 such operations performed every year were clearly in the interests of the patient.[47] A 1990 study in the *New England Journal of Medicine* reached similar conclusions about several other kinds of operations and found that physicians who specialized in a particular operation were more likely than other surgeons to perform it unnecessarily.[48]

American physicians are also poorly distributed in terms of ethnic group and gender. Like the members of other lucrative professions, most physicians have traditionally been white males. Although the last decade has seen a significant increase in the number of female doctors, they still make up only about 16 percent of the profession and are particularly underrepresented in the most prestigious specialties. Most ethnic minorities are even more scarce. Currently only 3.2 percent of American physicians are black and 4.5 percent are Hispanic.[49] It may appear that the personal background of physicians makes little difference to the quality of care they give as long as they are well trained. But imagine the difficulties of a Spanish-speaking patient whose physician cannot understand what he is saying, or the embarrassment of a female patient who would rather not discuss the intimate details of her sex life with a male physician.

Physicians are also far too heavily concentrated in the affluent neighborhoods of big cities and suburbs, leaving many low-income and rural areas with a critical shortage. Wealthy states such as Massachusetts and Connecticut have twice as many physicians per person as do poor states such as Alabama or Arkansas. As Howard D. Schwartz puts it, "two-thirds of American physicians treat the one-third of the population that is most able to pay."[50]

Once a patient gets in to see a doctor, his or her problems may be just beginning, for patients are often hurt rather than helped by their physician. A 1981 study of a major university hospital found that more than one out of every three of its patients suffered from some sort of physician-caused disease—most commonly, an adverse reaction to the medications they were given. Others estimate that anywhere between 5 to 15 percent of hospital patients develop medically induced infections unrelated to their original health problem.[51] And, of course, there are the numerous deaths caused by the unnecessary surgery already discussed.

Why do such problems occur? No matter how well trained they are, doctors and nurses are only human, and some make mistakes that cost patients their health or their lives. But in addition to the inevitable errors, some physicians and nurses are simply incompetent. Because neither patients nor government officials are as well qualified as physicians to judge professional competence, the burden of protecting the public has fallen on the medical profession itself. But physicians have failed to live up to this important responsibility. The subculture of their profession strongly discourages one physician from criticizing another, and only the most grossly incompetent doctors are forbidden to practice. Of the approximately 320,000 physicians in the United States, 16,000 are believed to be incompetent or unfit, but an average of only 72 medical licenses are revoked each year.[52] Another source of serious trouble is that our health care system provides too few doctors, nurses, and hospitals to care for the poor and the uninsured.

Physicians are the elite of the medical profession, while nurses are its "working class." The doctors make the diagnosis and prescribe the treatment, but it is generally the nurses who carry out those instructions and do the other work necessary for the day-to-day operation of the hospitals and other treatment facilities. In many ways, the relationship between doctors and nurses mirrors the relationship between men and women in our society. Doctors, who are mostly male, make the important decisions and enjoy most of the prestige, while nurses, who are usually women, work under the authority and control of the doctors.

Many nursing jobs require long hours and entail enormous responsibilities that may mean life or death to a patient. Nurses are also the ones who must try to meet the emotional needs of patients who are away from home under unpleasant and often fearful circumstances. Yet nurses seldom receive the recognition or the pay that such important work warrants. On the average, a physician makes almost five times the salary of a nurse and, of course, enjoys better working conditions and far higher prestige. It is not surprising, then, that at a time when many new career opportunities are opening up for women, there is a critical shortage of nurses. The output of America's nursing schools is actually declining, while the demand has steadily increased.[53]

The Hospitals Hospitals were originally hospices, a place of refuge where the poor could go to die. Not until modern times did the hospital become a place where sick and injured people were given medical treatment. Today hospitals are the nerve centers of the medical profession. A hospital determines which physicians will be allowed to use the hospital and thus which patients will be admitted. Some hospitals are deeply involved in teaching and research, and an increasing number offer a wide range of outpatient services through clinics and emergency rooms.

In most industrialized nations, hospitals are either owned directly by the government or are operated under tight government controls. In the United States the ownership and control of hospital services rests in many different hands. The federal government has special hospitals for military personnel and veterans, and many counties operate their own hospital systems, which often carry a heavy share of the burden of providing health care for the poor. Most hospitals, however, are owned by such diverse private groups as universities, religious organizations, physicians, health plans, and charities. Of all types, the fastest growing are the large corporate hospital chains, which now run more than one of every five American hospitals.

This rapid shift toward corporate ownership has had some beneficial effects. Hospital chains often provide more comfort and convenience for patients and have introduced computerized billing facilities and other efficient management practices. Moreover, many of these chains have set up "emergency centers" in suburban malls and business districts that often provide faster and more convenient care at lower cost than traditional health care services.

Yet on the whole, this trend is a worrisome one. One fear arises from the shift in control that goes with corporate ownership. Traditional hospitals are usually run by their physicians, but the corporate chains are controlled by professional managers who are likely to have far less understanding of medical practice and the needs of patients. But the greatest concerns center on finances. Although the corporate hospitals provide more services to patients, they also charge higher rates than the traditional nonprofit hospitals.[54] Moreover, the corporate hospitals have tended to ignore the enormous health care needs of the poor and focus on the people with good health insurance who are already well cared for. These hospitals have often been charged with performing "wallet biopsies" before admitting any patient who does not have a dire need for emergency care. In 1983, the attorney general's office in Kentucky actually had to file suit against one of the nation's largest hospital chains, because it refused to let parents take their newborn babies home until they paid their bill.[55] Even the lower-cost emergency-care centers often take Visa and Mastercard but not medicaid (the government health care program for the poor). Defenders of the corporate hospitals argue that they have no more responsibility to provide free services to the poor than any other business, and that it is up to the nonprofit hospitals to carry that cost. The problem with that argument is that the corporate hospitals are skimming off the most lucrative business that the nonprofit hospitals once used to cover their losses from treating the poor. As a result, more and more nonprofit hospitals are going bankrupt—often to be bought up by the corporate chains and closed to the poor. And that, of course, creates acute overcrowding and an inevitable decline in the quality of care at those hospitals that still try to meet the needs of all people.

The growth of corporate medicine is not, however, the only reason that many hospitals are having financial troubles. Another major problem is that the cost of medical technology has continued to escalate, while cost-containment efforts by the government and private insurers have made it more difficult for less efficient hospitals to pass along all their expenses. New government restrictions on payments by medicare and medicaid, for example, have meant that nearly half of U.S. hospitals lose money treating the elderly and the poor.

Mental institutions have always been different from other hospitals. Most hospitals focus on short-term treatment for those with acute medical conditions. But because physicians are unable to "cure" most mental disorders, mental hospitals, like nursing homes, provide long-term treatment and custodial care for chronic patients. Moreover, sociologists have long questioned the wisdom of sending psychologically troubled people into large, impersonal institutions in order to help them resolve their problems. For example, Erving Goffman's classic study of life in the "asylum" uncovered a host of difficulties that beset the institutionalized mental patient.[56] For one thing, patients often come into the institution with a sense of betrayal, believing that they have been tricked and manipulated by their friends and family. Upon admission, they are subjected to a variety of what Goffman called "degradation rituals" that strip them of their dignity and their identity. Familiar clothing and personal possessions are taken away; they are poked, prodded, and classified by medical personnel; and, worse of all, they are locked up and denied the freedom to move about as they please.

As a result of such stinging criticisms and the desire of politicians to reduce the costs of supporting these institutions, a widespread movement to deinstitutionalize mental patients developed. The goal was to treat those with mental disorders in community facilities and get them out of the large mental institutions. From 1955 to 1990, the number of patients in state mental facilities dropped from 552,000 to only 119,000, despite a more than 50 percent increase in the American population.[57]

Critics of deinstitutionalization argue that it is merely a convenient justification for ignoring the problems of the mentally disturbed. It is estimated that about a third of the nation's growing body of homeless men and women suffer from serious mental disorders. Former mental patients are commonly seen wandering aimlessly in city streets, eating food from garbage cans, and sleeping in alleys and parks. Although there seems little doubt that these people need more help than they are receiving, defenders of deinstitutionalization point out that the original intent of the reforms was never carried out. The idea behind deinstitutionalization was to treat fewer mental patients in hospitals and more in the community. But most of the mental patients who were released from the hospital never received adequate treatment on the outside. It is estimated that about 2,000 community centers were needed to support deinstitutionalized mental patients, but only about 700 were ever built. Although about 63 percent of the persons with serious mental disorders are now at large in the community, two-thirds of state and local funding still goes to mental institutions.[58]

Who Pays? Traditionally, Americans have bought medical care the way they buy beans, pork chops, and cars: purchasing what they desire and can afford. But these direct payments by patients have been supplemented by government programs and private insurance, which now pick up most of the tab. But these changes were carried out in a haphazard way, and, as a result, the current system is highly inequitable.

Government pays the biggest share of the health care bill—currently about 41 percent. Insurance companies pay about one-third of the bills, and consumers pay a little less than a quarter of the cost directly. The critical problem with this system of financing is that while some people are almost entirely shielded from the potentially crushing costs of medical care, others have only spotty protection, and an estimated

31 to 37 million Americans have no protection at all. They must pay for whatever medical care they need entirely from their own pocket. It is not surprising, then, that a 1990 poll conducted by the *Los Angeles Times* found that 48 percent of all Americans believed that they could not afford quality care if they became critically ill.[59]

Those lucky enough to have good insurance coverage pay little or nothing for even the best medical care. While most Americans have some kind of private insurance, there are usually significant gaps in coverage. Some policies have little or no coverage for office visits or preventive care, while others require patients to make large deductible payments before the insurance company contributes. Most policies also limit the total amount the insurer will pay for any illness. Thus, those with serious medical conditions may find that their coverage has run out or that their insurance company has canceled their policy and refuses to pay for any future illnesses.

Aside from this inadequate coverage, the private insurance system has another critical fault: it is extremely wasteful and inefficient. Estimates of how much the insurance companies spend on overhead and administration vary from source to source, but all the figures indicate that private insurance companies are far less efficient than government programs. A report by one consumer group estimated that private insurance companies spend 33.5 cents on administration, marketing, commissions, and other overhead for every dollar they pay out for medical care, while medicare's administrative costs were only 2.3 cents and the administrative costs of national health care in Canada were about 3 cents per dollar. *Consumer Reports* puts the administrative cost of the Canadian system at 1 to 2.5 percent and of private insurance at 10 to 11 percent.[60] Whichever estimate is most accurate, the conclusion is clear.

Such inefficiencies are making private insurance an increasing burden on American business. Since employers usually pay a large part of the cost of employees' health insurance, runaway medical expenses make American business less competitive in the world market. Chrysler Corporation, for instance, estimates that its workers' health insurance adds about $700 to the price of every car it produces—a far greater amount than its Japanese competition. Employers' efforts to cut back coverage to reduce those costs have made health insurance a major bone of contention in three of every four recent strikes. Moreover, there is evidence that insurance companies have been blacklisting many types of small businesses, so that those employers are often unable to provide insurance coverage for their employees even if they want to do so. For example, many companies attempt to avoid insuring beauty salons, interior design firms, and other places they presume will have a higher percentage of gay workers who might be infected with the AIDS virus.[61]

The government's health care payments come primarily from two programs: medicare and medicaid. **Medicare** buys medical services for people 65 and older, while **medicaid** is designed to help the poor, the blind, and the disabled. The medicare program is relatively uniform throughout the nation. Medicaid, however, is administered by the states, and each state has its own standards of eligibility and levels of benefits.

There are major gaps in the coverage of these various programs, and they are growing wider year by year. The worst off are increasing numbers of the poor and near-poor who are not eligible for medicaid and cannot afford private insurance.

When medicaid was first established, in the mid-1960s, it covered about 70 percent of those with incomes below the poverty line. Today, only about 38 percent of the poor are covered.[62] In addition to cutting many poor people out of the program entirely, state and federal governments have been placing tighter limits on the assistance they receive. States have been creating more restrictive lists of the kinds of treatment they are willing to pay for, bringing charges that they are rationing health care for the poor. For example, in 1987 the state of Oregon decided that medical procedures such as organ and tissue transplants were too expensive, and that poor people who needed them would either have to get them from charity or do without. But the most common approach has been to limit access to care informally by making it difficult and unattractive for physicians and hospitals to treat welfare patients. For one thing, the states pay far less for most medical procedures than physicians and hospitals usually charge. And on top of that, states often impose a bewildering array of bureaucratic barriers that must be overcome before a physician can actually be paid. Consequently, most physicians simply refuse to accept medicaid patients. Nathan Shapell, chair of a California commission that investigated that state's medicaid program, summarized its findings this way: "The result is similar to a lottery. If you're lucky enough to have your number come up, you'll get health care. If you're not, you'll suffer frustration and delays, while facing an endless line of closed doors to vital medical care."[63]

Medicare coverage for the elderly is far less restrictive than medicaid—almost everyone 65 and over qualifies. But medicare still has some glaring omissions, especially its failure to cover the costs of care in a nursing home. A report from the House Subcommittee on Aging concluded that half of all elderly couples with one member in a nursing home are driven into poverty within six months, and that 90 percent of single people in nursing homes are impoverished within a year.[64]

The Crisis in American Health Care   The picture of the American health care system drawn in these pages is certainly not a bright one. Despite the efforts of some of the most dedicated and capable health care workers in the world, the problems of the American system remain serious and deep-seated, and all the trends seem to be pointing in the wrong direction. The American system is failing the poor, women, and the elderly, at the same time that its overall cost continues to escalate out of control. As the crisis intensifies, it seems increasingly unlikely that anything short of a basic reorganization of the entire system can solve its problems.

Failing the Patients: The Poor, Women, and the Elderly The American health care system's most glaring defect is its failure to meet the needs of poor and low-income Americans. As we have seen, poor people's access to health care is often severely restricted, and the problem is not limited to those below the poverty line. The 1990 poll mentioned earlier found that almost one of every four Americans had put off some medical treatment in the last year because he or she could not afford it. And this situation is not only unjust; it is foolishly shortsighted. When people delay medical treatment until their condition is so severe that they have no choice but to seek help, the total costs are likely to be far greater than timely preventive treatment. The cost of the prenatal care denied so many poor women is, for example, far less than the hundreds of thousands of dollars often necessary to help their gravely ill infants.

Lack of prenatal care is, moreover, only one of the ways the medical system neglects women's health needs. Until recently, women were systematically denied entry into the upper levels of the medical profession, and today, as we have noted, the vast majority of physicians and medical researchers are still men. This male bias is reflected in many other aspects of the health care system as well. The fact that women are twice as likely as men to be given prescription tranquilizers reflects the continuing strength of the old stereotype that women are more likely to present hysterical symptoms that have no organic cause. Similarly, medical researchers have often excluded women from their studies, leaving physicians unsure if new medical findings apply to their female patients. Most clinical research on heart disease, for example, has used only male subjects. This practice is often justified on the grounds that heart disease is more common in men—although it is still the leading cause of death in American women as well as men. Moreover, the same male-only approach to medical research is used for conditions that clearly affect women as much as men. For example, in 1958 the National Institute on Aging began a major study of the problems of aging, but women were not included among the subjects until 20 years later.[65]

In some ways, the low-income elderly are better off than their younger counterparts, since at least some of their medical expenses are covered by medicare. But their total need for health care is also much greater, and in recent years medicare coverage has failed to keep pace with the rapid increase in costs. As we have seen, moreover, the exclusion of extended nursing home care from medicare and most private health insurance plans has led to the impoverishment of many American families. And even in strictly medical terms, the health care system is far better equipped to deal with the acute problems typical of younger patients than the chronic problems that trouble the elderly (see Chapter 9).

Runaway Costs Not only is the American health care system the most expensive in the world, but the cost of health care is growing at more than twice the rate of inflation. Every year health care takes a bigger and bigger bite of the economic pie (see Figure 8.3). In 1950, the United States spent 4.4 percent of its gross national product on health care; by 1989, that figure was 11.6 percent.[66] The specter of runaway medical inflation led to new measures by the government and the private insurance companies to place stricter limits on the amount they will pay for each medical procedure. After years of double-digit inflation, this effort brought the yearly increase in medical costs below 10 percent during the middle 1980s. But physicians and hospitals responded by increasing the number of services performed, switching to more costly types of services, and even hiring specialists in "doctor reimbursement and coding" to teach them how to beat the cost controls. As a result, this attempt to rope in costs without making fundamental changes in the health care system was ultimately a failure. In 1988, medical inflation again hit double digits (10.5 percent), and in 1989 it was over 11 percent.[67]

There are at least three main reasons for the runaway costs. The first is the way the health care industry is financed. Because most physicians are paid on a **fee-for-service** basis, there are strong financial incentives to perform as many medical pro-

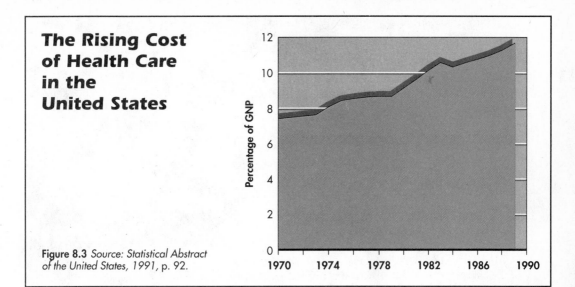

The Rising Cost of Health Care in the United States

Figure 8.3 *Source: Statistical Abstract of the United States, 1991, p. 92.*

cedures on each patient as possible. A study of the amount of surgery performed on government employees covered by different health insurance plans revealed some startling facts. Employees covered by Blue Shield insurance, which pays doctors on a fee-for-service basis, had more than twice as much surgery as employees with group medical plans offering doctors no financial incentives for unnecessary operations.[68] Obviously, some physicians' decisions to operate are based on the profit to be gained rather than on the needs of their patients. Moreover, the fact that less than 30 percent of health care costs are paid directly by patients means that they have fewer incentives to look for the least expensive care or take other steps to hold costs down.

A second important cause of increasing costs has been the development of expensive new drugs and medical techniques. Such procedures as organ transplants and renal dialysis (the use of artificial kidney machines) are extremely costly and tend to drive up the overall price tag for health care. A third factor is that patients have discovered that they can sue doctors for malpractice and win. As a result, the number of those suits has quadrupled since the late 1970s. All doctors—competent or not—now must pay large fees for malpractice insurance. The cost of this insurance increased tenfold between 1965 and 1975 and that much again between 1975 and 1990.[69] The increasing number of malpractice suits has driven up health care costs in an indirect way as well. The fear of being charged with malpractice has forced many doctors to practice *defensive medicine*—that is, they order a large number of costly tests that are not really needed because they do not want to be accused in court of having forgotten something important.

Finally, although the full impact of the AIDS epidemic has yet to be felt, it is already a heavy burden on the health care system. While there is no known cure, some drugs can extend the life of AIDS patients. But their price is extremely high, and, of course, the longer AIDS patients survive, the higher the bill for their medical services will be.

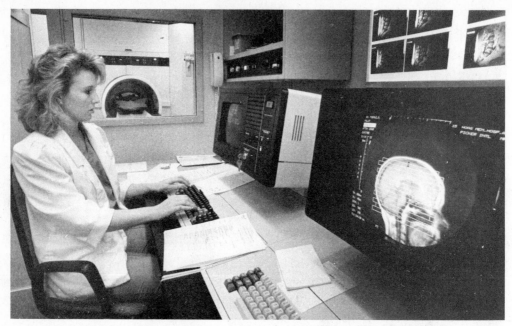

The development of complex and expensive new techniques has been a major factor in the rapid increase in the cost of medical care.

Today, the cost of hospitalization for a single AIDS patient runs from $40,000 to $140,000, and that figure is likely to grow in the future.[70] Since most of the hundreds of thousands of people now infected with the AIDS virus will almost certainly contract the disease, this epidemic may push the health care system to its financial limits.

NATIONAL HEALTH CARE: CANADA AND BRITAIN

In all the industrialized nations except the United States, the government has created a system of national health care with more or less universal coverage. The fact that the government pays most of the cost of health care does not make it "free," as is sometimes claimed. Obviously, citizens must be taxed to pay for those services. But national health care does have three major advantages over the American system. First, it is more fair, since the wealthy can be made to pay for the health care of those who cannot afford it. (Medicaid and medicare help the very poor and the elderly, but other needy Americans are ignored.) Second, national health care provides far better service for the less fortunate. Third, it is cheaper. It would be a mistake, however, to look at all national health care systems as if they were basically the same. Every nation takes its own approach to providing health care for its citizens. A look at two other English-speaking nations—Britain and Canada—shows us two different ways of organizing a national health care system.

Great Britain   In England, Northern Ireland, Scotland, and Wales, most medical care is provided at very little direct cost to the patient. The government owns the hospitals and pays most of the physicians. It also pays most of the costs of dental care and drugs. The National Health Service operates a two-tiered system of health care. Everyone signs up with a general practitioner, who is the one patients go to first with any ailment. Most general practitioners have about 2,000 patients. They are paid on the basis of how many patients they have on their list, not on how many procedures are performed, and as a result there is no financial incentive for "overdoctoring." When patients need special services, they are referred to a consultant in a hospital. The consultants are paid a fixed salary that doesn't depend on the number of patients or the procedures performed. Many consultants work only part time for the National Health Service and also have a private practice in which they charge fees directly to their patients.

In many ways the British system is more efficient than the American one. Britain spends only about 6 percent of its national income on health care, while the United States spends twice as much; yet the death rates for most age groups in the two countries are very similar. The British system is clearly superior in providing health care for the poor, since everyone has equal access to the National Health Service. On the other hand, financial restraints mean that expensive procedures are often informally rationed, so that there may be delays in receiving some kinds of treatment that can be safely postponed. Moreover, Britain, like all other industrialized nations, is having trouble meeting the needs of an aging population and coping with the exploding costs of medical technology. In the last decade, the Conservative government has failed to provide sufficient funding to meet these new expenses. And as a result, there are increasing delays before a patient can receive a needed operation, and about 10 percent of the British people have now taken out private insurance to supplement the public system. Thus, the gap between the quality of health care for the rich and the poor has grown wider in recent years.[71]

Canada   Although the Canadian and American cultures are similar, Canadians have always been more enthusiastic than their neighbors to the south about government social programs. As a result, Canada became involved in government-supported health care much earlier and to a much greater extent than the United States. As far back as 1914 the province of Saskatchewan established a hospital insurance program and followed it with comprehensive health insurance in 1948. By the end of the 1950s, hospital insurance had gone nationwide, and, in 1966, the Medical Care Act provided government-funded medical care for all Canadians. At the same time, the country also outlawed all private insurance for services covered by the government plan.

The Canadian system of national health care is quite different from the British one. For one thing, it is more decentralized, with the federal and the provincial governments sharing in the control and the financial responsibility. Another difference is that although Canadian hospitals are funded by the provinces, their ownership remains in private hands. But one of the most important dissimilarities is in the way physicians are paid. Like their American counterparts, most Canadian physicians are paid on a fee-for-service basis rather than a fixed salary. But unlike the United States, there is only a single fee schedule for each province which is negotiated between the provincial government and the local medical association. Although physicians' incomes are somewhat lower than in the United States, doctors are still among the highest paid of all Canadians. The average Canadian physician earns four to five times more than the average industrial worker, while that ratio is five or six to one in the United States.[72]

The growing cost of health care is a problem in Canada as it is in the United States, but Canadian officials have been far more effective in containing it. Twenty-five years ago, before the start of national health care, Canada and the United States both spent about 6 percent of their gross national product on health care. Today, that figure is a little less than 9 percent for Canada, but almost 12 percent for the United States. There are several reasons for Canada's success. Because physicians' fees and hospital budgets must be negotiated directly with the provincial governments, they have far more leverage to hold down prices. The province of Quebec has gone a step further by restricting the total amount any physician can earn no matter how many procedures he or she performs. Another major saving is in the reduction in paperwork. Because all the costs are paid by the government, physicians and hospitals do not have to worry about collecting bills from patients, and the duplication of services and high executive salaries typical of the private insurance industry are eliminated. One estimate holds that a Canadian-style national health system would save the United States more than $21 billion a year in overhead costs alone.[73]

The Canadian system clearly costs less, but how good is the care? Critics point out that provincial restrictions on hospital budgets have slowed the purchase of the equipment needed to handle expensive new procedures such as heart transplants. But if the Canadian system does not do quite as well in providing the most expensive medical innovations, it does a far better job of supplying the everyday health care most people need. Because medical services are provided without cost to the patients, low-income Canadians get far better care than they would in the United States. And equally important is the fact that Canadians are free to go to their doctors for minor problems or preventive care, before they develop serious complications. Infant mortality is significantly lower in Canada than in the United States, and overall life expectancy is higher.[74] But the final proof of the superiority of the Canadian system lies in the opinions of its clients. In one recent poll, nine out of ten Americans felt that their health care system needed "fundamental changes," while in a different poll a similar number of Canadians agreed that their health care system is "one of the things that makes Canada the best country in the world in which to live."[75]

ETHICAL DILEMMAS

To most outsiders, the moral responsibility of the medical profession seems clear: to save lives and help patients be as healthy as possible. But the increasing power of medical technology has created perplexing ethical dilemmas for which we have yet to find satisfactory answers. One such issue concerns the so-called heroic efforts physicians use to extend the lives of dying patients. Medical costs mount rapidly in the final weeks of a patient's life as great efforts are needed to prolong life. One-third of medicare's entire budget is spent on people in the last year of life.[76] Most of us would say that cost should not be the standard to decide who lives and dies. But in

D E B A T E

Should Abortion Be Legal?

YES To deny a woman the right to have an abortion is to deny her control of her own body. The government has no right to force a mother to have a child she does not wish to bear. Those who demand that the government stop all abortions are urging us down the road to a totalitarian society where the police and the courts control our most personal decisions.

Those who oppose abortion claim that a fetus is a fully formed human being and to abort it would be murder. Such claims lack any scientific support. A fetus is not an independent living creature and can survive only as long as it is attached to its mother's body. If it is murder to abort a fetus that cannot live on its own, then it is murder to practice birth control and cut off the unfertilized egg's chance of survival.

In addition to the obvious danger of giving the state authority over the private workings of our bodies, there is another important reason to keep abortion legal. The laws prohibiting abortion never stopped such operations. What they did do was to force hundreds of thousands of women to go to incompetent, untrained abortionists, and many of them paid with their lives. If the antiabortion crusaders are successful, the black-market abortionists will be back in business, and thousands of women will be their victims.

NO Abortion is murder, plain and simple. When a fetus is aborted, a human life is ended. An aborted fetus dies just as surely as a baby shot with a gun. A society that claims to respect human life cannot allow the continuation of this slaughter.

The supporters of abortion claim that the old antiabortion laws created a flourishing business in illegal abortions that injured or killed many of its customers. They are certainly right in pointing out the harm the illegal abortionists did to many of these women. But they ignore the harm that abortions—legal or illegal—do to innocent fetuses. The way to stop the black-market abortion business is not to legalize it but to demand tougher law enforcement to stamp it out.

There is another important reason to make abortion illegal again: to preserve the sanctity of the family and to reinforce our society's support of the fundamental value of human life. When society permits a mother to take the life of her unborn child, it tells us all that human life is a cheap commodity to be thrown away for the sake of mere convenience. Mothers should be required to carry their babies the full term necessary for their survival. Unborn babies have a right to life.

a world in which millions of people starve to death every year, the money we use to keep one dying patient alive for another month could save a thousand hungry babies in the Third World. Is this fair? And what about all the American babies who die because their mothers never received a few hundred dollars' worth of prenatal care?

Even if we ignore the costs, serious ethical issues remain. When people die, all their life-sustaining systems usually fail at about the same time, but medical equipment can take over the functions performed by the heart and lungs, thus keeping some gravely ill patients alive almost indefinitely. But although such patients are alive, the quality of their life is often pitifully low. They lie trapped in a hospital bed connected by wires and tubes to a machine upon which they totally depend. If the patient wishes to continue under such conditions, there appear to be few ethical problems. But in most cases the patient is unconscious and unable to make any sort of decision. Some people now make out "living wills" that spell out how far they wish their physicians to go in using heroic means to extend their life if they become gravely ill. Yet even the principle of self-determination implied in such wills is not universally accepted in our society. Many hospitals refuse to turn off patients' life-support machines, even if they request it. In fact, under the current law, a physician who helps a dying patient end a life full of pain and discomfort can be charged with murder.

Just as many perplexing ethical questions surround the beginning of life as its end. One of the most controversial ethical issues of our time concerns abortion. This difficult matter revolves around two separate issues that are often confused. On a personal level, the issue concerns when a woman is justified in deciding to have an abortion; and on the sociological level, the question, which is argued in this chapter's debate, concerns the role the government should play.

While the abortion debate has been going on for decades, advances in medical technology are also creating new dilemmas about human reproduction. The technique for artificially inseminating a woman without sexual contact has been used for decades to help women with infertile husbands become pregnant. But the practice of **surrogate mothering**, in which a woman is hired to take the place of an infertile wife, has raised a storm of protests. Although the surrogate mother signs a contract agreeing to give the child to the biological father and his wife, bitter legal battles have arisen when surrogates have attempted to void those contracts and claim legal custody of the child. Obviously, there are no simple answers to these troubling ethical questions, yet society must somehow formulate social policies to guide the medical profession in making these ethical decisions.

RESPONDING TO PROBLEMS OF THE SICK AND THE HEALTH CARE SYSTEM

There are two approaches to the problems of the sick. The first is to try to prevent health problems by changing life styles and eating habits, reducing pollution, and increasing the use of preventive medicine. The second aims at improving care for people after they become sick. The latter approach includes proposals designed to create equal access to health care regardless of income and to improve the overall quality of these services at less cost.

Preventive Medicine   The old saying that "an ounce of prevention is worth a pound of cure" is as true today as it was 100 years ago. As we noted earlier, improvements in sanitation and nutrition have saved more lives than all hospitals combined. Yet our health care systems continue to emphasize treatment rather than prevention of disease. A delicate heart operation is much more dramatic than the dull business of educating people to avoid heart trouble through proper diet and regular exercise. Yet the sec-

Regular exercise is an important component of healthy living, and growing numbers of people are making an effort to incorporate more physical activity into their lives.

ond approach is both cheaper and more effective. In its broadest sense, **preventive medicine** includes a wide range of programs to encourage healthier living, including school courses in nutrition, personal hygiene, and driver training, as well as campaigns against excessive use of tobacco, alcohol, and other drugs.

This approach has a long history in non-Western medical traditions. Wealthy Chinese commonly placed a practitioner of traditional medicine on a monthly salary to overlook the welfare of their family. The physician would make regular visits to check dietary and personal habits, dispense advice and medicines to help prevent illness, and generally keep abreast of the state of health of each family member. If anyone fell seriously ill, the payments were stopped until the physician had nursed the patient back to health.[77]

There is no question that Western medicine has made enormous progress in curing disease. But many critics charge that today's physicians focus so heavily on the symptoms of disease that they have forgotten the patients who suffer from them. Drawing heavily from the approach of traditional Chinese and Indian physicians, practitioners of **holistic medicine** focus on the patient's overall mental, emotional, and physical condition. The goal is not to cure the symptoms of disease but to improve the general state of the patient's health. But whether or not most medical practitioners follow the holistic approach and adopt specific techniques borrowed from the non-Western traditions, they clearly need to pay more attention to their patients' life style and mental outlook and not just to the symptoms of their disease.

Medical Personnel The United States needs to train more general practitioners, pediatricians, and nurses. By restricting the number of students in overcrowded specialties such as surgery, medical schools could help move physicians into fields where they are badly needed, particularly general practice. Medical schools could also train more paramedics: medical personnel who, although less broadly trained than MD's, are qualified to perform many services that are now restricted to physicians. Significant progress has, nonetheless, been made in one area. Today almost one-third of medical school graduates are women compared with only 5 percent in 1960.[78]

One of the best ways to improve the quality of our medical personnel would be to offer higher pay and more professional authority for nurses. Not only would this attract more people into the nursing profession, but it could save money if nurses were allowed to do more of the services now carried out exclusively by physicians. During the last two decades the nursing profession has been moving in this direction with the development of a new category of nurse, known as a nurse practitioner, whose duties and responsibilities are halfway between those of the traditional nurse and the physician. Although the first nurse practitioners did not graduate until the early 1970s, they have been providing effective low-cost care, and their numbers have been increasing rapidly in recent years. However, regulations concerning nurse practitioners vary greatly from state to state, and they have had to fight numerous battles with physicians who see them as a threat to their professional status.[79]

National Health Care As we have seen, the United States is the only developed nation that does not have some form of government-financed medical care available to its entire population. Although poll after poll has found that over 60 percent of the American public would also prefer a system of national health care, the medical establishment has succeeded in blocking the road to change. The strongest barrier is the American Medical Association, which has over 270,000 of America's best-paid professionals as members. The AMA has waged a battle against what it calls "socialized medicine" for decades. Statistics for the period from 1989 to early 1990 show the AMA to be the second largest spender among all the political action committees in the United States. In the 1988 congressional elections alone, the AMA spent $5.3 million to elect candidates favorable to its point of view. State medical associations are also in the front lines of the war against national health care. From early 1989 to March 1990, they spent over $4 million on political causes. In addition, four companies in the medical insurance business are also on the list of the top 50 corporate campaign contributors.[80]

As a way of avoiding the opposition of the medical industry, some advocate new laws requiring all employers to provide private health insurance for their workers or pay into a special government fund for that purpose. Such proposals, often known as "play or pay," would help extend medical benefits to full-time workers who are not currently covered by health insurance; but most of them remain halfway measures, since part-time workers and the unemployed are not usually included. Moreover, this approach offers no effective response to runaway medical inflation or the high overhead costs of the private insurance system.

Another common suggestion is that the United States create a national health care system patterned on the Canadian model. Given the political power of the insurance industry, it seem unlikely that the United States would ban private health insurance, as the Canadians have. But a system in which mandatory government insurance covers the cost of basic medicine, and private insurance may be added to cover extras such as private rooms or special home visits, would make good sense. Since many physicians would probably still be paid on a fee-for-service basis, the financial incentives for "overdoctoring" would remain, but the reduction in overhead and the increased bargaining power of a centralized system should make it more cost-effective. Moreover, an effort to encourage more patients to join *health maintenance organizations*, which pay physicians a fixed salary and not fee-for-service compensation, could further reduce costs. In any case, such a national health care system is almost certain to provide better care for the poor and those who are now uninsured.

Community Mental Health Treatment   Despite the problems created by the movement to deinstitutionalize mental patients, well-run community-based care is still the best way to treat all but the most severely disturbed individuals. Patients who remain in their community during treatment avoid the shock of being taken out of their normal environment. They also escape the labeling, humiliation, and feelings of powerlessness that are bound to accompany institutionalization, as well as the painful readjustment period that follows it.

Community mental health centers usually offer five basic services: short-term hospitalization, partial hospitalization that allows patients to return home at night or on the weekends, outpatient therapy, emergency care for special problems, and consultations and educational services for the community at large. These centers thus provide a broad range of services, many of which are likely to be unavailable from other sources. The major problem with today's centers is simply that there are not enough of them, and those that do exist are too often underfunded and understaffed.

In addition, other kinds of community programs can help deal with the problems of the mentally disturbed. For example, physicians, teachers, police officers, and others who are likely to come into contact with people who need mental health care should be taught the best ways of handling those individuals and should be familiarized with agencies that can provide help. Many private organizations can also help meet community mental health needs. Citizens working without pay for agencies such as Hotline answer phone calls from people in need of help, refer them to appropriate agencies, try to head off suicides, or merely lend a sympathetic ear to lonely voices.

SOCIOLOGICAL PERSPECTIVES ON PROBLEMS OF HEALTH AND ILLNESS

Concern about the increasing gap between the high-quality health care that modern medicine can provide and the care that most people receive has made health care an important social problem. Social scientists of every persuasion have tried to explain why the social organization of health care is not better, given the fact that it is now a multibillion-dollar business with the knowledge and technology necessary to provide excellent services for everyone.

The Functionalist Perspective Viewed functionally, the jumbled health care system is a result of the rapid development of medical technology and the changes in public attitudes about medical care. In the nineteenth century, medical knowledge was so limited that private doctors could handle almost all demands for health care. Rapid growth of medical knowledge and techniques greatly increased the kinds of services doctors had to offer. Because these services were effective, the demand for them boomed. People came to see good health care as a fundamental right, but the American system of health care was unable to adapt efficiently. The idea that health care is a commodity, to be bought the way one buys a sack of potatoes or hires a carpenter, is still with us, as is the conviction that medical care should be provided by a private practitioner and not by a corporation, a group practice, or a government bureau.

Because of this lag, functionalists say, the U.S. health care system is failing to do its job efficiently. Health care services are still sold privately. But this individualistic "free-enterprise" system has been supplemented, in patchwork fashion, by a great variety of cooperative organizations: clinics, hospitals, group practices, and health maintenance organizations. It has also been supplemented by many new sources of funding: employers, unions, insurance companies, and a host of government agencies.

In short, the U.S. health care system is disorganized because it has grown rapidly and haphazardly, without proper planning. Obviously, the solution to this problem is reorganization. But functionalists do not agree on the form this reorganization should take. Some would have us return to complete free enterprise in the health care business. Such a system would allow physicians to sell their services at whatever price the market will bear, and let those too poor to pay that price turn to private charity or go without. Others believe that we should merely streamline the present system. They call for reallocating medical personnel, reducing fraud and malpractice, lowering costs, and training more nurses and other medical personnel. Still others advocate a Canadian- or British-style national health care system.

The Conflict Perspective Conflict theorists see the U.S. health care system in a different light. They argue that its problems and deficiencies stem from the fact that it is designed to serve the needs of the rich and powerful (including doctors themselves), thus neglecting the needs of low-income groups. Health care is dominated by businesspeople with medical degrees who try to sell their services at the highest price. Because physicians have a legally enforced monopoly on medical services, they are in a position to rig prices. Their services are sold at inflated prices that only the rich or well insured can pay, and programs that would reduce profits or require physicians to provide cheap health care for the poor are opposed. Further, conflict theorists claim, physicians have created an aura of mystery about their profession in order to boost their occupational prestige and cover up their shortcomings. In this atmosphere, patients are not expected or allowed to judge the quality of the medical care they are receiving—"the doctor knows best." Incompetents and profiteers are not weeded out because patients are kept in the dark about the true nature of the medical care they are receiving.

Sociologist Paul Starr's research has shown that the U.S. health care system's reliance on unrestricted fee-for-service payments by insurance companies and government agencies was created by powerful interests in the medical industry itself.[81]

According to Starr, the largest, most important health insurance company, Blue Cross/ Blue Shield, was intended to protect the interests of hospitals and physicians. Blue Cross, which originally covered only hospital expenses, was started in response to the financial crisis of U.S. hospitals during the Great Depression, and was directly controlled by the hospital industry. Blue Shield, which originally covered doctors' expenses, was created and controlled by physicians. Starr also argues that the generous system of medical payments in the original medicare legislation was put there as a result of pressure from the medical lobby.

Conflict theorists would resolve the health care problem by reducing the medical profession's control over the financing and organization of the health care system. This power would then be transferred to the government to ensure good medical care for all citizens regardless of their ability to pay. Most conflict theorists call for government-financed health care that is available without charge to individual patients. They also argue that such changes will come about only if those who receive inadequate health care organize themselves to counter the tremendous power of the health-care establishment.

Social Psychological Perspectives   Health and health care are obviously of tremendous psychological importance to every individual. Although social psychologists rarely deal directly with the organization of health care services, they have made significant contributions to the health care field. They have shown, for example, that the socialization process in medical schools often has unanticipated consequences, making doctors into something less than the humanitarians many medical students aspire to be. They have shown, further, that people learn to be "sick" (to play the role of sick people) just as they learn to be parents, factory workers, or lawyers. It follows that health care services sometimes make people sick rather than well.

Social psychological research is the foundation for the popular notion that effective medical care should meet patients' emotional needs as well as their physical needs. The oft-heard calls for more "family medicine" and general practitioners are a response to current medical practice which relies on specialists and large clinics and treats patients more like objects than people ("the ulcer in room 12," "the pregnancy in the waiting room"). Impersonal bureaucracies, including mental hospitals, are poorly suited to meet an individual's emotional needs.

Behaviorists and interactionists are concerned with the ways we develop unhealthy habits and life styles. Attitudes toward exercise, diet, smoking, and drinking are learned from our primary groups and reflect the attitudes of our culture as well. Social psychologists point out that unhealthful behavior is often encouraged by the mass media, business, and even the government. Expensive advertising campaigns designed to sell junk food, cigarettes, and alcohol are good examples. The competitive pressures of our economic system are also a major factor in health problems resulting from stress and tension.

Many social psychologists believe that significant improvements can be made in public health through a concerted campaign of education and social change. First, there must be greater awareness of the damage caused by unhealthy life styles and poor diet. Second, there must be changes that will encourage everyone to follow the principles of good health. The ideal of the successful, hard-driving achiever will have to be modified to permit a new emphasis on cooperation and mutual support. It is also important that businesses take greater social responsibility for the products they sell. A new social climate must be created in which it is no longer acceptable for corporations to spend millions of dollars advertising children's breakfast cereals that are mostly sugar, developing new cigarettes with more "sex appeal," or promoting other dangerous products.

SUMMARY

In the past 100 years there has been a tremendous drop in the death rate. Improved health care and new treatments for deadly diseases contributed to this decline, but it was largely due to improvements in living conditions—better food, housing, and sanitation.

Although industrialization and technology have helped increase food supplies and reduce epidemic disease, they have also created new health problems. The stress of modern-day living and the decline in physical exercise have increased the frequency of a variety of heart and circulatory diseases, and our diet is often unhealthy. Occupational hazards, smoking, and environmental pollution are now major causes of death and injury. And as the AIDS crisis has shown us, even the problem of epidemic disease is far from over. On the average, poor people have more health problems and a shorter life span than others. Many factors contribute to these problems, including stress and worry, dangerous occupations, poor diet, and inadequate medical care.

There are significant disagreements about the true nature of mental disorder. Some see it as mental illness, others as a problem of personal adjustment, and still others as a label given to deviant behavior. Like the physical illnesses, mental disorders are more common among the poor. There are many different theories about the causes of mental disorders, including the notion that they stem from an inherited biological predisposition, that they result from difficulties in early childhood development, and that they come from problems in the individual's environment.

The American system of health care is unique among all the industrialized nations, because it is organized and run like a private business. Despite medical welfare programs, poor people receive inferior care, and there are about 34 million Americans who are not covered by welfare programs or private insurance. At the same time, the inefficiency and high overhead costs of this system make it the most costly in the world. The physicians practicing in the United States are poorly distributed among the various specialties and geographic regions, and there is a shortage of nurses. Financial incentives provided by the fee-for-service method of payment encourage "overdoctoring," and critics charge that it is too difficult to stop incompetent physicians from practicing. Traditionally, most American hospitals were privately owned but operated as a nonprofit business. In recent years, however, hospital chains run by large corporations have sprung up rapidly, skimming off the most lucrative business and neglecting the needs of the poor and the uninsured. Another important change has been the deinstitutionalization of mental patients since the 1950s. American medicine is financed by an inefficient combination of private health insurance, government welfare programs (medicaid and medicare), and direct payments by patients.

The main alternative to this approach is some kind of government-funded national health care system. In Great Britain almost all health care costs are paid directly by the government. Citizens sign up with the general practitioner of their choice, and the physician is paid by the number of patients served, not by the number of tests or treatments performed. In Canada most health care services are also financed by taxpayers rather than by individual patients. However, the Canadian health care system is much more decentralized than the British system. Each province directs its own health care program, and the federal government underwrites part of the cost. Unlike Britain, hospitals remain in private hands, and physicians are paid on a fee-for-service basis.

There are two ways of dealing with the problems of the sick. One is to prevent health problems before they start. Another approach is to improve the quality of health care services for people who have become ill. This includes proposals for improving medical personnel and for setting up a government-funded national health care system in the United States.

Functionalists contend that the health care system is disorganized because the ways and means of delivering medical services have not adjusted to changes in the medical services themselves. Conflict theorists argue that because the U.S. health care system is controlled by medical professionals and the rich, it serves their interests and neglects the poor. Social psychologists point out that unhealthful life styles are learned from others, and call for a program of education and social change to improve our way of living.

KEY TERMS

acquired immune deficiency syndrome (AIDS) A fatal disease that attacks the body's defenses against illness.

fee-for-service compensation A form of compensation in which a physician receives payment for each service rendered.

health A state of physical and mental well-being.

medicaid A medical welfare program for the poor, blind, and disabled.

medicare A medical welfare program for the elderly.

mental disorder A condition that makes it difficult or impossible for a person to cope with everyday life; sometimes seen as an illness, a problem in adjusting to the environment, or just a label for those who violate social rules.

preventive medicine An approach to health care that attempts to stop potential problems before they start.

FURTHER READINGS

"The Crisis in Health Insurance," *Consumer Reports* 55 (Sep. 1990): 608–617. An excellent report on the serious deficiencies in the way the United States organizes its health care system; also contains a useful comparison with the Canadian system.

Andrew C. Twaddle and Richard M. Hessler, *The Sociology of Health*, 2nd ed. (New York: Macmillan, 1987). A good general text examining the issues of health and health care from a sociological perspective.

Paul Starr, *The Social Transformation of American Medicine* (New York: Basic Books, 1982). An extremely influential book tracing the origins and development of the American health care system.

David Mechanic, *Mental Health and Social Policy*, 3rd ed. (Englewood Cliffs, N.J.: Prentice-Hall, 1989). An examination of the problems of mental health and mental disorder by a well-known medical sociologist.

Erving Goffman, *Asylums: Essays on the Social Situation of Mental Patients and Other Inmates* (New York: Doubleday, 1961). A classic exploration of the social psychological effects of life in a "total institution" (mental hospital, prison, etc.).

chapter 9

The Old and the Young

- How does society respond to the process of aging?
- Is there an "erosion of childhood?"
- Why is adolescence such a difficult time of life?

- What problems do the elderly face in today's society?
- How should society respond to the problems of the young and the old?

From the time we are born until the time we die, we are constantly aging. Most people see this strictly as a biological process, but aging is a social process as well. Although the problems of aging are rooted in the physiological changes we all experience, society tells us what these changes mean and what is expected of people of any particular age group. Thus, the problems of aging are social problems. For example, many of the tragic difficulties the elderly face in our society stem from the fact that they receive little of the respect and consideration that elderly people enjoyed in the past. In Colonial times, Americans dressed to make themselves look as old and dignified as possible; today there is a multibillion-dollar industry devoted to making us look younger than we really are. Yet at the same time that we idolize youthful beauty, we seem to be indifferent to the real needs of the young. Compared with older people, the younger are far more likely to be poor. They are also far more likely to suffer from a deep confusion about who they are and where they are going. Society cannot eliminate the need to adjust to the changes brought on by such things as sexual maturity or the physical deterioration of old age. But we can do a far better job of dealing with the social and biological realities of aging.

AGING AND THE LIFE CYCLE

Everyone is familiar with the biological changes that we experience as we age. They occur most rapidly in our earlier years, as we grow from a baby, to a child, to a sexually mature adult. The changes occur more slowly after physical maturity, but they never stop. As we grow older, most of our physical abilities eventually decline. The most obvious signs are the external ones—the graying of the hair and the wrinkling of the skin—but the changes are much more far-reaching than that. Such things as hearing, eyesight, muscular strength, reaction time, and heart and lung capacity all decline. But although the physical changes aging brings are inevitable, the rate at which they occur is profoundly affected by such social factors as diet, exercise, medical care, and life style. Not only have the improvements in diet and public health made us taller and healthier than our ancestors, but children today reach their full height and mature sexually at an earlier age than they did in past generations.[1] The physical deterioration associated with advancing age is subject to the same kind of social influences. Exercise and a good diet can help slow down the process of deterioration. Research even shows that new opportunities and new stimulation increase the IQ scores and mental abilities of elderly people.[2] But our social environment can have the opposite effect as well. Skid-row alcoholics and homeless transients, for example, often seem 10 or 15 years older than they actually are.

In addition to its influence on the physical process of aging, society tells us what we have to do to "act our age." Every society is divided into what anthropologists call **age grades**: groups of people of similar age. The **life cycle**, then, consists of a series of passages between the social roles expected of people in different age grades. As we progress from one age grade to another, we are presented with a predictable set of new social expectations and a new set of problems that go with them.

The transition itself may also present a difficult challenge of its own. On the one hand, people experiencing such transitions must cope with the feeling of loss at seeing an end to a major period of their lives. On the other, they must face the difficult task of learning new roles. Young adults must conquer their fears and learn how to shoulder the new responsibilities expected of them. The elderly must learn how to reorganize their lives after the stability of child rearing and employment is torn away.

Most cultures have what are known as **rites of passage** to mark transitions from one stage of life to another. These ceremonies provide individuals who are in transition with group support and symbolic confirmation of their new status. Although our culture still maintains a few rites of passage, such as marriage, confirmation, and bar mitzvah ceremonies, most people do not receive much social support when making critical transitions from one age grade to another.

Age grades and the behaviors associated with them vary tremendously from one society to another, and even within a single society over the course of history. Our current ideas about age and what it means are very complex, and experts see the stages of aging in different ways. There are four broad age grades typical of contemporary industrialized society—**childhood**, **adolescence**, **adulthood**, and **old age**—but each one of these can also be subdivided into two or more smaller categories.

The remainder of this chapter will focus on the problems of those at the two ends of the life cycle: the young and the old. By most sociological standards, those in their middle years are an advantaged group and do not require special attention here. But despite the fact that those in mid-life have higher incomes, more prestige, and more power than others, there is growing recognition that these advantages do not necessarily translate into personal happiness. For one thing, those in mid-life are often responsible for the care and support of their children *and* their parents, and they often find those responsibilities to be a heavy burden. The cost of raising a family and supporting aging parents leaves many adults with little to show for the wages they earn. About three-fourths of those caring for the elderly are women, and the demands on their time and their emotional reserves can be overwhelming. A recent report to the U.S. House of Representatives found that the average American woman will spend 17 years raising children and 18 years helping to care for aged parents.[3]

Another common problem for those in their middle years is the acute psychological predicament that has come to be known as the **mid-life crisis**. This crisis typically occurs in the late 30s or 40s when persons in mid-life grapple with the reality that their youth is gone and that death is the inevitable end of their journey. Those devoted to a career must often come to terms with the fact that their dreams of success may never come true, or the even more difficult conclusion that success itself was an empty goal that has left them unfulfilled.[4] Thus, the adjustment to mid-life can be as difficult as any other role transition, even if it is not aggravated by as many economic and social restrictions.

PROBLEMS OF THE YOUNG

Childhood   To most of us, childhood conjures up memories of a carefree time that we would love to relive. But although adolescence is usually the most difficult period of a young person's life, children face some very real problems as well. The important issues of child abuse and molestation (see Chapters 5 and 11) have been the subject of increasing national concern. But the economic problems faced by our children have unfortunately received far less attention. In 1989 the poverty rate for children under 16 was more than 50 percent higher than the national average and double the rate for those in their middle years. About one in every five American children now lives in poverty.[5]

At the same time that the poverty rate was soaring among the young, the government seemed to turn its back on their needs. School lunch programs were slashed, eligibility requirements for Aid to Families with Dependent Children were raised, and federal support for education was cut. Between 1978 and 1987, spending for programs for the elderly rose 52 percent while spending on children dropped 4 percent.[6] The plain fact is that unlike the elderly, the young cannot vote and have virtually no political power.

The sweeping changes in the family system examined in Chapter 5 have caused serious problems for many children. Significant increases in the divorce rate and the number of babies born to single women mean that a quarter of today's children live in single-parent homes. Moreover, 56 percent of mothers with children under the age of 6 now work outside the home, so even children who live with both parents often have less contact with them than they would have in the past. Over 40 percent of children from kindergarten through third grade are at least occasionally left alone to care for themselves, and, of course, the percentages are much higher for older children.[7] A different kind of trouble for today's children comes from their parents' abuse of alcohol and other drugs. It is estimated that 300,000 babies a year are born with serious neurological damage because their mothers used drugs during pregnancy, and there has been a sharp rise in the number of children placed in foster homes because of their parents' drug use.[8]

There is also growing concern about the "erosion of childhood": the deterioration of the special protected status accorded childhood. There are still strong restrictions on child labor (as much to protect the jobs of older people as the welfare of children). But the ever-increasing importance of education and the relentless materialism of the consumer revolution have made many children's lives highly competitive ones, while changes in the family structure have forced many children to take on adult roles and responsibilities at an earlier age than they did in the recent past. Another important contributor to the breakdown of the protective barrier around the world of childhood is television. It is estimated that the average child has watched 5,000 hours of television before he or she enters the first grade, and 19,000 hours by the end of high school.[9] In the past, parents controlled their children's access to information about such things as sex, crime, and the injustices of life. But the media now bring the harshest adult realities onto the television screen and thereby into the world of childhood. In the early days of television, programs were carefully examined to make sure that they were appropriate for family viewing. The results may often have been bland and boring, but they did protect the sheltered world of childhood. Today, however, the media is straining to win the lucrative "baby boom" market, and even early-evening programs are often filled with sex and violence.[10]

Adolescence Of all the stages in the life cycle, society has the most contradictory expectations for adolescents. No longer children but not yet adults, adolescents live in a kind of limbo between two worlds. On the one hand, they are told that they must act their

DEBATE

Are We Turning Our Backs on the Problems of the Young?

YES We were far more concerned about the problems of our children a generation ago than we are today. Television was tightly regulated to make sure that its programs were suitable for even the youngest viewers. The movies contained only the tamest sex and far less graphic violence than they do today, and pornography was banned from all respectable newsstands. Even parents seemed more willing to sacrifice their own happiness and stay together for the sake of their children.

Perhaps some of these changes were the inevitable result of historical trends, but even the government seems to have forgotten about the needs of our children. The funding for education is grossly inadequate. Federal programs to provide such things as free school lunches and welfare benefits to poverty-stricken families have been slashed, parks and playgrounds in hundreds of cities have been shut down, and nothing is being done to stop the advertisers' shameless exploitation of the young. Commercials tell our children that processed breakfast cereals laden with sugar are part of a nutritious breakfast and urge them to buy everything from ice cream and candy bars to war toys, and the government just looks the other way.

The babies that used to be considered a "bundle of joy" are now more often seen as a noisy, messy nuisance. Parents are glared at when they bring their infants into a movie or a restaurant, "adults-only" apartment buildings have sprung up across the country, and the birthrate itself has plummeted as more and more young couples decide that extra spending money is more important than children. Today's children

NO Today's society is a far better place for children than it ever was before. Improvements in public health, sanitation, and medicine have slashed the infant mortality rate and allow more children to grow into healthy adults. The number of years an average child attends school has gone up and illiteracy has gone down. Children are now more likely to have braces on their teeth and vaccinations against serious diseases, and their parents generally keep a much closer watch on their diet and their physical safety than they ever did in the past.

The increase in sexually oriented material in the media has nothing to do with our attitudes about children. It is a result of changing attitudes about sex. Similarly, the increase in divorce is not the result of a lesser concern for children but a decline in the belief that keeping an unhappy marriage together is really good for the children.

Far from turning its back on children, the government is much more involved in protecting their welfare than it ever was before. The safety of toys, for example, is much more tightly regulated, and many popular toys from the 1950s and 1960s can no longer be sold at all. We used to all but ignore the problems of child abuse and molestation, but today they are major social concerns. The public is more vigilant, the police more willing to investigate, and the courts more likely to send the offenders to prison than at any time in the past. A hundred years ago, children commonly worked long hours in dirty sweatshops and dangerous factories, and severe beatings were accepted as normal discipline; but today all that is against the law. There are the forgotten Americans. Their needs clearly come last on our list of national priorities.

simply is no doubt that we are more, not less, concerned with the welfare of our children than we were in the past.

---

age and behave in a responsible and mature manner; but at the same time, they are told that they are not old enough to get married, have sex, drink, vote, or hold down a well-paying job. It is therefore hardly surprising that psychologist Erik H. Erikson concluded that the **identity crisis**—the pressing need to figure out who we are and how we fit into the scheme of things around us—is the central problem of adolescence.[11]

Adolescents must also face a host of difficult decisions that will shape the rest of their life. Children have most of their decisions made for them, and those later in life are more likely just to follow a long-established course. But the adolescent must decide critical questions about such things as relationships with the opposite sex, marriage, school, and career, with little previous experience to fall back on. Another problem that springs from adolescents' position in contemporary society is their sense of powerlessness. Although they feel themselves to be physically mature and capable of running their own lives, they are constantly under the authority of their elders, whether parents, teachers, or the local police.

In response to their unique problems and experiences, adolescents in most industrial societies have created their own subculture. Many of the characteristics of this so-called **youth culture** can be seen as a reflection of teenagers' pressing need to create a viable identity.[12] The constantly changing fashions in speech, clothing, and music provide a sense of belonging and a way for the followers of such fashions to gain status and feel a part of an in-group. These symbols also allow teens to see themselves as separate and somehow "cooler" than the adults that exercise such power over their lives.

This symbolic rejection of the adult world becomes a much more direct and violent challenge in the delinquent subculture that has long made up an important current within the overall youth culture. This subculture, along with the drug culture, certainly contributes to the fact that the arrest rate for 16- to 21-year-olds is higher than for any other age group. One large survey conducted in 1989 and 1990 found that a little more than one in ten high school juniors admitted having stolen from a store or been in trouble with the police two or more times in the previous year. The use of alcohol and other drugs is another distressing issue. Two of every five high school seniors acknowledged having had a "drinking binge" (five or more drinks in a row) in the last two weeks, one of five smoked daily, and, perhaps most disturbing of all, a third admitted drinking and driving in the last year.[13] Of course, all these problems are not the result of deviant subcultures or even a sense of youthful rebellion. Adolescence is a time of exploration and experimentation, and it is hardly surprising that young people try out as many options as they can. If nothing else, they are less likely to have the responsibilities of a well-paying job or a family to support and therefore have far less to lose if caught breaking society's rules.

Adolescence is a time of conflicting demands, as an individual makes the transition between the dependency of childhood and independent responsibilities of adult life.

While some teenagers respond to their difficulties with delinquency and rebellion, others give in to depression or other mental disorders. A recent report by the Institute of Medicine concluded that as many as 12 percent of young people suffer from some form of psychological illness.[14] One of the most disturbing manifestations of this problem is the sharp increase in suicide: the survey mentioned above found that 15 percent of high school students admitted making at least one suicide attempt. While most such attempts are unsuccessful, the death rate from teenage suicide has more than quadrupled since 1950.[15]

One of the most difficult problems adolescents must face is coming to terms with their sexuality. If anything, society's norms and expectations for adolescent sexual behavior are even more confusing than they are for other aspects of their lives. Teenagers are bombarded with books, movies, and advertising emphasizing the importance of being sexy and attractive. Everything from soft drinks to jeans is given the sexual sell. Yet at the same time, parents, teachers, and religious leaders tell young people that they are not ready for sex and all the complications it involves. Unlike young people in most European countries, American teenagers are also strongly discouraged from using birth control. Sixty percent of high school seniors surveyed in 1989–1990 said they were sexually active, and the majority of them (53 percent) said that they did not always use contraceptives.[16] As a result of all this, unmarried teenagers in the United States have the highest birthrate of any country in the industrialized world (see Chapter 11).

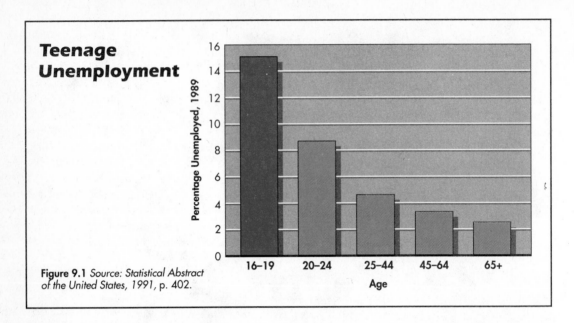

Teenage Unemployment

Figure 9.1 *Source: Statistical Abstract of the United States, 1991, p. 402.*

Finally, something must be said about the serious economic problems faced by many adolescents. Most teenagers still derive their economic status from their family, and because poor people have larger families, a disproportionate number of teenagers are trapped in poverty. The poverty rate for teenagers is higher than for any other age group in the United States except those under 13. Teenage males who work in full-time jobs still make less than a third as much as those in their peak earning years, but despite their low wages, those working teenagers are the lucky ones. The unemployment rate for teenagers was three times higher than the national average in 1989 (see Figure 9.1).[17] In many ghetto neighborhoods, teenagers looking for work are more likely to end up unemployed than in a job.

PROBLEMS OF THE ELDERLY

In traditional societies with extended family systems, increasing age is usually accompanied by increasing prestige. But with the breakup of the extended family, the status of the elderly has suffered a severe decline. No longer are old men and women the respected heads of an ongoing social unit. Rather, they are increasingly isolated and alone. Youth and vigor are cultural ideals in North America, and there is widespread belief that older people have little or nothing left to contribute. In a common phrase, the elderly are said to be "over the hill."

The problems of the elderly have been drawing considerable attention in recent years, probably because there are more old people than ever before. Since 1900, the average life expectancy in the United States has risen by 24 years, and the percentage of the population over age 65 has more than doubled. There are now almost 31 million people age 65 or older, about 12.5 percent of the U.S. population,[18] and projections indicate that the elderly population will continue to grow rapidly in the years ahead.

Within about four decades, the elderly are expected to make up a quarter of the Canadian population—more than double their present percentage.[19]

Health   Of all the problems that trouble older people, health seems to concern them the most. There is good reason for this concern: the elderly have more severe health problems than other age groups. But although most Americans over age 65 have at least one chronic illness, such as arthritis or heart disease, elderly people actually have fewer acute illnesses (such as colds and infectious diseases) than others. However, their recovery time from such illnesses tends to be much longer than that of younger adults. Despite the prevalence of chronic illness among the elderly, only 15 percent are too sick to care for themselves, and only about 1 out of every 20 people over 65 lives in an institution. Most elderly people say that they are in reasonably good health, perhaps because they have learned to put up with illness and physical impairment as an inevitable part of the aging process.[20]

The elderly have trouble getting care and treatment for their ailments. Most hospitals, designed to handle injuries and acute illness that are common in the young, are inadequate to treat the chronic degenerative diseases of the elderly. Many doctors are also ill prepared to deal with such problems. As Fred Cottrell points out, "There is a widespread feeling among the aged that most doctors are not interested in them and are reluctant to treat people who are as little likely to contribute to the future as the aged are reputed to."[21] And even with the help of medicare, the elderly in the United States often have a difficult time paying for the health care they need (see Chapter 8).

Money   For most of this century, the elderly were much more likely than other people to be poor. Recent statistics reveal a remarkable turnaround in the general financial condition of older people. In 1989, 11.4 percent of persons over 65 were below the poverty line, while that figure was 12.8 percent for the entire population and 20.1 percent for children under 16.[22] One of the main reasons for this improvement is that, since 1970, social security benefits have automatically been adjusted for inflation. In the late 1970s and early 1980s, when prices were rising at a record pace, the income of social security recipients was growing considerably faster than the income of wage earners. Inflation helped more affluent elderly people in another way as well. Unprecedented increases in the cost of real estate produced enormous profits for older people who had purchased a home in the days when prices were low. Households headed by someone over the age of 60 now have more than ten times the average net worth of households headed by someone under age 35.[23] But the financial condition of the elderly is not as rosy as these figures might suggest. Poverty among the elderly is still higher than it is for those in their middle years, and there are some serious pockets of poverty among older people, especially among widows and members of minority groups. Also, government statistics underestimate the amount of poverty among the elderly because such data do not acknowledge the fact that older persons need more money than younger persons to enjoy the same standard of living. Medical bills increase, and as the elderly grow more feeble, they must hire others to do many of the heavy chores they once did themselves.

One source of these financial problems is that as people grow older, they are less likely to be employed. Most older people look forward to retirement and the escape it offers from the pressures of the working world, but some find they must retire because they can no longer muster the stamina that their jobs require. Another employment problem for older people arises from technological changes that may suddenly make the skills that older workers have acquired over a lifetime obsolete. Older people who know only how to bake bread or build fine cabinets or repair shoes are bound to have a tough time as bakeries become bread factories, cabinets are made of plastic, and cheap shoes are imported in huge quantities. They cannot even get unskilled jobs because employers want the energy of youth. Employee training programs that might lead to new skills are often closed because training directors believe that older men and women will not work long enough to repay the cost of the training.

Discrimination in hiring and promotion is a fact of life for the elderly. Employers give a variety of reasons for their reluctance to hire senior citizens. They fear that older workers will take longer to learn a new job, will work fewer years on the job, will demand higher pay and be less willing to accept the authority of supervisors younger than themselves, and will be sick more often than their younger counterparts. Although such fears are not entirely groundless, they certainly do not apply to all older workers. Yet all older workers are potential victims of age discrimination.

Retired men and women receive income from a variety of sources, including pensions, social security, and personal savings. Most workers dream of retiring on a "fat pension," but only a minority of the retired receive any pension at all, and such pensions are seldom "fat." The single most important source of income for elderly people in the United States is the payments from Old Age and Survivors' Insurance, commonly called **social security** benefits. More than 90 percent of all elderly people in the United States collect social security or public assistance, and over half the elderly have no other source of income.[24] About 60 percent of the elderly in the United States would be living in poverty if they did not receive social security. Still, social security benefits are hardly extravagant, despite the automatic cost of living adjustments. In 1989 the average retired worker received $567 a month in social security payments, and an average couple received $966.[25]

Housing Decent housing is especially important to the elderly because they spend so much time at home. For personal comfort the elderly need higher room temperatures than the young require, but housing for the elderly often lacks proper heating. Those who are physically handicapped or disabled also need wheelchair ramps, elevators, and other special facilities. Even owning a home is not easy for many elderly people. There may still be mortgage payments to meet, and rising taxes and insurance must also be paid. Because many of the homes in which the elderly live were built before World War II, they are old by U.S. standards. New roofs and other needed repairs may be left undone because many elderly people are unable to do the work themselves and cannot afford to hire outside help.

So-called retirement communities can be a very effective way to meet an elderly person's special housing needs. But unfortunately, most of these are private, and, thus, the better ones are available only to people with substantial means. Often built in sunny climates, these complexes of houses or apartments are designed for the elderly and usually include special recreational facilities. Some are run like hotels or make hotel-like arrangements for residents who can afford them. Retirement communities have often been criticized because they weaken the ties between generations and create a kind of "old people's ghetto." Nevertheless, many older people move to retirement communities precisely because they seek the companionship of others who share their interests and experiences.

Only about 5 percent of people over 65 live in an institution, but that percentage increases sharply with advancing years. Almost a quarter of all Americans over the age of 84 live in a nursing home.[26] Most of these institutions, privately owned and managed, are profit-making businesses. Many that charge high fees give excellent service, but some of these, and most of the less expensive ones, do not do much "nursing" and are in no sense "homes." The worst of these facilities are old, overcrowded, unsanitary firetraps. There are not enough toilets, the sewers back up, and the light switches don't work. Residents complain that they are served only the cheapest foods and do not get a balanced diet. And even those who live in good nursing homes may face serious psychological problems, for many people feel that entering a nursing home is a disgrace—a sign of final rejection by friends and family and proof that no one really cares.

Problems of Transition Elderly people somehow learn to adjust to the profound role changes that are thrust upon them. But the transition to old age is a difficult one because it usually involves the loss of status, while role changes for younger people are likely to involve increasing prestige and responsibility. The three most significant personal transitions that the elderly must face are retirement, the loss of friends and loved ones, and their own death.

After a person has been employed for decades, the transition to retirement can be painful. The daily routine that has given direction to the worker's life is suddenly yanked away. This transition is not just a matter of finding new things to do but requires major psychological adjustments. Retirement demands a new answer to the first question strangers are likely to ask each other: "What do you do?" An old saying held that "it is better to wear away than to rust away." People who are perceived to be rusting away on park benches and shuffleboard courts are seen as useless and perhaps a little immoral as well. To make matters worse, retirees usually suffer a drop in income and can no longer afford many of the things that they were used to buying—another sign of "failure." But despite these problems, studies show that most retired people are satisfied with their lives. When a Harris poll asked a sample of retired people, "Has retirement fulfilled your expectations for a good life or have you found it less than satisfactory?" 61 percent of the respondents said that retirement had fulfilled their expectations, while only a third felt that it was less than satisfactory.[27]

The social world of the elderly tends to shrink as the years accumulate. There are fewer social contacts as friends and relatives die, and moving from place to place becomes increasingly difficult. Old social roles are dropped, and even sex differences decline. Old people look and behave differently from others, and may be increasingly shunned by the young. If they have children or sisters and brothers, they are fortunate,

As people grow older, their environment changes and friends and loved ones die. One result may be loneliness and isolation.

for ties with surviving family members normally remain strong. Those without close living relatives find their world growing smaller and smaller.

Sooner or later old people die. When one member of a married couple dies, the survivor must cope without a partner. Most survivors are women, both because most wives are younger than their husbands and because women tend to live longer than men. Normlessness, isolation, and loneliness can be particularly severe in widowhood. The older the widow, the greater the problems. There is often no sex, no love, no help with daily tasks, and less income. Problems of transition begin immediately after the husband's death. The woman who depended on her husband to make the decisions and handle financial affairs must, in the midst of her grief, work her way through a maze of medical bills, insurance claims, funeral expenses, and tax payments. She is likely to discover that she is eligible for little or none of her husband's pension benefits, and may have to choose between looking for a job, trying to live on social security, or remarrying. Remarriage is not likely to be easy, however, for there are not enough eligible older men. Moreover, after living with one man for most of a lifetime, the idea of taking up with another may not be attractive.

Becoming a widower has its problems too. Should the elderly widower desire to remarry, his chances of finding a mate seem brighter because there are more elderly

19th-Century Social Problems

Died, September 20th, 1892, at his home in Sechlerville, Wisconsin, Samuel McWilliam, in the 84th year of his age. The death angel hovered over the home of Uncle Sammy for many months, threatening and retreating until gently and silently it wrapt its dark mantle around his wasted form and winged its flight to that bourn from whence no traveler returns. Born in . . . 1809, the deceased . . . was the father of 8 children, 6 of whom (2 sons and 4 daughters) remain to comfort the last days of their widowed mother. . . . His sufferings were such as only those with cancer endure. He longed for release. His eyes, closed in the darkness of here, [have] opened (we trust) in the brilliant presence of his Redeemer.

September 29, 1892

Alexander Gardapie, aged 90 years, died at Prairie du Chien. He walked into a saloon, drank a glass of gin, asked the time of day, sat down, and died.

January 31, 1895

These selections, which appear throughout the text, are from the *Badger State Banner*, a newspaper published in Black River Falls, Wisconsin.

women than men. But if he does not remarry, his life may become more difficult. In most families it is the wife who keeps up contacts with friends and relatives, arranges parties, and runs the household. Consequently, a man who loses his wife is likely to lose touch with many of his friends as well. Further, although some widows can fall back on their maternal roles, widowers generally have weaker ties to their children and therefore are likely to be lonely and isolated.

But whether married or not, all elderly people come to terms with their own mortality. In the rich industrialized nations where death rates are low, we often pretend that death is an accident. When it occurs we grieve, but we imagine that it is avoidable, like automobile collisions or flunking out of college. The dying pay the price for this denial of reality, for they are avoided as deftly as our thoughts of death. Most people in the industrialized nations die in a hospital or other institution, shut away from the familiar surroundings of home. As a result, feelings of rejection and loneliness are common among the dying. Even the friends, relatives, and medical personnel who have contact with the dying engage in a kind of "conspiracy of silence." Everyone tries to avoid the subject of death and to pretend that nothing is really going to happen to the patient.

RESPONDING TO PROBLEMS OF THE YOUNG AND THE OLD

The problems of the young and the old may seem very different, and in some respects they are. But these age grades experience two difficulties in common. They both have lower incomes than those in their middle years, and as a result they both are often dependent on government assistance. Culturally, both groups are shut out of the mainstream of social life and are seen to be a burden on those in their middle years.

Employment   Both aging workers and adolescents suffer from high levels of unemployment. The most effective way to deal with this problem is to improve the economic conditions of all workers. If the unemployment rate were lower, employers would have to hire the many capable older workers who are available and give more teenagers a chance at their first job.

The United States, like other nations, has tried to deal with the problem of age discrimination by passing laws against it. The Federal Age Discrimination in Employment Act of 1967 prohibits many types of age discrimination. As a result, the most blatant signs of such bias have decreased significantly. But more subtle forms of discrimination continue. Laws of this type are difficult to enforce because it is hard to prove why an employer hired or promoted one person rather than another. In actual practice, the law is enforced on a hit-or-miss basis because there isn't enough money to enforce it across the board. Moreover, the current laws are far too narrow, and do not include discrimination against young workers. Although legislation of this kind can never be a complete answer to the problem, a revision of the law to include all kinds of age discrimination and a significant increase in the funding to enforce the law would certainly be a step in the right direction.

Social Welfare   As we have seen, the government substantially reduced its commitment to young people during the last decade. Although such short-sighted policies may achieve some immediate saving, in the long run their social and financial costs are likely to be staggering. The problems of neglected youth do not simply go away but grow progressively worse and more costly as the years go by. For example, the cost of a measles shot is only $8, but hospitalization for a child with measles runs about $5,000.[28]

The obvious way to reaffirm our commitment to the young is to increase the government's support for children and their families. A school lunch program to provide at least one nutritious meal to every child every day, free health care for any child who needs it, an increase in the tax exemption allowed for dependent children, and a national system of top-quality day care at no cost to middle- and low-income parents would contribute significantly to the welfare of our children. But a real commitment to the young must go beyond providing the necessities for survival. Our young people desperately need a better system of education, and that will require the kinds of costly reforms discussed in Chapter 4. And we should take more interest in the social needs of the young. The financial problems of local governments have resulted in the closing of many parks and the elimination of sports programs. A new commitment to the young would mean a reversal of this trend and a greater effort to see that young people are given positive, healthful outlets for their energies.

Although the government programs designed to help the elderly are different from those for the young, their goals are much the same: to assist a group of people who cannot always provide for themselves. Social security is the major source of income for most elderly Americans. Although it is one of the most popular and widely accepted social programs in the United States, social security is experiencing some serious difficulties. As we have seen, benefits are too low to support some elderly people, yet the system is having trouble meeting the financial commitments to an aging population. Moreover, similar problems are occurring in the other industrialized nations. The Canada Pension Plan, for example, is expected to run out of money early in the next century unless contributions are significantly increased.[29]

The original idea behind the social security system was that all workers would contribute part of their income to a pension fund, and those contributions would be matched by the employer. When workers retired, they would be entitled to regular payments from these savings. In practice, however, the contributions of workers have not been saved up; they have been paid out as needed. Thus, the increase in the number of retirees means that today's workers must pay higher social security taxes than in past decades (see Figure 9.2). This burden is particularly heavy on low- and middle-income people because the social security tax rate does not increase with increasing income (as income tax rates do), and those with high incomes do not pay taxes on their entire earnings but only on the portion below a fixed level. Thus, one way to ensure adequate benefits and keep the system on sound financial footing is to institute a progressive social security tax that goes up as income increases.

The elderly could benefit from a variety of other programs as well. One of the most pressing needs is for more government-subsidized housing for those who are too poor to own their own home or live in a retirement community. To help middle-income retirees squeezed by inflation and health care costs, several states allow the elderly to defer their property taxes until after their death, when the equity in their

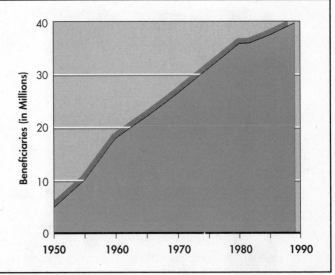

Figure 9.2 *Source: Statistical Abstract of the United States, 1991, p. 363.*

house is used to pay the taxes due. Finally, a universal program of national health insurance that contained effective cost-control measures would help the elderly, the young, and many of those in their middle years as well (see Chapter 8).

Cultural Change   The problems of the elderly and the young are rooted in the cultural traditions of our society. There is, for example, a strong negative stereotype of elderly people. A public opinion survey sponsored by the National Council on Aging found that older people consistently described themselves in more positive terms than those used by the general public. For instance, people over 65 were almost three times as likely as those under 65 to say that the elderly are "very open-minded and adaptable." The general public also saw the elderly as much less active and more bored than the elderly saw themselves. Those under 65 were more than twice as likely to believe that the elderly spend a lot of time sleeping or doing nothing, and they were four times as likely to say that "not having enough to do" is a serious problem for the elderly.[30] Such stereotypes become self-fulfilling prophecies that lead to the exclusion of the elderly from employment opportunities and other forms of social involvement.

The most effective way to change this situation is to encourage the elderly to participate in community life, putting their wealth of wisdom and experience to work for the good of others. A number of government programs are aimed toward these ends. For example, the Foster Grandparent Program helps the young and the old at the same time by paying older people to work part time at child care centers and institutions. The elderly get meaningful work and additional income, and the children receive the benefits of personal attention and concern. Senior citizens' centers, which are funded by public and private sources, also employ older people in community projects. Perhaps more important, these centers provide a place where the elderly can congregate, make new friends, and get a hot meal.

The problems of adolescents stem less from negative stereotypes about them— although these certainly abound—than from the contradictory demands and expec-

Many in our culture view old people as useless and incompetent, but few of the elderly actually fit this stereotype. The store of information and wisdom accumulated by the elderly is especially useful to the young as they are growing up.

tations of the adult world. If we are to significantly reduce juvenile delinquency, drug and alcohol use, suicide, and the general sense of boredom and aimlessness among the young, we must provide a more clear-cut set of expectations for their age grade, and more rewarding and worthwhile things for them to do. In the past, teenagers were considered adults and given adult responsibilities. If industrial society continues to deny adolescents full adult status, young people must at least be encouraged to see themselves as respected and worthwhile members of their community. Providing jobs for young workers who need them would certainly make a big difference. But adolescents need something more than just a regular source of income. Of all age grades, they are the most idealistic, and they need to feel that they are contributing to the world around them. It is up to society to tap this youthful idealism and channel it into worthwhile projects. Not only can such endeavors give purpose and meaning to those involved; they can produce real benefits for the society as a whole.

SOCIOLOGICAL PERSPECTIVES ON PROBLEMS OF THE LIFE CYCLE

Each of us must come to terms with the realities of growth, aging, and death as we pass through the stages of the life cycle. This may appear to be a lonely struggle, but it is not. Although the major sociological perspectives focus on different issues, they all show us how such seemingly individual problems are inextricably bound up with the social order in which we live.

The Functionalist Perspective   Functionalists see much confusion in the institutions and agencies that are supposed to meet the needs of our youngest and oldest citizens. At the root of the problem are the changes that continue to transform Western culture. In the past, death came at an early age, and there were relatively few elderly people. Most of those who did grow old were cared for by their families. But with the improvements in sanitation and food supplies brought about by industrialization, the percentage of elderly people in the population has increased enormously. At the same time, economic changes caused a breakdown in the traditional extended family, leaving many older people alone and unable to support themselves.

These developments are, moreover, having just as profound an effect on children and young adults as on the elderly. The weakening of the family has created severe problems for the growing number of children who come from broken or conflict-ridden homes. At the same time, changes in the economic system that slashed the demand for unskilled workers have fundamentally transformed the social role of teenagers as they have been squeezed out of the mainstream of the labor force and into a marginal position. The creation of the new age grade of adolescence stemmed at least in part from an attempt to deal with the special problems of this group, yet society continues to hold highly contradictory expectations for its young people.

From the functionalist perspective, it is necessary to reorganize the social institutions that traditionally cared for the young and the elderly or to develop new agencies that can do so more effectively. The fact that the government has been taking increased financial responsibility for the elderly can be seen as an attempt to get the machinery of society running smoothly again. But there is a great deal of disorganization in the administration of government programs for the elderly, just as there is disorganization in the far smaller programs for the young. These programs are often cumbersome and inefficient, and they spend far too much on administrative costs. But the most serious problem is that these agencies often do not have enough money to meet the needs of the people they serve.

There are signs that society is at least beginning to come to terms with the problems of the elderly. Stereotypes about the elderly are beginning to change, and senior citizens' centers, retirement communities, and other organizations designed to meet the needs of the elderly are becoming more common. But our efforts to deal with the problems of the young seem to be less successful. Some of the functions formerly performed by the family have been shifted to the schools and the criminal-justice system, but generally they remain a poor substitute for a supportive family environment. Moreover, at the present time at least, there seems to be little willingness by society to make the kind of financial and psychological commitment to take effective action to attack these problems.

The Conflict Perspective   Many social scientists are convinced that the government's seeming indifference to the problems of the old and the young is no accident but a product of class conflict. They argue that the wealthy and powerful have blocked efforts to help these groups because it is not in their best interests to do so. The wealthy do

Conflict theorists are convinced that political activism is the most effective way to solve the problems of our youngest and oldest citizens.

not need government assistance for their children or their old age, and do not care to pay for such help for others.

Value conflicts also play an important part in these problems. Ideas about the value of competition, self-reliance, and personal responsibility clash with the effort to care for people who are not productive. Thus, the ideology of individualism (see Chapter 6) blames the elderly for their poverty, assuming that they deserve to suffer because they have failed to provide for their future. Similarly, single parents are blamed for their failure to follow traditional family patterns. Ignoring their complex financial and social problems, single mothers are told to simply go out and get a job. On the other side of this conflict are those who hold to the values of community and collective responsibility. These people see the problems of the life cycle as the product of social forces beyond the control of any individual; and if these problems are created by society, it follows that society should do something to resolve them.

From the conflict perspective, the most effective response is political action. And in fact, senior citizens have already organized themselves into an effective lobby. Acting through such organizations as the American Association of Retired Persons, senior citizens have been able to protect social security from the kind of cutbacks that hit most other social programs in the 1980s and early 1990s. Children and adolescents are, however, in a much weaker position. They lack political experience, have little money, and cannot vote. Their only hope for political representation lies with concerned adults who are willing to fight for their interests.

Social Psychological Perspectives   Social psychologists who take the biosocial perspective emphasize the importance of the physical changes we undergo as we age. Some argue that the high rates of crime and violence among young people are the direct result of the intense sex drive and physical vigor characteristic of this age group (see Chapter 13). Similarly, the emotional problems of the elderly are linked to the physiological deterioration brought on by advancing age. Although few have proposed biological treatments for the problems of the young, some scientists feel that medical breakthroughs may make it possible to slow the process of degeneration that accompanies aging. But whatever the future may hold, it is clear that some of the physical degeneration of the elderly results from improper diet, inadequate heating and shelter, and lack of exercise—conditions that are social rather than biological. Thus, major scientific discoveries are not necessary to improve the health of older people.

Most social psychologists are concerned more with the social than the biological process of aging. Both behaviorists and interactionists emphasize the point that social behavior is learned from other people. As people reach different age levels, their group memberships change and they assume new roles. The key to negotiating these role transitions lies in the nature of the new groups. If one is accepted by his or her new peers and given some positive ideal to emulate, the transition is likely to be an easy one. But those entering adolescence are often confronted with a confusing barrage of competing groups with conflicting ideals and expectations, and as a result they find it difficult to discover their own direction. On the other hand, people entering old age find that their previous roles disappear, along with friends and loved ones, but that their new role is poorly defined. There are far fewer expectations of any kind placed upon them and fewer goals to pursue. Although this can be a liberating experience, feelings of aimlessness and apathy are the more common result.

Most social psychologists recommend the same general kind of solution to the problems of young and old alike: help integrate them into supportive social groups that offer a constructive role to play in society. But though this conclusion is almost universally accepted for adolescents, there are some who feel that it is less appropriate for the elderly. The majority of social psychologists adhere to what is known as **activity theory**, which urges older people to remain active and involved in community life. However, **disengagement theory** rejects this recommendation and holds that old age is best handled by accepting the inevitable contraction of one's social world and gradually disengaging from social involvements and responsibilities as death comes nearer. While the idea of disengagement clashes with the activist bent of Western culture, it is the ideal of many Asian cultures that the elderly should withdraw from everyday activities and focus their attention on spiritual pursuits.

SUMMARY

Aging is a social as well as a biological process. All societies divide their members into age grades—groups of people of similar age—and the members of the various age grades have different rights and duties. Sociologically, the life cycle is a series of transitions from one set of social roles to another, and such role transitions are difficult. The individual making such changes must adapt to a new set of expectations and leave behind the rewards and security of earlier roles. The four principal age grades in industrial societies are childhood, adolescence, adulthood, and old age.

Although childhood is seen as a carefree time, children still face significant problems in today's society. There is a great deal of concern about child abuse and molestation, and the poverty rate is higher for children than for any other age group. Moreover, the sheltered status children have enjoyed in most of the twentieth century seems to be eroding. Changes in family structure have forced many children to assume adult responsibilities at an earlier age, and television and the other mass media are bringing adult attitudes and problems into the world of childhood.

Adolescents are seen neither as children nor as adults, and society's expectations for them are probably more contradictory than for any other age grade. Adolescents face many difficult problems, including constructing a viable personal identity, dealing with their awakening sexuality, and making critical decisions about education and jobs. To make matters worse, adolescents have a higher poverty rate than any other age group except young children. One response to this situation is the youth culture, which provides adolescents with a group identity and supplies some common answers to these perplexing questions.

Because Western culture puts high value on beauty and vigor, it fails to give the elderly the prestige and respect that they receive in many other cultures. Elderly people have more chronic diseases and poorer overall health than the general population, but most elderly people say that they are in reasonably good health. Money worries are common among the aged. Most elderly people are not eligible for a private pension, and the private pensions that the elderly do receive are usually inadequate. Over half of all the elderly people in the United States live almost entirely on social security payments or public assistance. Because the elderly lose old friends and relatives as well as most of the social roles they once performed, they are more likely to be lonely and isolated. The death of a spouse makes matters worse. After a brief period of support and sympathy, the new widow or widower must take up a new life. Widows have some special problems of adjustment because their incomes are often greatly reduced and their chances for remarriage are slim. And all elderly people are faced with the reality that their own death is drawing near.

Many different responses to the problems of our youngest and oldest citizens have been suggested. A program to create more jobs would help all workers regardless of age. A broader prohibition against age discrimination, a reform of social security financing, free school lunches, and a comprehensive national health insurance program are commonly suggested ideas, as are making cultural changes that give both the old and the young a more positive role to play in our society.

Functionalists see the problems of the old and the young as one more product of the disorganization that follows rapid economic and social change. From this perspective, it is necessary either to restore the extended family or to develop new organizations to take its place. Conflict theorists are convinced that those groups suffer because the wealthy and powerful profit from their misery. They advocate more and better organization for political action by these groups and their supporters. Social psychologists study how age-graded roles are learned and emphasize the need of all people to be integrated into supportive social groups.

KEY TERMS

adolescence The age grade of persons who have reached puberty but have not been given full status as adults.

adulthood The age grade of persons who have reached full social and physical maturity.

age grade A group of people who have a similar social status because of their age.

childhood The earliest age grade, lasting from birth to the onset of puberty.

mid-life crisis A psychological predicament commonly experienced by persons in their middle years when they face the passing of their youth and the limitations on their future.

old age The last age grade, usually considered to start around age 65.

youth culture The distinctive subculture created by adolescents in industrial societies.

FURTHER READINGS

Matilda White Riley, "On the Significance of Age in Sociology," *American Sociological Review* 52 (Feb. 1987): 1–14. A discussion of the sociology of aging by a highly respected gerontologist.

Joseph M. Hawes and N. Ray Hiner, eds., *American Childhood: A Research Guide and Historical Handbook* (Westport, Conn.: Greenwood Press, 1985). A good resource for those interested in taking a closer look at childhood in American society.

Beth B. Hess and Elizabeth Markson, eds., *Growing Old in America*, 3rd ed. (New Brunswick, N.J.: Transaction Books, 1985). A collection of articles examining the sociological aspects of aging.

Hans Sebald, *Adolescence: A Social Psychological Analysis* (Englewood Cliffs, N.J.: Prentice-Hall, 1984). A general text on adolescents and their position in contemporary society.

Elisabeth Kübler-Ross, *Questions and Answers on Death and Dying* (New York: Macmillan, 1985). A general work by the most influential student of the process of dying.

chapter 10

Women and Men

- What are the differences between male and female gender roles?
- Are the differences in the behavior of males and females caused by biology or culture?
- How do we learn gender roles?
- What forms does the discrimination against women take?
- How can sexual inequality be reduced?

A generation ago, people would have been shocked to hear of a young husband who stayed home to care for the kids while his wife went off to work. And the idea of a female police officer walking a beat in a big city would have seemed an impossibility. Both examples violate traditional gender role expectations, which most people accepted almost without question. But new economic and social conditions are forcing us to rethink those traditional attitudes. Women are moving into the "man's world" of employment and competition in record numbers, and men are beginning to explore the "woman's world" of family and children. Indeed, this redefinition of what it means to be a woman or a man may be one of the most significant developments of modern times.

Although traditional gender roles were clearly based on the subordination of women, it was not until they began to change that **gender inequality** came to be seen as a social problem. Today, everything from popular magazines to daily talk shows discuss the problem of sexism and debate the proper role of women and men in our society. But too much of this dialog is carried out in a sociological and historical vacuum. To understand this issue more deeply, we must first explore the nature and origins of gender roles and the ways gender inequality is built into the structure of our social institutions.

GENDER ROLES

Like veteran actors, each of us plays many roles. The list is almost endless—parent, child, student, worker, pedestrian, automobile driver, shopper, consumer. **Gender roles** are assigned to us on the basis of our biological sex. These roles contain sets of expectations both for what we are supposed to do and what we are not supposed to do. A woman who spends hours dyeing her hair and applying just the right makeup before going out meets our gender role expectations; a man who does the same thing violates those expectations.

Gender roles are assigned early in life. Children quickly learn that they are girls or boys and act accordingly. Nevertheless, adult gender roles are complex, involving both personality and behavioral characteristics. Women are expected to be passive, warm, and supportive. In contrast to men, who are expected to suppress their feelings, women are encouraged to express emotions openly. Men are supposed to be active, independent, and self-controlled, while women are thought to be more dependent and in need of emotional support. A man's role centers around his work and his responsibilities as breadwinner and provider of financial security. The traditional role of women, on the other hand, is to run the home and rear the children.

The movement of women out of the home and into the workplace has led to a vigorous challenge to those old notions about the natural differences between the sexes. In the past, people who did not fit the expectations for their gender were shunned and laughed at. Today, some argue that the healthiest individuals display both strong masculine and strong feminine characteristics, and that the new ideal should therefore be a single **androgynous** one combining traits traditionally assigned to different genders.[1] Others hold that the distinction between masculine and feminine characteristics is harmful and should be abandoned altogether.[2] Nonetheless, these traditional roles and stereotypes are still a powerful force in our society, and their consequences will be with us for a long time to come.

Nature or Nurture?   Where do these gender roles come from? Why do we see such differences in the way men and women act? As with so many other issues in the social sciences, such questions reflect the long-running debate about the relative importance of nature (biology) and nurture (learning) in human behavior.

The two most significant biological differences are clearly the greater size and strength of the male and the female's ability to bear and nurse children. In physical contests most males have a clear advantage. Not only is the average male taller than the average female, but testosterone, a male sex hormone, promotes muscular development and strength. The female has a much closer biological tie with the process of reproduction. Childbearing is, of course, the exclusive domain of the female. And before the development of baby bottles, only the female could feed the child for the first months of its life. Because a sexually active woman who lives in a farming society will become pregnant about once every two years without the use of contraceptives, the average woman in most agricultural societies was either pregnant or nursing a small child during most of her adult life.[3]

Despite the male's advantage in physical strength, females are clearly the healthier sex. Males are subject to a variety of sex-linked genetic defects, including hemophilia and color blindness. They are also more susceptible to some diseases, and they mature more slowly than females. Although more male infants are born, their rate of death is significantly higher. Females have longer life spans in all modern societies.[4]

The relationship between sex hormones and behavior is a highly controversial issue. Numerous researchers have attempted to show that male hormones are linked

Changes in life style have significant effects on physique. Muscular strength used to be considered "unfeminine," but such attitudes are now changing.

to such things as aggression and dominance, and female hormones to mothering and nurturant behavior. Studies have been made of children exposed to high levels of male hormones in the womb because of a hereditary defect in the function of the adrenal gland (adrenogenital syndrome), and of children exposed to high levels of a female hormone (progesterone) given to mothers because of difficulties in pregnancy. In general, these studies have found girls exposed to male hormones to be more "masculine," and males exposed to female hormones to be more "feminine." However, the interpretation of these results is far from clear. The cause of the lower levels of aggression and physical activity in the "feminized" boys may have been their mothers' problems during pregnancy and not the drug prescribed to deal with those problems. Similarly, the "masculinized" behavior of girls with adrenogenital syndrome may have been the result of the regular doses of cortisone (a drug that can cause hyperactive behavior in adults) prescribed by their physicians, or the expectation of parents and friends that they will be more masculine than other girls (at birth their genital organs may appear to be those of a male).[5]

Other researchers have sought to demonstrate a correlation between high levels of the male hormone testosterone and aggressive behavior in adult men. But such studies have produced mixed results. Some have shown a significant correlation between high levels of testosterone and aggression and hostility, but most have not. But even if a correlation between the two were clearly established, that would still not prove that the hormone causes aggression. Numerous studies have indicated that testosterone levels are strongly affected by an individual's environment and emotional state. For example, researchers have found that men's testosterone levels go up after winning a tennis match and down after losing one. Moreover, the practice of castrating prisoners or giving them drugs that neutralize male hormones have proven to have little effect in preventing violence.[6]

If gender roles are determined solely by biology, it is logical to assume that they should be the same in all cultures. Most researchers agree that some degree of male dominance is a characteristic of all known societies.[7] But anthropological studies have shown that there are still enormous differences in the gender roles of different cultures, and historians have found that gender roles change within the same culture over time. For example, in many hunting and gathering societies, both males and females are peaceful and cooperative, and in other societies, such as the Mundugumor of New Guinea, both males and females are highly aggressive and competitive.[8] Further evidence against the biological determination of gender comes from the study of people who have been raised as members of the opposite sex. This usually occurs because of a physical abnormality of the genitals, but it occasionally happens for other reasons as well. The general conclusion from this research is that a woman raised as a man will act like a man, and that a man raised as a woman will act like a woman.[9] In other words, people act the way they are taught to act; their behavior is not predetermined by a biological program.

Two conclusions seem justified from the evidence. First, gender roles themselves are social creations. The gender roles we learn are determined by society, not biology. Second, the gender roles that society creates are nonetheless strongly influenced by biological considerations. Because men tend to be stronger and larger than women and do not bear and nurse children, it is not surprising that they are assigned more activities that involve strength and travel, or that women are more concerned with childbearing and the responsibilities of the home. The typical pattern of male dominance can be seen as a result of the greater physical strength of the male. The typical "family-oriented" female pattern can be seen as a consequence of childbearing and breast feeding. But as we will see in the next section, the influence of these biological considerations has been greatly diminished in modern industrial societies.

The Historical Development of Gender Roles   Throughout human history, the roles that women and men played have been shaped by the demands of their environment and their economic system. In the earliest societies, people lived in nomadic bands and got their food by gathering edible plants and hunting animals. Judging by the hunting and gathering societies that still survive today, it appears that these early human cultures were highly egalitarian, with few fixed distinctions of status or wealth. Leaders would emerge in response to specific problems and then be absorbed back into the groups when the problems were solved. The economic contribution of men, who did most of the hunting, and women, who focused more on gathering and child care, were both essential to the survival of the group. Although some anthropologists feel that men's monopoly on the hunting of large animals gave them a source of prestige not available to women,[10] others hold that women provided other services of equal

There are wide variations in sex roles among the various cultures of the world. Hunting-and-gathering societies, such as the one pictured here, generally have egalitarian relationships between the sexes.

social value to the meat from the hunt.[11] Despite such disputes, anthropologists generally agree that the relationships between the sexes, like other relationships in hunting and gathering societies, tend to be egalitarian.

A major change in human society occurred with the discovery that plants could be grown specifically for human use. In the earliest farming societies, women and men often shared the work of cultivating the fields, while women did most of the child rearing and men fought the wars (hunters and gatherers generally do not engage in warfare). But as agricultural technology was improved by complex irrigation systems and the use of the plow, men's responsibility for agricultural labor increased, and the status of women generally declined. The growth of the state further strengthened male dominance as men came to monopolize government and religious bureaucracies.[12]

The industrial revolution once again brought profound changes in human society and in the relationship between the genders. As noted in Chapter 5, the extended family broke down and the nuclear family became the norm. Economic changes that made children a financial burden instead of an asset led to fewer births and a smaller number of children. Industrialization reduced the importance of physical labor, and women joined the work force in increasing numbers.

This transformation of the family and the economic system had a significant impact on gender roles. Because technological and social development sharply reduces the importance of the biological differences between the sexes, their roles change as societies industrialize. The male's greater size and strength means much less in an age of machines and automation. The qualities necessary for economic success are now related more closely to personality and intelligence than to physique and are possessed equally by women and men. At the same time, birth control, smaller families, bottle feeding for babies, and the great increases in life span mean that child rearing no longer takes up most of a woman's adult life. But though there have been significant improvements in the status of women in industrial societies, cultural change still lags behind technological change. The ideal of equality between men and women has gained increasing acceptance in the industrialized countries, but the realities of women's lives are still often those of subordination and oppression.

GENDER SOCIALIZATION

Socialization is the process by which we learn the essentials of life in our culture. Customs, behavior, mores, values, how to speak, even how to think—all these are learned in the course of socialization. **Gender socialization** is part of this process. It is the way we learn the behavior and attitudes that are expected of the members of our sex. **Sexual stereotyping** starts almost from the moment of birth, when boys are wrapped in blue blankets and girls in pink ones. Girls' and boys' bedrooms are often decorated differently and contain different kinds of toys. Researchers have found that boys are given a wider variety of toys than girls, and that the boys' toys are more likely to encourage activities outside the home.[13] But the most important differences are learned as children begin to master a language. For one thing, most languages require the speaker to make frequent distinctions between the sexes. The use of the words *he* and *his* or *she* and *hers* continually draws the child's attention to the importance of gender differences. In addition, the structure of every language conveys social assumptions about the nature of the differences between the sexes. The child quickly learns that male is given first-class status, while the female takes second place. In English, for example, male pronouns and adjectives are used to describe people whose gender is unknown ("No person shall be compelled in any criminal case to be a witness against himself"). When one is referring to the entire human race, the term *man* or *mankind* is often used. The male is primary in our language, the female a vaguely defined "other."[14]

The older children become, the greater the differences in the family's expectations for boys and girls. Because the male role is more narrowly defined, young boys come under some particularly intense pressures. They are continually told not to be "sissies" and not to "act like a girl." A boy who playfully puts on a dress and lipstick is likely to receive a hostile and even panicky reprimand from his parents. The root of many of these attitudes is the deep-seated homophobia (fear of homosexuality) in Western culture. Some argue that the training boys receive to repress their feelings of love for other males eventually leads to a repression of all sorts of emotional expression, and there is little doubt that most boys learn to reject and even fear the feminine at an early age.[15] But with the coming of adolescence, it is the girls who find their lives increasingly restricted by the demands of their gender role. While the boys are allowed and even encouraged to "sow some wild oats," girls are usually denied such freedom. Not only are they far more closely watched, but they quickly learn that appearing too assertive will make it more difficult to form the marital relationship that traditional standards hold to be so critical to the rest of their lives.

From their earliest years, girls are taught the vital importance of personal relationships, and they are encouraged to develop the traits that promote them: empathy, expressiveness, and sensitivity to others. Boys, on the other hand, are urged to be self-reliant, assertive, and achievement-oriented. The results of this differential socialization are reflected in the relationships that girls and boys create. Girls tend to have fewer, more intense friendships, whereas boys form larger and therefore less intimate groups.[16]

Boys generally have more trouble adjusting to school than do girls. Because boys mature more slowly, they are often less able to live up to the expectations of the school than girls of the same age. Since boys are given much more encouragement to be independent and assertive, they also tend to find the docile, cooperative behavior expected of schoolchildren far more frustrating than girls. Boys are therefore more likely to act up and get into trouble.[17] Perhaps for this reason, studies of teacher-student interaction have found that boys get more attention, both positive and negative, than girls. As Myra Sadker and her associates put it: "Boys are the central figures . . . and girls are relegated to second-class participation."[18]

Research shows that teachers' expectations have a powerful influence on the way students perform in the classroom (see Chapter 4). This creates a serious problem for girls, because most teachers accept the sexual stereotypes so common in our society. Teachers expect a good male student to be active, adventurous, and inventive, whereas good female students are expected to be calm, conscientious, and sensitive.[19] These expectations also involve more specific abilities. For example, John Ernest found that 41 percent of the teachers he interviewed believed that boys were

Gender role socialization begins almost from the moment of birth. As children grow older, boys are encouraged to develop "masculine" attributes while girls are taught "feminine" qualities. By the time most people reach adulthood, gender role socialization has produced significant differences between men and women.

better than girls at math, and none felt it was the other way around.[20] Moreover, Alison Kelly found that most teachers actually believed that those differences were genetic.[21] Teachers who believe that girls are genetically inferior at math are bound to have lower expectations for them and convey that message to their students. Thus, such expectations become a self-fulfilling prophecy.

The mass media also have a profound effect on the definition of personal gender roles. A variety of research studies show that television, motion pictures, radio, books, and magazines all tend to reinforce traditional gender role stereotypes. Children's television programs, which are particularly important in the early socialization process, consistently depict men and women in stereotyped ways. Male characters are shown in such active and prestigious occupations as physician, lawyer, and police officer, while women are more likely to be relegated to secondary roles such as mother, secretary, and helper. Commercials also reflect the same biases. J. H. Feldstein and S. Feldstein found that boys are overrepresented in advertisements for every type of toy except dolls, and that the girls who are shown are far more likely to be given only a passive role.[22] Even children's cartoons are stereotyped. One study found that male cartoon characters outnumbered female characters by three to one.[23] But beyond simply showing more males, the cartoons depict males as being more powerful and having a greater impact on their environment than females do.[24]

Of course, sexist stereotypes are not limited to children's television. The advertising aimed at adult audiences reveals the same bias. Women are used to attract attention to a man's sales pitch—perhaps wearing a bikini while sipping a new drink, wearing a silk gown while slithering into a sports car, or staring seductively at a man who uses the right brand of shaving cream. The prime concern of the "good housewife" is the whiteness of her wash and whether she can see her face reflected in her dinner plates. Research on the contents of popular books, movies, and magazines points to much the same conclusion: women are consistently portrayed as sex objects, passive bystanders, and willing assistants, whereas men are more often active, aggressive, and dominant.[25]

GENDER INEQUALITY

In Western society the traditional roles of females and males are not only substantially *different* but also *unequal*. As we have seen, the male is given the dominant position. In a sense he is the star actor, whereas the female often plays only a supporting role. The male is expected to have superior strength, greater stamina, higher intelligence, and better organizing ability. Psychologically, the male is trained to play the role of decision maker, whereas the female is encouraged to be submissive and obedient. This same gender inequality is reflected in our basic institutions. In education, employment, and political power, women clearly are treated as inferiors. They are victims of **sexism** (sexual stereotyping, prejudice, and discrimination) in much the same way that blacks are victims of racism.

Education   In the past, women faced open discrimination in almost every aspect of our educational system. Far more boys than girls were enrolled in primary and secondary schools, and most of the best colleges did not admit women at all. Changing cultural expectations and new antidiscrimination laws broke down most of these barriers, and great progress has been made. Today, more females than males graduate from high school and from college.

Yet men still maintain some important educational advantages. For one thing, men receive almost two out of three professional degrees and PhD's.[26] There are also important differences in the majors women and men pursue. More females are in the liberal arts and humanities, while more men major in fields, such as science, mathematics, and engineering, that are most likely to lead directly to high-paying careers. Although the reasons for these differences are not entirely clear, several factors appear to be important. It seems that traditional gender role stereotypes no longer stop females from pursuing an education, but women are discouraged from going into academic areas that are overwhelmingly dominated by males. For example, recent studies show that the lack of female role models among faculty members in mathematics, science, and engineering subtly conveys the message to young women that those fields are not for them.[27] Women's preference for a more general liberal education may also reflect the fact that women expect to carry more child-rearing responsibilities than their male counterparts. As a result, they may shy away from majors leading to demanding careers that would interfere with those responsibilities.

Employment Women's role in the work force has undergone a remarkable change. Fifty years ago, fewer than a quarter of all adult women in the United States worked outside the home. Today, that figure has more than doubled, and the number of working women continues to increase.[28] In the next decade, six of every ten new workers in the United States are expected to be women.[29] A similar trend is evident in Canada, where 55 percent of all women now work, and both North American countries are behind such European nations as Denmark, Finland, and Sweden.[30]

Although the gap between men's and women's pay has narrowed in recent years, it continues to be a large one. In 1975 a woman working full time for the entire year earned about 59.5 percent as much as a man working full time. In 1991, that figure was 72 percent.[31] Unfortunately, this change was caused more by a decline in men's earnings than by an increase in women's pay. Moreover, women's wages are still far below those of their male counterparts (see Figure 10.1). A woman with a college degree earns only a little more than a male high school dropout, whereas a male college graduate earns half again as much.[32]

Many women receive lower paychecks than men because they enter lower-paying occupations and hold lower-ranking jobs within their occupation. Yet there are substantial differences in pay even between men and women who do the same type of work. A recent *Business Week* survey found that the starting salaries of male graduates of the best MBA programs in the United States are 12 percent higher than the starting salaries of female graduates.[33] Even when workers break out of the traditional occu-

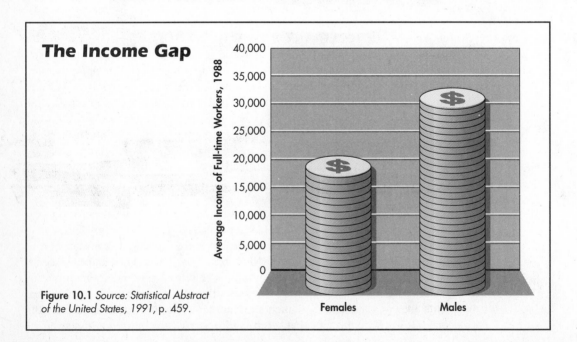

Figure 10.1 *Source: Statistical Abstract of the United States, 1991,* p. 459.

D E B A T E

Should Federal Legislation Be Enacted to Require That Women Be Given Comparable Pay for Comparable Work?

The law now prohibits employers from paying a woman with the same qualifications less than a man who does the same work. Many advocates of women's rights would like to see the law expanded to guarantee that the jobs in which most of the workers are women are paid at roughly the same rate as comparable jobs in which most of the workers are men.

YES Virtually everyone agrees that women deserve equal pay for equal work. Despite the inadequacies in the enforcement process, our antidiscrimination laws have done a great deal to promote the ideals of social justice. But women are now confronting another major economic barrier that is not covered by existing legislation. Study after study has shown that job categories dominated by women receive substantially lower pay than less demanding, lower-skilled jobs performed primarily by men. For example, skilled nurses are commonly paid less than the grounds keepers who trim the hospital trees, and executive secretaries on whose skills an entire firm's future may rest are paid less than the plumbers who unclog the drains. This double pay scale demeans women and violates the most fundamental principles on which our society claims to be based. Justice demands that it be ended once and for all.

The only real issue is how to eliminate such discrimination. Some people say that women should simply change to traditional male jobs that offer higher pay and better chances for advancement. But such claims are so unrealistic they can hardly be taken seriously. How are the millions of secretaries, nurses, and saleswomen suddenly going to develop new skills, and where could they all possibly find jobs if they did? Other critics say that legislation requiring comparable pay would only create another cumbersome bureaucracy, one that would raise

NO There is now strong social support for women's demands for equal pay. Both private and government employers are making vigorous efforts to implement this new policy. But the demand that the government somehow analyze every job in the country, decide which ones are comparable, and then require that their pay be equalized is, in the words of former President Ronald Reagan, "a cockamamie idea."

The most obvious drawback of the proposal for comparable worth legislation is that such a law would be impossible to enforce. How can anyone determine if a welder's job and a respiratory therapist's job have comparable worth? The only efficient way to make such decisions is through the operation of the free market. If one job is overpaid, more people will be attracted to it and wages will decline. If another job is underpaid, employers will not be able to hire the people they need and wages will improve. The intrusion of government into this system would create a bureaucratic nightmare. You can be sure that politically sensitive government employees would never order anyone's salary cut, so the final result of such legislation would be big pay hikes for many workers and a huge jump in inflation that would seriously hurt our already precarious position in world markets. Such legislation would require that the government set salaries without regard to market conditions. How would we make adjustments between the costs of business and make us less competitive in world markets.

The same argument could also have been used against the abolition of slavery. Legislation requiring equal pay for equal work did not harm our international competitiveness, and neither will legislation requiring comparable pay for comparable work. The enforcement of such legislation would certainly require some bureaucracy, but it need not be cumbersome or inefficient unless its opponents try to make it that way. When all is said and done, there is no other way to give women an equal chance in our society. We must enact comparable pay legislation, now!

the kinds of work people desire and the needs of the economy? Hundreds of thousands of people would scramble to get the overpaid jobs, while the underpaid ones would go begging. The net result would be economic chaos that would benefit neither men nor women. Comparable pay for comparable worth is another of those ideas that sounds good in theory but would be a disaster in practice.

---

pational stereotypes, women still come up short. Although 94 percent of all registered nurses are female, male nurses earn about 10 percent more than their female co-workers. But women who cross the gender barrier to join the building trades earn about 25 percent *less* than male construction workers.[34]

Employers traditionally justified this inequality by claiming that men need higher pay because they must support their families and that women just work for "extra" money. Few employers openly use such rationalizations anymore, but they nonetheless persist in paying men higher wages. Some economists explain this income gap by pointing out that the average male worker has more years of experience than his female counterpart. Others argue that women are more likely to put the demands of their family ahead of their job. A *Time* magazine poll, for example, found that a happy marriage was the single most important goal for most young women, while young men rated career success as their number-one objective.[35] Although such factors are significant, sexism and discrimination are still of central importance as causes of the income gap. Employers pay women less for the same work because they can get away with it: they know that the prevailing wages are lower for women, and that their female workers probably cannot get another job at "men's wages."[36]

Many occupations are clearly "sex-typed": that is, they are considered either men's jobs or women's jobs. Almost two-thirds of all university professors are men, as are 87 percent of all police officers and 92 percent of all engineers. In contrast, 73 percent of all primary and secondary teachers, 87 percent of all librarians, and 99 percent of all secretaries are women.[37] "Women's jobs" almost always have lower pay and lower status than comparable "male" positions (see Figure 10.2). The nurse (usually female) is subordinate to the doctor (usually male), just as the secretary (usually female) is subordinate to the executive (usually male). Jobs that are relatively autonomous are usually typed as male, as in the case of truck drivers or traveling sales personnel.

"Women's jobs" also offer less chance for advancement. The secretary does not become a top executive, nor the nurse a doctor. Although there are now far more

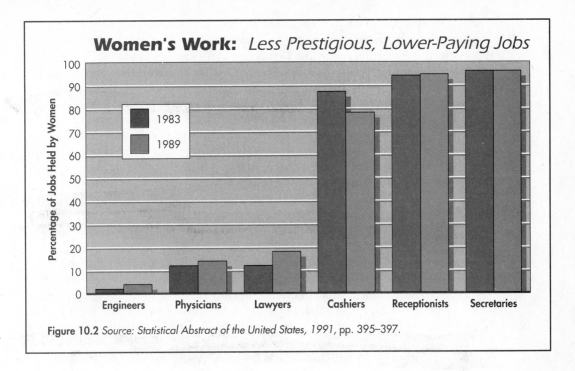

Women's Work: *Less Prestigious, Lower-Paying Jobs*

Figure 10.2 *Source: Statistical Abstract of the United States, 1991, pp. 395–397.*

women in middle management, they still are more likely to be in dead-end positions (such as administering affirmative-action programs or supervising the hiring process) than in the production and financial posts that lead to the top corporate jobs. After years of progress at other levels, women still hold only 3 percent of top corporate positions in the United States.[38] And even governments follow this pattern of discrimination. A typical example is the Canadian federal government, where women hold only 12 percent of the senior civil service positions.[39] Even successful female executives often complain about an invisible "glass ceiling" that seems to lock them out of the key positions of power. One study based on interviews with 100 male and female executives from three major U.S. corporations concluded that there was a clear double standard in promotions, and that women had to perform significantly better than their male counterparts in order to get ahead.[40]

There are, nonetheless, some hopeful signs. As Francine D. Blau and Marianne A. Ferber point out, there has been a slow but steady decrease in occupational segregation since the 1960s, and many women have managed to breach the walls that kept them out of better-paying "men's jobs."[41] In 1960 only about 6.5 percent of U.S. physicians were women; today that number is nearly 18 percent. Women have made even greater strides in the legal profession: in 1960, fewer than 1 out of 20 lawyers and judges was a woman, but today the ratio is more than 1 in 5.[42]

Political Power   Politics has been considered a man's business in almost all societies throughout the world. Women were not even allowed to vote in most democracies until this century. The few women who have gained power have often had the benefit of family connections to overcome objections to their sex. India's Indira Gandhi, Corazon Aquino in the Philippines, and the hereditary European monarchs such as Queen Elizabeth II in England are good examples. Neither the United States nor Canada has ever had a female head of state.

In 1990, only 2 percent of the members of the U.S. Senate, 6.4 percent of the House, and 6 percent of the state governors were women.[43] No woman has ever held a key position of power in Congress, such as majority leader or Speaker of the House, and women are still locked out of the inner circles of power in the White House—including, of course, the presidency itself. In the judicial branch, only one woman in the history of the United States has ever been a Supreme Court justice. Moreover, the story is much the same in other democratic nations. Women have the greatest representation in the Scandinavian countries and the lowest in Canada, the United States, and Japan, but they are greatly underrepresented in the legislative bodies of all the industrialized countries.[44]

Nonetheless, women have enormous political potential. Most of the volunteer workers essential to political campaigns are women. Even more significant is the fact that women outnumber men and could easily outvote them. Until recently, women voted much as their husbands did. But in the last decade a significant "gender gap" between the voting patterns of men and women has developed. Polls show that women look more favorably on welfare programs and environmental protection and are more likely to oppose military spending and an aggressive foreign policy. In the last three presidential elections, substantially more women than men voted for the Democratic candidate.[45] So far, the gender gap has not been a decisive factor in U.S. politics, but the potential is certainly there.

Social Life   Sexism in education, employment, and politics is obvious to anyone who cares to look. But women and girls are also victims of more subtle forms of discrimination. They are told in many subtle ways that they are second-class citizens. They are seen as emotional, unstable, and unable to direct their own lives. Women are taught from childhood that beauty and sex appeal are the keys to happiness. Success comes not from their own efforts but from the ability to appeal to the right man. Women are more likely to be seen as wives and mothers of important people than as significant individuals in their own right.

Women are routinely expected to repress their desires and ambitions in ways that are seldom demanded of men. Studies of dual-career families (in which both husband and wife work) reveal that it is usually the wife who must sacrifice her career if it interferes with that of her spouse. The working woman is also expected to carry most of the homemaking and child-rearing responsibilities in addition to her job (see Chapter 5).

Women are often expected to repress their sexuality in the same way that they are expected to repress their career ambitions. During the Victorian era women's sexuality was almost entirely denied. The "good" woman did not enjoy sex; she put up with it for her husband's sake. Recent research shows that although the **double standard** for sexual behavior has weakened in recent years, it is still very much with us. Young men are expected to "sow their wild oats," but the "slut" is still condemned. And those who berate an unfaithful wife often condone a husband's infidelities with a wink (see Chapter 11).

The growing entry of women into the work force has focused attention on another kind of problem—**sexual harassment**. Since 1975, a flood of complaints has come in from women who were the victims of unwanted sexual pressures at work.[46] In California, for example, charges of sexual harassment now make up 20 percent of all complaints to the state's Department of Fair Employment and Housing. A recent survey of 13,000 federal employees found that 42 percent of the females reported experiencing some kind of sexual harassment on the job.[47] Sexual harassment has also become a major issue on campus, where a growing number of students who have been the victims of sexual advances are recognizing their right to stand up and protest.[48]

Although definitions of sexual harassment vary, it includes everything from unwanted sexual comments and gestures to direct physical assaults. There are two generally recognized types of sexual harassment. The first, which lawyers term *quid pro quo* harassment, includes sexual comments and advances aimed directly at a particular individual. This kind of harassment involves an implicit or explicit threat,

The fact that Judge Clarence Thomas was confirmed to a seat on the U.S. Supreme Court, despite dramatic testimony from Anita Hill charging him with a long-term pattern of sexual harassment, spurred a wave of public indignation and a national debate about this serious problem.

such as loss of a job, or a reward, such as a better grade, if the victim goes along. Obviously, a woman whose boss makes sexual advances is in a very difficult position. She must often choose between a physical relationship she doesn't want and a job she can't afford to lose. The second type of sexual harassment is known as "hostile environment" harassment. This offense involves a workplace in which such things as unwelcome sexual comments, gestures, and explicit photographs create an offensive or intimidating environment for female employees. This kind of harassment may be unintentional, or it may be part of an explicit effort by male employees to drive females out of jobs that they consider to be men's work.

Women are not alone in suffering from the stereotyping of traditional gender roles, however. Although the male role often has higher status, it is also more narrow and restrictive, and many men find the demand to repress natural "feminine" behavior an extremely heavy burden. And while women frequently complain about being only sex objects in the eyes of men, an increasing number of men are complaining that they are only "success objects" for women. Seventy-seven percent of the young women, but only a quarter of the young men, polled by *Time* magazine said that a well-paying job was an essential requirement for a spouse.[49] Obviously, 77 percent of all men will not have well-paying jobs, and, in fact, the income of young men has been declining faster than that of any other group in our society (see Chapter 2). There is also a rising rate of suicide among men, who are now about four times more likely to take their own life than women are.[50] Another common complaint among men is that although they are being encouraged to take a greater role in child rearing, the deck is still stacked against them when it comes to child custody after a divorce. The average divorced man in the United States is able to spend only two days a month with his children.[51] Finally, there is an increasing tendency in the media to reinforce negative stereotypes about men. A recent study of 1,000 television commercials in which there was a negative portrayal of one side of a male-female interaction found that the male was cast as the "bad guy" in every single case.[52]

RESPONDING TO PROBLEMS OF GENDER INEQUALITY

Political Activism The inequality between women and men has been the subject of intense debate in the last two decades. But to understand the current controversy over how to respond to this problem, it is necessary to understand the history of the women's movement. In North America, its origins are usually trained to the nineteenth century and the struggle to free the slaves. Many idealistic women who were involved in the abolitionist movement came to realize that they too were part of an oppressed group. These early feminists made wide-ranging demands for sexual equality, but the movement they created eventually came to focus on a single issue: women's right to vote. After years of struggle, these "suffragettes" built themselves into a powerful political force and won their battle for the right to vote. But after that success, the movement began to fade. It was not until the 1960s, when the civil rights movement was once again calling attention to the racial injustices of North American society, that the feminist movement was reborn.

The feminist movement has a long history in North America, dating back to the struggle for women's suffrage. Today's feminists are seeking complete equality between the sexes.

The modern feminist movement has scored some remarkable successes. Women's liberation and sexual equality are now widely discussed, and more and more women are entering occupations that were formerly closed to them. Through effective court and legislative action, feminists have successfully attacked employment and promotion practices that discriminate against women. Government-sponsored affirmative-action programs now require employers to hire and promote more women and members of minority groups. Feminists have even made some inroads on the sexual biases built into the English language. Women are increasingly identifying themselves as *Ms.* rather than *Miss* or *Mrs.*, and new sexually neutral words such as *chairperson* and *humankind* are replacing the traditional masculine terms. But as we have seen in this chapter, we are still a very long way from full equality.

As in other social movements, all feminists do not agree on the best ways to win their objectives. The liberal feminists are the largest group in the movement, and their approach is the predominant one in the National Organization for Women (NOW). Drawing on the values of freedom and individual liberty central to the liberal tradition, these feminists call for a vigorous government attack on all forms of prejudice and discrimination. The liberal feminists nonetheless have their critics both inside and outside the movement. To the left are the socialist feminists, who argue that the exploitation of women arises from the capitalist system and that only fundamental changes in our economic institutions can liberate women. Radical feminists focus more on the social arena, calling for a "women-centered" culture to replace the current pattern of **patriarchal** (male-dominated) **society**. At the same time, all feminists are criticized by those who feel that they are undermining the family and traditional social values.[53]

Although still much smaller and weaker, there is also a growing "men's movement" that has its own critique of today's gender problems. In general, the men's movement is sympathetic to the feminist perspective and its call to redefine our gender relations. Advocates of the men's movement argue that current gender roles are just as harmful to men as they are to women, but in different ways. They particularly object to the ideal of masculinity that holds that "real" men must always be strong, self-controlled, and successful. The effort to live up to this impossible ideal (or at least to appear to live up to it) leaves many men anxiety-ridden and isolated. However, the men's movement does voice one major criticism of the feminists—what they see as their tendency toward "man bashing." That is, some supporters of the men's movement feel that feminists perpetuate negative stereotypes of men and blame men for problems that are actually created by historical forces beyond the control of any person or group.

Social Change   Two general types of responses are commonly proposed to deal with the problems of gender inequality. One approach aims to eliminate sexual discrimination, the other to restructure sex roles. Proposals for eliminating obvious discrimination often win wide support. Few people openly approve of such practices as paying women less money than men for the same work, refusing to grant them financial credit, or denying them jobs and promotions simply because they are women. The values of democratic society make it very hard to justify such practices, and many of the feminists' most important victories have been against this kind of discrimination.

As the most obvious forms of sexism are eliminated, however, the movement for social change must challenge more entrenched institutional structures, and further progress becomes increasingly difficult. For example, the law has long required employers to pay men and women the same pay for the same work, yet it remains perfectly legal to pay secretaries, nurses, and others in "women's jobs" far less than comparable jobs that are filled mainly by men. Proposals to require comparable pay for comparable work (see this chapter's debate) have run into fierce opposition because they threaten the interests of businesses that benefit from the low cost of women's labor. There are, nonetheless, several useful proposals that have a wide base of support. Stronger enforcement of the laws banning sexual harassment and tougher sentences for rapists and other sex offenders are two of those. Another popular idea is the creation of government-supported day-care centers to help relieve some of the heavy burdens on working mothers (see Chapter 5).

Proposals for restructuring sex roles have run into even greater opposition. Attitudes and expectations about sex roles are formed early in life, and many people feel threatened when such basic assumptions are challenged. The more vicious attacks on feminism can be seen as a response to these threats. But despite the fear and hostility produced by rapid change, sex roles in industrial societies are undergoing a revolutionary transformation. While it is impossible to say what roles will finally develop, there is no reason to suppose that sexual equality would mean that men and women would become socially identical. Some of the differences in behavior between men and women already have diminished but the development of a "unisex" remains a prospect for the distant future, if at all. What does seem possible, perhaps even likely, is a further weakening of the rigid gender role expectations of the past. Thus, women and men would be freer to act in ways that suit them as individuals, instead of being compelled to follow along in the life course expected of their gender.

SOCIOLOGICAL PERSPECTIVES ON PROBLEMS OF GENDER

Every society assigns different roles to women and to men. In the past, these social arrangements were usually accepted as the will of God or an inevitable result of biological differences. But such justifications are no longer as convincing as they once were, and there is a significant gap between the ideal of equality and the reality of male domination over females. The major sociological theories provide us with different perspectives on why this gap exists and what should be done about it.

The Functionalist Perspective   Functionalists say that the problems of gender roles stem directly from the historical changes discussed earlier in this chapter. Traditionally, gender roles were based on biological differences between the sexes: women were concerned primarily with child rearing and men with providing economic support. But changes brought on by the industrial revolution threw this arrangement out of balance. The decline in infant mortality and the spread of effective methods of birth control made it possible to depart from traditional roles. It was no longer necessary for women to devote most of their adult lives to the raising of small children, and automation wiped out the importance of the male's greater strength in most types of work. However, attitudes and expectations about the proper role of women have changed much more slowly than social and economic conditions. This cultural lag is therefore the principal source of today's problems.

To resolve these problems, most functionalists suggest that expectations be made to conform more closely to actual conditions. Some advocate a return to the stable past, believing that too great a shift toward sexual equality is dysfunctional. They note that the traditional division of labor between men and women was highly efficient, enabling society to train people for specialized roles that meshed together in stable families. Other functionalists, however, advocate a redefinition of sex roles to bring them into line with changed economic, political, and social conditions. Although these functionalists do not agree on the exact form the proposed changes should take, they do agree on the need for a shift toward full sexual equality and a reconstruction of women's roles to encourage economic competition and achievement. Along with this change, basic institutions would also have to be modified to eliminate sexual discrimination. The current family system, for example, would have to undergo extensive changes to accommodate new roles for both men and women.

The Conflict Perspective   Prejudice and discrimination against women come as no surprise to conflict theorists, since they see exploitation and oppression as universal human problems. Conflict theorists say that men first used their greater size and strength to force women into a subordinate position. Then, like any other dominant group, they created institutions that serve to perpetuate their power and authority. Men gain economic advantages by paying women low wages and excluding them from positions of economic control and political power. Men also benefit from women's subordinate role in the family. The "good" woman, we are told, blindly serves her husband and obeys his will like a domestic servant. The traditional wedding vows reflect the strong social support for the subordination of women. Only the bride must pledge to love, honor, and *obey* her spouse. Even the structure of our language serves to reinforce the belief in male dominance. Conflict theorists hold that the position of women in most societies today is similar to that of a subordinate ethnic minority, such as African Americans in the United States.

There are many indications, however, that the traditional male advantages are declining in importance. The superior strength of the male means little in a highly mechanized society. The real barriers to women's liberation are now the institutions and attitudes that were established in the days of unquestioned male dominance. An increasing number of women are coming to realize this fact, and they are organizing themselves to break these barriers. According to the conflict perspective, the feminist movement is thus both a reflection and a cause of the growing strength of women in industrial societies. Conflict theorists advise women to continue publicizing their grievances, bring all women and sympathetic men together in a unified movement, and solicit the support of other dissatisfied social groups as well. For the conflict theorist, social action is the road to social change and a just society.

Social Psychological Perspectives   Social psychologists see gender roles, and the sense of identity we derive from them, as critical components of human personality. Most social psychologists are convinced that sexual identity develops in the early years of childhood in interaction with parents, peers, teachers, and the mass media. Once formed, these ideas and concepts are quite durable. Social psychologists note that prejudice and discrimination against women arise from differences in socialization. Females are conditioned to be passive and dependent and are therefore less dominant than males, who are trained to be more aggressive and independent. Thus, both sexes are often taught to see females as inferiors.

Biosocial theorists, however, are yet to be convinced that gender role differences are simply a product of socialization. They argue that the personality and social differences between men and women are biological in origin. Clearly, there are differences in physical and biochemical makeup between men and women that cannot be ignored, but it is not clear how important they are in contemporary society. If gender roles are determined mainly by biology, there may be little that can be done to change them or to reduce sexual inequality.

Behaviorists, personality theorists, and symbolic interactionists are more optimistic. They are convinced that gender roles and the inequality they promote can be changed if the content of the socialization process is altered. These theorists argue that girls should be encouraged to be more aggressive and that boys be urged to accept the passive, dependent side of their nature. Because parents have been socialized into traditional gender roles, persuading them to teach their children to behave differently is extremely difficult. Schools, which are an increasingly important influence in socialization, can be changed more easily. Feminists are already pressing to remove sexual stereotypes from schoolbooks and lectures and to promote higher educational and occupational aspirations for talented girls. The media, particularly radio, television, and film, could also promote these changes. Showing women as powerful, assertive figures and allowing men who do not live up to the code of male dominance to be heroes equal to the "he-men" idealized in so many adventure films would do much to foster equality between men and women.

Most social psychologists also hold that greater tolerance of human differences is also needed. No matter what characteristics a culture attributes to the ideal woman or the ideal man, many people of both genders will not live up to those standards. The nonconformist must often pay an enormous personal price for being a little different. There is no reason, aside from prejudice and bigotry, that society cannot recognize the range of human diversity as a normal and healthy phenomenon.

SUMMARY

Gender roles (sets of expectations about the proper behavior for each sex) are basic components of individual personalities as well as of the larger social system. The male role has traditionally been centered on work and providing for the family. The male is expected to be more aggressive than the female and to have tighter control over his emotions. The female role has centered on child rearing and the family. Females are expected to be emotionally expressive, dependent, and passive. Gender roles show a wide range of variation among cultures, and in our culture, as in others, the behavior of many men and women does not fit the expected patterns.

Two important conditions seem to have influenced the development of gender roles: biology and culture. The fact that females bear and nurse children has had an obvious influence on the definition of sex roles, as has the fact that males tend to be larger and stronger than females. Despite the importance of biology in the origin of gender roles, the individual's role is determined primarily by culture. Some cultures assign what we consider "feminine" traits to both sexes, while others assign "masculine" traits to both.

In early hunting and gathering societies the relationships between men and women were generally egalitarian. With the coming of agriculture, the power of women declined because their contribution to food production was reduced. But the economic and social conditions accompanying industrialization neutralized many male advantages. Mechanization made physical size and strength less important, and the sharp drop in infant mortality and the spread of birth control reduced women's child-rearing burdens.

Gender socialization is the process by which children learn the behaviors and attitudes expected of their sex. The family plays a critical role in this process. Parents begin treating boys and girls differently almost from the moment of birth. Schools reinforce the traditional gender roles learned at home. Teachers encourage high aspirations in boys and discourage them in girls. Radio, television, and motion pictures also convey sexual stereotypes.

The roles we assign to each sex clearly promote gender inequality. Men are given the dominant position, and a variety of evidence reveals a clear pattern of discrimination against women in education, employment, politics, and social life.

The feminist movement emerged when women organized to protest against discrimination and to work actively for their economic, political, and social rights. Liberal feminists advocate a vigorous attack on all forms of discrimination against women, and laws that guarantee comparable pay for comparable work, reproductive rights, and government-supported child care. Other feminists criticize the liberals for failing to recognize the connection between the discrimination against women and the social institutions that create it. Traditionalists accuse all feminists of undermining essential social values. The small but growing men's movement points out that our current system of stereotyped gender roles has many negative consequences for men as well as for women.

Functionalists see the problems of present-day gender roles as stemming from economic changes that upset the traditional cultural pattern. They advocate a reduction in the gap between expectations and actual conditions. Conflict theorists are convinced that these problems arise from domination and exploitation of the weak by the strong. They advise women to organize and to use political power to gain equality. Most social psychologists are convinced that gender roles and sexual identity are learned in the process of socialization, but biosocial theorists emphasize the biological origins of gender differences. The consensus among most social psychologists is that sexual inequality can be reduced by changing gender roles, and that gender roles will change if the content of the socialization process is changed.

KEY TERMS

double standard A set of norms requiring different behavior for women and men, especially in regard to sexual activity.

gender role A social role assigned on the basic of biological sex.

gender socialization The process by which a person learns the behaviors

and attitudes that are expected of his or her gender.

sexism Stereotyping, prejudice, and discrimination based on gender.

sexual harassment Unwanted sexual comments, gestures, or physical advances, especially in the workplace.

FURTHER READINGS

Laura Kramer, ed., *The Sociology of Gender* (New York: St. Martin's Press, 1991). A useful collection of articles on gender and gender inequality.

Laurel Richardson, *The Dynamics of Sex and Gender: A Sociological Perspective* (New York: Harper & Row, 1988). A general text examining the role of men and women in contemporary society from a sociological perspective.

Josephine Donovan, *Feminist Theory* (New York: Ungar, 1985). A good book for students interested in learning more about feminism.

Sam Keen, *Fire in the Belly: On Being a Man* (New York: Bantam Books, 1991). One of the most thoughtful of the recent books about being male in contemporary society.

Mark Aldrich and Robert Buchele, *The Economics of Comparable Worth* (Cambridge, Mass.: Ballinger, 1986). A thorough examination of the pros and cons of comparable worth legislation.

PART THREE

Conformity
and Deviance

chapter 11

Sexual Behavior

- Was there really a "sexual revolution?"
- How have attitudes toward sexual behavior changed?
- What causes someone to become heterosexual or homosexual?

- Why do so many unmarried teenagers become pregnant?
- Should prostitution and pornography be considered social problems?

Few things seem more personal than our sexual behavior, yet it is shaped by the same social forces as any other human activity. Society defines what is attractive and what is ugly. Our social groups tell us when sex is acceptable, when it is forbidden, and when it is required. Popular culture creates powerful expectations about our sex lives, and those who cannot live up to those expectations are often left feeling frustrated or shameful.

In the past, Western culture held some of the most negative attitudes toward sex found anywhere in the world. The Puritans, who played such an important role in the colonization of North America, condemned all sexual activity outside of marriage and even disapproved of sexual relations between husbands and wives except as a means to have children. Not surprisingly, society's main problem with sexual behavior was how to restrict it within those narrow limits.

Tremendous changes in values and attitudes have taken place since Puritan times. The old consensus about what is right and wrong has broken down, but no new standard has won universal acceptance. What is normal and natural to some people is still sinful to others. The consensus that such things as homosexuality and prostitution are harmful to society and deserve strong punishment has broken down. But many of the old laws remain on the books, and people continue to be harassed, even jailed, for private sexual activities that are perfectly acceptable to large segments of society.

To make matters worse, many businesses take advantage of our sexual interests and fears for a quick profit. Images of bathing beauties and muscular young men are used to sell everything from automobiles to dish soap. Television, books, and movies routinely depict a kind of fantasy sex devoid of real-life consequences while promoting a virtual cult of glamour and sex appeal. Advertisers play on the insecurities these attitudes create, telling us that such products as deodorants, mouthwash, and cosmetics are essential if we are to attract the opposite sex. In such an environment many young people become involved in sexual activities before they are emotionally prepared for them, perhaps ending up with an unwanted pregnancy; and people of all ages may feel inadequate when they are unable to match the impossible sexual ideals promoted by the mass media.

HUMAN SEXUALITY

Although many people believe that the sexual acts that are acceptable in our society are the only natural ones and that other acts are violations of "human nature," anthropological studies have revealed a wide range of sexual customs and behavior in cultures around the world. Indeed, almost every form of sexual behavior is considered normal somewhere under some circumstances. Historically, Western culture has been sexually conservative. Clellan S. Ford and Frank A. Beach found that only 10 of the 190 societies they studied share our traditional disapproval of both premarital and extramarital sex.[1] The Polynesian peoples of the central Pacific, for example, have long been noted for their free sexual attitudes. Before the growth of Christian influence, Tahitians worshiped physical beauty. Young people of both sexes were encouraged to engage in masturbation and premarital intercourse, and both activities were openly discussed and practiced.[2]

Although North Americans are shocked by the thought of sexual activity among children, it is encouraged in some places. In some cultures intercourse is believed to be necessary if preadolescents are to mature sexually. The Trukese of the Caroline Islands build small huts especially for this purpose. Among the Alorese of Indonesia, mothers routinely masturbate their children in order to relax them.[3]

Yet such liberalism is far from universal. The men of Yap Island believe that intercourse causes physical weakness and reduces resistance to disease. At one time Yap attitudes toward sex were so negative that the Yap people almost became extinct. The Manus of New Guinea consider intercourse degrading—a disgusting act that a woman must endure in order to produce children. The neighboring Dani tribe do not have sexual relations until two years after marriage, and refrain from sex for five years following the birth of each child. Closer to home, the Shakers, a Protestant sect founded in New England, banned all sexual activities, acquiring children only by adoption. Rural Ireland is also notable for its repression of sexuality. Men and women are segregated in public places, and there is a strong taboo against the discussion of sexual matters. Women's capacity to experience orgasm is denied by some and considered deviant by others.[4]

The kinds of sexual behavior that are considered deviant also vary widely from culture to culture. The use of force to obtain sexual favors is strictly forbidden in our culture and in most of the rest of the world. But among a tribe living in southwestern Kenya, normal intercourse is a kind of ritualized rape.[5] Women are encouraged to frustrate men with sexual taunts, and the men overcome this resistance with force, often inflicting pain and humiliation in the process. Attitudes toward homosexuality also show enormous variation. Heterosexuality is preferred over homosexuality in most societies, in part because of its essential role in reproduction. Yet there are at least two societies in New Guinea in which homosexuality is more highly valued. The Marind-anim people are so strongly homosexual that they must kidnap children from other tribes to maintain their population.[6] At the opposite extreme are such peoples as the Rwala Bedouin, who consider homosexuality so base that it is punishable by death. Even the **incest taboo** (the prohibition of sexual relations between parents and their children or between the children themselves), which is certainly the most common restriction on sexual behavior, is not universal.

There is clearly nothing innate in human beings that makes certain types of sexual behavior normal and other types abnormal. The distinction between "normal" and "deviant" sex comes from society, not biology. We are all born with a sex drive, but it can be satisfied in a great variety of ways. We learn to channel our sexual energy into one type of behavior and not another in the same way that we learn to satisfy our hunger with socially acceptable foods and not with dog meat or human flesh.

CONTEMPORARY SEXUAL BEHAVIOR

The study of sexual behavior is a difficult and confusing task. Social scientists have repeatedly found that many people do not care to describe their sexual behavior even to the most objective investigators. As a result, it is impossible to say how common various forms of sexual behavior actually are. North American researchers find it hard even to describe public attitudes toward sex because there are such deep conflicts over sexual morality. At the heart of the matter is the conflict between restrictive traditional standards and the growing belief in the value of individual choice and personal freedom. Many religious groups continue to advocate the traditional values, while the media pour out an increasing stream of sexually arousing advertising and entertainment. Because of this confusion and uncertainty, sex researchers have found themselves in the uncomfortable position of influencing as well as describing contemporary sexual standards. Some people evaluate their own sexual behavior by comparing it with the findings of the sex surveys, apparently assuming that unusual sexual behavior may be wrong but that "if everyone else is doing it, it must be all right."

A Historical Sketch After the fall of the Roman Empire, Western society adopted a very restrictive sexual morality. In general, sexual relations have been approved only between a husband and wife, often only for the purpose of reproduction. The origins of this attitude are to be found in the Judeo-Christian religious tradition, particularly the New Testament teachings of Saint Paul and the lectures of early Christian leaders such as Saint Augustine. These leaders held sexual abstinence to be the ideal but allowed that "it is better to marry than to burn." Sex was seen as something evil and degrading, to be avoided as much as possible. Although such standards continued to be supported by religious and secular leaders for centuries, it is doubtful that more than a small percentage of the population adhered to them.

The Puritans of the seventeenth century reemphasized the strict moral code of the early Christians and demanded almost complete repression of sexuality. Puritan immigrants in North America helped establish this rigid code as a dominant force on the new continent. The Victorian era, in the nineteenth century, was also noted for its repression of sexuality. Victorians avoided discussion of anything that could be considered even remotely sexual. Legs became limbs, sweat became perspiration, and underwear became "unmentionables." Masturbation was believed to cause everything from mental disorders to blindness. The double standard was so strong that female sexuality was almost entirely denied. The surgeon general of the United States reflected the prevailing opinions of the time when he said that "nine-tenths of the

19th-Century Social Problems

Young men who have become the victims of solitary vice, that dreadful habit that sweeps annually to an untimely grave thousands of young men of exalted talent and brilliant intellect, can call with confidence. [front-page ad about masturbation]

August 5, 1897

These selections, which appear throughout the text, are from the *Badger State Banner*, a newspaper published in Black River Falls, Wisconsin.

time decent women feel not the slightest pleasure in intercourse.''[7] But the Victorian era is noted for its hypocrisy as well as its sexual repression. Prostitution and pornography flourished, and there appears to have been a wide gap between what people said and what they did.

A Sexual Revolution?   There is no doubt that sexual attitudes and practices have become much more liberal since the time of the Victorians, but such changes are difficult to measure precisely. One notable development is that the media now make far more use of sexual material than ever before. Not only has there been explosive growth in such things as ''X-rated'' videotapes; but more importantly, mainstream magazines, movies, and television programs are now far more explicit sexually. Even our newspapers and billboards are full of sexually oriented advertising.

Methodological problems make it difficult to measure the extent of the actual changes in sexual behavior. Sex surveys such as the pioneering studies conducted by Alfred Kinsey and his associates in the 1940s and 1950s are the best sources of data available, but they still have serious methodological weaknesses.[8] Kinsey interviewed volunteers, including people in social clubs and prisons, and it is doubtful that his subjects were representative of the overall population. More recent research has avoided some of the problems of Kinsey's work but has serious shortcomings of its own. Scientific studies of sexual behavior seldom have strong financial backing, and they therefore tend to use small local samples of high school or college students and neglect the rest of the population. Magazines often rely on responses from whoever happens to answer their published questionnaires, and even broad surveys that use normal sampling techniques are flawed in that an unusually high number of people refuse to respond to their questions. As a result, there are probably important differences between those who respond to sex surveys and those who do not. And because of the sensitive nature of the subject, many respondents are undoubtedly less than honest in their replies. Despite all these methodological drawbacks, conclusions based on these studies are still vastly superior to the unsupported opinions and generalizations voiced by so many people. But it should be kept in mind that the percentages given in this chapter are just rough estimates and may be very wide of their mark.

When Kinsey's report on male sexual behavior was published in 1948, it shocked the nation, and his later study on female behavior had much the same effect. Kinsey concluded that 85 percent of all American men had experienced premarital intercourse, 70 percent had visited a prostitute, and over one-third had participated in at least one homosexual act. Kinsey's data suggest that the first wave of sexual liberation in the United States occurred much earlier than is usually believed, probably in the generation that came of age after World War I. His study found that only 8 percent of white women born before 1900 had had premarital intercourse by age 20, but that among those born between 1910 and 1929, the figure was 22 percent. Later surveys indicate that a second wave of liberation occurred in the late 1960s and early 1970s.[9]

An important part of these changes was the decay of the double standard, discussed in Chapter 10. Traditionally, both sexes were supposed to refrain from ''sinful'' sexual activities, but violating this taboo was considered a greater sin for women than for men. To be a ''loose woman'' or an unfaithful wife was a social disgrace, but young

Kinsey's research indicated that, contrary to popular belief, the first wave of sexual liberation occurred in the generation that came of age in the "roaring twenties."

men were expected to gain sexual experience before marriage, and a husband's carousing was often passed over with a wink. A century ago the "good" woman was not supposed to enjoy sex; she was merely to tolerate it for her husband's sake.

Although the double standard has not disappeared, it has certainly weakened. There has been some increase in the amount of premarital sexual experience reported by males since the 1940s, but the change was much more dramatic for females. Only one-third of all the women in Kinsey's original sample reported having engaged in **premarital intercourse** by age 25. But according to the Centers for Disease Control, in 1970 about 40 percent of 18-year-old females had experienced premarital sex, and by 1988 that figure had risen to about 70 percent.[10] (The Kinsey Institute, founded by the pioneering sex researcher, now estimates that the average American becomes sexually active around age 16 or 17.[11])

One should not conclude, however, that because women are enjoying more of the freedoms formerly reserved for men, the double standard no longer exists. It is still with us. Most surveys show that females are still less likely to engage in premarital and extramarital sex. For example, while the current estimates of the frequency of extramarital affairs by the Kinsey Institute and the National Opinion Research Corporation (NORC) are widely divergent, they both find that extramarital sex is more common among husbands than wives. The Kinsey Institute estimates that 29 percent of wives and 37 percent of husbands have had at least one other partner during their marriage, while the NORC survey puts those figures at 35 percent for wives and 70 percent for husbands.[12]

The surveys indicate that there is more sexual activity within marriage as well as outside it. Particularly striking is the sharp increase in oral-genital sex. The original Kinsey survey found that only 40 percent of the married males surveyed had ever engaged in oral sex with their wives; current surveys put that figure around 90 percent.[13] There is also evidence that married couples have intercourse more often than they did in the past, and that masturbation is more common among both married and single people.[14] However, not all forms of sexual behavior have become more common. There is no evidence that male or female homosexuality has increased,[15] and several studies indicate that, as women have become more sexually active, prostitution has actually declined.[16] And surprisingly, the NORC survey found that more than one in five adults reported having no sex at all in the last year.[17]

The rise in sexual freedom described in these surveys is one result of the sweeping cultural changes of the twentieth century. The weakening of the influence of traditional religious morality has lowered the barriers that once prevented many kinds of sexual activity. There has been a significant erosion of the double standard. As women have gained economic and political power, they have achieved greater equality in sexual matters as well. A very important factor was the development of more effective birth control techniques that reduced the fear that sexual relations would lead to an unwanted pregnancy. Growing emphasis on individual freedom and self-determination in all aspects of our lives has made many people more willing to challenge traditional sexual ideas and customs. The use of erotic materials to entertain and to sell products has also exerted an influence in many subtle ways. Finally, sexuality itself seems to be undergoing a basic redefinition. Although sinful and degrading to Victorians, sexual activity is increasingly seen as a normal part of daily life.

Homosexuality   Of all types of sexual behavior, homosexuality is one of the least understood. Popular stereotypes hold that male homosexuals all put on a flashy display of femininity and that female homosexuals all lift weights and dress like men. In fact, most homosexuals look and act like everyone else. The few who fit the popular stereotype are just more noticeable. Another common myth is that homosexuals and heterosexuals have different personality characteristics. An experiment by Evelyn Hooker, however, showed that even experienced clinical psychologists were unable to identify the sexual orientation of a mixed group of subjects by examining their responses to a battery of psychological tests. Nor were any differences found in personal adjustment.[18] Some people believe that homosexuals endanger children, but there is no evidence to indicate that homosexuals are more likely than others to be child molesters. Finally, many people are not aware that many homosexuals form stable, long-term relationships, just as heterosexuals do.

A major source of confusion about homosexuals is the tendency of many people to see sexual orientation in absolute terms. Most people assume that individuals are sexually attracted either to members of the opposite sex (and thus are heterosexual) or to members of the same sex (and thus are homosexual). In reality, most people have both homosexual and heterosexual urges at one time or another. The differences among **homosexuals**, **bisexuals**, and **heterosexuals** are a matter of degree. Many heterosexuals briefly engage in homosexual activities during their adolescent years, and surveys show that a large majority of those who identify themselves as homosexual have had some sexual relations with members of the opposite sex.[19]

Causes There are many theories about the causes of homosexuality but little conclusive evidence. One popular explanation is that homosexuals are "born that way." The strongest evidence to support the contention that homosexuality is hereditary comes from studies of twins. Several investigations have found that identical (one-egg) twins are more likely to show the same sexual preference than fraternal (two-egg) twins.[20] However, the problem with such studies is that identical twins are more likely to be treated alike by family and friends; thus, their similarities may be the result of environment, not heredity.

Some biological theorists argue that homosexuality is determined by sex hormones. Although no significant differences have been found in the levels of sex hormones in homosexual and heterosexual adults, some researchers claim that there may be differences in receptivity to those hormones or in exposure to them before birth. In a recent study, Simon LeVay conducted autopsies on a small number of men and found some significant differences in brain structure between those who were homosexual and those who were not. But much more research will be needed before we can evaluate the importance of this study. Moreover, all biological theories of homosexuality have difficulty explaining the significant differences in the extent of homosexuality in various cultures and the reasons that some people are homosexual during one period of their life and heterosexual during others.[21]

Classical psychoanalytic theory views homosexuality in males as the result of an excessively close relationship with the mother and a distant and rejecting father. Numerous studies based on interviews with heterosexuals and homosexuals have generally supported this conclusion, although a study by the Kinsey Institute did not. Surveys also show that lesbians report much more fear and hostility toward their fathers than heterosexual women.[22] It may be, however, that some of this parental rejection is the result of the behavior of the children, not its cause. In one of the few long-term studies of the same group of subjects, psychiatrist Richard Green found that a homosexual orientation begins long before adolescence. Three-fourths of the "feminine" boys he studied went on to homosexual lives as adults, while only one of the "masculine" boys became involved in homosexual activity.[23]

Sociologically, homosexuality is explained by examining the conditions in which it is learned. Given the enormous range of sexual behavior in the cultures of the world, it would actually be much harder to explain the absence of homosexuality in diverse societies such as the United States and Canada than to explain its presence. Although a strong social condemnation of homosexuality discourages homosexual tendencies, homosexuality is encouraged in many other ways. For instance, when adolescents first begin to feel strong sexual urges, society forbids them to engage in heterosexual intercourse. Young males and females are not permitted to sleep or shower together, but these activities are acceptable for members of the same sex. The encouragement of specific sex role differences, combined with the pressures of mate selection, makes association with the same sex less painful and embarrassing than association with the opposite sex. Some adolescents can carry on homosexual activities without arousing the suspicion of their parents, when heterosexual activities would be out of the question. Further, the widespread belief that one is either homosexual or heterosexual often causes individuals who engage in exploratory homosexual behavior to define themselves as homosexuals. And once such a self-concept takes hold, it is likely to persist, perhaps for a lifetime.[24]

The Homosexual Community There is considerable disagreement about how common homosexuality actually is. The various surveys of sexual behavior that have been done over the years have reached widely different conclusions. The most commonly accepted estimate puts the number of men who have had extensive homosexual experience at about 10 percent of the total population, with somewhere around 1 to 4 percent of all men being primarily or exclusively homosexual. Almost all the surveys show less homosexuality among women. Most estimates indicate that women are only about half as likely as men to engage in homosexual activities.[25]

Unlike many other minorities, homosexuals can conceal their differences from the public if they choose to do so. There is even a common slang term—the "closet

Only a small percentage of homosexuals make a showy display of the characteristics usually associated with the opposite sex; most homosexuals look and act like everyone else. Demonstrations such as the one shown here are part of the efforts of homosexuals to win greater social acceptance.

queen"—for gay men who disguise their sexual preference and pass as heterosexuals. But such deception places the homosexual under great emotional stress. Discovery and possible blackmail are constant dangers. In the last two decades there has been a growing trend among homosexuals to "come out of the closet" and openly participate in the homosexual community. But "coming out" means more than just publicly admitting one's homosexuality; it also means admitting it to oneself.

From the 1960s homosexuals had been making steady progress against the prejudice directed at them for so many years. However, the epidemic of AIDS among male homosexuals has been a severe blow to the liberation of the homosexual community. Irrational fears that one might catch that fatal disease from casual contact with a homosexual have led to a new wave of hostility toward gays. The National Gay and Lesbian Task Force found 7,031 reported incidents of antihomosexual violence in 1989, and, of those, about 15 percent were AIDS-related in one way or another.[26] And at the same time, gays themselves have to live with the fear that any new sexual contact might be a fatal experience, or the even more frightening thought that they may already have an undetected case of the disease. The AIDS epidemic has produced major changes in sexual behavior among male homosexuals. Many "bath houses," which served as sex clubs, have been closed, and there has been a sharp decline in all sorts of casual sexual contact.

Homosexuality and the Law The Judeo-Christian religious tradition has long condemned homosexuality as a sin, and Western nations have acted accordingly. During the Middle Ages homosexuals were commonly tortured to death. In Britain homosexual activities were punishable by life imprisonment until 1956.[27] But the recent trend has been toward repeal of legal penalties for homosexuality. Britain canceled its most repressive laws in 1965, and most other European nations followed suit. Canada passed a law similar to Britain's in 1969, but some official harassment of homosexuals has persisted.

The trend toward legalization has developed more slowly in the United States. Twenty-five states have legalized homosexual acts between consenting adults, but others continue to threaten homosexuals with penalties as severe as life imprisonment. However, in states where homosexuality remains a crime, the laws are not vigorously enforced. Only a few unlucky or unwise individuals are arrested, prosecuted, or punished. Moreover, enforcement efforts are directed almost exclusively against gay men. Lesbian activities are usually ignored. And even in jurisdictions where criminal penalties have been reduced or abolished, homosexuals still suffer from open legal discrimination. In some places the professions of law, medicine, and teaching are closed to homosexuals, and the U.S. military still refuses to accept homosexuals as recruits.

Like many ethnic minorities, homosexuals have been organizing and demanding an end to the discrimination against them. The American Psychiatric Association was persuaded to drop homosexuality from its list of mental disorders; television stations have been pressured to stop programs that cast homosexuals in an unfavorable light; and a number of cities—including Los Angeles, Minneapolis, and Seattle—have passed legislation protecting homosexuals from various forms of discrimination. However, the movement has had its failures as well. The United States Supreme Court refused to ban prosecution and imprisonment of people for homosexual activities, even if those activities were conducted in private between consenting adults. And the gains of homosexual activists have often stirred savage counterattacks by religious fundamentalists who continue to see all homosexual relations as sinful.

PROBLEMS AND ISSUES

Considering the conflict about sexual morality in the twentieth century, it is hardly surprising that many people do not agree about which sexual behaviors are a social problem and which are not. The issues discussed in this section fall into three general groups. The first are unintended problems that arise as a consequence of sexual activities, such as unwanted pregnancy and sexually transmitted disease. The second group involve the sexual victimization of one person by another, as in child molestation and rape (which will be discussed in Chapter 13). Finally, there are prostitution and pornography, in which everyone involved is usually participating voluntarily. Problems in the first group (unwanted pregnancy and sexually transmitted disease) are generally not considered criminal matters; activities in the second category (child molestation and rape) are almost universally condemned as serious crimes; but there is great variation in the legal response to such things as prostitution and the use of erotic material in the media.

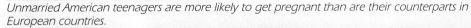

Unmarried American teenagers are more likely to get pregnant than are their counterparts in European countries.

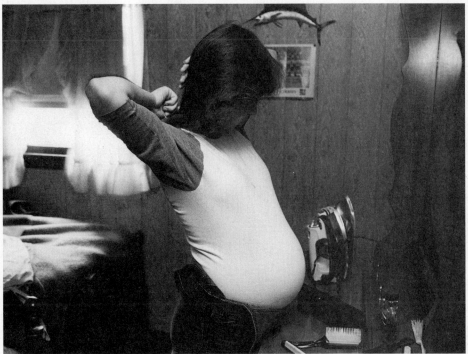

Adolescent Sex and Unwanted Pregnancy   Many surveys have been done about adolescent sexual behavior, but their results have not been consistent. In the eight studies reported by Gerald R. Adams and Thomas Gullotta in 1983, the percentage of females from age 16 to 19 who report having had intercourse ranged from 18 to 57 percent, and for males the range was 21 to 72 percent.[28] More recently, two studies of 15- to 19-year-olds put that figure at 51 percent for females and 56 percent for males.[29] There is, however, general agreement about one point: young people are having sex at a somewhat earlier age than they did in the past. This is just one part of an overall trend toward more liberal sexual attitudes and behaviors, but it also poses some special problems. In the erotically charged atmosphere of today's society, young people are often confused about how to deal with their own sexuality. They see the overwhelming importance given sexual attractiveness in the media, yet they also hear their parents and religious advisers telling them sex is wrong. As a result, many young people begin having sex without really intending to and without taking proper precautions against pregnancy.

In 1960 only about 15 of every 1,000 unmarried teenage girls (age 15 to 19) in the United States gave birth to a child, but by 1988 that number had increased to almost 35 births per 1,000 (see Figure 11.1; also see Chapter 5 for a discussion of the difficulties these young women are likely to face).[30] Teenagers in other industrialized nations, however, have far lower pregnancy rates. Some of this difference can be attributed to the high pregnancy rates of black teenagers in the United States. But white American teenagers are still twice as likely to become pregnant as British or French teenagers, and six times more likely than Dutch teenagers. The cause of this difference is clear. Although studies show that American teenagers are no more sexually active than their European counterparts, they are far less likely to use contraceptives.[31]

The Rising Birthrate Among Single Teenagers

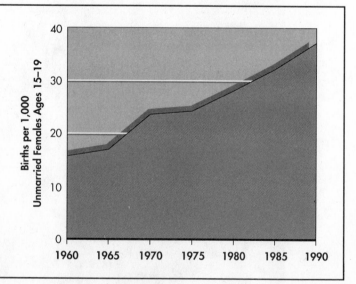

Figure 11.1 *Source: Statistical Abstract of the United States, 1988, p. 62; Statistical Abstract of the United States, 1991, p. 67.*

Why don't more sexually active teenagers use contraceptives? In some cases they actually want to have a child, but most of the time a teenage pregnancy is an accident.[32] Many teenagers are simply ignorant about sexual matters and believe such myths as "you can't get pregnant the first time" or "you won't get pregnant if you only have sex once in a while." Teenagers are also influenced by parents and religious leaders who tell them to abstain not only from having sex but from using birth control as well. It is certainly far easier to abstain from the second than from the first. Many teenage girls feel that planning a sexual encounter is immoral but that if you are swept off your feet and are unable to stop, you can't be blamed for your actions. Finally, teenagers often do not know how to get birth control devices or are afraid that their parents will get angry if they do.

AIDS

Sexually transmitted disease (diseases passed from one person to another during intercourse) is an old problem. Descriptions of such diseases have been found in records dating back thousands of years. The first sexually transmitted diseases to be widely recognized were syphilis and gonorrhea—both caused by bacteria. More recent medical research has added numerous others to the list, including chlamydia and such viral diseases as genital warts and herpes. Although syphilis is the only one of these that is a killer, the diseases caused by viruses are the most difficult to treat.

But the problems caused by these diseases pale in comparison with the devastating effects of acquired immune deficiency syndrome. The first reported case of AIDS did not occur until 1981, and the illness is apparently caused by an entirely new virus. The World Health Organization estimates that 70 to 80 percent of AIDS cases start from sexual contact, so in roughly a quarter of the cases it is not a sexually transmitted disease at all (see Chapter 8).[33] Worldwide, heterosexual intercourse is the most common way AIDS is transmitted, but in the wealthy industrialized nations, AIDS is much more widespread among gay men. For example, it is estimated that of the 56,000 gay men living in San Francisco at the start of the AIDS epidemic, about 12 percent have died from AIDS and 35 to 40 percent are now infected with the human immunovirus (HIV) that causes AIDS.[34] No one is sure why there is such a big difference in the way AIDS is spread in the rich and poor nations. The evidence shows that AIDS is more easily transmitted in anal than vaginal intercourse, but the difference may not be as great among Third World people, who are already in poor health.

There have been about 170,000 reported cases of AIDS in the United States and about 5,000 in Canada, and it is estimated that between a million and a million and a half North Americans are infected with the HIV virus.[35] (See Figure 11.2.) Because the virus typically lies dormant for seven to ten years after the victim is first exposed, many people carry the disease and pass it on to others without ever knowing that they are infected. Another problem in arriving at any firm statistics is that the HIV virus attacks its victims' immune system, leaving AIDS patients vulnerable to a host of other diseases. Thus, the direct cause of death is often some other illness that flourishes because the victim's immune system is too weak to fight it off.

The new epidemic has touched off a near-panic among some people. Unfounded fears that one can get AIDS from casual contact with an infected person are common. Yet at the same time, many people are failing to take reasonable precautions to protect

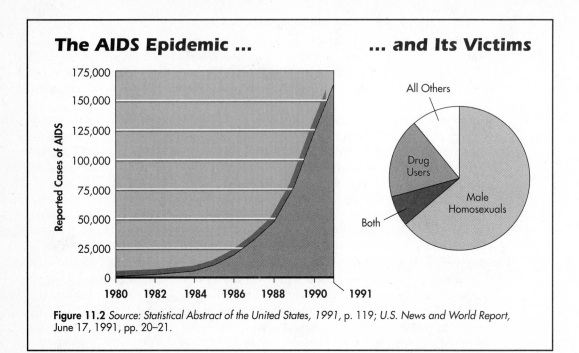

The AIDS Epidemic ...   **... and Its Victims**

Figure 11.2 *Source: Statistical Abstract of the United States, 1991, p. 119; U.S. News and World Report, June 17, 1991, pp. 20–21.*

themselves. Reports indicate that the biggest behavioral changes have been among gay men—who, of course, have borne the brunt of the epidemic. In contrast, a recent survey found that only one sexually active single woman in three had changed her behavior to lower the risks of getting AIDS.[36] The use of a condom lubricated with a spermicidal gel, such as nonoxynol-9, that also kills the HIV virus can greatly reduce one's chances of contracting AIDS. But too many people still fail to take this simple precaution.

Child Molestation   There are few kinds of deviant behavior more repugnant to the general public or more frightening to parents than the sexual molestation of a child. But the image most people have of the child molester as a demented stranger who seizes a child and forces her to have intercourse with him is highly inaccurate. It is generally estimated that 50 to 80 percent of **child molestations** are committed by family friends, relatives, or acquaintances.[37] Most cases of child molestation do not involve actual intercourse but such things as exposure, fondling, and masturbation. A. C. Jaffe found that only 11 percent of victims were physically penetrated by the offender,[38] and Charles H. McCaghy concluded that physical violence is used in no more than about 3 percent of molestation cases.[39] The only accurate part of the popular stereotype is that most offenders are male and most victims are female, but even that is not always the case.

Accurate measurement is even more difficult for child molestation and incest (sex between persons with a close biological relationship, such as a father and daughter) than for other types of sexual behavior. In a survey in the 1980s, one in ten Boston couples reported that their child had been the victim of sexual abuse or attempted sexual abuse, and 15 percent of the mothers and 6 percent of the fathers said that they themselves had been abused as children.[40] A nationwide study published in 1991 that went to unusual lengths to assure the anonymity of the respondents concluded that one in seven Americans had been sexually abused as children.[41] Although some claim that there has been a big increase in child molestation in recent times, there is no convincing evidence to support this assertion. The estimates produced in the original Kinsey studies, for example, were within the same range as the later research. One thing that has increased is the willingness to acknowledge the problem and talk about it, and as a result the number of cases of child molestation reported to the police has gone up in the last few years.

Child molestation stems from complex social and psychological causes, and no single theory explains them all. Most psychologists depict child molesters as insecure and sexually inadequate. They turn away from adult sexual relationships to seek out children, who are less threatening and more easily controlled.[42] However, some child molesters are married people with adult sexual relationships, and most people with feelings of sexual inadequacy never become child molesters. There is mounting evidence that child molesters often learned that behavior in their own childhood, when they themselves were the victims of sexual abuse. Other evidence indicates that father–daughter incest most often occurs in disturbed families. Often there is no sexual relationship between the parents, and the father forces his daughter to assume that part of his wife's role.[43]

Prostitution   **Prostitution** has declined dramatically in the past half-century. Kinsey's data suggested that prostitution had begun to decline in the 1940s. Morton Hunt's survey in the 1970s found that prostitution had decreased by over 50 percent since the time of the Kinsey report, and more recent studies show the same trend.[44] It appears that the demand for prostitution has decreased as sexual freedom has increased. Nevertheless, it is unlikely that prostitution will disappear by itself, and repeated efforts to stamp it out have been remarkably unsuccessful.

Prostitutes are condemned by "respectable" people, but within their own world they have a status hierarchy like those of other professions. Call girls are the best paid and the most respected. They are highly selective about their customers, charge high fees, and see the same clients again and again. Because they seldom accept unknown customers, their chances of arrest are low. The woman who works in a house of prostitution is a step below the call girl in status. The "house girl" does not have to walk the streets in search of customers, but neither can she screen her customers. She must service a large number of clients each night and split her fees with the operator of the house, who is usually known as a madam. Streetwalkers are on the bottom rung of the status ladder. They must prowl the streets in search of clients, often rob their customers, and are themselves highly vulnerable to assault, robbery, and arrest. Most streetwalkers work for a pimp, who takes most or all the income. In return, the pimp pays for the prostitute's apartment, buys her clothes, arranges legal services, provides protection, and gives her emotional support and affection.

Many people think that all prostitutes are women, but male prostitution is also common. Male prostitutes sometimes have female clients, but most of their business

Streetwalkers, both female and male, are the lowest status prostitutes. Those who work in a house of prostitution are somewhat better off, while the call girl (or call boy) has the highest status and the best working conditions.

comes from other men. In his interviews with male prostitutes in Chicago, David F. Luckenbill found another clear-cut occupational hierarchy. At the bottom are the ''street hustlers,'' similar to female streetwalkers except that they do not work for a pimp. Next are the ''bar hustlers,'' who find their customers in bars, and at the top of the hierarchy are the prostitutes who work for an ''escort service.''[45]

A hundred years ago prostitution was widespread in North America. It was illegal, but it was carefully ignored by most police departments. At that time most prostitutes worked in brothels (houses of prostitution) concentrated in the ''red-light'' districts of larger cities. Madams paid police officers to leave their girls alone, and they were not disturbed as long as they did not venture out of their district. In the early part of the twentieth century, this cozy arrangement was upset by a wave of vice crusades. The American Society of Sanitary and Moral Prophylaxis, the American Purity Alliance, the YMCA, and other organizations mounted a powerful offensive against prostitution. One by one the red-light districts were closed down, and increasing numbers of prostitutes became streetwalkers instead.

The laws that were intended to solve the problems of prostitution have on the whole made them worse. Closing houses of prostitution increased the number of streetwalkers, who pose a more serious problem than ''house girls'' because they solicit men who are not interested in their services, ply their trade in areas in which they are not welcome, and are often involved in criminal activities such as robbery and narcotics dealing. The prohibition of prostitution also encourages organized crime to enter the business because of the enormous potential for tax-free profits.

Pornography Strictly speaking, **pornography** is not a form of sexual behavior. It consists of obscene books, pictures, sights, and sounds. But the attempts to clearly define what is obscene have ended in failure and confusion. One popular definition holds that any material that is intended to be sexually arousing is obscene and, thus, pornographic. But by this definition a large percentage of all advertising, books, and movies would be pornographic. According to the Supreme Court, sexually explicit materials are not obscene unless they (1) appeal to "prurient" (lewd, lustful, indecent) interests, (2) are contrary to community standards, and (3) lack all "redeeming social value."[46] But although these criteria appear to be clear and precise, they are impossible to apply objectively. Any book, magazine, or film can be said to have some social value. In fact, in 1970 the President's Commission on Obscenity and Pornography found that 60 percent of all Americans believe that exposure to erotic materials provides information about sex and entertainment, both of which appear to be of "redeeming social value." A 1985 survey by *Newsweek* found that only one out of five Americans favored a ban on magazines that show nudity, and less than one out of three favored a ban on rentals of X-rated films.[47]

Critics of sexually explicit materials charge that they lead to immorality and social decay. However, standards of sexual morality differ so widely that it is difficult for sociologists even to determine what is or is not considered immoral, much less to decide whether or not pornography encourages it. There is, moreover, considerable evidence to support the argument that looking at "dirty" books and pictures does not lead the viewer to rape, child molestation, or other sex crimes. W. Cody Wilson found that his sample of sex offenders had had less exposure to pornographic materials than the average citizen, and this finding has been confirmed by other researchers.[48] Even more telling evidence comes from Denmark, the first European nation to repeal its pornography laws. Studies revealed a substantial reduction in exhibitionism (58 percent), peeping (80 percent), and child molesting (69 percent) as erotic materials became more easily available. Examinations of criminal statistics show no relationship between the amount of pornography available in a state and its rate of forcible rape.[49]

Critics of such studies, however, point out that they often fail to consider the important distinctions between the types of materials that are labeled as pornography. A nude photograph or an explicit love scene is a far cry from a graphic videotape showing a woman being raped and murdered. There is good reason to believe that violent pornography contributes to violent sex crime. For one thing, laboratory studies have found a correlation between exposure to violent pornography and favorable attitudes toward rape[50] and a greater willingness to inflict suffering (electric shocks) on other experimental subjects.[51] Moreover, the much more extensive research on television violence indicates that it does encourage violence in real life (see Chapter 13). After a thorough review of the available literature, Edward Donnerstein, Daniel Linz, and Steven Penrod concluded that the scientific evidence generally supports the idea that violent pornography promotes sexual violence. On the other hand, they found only weak and inconclusive evidence that materials showing "degrading" sex (for example, a film showing a woman having sex with numerous men in a short period of time) promote violence or other criminal behavior, and they concluded that depictions of "nondegrading" sex and simple nudity do not promote illegal activities.[52]

These findings are consistent with the attitudes of the general public. Polls show that most Americans believe that violent pornography and so-called kiddie porn (sexually oriented materials involving children) should be banned, but that other kinds of erotic material should not be prohibited. Seventy-four percent of the subjects in the *Newsweek* poll mentioned earlier favored a total ban on magazines that show sexual violence, and 68 percent favored a ban on movies that depict sexual violence.[53] Research shows, however, that most hard-core, X-rated movies actually contain very little violence. It is the R-rated "slasher" movies that are the worst offenders.[54]

It is also important to keep in mind that any type of restriction on freedom of the press creates its own problems. Censorship has a chilling effect on personal freedom as well as on artistic expression. Works ranging from Shakespeare's plays to *Alice in Wonderland* have been banned at one time or another. If censors are given broad powers to prohibit "pornography," many works of art will be affected as well. Because pornography is so difficult to define, there is also a real danger that the decision to ban a particular book or picture would be based on political considerations and that authors who threaten powerful special interests would be more likely to have their works censored.

RESPONDING TO PROBLEMS OF SEXUAL BEHAVIOR

The diverse problems and issues surrounding sexual behavior obviously require different kinds of responses. But most proposals for dealing with them can be put into one of two categories: those that rely on education and prevention, and those that advocate changes in the laws and the criminal-justice system. One set of proposals in the first category aims to correct the irresponsibility of the broadcast media. According to a study sponsored by Planned Parenthood, in the 1987–1988 television season the average viewer saw about 14,000 references to sex but only 165 references to such things as birth control, abortion, sexually transmitted diseases, or sex education.[55] The three major networks not only refuse to run public service announcements to inform sexually active teenagers about the importance of birth control but will not even accept paid advertising from the manufacturers of birth control products.[56] Given this attitude—that sexual titillation is fine but that birth control is dirty—it is hardly surprising that so many American teenagers have unwanted pregnancies. A law requiring televison stations to run public service birth control announcements would help change the message that we are giving to young people. Such announcements could also be a major force in the fight against AIDS and other sexually transmitted diseases if they forcefully promoted the use of condoms—the only technique of birth control that is also effective in the prevention of disease. Unfortunately, such proposals are opposed by powerful groups that confuse the advocacy of birth control and safe sex with the advocacy of promiscuity.

Another common proposal to reduce teenage pregnancy is to create a more comprehensive program of sex education in the schools. A study by the Urban Institute concluded that the average high school student receives less than five hours of sex education a year. However, research by Douglas Kirby found that it was much more effective to create clinics on school campuses to distribute contraceptives to students than it was to increase educational programs. Several such clinics now operating in the United States have reduced the number of pregnancies in their schools by over

DEBATE

Should the Schools Provide Free Birth Control to Teenagers?

YES The time has come to face facts. We may not want teenagers to have sex, but they are having it. We continue to pretend that "good girls" don't use birth control, and the result is that our unmarried teenagers have a higher birthrate than in any other industrialized nation. These young mothers often drop out of school and into years of welfare dependence. Many of their children are raised in poverty by a single parent unready for the burdens of motherhood. Too often the ultimate result is a negligent and abusive parent, and a disturbed child who grows into a troubled adulthood.

Fortunately, there is an effective and inexpensive way to deal with this problem: realistic sex education and free birth control provided directly in the schools. This kind of program has already been tried and proven effective in numerous schools, and if applied nationwide, it could slash the birthrate among single teenagers. Critics say that such programs encourage teenagers to have sex, but there isn't a shred of evidence to support such a claim. Surveys show that adolescents in European countries that provide access to birth control are no more sexually active than in the United States. And studies of the U.S. schools that already have these programs show no increase in sexual activity among the students. The real reason that there is such vehement opposition to effective birth control programs is that self-righteous moralists want to make these girls suffer for their "sins." What these young mothers really suffer from is our short-sighted birth control policies, and it is time for a change.

NO The proposal that the schools should give out condoms and birth control pills like popcorn in the movies is offensive and wrong. The way to deal with the shocking increase in illegitimate births among teenagers is to return to the traditional values that have made our society strong. You stop illegitimate births by convincing teenagers to wait until they are married to have sex, not by helping them violate one of the most sacred commandments in the Judeo-Christian tradition.

A program to allow the schools to give out birth control information and devices would be a highly unwelcome intrusion of government power into the private lives of millions of families. If parents do not want their children to use birth control, what right does the government have to go ahead and give it to them anyway? One of the most important of all parental duties is to teach their children how to tell right from wrong. But what chance do parents have to instill a strong sense of sexual morality when the government steps in and helps teenagers behave in an immoral way?

The problem of unmarried mothers is indeed a serious one, but pursuing a policy that will encourage sexual promiscuity is certainly not the way to deal with it. All this classroom discussion of sex and the easy availability of contraceptives would certainly encourage many students to become sexually active and might well result in more, not less, illegitimacy. But even if it prevents a few illegitimate births, the moral damage such a program would cause is far too high a price to pay.

50 percent—a record unmatched by any other type of program. Moreover, recent studies indicate that, contrary to fears of some parents, such programs do not encourage teenagers to engage in sexual activity. The evidence shows that girls in schools that provide birth control programs actually begin sexual intercourse at a somewhat later age than girls in schools without such programs.[57]

The criminal-justice system's response to society's about sexual behavior has been criticized from two different directions. The main complaint concerning the crimes in which there is a clear-cut victim—such as incest, child molestation, and rape—is that the criminal-justice system is not enforcing the law strictly enough. (See Chapter 13 for a discussion of ways to improve the efficiency of the criminal-justice system.) But when it comes to sex crimes without victims, many critics take the opposite approach, arguing that the criminal-justice system has no business interfering in private sexual acts between consenting adults. The most universal prohibition of this kind is on prostitution, but homosexuality, adultery (sex with someone other than one's spouse), fornication (sex between unmarried people), and cohabitation (living with someone of the opposite sex to whom one is not married) are still crimes in many states. Of course, many of these laws are seldom enforced, but that very fact can create a problem. When unenforced laws stay on the books, they can still be dusted off and used to attack some person or group that is politically unpopular. Moreover, the prohibition on homosexual acts serves to stigmatize gays and lesbians and to encourage occupational and social discrimination against them. The laws against prostitution are more commonly enforced than the others, and critics charge that the result is not only to create a thriving deviant subculture among prostitutes but to prevent any effective regulation and control of the prostitution industry. Many criminologists therefore believe that the legalization of all private sexual acts between consenting adults would not only remove an unnecessary burden from the criminal-justice system but would help reduce the rampant discrimination against homosexuals, and allow government regulation of prostitution in order to reduce the spread of sexually transmitted disease.

SOCIOLOGICAL PERSPECTIVES ON SEXUAL BEHAVIOR

Because sexual behavior is deeply rooted in human biology, many people lose sight of the fact that it is socially controlled and directed. Instead, they believe that the sexual standards of their social group are a part of human nature and that those who do not follow those standards are abnormal or unnatural. Such ethnocentric attitudes help to make sexual behavior a social problem by fostering concern about "abnormal" sexual activities and by encouraging campaigns to stamp out sexual deviance. These problems are particularly severe in North America because there are so many different cultures and subcultures with contradictory standards of sexual behavior. The conflicts between moral standards and the rapid changes that have occurred in sexual attitudes have made sexual behavior a controversial social issue.

The Functionalist Perspective Kingsley Davis's early analysis of prostitution set the pattern for most of the functionalist work on this subject.[58] Following Davis's lead, most functionalists hold that prostitution is inevitable. As long as there are sexual restrictions in a society, the argument goes, sex will be for sale. Functionalists also note that prostitution benefits society by creating jobs for people with few skills, by providing a sexual outlet for people who would otherwise be without one, and by reducing the risk that frustrated, hostile men might use violence to satisfy their sexual desires. Consequently, many functionalists, including Davis, advocate the legalization of prostitution.

At the same time, however, other restrictions on sexual expression are considered functional. Thus, the prohibition of premarital and extramarital sex is seen as a device to keep society's kinship system intact, ensuring a clear knowledge of a child's paternity and facilitating the transmission of money and power from parents to children. Sexual restrictions in general are considered to be functional because they direct individuals' energy away from personal pleasure seeking and into more socially beneficial activities. Pornography is held to be dysfunctional because it encourages extramarital affairs and therefore threatens an essential social institution: the family. Similarly, many functionalists believe that homosexuality should be banned because this sexual outlet does not contribute to society's need for new members. In other words, homosexuality is dysfunctional because it does not contribute to reproduction. But considering the current overpopulation of the world, it can now be argued that some amount of homosexuality has actually become functional.

The Conflict Perspective It is obvious that many of the problems of sexual behavior stem from conflicting ideas about sexual morality. There are numerous standards of sexual behavior, but supporters of traditional standards have the lion's share of the power and have been able to write their convictions into law. Those whose sexual morality differs from the values of dominant groups are made into criminals and threatened with imprisonment. Conflict theorists see such actions as part of a larger effort by traditional groups to maintain their cultural dominance by controlling the criminal law. The same power struggle leads to the imprisonment of marijuana smokers, bigamists, political radicals, and others who challenge the beliefs and customs of dominant groups.

Conflict theorists see attempts to stamp out prostitution and homosexuality as the oppression of "sexual minorities," similar to the oppression of ethnic minorities by segregation laws. Aside from noting the obvious injustice of such policies, conflict theorists point out that such oppression causes secondary problems, such as the creation of a black market for the forbidden goods and services and a burning hostility among these groups to the current social order.

Conflict theorists recommend that homosexuals, prostitutes, and other so-called sexual deviants organize and agitate for social change, as they have already begun to do. In addition, conflict theorists encourage them to form alliances with other oppressed groups such as drug users and religious and ethnic minorities. The "problem" of sexual behavior would be far less severe, according to conflict theorists, if we repealed laws prohibiting sexual acts between consenting adults and instead passed laws banning discrimination against homosexuals and others who engage in unpopular sexual activities.

Social Psychological Perspectives Biosocial theorists point out that humans are the most sexually active animals on earth. The human female is unique because she is sexually receptive at all times, whereas the females of other species are receptive only around their periods of fertility. Nonetheless, human males are still far more likely to desire a large number of sexual partners and to force others to have sex with them. Biosocial theorists often attribute this difference to evolutionary forces. According to one widely accepted theory, men have a higher sex drive and are naturally more promiscuous because sexual contact with a large number of women increases a man's chances of passing his genes on to the next generation. The more women a man has sex with, the more children he is likely to father, and the more descendants he is likely to leave. However, a woman's reproductive success is not enhanced by having sex with numerous men but by attaching herself to a single man who will protect the children she bears, and women therefore tend to be more monogamous and less likely to force sexual relations on an unwilling partner.[59] Critics of this theory point out that even monkeys must learn how to have sex or they will be unable to reproduce, and humans have a far greater capacity for learning than monkeys. Moreover, the critics charge that the rigid programming of sexual behavior hypothesized by some evolutionary theorists would actually be maladaptive for a species whose survival is dependent on effective cultural adaptation to a changing environment.

Many social psychologists have become concerned about the effects of the constant use of sex to sell consumer goods and to boost television ratings, motion picture receipts, and magazine sales. This erotic bombardment creates serious psychological problems for many people who cannot live up to the demands for sexual attractiveness and instant fulfillment generated by the media. Although such problems are common among people of all ages, they are particularly prevalent among the young, who have little sexual experience and are more likely to uncritically accept the expectations fostered by the media. The mystique of sexuality used to sell products and attract audiences has also contributed to the extremely high rate of pregnancy among teenagers. In response to this problem, social psychologists recommend more effective sex education in the schools, therapy and counseling for those with sexual problems, easier availability of contraception, and greater social responsibility on the part of advertisers and the media. The resolution of these problems seems unlikely in the short run, but many social psychologists are optimistic that a healthier, more matter-of-fact attitude toward sex will eventually replace the current state of confusion.

SUMMARY

In view of the enormous range of sexual customs and beliefs found in different cultures, it is clear that all sexual behavior is not biologically determined. It derives from a biological drive, but a drive that is channeled, directed, and controlled by social forces.

Traditionally, Western culture has been sexually conservative. Intercourse was permissible only between a husband and wife, and then only for reproduction. But these attitudes and values have changed. Comparison of surveys taken over the past four decades shows that there has been a substantial increase in many types of sexual activity. The double standard has weakened but has not disappeared; premarital and extramarital sex have increased significantly, as has sexual activity between married couples. The same surveys show no change in the incidence of homosexuality and a decrease in prostitution. A number of forces have contributed to the rise in sexual activity, including changing attitudes about sex, a weakening of the power of families to control the sexual behavior of their children, and improvement in birth control techniques.

Homosexuality is an often misunderstood form of sexual behavior. Contrary to popular belief, the differences between homosexuals, bisexuals, and heterosexuals are not absolute but are a matter of degree. Biosocial theorists feel that homosexuality is hereditary. Psychologists often argue that homosexuality is learned in the early years of childhood, but strong prohibitions against adolescent heterosexuality also encourage homosexual experimentation. In the past, most homosexuals concealed their sexual preference, but now many are "coming out," publicly acknowledging their sexual preference. Most European countries, Canada, and 25 states have repealed their antihomosexual legislation, but homosexuals are still subject to both occupational and social discrimination.

Single teenage girls in the United States have sex about as often as do single teenage girls in other industrialized nations, but because they are less likely to use birth control, they are more likely to get pregnant. Another unintended complication of sexual activity may be the exposure to a sexually transmitted disease—the worse of these is, of course, acquired immune deficiency syndrome (AIDS).

Child molestation is a different kind of problem: the intentional sexual victimization of one person by another. Contrary to popular opinion, most cases of child molestation involve sexual behaviors that stop short of intercourse, and the offenders are not usually strangers but family friends or relatives. Psychologists argue that child molesters are usually sexually inadequate people who turn to children because they cannot handle adult sexual relations. Sociologists point out that many child molesters learned that behavior when they themselves were victimized as children.

Prostitution has declined in this century, but it is unlikely that it will ever disappear. Prostitutes have an occupational prestige system. The call girl has the highest rank; next is the woman who works in a house of prostitution; and at the bottom is the streetwalker, who must search out her customers in public. Although most prostitutes are females, there are a substantial number of men in the profession as well. Legal efforts to restrict prostitution have often aggravated the situation. Closing houses of prostitution created more streetwalkers, who are a far greater social problem than the "house girls" they replaced.

Legally, pornographic material must be lewd, contrary to community standards, and without redeeming social value. But applying these standards is quite difficult, especially because almost any book or picture can be shown to have some redeeming value. Many believe that all sexually explicit materials promote sex crimes, but scientific evidence suggests that most is harmless. Sexually explicit materials that contain violence or use children as sexual objects do, however, have damaging social consequences.

Several different responses to the social problems created by sexual behavior are commonly suggested, including (1) an effort to balance the unrealistic image of sexuality presented in the media with public service announcements promoting birth control and the use of condoms to prevent sexually transmitted disease; (2) more sex education in the schools and easier access to contraceptives for teenagers; (3) better enforcement of laws protecting children and other victims of sexual aggression; and (4) legalization of all sexual behavior between consenting adults in private.

Many functionalists feel that prostitution is functional for society and should be legalized. But other restrictions on sexual expression are generally considered to be functional, since they help protect a vital social institution—the family. Conflict theorists say that problems of sexual behavior stem from value conflicts and from efforts by powerful groups to force their morality on others. Biosocial theorists argue that a great deal of our sexual behavior has been biologically predetermined by the process of evolution. Many social psychologists are concerned about the harmful effects of the media's exploitation of sex to maximize profits.

KEY TERMS

child molestation The sexual abuse of a child by an adult.

heterosexual Someone who prefers sexual relations with members of the opposite sex.

homosexual Someone who prefers sexual relations with members of the same sex.

pornography Films, photographs, literature, or other forms of expression judged to be obscene.

premarital intercourse Sexual relations before marriage.

prostitution The act of engaging in sexual relations for money.

FURTHER READINGS

June M. Reinisch, *The Kinsey Institute New Report on Sex* (New York: St. Martin's Press, 1990). A wealth of information on sexual behavior, presented in a simple question-and-answer format. Some answers, however, uncritically accept questionable conclusions from the original Kinsey surveys.

Barbara Ehrenreich, Elizabeth Hess, and Gloria Jacobs, *Remaking Love: The Feminization of Sex* (New York: Anchor/Doubleday, 1988). An interesting feminist analysis of the changes in our sexual attitudes and behaviors.

Joseph Harry, *Gay Couples* (New York: Praeger, 1984). A report based on a survey of male homosexual couples in the Chicago area.

Edward Donnerstein, Daniel Linz, and Steven Penrod, *The Question of Pornography: Research Findings and Policy Implications* (New York: Free Press, 1987). A comprehensive examination of the pornography issue. Contains an excellent review of the research on the effects of pornography.

Eleanor Miller, *Street Woman* (Philadelphia: Temple University Press, 1986). A study of the social world of street prostitutes.

chapter 12

Drug Use

- Is drug use increasing or decreasing?
- Which drugs create the most serious problems?
- Why do people use drugs?
- How has legal repression affected drug use?
- How can we deal with the drug problem?

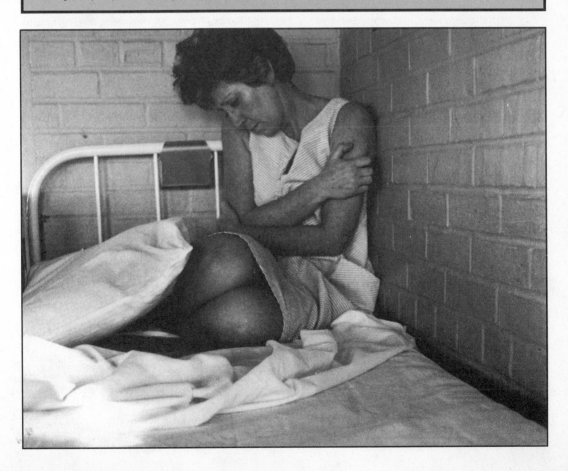

Few other social problems are surrounded by more myths and misinformation than drug use. The confusion starts with the very meaning of the term, for many people mistakenly believe that only illegal substances like heroin, cocaine, or marijuana are drugs. But alcohol and tobacco alter the minds and moods of those who use them and can be just as dangerous as the illicit drugs. Nor is drug use confined to a few ragged deviants on the margins of society. Drugs are a big business. Americans spend billions of dollars a year for coffee, tea, cocoa (which contains the stimulants caffeine and theobromine), tobacco, and alcohol, and the manufacturers of these products have a respected place among the corporate giants of today's economy.

One of the most widespread myths is that we are in the midst of a rising "drug epidemic." It is true that the use of most drugs increased rapidly in the 1960s and 1970s, but drug use has been declining in the last decade. While the amount of beer and wine consumed by the average American showed little change during the 1980s, there was a 20 percent drop in the use of distilled liquors such as whiskey and vodka.[1] The percentage of tobacco smokers in the population declined from 37 percent in 1970 to 29 percent in 1988.[2] Surveys show that the use of marijuana peaked in about 1979 and has been falling steadily since then, and the use of other illicit drugs has also been going down in the last decade. Cocaine was the one exception. It showed a big jump in popularity in the early 1980s, but apparently peaked in the middle of the decade and dropped sharply after that. Surveys by the Department of Health and Human Services indicate that cocaine use decreased 72 percent from 1985 to 1990.[3]

One commonly held belief about the drug problem that is certainly not a myth is that it is widespread and extremely costly. According to the National Safety Council, about 60 percent of all drivers killed in automobile accidents had drunk enough alcohol to impair their driving skills. Alcohol abuse is estimated to cost anywhere between $43 billion and $120 billion each year in lost workdays, medical expenses, and accidents.[4] But some of the most tragic problems occur among adolescents who turn to drugs to escape the intense emotional problems that they face (see Chapter 9). According to government surveys, about 25 percent of Americans from age 12 to 17 use alcohol at least once a month, 6 percent use marijuana, and 1 percent cocaine.[5]

DRUGS AND DRUG ADDICTION

While everyone uses the terms *drug addiction* and *drug addict* at one time or another, *addiction* is a technical term that is difficult to define. In the broadest sense addiction refers to an intense craving for a particular substance. But this definition can be applied to almost any desire or craving, whether it is for ice cream, potato chips, or heroin. To avoid this confusion, drug addiction is sometimes erroneously defined as the physiological dependence that a person develops after heavy use of a particular drug. Most addicts, however, experience periods when they "kick" their physical dependence, yet their psychological craving continues undiminished and they soon return to drugs. It is therefore more useful to define **addiction** as the intense craving for a drug that develops after a period of physical dependence stemming from heavy use.

Two essential characteristics of an addictive drug are tolerance and withdrawal discomfort. **Tolerance** is another name for the immunity to the effects of a drug that

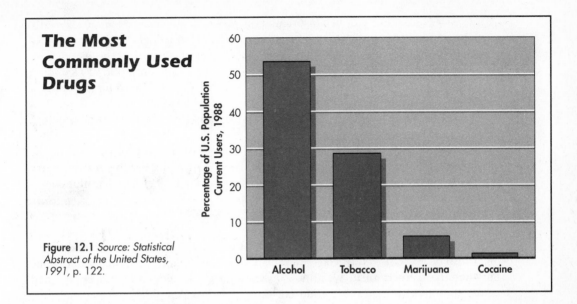

The Most Commonly Used Drugs

Percentage of U.S. Population Current Users, 1988

Alcohol Tobacco Marijuana Cocaine

Figure 12.1 *Source: Statistical Abstract of the United States, 1991, p. 122.*

builds up after heavy use. For instance, if someone takes the same amount of heroin every day for a month, the last dose will have much less effect than the first. If the user wants the same psychological effect at the end of the month, the dosage must be increased. **Withdrawal** is the name given to the sickness that habitual users experience when they stop taking drugs. Addictive drugs produce both tolerance and withdrawal distress. Drugs that produce tolerance but no withdrawal discomfort, such as LSD, are not addictive.

Drug addiction is not solely a physiological matter, however. Psychological craving supplements biological dependence. Moreover, the behavior of those who use specific drugs is influenced by cultural expectations that are quite independent of the drug's physiological effects. For example, anyone who drinks a large quantity of alcohol will pass out—a physiological reaction. But behavior while drunk but not dead drunk varies greatly from culture to culture and even from group to group within a culture. For example, people in some cultures become more violent and aggressive when they drink, but in other cultures such a reaction is rare.[6]

Alcohol The use of alcohol is an accepted part of our culture. Businesspeople make deals over a three-martini lunch, college students escape the pressures of final exams with a keg of beer, restaurants offer champagne brunches and expensive wine lists, and, of course, there are the neighborhood bars that serve as social centers for many local residents. The fact that alcohol is so widely accepted and so widely used means that it creates more problems than other drugs.

Alcohol, like most other drugs, is rather harmless when used in moderation (except in the case of pregnant women) but is extremely dangerous when used to excess. Alcohol is called a **depressant** because it depresses the activity of the central nervous system and thereby interferes with coordination, reaction time, and reasoning ability.

Large doses of alcohol produce disorientation, loss of consciousness, and even death. The psychological reaction to alcohol varies from person to person, but the physiological effects of alcohol clearly increase as the level of alcohol in the blood rises. The effects of alcohol first become apparent when the concentration of alcohol in the blood reaches about 0.05 percent, and most states hold 0.10 to be the point of legal intoxication. Extreme intoxication occurs between 0.20 and 0.30 percent. A user with over 0.4 percent blood alcohol is likely to pass out, and concentrations over 0.6 percent are usually fatal.[7]

Prolonged heavy drinking may generate a number of health problems. Alcoholic beverages are high in calories but have little other food value. For this reason, heavy drinkers often lose their appetite and suffer from malnutrition. The harmful effects of excessive drinking on the liver are well known; the end result may be cirrhosis, a condition in which liver cells are destroyed by alcohol and replaced by scar tissue. Heavy drinkers are more likely than others to have heart problems, and there is evidence that they suffer from a higher rate of cancer as well. The problem drinkers may also be a problem to their children. Studies show that the children of alcoholic mothers have lower birth weights, slower language development, lower IQs, and more birth defects than other children.[8]

Alcohol will produce addiction if used in sufficient amounts over a long period. The so-called DTs (short for *delirium tremens*) are actually symptoms of alcohol withdrawal. These symptoms commonly include nausea, vomiting, and convulsions; sometimes they involve hallucinations and coma as well. Death from heart failure or severe convulsions occurs in about 10 percent of victims of the DTs. A much more common cause of death is the use of alcohol in combination with other depressant drugs. Many people have, for example, unintentionally killed themselves by taking sleeping pills after an evening of heavy drinking. Death occurs because two depres-

19th-Century Social Problems

The beer garden recently started on this side of the river, by permission of our town board, continues to grow offensive. The rabble from the city and the country meet there and sometimes form nothing less than drunken mobs. It is not safe for women to pass along the road near this place. Bloody fights are of a daily occurrence and drunken men may be found lying around in the bushes on all sides. Wife whipping has come into vogue since the new institution was forced upon us.... What it may end in need hardly be conjectured.

July 10, 1890

These selections, which appear throughout the text, are from the *Badger State Banner*, a newspaper published in Black River Falls, Wisconsin.

sant drugs taken together have a *synergistic* effect. That is, the strength of the effects of the two drugs is much greater than that of either drug taken alone.

Over 90 percent of the Americans surveyed in a Harris poll agreed that heavy drinking was a serious problem in the United States, and one out of five persons questioned told the Gallup poll that drinking had been a source of distress in their own family.[9] It is doubtful that all the people who cause such problems should be considered alcoholics, but the term is often used so loosely that anyone who takes more than an occasional drink might be included. For the purposes of this book, we will define an **alcoholic** as a person whose drinking problem disrupts his or her life, interfering with the ability to hold a job, accomplish household tasks, or participate in family and social affairs. Although many people use alcohol as a means of improving their self-esteem, in the long run it usually has the opposite effect. Statistics suggest that alcoholics can expect to die 10 to 12 years sooner than other people and are more likely to suffer from a variety of serious health conditions. Estimates of the number of alcoholics in the United States range from 8 to 25 million, more than the total number of users of most illicit drugs.[10]

It is often said that drunk drivers cause half the 50,000 or so traffic fatalities that occur in the United States every year,[11] but at best, such figures are only a rough estimate. What we do know with some accuracy is the percentage of drivers killed in traffic accidents who had been drinking. In 1988, 37.4 percent of such drivers were legally intoxicated, and another 8.7 percent had some alcohol in their blood.[12] In recent years, the victims of drunk drivers and other concerned citizens have banded together in such organizations as MADD (Mothers Against Drunk Drivers) and SADD (Students Against Drunk Drivers) to publicize the problem and push for stiffer punishments. Their efforts seem to be having some positive effects. Those 1988 figures on the intoxication rate of fatally injured drivers actually reflect a 14.6 percent decline since 1982, and research by Hanson and Engs found a similar decline in the percentage of college students who reported having driven after drinking too much.[13]

When asked by survey takers, a little more than half of all Americans say they have had at least one drink in the last month.[14] But after years of steady increases, the use of alcohol by both juveniles and adults has now begun to decrease. The prevalence of drinking varies widely among different social and ethnic groups. Most studies indicate that more men drink regularly (about 60 percent) than women (about 48 percent), but that drinking has been increasing among women as they have gained more freedoms and taken on more financial burdens.[15] The prevalence of drinking is greatest among the college-educated and those with higher incomes. It is estimated that about 80 percent of all college students drink, and student alcoholism is a serious problem on campuses throughout North America.[16] Despite their visibility, alcoholics who live on the streets or in flophouses make up fewer than 1 of every 20 alcoholics.[17]

Tobacco About 29 percent of Americans over the age of 17 smoke cigarettes, and the percentage of smokers between 12 and 17 is about half that number. Men smoke more than women, but the use of tobacco has been declining more rapidly among men (see Figure 12.2.), and teenage girls are now actually more likely to smoke than teenage boys. About 70 percent of all smokers have more than 15 cigarettes a day, making tobacco one of the few drugs that addicts use practically every waking hour

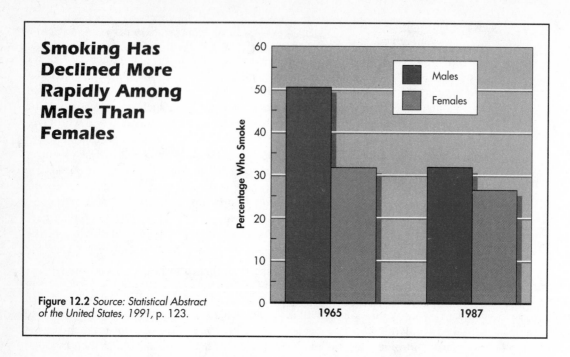

Smoking Has Declined More Rapidly Among Males Than Females

Figure 12.2 *Source: Statistical Abstract of the United States, 1991*, p. 123.

of every day. The sales of tobacco, like those of alcohol, have been falling in recent years. Since 1981 the number of cigarettes sold in the United States has decreased more than 2.5 percent a year.[18]

The principal drug in tobacco is nicotine, which is clearly addictive. Withdrawal symptoms include drowsiness, nervousness, anxiety, headaches, and loss of energy. Nicotine is a **stimulant** that raises blood pressure, speeds up the heartbeat, and gives the user a sense of alertness. However, nicotine also seems to have the contradictory effect of producing a feeling of relaxation and calm in the user. Some claim that this relaxation is due to the ritual of smoking and not to the drug itself, but the issue remains unclear.[19]

In 1964 the surgeon general's Advisory Committee on Smoking and Health issued its famous report concluding that smoking is hazardous to health, and since then the annual report issued by the federal government has painted an ever-bleaker picture of the effects of smoking on health. Commenting on the particularly detailed 1979 report, the Secretary of Health, Education and Welfare said that it "reveals with dramatic clarity that cigarette smoking is even more dangerous—indeed, far more dangerous—than was supposed in 1964."[20] In issuing the 1988 report, the surgeon general took another major step by forcefully acknowledging the addictive properties of nicotine and its similarity to heroin and other illegal drugs.[21]

Cigarette smoking has been linked to cancer of the larynx, mouth, and esophagus, as well as to lung cancer. Other diseases linked to smoking include bronchitis, emphysema, ulcers, and heart and circulatory disorders. It is estimated that smoking more than two packs a day reduces normal life expectancy by eight years and that light smoking (half a pack a day or less) reduces it by four years. The babies of women who smoke weigh less than other babies and have slower rates of physical and mental growth.[22] And even nonsmokers are at risk, if they live or work in a smoke-filled environment. A 1991 report by the Environmental Protection Agency, which some of its own officials tried to cover up, estimated that 53,000 Americans a year die from "passive smoking."[23] Jeff Bingaman estimates that smoking causes one of every six deaths in the United States, but whatever the exact figure, tobacco certainly kills far more people than all other drugs combined.[24]

Why, then, do so many people smoke? One reason is that cigarette smoking is addictive and most smokers find it difficult to stop. But what about the substantial number of young people who begin smoking for the first time every year, despite medical warnings? Youthful rebelliousness is certainly part of the reason. But another factor is the tobacco industry's success in establishing an association in the public mind between smoking and maturity, sophistication, and sexual attractiveness. Cigarette manufacturers spend billions of dollars a year advertising their products, and the smokers in those ads are invariable young and good-looking. As the sales of cigarettes have decreased in recent years, the tobacco industry has responded with ever more sophisticated marketing campaigns targeted at specific groups. The popularity of smoking among women is certainly related to the special efforts the tobacco companies have made to encourage them to smoke, and similar campaigns have been directed at blacks and Hispanics. Not surprisingly, the rates of lung cancer and other respiratory diseases have shown an alarming increase among these groups in recent years.[25]

Marijuana Marijuana is the most widely used illegal drug. About 1 in 3 Americans acknowledged having tried marijuana, but only about 1 in 20 is classified as a current user (that is, reported using the drug at least once within the previous month).[26] Marijuana use is most frequent among those between 18 to 25 years of age and drops off sharply after age 35. Marijuana is more popular among males than females and among those who live in the Northeast and on the Pacific Coast.[27] The use of marijuana increased sharply during the 1960s and 1970s, but, as with most other drugs, its use has been decreasing since the early 1980s.

The health hazards of marijuana are still the subject of an emotional debate that has often had more to do with politics than with objective scientific research. Numerous claims made about the damage caused by marijuana have later proven to be false. The current evidence indicates that the main health hazard in marijuana use is the risk of cancer and other lung problems caused by inhaling the smoke. Some studies show that the way marijuana is usually smoked (deep inhalations that are held for a long time) makes it more damaging than tobacco, puff for puff.[28] However, this effect is offset by the greater number of cigarettes smoked by tobacco users. Two or three "joints" a day is heavy marijuana use (the fact that marijuana is usually shared among a group of people means that each user smokes less), whereas many heavy tobacco users smoke more than 50 cigarettes a day. There is also evidence that marijuana may harm a user's unborn baby, and pregnant women should not use the drug. Thus, those who claim that marijuana is harmless are wrong: there are clearly significant health hazards involved in the excessive use of marijuana. However, on the whole marijuana is probably less dangerous than most of the other widely used recreational drugs.

The psychological effects of smoking marijuana are strongly influenced by the social environment and the expectations of the users. Howard S. Becker has shown that users must learn from their peers how to identify the effects of the drug before they actually get "high."[29] Descriptions of the drug's psychological effects vary considerably from one person to another. Typical effects include relaxation, increased sensitivity, and hunger. Studies show that a marijuana "high" impairs reaction time and coordination and therefore makes driving or operating other machinery more dangerous.[30]

Opiates The **opiates** are a group of natural (opium, codeine, morphine, and heroin) and synthetic (meperidine, methadone) depressants, all of which are all highly addictive. Users rapidly develop a tolerance and must continually increase their dosage to get the same effects. Although the intensity of opiate withdrawal varies with the amount taken and with the individual involved, withdrawal seldom causes the screaming agony depicted in so many books and movies. Withdrawal distress usually resembles a bad case of the flu accompanied by a feeling of extreme depression. In some cases, however, it can be much more severe.

Opiate addiction has serious consequences for the health of the addict. Ironically, most of these problems come not from the drug itself but from the way in which it is used. The opiate addict's life style, as well as impure drugs and infected needles, produces most of the severe health problems. Addicts often share the same needles without proper sterilization, and this practice spreads disease. Until recently, hepatitis, a serious liver infection, was the most serious risk. But intravenous drug users are now stalked by a much more deadly disease: AIDS. Almost a quarter of all AIDS sufferers are intravenous drug users, and a majority of the addicts in some cities are believed to be infected with the virus.[31] Overdose is another threat to the addict's survival and is a major cause of death among young males in many American cities.

19th-Century Social Problems

We are about to have a gold cure institute in this city. Dr. A. E. White and E. Krohn have purchased the right for this section to use the celebrated improved "Tri Chloride of Gold Cure" and are about to establish here an institution for the cure of the liquor, opium, morphine, and tobacco habits. . . . They guarantee a cure for a stipulated fee. The time required for treatment is 3 weeks. The patient is required to deposit the full fee in the bank, payable to the doctors when a cure is perfected, the patient agreeing to follow directions strictly. Medicine is taken internally every 2 hours, and 4 hypodermic injections are given each day. . . . We presume they will have few patients for the cure of other than the liquor habit.

June 2, 1892

In many cases, however, death can more properly be attributed to the combination of opiates with other depressant drugs such as alcohol.

Despite all the publicity, opiate use is actually quite rare. Only 1 of every 1,000 respondents in the 1988 survey by the National Institute on Drug Abuse acknowledged having used heroin in the last month.[32] Well over half of all heroin addicts in the United States live in its three largest cities, with the heaviest concentration in New York City. Addiction is an urban phenomenon in Canada as well, with its major center in Vancouver. Despite some increase in heroin use among middle-class people, most addicts are young males from the poorest segments of society.

Almost everyone has seen or read about the skinny, haggard "junkie" prowling the streets in a desperate search for the money to buy his next "fix" (injection of heroin). Although most fictional descriptions of junkies are greatly distorted, the stories contain a grain of truth. Most heroin addicts depend on crime to support their habits, and some will do almost anything to get a fix. However, all heroin users do not fit this stereotype. There are more addicts in the medical profession than in any other occupation, yet they are seldom involved in crime or violence.[33]

Psychedelics The physical effects of the most popular psychedelic drugs, such as LSD, mescaline, and MDMA, are generally minor. However, taken in large doses, they produce some of the most sweeping psychological effects of any drugs, including profound changes in emotion, perception, and thought. Although the psychedelics rank third in popularity among the users of illicit drugs, it is a rather distant third. (The use of cocaine, which is the second most popular illicit drug, is more than three times as common as that of the psychedelics.)

Mescaline was probably among the first psychedelic drugs used in North America. The consumption of the peyote cactus (which contains mescaline) was apparently an important element in some Native American religions long before the Europeans came to the continent. Peyote use continues today as a central part of the ritual of the Native American Church of North America, which claims 250,000 members from various tribes.

In the other extreme is MDMA (methylenedioxymeth-amphetamine), which is one of the newest arrivals on the drug scene. Sometimes known as "ecstasy" when sold on the streets, the drug is the center of a controversy between some psychiatrists, who believe that it is a useful therapeutic tool, and drug enforcement officials, who have succeeded in banning its use.

LSD is probably the best known of the psychedelic drugs. A tiny dose of the colorless and tasteless drug produces a tremendous psychological effect that is highly unpredictable. Some users report an intensely beautiful experience, whereas others find it the most frightening experience of their lives, and still others swing from one extreme to the other on the same "acid trip." Aside from such profound emotional changes, LSD also produces hallucinations and perceptual distortions. Colors and smells often appear more intense under the influence of these drugs.

Users of psychedelic drugs rapidly develop a tolerance, but most of these drugs produce no withdrawal symptoms. Few people become heavy psychedelic users (once a week or more), and those who do usually give up the drug after a few years. Although some have charged that LSD produces brain damage and birth defects, there is little evidence to support this claim.[34]

The greatest dangers of psychedelic drugs are psychological rather than physical. The "bad trip"—a terrifying experience that often throws the user into a panicky state—is always a possibility, especially among inexperienced users. Such bad trips have apparently brought on serious mental disorders in some susceptible persons. However, the average dose of LSD used today is only a quarter to a half of what it was during the drug's first wave of popularity, in the 1960s. As a result, the intensity of the psychological effects and the likelihood of a bad trip are both reduced.[35] Because the environment is so important in determining whether a psychedelic experience is wonderful or terrifying, many users take the drug with a "guide" who understands the effects of the drug and can help point them in the right direction.

Sedative-Hypnotics   **Sedative-hypnotics**, such as barbiturates and tranquilizers, depress the central nervous system. In moderate doses, these drugs slow down breathing and normal reflexes, interfere with coordination, and relieve anxiety and tension. Speech becomes slurred, the mind clouded. In larger doses, they produce drowsiness and sleep. Medically, these drugs are used to produce two effects: relaxation (sedation) and sleep (hypnosis).

Among recreational users, the barbiturates are the most commonly used of the sedative-hypnotics. The psychological effects of barbiturates are similar to those of alcohol. Indeed, the state of intoxication that barbiturates produce is often indistinguishable from alcoholic drunkenness. And, like alcohol, the barbiturates are addictive. Repeated doses produce a growing tolerance, and heavy use can create severe withdrawal distress. Addiction to barbiturates differs from addiction to opiates in two significant respects. First, physical dependence develops much more slowly. Second, withdrawal symptoms are more severe and may cause hallucinations, restlessness, and disorientation. Barbiturate withdrawal is fatal for about 1 in every 20 persons who abruptly terminate their habit. Alcohol and barbiturates are similar enough that the use of one will prevent the withdrawal symptoms caused by the other. When taken at the same time, these drugs have a synergistic effect that makes their combination much more dangerous than either taken alone.[36]

Methaqualone, known under the brand names of Quaalude and Sopor, is not chemically a barbiturate, but its effects are similar. A decade after methaqualone was synthesized in the 1950s, a heavy advertising campaign promoted it to physicians as a safe, nonbarbiturate sleeping pill. The result was a massive increase in prescriptions for what physicians believed to be a nonaddictive aid to sleep. The drug soon caught on among recreational users in the black market as well. In reality, however, methaqualone is as highly addictive as the barbiturates, and the loss of coordination it produces is even greater. In the 1980s methaqualone declined in popularity as its dangers became more widely known and law enforcement cracked down on its use.[37]

A large number of tranquilizers are now on the market that are prescribed for various psychological problems. Some are so strong that they are seldom used except in the treatment of severely disturbed mental patients, but "minor" tranquilizers are widely used by the public to reduce tension and to relieve anxiety. Librium and Miltown are well-known brand names of minor tranquilizers, and they are sometimes used for recreational as well as medical purposes. Valium has become particularly popular among drug users. Although many people believe this drug to be harmless, it actually has many of the same effects and dangers as the barbiturates. Valium is addictive and will produce a withdrawal syndrome when heavy use is discontinued.[38]

Amphetamines   The amphetamines are a group of synthetic stimulants that includes benzedrine, dexedrine, and methedrine. These drugs were once widely marketed as "diet pills," although physicians are now much more likely to use other methods to help patients lose weight. They reduce the appetite, increase blood pressure, and step up the rate of breathing. In moderate doses they generate heightened alertness, even excitement. Continuous heavy doses of an amphetamine produce a psychosis-like state that is often indistinguishable from schizophrenia. Fear and suspicion are common symptoms, and fits of violent aggression may occur. Hallucinations, delusions, and general personal confusion are also common. Repeated use of amphetamines leads to tolerance, and withdrawal symptoms, mainly severe depression, also occur.

Most amphetamine users take the drug in pill form, but some inject it directly into the bloodstream, producing a brief but extremely intense high, or "rush." Such heavy use takes a tremendous toll on the health of the user, and so-called speed freaks often go on "runs" lasting several days, during which they get no sleep or proper nutrition. Long-term users lose their hair, teeth, and a large portion of their normal body weight. And, of course, the amphetamine-induced psychosis becomes increasingly severe.[39] There is evidence that the crackdown on the cocaine trade has caused some users to switch to amphetamines—a lower-priced drug that is relatively easy for black market chemists to produce.

Cocaine   Cocaine is a natural stimulant derived from the leaves of the coca plant, which Peruvians have chewed for at least 1,500 years. Until 1906 it was a major ingredient of Coca-Cola and a number of patent medicines. The effects of cocaine are similar to those of amphetamines except for two differences. First, cocaine is a powerful local anesthetic; second, the effects of cocaine do not last as long. This means that cocaine users often repeat their doses every hour or so as the effects wear off. Heavy cocaine users may experience the same personality change and psychotic episodes as heavy amphetamine users, but the most frequent psychological effect is the irritability and depression that occur after the drug wears off. The easiest way to avoid those discomforts is, of course, by taking more, and compulsive cocaine use is a widespread problem. Many wealthy cocaine users report having spent hundreds of thousands of dollars on their drug habit.

Most users sniff cocaine powder into their nose through a tube or straw. Heavy users who "snort" cocaine in this way often suffer damage to the nasal passages and a constantly runny nose. Smoking cocaine has become popular because it produces an intense and immediate high, but it also has the potential to cause severe lung damage as well as a host of other serious health conditions. Street cocaine cannot, however, be smoked unless it is chemically treated in a process known as freebasing. In response to the rising popularity of freebasing, dealers introduced "crack": a special form of cocaine that comes in a small "rock" that can be smoked immediately, without further chemical treatment. The enormous popularity of this drug among hard-core users has created serious problems both for the communities in which users live and for law enforcement agencies. Users inflict great damage to their health, and

Crack—a form of cocaine designed specifically to be smoked—was a major contributor to the drug problem in the last decade.

many cities have experienced gang wars between groups trying to control the lucrative trade in crack.[40]

In the early part of this century, cocaine use was concentrated mainly among poor blacks, but the demographics of cocaine use have changed dramatically since then. In the 1970s and early 1980s, cocaine became known as a "rich man's drug" because of its high cost and popularity among some middle-class professionals. However, the popularity of crack in the underclass, as well as more negative attitudes about cocaine in the middle class, seems to be reshaping the demographics of cocaine use once again. Surveys of young people and of the general public indicate that cocaine use has plummeted in the last five years.[41] However, such studies generally miss large segments of the underclass, and it is quite possible that their behavior is not following the national trend.

Steroids The anabolic steroids are synthetic derivatives of the male hormone testosterone. They are unique among the drugs discussed here because they are taken not for their psychological effects but for building muscle and increasing athletic performance. (Steroids also have legitimate medical uses, but it is their use as a performance booster that makes them a social problem.) Although there is no evidence that simply taking the drug produces athletic benefits, it does heighten the effectiveness of training programs designed to enhance muscularity and strength. But such benefits carry a heavy price, which may include elevated cholesterol levels, high blood pressure, heart problems, irritability, liver damage, and sterility. In males, heavy steroid use may cause an atrophy of the testicles, and heavy female users may develop some male characteristics such as a deeper voice and more body hair. Steroid use by adolescents may also disrupt normal growth patterns. Thus, young steroid users who seek to build muscle may also be stunting the growth of their skeletal system.[42]

Although steroids are banned by virtually all reputable athletic organizations, including the International Olympic Committee, their use is still extremely common. In the ultracompetitive atmosphere of today's sports, many athletes feel they need every advantage possible. There are numerous reports that coaches as far down as the high school level have ignored the rules and encouraged their athletes to take these drugs. In some cases, coaches even act as drug dealers by providing steroids to their athletes. There is also disturbing evidence of increasing steroid use among teenage boys—both for sports and for muscle building. A recent survey by the Department of Health and Human Services estimated that about 3 percent of the boys in grades 7 through 12 have taken steroids.[43]

WHY USE DRUGS?

Researchers seem to be fascinated with the question of why we use drugs. Tremendous effort has gone into the investigation of this topic, much of it on the assumption that if we can find out why people take drugs, we can find ways of preventing them from doing so. Most of these explanations are based on one or more of the social psychological perspectives.

Biological Theories Many believe that drug problems are caused by the nature of the drugs themselves: once someone takes too much of a drug, he or she becomes addicted and is simply unable to stop. Although such theories are probably most popular with the general public, biological explanations of drug problems have also won increasing attention from scientists in the last decade. For example, a Danish study found that 65 percent of people whose identical twin was an alcoholic became alcoholics themselves, compared with only 25 percent for nonidentical twins. Although much of this difference may stem from the fact that identical twins are treated more similarly than fraternal twins are, some studies indicate that alcoholism in adopted children correlates more closely with the alcoholism of biological parents than with the alcoholism of adoptive parents.[44] In one of the best-known biological theories of alcoholism, E. M. Jellinek argued that it is a disease with a consistent pattern of symptoms and not voluntary behavior.[45] Some studies have attempted to find the exact biochemical reason that one person is more susceptible to alcoholism than another. The evidence shows that alcoholics have higher levels of a chemical (acetaldehyde) that is produced by the metabolic breakdown of alcohol in the body. Some researchers hold that these high levels of acetaldehyde are the result, not the cause, of alcoholism. But others argue that persons who are better able to metabolize alcohol are more likely to become alcoholics. Because they show a higher tolerance to the effects of alcohol, such persons drink more heavily, which in turn produces more of the chemicals that create the physical addiction to alcohol.[46]

We must, however, be careful not to let the impressive findings of the new bio-logical research lead us to unwarranted conclusions. Although there apparently is a genetic predisposition toward particular drug problems in some individuals, drug use is still learned behavior that is created and controlled by society. There are no alco-holics or heroin addicts in cultures where the use of those drugs is unknown or is practiced only in tightly restricted ritual situations. Drug problems are now so much more severe than they were two centuries ago because of the wrenching changes brought on by industrialization, not because there has been a genetic change in our population. But although biological theories cannot explain the historical changes in drug consumption or the reasons that drug problems are so much worse in big cities than in traditional small towns, they do help us understand why one person develops a drug problem while another person with similar experiences and background does not.

Behavioral Theory Psychologists have done extensive studies of the effects of drug use on animals. They have found that animals can be trained to use drugs and that some become habituated. Behaviorists argue that such experiments show that drug use is learned through a process of conditioning. Taking a drug often provides a reward (positive reinforcement), and when experimental animals or humans use a drug and find it pleasurable, they are likely to use it again.

Alfred Lindesmith, on the other hand, turned this behavioral theory on its head.[47] Rather than being attracted to an enjoyable experience, he said the addict is trying to escape the unpleasant experience of withdrawal distress (negative reinforcement). According to Lindesmith, addicts use drugs so frequently to relieve withdrawal dis-comfort that they begin to associate the drug with the relief it brings. They continue to use drugs even when there is no physiological dependence because they associate drug use with the elimination of discomfort and pain.

Critics complain that the basic idea behind behavioral theory—that people use drugs because they find them pleasurable and continue to use them because doing so prevents withdrawal distress—is nothing new. But whether the concept is old or new, there is little doubt about the importance of this kind of reinforcement in de-veloping a drug habit.

Personality Theories Many psychologists have tried to explain drug problems by investi-gating users' personalities. However, there is no general agreement among psychol-ogists about the personality characteristics of addicts and drug abusers. Drug addicts have been classified as narcissists, psychopaths, sociopaths, dependent personalities, immature, schizophrenic, neurotic, and character-disordered, to list only a few of the labels used.

The most common theory is that alcoholics and drug addicts have weak person-alities and low self-esteem and therefore turn to drugs to try to escape their problems. G. E. Barnes, for example, argued that there is an "alcoholic personality" that displays such characteristics as "neuroticism, weak ego, stimulus augmenting [a hypersensi-tivity to the environment that results in fear and anxiety], and field dependency [a passive-dependent orientation to life]."[48] Because these traits may be a response to alcoholism rather than its cause, psychologists also talk about a "prealcoholic personality." The characteristics that are believed to lead to alcoholism include impulsivity, gregariousness, and nonconformity.[49] Isador Chein and his associates reached similar conclusions about their sample of heroin addicts.[50] They found that heroin addicts have major personality disorders originating in the addicts' early family histories. The mother was usually the most important parent figure to the child, with the father cold or even hostile. Children from these homes were found to be over-indulged or frustrated and were uncertain of the standards they were expected to observe. These conditions were said to produce such personality traits as passivity, defensiveness, and low self-esteem.

Critics of these studies charge that they are little more than a reflection of the popular stereotypes that condemn those who suffer from drug problems. They argue that heavy drug users have as many diverse personality characteristics as any other group of people, and that the findings of these psychologists are based on their own prejudices and the fact that those with inadequate personalities are more likely to come to them for treatment. Support for this position comes from an unusually comprehensive 40-year longitudinal study of 660 young men drawn both from Harvard University and from an inner-city slum. Although the study found a strong correlation between alcoholism in parents and children, no personality differences were found between those who became alcoholics and those who did not.[51]

Despite the weaknesses in these theories, there is no question that personality plays a critical role in an individual's decision to use a drug. There is no single type of personality that is most likely to lead to drug problems, however. A great number of learned behavior patterns and personality traits interact in a given environment either to promote or to discourage drug use.

Interactionist Theory Most social psychologists see drug use simply as one more behavior pattern that is learned from interaction with others in our culture. They observe, for example, that most people in our society who drink alcohol do so not because they have some personality defect or a biological urge to drink but because drinking is a widely accepted cultural pattern. Most children see adults drink, and they learn attitudes, beliefs, and definitions that are favorable to alcohol use. When such children reach adulthood, they are likely to use alcohol just as their parents did.

Interactionists hold that the use of illegal drugs is also culturally learned, although in a slightly different way. Because the dominant culture encourages negative attitudes toward illegal drugs, some contact with a drug subculture is necessary before most people start using such drugs. The longer and more intense a person's contact with a drug subculture, the greater the likelihood that he or she will accept attitudes and definitions that are favorable to drug use. A person who actually begins to use an illicit drug is likely to grow closer to other drug users and to become more deeply committed to the values of the drug subculture. In fact, some people use drugs for the companionship of other drug users as much as for the effects of the drugs themselves.

The key point in interactionist theory is that drug use is determined by individuals' attitudes toward drugs, the meaning drug use has for them, their overall worldview, and their system of values—all of which are learned from interaction with people in a certain culture or subculture. Drug users, according to interactionist theory, quit

Drugs are used in many social settings. According to interactionist theory, people use drugs because of the attitudes and values they learn in their daily contacts with other people.

only when their attitudes and values change and the drugs involved are redefined in negative terms.[52] Labeling theorists point out that such changes are much more difficult when a drug user has been discovered and publicly labeled "addict," "alcoholic," "junkie," or "pill head." Those who have been branded in this way often find that they are excluded from contact with groups and individuals who might support their attempts to reform.

DRUG CONTROL IN NORTH AMERICA

European colonists who came to North America brought their drinking customs with them. Before 1700 most drinking was moderate and socially accepted. The most common beverages were beer and wine. Strong religious and family controls limited drunkenness and disorderly conduct. However, as westward expansion continued, drinking patterns changed. The traditional restraints of family and religion were ineffective among rugged pioneers, and heavy consumption of distilled spirits became commonplace. This type of drinking, often accompanied by violent, destructive behavior, was the first alcohol problem to gain widespread social attention. At the same time, total abstinence was becoming more popular among rural farmers.

By the nineteenth century there were two different drinking patterns among Americans. Rural middle-class people were largely abstainers, while settlers on the frontier and the thousands of immigrants in the big cities tended to be alcohol users. Three waves of state prohibition laws swept the United States as small-town dwellers tried to stamp out the customs of urban drinkers. The last wave resulted in the passage in 1919 of the Eighteenth Amendment to the Constitution, which prohibited the manufacture, sale, and transportation of intoxicating liquors. This amendment was repealed in 1933 by the Twenty-first Amendment.

Just as the drive against alcohol intensified in the nineteenth century, so also did the drive against the use of other drugs, particularly the opiates. At that time, opium was sold legally in over-the-counter patent medicines as a cure for everything from diarrhea to whooping cough, and most opiate habitual users were middle-aged, middle-class women who were no more involved in crime or deviant behavior than other people.

By the turn of the century, however, the public had come to see opiates as dope, not medicine. All nonprescription use of the drugs was prohibited in Canada in 1908 and in the United States in 1914.[53] This prohibition produced a sharp drop in the number of opiate users. However, users who were unwilling or unable to quit were placed in a very difficult position. They found themselves labeled "dope fiends" and were virtually forced to associate with smugglers and other criminals if they were to obtain supplies of the drug. This small group of opiate users was the beginning of the subculture of opiate addiction that was to become such a problem in the years ahead. The price of illicit opiates rose steadily, and so did users' need for money. The method of consumption changed from drinking opiated medicines to injecting morphine and heroin. Within a few decades after opium prohibition, the modern junkie emerged: predominantly young, predominantly male, and often deeply involved in crime.[54]

Alcohol prohibition had equally negative effects on American society. While the prohibition law was in effect, Americans witnessed an unprecedented wave of crime and gangsterism. The drinking public was not willing to give up alcohol, no matter what the law said. They turned to illegal sources of supply, thus creating a huge illicit market for alcohol. Members of organized crime and many independent operators jumped into the alcohol business, and speakeasies (illegal bars) sprang up in every city.[55]

Marijuana was the last major drug to be prohibited during this "era of temperance." As late as 1930, only 16 states had laws prohibiting marijuana use, and these laws were not vigorously enforced. A single government agency, the Federal Bureau of Narcotics, played the key role in bringing about the prohibition of marijuana in the United States. This agency was set up to enforce opium prohibition in 1930, and its director became convinced that marijuana use was an area of wrongdoing that should be under his jurisdiction. Accordingly, the bureau began an intensive program of lobbying for the prohibition of marijuana. It also circulated a number of phony horror stories about the effects of marijuana, but virtually no one challenged the Bureau's distortions and outright lies. In 1937, Congress passed the Marijuana Tax Act, which was designed to stamp out use of the drug, and every state eventually passed an outright prohibition of its own.

Most of the new drugs that have become popular among recreational users in the twentieth century have been produced by the pharmaceutical corporations, and many were initially promoted with erroneous claims that they were less addictive than their predecessors. Heroin was synthesized in 1874 and first placed on the market by Bayer Laboratories in 1898. It was widely promoted as a safe substitute for codeine and a cure for morphine addiction. The first barbiturate was clinically tested in 1903, and by the 1930s the barbiturates were in common use. Although references to barbiturate intoxication and withdrawal convulsions were made as early as 1905, it was not until 1950 that a controlled study was done to prove their addictive properties. Methaqualone was, as we have seen, falsely advertised as a safe substitute for the barbiturates that were coming to be recognized as a major drug problem. LSD was first created in 1938. Although it was never promoted as a prescription drug, the Sandoz laboratories did give LSD samples to a wide variety of scientists from 1953 to 1966. (It has now come to light that the Central Intelligence Agency and the U.S. Army conducted experiments with LSD during this period that included dosing unsuspecting citizens with the drug to observe its effectiveness as a combat weapon.[56]) Of course, the pharmaceutical companies never sold these drugs directly to recreational users. But drugs legally produced for the prescription market are often diverted into the black market, and once a particular drug gains popularity with recreational users, illegal laboratories soon spring up to meet the demand.

During the second half of the 1980s, American society began to focus on the problem of drug abuse more intensely than ever before. Drug use became a powerful public symbol for a host of social ills from the decline of the work ethic to the decay

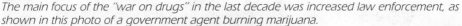

The main focus of the "war on drugs" in the last decade was increased law enforcement, as shown in this photo of a government agent burning marijuana.

of the traditional family structure. In the frenzy that followed, politicians from all sides of the political spectrum seemed to be competing to outdo each other with their con... s of drug users, and the federal government launched what was ... antidrug campaign ever. This so-called war on drugs involved ... its principal focus was tougher enforcement. Unprecedented ... billions of dollars were devoted to the antidrug campaign, and ... overflowing with drug offenders. Supporters of this enforce- ...ed that it was responsible for the decline in drug use during ...ver, this seems unlikely because, as we have seen, drug use ...own well before the big increases in funding for drug enforce- ...bacco and alcohol (which were obviously not affected by the ...ght along with that of the illicit drugs. Rather, most sociolo- ...ese changes to the aging of the population and to a natural ...xcesses of the 1960s.

...UG PROBLEM

...t the best way to deal with drug problems is to discourage ...drugs before they start. But how is that to be done? One ...y to frighten them by presenting horror stories in "drug ...tempts seriously underestimate the awareness and intelli- ...r or later they discover that they have not been told the ...even come to doubt the accurate information they have ...lems. A more reasonable approach is to present the best ...regardless of whether it is likely to discourage students ...ducational programs argue that so much talk about drugs ...ome teenagers' interest in trying them. Richard H. Blum, ...ncluded that students exposed to drug education pro- ...likely than other students to experiment with drugs, ...moderate fashion. In contrast, less informed students ...ither abstainers or heavy drug users.[57] Education pro- ...administered exclusively by the schools. Another ap- ...advertising about alcoholism, lung cancer, and other ...to prohibit the advertising of drugs such as alcohol

...n programs are doomed to failure because such pro- ... These critics think that a certain amount of drug ... and insecure society and that the goal therefore ...ourage moderation, not total abstinence. Most research indicates that moderate drug use does not usually cause serious psychological or physical problems. For example, a ground-breaking UCLA study published in 1988 tracked 739 young people from junior high until young adulthood and concluded that the harm caused by drugs depends largely on the level of use. No measurable harm was found from moderate drug use, but as use increased, so did its damage.[58]

Many, therefore, advocate more balanced educational programs that allow students to make a rational choice based on all the available information. In this view, the best way to prevent drug problems is to openly accept a certain level of use but encourage the creation of clear social standards about how much is too much. Researchers have found, for example, that the rate of alcoholism is low among Italians (and Italian Americans) even though their per capita alcohol consumption is significantly higher than in most countries. Italian culture does not condemn drinking but contains clearly defined norms that limit total alcohol consumption to mealtimes and other social occasions. On the other hand, alcohol use was not part of the traditional culture of American Indians, and their high rate of alcoholism today is often attributed to the weakness of the norms regulating alcohol use.[59]

Treatment The treatment approach, like prevention programs, tries to discourage drug use. The difference is that treatment programs attempt to help people stop using drugs after they have already developed a drug problem. A variety of treatment programs have been tried, but no single program works for everyone. Many drug users go through several programs before kicking the habit.

"Individual psychotherapy" has proven to be one of the least successful approaches to drug problems.[60] No matter how much psychiatric care most drug users receive, strong social support is needed to motivate them to give up the drug habit. "Aversive therapy" is designed to associate the effects of the drug with some unpleasant sensation such as an electric shock or nausea. Aversive techniques are widely used to discourage smoking, but they have been less successful with other drugs such as alcohol and heroin.

Many social scientists believe that treatment programs are the most effective way to deal with the problems created by the use of alcohol and other drugs.

19th-Century Social Problems

Thomas Galt died at his home in this city Friday night last ... from the effects of the Ackerman anti-dipsomania gold cure which he was taking. He was 37 ... he contracted the drink habit and it so obtained the mastery of him that he was much of the time incapacitated for labor. He was so anxious to break the fetters that enslaved him ... that he risked and lost his life.... He was a great sufferer throughout the treatment.

November 16, 1893

The most successful treatment programs involve some kind of group support. Alcoholics Anonymous (AA) is one of the oldest such groups and is now a worldwide organization. Treatment takes the form of meetings at which members give accounts of their troubles with alcohol and the help they have found in Alcoholics Anonymous. Members are encouraged to call on one another for help when they feel a desire to start drinking again. The AA program is religiously oriented, but its success seems to derive primarily from its system of encouraging each member to try to reform others, thus reinforcing the reformer's own nondrinking behavior. There are also successful nonreligious programs, such as Rational Recovery (RR) and the Secular Organization for Sobriety (SOS), that follow the same principles but emphasize individual responsibility instead of the reliance on a "higher power," as AA does.[61]

More intensive than AA-style programs are the "therapeutic communities," in which the patients live together in a special house or dormitory and are under virtual 24-hour supervision. The first of these communities was Synanon, founded in Santa Monica, California, in 1958. Synanon members were ex-users who maintained strict discipline, prohibited all drug use, and helped each other avoid drugs. Frequent group sessions were held in which members discussed their problems and criticized individuals who failed to live up to the expectations of the group.[62] Although Synanon has changed drastically in recent years, other therapeutic communities still follow its original principles.

Most therapeutic communities claim high rates of success but have seldom conducted rigorous research to support their claims. One major drawback is that these programs appeal only to drug users who can accept their ideology and discipline. It has been estimated that only 10 to 20 percent of those who join these communities finish the program, but at least a majority of these individuals remain drug-free.[63] Another problem with some therapeutic communities is that those who complete the program successfully often have great difficulty leaving. Many who do manage to leave become "professional ex-addicts" working in halfway houses or other drug programs.

Legal Repression When the use of a particular drug comes to be seen as a problem, the most common response has been to make it a crime, usually by prohibiting the manufacture and sale of the drugs and punishing the users. This approach has been tried with almost all psychoactive drugs except caffeine and nicotine. The idea is that people will not use drugs if they are threatened with jail or there are simply none available, but it is difficult to evaluate the success of this approach. For example, opiate use declined sharply after it was declared illegal, but marijuana use has increased enormously since its prohibition. Supporters of this approach argue that its failures are due to a lack of tough laws and enough money to enforce them. It does seem fair to conclude that the prohibition approach usually does reduce (but not eliminate) the use of the condemned drug. However, the matter is a good deal more complex than that. For one thing, the cost of effectively repressing a popular drug may be far more than society can afford. As the drug becomes more scarce, the price is driven up and drug dealers have more money to offer in bribes and corruption (a key reason for the frequent failure of this approach). Political factors also obstruct the enforcement effort. Evidence has emerged showing not only that the Central Intelligence Agency has been involved with drug-dealing schemes to help finance its secret operations but that several presidential administrations have intentionally ignored drug-running activities by their allies in volatile Third World countries. But even if the enforcement effort could somehow dry up the supply of illicit drugs, this approach would still have unintended side effects. A policy that completely removed all popular drugs from the black market, while allowing almost unrestricted over-the-counter sales of alcohol, seems likely to achieve little more than the substitution of one dangerous substance for another.

In the real world, of course, a black market almost certainly would remain, and that fosters the growth of organized crime. When a drug is prohibited by law, legitimate businesses are forced out of the market. The demand for the drug is still there, however, and criminals organize to meet it. Because such criminals have no competition from legitimate enterprise, legal prohibition guarantees them huge profits. The classic example of this process is the prohibition of alcohol in the United States during the 1920s and early 1930s. As many Americans sought new sources of alcoholic beverages, gangs of criminals began to supply them. The result was widespread gangsterism and disrespect for the law. Gang bosses like Al Capone, who built his illegal empire by bootlegging alcohol, virtually controlled some American cities.

In addition to organized crime, drug prohibition encourages the growth of deviant subcultures among users who band together to share their experiences and defeat the government's efforts to cut supplies of their drug. Many marijuana users report that they originally were more attracted to the camaraderie and friendship of other drug users than to the effects of the drug itself. And finally, the enforcement effort poses a serious threat to civil liberties. Drug offenses seldom have victims who call the police. Law enforcement agencies must therefore resort to such questionable techniques as the employment of wiretaps, undercover agents, and spies to flush out violations.

Of course, these criticisms do not necessarily mean that the enforcement approach should be abandoned, for the results may be judged to be worth the price. But they do suggest that it is far more preferable to reduce the demand for drugs through education and treatment.

DEBATE

Should We Prohibit Involuntary Drug Testing?

One of the newest ideas to deal with the drug problem is to require workers to be periodically tested for illegal drugs, and either fire violators or force them into drug treatment programs. A recent survey found that 63 percent of American corporations now have some kind of drug testing program (see Chapter 3).

YES The phony "drug epidemic" whipped up by politicians and sensationalistic journalists has reached hysterical proportions and threatens to sweep away our most cherished civil rights. The fact of the matter is that drug use is going down, not up. But no matter what the latest trends may show, it is intolerable to allow the government and the corporations to dictate the standards by which we must lead our personal lives.

Employers have every right to fire employees whose drug use interferes with their work. But what right does an employer have to fire someone who is doing a good job, because he or she smoked marijuana at a party on Friday night? Another injustice inherent in drug testing comes from the tests themselves, which are highly inaccurate and often give false results. Moreover, they are not equally sensitive to all drugs. Marijuana, a relatively harmless drug, can be detected weeks after it has been used, whereas more dangerous drugs such as heroin cannot. Thus, marijuana smokers might be encouraged to change to cocaine, heroin, and other more hazardous drugs. And what about alcohol? If we are going to fire marijuana smokers, shouldn't we fire alcohol drinkers too? And for that matter, what about tobacco smokers, caffeine drinkers, unfaithful husbands, or political radicals? The new programs of involuntary drug testing are a step toward a totalitarian police state and must be stopped now!

NO Drugs are a menace to the very survival of our society. Drugs corrupt children, break up families, and lead hundreds of thousands of people to an early grave. Mandatory drug testing is a serious measure, but only serious measures can solve this frightening problem.

Because drug use has become so widespread in our society, mandatory testing is the only way to ensure that our aircraft pilots, railroad engineers, police officers, and other vital personnel are fit to do their jobs. Without drug testing we can expect to see thousands of innocent people lose their lives in drug-related accidents. But the economic consequences of drug abuse are just as serious as its toll of deaths and injuries. One of the major reasons that our products and our businesses are doing so poorly in world trade is that so many of our workers have drug problems. The workers in Japan and South Korea do not use drugs, and mandatory drug testing is the only way that we are going to remain competitive and ensure a drug-free workplace.

Of course, it would be preferable if workers simply refrained from using drugs without being tested. And if we crack down on drugs now, someday we may reach that goal. But until we do, mandatory drug testing is the most effective weapon we have in the battle against the drug menace, and we must use it.

Increased Social Tolerance An alternative approach to the drug problem is to increase social tolerance for drug use. This approach includes a variety of proposals, ranging from reductions in penalties for some types of drug offenses to full legalization of all drugs. Advocates of such proposals claim that a less punitive reaction to drug use would reduce the negative side effects stemming from legal repression and, in the long run, reduce the need for treatment. If drugs could be obtained legally, it is argued, their attractiveness as "forbidden fruit" would decrease. Further, legalization would take the profit out of drug distribution, thus taking drugs off the street. But even if this approach failed to reduce drug use, its advocates assert that it would still reduce the drug problem by reducing organized crime, destigmatizing drug users, undermining drug subcultures, and eliminating the need for addicts to commit crimes to pay for high-priced illegal drugs.

Legalization Proponents of **legalization** believe that attempts at legal repression of drug use have been so disastrous that the problem can be solved only by taking the government out of the drug-law enforcement business. In practice, regulation by government agencies would undoubtedly continue, as it does in the case of alcohol. Minors would be prohibited from purchasing drugs, and taxation and regulation of quality standards could be expected.

Most proponents of legalization do not advocate over-the-counter sales for all drugs. In fact, marijuana is the only drug for which full legalization has widespread support. Those who do advocate the legalization of all drugs often base their arguments on philosophical opposition to government interference in individuals' lives. The psychiatrist Thomas Szasz, for instance, feels that the decision to use a drug is entirely an individual matter in which the government has no legitimate concern.[64]

Decriminalization A step halfway between prohibition and full legalization is **decriminalization**. Its advocates argue that the penalties for possession and use of a given drug, usually marijuana, should be dropped but that the sale of the drug should continue to be illegal. The aim is to stop punishing those who use illicit drugs but to discourage such use by forbidding sales. Critics of this policy point to the contradiction between allowing legal possession and penalizing sale or purchase. Its advocates, who fear that legalization would encourage a new wave of drug use yet want to reduce the repression of users, propose decriminalization as a compromise. Decriminalization of marijuana use, or reduction of penalties for possession and use of marijuana, has at various times been endorsed by American and Canadian commissions on drug use, the American Medical Association, and the American Bar Association. Eleven states decriminalized possession of small amounts of marijuana during the 1970s. But the new wave of concern about drug abuse has stopped this trend, and no new states have joined them.[65] A 1986 poll found that 57 percent of those questioned opposed the decriminalization of marijuana and 36 percent supported it.[66]

Maintenance Through **maintenance programs** addicts or habitual users can be supplied with a drug while it is still prohibited among the public at large. This approach is usually advocated for the opiates, but it could also be applied to other addictive drugs. The only widely used maintenance program in the United States or Canada is the distribution of methadone (a synthetic opiate) to heroin addicts. Although methadone maintenance is often called treatment, it has little in common with real treatment programs. In essence, these programs simply provide a restricted legal supply of an opiate to people who otherwise would obtain opiates illegally.

Supporters of methadone maintenance programs believe that methadone has several advantages over heroin: its effects last longer, it can be given orally, and it does not generate the intense high that is produced by heroin. However, many heroin addicts refuse to participate in methadone programs because they prefer heroin. Critics, including some ex-addicts, argue that methadone is just another narcotic and that dispensing it to heroin users does nothing to solve the addiction problem.

Another issue concerns the method used to distribute methadone. In current programs the addict must go to a special clinic and is given only a small dose. This technique is designed to minimize the diversion of methadone into the black market. Critics say that these programs throw addicts into association with one another just when they are trying to escape the culture of addiction, that they unreasonably restrict addicts' freedom to travel, and that they are demeaning because they require addicts to wait in line for their daily handout. Some have proposed that a different kind of maintenance program be established, one that allows individual physicians, rather than government clinics, to distribute any opiate the patient needs, including heroin.[67]

The Dutch Approach Some advocates of a new approach to the drug problem point to the Netherlands as a possible model. Dutch drug policy is an interesting combination of four elements. The first is the official tolerance of "soft drugs" (marijuana and hashish). Although technically illegal, many cafés openly sell marijuana without fear of arrests or fines. The second is a tough enforcement effort aimed at the dealers of hard drugs, such as heroin and cocaine, that are often smuggled into Rotterdam—the world's largest port. The third element of Dutch policy is the decriminalization of all users. No one is jailed for merely possessing or using any drug. Finally, the Dutch have made treatment and maintenance programs easily available for all addicts.

Dutch officials have attempted to drive a wedge between hard and soft drug users by closing down clubs that tolerate hard drugs, while allowing the use of soft drugs to continue unmolested. Those addicted to hard drugs are encouraged to register with the government, and "methadone buses" travel around Amsterdam distributing maintenance doses to addicts. There are also free needle exchanges that encourage addicts to trade in their used needles for sterile ones in hopes of discouraging the spread of AIDS and other diseases.

In the last decade, Holland has seen both a sharp decline in the number of heroin addicts and an increase in their average age (indicating that fewer young people are starting the habit). Equally impressive is the fact that the Netherlands never experienced the cocaine epidemic that created such a crisis in North America. But despite these successes, the critics of increased tolerance for drug users remain unconvinced. They argue that the Dutch experience is not applicable to the United States, because the Netherlands has no large ethnic ghettos and a much more generous welfare system that makes poverty far less severe.[68]

SOCIOLOGICAL PERSPECTIVES ON DRUG USE

The Functionalist Perspective Functionalist theory does not attempt to explain the specific reasons why individuals use or do not use drugs. It concerns itself with the social conditions that have caused the tremendous increase in drug use in industrial society. Many functionalists assume that drug use is a means of escaping from difficult and unpleasant social circumstances. Consequently, drug abuse is seen as a response to other social problems, such as poverty, worker alienation, and racism. To these functionalists, the way to reduce substance abuse is to deal with the underlying problems that cause it. This is obviously no simple matter, but the functionalists have numerous proposals for improvements, many of which are described in the other chapters in this book.

Other functionalists, however, look at the causes of drug use in a different way. They feel that the use of drugs is inherently pleasurable and that, despite the serious consequences, people will take them unless prevented from doing so. The steep increase in drug consumption in the twentieth century is seen as the result of the weakening of the family and religious institutions that formerly kept antisocial behavior in check. The most direct way to deal with the drug problem is therefore to strengthen these institutions. But many functionalists feel that the historical developments that have occurred are irreversible, and that industrial societies must rely on formal mechanisms of social control—that is, the criminal-justice system. These functionalists often criticize the disorganization of our system of justice. They argue that the inefficiency, inadequate funding, and payoffs and corruption that characterize so many of our criminal-justice agencies must be halted if we are to solve the drug problem.

The Conflict Perspective Some conflict theorists also assume that drug users are escapists and agree that drug use is caused by other social problems. However, they hold that these social problems, such as unemployment, stem from exploitation and injustice rather than from social disorganization. Like their counterparts among the functionalists, these conflict theorists advocate a direct attack on the primary problem—exploitation—rather than on the symptoms of the problem—drug use. They argue that drug use will decrease only after a just society, free from racism, poverty, and oppression, is created.

Other conflict theorists strongly disagree, asserting that drug use itself is neither escapist nor a social problem. Rather, it is normal behavior that occurs in all societies around the world. According to these theorists, drug use becomes a problem only when groups who oppose drugs use the power of the state to force their morality on everyone else. The inevitable result of such actions is social conflict, violent repression of drug users, and a booming black market.

Most conflict theorists argue that people should not be jailed for using drugs if their behavior causes no danger to others. Conflict theorists also say that the attempt to repress drug use creates secondary social problems, such as organized crime and a seething discontent with the legal system. Those who hold this viewpoint advocate a simple solution to the drug problem: legalize the prohibited drugs and stop jailing people who have done nothing worse than refuse to accept the dominant society's idea of what is good for them. If drug users victimize others to support their habit, they should be sent to prison; otherwise they should be left alone.

Social Psychological Perspectives   Most research into the causes of and solutions to the drug problem has been at the social psychological level. As our previous discussion has suggested, each of the four major social psychological theories has its own explanations of drug use and its preferred treatments. Biosocial theorists say that drug addiction is a physiological problem and recommend more research to develop a biochemical cure. Personality theory holds that addiction is caused by defects in the addict's personality and recommends psychotherapy. Interactionists and behaviorists agree that drug addiction is learned behavior and recommend treatment programs designed to help addicts learn less destructive patterns of behavior.

SUMMARY

Many people have mistaken ideas about drug use. For example, it is widely believed that alcohol and tobacco are not drugs because they are legal, but there is actually little difference between these drugs and the illegal ones. Another misconception is that drug use is a new epidemic that is sweeping through our society. Surveys and sales figures indicate that total drug use has actually gone down sharply in the last decade.

Many drugs are habit-forming, meaning that continual use produces tolerance and that the user becomes sick when the drug is withdrawn. Addiction is the strong craving that often develops when one uses habit-forming drugs.

Alcohol is the most popular recreational drug, and it also creates the most problems for society. It is a depressant and is addictive if used in excess. Tobacco is another widely used legal drug. Cigarette smoking has been shown to be highly dangerous, yet large numbers of people start smoking every year.

Marijuana is the most widely used illegal drug, although its popularity has declined in recent years. The opiates are all highly addictive. Although the drugs themselves do not appear to cause great physical harm, the way they are used and the life style of most addicts make these drugs extremely dangerous. Mescaline and LSD are two of the most popular psychedelic drugs, and both produce powerful psychological changes in the user that may be positive or negative. The psychedelics produce few health problems but may create serious emotional disturbances in some users. The sedative-hypnotics depress the central nervous system and are frequently prescribed by physicians, but there is also a flourishing black market for many of these drugs, which have effects similar to alcohol.

The amphetamines are stimulants. Excessive amphetamine use can produce a psychotic state as well as considerable physical damage. Cocaine is a natural stimulant with effects similar to those of the amphetamines. It is one of the few drugs that increased in popularity in the 1980s.

Biological theories hold that some people have an inherited predisposition toward alcoholism or drug addiction. Behavioral theory sees drug use and addiction as products of conditioning: people use drugs because they find the experience to be rewarding, and addicts continue to take drugs because they want to avoid painful withdrawal. Personality theorists argue that individuals who use drugs have inadequate or impulsive personalities. According to interactionist theory, drug use stems from attitudes, values, and definitions favorable to such behavior, often learned in drug subcultures.

The early North American colonists had few problems with drugs. Later, heavy drinking patterns developed among single men on the frontier, while more respectable farm families began to give up drinking. Several prohibitionist movements swept North America in the early twentieth century and resulted in the banning of alcohol, opiates, and marijuana. Prohibition of these drugs fostered drug subcultures among some users, who were branded as criminals.

Proposals for dealing with the drug problem fall into four main categories. The first consists of prevention programs designed to stop people from getting involved with drugs or using them to excess. The second approach is to treat drug users to help them stop using drugs. The most successful treatment programs use some form of group support. A third set of proposals aim to increase legal repression of drug use. This approach discourages drug use but has damaging side effects, including the growth of organized crime and drug subcultures. Increased social tolerance of drug use is a fourth alternative. Included in this category are legalization, decriminalization, and maintenance programs, as well as the multifaceted approach used in the Netherlands.

Functionalists generally assume that drug use is a means of escaping from unpleasant social conditions that have arisen as society has become disorganized. Some conflict theorists also assume that drug users are escapists, but they are convinced that the tensions drug users seek to avoid stem from exploitation rather than from social disorganization. Other conflict theorists consider drug use to be normal behavior and argue that the problem lies in the state's attempts to repress it.

KEY TERMS

addiction The intense craving for a drug that develops after a period of physical dependence.

alcoholic A person whose work or family and social life is disrupted by heavy drinking.

decriminalization Repeal of the penalties for possession and use of a drug. The penalties for sales, however, generally remain.

depressant A drug that slows the responses of the central nervous system, reduces coordination, and decreases mental alertness.

stimulant A drug that arouses the central nervous system, increases the metabolic rate, and reduces drowsiness.

FURTHER READINGS

Richard G. Schlaadt and Peter T. Shannon, *Drugs*, 3rd ed. (Englewood Cliffs, N.J.: Prentice-Hall, 1991). An up-to-date text covering a broad range of drugs and drug problems.

Ronald Hamowy, ed., *Dealing with Drugs: Consequences of Government Control* (San Francisco: Pacific Research Institutes for Social Policy, 1987). A good collection of articles examining the effects of current legal policies toward drugs.

Jay Stevens, *Storming Heaven: LSD and the American Dream* (New York: Atlantic Monthly Press, 1987). A fascinating account of the history of the use of LSD in the United States.

Edmundo Morales, *White Gold* (Tucson: University of Arizona Press, 1988). A Peruvian sociologist examines the impact of the cocaine trade on the villagers of the Andes Mountains.

Joseph Gusfield, *Symbolic Crusade: Status Politics and the American Temperance Movement* (Urbana: University of Illinois Press, 1963). By now a classic work on the historical origins of the drive to prohibit alcohol use in the United States.

chapter 13

Crime and Violence

- What are the most serious types of crime and violence?
- What do statistics tell us about the crime problem?

- What are the causes of crime?
- How does society deal with crime?
- What can be done to reduce crime?

The fear of crime and violence haunts the great cities of North America, and it seems to be spreading out to the suburbs and towns as well. One in every five American households is touched by crime every year, and the total losses run to billions of dollars.[1] Although only a small percentage of those crimes are violent ones, many people are so terrorized that they are literally afraid to leave their homes. As many as 59 percent of American women and 44 percent of Canadian women say they are afraid to walk outdoors at night even in their own neighborhood.[2] Yet despite an overwhelming public concern, the average citizen is poorly informed about the nature of the crime problem and is frequently misled by sensationalistic news reporting and the claims of opportunistic politicians. During the 1980s, for example, those who believed that crime was increasing outnumbered those who felt it was decreasing by from 2 to 1 to as many as 13 to 1.[3] But as we will see, the evidence shows that crime was actually going down.

THE NATURE OF CRIME AND VIOLENCE

Any act that is intended to cause physical pain, injury, or death to another is violent. **Violence** therefore includes everything from spanking a child to a thermonuclear war. However, the focus of this chapter is on crime (whether violent or not); warfare and terrorism will be covered in Chapter 18. **Crime** is usually defined as a violation of the criminal law. No matter how indecent or immoral an act may be, it is not a crime unless the criminal law has listed it as such and provided a punishment for it. In practice, of course, it is not always easy to tell whether a specific act is or is not a burglary, a robbery, a rape, or some other crime. Roscoe Pound, a famous American legal scholar, once pointed out that there is a great difference between "law on the books" and "law in action." In other words, what the criminal law says and what police and the courts do are often quite different. For example, some old laws—such as those outlawing certain sex acts—remain legally valid but are almost never enforced, and other laws such as those making it a crime to go nude on a beach are sometimes enforced and sometimes ignored. But even the most widely accepted laws are still enforced selectively. This means, for example, that an act might be called burglary if it is committed by a poor person—especially one with a criminal record—but might be called trespassing or some other minor offense if it is committed by someone who is more "respectable."

Because such a confusing hodgepodge of different behaviors may be considered as crimes, much effort has gone into an attempt to classify them in some orderly way. Legally, the most serious offenses are classified as **felonies** and the less important ones as **misdemeanors**. Generally speaking, the more serious the crime, the less frequently it occurs. The police are about 400 times more likely to make an arrest for drunkenness, disorderly conduct, or driving under the influence than for murder.[4] For statistical purposes, crimes are usually classified as offenses against persons (violent crime), crimes against property (property crime), and crimes against public decency and order (victimless crime). This approach is useful for sociologists, because it groups similar types of offenses together, but it is still necessary to break down those large categories into smaller ones. The two most important victimless crimes have already been examined. Forbidden sexual practices such as prostitution and pornography were discussed in Chapter 11, and the use of illicit drugs in Chapter 12. The FBI lists four major violent crimes—murder, assault, rape, and robbery—but because of their similarity, we will consider murder and assault together. Rape will be covered separately, and robbery is included in the section on property crime. Finally, three crimes that are directed against both persons and property will be explored: juvenile delinquency, syndicated crime, and white-collar crime.

Murder and Assault   **Murder** is not the same as **homicide**. Homicide is the killing of any human being. Murder is an illegal homicide committed with what lawyers call "malice aforethought." Thus, the killing of enemies in wartime, killing in self-defense, and killing in lawful execution of a judicial sentence are all homicides but not murders, because they are neither malicious nor unlawful. **Manslaughter** is the unlawful killing of another person without malice aforethought, as in a traffic accident caused by a reckless driver.

An **assault** occurs when one person attacks another with the intention of hurting or killing the victim. There is little difference between some murders and some assaults. The fact that the victim of an armed attack got to a hospital in time to be saved may spell the difference between one crime and the other. Most assaults do not involve deadly force, however. A punch in the belly is an assault. So is a slap in the face. But the essence of assault is the intention to do harm. If your professor raises his fist at you in a menacing manner, you have been assaulted. You are also assaulted by anyone who takes a swing at you and misses. An "aggravated assault" usually involves a more serious injury than a "simple assault."

Newspaper and television reports focus on dramatic crimes such as mass murders, "gang war," and particularly brutal and vicious attacks. Such media coverage misleads the public. The fact is that few people are attacked or killed by a demented stranger. We are actually far more likely to be killed by a relative, friend, or acquaintance. Indeed, the closeness of the relationship may add to the violence of the attack when someone feels betrayed or insulted.

Marvin E. Wolfgang's classic study of murder in Philadelphia found that only 15 percent of the 550 murders he analyzed occurred between strangers; almost 60 percent occurred between relatives or close friends.[5] More recent data show much the same picture. Only about 19 percent of the murders for which we had information in 1989 were committed by strangers.[6] Studies of assault show that victims are less likely to know their attackers but are still acquainted in almost half of the cases.[7] One's chances of being assaulted or killed, therefore, depend more on one's relationship with relatives and friends than on the whim of some predatory stranger.

Alcohol is frequently an important contributing factor in murders and assaults, as it is for violent crime in general. Slightly over half of all those in prison for violent crimes report they were under the influence of alcohol or other drugs at the time of their offense.[8] Gender also plays a major role—both assault and murder are much more common among men than women. Not only are the large majority of the offenders men, but so are most of their victims. Men are more than twice as likely as women to be the victims of an aggravated assault, and three times more likely to be murdered. However, a woman is about 30 percent more likely to be killed by someone she is romantically involved with than a man, and over a quarter of all the women who are murdered in the United States are killed by their husband or boyfriend.[9]

Rape   Although the laws differ from place to place, **forcible rape** is usually defined as sexual intercourse forced upon a person without consent. So-called **statutory rape** is not a violent crime, but is sexual intercourse between an adult and someone below the legally defined age of consent, which is usually 16 to 18 years old. Many jurisdictions now use the more appropriate term *illegal intercourse* for this offense.

Studies show that there are two distinct patterns of forcible rape. In the first type, the rape arises from the social interaction between friends or acquaintances, often on a spur-of-the-moment basis. This type of sexual assault is sometimes known as *date rape*; however, that term is misleading because this kind of offense occurs in many other circumstances as well. The other pattern of rape usually takes place between strangers. The rapist, often a repeat offender, actively seeks out a victim with the prior intention of raping her. The rapist may wait on a dark street for a lone woman to walk by, search for an unsuspecting hitchhiker, or break into a woman's home. Because the first type of rape is less likely to be reported to the police, it is difficult to determine which pattern is more common. About two-thirds of the persons who told the National Crime Survey that they had been raped knew their attacker, but other research has not provided consistent support for this or any other conclusion on this issue.[10] According to the National Crime Survey, rape is equally likely to occur in the home of the victim or a friend, or in a public place such as a parking lot or a street.[11]

It is extremely difficult to measure the amount of rape accurately. The National Crime Survey puts the rate of victimization at about 1.2 rapes for every 1,000 women over the age of 12, but other research, using different methodology and different definitions of rape, has put the figure far higher. Studies of college women, for example, have found that somewhere between 11 and 25 percent report having been forced to have sexual intercourse by a date or a boyfriend.[12] Whatever the exact number, the fear of rape has a profound effect on the way most women live their lives, forcing them either to severely restrict their freedom of action or to run the constant risk of victimization. As one woman put it: "I know what I can't do and I've completely internalized what I can't do. I've built a viable life that basically involves never leaving my apartment at night unless I'm directly going someplace to meet somebody. It's unconsciously built into what it occurs to women to do."[13]

Unlike the victims of other violent crimes, most rape victims are female. For every male who reported being the victim of a rape to the National Crime Survey, there were 12 females. The attackers, on the other hand, are overwhelmingly males. Only about 1 in 50 victims who had been attacked by just one person reported that the attacker was a female.[14] Thus, even most male victims are raped by other men. Those who are 16 to 19 years old are at greatest risk of being rape victims, and the rate of victimization drops off sharply after age 34. In 1988, those with family incomes under $15,000 a year were more than 20 times more likely to report being raped than those with family incomes above $30,000, and blacks were almost three times more likely to be victimized than whites.[15] Data from the National Crime Survey indicate that victims who physically resist their attackers are often successful in preventing the completion of the rape. The attacker completes the rape in only 32 percent of the cases in which the victim resists, but in 56 percent of the cases where she does not. However, resistance by the victim is also related to an increase in the probability of such injuries as black eyes and cuts.[16]

Property Crime Although most people are much more worried about being the victim of violence than of a property crime, the latter is nearly ten times more frequent. **Theft**—taking the property of another—is by far the most common property crime. (Legally, this crime is called *larceny* in many jurisdictions.) Many thefts are related in one way or another to the automobile. According to FBI figures, stealing something from an automobile (or truck) is the most widespread type of theft reported to the police. Taking the whole vehicle is the second most common, and the theft of motor vehicle accessories such as stereos or wheels is third. Motor vehicle crimes are followed by thefts from buildings (such as homes or factories), shoplifting, and bicycle theft.[17] Although **robbery**—theft by force—is officially classified as a violent crime, for sociological purposes it is best grouped with the property crimes. Unlike most other violent crimes, robbery is seldom a crime of passion and the offenders and their victims are unlikely to know each other. **Burglary**—the unlawful entry into a structure with the intent to commit a felony—is legally separate from theft. In most cases, however, the crime the burglar intends to commit is in fact a theft. A **fraud** involves trickery and deception rather than just walking off with someone's property. Fraud is common in the business world; offenses of this sort will be discussed in the section on white-collar crime. Off the job, the most common forms of fraud involve checks and credit cards. Contrary to popular belief, it is a crime to write a check when you know that you do not have sufficient funds to cover it. Finally, **arson** is the intentional burning of a structure or other property and is often part of some kind of insurance fraud. It is estimated that 30 percent of all losses from fires are caused by arson.[18]

The key to understanding these crimes is to recognize the diversity in the offenders' motivations and techniques. On one end of the spectrum are the occasional criminals who steal something only when they are short of money or happen to stumble on an especially attractive opportunity—a woman's purse sitting on the seat of an unlocked car or a store left untended while the clerk runs out to get coffee. The occasional criminal is not usually very skilled and lacks a wide range of criminal contacts. On the other extreme are the highly skilled professional criminals, such as safe crackers and counterfeiters, who know the fences who pay the best price for stolen merchandise, the lawyers who might be able to "fix" a case, and the latest technology used to deter them. Amateur criminals usually commit crimes with a relatively small take—often stealing things for their own personal use or, in the case of juveniles, just to prove they have the guts to do it. The professional thief looks for the highest possible cash return and is far less likely to be deterred by such things as dead-bolt locks or burglar alarms. The skills of professional criminals make it far less likely that they will be caught for any one crime, but, because they repeat their offenses so often, the odds are that their luck will eventually run out.

Syndicated Crime From the Yakuza of Japan to the South American cocaine cartels, **syndicated crime** is a worldwide problem. In North America, the most famous criminal syndicate is the Italian-Sicilian organization sometimes known as the Cosa Nostra or Mafia, but this old-time criminal organization is being strongly challenged by new black, Hispanic, and Asian groups. Although such criminal syndicates are more frequently referred to as *organized crime*, that term is misleading, since many other types of crime are also highly organized.[19] What sets syndicated criminals apart from other criminals is that they work together in large groups. As a result, they have far more power to threaten their enemies and to buy protection from law enforcement agencies. In fact, it is often said that large-scale syndicated crime would be impossible without the widespread corruption it creates.[20]

Criminal syndicates are, in many ways, very much like legitimate businesses (and, as we will see, many legitimate businesses also have their similarities to the criminal syndicates). Like most businesses, their principal source of income is selling goods and services to the public. The main difference is that the criminal syndicates sell illegal goods such as drugs and provide forbidden services such as gambling, loan sharking, and prostitution. In the beginning, a new criminal syndicate is usually run by violent young toughs who operate in a small area. If the group grows and prospers, it is likely to come into greater contact with the legitimate world, seeking to corrupt law enforcement, curry favor with politicians, and hide its profits in legitimate investments. Eventually, such syndicates may come to operate a number of legitimate businesses along with their criminal operations.

White-Collar Crime   White-collar crimes cost more money and more lives than all other types of crimes put together. Although accurate tallies of the financial burden of white-collar crime are hard to come by, a conservative estimate would place the yearly losses from 20 to 30 times higher than the losses from street crime.[21] For example, in 1988 the average robbery netted $631 and the average theft $426.[22] The collapse of the savings and loan industry, on the other hand, is expected to cost as much *$500 billion*, and estimates are that outright fraud accounts for anywhere between 40 to 80 percent of those losses.[23]

Most people do not think of white-collar offenses as violent crime, and it is true that the criminals seldom intend to injure or kill anyone. Nonetheless, the yearly death toll from unsafe products, worker safety violations, the illegal dumping of toxic wastes, and other corporate crimes is far higher than that from murder. The cover-up of the deadly hazards of asbestos by its manufacturers will probably cost as many lives as all the murders in the United States for an entire decade. And in addition to our lives and our money, white-collar criminals threaten something else as well: political freedom. The assassinations of foreign political leaders, the illegal surveillance and harassment of groups opposed to government policy, election fraud, and the kind of political dirty tricks involved in the Watergate scandal are all important white-collar crimes.[24]

Edwin H. Sutherland originally coined the term *white-collar crime* to call attention to the weaknesses in theories that say crime is due to personal pathologies or poverty (such theories obviously cannot account for most criminal activities among the upper classes). He defined **white-collar crime** as any "crime committed by a person of respectability and high social status in the course of his occupation."[25] There are two basic types of white-collar crime. **Organizational crimes** are committed by people

White-collar crime costs the public far more than any other type of offense. Michael Milken, the convicted white-collar offender shown in this photograph, is reported to have made more than half a billion dollars in a single year through illegal activities.

who are acting on behalf of the organization for which they work. **Occupational crimes** are committed solely to advance the personal interests of the criminal. For example, when employees embezzle money from a bank, the crime is occupational because the employees are obviously not working for the interests of their employer. But when an executive of a pharmaceutical company covers up negative findings from its research lab and claims that a potentially dangerous new drug is perfectly safe, it is an organizational crime because the offense was committed to benefit the company.

There are white-collar criminals in every type of occupation, from accounting to zoology, and in every type of organization, from the corner grocery store to huge government bureaucracies. Many of the victims of such criminals do not know that they have been victimized and therefore do not complain to the police or anyone else. For this reason the public is often unaware how serious the problem of white-collar crime really is.

Numerous studies have also shown that those charged with white-collar crimes are less likely to be prosecuted and convicted than those charged with comparable "street crimes." And when the defendants in white-collar cases are convicted, they receive a lighter sentence.[26] But the most leniency goes to the big corporations. The famous University of Wisconsin study of corporate crime headed by sociologist Marshall B. Clinard found that the major corporations were seldom given any real punishment for their illegal activities. Almost half of the "penalties" given to the 477 largest manufacturing firms in the United States for their illegal activities were merely warnings. The corporations were fined for fewer than a quarter of their offenses, and those fines averaged only about $1,000—hardly a significant punishment for a multibillion-dollar business.[27]

There are several reasons why white-collar criminals receive such lenient treatment. For one thing, their status and respectability make many people—law enforcement officials included—reluctant to believe they are criminals. And of course, if they are charged with a crime, they can afford the best defense available. In the case of corporate crimes, the defendants can overwhelm the enforcement agencies, which are almost always underfunded and understaffed. Their enormous economic and political power also enables many corporate criminals to bring almost irresistible outside pressures to bear on enforcement agents. Even the laws themselves are often written to reflect the interests of the corporate offenders and not the general public. Finally, the thousands of victims of such white-collar crimes as false advertising and price fixing lose only a few dollars each; so there is less public resentment than when a criminal strikes more heavily at a few individual victims. Indeed, many of the victims of white-collar crimes never know they have been victimized.

Juvenile Delinquency The difference between crime and **juvenile delinquency** is not simply a matter of age. It is true that adults who violate criminal laws are called criminals, while juveniles who do the same things are called delinquents. But this is only part of the story. A substantial portion of all juvenile delinquents have never even been accused of doing anything that would be against the law if they were adults. Runaways, truants, and violators of curfew laws, for example, are delinquents only because they have broken laws pertaining to the behavior of juveniles.

Anthony Platt has shown that the concept of delinquency was created in the latter part of the nineteenth century by middle-class reformers he calls the "child savers."[28] Despite their good intentions, Platt argues, the child savers' efforts to create a special juvenile justice system to deal with delinquency introduced government controls over juveniles who did nothing more than violate middle-class standards of propriety. In the 1960s, civil libertarians began voicing strong objections to the practices of the juvenile courts. In theory, the juvenile courts were allowed to operate with fewer legal safeguards because they were intended to help, not punish, young people. But the civil libertarians argued that the juvenile courts were actually just as punitive as the adult courts. They eventually persuaded the Supreme Court to go along, and the juvenile courts are now run much more like their adult counterparts. For instance, many states no longer define running away, incorrigibility, and other **status offenses** (juvenile offenses that do not violate the criminal law) as delinquency. At the same time, juveniles are increasingly being prosecuted for their delinquencies in the same ways as adults are prosecuted for their crimes.

Juvenile delinquency—at least the acts of juveniles that would be crimes if committed by adults—has probably been studied more carefully than any other category of crime. The principal explanations of crime were developed from the study of delinquency as well as adult criminality, and all of them are used to understand delinquency as well as crime. Nevertheless, juveniles have special problems and should not be considered merely young criminals. For one thing, the influence of the family is certainly greater in the lives of juvenile delinquents than of adult criminals. A number of studies show that children are much more likely to become delinquent if one of their parents is a criminal. Self-report studies show that children from all economic backgrounds commit minor acts of delinquency at about the same rate, but that children from poor homes are much more likely to commit serious criminal acts.[29] Delinquency also occurs more often among children in single-parent families. After a careful review of 50 different studies on this subject, L. Edward Wells and Joseph H. Rankin concluded that the prevalence of delinquency was 10 to 15 percent higher among children from broken homes. However, it seems to make no difference if the family is dismembered by a divorce or by the death of a parent.[30] Another unique problem of juvenile offenders is youth itself (see Chapter 9). In traditional cultures people go directly from being a child to being an adult. But in industrialized nations there is an extended in-between period of adolescence in which difficult demands are placed on young people. Adolescents are not considered old enough for marriage and family responsibilities of their own, yet they are too old to remain totally dependent on their parents. In a sense they are between two worlds and part of neither.

Finally, the problem of juvenile gangs deserves mention. Adolescents all over the world form groups based on friendship and mutual interests. When these groups meet social approval, we call them clubs; but when the community condemns them, they are called gangs. Juvenile gangs of streetwise young toughs roam the streets of most urban slums and ghettos. The primary motivation of the "fighting gang" is to control their "turf" (territory) and defend their honor, sometimes to the death. Some of these gangs have long histories, going back 30 or 40 years, and gang fights and killings have been a fact of life in some urban neighborhoods for generations. Some juvenile gangs, however, are more concerned with making an illicit profit than fighting gang wars, and they bear a closer resemblance to the syndicates of adult criminals.

MEASURING CRIME AND VIOLENCE

One of the first steps toward understanding crime is to measure it accurately, but that task is much harder than it sounds. Criminals are often unwilling to talk about their activities, and the general public's knowledge about their own victimization is frequently inaccurate. For example, a homeowner who develops cancer may not know that the cause was toxic waste illegally dumped on a nearby lot, or a man who loses his wallet may mistakenly believe it was stolen.

Criminologists use four principal means of measuring crime, each with its own strengths and weaknesses. The first source of statistics available to criminologists were the crimes reported to the police. Since the 1930s, the FBI has published a summary of all the crimes reported to police agencies in the United States, and other industrialized nations now have similar publications. These FBI statistics, known as the **Uniform Crime Reports**, or UCR, were virtually the only source of nationwide data on crime until the 1970s, when the federal government began conducting a yearly crime survey. This **National Crime Survey** (NCS) asks a random sample of Americans to report information about any crimes of which they were the victim in the last year. Of the two, the National Crime Survey is generally considered the more accurate because many victims are either afraid to report their problem to the police or simply don't want to take the time. The National Crime Survey's reports show about twice as much crime as the UCR.

But neither the victimization surveys nor the tallies of the crimes reported to the police contain very much direct information about who commits those crimes. For that, criminologists often use **arrest statistics**. Such figures gives us a variety of information about the characteristics of those who are arrested (sex, age, ethnic group, etc.), but they have one major flaw. Everyone who commits a crime does not have an equal chance of being arrested, and therefore these statistics may not paint an accurate picture of the typical criminal. To try to solve this problem, some criminologists conduct what are called **self-report studies**. That is, they ask a sample of people to report anonymously on the crimes they themselves have committed. The obvious drawback in this approach is that despite the assurance of anonymity, many people are still afraid to describe their criminal activities honestly, especially their more serious offenses.

Is There a Crime Wave? Many people throughout the industrialized world are convinced that we are in the midst of a massive crime wave that is threatening their property and their personal safety. In the United States, the main support for this belief comes from the Uniform Crime Reports. Except for a brief decline from 1980 to 1984, the UCR shows a steady increase in crime for the last three decades.[31] However, there are serious questions about how accurate those data are. Greater confidence in the police, quicker and easier ways of reporting crime, improved record keeping, and the growing popularity of theft insurance (which requires victims to report a crime in order to collect) have all tended to artificially boost the number of crimes that are reported. Moreover, many criminologists believe that some police departments intentionally exaggerate the increases in crime in order to justify their requests for more money and more personnel. On the other hand, data from the National Crime Survey indicate that crime has actually been declining. From 1973 to 1989, the overall crime rate reported by the NCS dropped by about 21 percent.[32] (See Figure 13.1.) Given the weakness of the Uniform Crime Reports, the most likely conclusion is that crime has been going down, not up, in recent years. There are, moreover, good reasons for believing that the crime rate should be declining. The average age of our population has been rising, and, as we will see in the next section, older people commit fewer crimes.

Who Commits Crime? Criminologists agree that three variables—age, gender, and geographic area—all have an important influence on the incidence of crime. In the United States, about 6 times as many men as women are arrested and about 18 times as many are sent to prison, and similar ratios exist in other nations as well.[33] Of course, some of this difference may stem from the fact that the criminal-justice system expects more men to be criminals and therefore watches them more closely. But when the respondents in the National Crime Survey are asked about the gender of the criminals who victimized them, their responses are generally consistent with the gender ratios

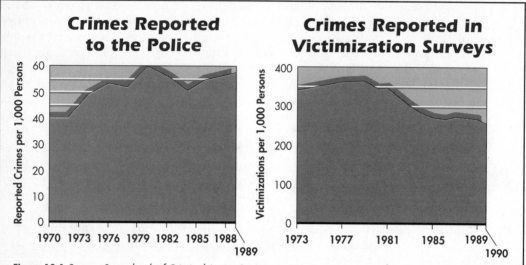

Figure 13.1 *Source: Sourcebook of Criminal Justice Statistics, 1990,* p. 353; Bureau of Justice Statistics, *Criminal Victimization, 1990.*

in the arrest reports.[34] The crime rate for women has, however, been growing faster than the rate for men. The biggest increases have been in the nonviolent property crimes, such as larceny (theft), fraud, and embezzlement, where 30 to 40 percent of the arrestees are now female. The rise in violent crime among women, on the other hand, has not been very significant. And even for the nonviolent property crimes, there are still some important differences in the kind of offenses committed by women and by men. The value of the take from women's crimes is generally much lower than from men's crimes, and women are more likely to act as a single individual rather than as part of an organized group.[35] (See Chapter 10 for an examination of the reasons men's and women's behavior often differs so sharply.)

Records of arrests and convictions show that teenagers and young adults have the highest crime rate. In the United States, the likelihood of arrest peaks in the 19- to 21-year-old age group and slowly declines after that. But contrary to the popular image of the violent teenage hoodlum, minors commit fewer violent crimes than young adults do. Over 20 percent of the property crimes solved by the police are attributed to minors, but for violent crime that figure is less than 9 percent.[36]

Both victimization surveys and police reports also show that the highest crime rates are found in the decaying inner-city slums and that crime rates decrease as one moves out from the central city to the wealthier residential areas. Crime is lower in the suburbs than in the cities, and lower still in the rural areas (see Chapter 15).

Most criminologists also believe that social class and ethnic group have a powerful effect on crime rates, but there is more controversy about this point. Arrest statistics show some significant differences among ethnic groups in the United States. Jews and Japanese have lower than average arrest rates, while blacks, Hispanics, and Native Americans have higher than average rates. Although African Americans make up about

There has been a big increase in the crime rate for women, but mostly for nonviolent offenses.

12 percent of the population of the United States, they account for about 30 percent of all those arrested. The difference is even more pronounced for violent crime. In 1989, 56 percent of those arrested for murder, 47 percent of those arrested for rape, and 65 percent of those arrested for robbery were African Americans.[37] Official statistics also show that poor people are more likely to be arrested and sent to prison than those from middle- or upper-class backgrounds. Two-thirds to three-fourths of the men and nine-tenths of the women in prison are from the poverty class or the working class. However, there is good reason to doubt that arrest and incarceration statistics are an accurate measure of the extent of crime among those groups, because poor people and members of ethnic minorities are probably more likely to be arrested and sent to prison for their crimes than others are. For one thing, money and influence often serve to protect someone from being arrested or incarcerated, and ethnic stereotypes may lead the police to watch minorities more closely than members of other groups.

Most of the other data, nonetheless, point to the same conclusion as the arrest statistics. At one time, some criminologists claimed that the self-report studies didn't indicate any consistent relationship between crime and social class,[38] but subsequent analyses have shown that to be true only for very minor offenses. Self-report studies that include serious offenses do reveal higher crime rates among the poor.[39] The victimization surveys also provide support for this conclusion. They show that the rates of victimization are highest in poor and minority areas, and the most probable explanation is that the crime rates are higher in those neighborhoods because more criminals live there.[40] According to studies of murder victims, African Americans are about seven times more likely to be murdered than other Americans, and we know from other studies that murderers and their victims are usually from the same ethnic group. Further, when the National Crime Survey asked respondents to identify the race of the criminals who victimized them, blacks were selected in roughly the same proportion as we would predict from the arrest statistics.[41] There is still one serious weakness in our data, however. We have no good measures of the true incidence of most white-collar crimes, because many of the victims of those crimes do not know they have been victimized. Since white-collar offenses are mainly committed by affluent individuals who are not from minority groups, it is impossible to be certain who has the highest overall crime rate. We can say that poor people and ethnic minorities commit more "street" crimes, such as murder, burglary and theft, but that is all.

America: Land of the Violent?   The question of which nations have the highest crime rates and how we can explain the differences among nations is an extremely important one. Unfortunately, though, the data are not good enough for us to draw many firm conclusions. Most other nations do not conduct victimization surveys comparable to the NCS, and variations in the laws and in the way police departments handle their record keeping make comparisons of the statistics on reported crime virtually meaningless. There is, however, one exception to this rule, and that is for the crime of murder. Murder is illegal in virtually all nations, and the seriousness of the offense and the existence of a dead body as evidence mean that most murders are in fact reported to the police.

Although a few Third World nations, such as Thailand and the Philippines, report higher murder rates, the United States has by far the highest rate of any industrialized nation (see Figure 13.2). According to the World Health Organization, the murder rate is five times higher in the United States than in Canada, and seven and a half times higher than in Europe. Data from the International Police Organization (Interpol) indicate that murder is three times more common in the United States than it is in Canada and five times more frequent than in Europe.[42] Although the statistics on rape and robbery are less reliable, there seems little reason to doubt that those crimes are also much more common in the United States.

American violence is often seen as a holdover from the rowdy days of frontier expansion. According to this view, violence became a way of life as an unending stream of settlers fought among themselves and with native peoples for land and profit. However, Canada and Australia were also settled by rough pioneers, and the citizens of those countries have apparently not passed down a violent frontier tradition. America was unique, however, in its extensive use of slave labor, and slavery's legacy of racism and resentment is a major contributor to the pervasiveness of violence. Furthermore, America is an extremely wealthy nation, but, compared with other Western countries, it has a bigger gap between the rich and the poor and inferior welfare and social programs (see Chapter 6). Thus, those at the bottom of

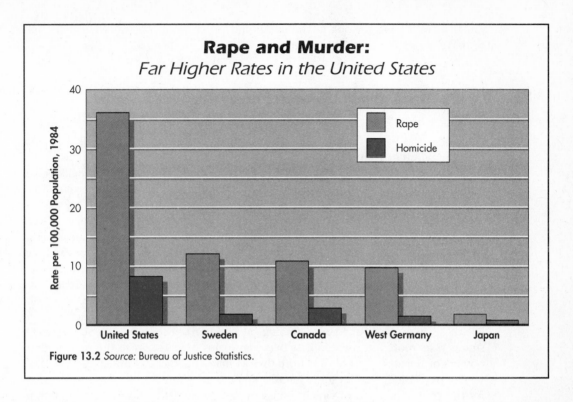

Rape and Murder:
Far Higher Rates in the United States

Rate per 100,000 Population, 1984

Rape
Homicide

United States   Sweden   Canada   West Germany   Japan

Figure 13.2 *Source:* Bureau of Justice Statistics.

the social hierarchy tend to be more frustrated and desperate and more resentful against the powers that be.

THE CAUSES OF CRIME AND VIOLENCE

The birth of modern criminology can be traced to 1764 and the publication of the Italian nobleman Cesare Beccaria's book *On Crimes and Punishments.* The great English philosopher Jeremy Bentham applied Beccaria's ideas to legislation, and these two men became the leaders of what came to be called the classical school of criminology. They thought that all people were guided by a rational desire to seek pleasure and avoid pain. According to the **classical school**, persons who commit a crime choose to do so. They weigh all the options and find that a crime will give them the most pleasure for the least amount of pain. This was regarded as a complete explanation of crime, and these early theorists saw no need for research on the economic, psychological, political, or social conditions associated with crime. The classical school has been heavily criticized for its view of human beings as something like rational calculating machines. Nonetheless, the idea that people violate the law because they feel it will maximize their pleasure and minimize their pain remains popular today. The contemporary proponents of this classical theory are, however, much more willing to look at the social and psychological factors that make one opportunity more attractive than another.

Biological Theories   The first real challenge to the classical school was mounted by an Italian physician, Cesare Lombroso, and his supporters in the last quarter of the nineteenth century. The "positive school" of criminology rejected classical theory's assumption that crime was based on free choice. Proponents felt that most criminals were biologically different from "normal" people and had easily identifiable physical traits such as sloping foreheads, small brains, overdeveloped jaws, and other apelike characteristics. Indeed, Lombroso believed that criminals were actually evolutionary throwbacks to our "savage" ancestors.

Although Lombrosian ideas about the physical characteristics of criminals have been discredited in the scientific community, different kinds of evolutionary theories are still used to explain violent behavior. Martin Daly and Margo Wilson, for example, argue that the basic motives and structure of the human psyche evolved to serve one evolutionary goal: the survival of our genes. Utilizing admittedly incomplete data, they argue that within the family we are most likely to kill those with whom we do not share common genes (for example, spouses and adopted children) and least likely to kill those who carry our genes (biological children). They see violence between strangers as rooted in the conflicts between males over access to the reproductive powers of females and the right to father as many children as possible. This "Darwinian psychology" raises some interesting new questions but is unable to account for the known patterns of violent behavior. We are actually more likely to kill ourselves than to commit a murder, and suicide obviously is an act that will greatly diminish our chances of passing our genes on to the next generation.[43]

Most of the current research in this area is not concerned with evolution but with the overall importance of biological factors as a cause of criminal behavior. The usual approach is to try to determine if those who have a close biological relationship to a known criminal are themselves more likely to be involved in crime. One technique is to compare the criminal records of identical twins (whose genetic makeup is presumed to be identical) to see if such records are more similar than those of fraternal twins. Although most of these studies have found that to be the case, the interpretation of that fact is unclear, because parents and friends tend to treat identical twins more similarly than other twins.

A better methodological approach is found in studies that compare the crime rates of adopted children with those of their biological parents. Once again, most of these studies have found higher crime rates among adopted children whose biological parents were criminals than among those whose biological parents were not. Barry Hutchings and Sarnoff A. Mednick's study of 1,145 boys adopted in Copenhagen, for example, found that having a biological parent as a criminal significantly increased a boy's chances of growing up to be a criminal and that the highest crime rates were among those boys whose adoptive and biological parents were both criminals.[44] But adoption studies still have serious weaknesses. For one thing, adoption agencies do not randomly assign babies to adoptive parents, as scientists would like. Rather, they match up parents and children with similar characteristics, and the social environment of the adopted children may therefore be far more similar to that of their biological parents than the researchers assume. Another problem comes from the fact that adoption agencies screen out those they consider undesirable parents. Since people in homes with conditions that are likely to encourage criminality are not allowed to adopt children, adoption studies are bound to underestimate the impact of the home environment on criminal behavior.[45]

A general problem with the biological theories is that they have yet to determine exactly what inherited characteristics contribute to criminal behavior. James Q. Wilson and Richard Herrnstein speculate that it might be low intelligence or an impulsive personality, but there is little conclusive evidence on the matter.[46] Criminality obviously cannot be directly inherited because crime is defined by legislators and politicians and the definition of what is criminal and what is not is continually changing. It seems likely that inherited traits are related to criminal behavior only by virtue of the fact that people have learned to react to them in a certain way. For example, a student with high intelligence will be more likely to do well in school and receive praise and support from teachers, whereas a student with lesser abilities is far more likely to feel rejected and rebel against school authorities.

Personality Theories There is a widely held belief that many criminals, especially violent ones, are mentally disturbed. After a particularly gruesome murder has occurred, we often hear the comment "A person would have to be crazy to commit a crime like that." Although such statements express understandable shock and disbelief, they don't really tell us much about the causes of crime. Psychiatric examinations of convicted criminals show that only a small percentage are psychotic, and official records indicate that most psychotics are not criminals and have not attacked or harmed other people.[47]

Some psychologists and psychiatrists feel that personality traits lie at the root of criminal behavior. Dozens of personality tests and rating scales have been used to compare criminals and noncriminals, but few significant differences have been found. For example, the most widely used personality test is the Minnesota Multiphasic Personality Inventory (MMPI), and numerous studies have been made of the differences between the scores of criminals and noncriminals over the years. Three comprehensive reviews of the studies using the MMPI or other personality scales—one by Karl Schuessler and Donald R. Cressey in the 1950s, a second by Gordon Waldo and Simon Dinitz in the 1960s, and a third by David Tennenbaum in the 1970s—have all concluded that there was little evidence to support the claim that criminals have distinctive personality characteristics.[48]

Many psychologists and psychiatrists who routinely examine convicted criminals have nonetheless concluded that they often have a **sociopathic personality**. This term is quite vague, but it refers to an inability to form close social relationships combined with a lack of moral feelings or concern for others. Some psychiatrists think that this personality type is hereditary, but the most common explanation is that it develops in early childhood. The method of diagnosing a sociopathic personality is not at all standardized. For this reason, the labels "sociopathic" and "sociopath" can be applied to almost anyone. It appears that the idea of causation is circular. People are labeled sociopathic because they have broken the law, and then it is claimed that people break the law because they are sociopaths.

Sociological Theories   There are dozens of sociological theories of crime and violence. In general, however, they either focus on the reasons an individual commits criminal acts or they examine the larger social forces that determine the overall rates of crime and violence.

The most common answer that sociologists give to the question of why someone becomes a criminal is that he or she has learned to act that way from others. One of the earliest and most influential of these learning theories is known as **differential association**.[49] This theory, developed by Edwin H. Sutherland, says that people become criminals because they are exposed to more people with attitudes and definitions that are favorable to a certain type of crime than are opposed to it. However, all associations and personal contacts do not have the same influence. The longer, the more frequent, the more intense, and the more important an association is to a person, the stronger its effect. Most criminal behavior, like most noncriminal behavior, is therefore learned in intimate personal groups and not from impersonal sources such as movies and television.

Numerous studies of violent behavior have shown that it is often learned from other family members. Murray A. Straus, Richard J. Gelles, and Suzanne K. Steinmetz found that men who grew up in families in which violence was prevalent were ten times more likely to beat their wives than men from nonviolent families.[50] A number of studies show that individuals who were abused as children are at greater risk than others to become child abusers when they grow up.[51] And two recent studies have found that even the physical punishment of children increases the probability that they will commit a violent crime as an adult.[52] The socialization into violence is especially pronounced for boys, who are expected to be tough, strong, and aggressive. A survey conducted by the National Commission on the Causes and Prevention of Violence found that 70 percent of Americans agreed with the statement "When a boy is growing up it is important for him to have a few fist fights."[53] Although they didn't ask about girls, it is unlikely that most parents would feel that a few fist fights would be good for their daughters. Straus, Gelles, and Steinmetz summarized the literature on violence well when they wrote that "over and over again, the statistics . . . suggest the same conclusion. Each generation learns to be violent by participating in a violent family."[54]

Crime and violence are also learned from contact with **deviant subcultures**—that is, groups that have developed perspectives, attitudes, and values that support criminality. The more someone is involved with the members of such a subculture, the more likely he or she is to join in its criminal activities. Many sociologists consider the culture of poverty to be a deviant subculture, since many of its attitudes and values seem to encourage criminal behavior (see Chapter 6). The drug subculture and the subculture of juvenile gang members are also distinctive perspectives on the world, and both reject at least parts of the conventional morality embodied in the criminal law. For a girl or boy from the underclass who is a drug user and a member of a juvenile gang, committing a crime of one kind or another is almost automatic.

Sociologists argue that criminal behavior is often learned from the subcultures to which the offenders belong.

Labeling theory has added to our understanding of the way crime is learned by exploring the process by which people are branded as criminals and the effects such labeling has on them. Contrary to popular opinion, labeling theorists hold that branding someone as a deviant usually encourages further criminal behavior. For example, take the case of an adolescent boy whose "play" includes breaking windows and stealing hubcaps. He might consider such activities as akin to the fun of Halloween, but to most adults his behavior is delinquent, and they soon demand that he stop it. If he continues, there is a shift away from the definition of the *acts* as delinquent to the definition of the *boy* as delinquent. The boy, realizing he is being branded as "bad," draws closer to others with the same problem. The community responds with punishment, counseling, and finally with commitment to an institution. The boy acquires a police record and eventually comes to define himself as he is defined: as a delinquent—by this time an incorrigible one committed to a long-term criminal career.

There is little doubt that most criminal behavior is learned, but critics claim that theories based on learning have significant weaknesses. For one thing, they are incomplete. Where do the behavior patterns that criminals learn come from in the first place? Learning theories provide no answer. A second common criticism is that these theories are so vague and general that they can be used to explain almost anything but are difficult to prove or disprove scientifically.

Another group of sociologists who take a different approach to criminology see crime as normal and natural. If all people are born with an "aggressive instinct" or automatically commit crimes for some other reasons, it is not very useful to ask why they commit crimes. It is more reasonable, according to this way of thinking, to ask why people do not commit crime. **Control theory** answers this question by saying that noncriminals are constrained by society and thus are prevented from breaking the law. Some control theorists emphasize the importance of the internal reins that society builds up in the individual through the process of socialization. They say it is a strong conscience and a sense of personal morality that stops most people from breaking the law. In this sense, Freud's psychological theory can be seen as a control theory. Other control theorists, such as Travis Hirschi, believe that what stops crime is the bond that individuals form to conventional social institutions. Still other control theorists have returned to the rationalistic assumptions of the classical school, arguing that most of us do not commit crimes because we are deterred by the fear of legal punishment. But these different versions of control theory are not mutually exclusive. In fact, the most convincing form of control theory sees all three types of controls working simultaneously.[55]

Critics point out that control theory, like the learning theories, is extremely broad and virtually impossible to prove or disprove. The critics have passed particularly harsh judgment on control theory's assumption that people "naturally" commit crimes. Like the religious idea that human beings are evil by nature, it is an assumption that is almost impossible to study scientifically.

To understand the rates and distribution of crime, sociologists must link these individual explanations of crime to the larger social forces that shape contemporary society. For example, sociologists have been trying for generations to explain why there is apparently more crime among the poor than the other social classes. Probably the most influential of these is Robert K. Merton, who developed what is often called **strain theory**.[56] Crime, according to this concept, is produced by the strain in societies that (1) tell people that wealth is available to all but also (2) restrict some people's access to the means for achieving wealth. Because lower-class people in such societies cannot legally obtain the things they are taught to desire, they may try to reach their goals by breaking the law.

The learning theorists, on the other hand, tend to emphasize the cultural characteristics of the lower classes that encourage crime. For example, Walter B. Miller argues that although the subculture of poverty may have originated from a process similar to the one described by Merton, strain and frustration are not the causes of the high crime rate in the lower class. Rather, it is the distinctive attitudes and values found among the poor.[57] Another explanation comes from control theorists who feel that the punishments that keep most people out of crime are less effective on the poor, because they are frequently less bonded to conventional social institutions and have much less to lose in material possessions and social prestige.

Of course, crime is not limited to the lower class, and another critical sociological question concerns the reasons our society as a whole has such a high level of crime. To answer this question, many sociologists turn to the pioneering work of Émile Durkheim, who saw the roots of the problem in what he termed **anomie**, or normlessness. According to Durkheim and his contemporary followers, modern industrial society has become so diverse and impersonal that consensus about what is right and wrong has broken down, and many people no longer belong to strong supportive groups that regulate their behavior. As a result, there is not only more crime but more frustration and suicide as well.[58] On the other hand, supporters of **critical theory** argue that it is the capitalist economic system that is the root cause of our crime problem. According to this school, capitalism fosters crime by encouraging, and even requiring, the exploitation of one group by another and by promoting the selfish quest for personal gain as if it were the inevitable goal of all human behavior.[59]

DEALING WITH CRIMINALS

The criminal-justice process reflects a conflict between two very different social goals. On the one hand, there is the need to stop crime and rid society of troublemakers. On the other hand, there is the need to protect, preserve, and nourish the rights and liberties of individuals. All societies pit these two needs against each other. Some are police states, in which the methods of crime control bulldoze citizens into submission. At the other extreme is chaos, in which individuals run wild. Democratic societies take a middle ground, tempering the need to repress crime with concern for the rights of their citizens. But even in democratic societies, few people agree on what the proper balance should be. Some North Americans favor what Herbert L. Packer called the **crime-control model** of criminal justice, a program for the speedy arrest and punishment of all who commit crimes. Others advocate a **due-process model** that tempers the rush to punishment with concern for human rights and dignity.[60] Speaking generally, those who fear the official abuse of power favor the due-process model, while those who fear crime more advocate the crime-control model.

The Police Police officers are on the cutting edge of the criminal-justice process. They are much more visible than other criminal-justice personnel, and they have more contacts with the citizenry. They have become the symbols of the whole system of justice. And in addition to their symbolic importance, police officers are the gatekeepers for the other criminal-justice agencies. They cannot possibly arrest all suspected lawbreakers. There aren't enough police, and, if there were, there wouldn't be enough courts to try the accused or enough jails to hold them. But equally important, it is not in the interests of justice to arrest everyone who has violated the law regardless of the circumstances. Thus, police officers must use a great deal of discretion in deciding how to carry out their duties, and those decisions, in turn, determine how much business there will be for the criminal-justice agencies down the line.

Contrary to popular opinion, only a small part of all the work done by a police department is directly concerned with fighting crime. For example, only 10 to 20 percent of the calls to most police departments require officers to perform law enforcement duties, and most of the incidents an officer handles on any given day are not criminal matters.[61] Outsiders who have observed police activities confirm the idea that the term *peace officer* describes the work of police personnel more adequately than *law enforcement officer*.

Although most police work is routine, even boring, there is always an element of danger for the officer on the street. At least partially for that reason, police officers form tightly knit groups that stick together. The effort to protect fellow officers is

Police officers spend more of their time providing public service than enforcing the law.

vital on the streets but is a serious barrier to controlling police misconduct. Time and again, efforts to investigate charges of racism, corruption, and brutality run into a wall of silence. As a result, no one can say how widespread this problem actually is, but there have been enough substantiated cases to know that it is indeed a serious one.

The Courts   After an arrest, police officers must take the suspect promptly before a lower-court magistrate (judge). If the magistrate decides that a suspect must come back to the lower court for further proceedings, the magistrate sets the conditions under which temporary release on bail can be granted. Under the American **bail** system, accused persons put up a sum of money to be forfeited if they do not show up for trial. In most courts, the accused can pay a relatively small fee to a bail bonder, who then provides the financial security (called a bail bond) necessary for release. It is a well-known fact that the bail system discriminates against the poor. The amount of money required is usually determined by the charge against the suspect rather than by the person's character and sense of responsibility. Poor people who cannot raise enough money stay in jail awaiting trial, sometimes for months, while the more affluent post their bail and go free.

Most people think that the defendant's fate is decided in a public trial, in which the prosecutor and defense attorney battle to prove their case. Actually, the trial plays a small part in the criminal-justice process. Only about one out of every ten defendants in the federal courts of the United States actually has a trial, and the percentages are similar for most of the state courts as well.[62] Most defendants make a deal with the prosecutor by agreeing to plead guilty in exchange for a reduction in the charges or some other consideration. This process, called **plea bargaining**, is much faster and cheaper than taking each case to trial. The state saves money, and the defendants receive more lenient punishment than they would if they had gone to trial and been convicted. Critics from both the left and the right have nonetheless passed disparaging judgments on the process of plea bargaining. Civil libertarians complain that it takes the process of justice behind closed doors, where violations of defendants' rights are hidden from the public view, and that innocent people are coerced into pleading guilty because they know that if they demand a trial and are convicted, they will receive much harsher punishment. Conservatives, on the other hand, complain that plea bargaining lets the guilty off with a lighter sentence than they deserve.

After the defendants have pleaded guilty or been found guilty, they are called back into court for sentencing. Until recently, judges were given wide discretion in deciding how severe a sentence to hand down. But complaints about what were perceived to be excessively lenient sentences have led to greater restrictions on judges' powers. In most cases, however, the judge must at least decide whether to give the defendant probation or sentence him or her to prison for the term prescribed by law.

Corrections   Originally, prisons were nothing but places to hold criminals until society could decide what to do with them (usually either execute them or inflict some form of torture). Prisons as places for the long-term confinement of inmates were originally established in order to achieve three goals, and they are still central objectives of today's prison system. The first is to get even (**retribution**). The public wants to make criminals suffer by depriving them of their liberty. The second is to scare potential criminals so much that they will be afraid to violate the law (**deterrence**). And the third is to protect the public from dangerous individuals by locking them up (**incapacitation**). In the 1940s and 1950s, an innovative new goal was added: to reform prisoners through such programs as job training and psychotherapy (**rehabilitation**). Unfortunately, this new objective often clashed with the prison's other goals. In most cases, prison officials adopted the language of rehabilitation (penitentiaries, for example, became ''correctional institutions''), but they continued to give the goal of reforming prisoners a low priority. As a result, few of the rehabilitation programs were effective, and many of them have been dismantled in recent years. However, the prisons have proven no more effective at deterring crime than they have been at reforming criminals. Although it is a matter of some dispute, the most commonly cited figure is that about two-thirds of those released from prison commit another serious crime within four or five years.[63]

Despite such evidence of failure, America's prison population is growing at an alarming rate—over 115 percent in the last decade alone[64] (see Figure 13.3). The United States now has a higher percentage of its population in jail than any other country in the world.[65] Even more disturbing are the results of a study that found that one in every four young black men in the United States is either in prison or on

D E B A T E

Will Sending More Criminals to Prison Solve the Crime Problem?

YES The spread of crime and lawlessness threatens the survival of our society. Yet the criminal-justice system is hamstrung by pointless rules and regulations and obsessed with safeguarding the rights of criminals. The result is that law-abiding citizens go unprotected. The maze of legal restrictions are so complex that it practically requires the service of a lawyer for the police to make a legal arrest. Criminals are commonly turned loose because of minor technical errors that are not related to their guilt or innocence. Even if they are brought to court, plea-bargaining arrangements allow many dangerous felons to plead guilty to minor crimes. Convicted criminals are freed by judges or parole boards after serving little or no time in prison. This leniency permits thousands of criminals to remain at large, threatening the lives and property of decent citizens.

Despite the claims of liberals, putting criminals in prison is an effective way of preventing crime. Criminals obviously cannot victimize the public when they are locked up. Therefore, more criminals in prison means more safety on the streets. Fear of imprisonment is also a powerful deterrent to crime. If criminals were given the tough punishment they deserve, more people would be afraid to break the law. But even if strict punishment failed to reduce crime, simple justice demands that the leniency in our criminal-justice system be ended. Law-abiding citizens are cheated when criminals go free. A crackdown on crime and lawlessness would make society better for everyone.

NO A larger portion of the population of the United States is in prison than in any other nation. The proposal to solve the crime problem by locking up even more people is foolish and misguided. Prison actually encourages more crime. To be locked up with hundreds of criminals is to enter a school for crime in which degrading and inhumane conditions generate bitterness and resentment. The inevitable result is more crime, as is shown by the high percentage of offenders who return to prison for a second, third, or fourth time. The answer to the crime problem will not be found in imposing even more severe punishment on criminals but in changing the economic and social conditions that cause crime.

Even if packing more people into our prisons would reduce crime, such a "get tough" policy poses an unacceptable threat to civil liberties. Many conservatives would dismantle the constitutional safeguards that regulate the criminal-justice process, in order to catch more criminals. Under such a system no one would be safe from the prying eyes of the government. Police could stop people and search them without reasonable cause; they could enter homes, tap telephones, or investigate our private lives. Can we trust the government with such unbridled power? Numerous government scandals prove that the answer is no. Sooner or later this enormous power would be turned to political ends. We cannot surrender our freedom to an oppressive state even if it promises to solve the crime problem.

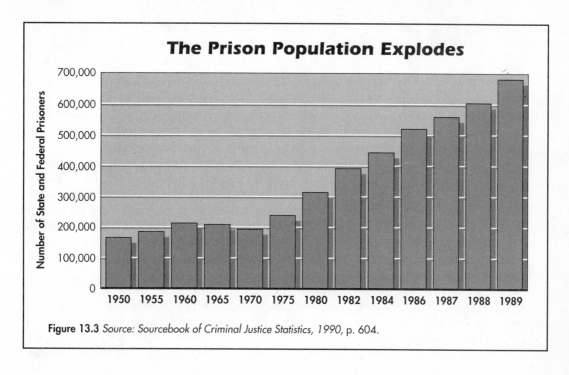

The Prison Population Explodes

Number of State and Federal Prisoners

700,000
600,000
500,000
400,000
300,000
200,000
100,000
0

1950 1955 1960 1965 1970 1975 1980 1982 1984 1986 1987 1988 1989

Figure 13.3 *Source: Sourcebook of Criminal Justice Statistics, 1990,* p. 604.

probation or parole.[66] Prisons are becoming increasingly overcrowded, and living conditions have gone from bad to worse. Murder, assault, and homosexual rape are everyday events in our prisons, and mere survival has become the primary goal of many inmates.

Probation, which allows convicted criminals to remain in the community under government supervision, is the principal alternative to incarceration. In theory, probation officers work to help offenders stay on the right track, while keeping close tabs on them to make sure they do not return to crime. In practice, probation is seldom very effective in achieving either goal, primarily because probation officers are given such a huge number of cases to handle. A Rand Corporation study of 1,600 probationers found that the majority are eventually arrested again for another offense; however, other research shows that those placed on probation are still less likely to commit new crimes than are those who are sent to prison.[67] But because the most hardened and dangerous criminals are not given probation, it is unclear whether current probation programs are really any more effective at stopping crime than is incarceration.

RESPONDING TO CRIME AND VIOLENCE

Everyone seems to have an idea about how to stop crime. Politicians, police officers, criminologists, sociologists, and ordinary citizens propose one solution or another almost every day. Many of these proposals are contradictory, but it would seem possible to combine the best features of each in one comprehensive program. The following are a few of the most frequently suggested alternatives.

Increasing Punishment   The United States punishes its criminals more severely than any other democratic nation. American criminals receive longer prison terms than criminals in other industrialized countries, and, as we have seen, a higher percentage of the U.S. population is in prison. Many Americans nonetheless believe that the solution to the crime problem is to get even tougher. These proposals generally have two parts. First, they demand that punishment be made more certain, even if such a practice requires some reduction in the legal protections against the abuses of government power. Second, they demand that punishment be more severe, that prison terms be lengthened, and that more criminals be executed. Such ideas are popular with the general public, and both kinds of proposals have been put into effect in the last decade. Prison sentences have been significantly lengthened and an increasingly conservative Supreme Court has cut back on the legal safeguards granted by earlier courts.

Supporters of these "get-tough" policies claim that they are responsible for the drop in the crime rate; however, critics point out that most of the decline is the natural result of an aging population. While most criminologists will grant that get-tough policies can produce some short-term reductions in crime, many argue that the long-term effects will be just the opposite. Sooner or later almost all prisoners are released, and their experience in jail is likely to leave them bitter and hardened in their criminal ways. Even more troubling is the enormous cost of these efforts and the threat they pose to civil liberties in a democratic society. The critics pass particularly harsh judgment on the "war on drugs" that has sent huge numbers of nonviolent drug users into our prisons, where they are cut off from their family, their community, and virtually all the other positive influences on their lives.

Focusing on Violence   An alternative approach to criminal-justice reform would focus the most severe punishment on the violent criminals who virtually everyone agrees are the greatest threat to the public. Prison sentences for such offenders as murderers, rapists, and business executives who knowingly endanger the public's safety would be significantly lengthened. At the same time, the use of prison for nonviolent property offenders could be reduced and greater reliance placed on restitution programs that force offenders to work to repay their victims. The primary response to drug users would be shifted from punishment to treatment and therapy.

Another reasonable response to the problem of violence is to enact stronger gun control laws. Some opponents of this idea claim that criminals would simply use other weapons if guns were not available, but even if that were so, the evidence shows that guns are far more lethal than other weapons. A study of violence in St. Louis, for example, found that a person attacked with a small-caliber gun was almost twice as likely to die than if attacked with a knife, and three times more likely to die if attacked with a larger-caliber weapon. Others claim that gun control simply wouldn't work. However, international comparisons indicate that the nations with the toughest gun control laws have the lowest level of gun ownership and the lowest percentage of criminals who use guns. For example, about 60 percent of all murders in the United States are committed with firearms, but in Canada, which has stricter gun control laws, that figure is only 31 percent.[68]

Although the regulation of firearms in the United States is extremely loose and ineffective, public opinion polls starting as far back as 1959 have repeatedly shown that Americans favor more gun control. A 1989 poll, for example, found that 70 percent of the people want stricter gun control laws, and that only 1 in 20 want to loosen them. Large majorities also favored universal gun registration and an outright ban on assault weapons and plastic guns (which cannot be discovered by metal detectors).[69] Why, then, aren't tougher laws passed? The major opposition comes from several powerful organizations funded by sports enthusiasts and firearms manufacturers that are known collectively as the gun lobby. Public opinion is apparently less influential than a well-financed and highly organized special-interest group such as the National Rifle Association.

Another controversial issue concerns the pervasive use of violence in the media. After conducting an extremely large number of studies using a variety of different methodologies, scientists have reached a consensus that media violence encourages real-life violence.[70] As Jeffrey H. Goldstein puts it, "After nearly three decades of research social scientists are now almost unanimous in their agreement that portrayed violence increases aggressive behavior."[71] However, it is also widely accepted that government censorship of the media poses a fundamental threat to democratic institutions. Some other way, therefore, needs to be found to reduce the huge amounts of graphic violence in the movies and on television. To date, public pressure has been to little avail. But organized minority groups have been successful in sharply reducing the racist stereotypes that were once common in the media, and if the public were concerned enough, there is no reason similar improvements couldn't be made in reducing gratuitous violence.

Attacking the Roots of Crime   Proposals for punishing criminals, increasing our defenses against criminal activities, and employing social intervention are all concerned with preventing crime. Crime is prevented when perpetrators are afraid to commit new crimes. It is also prevented when criminals are killed or kept behind bars, and when citizens lock up their valuables and themselves, thus frustrating people who would behave criminally. Finally, crime is prevented when the personal and social situations of criminals are improved or when the economic, political, and social order that generates high crime rates is modified so that it no longer does so.

Of the three methods, social intervention is, or could be, the most effective procedure. We have seen that crime is rooted in the economic, political, and social order. Most social scientists realize that it is foolish to leave this situation the way it is and then try to reduce crime by punishing criminals or defending against them. But relying on punishment and defense are easier than carrying out some of the sweeping social changes that have been proposed—eliminating poverty, unemployment, and discrimination, for example. In the long run, however, genuine crime prevention—changing the conditions that cause crime—will be both cheaper and more effective.

SOCIOLOGICAL PERSPECTIVES ON CRIME AND DELINQUENCY

The Functionalist Perspective Functionalists study crime rates rather than individual criminal behavior. They hold, generally, that a certain amount of crime is inevitable in any society because crime makes a contribution to social order. For instance, crime is said to promote the solidarity of the group, just as war does, by providing "common enemies" (in this case criminals). It is also argued that crime is functional because it provides an "escape valve" for the pressures arising from unjust laws or excessive conformity. But although some crime is natural and even healthy, too much crime is highly dysfunctional. Today most functionalists, like the general public, feel that current levels of crime pose a major social problem.

Functionalists argue that the high crime rates in the industrialized nations have been caused by the hectic pace of social change in the twentieth century and the social disorganization it created. Old traditions have been shattered, but a new consensus has not developed to take their place. The weakening of such institutions as the family and the community has left many people isolated and loosened their bonds to the social organizations that are supposed to regulate their behavior. As a result, many people feel alienated from society and frustrated by the conditions of their lives. Some lash out in bursts of violence, and others simply drift into criminal activities because society is too disorganized to prevent it.

To deal with these problems, functionalists often call for greater social integration and a return to the traditional values of the past. Many functionalists believe that crime and violence would be reduced if people were encouraged to commit themselves to primary groups such as the family, religious organizations, social clubs, and political groups. Functionalists also recommend a thorough reorganization of the criminal-justice system so that criminals can be handled more quickly and efficiently, and a greater effort by the schools to deal with the problems that promote delinquency among their students. Much more difficult to carry out are their calls for a return to a more stable family system and the traditional values on which it was based.

The Conflict Perspective Conflict theorists emphasize the fact that both crime and the laws defining it are products of a struggle for power. They argue that a few powerful groups control the legislative process and that these groups outlaw behavior that threatens their interests. For example, laws outlawing vagrancy, trespassing, and theft are said to be designed to protect the interests of the wealthy from attacks by the poor. Although laws prohibiting such things as murder and rape are not so clearly in the interests of a single social class, the poor and powerless are still much more likely to be arrested if they commit such crimes.

Conflict theorists also see class and ethnic exploitation as a basic cause of many different kinds of crime. Much of the high crime rate among the poor is attributable to a lack of legitimate opportunities for improving their economic condition. This exploitation of the poor and ethnic minorities creates a sense of hopelessness, frustration, and hostility. Such feelings often boil over into acts of violence that are aimed not only at the system that oppresses the underprivileged but also at their friends, relatives, and neighbors. More generally, many conflict theorists hold that the greed and competitiveness bred by our capitalist consumer culture encourage crime among all social groups. Every day we are given countless subtle and not-so-subtle messages that wealth is the measure of a successful woman or man. It is therefore hardly surprising that even our richest citizens are often willing to break the law to enhance their fortunes and outdo their competition.

Violence plays an especially important role in the exploitation of another group— women. Conflict theorists point out that violence has always been one of the principal means of enforcing male dominance. Many feminists charge that as industrialization and technology eroded the underpinnings of male privilege, violence has become an increasingly important tool in keeping women "in their place." Rape and physical brutality continue to be used as a means for men to degrade women who challenge their sense of superiority and to express their rage against women in general. As a result, fear of violence forces women to change their ways of living, acting, and dressing, and thus deprives them of many basic freedoms.

Conflict theorists believe that crime will disappear only if inequality and exploitation are also eliminated. But because that is obviously a distant goal, they advocate more limited responses to the crime problem as well. For example, they ask that the police and the courts treat different classes and ethnic groups more equally. Thus, they want to see more attention given to white-collar crime, they support bail reform and programs to provide better defense lawyers for the poor, and they call for the elimination of class and ethnic discrimination by law enforcement officers. They also advocate a major effort to combat the domestic violence that oppresses so many women. The repeal of laws that enforce one group's cultural dominance over another is also supported by conflict theorists. Thus they support repealing laws prohibiting the use of marijuana, private sexual acts between consenting adults, and such activities as bigamy and gambling.

Social Psychological Perspectives   Most social psychologists regard criminal behavior as a product of primary-group interaction. As we have seen, however, they have developed different theories about the specific kinds of interactions that produce crime. Personality theorists focus on personal traits that encourage criminality, as well as on family environments that promote the development of such characteristics. Behaviorists argue that people commit crimes because they are rewarded for doing so: a bank robber is rewarded with money, a rapist with sexual gratification, and so on. Interactionists believe that people commit crimes because they learn attitudes and motivations that are favorable to crime: a boy who associates with other boys who believe that stealing is exciting is likely to adopt that attitude and start to steal.

The social psychological perspective helps us understand why one 18-year-old ends up in prison while another ends up in college. But the conditions producing criminal behavior are hard to change. The government in a free society cannot intervene significantly in child-rearing practices and can hardly change the character of a person's associations. The social psychological approach does have something practical to say about how to deal with criminals, however. For instance, it notes that punishment is not necessarily bad: if used sparingly and intelligently, it contributes to learning. Also, care should be taken to avoid the contagion of youngsters by confirmed criminals, as sometimes happens in juvenile halls and prisons. Finally, offenders should be integrated into primary groups that strongly discourage criminal behavior. Ideally, this is the aim of good probation programs. Social psychologists argue that the many programs that aim merely to keep tabs on probationers must be reorganized to meet this goal.

SUMMARY

A crime is a violation of the criminal law. Violence includes any behavior intended to cause physical harm to a person. Murder is the unlawful killing of a human being with malice aforethought. Research shows that the victims and attackers in most murders are friends or relatives. An assault occurs when one person physically attacks another; it differs from a murder in that the victim does not die. Sexual intercourse forced upon someone without consent is known as forcible rape. There are two types of forcible rape. The first kind occurs on a date or in the course of some other social contact; in the second type, the rapist simply selects a victim and attacks her (or him). Property crime includes a wide variety of offenses such as theft, burglary, arson, and fraud. Although robbery (theft by force) is officially classified as a violent crime, for sociological purposes it too is best considered a property offense. Offenses committed by highly organized groups of professional criminals are known as syndicated crime. White-collar crime is defined as a crime committed by a person of high status in the course of his or her occupation. Such crimes probably cost more than all other crimes put together. Juvenile delinquency includes a broad range of deviant behaviors committed by young people, some of which would also be against the law if committed by adults and some of which would not.

Although the rate of reported crime has been increasing for some time, most criminologists have more confidence in the victimization surveys, which indicate that the crime rate has actually been decreasing. The data show that crime is most common among males, young adults, and those who live in cities. For most types of crime, the poor and the minorities are also most likely to be the offenders; however, that is not true of the white-collar crimes. International comparisons show that the United States has the highest rate of violent crime of any industrialized nation.

The classical school holds that criminals choose to violate the law because that is the easiest way to get what they want. Biological theories see crime to be rooted in human nature and often look to the process of evolution to explain it. Psychologists and psychiatrists argue that crime is caused by the personality of the criminals. Some sociologists hold that crime is simply learned from others (differential association), while others see it as a result of society's failure to prevent it (control theory). Still other sociologists feel that our high crime rates are a result of the social and economic structure of contemporary society.

The police are the first to respond to most individual crimes, and how well they do their job has an enormous impact on the effectiveness of the rest of the criminal-justice system. If the police make an arrest, the suspects are usually held in prison until they can raise bail. If their case is not dropped, most defendants participate in a process called plea bargaining, under which they agree to plead guilty in exchange for some form of leniency from the prosecutor. In most cases, the judge sentences offenders either to prison or to a period of probation, during which they are allowed to remain free under official supervision. The huge increase in the inmate population of the United States has created serious overcrowding and deteriorating prison conditions.

There are many different proposals for dealing with the crime problem. Although the United States already has the highest percentage of its population in prison of any country in the world, some say we should get tougher still. Others propose focusing on violent criminals by lengthening their prison sentences but relying on other alternatives such as restitution and drug treatment for nonviolent offenders. Probably the most popular approach among criminologists is to attack the underlying causes of crime, such as poverty, unemployment, racism, and a deteriorating family structure.

Functionalists argue that the growing crime rate is but one symptom of increasing social disorganization. Conflict theorists emphasize the role of exploitation and inequality in promoting crime. Social psychologists generally focus on the ways individuals become involved in crime and violence.

KEY TERMS

control theory A theory that holds that people commit crimes because of the failure of the social controls on criminal behavior.

classical theory A concept that holds that people commit crime because it offers more pleasure and less pain than their other possible options.

differential association theory Holds that people commit crimes because they have more and stronger associations with those who favor criminal behavior than with those who oppose it.

juvenile delinquency Behavior by young people that is in violation of the criminal law or the special standards set for juveniles.

syndicated crime A crime committed by an organized group of professional criminals.

violence Behavior intended to cause pain, injury, or death to another.

white-collar crime A crime committed by someone of respectability and high social status in the course of his or her occupation.

FURTHER READINGS

Ronald J. Berger, ed., *The Sociology of Juvenile Delinquency* (Chicago: Nelson-Hall, 1991). A collection of articles that provide a comprehensive look at the problem of delinquency.

James William Coleman, *The Criminal Elite: The Sociology of White Collar Crime*, 2nd ed. (New York: St. Martin's Press, 1989). An examination of the problem of white-collar crime by the author of this text.

Liz Kelly, *Surviving Sexual Violence* (Minneapolis: University of Minnesota Press, 1989). An exploration of the causes of violence against women and the best strategies to cope with it.

Herbert L. Packer, *The Limits of Criminal Sanction* (Palo Alto, Calif.: Stanford University Press, 1968). A law professor's classic case against the legislation of morality.

Joseph F. Sheley, *Criminology: A Contemporary Handbook* (Belmont, Calif.: Wadsworth, 1991). A collection of essays on key issues in criminology by specialists in each field.

PART FOUR

Problems of a Changing World

chapter 14

The Global Divide
Problems of the Third World

- What are the economic differences between the industrialized nations and the Third World?
- What is it like to live in a Third World country?
- How do sociologists explain the huge gap between the rich and the poor countries?
- What can be done to make life better for the peoples of the Third World?

The images of Third World poverty are becoming more familiar every day: the tiny famine victim with stick legs and bulging eyes, a desperate young mother begging for food, a crowd of refugees fenced off in a pen like cattle. Bit by bit, media coverage is helping the people of the rich countries to realize how fortunate they are. But the media focuses only on the dramatic problems and the most desperate poverty. The average person's concept of the Third World, therefore, remains vague and poorly defined, and only a few have much of an idea about the causes of Third World poverty or what to do about it.

The question of why the countries of the world are so sharply divided into an affluent minority and a poor majority is one of the most controversial, and most closely studied, in all social science. This chapter will examine the most common explanations for this global divide and the kinds of solutions they each imply. But before we attempt to explain the problem, it must first be described.

GLOBAL INEQUALITY

Each of the more than 170 nations on this planet has its own unique economic, political, and social institutions, yet at the same time, all these countries are growing increasingly interdependent.[1] Some are fabulously wealthy, while others are mired in seemingly hopeless poverty. A few exercise awesome global power, but others are hardly noticed on the world stage. One of the best ways to make sense of this bewildering complexity is to think of the nations of the world as making up a kind of international class system, similar in many ways to the classes found within individual countries. A century ago the industrialized world, which makes up the "upper class," included only the United States and a few Western European nations, but today it encompasses countries as far away as Japan and Australia. The countries in the "lower class," collectively known as the **Third World**, are concentrated in the southern two-thirds of the planet, in Latin America, Africa, and much of Asia. Although they have some manufacturing industries, they are more likely to depend on agriculture and the sale of raw materials to get by.

Between these two extremes are a smaller group of nations, like South Korea, Taiwan, and Mexico, that have characteristics of both kinds of societies. They are more industrialized and have higher standards of living than the poorest nations, but they are still a long way from the affluence enjoyed by the established industrialized powers. More often than not, these "middle-class" nations are still counted as part of the Third World. It is important to remember, however, that there is a broad spectrum of nations on both sides of the global divide, and there may not be a great difference between the most prosperous Third World nations and the least affluent industrialized ones.

Just as individuals occasionally move up or down in the class system of a nation, so the status of the nations themselves also changes. Some of the countries in the world's "middle class" seem likely to become full-scale industrial powers, but others do not. Several nations have been knocked out of the elite club of industrial powers by wars or internal chaos but later rejoined it. Still other countries appear to be permanently stuck at the bottom of the heap.[2]

Wealth and Poverty Many people look at the differences between the industrialized nations and the Third World as simply a matter of money. And when seen in these terms, the gap is certainly enormous. In 1989, the average industrialized nation produced about $17,000 in goods and services for each of its citizens (known as the per capita gross national product), while the average Third World nation produced only $750 per citizen—a difference of more than 20 to 1 (see Figure 14.1).[3] But as we will see, the differences go far beyond money. Moreover, dollars, marks, and yen are not necessarily the best way to measure wealth. The cost of living varies greatly between one country and another; so, for example, a dollar's worth of rupees may buy two or three times more goods in India than a dollar's worth of lira does in Italy. To complicate matters further, many people in the Third World depend more heavily on the barter system—trading one thing directly for something else they want—and goods that are informally traded often do not show up in statistics such as the ones given here.

Another way to compare the industrialized countries and the Third World nations is to look at how much wealth they have accumulated. Some of this wealth is kept in dollars or pounds, but more important are the physical assets of a nation—its roads and bridges, its power plants, its sewers and canals, its supply of housing, and its factories. The simplest way to make this comparison is just to look around. The industrialized nations are crisscrossed with telephone and electric lines, and with highways full of cars and trucks. Their buildings are modern and are equipped with running water and indoor plumbing. Almost everyone has shoes to wear, and during

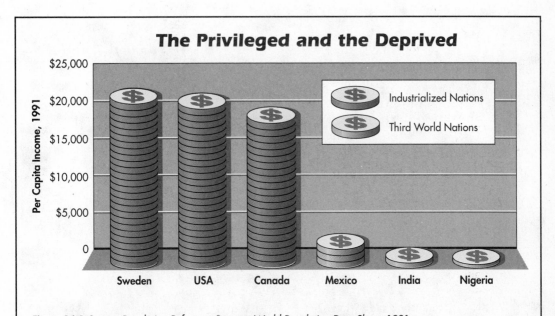

Figure 14.1 *Source:* Population Reference Bureau, *World Population Data Sheet, 1991.*

the cold months most people have warm clothing. In the Third World, such conveniences and comforts are far less common, and only a privileged few enjoy the affluent life style taken for granted by so many North Americans. Most Third World nations have paved roads connecting their major cities, but they are likely to be much smaller than those in the industrialized nations and in a poor state of repair. Access to smaller towns is often only by footpaths or dirt roads that become very hard going when it rains. Most rural areas are further isolated by a lack of telephones and the electricity necessary to run radio transmitters. Even on major highways, the traveler will see far fewer private cars, and the trucks and buses are usually primitive, noisy, and polluting. These motor vehicles must also share the road with a host of ox carts, horses, bicycles, and pedestrians.

Sanitation is often primitive, with open fields or shallow outhouses serving as the only toilets. In the cities and crowded villages, human waste may flow down the sides of streets in open sewers. Underground plumbing is now more common, but untreated sewage is still usually dumped directly into rivers and lakes. The quality of housing varies enormously in the Third World. The wealthy live in sumptuous mansions with servants and all the latest conveniences. But in most big cities of the Third World, hundreds of thousands of people live on the streets with no permanent shelter, and huge shantytowns of squatters have grown up on whatever vacant land is available. Since these squatters have neither the legal rights to the land they occupy

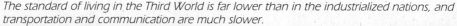

The standard of living in the Third World is far lower than in the industrialized nations, and transportation and communication are much slower.

nor the money to build a home, their structures are primitive affairs. Often lacking electricity and plumbing, these shacks typically provide poor protection against the elements (see Chapter 15). Most villagers at least have the legal rights to live where they do. But construction techniques are still primitive—buildings often have walls of mud bricks and thatched or corrugated iron roofs—and the basic amenities are still lacking.

One of the most fundamental problems of the Third World is the absence of economic opportunities for its young people. Rapid population growth (see Chapter 16) and a weak educational system mean there is almost always a large surplus of unskilled labor. In the past, these young people would have just gone to work on the family farm, but because so many more children now reach adulthood, there is often not enough land to support them all. To make matters worse, birthrates are the highest in the poorest countries and among the poorest people within each country. Young people from throughout the Third World are therefore migrating to the cities in search of work, but only the lucky find a permanent job. Most become part of what is sometimes called the urban subsistence economy. They work a few temporary jobs, trade their labor for the help of other poor people, receive an occasional handout from the government or a relief agency, and in some cases turn to begging or crime to make ends meet.

Health and Nutrition There is nothing more fundamental to the quality of life than good health, and the health statistics show the same global divide as the economic statistics. A baby born in the Third World is at least five times more likely to die in its first year of life than a baby born in a wealthy nation (see Figure 14.2). Overall, demographers

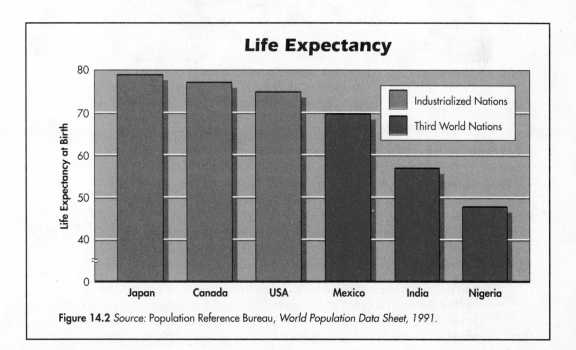

Figure 14.2 *Source:* Population Reference Bureau, *World Population Data Sheet, 1991.*

Good health care can be hard to come by in Third World countries, and educational facilities, where they are available, are often primitive affairs (see opposite page).

say that the people of the industrialized world can expect to live 12 years longer than their counterparts in the poor nations.[4]

Many of the causes of these staggering differences can be traced to the economic conditions we have already discussed, especially poor sanitation and lack of clean drinking water. Waterborne diseases such as typhoid and cholera, almost unknown in the wealthy countries, sweep through the Third World in epidemic after epidemic, taking millions of lives every year. Although malaria, which is another of the world's most lethal diseases, is transmitted by insects and not water, poverty is still a major contributor. Many poor nations simply cannot afford the expensive mosquito eradication programs that are the best way to deal with the disease. And when people get sick in poor countries, they may not be able to find a doctor to help. For every 1,000 people in the United States and Canada, there are 5 times more physicians than in India, and over 13 times more than in the Philippines.[5] Moreover, there is an acute shortage of medical care in rural areas of most Third World countries. Even those

lucky enough to find a doctor are likely to have their treatment hampered by shortages of everything but the least expensive medicines and equipment.

Food is, of course, another basic factor in determining our health. Lack of refrigeration and poor sanitation mean that food itself is often a cause of illness in the poor countries. But the biggest health problem related to food is simply the lack of it. According to United Nations figures, the average person in an industrialized nation consumes about 40 percent more calories and two-thirds more protein a day than someone in the Third World.[6] Of course, those are just averages, and many people in the rich nations eat more than is good for them. But people in the Third World who fall below the average may be in for serious trouble. It is estimated that 10 to 20 percent of the world's people suffer from chronic malnutrition and that millions die of starvation every year.[7]

Education and Culture Another major economic advantage of the industrialized nations is that the vast majority of their people can read and write. In most industrialized nations, less than 1 percent of the population is completely illiterate. But in many of the poorest Third World countries, such as India and Egypt, the majority are illiterate, and only a few Third World nations, such as Cuba and Chile, have brought their illiteracy rate down to under 10 percent.[8] Moreover, workers in the industrialized countries are far more likely to have specialized skills—for example, in word processing or automobile mechanics. Their labor force also contains large numbers of physicians, engineers, scientists, and other highly trained specialists. Moreover, many of the skilled professionals the poor nations do produce migrate to the industrialized countries, where the wages are far higher.

The system of universal education in the rich nations also serves as a kind of social cement to hold them together. Even children of widely different backgrounds acquire similar values and attitudes as they learn the history of their nation and read its literature. Mass communications contribute to the sense of national unity, because people who read newspapers and watch television programs produced in their country tend to develop a similar perspective on the world. In contrast, the illiterate masses in the poorest nations are shut out of the political life and social discourse of their nation. They know little of the history or politics of their country, they can't read the newspaper, and even televisions are few and far between (see Figure 14.3). To complicate matters, ethnic and linguistic differences are often far more pronounced in Third World countries. Thus, these nations must deal with traditional animosities

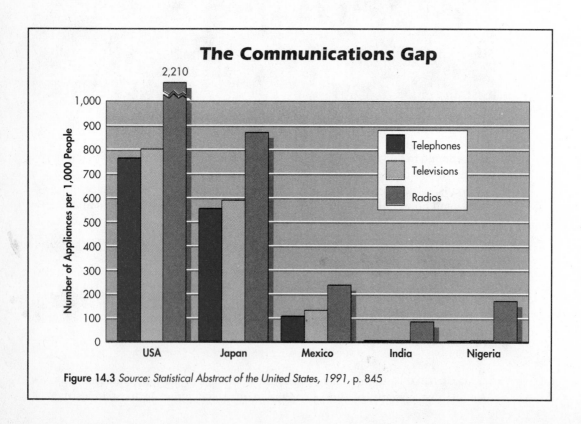

Figure 14.3 *Source: Statistical Abstract of the United States, 1991, p. 845*

and suspicions without the benefit of the strong mass institutions that help hold the wealthy nations together.

Social Structure Underlying the disparities in the quality of life are fundamental differences in the structure of rich and poor societies. The class system, political institutions, and economic structures are all markedly different in the Third World and the industrialized nations. For example, farming is only one of dozens of industries in the wealthy nations, but it is still the most common way people make their living in Africa, Latin America, and parts of Asia. Despite the rapid urbanization of recent years (see Chapter 15), two-thirds of the people in the Third World still lived in rural areas in 1991.[9] Many of these nations depend heavily on the exploitation of natural resources such as petroleum, timber, copper, and uranium—if they are lucky enough to have them. A third major source of employment is low-wage jobs in industries that require large amounts of relatively unskilled labor. Sometimes the factories are owned by local businesspeople or governments, but more often they are branches of huge multinational corporations run from headquarters in one of the industrialized nations. And as was already mentioned, rapid population growth and weak overall economies mean that there is a very large group of workers without steady jobs.

Another important difference between the rich and poor nations is in their class systems. Both types of societies have a relatively small upper class that commands a disproportionate share of the wealth and power. But the industrialized nations also have a large middle class, which had the skills necessary to keep the technological economy going. In Third World nations, the middle class is much smaller and weaker. Moreover, the gap between the rich and the poor is far larger. Consider two typical examples, one from Latin America and the other from Africa. The income of the richest one-fifth of the Mexican population is about 20 times that of the poorest one-fifth, while in the United States that ratio is about 8 to 1.[10] In Kenya, the top 10 percent of the population receives twice as big a share of the national income as does the top 10 percent in the United States.[11] There is one exception to this rule, however, and that is among the remaining communist nations of the Third World. Although reliable statistics are hard to come by, nations such as China and Cuba clearly have a smaller gap between the rich and the poor—not so much because they have a larger middle class but because the government does not provide as lavish an income for those in the upper class.[12]

Nations on the two sides of the global divide also have significant differences in their political institutions. The most obvious is that industrialized nations have stable democratic governments, while Third World countries are much more likely to have some type of dictator or a small group of bureaucratic rulers who are not elected by the public. Although there has been a trend toward more democracy in the Third World, those governments are usually fragile affairs. Elected leaders often face the constant threat of a military coup if they make the wrong move.

But whether dictatorships or democracies, governments in the Third World tend to be weaker and more unstable than their counterparts in the wealthy nations. For one thing, sharp ethnic and class differences and the lack of strong unifying institutions produce a high level of conflict in many poor nations. Popular discontent often leads to a succession of new governments that seem unable to get at the root of

Most industrialized nations have stable democratic governments, while Third World nations are far more likely to be ruled by a small clique or even a single person. Iraq's president, Saddam Hussein, is one of the Third World's most notorious military dictators.

national problems, or to an entrenched dictatorship that digs in and ignores public opinion. Significant parts of some Third World countries are not actually controlled by their central government at all but by bands of organized rebels. But even relatively stable Third World governments are hopelessly outmatched by the military and economic power of the industrialized nations. No matter how independence-minded Third World leaders may be, they often find that their destiny is determined by decisions made in Washington, Tokyo, or Paris.

EXPLAINING THE GLOBAL DIVIDE

In the distant past, when all human societies were based on hunting and gathering, the inequalities among the peoples of the world were fairly small. The transition to an agricultural economy greatly increased social inequality, but the beginnings of today's global divide can be found in the industrial revolution and the capitalist economic system that made it possible (see Chapter 2).[13] This new kind of society was based not on farming but on trade, commerce, and manufacturing, and as it took shape in Western Europe, it stimulated one technological advance after another at an ever-quickening pace. And the European countries soon used their technological superiority for political gains as well. They built huge colonial empires throughout the world, and used their economic and military might to dominate the remaining independent nations. From the beginning of the colonial period (around the end of the fifteenth century), the standard of living of the European nations grew at an unprecedented rate, while the rest of the world remained mired in poverty and stagnation. Although European colonialism lasted well into the twentieth century, its days are now over. Nonetheless, the economic inequality between the rich and poor nations is still growing larger year by year.[14]

Today's global inequalities clearly stem from the fact that some nations have undergone a full process of industrialization while others have not. The key question is why. In the early days of their colonial expansion, most Europeans simply assumed that their technological advantage was the result of the biological and religious inferiority of other peoples. Although such ethnocentric ideas are certainly still around, few social scientists take them seriously. But the effort to explain these differences scientifically has been a long and difficult process. Many of our greatest sociologists and historians have struggled with this crucial question, and, even today, opinions remain sharply divided along political lines. In this chapter, we will examine two broad theories—modernization theory and world system theory—that both seek to explain this global divide. The aim of this section is to present each approach in a clear and coherent form. But it is important to keep in mind that there are many disagreements among those who support the same theory, and that many social scientists freely combine the insights from both approaches.

Modernization Theory This theory, which borrows heavily from the classic sociological work of Max Weber (1864–1920), was developed in the 1950s and 1960s by a group of functionalist theorists who saw industrialization as part of a process of social evolution they called **modernization**.[15] According to these social scientists, modernization is the result of the build-up of the numerous improvements in the structure and function of social institutions. The most obvious are the technological innovations that have been made throughout the course of human history. Modernization also involves what economists call capital accumulation—that is, the build-up of wealth. The important thing is not so much amassing money, which is only a symbol of wealth, but increases in real assets such as roads, buildings, and power plants, and the improvements in the education and skill of the work force. There are also important changes in the organization of society as its institutions become more specialized and more efficient. For example, in most agricultural societies the extended family serves as the school, the employer, the welfare agency, and the punisher of deviant behavior—all rolled into one institution. As part of the process of modernization, a great deal of the responsibility for these functions is transferred to more specialized social institutions such as the criminal justice system.

Although modernization takes place as a result of the build-up of one improvement upon another, this process does not necessarily occur at a steady pace. In fact, the economist Walter W. Rostow has shown that industrialization in the Western nations took place in distinct stages, and he argues that today's Third World nations will eventually follow this same road to development.[16] According to Rostow, all nations begin at the traditional stage, in which people cling to their old ways and are very reluctant to change. As a nation enters the "take off stage," there is a slow but steady accumulation of wealth, assets, and skills, until the nation reaches a kind of critical mass. Once it reaches this third stage, which Rostow terms the "drive for technological maturity," society undergoes a very rapid process of industrialization and social change. A more stable balance returns in the fourth and final stage, as the society emerges as a mature industrial power. This process of transition is a tumultuous one, and Rostow maintains that the instability it causes may leave the developing nation vulnerable to communism or some other totalitarian system.

Why are some nations so much further ahead in the process of modernization than others? Many modernization theorists put the blame on the "traditionalism" of Third World nations, which has made them resist the kind of changes necessary to create a modern industrial society. Rostow, for example, argues that Third World countries tend to have a religious, rather than a scientific, cultural orientation that makes it more difficult to develop and utilize modern technology. According to this view, people in Third World countries often cling to their traditional way of doing things and resist the innovations that inevitably go with the process of modernization. Rostow and other modernization theorists also cite the centralization of wealth and power in the hands of a small elite, the numerous restrictions on competitive markets, and the low overall level of education as other important barriers to modernization.[17] Max Weber, whose work focused on the historical development of the modern world, pointed out several unique conditions in Western Europe that helped make the industrial revolution possible. Weber argued that the spread of Puritan religions that placed an enormous value on hard work and frugality stimulated the accumulation of wealth necessary for industrialization. He also felt that the political disunity of Europe and the independence of its cities and towns prevented its feudal rulers from repressing the development of capitalism as they did, for example, in China.[18]

World System Theory   The perspective known as world system theory is one of the newest and fastest-growing theoretical schools in contemporary sociology. While modernization theory has its source in the functionalist perspective, world system theory is clearly a conflict theory that can trace its roots back to Karl Marx. The immediate origins of this theory are often credited to Andre Gunder Frank's studies of Latin America,[19] but it was Immanuel Wallerstein who actually created world system theory.[20] Much of the inspiration for this approach came from the criticism of the modernization theory as ethnocentric and biased in favor of the status quo. Some world system theorists nonetheless accept many of the basic points of modernization theory, and many have also been heavily influenced by the works of Max Weber. But they all agree that modernization theory leaves out the most fundamental cause of Third World poverty—exploitation by the rich industrialized powers.

The primary tenet of this new perspective is that industrialization does not take place in isolated individual nations but within a complex web of international economic and political relationships known as the **world system**. In its beginnings, the modern world system was a rather small affair limited to a part of northern Europe, but it eventually grew into the global financial and political network that now dom-

DEBATE

Are the Industrialized Nations Exploiting the Third World?

YES All you have to do is look around any Third World country. The evidence of victimization is everywhere. The children are sickly and malnourished, while their parents are often tired and hopeless. Those who live in mud huts and crowded tenements are actually the lucky ones, for whole families often sleep in the streets. Most Third World cities are jammed with legions of unemployed young men and women who have little real chance of ever finding a steady job. Yet the poverty and deprivation occur in the shadow of the incredible abundance of the industrialized nations. The per capita income in the world today is far higher than it has ever been before, but most of that wealth stays in the hands of a privileged few.

Exactly how do the rich nations take advantage of the poor countries? First, Third World people are exploited for their labor. The Third World is now dotted with factories producing consumer goods for the rich nations. The wages paid by the multinational corporations that own most of these factories are pitifully low—often less than a dollar a day. But not only is the pay low and the hours long, but the factories are hot, polluted, and dangerous. Hundreds of thousands of workers die every year from working conditions that would never be tolerated in the wealthy nations. Second, Third World nations are exploited for their natural resources. Their forests are stripped, their petroleum pumped out, and their mineral deposits depleted in order to satisfy the core nations' voracious appetite for raw materials. Although the peripheral countries receive some money for these commodities, the economic monopoly of

NO It's human nature to try to find someone to blame our problems on. When we compare the poverty of the Third World with the affluence of the industrialized nations, it is natural to blame one on the other. But when we place these problems in historical perspective, it is apparent that the industrialized nations have actually helped to improve the standard of living in the Third World. The most useful comparison is not between the rich and poor nations of today's world but between the Third World today and the way most countries in Africa, Asia, and Latin America were before they were influenced by the industrialized powers. When seen in these terms, there is simply no question that the people of the Third World are far better off as the result of their contacts with the industrialized nations. Their average income and standard of living are much higher than they used to be. And even though most people in the Third World do not have all the latest technological innovations, they still have electric lights, radios, bicycles, and other scientific inventions created in the industrialized nations. Health conditions have vastly improved—infant mortality has plummeted and the average life expectancy in the Third World is probably double what it was five centuries ago. Although there are a lot of complaints about "political meddling" in the Third World, the industrialized nations have actually been a vital force encouraging democracy and fighting communism and other totalitarian systems. Five hundred years ago, there wasn't a single democracy in the entire world; today democracy is flowering in even the poorest nations.

The charges that the industrialized nathe industrialized nations enables them to keep the price of raw materials far below their real value. Third, the poor nations are forced to follow political and economic policies dictated by the rich ones. Through the careful use of bribes, covert operations, and outright military force, the core keeps the poor nations from mounting an effective challenge to the world order that exploits them. In addition, a new form of exploitation is developing, as the southern part of the planet becomes the dumping ground for toxic wastes and unsafe products manufactured in the core.

The next time someone tells you how much good our corporations and our governments are doing in the Third World, stop and think for a moment. Picture Europeans and North Americans dying from the clogged arteries that come from overeating, while millions of people starve to death in the Third World. Or picture a Third World dictator slaughtering his people with the guns, tanks, and aircraft supplied by his supporters in the core nations. The truth will soon become obvious.

tions are exploiting the Third World are just ideological rhetoric intended for political purposes. When revolutionary leaders come to power and cut their nation off from "foreign influence," their standard of living goes down, not up. It is easy to complain about the low wages of the workers in the Third World. But the economic fact is that these workers are less educated and less productive than the workers in the industrialized nations. If their wages are raised too much, Third World factories would no longer be competitive with those in the industrialized nations. Besides, the Third World workers employed by foreign multinationals are actually the lucky ones, because they earn far more than they could in almost any of the other jobs available to them. Of course, none of this means that the multinationals or the governments of the industrialized nations never take advantage of the people in the poor nations; the real world is not that simple. But it is clear that the industrialized nations have done far more to help than to hurt the Third World.

inates the planet. At the center of the world system are the rich and powerful industrialized nations, known as the **core**. These core nations are surrounded by a much larger number of poor nations, called the **periphery**. The core nations exploit the periphery for its natural resources and cheap labor, while using their military and economic power to prevent peripheral nations from growing strong enough to challenge the interests of the core. Between these two extremes is the **semiperiphery**. Countries in this category are more industrialized than the peripheral nations but are far behind the core. Although they are still subject to the economic and political domination of the core, the semiperipheral nations are themselves able to exploit their poorer neighbors. World system theorists disagree about how to classify the communist nations. But the most common view is that communism represents an effort by exploited nations to pull out of the world system and industrialize on their own, without foreign interference. The collapse of European communism is seen as evidence of how powerful the capitalist world system is and how difficult it is for any nation to challenge it.

World system theorists have found that the core often has a single **hegemonic power** that is far stronger than the other core states and assumes leadership of the world system. The first hegemonic power was Holland, followed by Great Britain and then the United States. However, the military and economic costs of protecting the world system impose a heavy burden on the hegemonic power, and many world system theorists argue that the United States is already slipping from its position of dominance, as Holland and Britain did before it.

According to world system theory, the fundamental cause of Third World poverty is not that the poor nations are too traditional but that the core nations have forced them into a position of economic and political dependence. While modernization theory sees Third World nations as simply places where economic development has yet to take place, world system theorists point out that Third World nations have in fact undergone enormous social and economic changes. But those changes have been dictated not by their own needs but by those of the core nations. Although many poor nations have huge mines, for instance, the factories that turn the minerals into finished products are in the core nations. Many poor nations have lush plantations, but their agricultural bounty is consumed by the people of the rich nations. Moreover, many of the most productive assets in the Third World are owned and operated by multinational corporations from the core nations.

Critics of world system theory complain that it is too ideological and that its supporters see only the bad side of capitalism. Such critics point out that the overall life expectancy and the standard of living in the Third World is actually much higher now than it was in the past. They argue that far from exploiting the Third World, the industrialized nations are in fact helping it. If capitalism and industrialization had never developed in Europe, the critics claim, the Third World would still be suffering under the horrible poverty and class exploitation typical of most agricultural societies. Defenders of world system theory respond that although the standard of living as calculated by economists has gone up, the quality of life has declined as the traditional life style of Third World people has been destroyed, and that conditions would certainly be much better in the Third World without foreign interference.[21]

Evaluation It may seem frustrating to students that the enormous amount of time and effort social scientists have spent analyzing global inequality hasn't produced more agreement about its causes. But behind the academic rivalry between these two theoretical camps, there are actually considerable areas of agreement. The naive version of world system theory would blame all the world's problems on the capitalist core nations, while naive modernization theorists see the "traditionalism" of the Third World as the cause of all its difficulties. But more sophisticated members of both camps recognize that no single factor can explain the complexities of the modern world. Traditional values, the lack of capital, low educational levels, weak government, and the other factors cited by the modernization theorists have certainly played a major role in creating today's global divide, but so has the exploitation of the poor nations by the rich ones. To understand our current problems, we must look at both the internal conditions in individual nations that impede development and the world system of economic and political relationships in which those nations are embedded.

RESPONDING TO THE PROBLEMS
OF THE THIRD WORLD

As we have seen, the nations of the Third World are faced with daunting and complex problems. Many social scientists and political leaders have a pet proposal they see as a solution to our global crisis. But just as there is no one cause of the global divide, so there is no single solution. This section will examine some of the most common suggestions, but there are still strong disagreements about the wisdom and the possible effectiveness of all these proposals.

The Industrialized Nations Although there are a number of ways the industrialized nations could help the Third World, there is a real question about whether they will make a serious effort to do so. Of course, virtually all the governments of the core nations say they want to assist the poor countries, but those fine words are seldom translated into effective programs. Many influential people in the industrialized nations simply don't care what happens in those far-off countries, while others may fear that the industrialization of the Third World would mean more economic and political competition for their own nation. Thus, the first step is to educate both the citizens and the leaders of the industrialized nations about the acute problems of the Third World and the international dangers posed by its poverty and political instability.

Dropping Trade Barriers Most wealthy nations use a complex system of import taxes, quotas, and other restrictions to protect their own industries and limit the flow of goods from the low-wage countries of Africa, Latin America, and Asia. When Third World leaders discuss the problems of economic development with their counterparts in the core nations, one of their most frequent requests is that those trade barriers be dropped and their goods be allowed to compete freely on the open market. Although the representatives of industries threatened by Third World competition often make dire predictions about what will happen if the trade barriers are removed, the impact on the core nations is likely to be relatively minor. A few industries that use simple technology and lots of labor would be hurt, but poor countries lack the technology and the skills to produce most of the high-quality products demanded by the industrialized nations.

Forgiving Debt One of the most serious problems facing the Third World today is what has come to be known as the debt crisis. The roots of this situation can be traced to the oil crisis in the early 1970s. When sharp increases in the price of petroleum sent hundreds of billions of dollars in new income to the Middle Eastern oil producers, Western banks were flooded with huge new deposits. But the oil crisis also created a severe recession in the world economy, so there were few attractive investment opportunities in the industrialized nations. The bankers' response was to make massive new loans to various Third World nations. Unfortunately, most of this money was simply spent to pay for higher oil bills or was wasted through corruption and inefficiency.

Today, many Third World nations are saddled with debts so large that they cannot even pay the interest, much less the principal, and as a result they are falling deeper and deeper into debt. For example, tiny Costa Rica is now about $4.5 billion in debt, Argentina owes about $65 billion, and Brazil over $111 billion.[22] Many poor nations have turned to the World Bank and the International Monetary Fund as their only possible source of capital to meet their debt payments. But in exchange for their money, those international development agencies typically demand that national governments take harsh austerity measures to balance their budgets and reduce imports. The effects of these government cutbacks fall hardest on the poor; whatever meager government assistance they receive is reduced or eliminated at the same time that the new economic policies drive their country into recession. This crisis has been particularly devastating in debt-ridden Latin America. In the past, Latin America was often one of the fastest-growing regions of the Third World, but in the last decade its per capita income *declined* by 10 percent.[23] The banks are obviously reluctant to write off their loans as bad debts, but sooner or later it must be done. Many of these nations simply have no way to pay back the money, and the human costs of the continuing demand for payment are far too great.

Foreign Aid Many Americans think that the government spends huge sums in foreign aid to help the developing nations. Actually, the United States contributed less than

The most effective foreign aid is often targeted to the specific needs of the recipient. This photograph shows part of a development program aimed at improving the productivity of Thailand's agriculture.

1 percent of its national income in foreign economic aid in 1989.[24] Although the American economy is twice as large as Japan's, the Japanese actually give more foreign aid. In fact, on a per capita basis, the United States is far down the list of donors. Norway gives almost six times more international assistance per person than the United States, and Canada more than twice as much.[25] Moreover, most American aid is not targeted to help the world's poorest people. The politically sensitive Middle East gets more American money than Latin America, Africa, and the Far East put together, yet of course it has only a tiny fraction of the world's people. It seems obvious that a serious effort on the part of the United States to help alleviate the poverty of the Third World should include a significant increase in the total amount of foreign aid and a change in the way it is allocated so that the assistance goes to the people who need it most. Nonetheless, foreign aid is certainly no cure-all for the problems of the Third World. For one thing, the governments of some countries are so corrupt that foreign aid only enriches the local elites and does nothing for the poor. Another problem is that handouts can inadvertently create a vicious cycle of dependency. For example, food from the core nations given out to help feed the hungry often drives down the prices paid local farmers, resulting in lower agricultural production and an even greater need for foreign aid the next year. Wherever possible, foreign aid should therefore be carefully targeted toward training, education, birth control, and other specific development projects.

Stopping Political Interference Many world system theorists feel that the best thing the core nations could do to help the peripheral countries is simply to leave them alone to run their own affairs. All the core nations have meddled in the internal affairs of the poor countries, but as the world system's current hegemonic power, the United States has been the most heavily involved. Since the end of World War II, the United States has fought three full-scale wars in the Third World (in Korea, Vietnam, and Iraq); invaded the Dominican Republic, Grenada, and Panama; organized and funded independent armies that attacked those perceived as America's enemies in such places as Nicaragua and Cambodia; made assassination attempts against Third World leaders; supported and even arranged numerous coups and revolutions, such as the one that brought the shah of Iran to power and the one that killed Salvador Allende, the leftist president of Chile; and given huge amounts of secret financial assistance to help one political cause or hurt another.[26] Defenders of these actions claim they actually benefited the countries involved, but the foreign policy of the United States is, after all, designed to advance America's own interests and those of its upper class—not those of the Third World.[27] The justification for most of these policies was America's overriding concern with defeating the communist challenge. With the end of the cold war and the collapse of Soviet communism, much of the rationale for such measures is also gone, and this would seem to be an ideal time for a fundamental reorientation of American foreign policy.

The Third World Nations Economic development of the poor nations is obviously a much more vital issue in the Third World than in the industrialized nations. But that does not mean that Third World nations do not have their own powerful vested interests that oppose significant changes. Elite groups that reap the benefits of the current system obviously have little interest in rocking the boat. Nonetheless, a growing num-

Troops from the industrialized nations have repeatedly intervened in the affairs of Third World nations, as seen in this photograph taken during the American invasion of Panama.

ber of Third World leaders realize that it is not a question of whether their societies will change but rather how they will change.

Those governments committed to major reforms face many perplexing issues. Some Third World leaders feel that the best path is simply to copy the nations that are already industrialized. But others, although attracted by the wealth and power of the Western nations and Japan, are also deeply disturbed by the threat industrialization poses to their traditional moral standards and way of life. In the Middle East, for example, many leaders advocate some kind of distinctive "Islamic" approach to development, but it is not clear exactly what that might be nor the chances such an approach would have for success. A related question concerns the role of the core powers. Should Third World leaders encourage foreign investment and accept the risk of domination it brings, or try to go it alone without much outside money? And no matter which option they select, funds are likely to be in short supply, and Third World governments will have to make difficult choices among competing options.

Population Control By itself, population control will not solve the problem of Third World poverty, but neither can the problem be solved without it. The current rate of population growth in Latin America and Asia is around 2 percent a year, which means that there must be at least 2 percent economic growth every year just to keep the standard of living from falling. And the situation is worse in the Middle East, where the growth rate is 2.7 percent, and in Africa, where it is a full 3 percent.[28] But it is not just an issue of making the economy grow faster than the population. There are concrete environmental limits on how many people can comfortably live in a given area. Even if the average income grows, the quality of life declines as overcrowding and pollution make conditions more and more difficult. An increasing number of Third World governments are coming to see excessive population growth as a serious national problem and are starting to take measures to control it.[29] But it remains to be seen how effective these programs will be (see Chapter 16).

Economic Development Practically all Third World leaders say they are committed to economic development, but that phrase has different meanings to different people. One of the biggest issues concerns priorities and goals. Those who want to emulate the industrialized nations tend to focus on large-scale development projects in urban areas. Typically, local governments use loans, foreign investments, or their own funds to try to build the kind of modern factories that exist in the core nations. Critics charge that such expensive factories with lots of labor-saving equipment make little sense in nations that are short on money but have vast resources of unused labor. They advocate simpler, "low-tech" industries that utilize inexpensive technology and local labor to turn out low-cost products. Others claim that the whole emphasis on industrialization is misguided and that the number-one priority of Third World governments should be rural development. They argue that since the majority of the people live in rural areas, an effort to increase farm production and prevent runaway urban growth will create the greatest benefits for the most people (see Chapter 15).

Most Third World leaders, nonetheless, want to see their nation grow powerful enough to compete on equal terms with the core nations, and that means industrialization. But how is that to be achieved? One key ingredient is capital—that is, the money to build the schools, roads, and factories necessary to an industrial economy. Unless a country is blessed with unusually rich natural resources, there are only two ways to get the capital they need—raise it locally or rely on foreign investment. The latter is often a far more attractive alternative to Third World leaders, because foreign investors can provide huge sums of money immediately without the sacrifices and political tensions necessary to raise significant amounts of local capital. However, a great deal of research indicates that although investment by foreign multinational corporations provides a short-term boost to a local economy, self-reliance is, in the long run, the more effective approach.[30] Investments by multinational corporations represent a quick infusion of cash, but once the factories are built, the flow of capital is reversed as the firms take their profits back home. Moreover, the more multinational investment a country allows, the greater the percentage of its economy that will be under foreign control. Time and again, the vast financial resources of the multinationals have enabled them to corrupt local officials and win economic concessions that benefit the corporations at the cost of the host economy.

But these generalizations do not mean that multinational investment cannot be beneficial in some circumstances. For example, nations so poor and disorganized that they have few sources of local capital may have no choice but to rely on foreign investors. At the other extreme, the most prosperous and well-organized Third World countries may be able to accept a certain amount of multinational investment and still maintain strict enough controls to ensure that they provide real benefits to their own economy.

Political Reform The nations that have industrialized in recent times, such as the United States, West Germany, and Japan, have all had a strong unified government.[31] The process of industrialization is a grueling one that creates enormous social pressures that cannot be effectively managed in a weak, divided country. Of course, it is easy to tell the people of Third World nations that they need to pull together and support a unified government, but how are they to do it? Some nations, such as Japan, had a long tradition of powerful government and obedience to authority that gave them a significant advantage from the beginning of their drive for industrialization. But as we have seen, Third World governments are more likely to be weak and deeply divided along class and ethnic lines. In some cases, democratic reforms can be extremely helpful, because they bring a much wider spectrum of people into the process of government and help create more popular support for the regime. New social movements based on religious or economic ideologies have sometimes served to bring a new sense of organization and purpose to floundering governments as well. At other times, violent revolutionary change is required before an unstable government is replaced by a strong one. Revolutions in the United States, Russia, and even Japan were necessary before those nations could launch an effective drive for industrialization. Even the current trend toward the fragmentation of large countries into smaller nations with more ethnic homogeneity may be beneficial if the end result is the creation of more unified nations with stronger governments. But once again, a unified and well-run government, or any other single factor, cannot guarantee economic success. The emperors of classical China used the authority of their government to prevent the merchant class from becoming prosperous enough to threaten the power of the feudal landlords, and thereby also prevented the growth of a modern economy. The powerful communist state in the Soviet Union was extremely effective in carrying out a crash program of industrialization, but the militarism and the rigid bureaucratic mentality of that regime eventually choked off its own economic growth.

SOCIOLOGICAL PERSPECTIVES ON THE GLOBAL DIVIDE

Most sociologists are convinced that in order to deal with social problems effectively, we must first understand their causes and then formulate our response based on that understanding. As we have seen, functionalism (by shaping modernization theory) and conflict theory (through its influence on world system theory) have played a major role in explaining the deep divisions in today's world, and each approach implies a different program of action. Social psychologists have given less attention to these problems, but they nonetheless have an important contribution to make to our understanding of global inequality.

The Functionalist Perspective Wherever functionalists look in the Third World, they see the problems of social disorganization. Under pressure from rapid economic change, the extended family is breaking down and its traditional power is slowly ebbing away. There is a growing cultural lag as people cling to traditional attitudes that were useful in the past but have now become a serious drawback. For example, most Third World people still place a high importance on having a large family, even though today's population explosion makes that an extremely dysfunctional attitude. Traditional religious beliefs are being challenged by secular ideas from the West and a rising tide of materialism. But the educational institutions that foster the scientific worldview are often so weak that they do not even reach large segments of the population. As we have noted, too, governments are ineffective and deeply divided. Perhaps most serious of all, the economic institutions have not made a smooth transition from an agricultural system to industrialism and often flounder somewhere between the two. A flood of immigrant villagers pour into cities that lack enough jobs, sanitation, and housing to support them. Thus, the functionalists see the Third World to be in a difficult state of transition from one kind of social and cultural system to another.

Since functionalists generally assume that Third World countries will ultimately end up as Western-style industrial nations, they feel that the best way to help is to speed up the process of transition, so these societies can regain their balance as quickly as possible. Functionalists therefore recommend a much stronger emphasis on education in Third World nations to teach the people the skills necessary in an industrial society. They advocate a strong program of family planning to help change dysfunctional attitudes favoring large families. Urban development programs must be launched to create enough housing for the expanding urban population. Since functionalists are not very concerned about the issue of economic exploitation, they often advocate more Third World investment by multinational corporations as a good way to spread modern attitudes and economic structures. Finally, Third World governments need to be made more democratic so that they can gain the support of their population for the difficult reforms that must be made.

The Conflict Perspective Where the functionalists see disorganization, the conflict theorists see the results of international exploitation. In the past, the exploitation was obvious. When the Europeans first colonized a new area, they would loot whatever gold and jewels they could find and then take over direct political control of the native peoples. Today the exploitation is more subtle, but conflict theorists are convinced that it is just as real. The Third World nations now have their own governments, but conflict theorists feel that the armies and the secret agents of the industrial powers are always waiting to punish any Third World leader who gets out of line. The people of the Third World are no longer forced to work as slaves in the mines and plantations, but they work for wages so low that they can barely survive. Foreigners no longer simply steal the wealth of the peripheral countries, but they buy up their precious natural resource at a fraction of the real value.

To the conflict theorists, the answer to the problems of the Third World is a simple one—end the economic exploitation that has victimized much of the earth's population. But exactly how that is to be done is a more difficult matter. Despite the failure of the communist government of the Soviet Union, many conflict theorists are still strong supporters of Third World revolutionary movements seeking to overthrow local governments. They urge the revolutionaries to create new regimes, free from foreign influence, that represent the interests of all their people, not just a small elite. Conflict theorists also encourage Third World nations to ban together in the struggle with the industrialized nations. They point to the success the Organization of Petroleum Exporting Countries (OPEC) had in increasing the price of oil, and they call for the creation of similar cartels for other raw materials. Many conflict theorists now feel that the key to liberating the Third World lies in the core nations. They argue that because workers in the industrialized nations are being exploited by the multinational corporations in much the same way as the workers in the Third World, the two groups must join together to demand the creation of a more just world order that will benefit everyone.

Social Psychological Perspectives   Social psychology's primary contribution to the study of global inequality has been through its efforts to understand the psychological consequences of modernization. Agricultural societies are characterized by mass poverty and a huge gap between the elite and the common people. Nonetheless, these tradition-bound societies provide their members with a sense of security and belonging seldom found in the industrialized world. Most people are born, live, and die in the same close-knit villages. The important transitions in life are all marked by religious rituals, and everyone holds a similar view of the world. Since poverty is the rule, not the exception, it holds no shame. The difficulty of social mobility and the absence of a profit-oriented economy minimize competition and the tensions it causes.

Sooner or later, the process of modernization shatters this traditional world. People leave their familiar village and move into an urban environment where few of the old rules seem to apply. Even if they can maintain strong family ties in this new world, the old sense of belonging is gone. The pressures of overpopulation and a changing economy create an intensely competitive environment in which those who fail may literally starve to death. Even those who remain in the villages are likely to find their lives changing in disturbing ways. Increasing levels of education and exposure to the media slowly spread the new commercial orientation, and economic dislocation and environmental deterioration make it harder and harder to make a living off the land.

The solutions to these problems must come from the kinds of proposals advanced by the macro-level conflict and functionalist theories (see Chapter 1), but social psychologists make two recommendations. First, they urge Third World governments to focus their efforts on improving the rural economy, so that people can stay in their villages and avoid the wrenching psychological changes that accompany urban migration. Second, they advise Third World leaders to learn from the mistakes of the West, and do their best to maintain strong family and community institutions.

SUMMARY

The nations of the world make up a kind of international class system, with a huge gap between the rich industrialized countries on the top and the poverty-stricken Third World nations on the bottom. The most obvious difference between these two groups of nations is in their wealth—in terms both of money and of accumulated assets such as buildings, roads, and factories. Because of runaway population growth and rapid urbanization, most Third World cities have a large number of homeless people and huge shantytowns of crude shacks. Inadequate nutrition and contagious disease make the life expectancy 12 years below that in the industrialized nations. Literacy rates are low, and because there is only a small middle class, the gap between the rich and the poor is usually a large one. Third World nations are more likely to have deep ethnic divisions and ineffective governments.

The enormous difference between the wealthy and the poor nations developed in the modern era as some countries underwent a rapid process of industrialization while others did not. Modernization theorists see industrialization as a universal process that has simply taken place more quickly in some parts of the world than in others. The less-developed countries have made slower progress because they have clung to traditional attitudes and values that impede industrialization. World system theory, on the other hand, sees industrialization as a global process, not a national one. All nations are seen to be part of a single world system dominated by the industrialized nations (the core), which exploit the poor nations (the periphery).

The rich countries can help the Third World by opening up their markets, forgiving the debts owed by the poor nations, increasing foreign aid, and ending their political interference in the internal affairs of the poor nations. The Third World nations themselves are faced with many difficult choices. Do they emphasize industrialization or rural development? Do they encourage multinational corporations to invest in their country or depend on their own resources? How are their limited development funds best spent? There are no simple answers to these questions, but it does seem clear that most Third World nations need better population control programs, a greater effort at economic development, and stronger governments.

Functionalists see today's global divide as the product of social disorganization in the Third World, and they recommend programs to speed up the transition to full industrialization in order to bring more stability to these societies. Conflict theorists see most of today's global problems as the direct result of European colonialism and the exploitative economic system on which it was based. They recommend an international effort by poor and working-class people around the world to create a more just international order. Social psychologists point out that the destruction of the traditional way of life in agricultural societies has also meant a great deal more insecurity and anxiety for the average person. They urge Third World leaders to work to keep their family and community institutions strong.

KEY TERMS

core The wealthy, industrialized nations that dominate the world system.

hegemonic power The strongest of the industrialized powers, which assumes leadership of the world system.

modernization The process by which a nation moves from a tradi-

tional agricultural society to an industrialized state.

periphery The poor nations of the world, which are subject to the economic and political domination of the core nations.

semiperiphery The partially industrialized nations that have characteristics

of both the core and the periphery.
Third World The poor nations of the world.

world system The network of economic and political relationships that link the world.

FURTHER READINGS

Daniel Chirot, *Social Change in the Modern Era* (San Diego: Harcourt Brace Jovanovich, 1986). One of the best sociological analyses of the nature and origins of the contemporary world order. Chirot deftly combines the framework of world system theory with the insights of other theoretical approaches.

Jeffry A. Frieden and David A. Lake, *International Political Economy: Perspectives on Global Power and Wealth*, 2nd ed. (New York: St. Martin's Press, 1991). A good collection of articles focusing on the economic problems of both the Third World and the industrialized nations.

Volker Bornschier and Christopher Chase-Dunn, *Transnational Corporations and Underdevelopment* (New York: Praeger, 1985). A comprehensive examination of the role of multinational corporations in the economic development of the Third World.

Thomas Richard Shannon, *An Introduction to the World-System Perspective* (Boulder, Colo.: Westview Press, 1989). A clearly written summary of world system theory and a useful analysis of its strengths and weaknesses.

Walter W. Rostow, *The World Economy: History and Prospect* (Austin: University of Texas Press, 1980). A detailed statistical analysis of the world economy by one of the most important modernization theorists.

L. S. Stavrianos, *Global Rift: The Third World Comes of Age* (New York: Morrow, 1981). A compelling history of the development of the Third World.

chapter 15

Urbanization

- How is life different in a rural area, a suburb, and a big city?
- What are the most serious problems created by the process of urbanization?
- How do the problems in the cities of the Third World differ from those in the industrialized nations?
- What are the best ways to deal with the problems of urbanization?

No social change in the last 200 years has had a more far-reaching impact than **urbanization**, the shift from rural to urban living. In 1790, only 1 in every 20 Americans lived in an urban area; today it is 15 in every 20. The same process has occurred in the other industrialized nations as well. Canada and Japan are slightly more urbanized than the United States (about 77 percent), while 90 percent of Germany's people live in its cities.[1] Most poor nations have only begun their urban explosion, but their cities are now growing much faster than those in the industrialized countries. Two-thirds of the people of the Third World still live in rural areas today, but it is expected that in just three decades or so, the majority will live in cities.[2]

The origins of the city can be found at the very beginning of recorded history, but the cities in agricultural societies were only small islands in a sea of rural farmlands.[3] It was not until the industrial revolution sent waves of immigrants to the cities in search of new jobs and new opportunities that the first urban societies emerged. Existing cities grew to an unprecedented size, and small satellite communities sprang up around their borders. The land between some cities has been completely filled in, creating what is known as a **megalopolis**—a large area in which cities fuse together to form one vast urban network. The largest megalopolis in North America is the unbroken stretch of cities and suburbs along the East Coast of the United States from Boston to Virginia. Another sprawling urban area is growing in California from San Diego to San Francisco, and a third runs from Milwaukee through Chicago to northern Indiana. In Canada, 60 percent of the population lives in a 600-mile strip from Quebec City to Windsor, Ontario. However, because these huge areas often have little overall political or economic integration, the U.S. Bureau of the Census uses a slightly more narrow concept, the **metropolitan statistical area** (MSA), which includes a central population center and the surrounding communities that are dependent on it.[4]

Although the nations of the Third World have yet to experience a complete industrial revolution, they are nonetheless undergoing a massive wave of urbanization. The principal motivation of urban migrants in the Third World is not so much the attractions of the city but the fact that rapid population growth and the spread of large export-oriented farming businesses have made it impossible for them to continue making a living on the land. The cities of Third World nations are now growing almost twice as fast as those in the industrialized countries. By the year 2000 there will be twice as many people living in the cities of the Third World as in those of the industrialized nations, and by 2025 there will be four times as many.[5] Yet the poor nations have little money for new housing, roads, water, sanitation, or electricity.

THE CITIES

Civilizations have always been centered in cities. Despite the recent flight to the suburbs, cities are more dominant in our social life than ever before. Huge corporations and government bureaucracies spread their influence outward from a few major cities. The large newspapers and broadcasting companies, which set our tastes and define our world, are based in cities and reflect their realities. The cities spawn and attract actors, artists, writers, and other intellectual innovators who set the cultural style of our age. There is a particularly big gap between the sophisticated Western-influenced cultural life found in the major cities of the Third World and the life of the tradition-bound villagers. Foreign visitors and immigrants stop in the great cities, rarely in country villages. In North America, new immigrants first occupy the run-down sections of the cities, then move to more affluent areas as they become accul-turated. This process has left the cities dotted with fragments of many different cul-tures—Irish, Italian, French, Chinese, Mexican, German, Russian, and more—thus adding to the diversity of city life.

But along with these attractions go a host of urban problems that include every-thing from traffic congestion to street crime, and public opinion polls show that most people in cities say they would rather live somewhere else.[6] Moreover, people in rural areas are almost two and a half times more likely to say that they are "completely satisfied" with their community than those in big cities.[7]

One of the most fascinating questions confronting urban sociologists concerns the nature of life in cities. Do urban people have a unique way of thinking, a special outlook on life? One of the first people to answer this question was the German sociologist Georg Simmel. In a classic essay published in 1903, Simmel noted that city dwellers are bombarded by a tremendous amount of "nervous stimulation."[8] Noise, traffic, crowds, the rapid pace of life, and dozens of other stimuli overload the urban resident. City dwellers simply cannot pay attention to everything that goes on around them, and as a result they become indifferent to their surroundings. Because urbanites deal with so many strangers, their relationships tend to be directed toward external

The modern city has a rich diversity of people, life styles, and architectures.

Beverly Hills of the North Pole

ction. On the whole, the city offers its people greater
e danger that they will be isolated and alone.
an sociology is Louis Wirth's "Urbanism as a Way of
rticle summarized much of the thought of the "Chi-
y, which developed at the University of Chicago in
th painted with a broader brush than Simmel, but he
ut the psychological impact of urban life. To Wirth,
nost important of the city's characteristics. According
ers are specialized in the work they do and in their
e. Being highly specialized, they know one another
nal ways. One person will be recognized as a bank
nd a third as a bus driver, but they are seldom known
nterests dominate this impersonal urban world. The
f people living close together but without deep emo-
en feels lonely and isolated even in the midst of vast
erate the attitudes and customs of other people, but
urity and instability as the normal state of the world.
ether to increase the incidence of what Wirth called
uding "personal disorganization, mental breakdown,
rruption, and disorder."
ists agree that city life is as dismal as Wirth pictured
s merely reflect small-town America's dislike of cities
and their rapid growth. For example, Herbert J. Gans noted that Wirth overlooked
the many city dwellers who have a strong sense of community, such as the affluent,
well-educated people who choose to live in the city because of its cultural life, or the
"ethnic villagers" who live in tightly knit ethnic neighborhoods.[10] Gans concluded
that social class and age have a greater effect on urban life styles than does city living
itself. And he argued that the kind of problems described by Wirth exist principally
among deprived groups, such as the poor and the ethnic minorities, and those who
are financially trapped in urban neighborhoods that have begun to decay.

THE SUBURBS

More Americans now live in **suburbs**—the part of an urban area that lies outside the
central city—than in cities or rural areas. The first suburbs can be traced back at least
as far as the 1760s. By the end of the nineteenth century, most American cities had
suburbs where the wealthy could live away from the congestion of the city. But the
fastest growth took place in the two decades after World War II, when millions of
Americans poured into suburban housing tracts. In one sense the big city, with its
congestion, crime, pollution, and decay, pushed them out. But in another sense the
suburbs pulled families out of the cities, offering space for growing families, good
schools, personal safety, and a pleasant environment at a price that they could
afford.[11]

But the suburbs did not simply spring into being because people wanted to live
there. The growth of the suburbs required three things: automobiles, highways, and
private homes. When the suburban explosion was just beginning, the "highway

lobby,'' composed of such diverse interests as the oil companies, automobile manufacturers, and truckers' unions, pushed through a massive program of freeway construction that laid the foundation for continued suburban growth. The government also spent billions of dollars subsidizing private homes for middle- and upper-class Americans. The biggest subsidy is the full tax deduction for interest paid on home mortgages. The government also worked to keep interest rates down on home mortgages, and even directly underwrote home loans through the Federal Housing Authority and the Veterans Administration.[12]

North Americans have a kind of love-hate relationship with the suburbs, seeing them as both a cause of social blight and its solution. The proponents of suburban living picture it as a refuge from the troubles of the big city. In this view, the neatly trimmed lawns and the well-ordered nuclear families of the suburbs stand in sharp contrast to the crime and confusion of city life. But the critics of suburbia picture it differently. They see the suburbs as an endless expanse of cracker-box houses that are so alike that it is difficult to tell one from the other. They say that because suburbanites are mostly from the white middle class, they lack individuality and diversity and are bland and dull.

Both these views are faulty, however, for they are based on an image of the suburb as a ''bedroom community'' for the affluent that is generations out of date. Although they started as residential areas for the wealthy, the suburbs are now heterogeneous and diversified. As people first moved to the suburbs, they were quickly followed by small shops and stores and eventually by huge shopping malls. Suburban retailers have grown steadily more prosperous, while sales in the central city have stagnated.[13] Along with the new jobs in retail has come a tremendous influx of manufacturing, wholesaling, and warehousing businesses that used to be found only in the central cities. Even the administrative offices of many major corporations have moved to the suburbs. There are now more corporate headquarters in the suburbs surrounding New York City than there are in the city itself. Overall, more than 70 percent of those who live in the suburbs of large metropolitan areas work in them too.[14]

As the suburbs have diversified economically, they have diversified socially as well. Because many older suburban neighborhoods have become less desirable and developers have put up more apartment buildings, less affluent people have been able to move in. The poor and the minorities are now the fastest-growing segment of the suburban population.[15] However, this trend has not led to a new era of integration but rather to the reproduction of the patterns of segregation found in the cities. About 86 percent of all suburban whites now live in segregated areas (areas in which less than 1 percent of the population is black).[16] And just as there are now black neighborhoods in the suburbs, so there are other neighborhoods populated mainly by those with a particular ethnic or economic background.

Today's suburbs are therefore a checkerboard of widely divergent communities, and as John R. Logan and Harvey L. Molotch point out, ''In the suburban milieu, as in the larger world system, the advantages adhere to the places of the rich and the disadvantages to the places of the poor.''[17] (See Chapter 14 for a discussion of the world system.) The rich neighborhoods have the best sanitation, fire, and police services, the best shopping, and the least pollution and crime. Because the process of suburbanization has fragmented the political control of metropolitan areas, the wealthy often live in their own towns and cities. One result is that their local taxes no longer go to help meet the pressing needs of the poor.

RURAL AREAS

Until the industrial revolution, most of the world's people lived in rural villages. Even today, the majority of the people in the Third World live in rural settlements, which tend to be traditional in their cultural outlook and skeptical of new ideas and attitudes. These villagers are not only isolated from world affairs and concerns; they generally have weak ties to their own nation. Illiteracy is still the rule, and because many Third World villages have no electricity, there is very little light after sunset, much less radio or television. The villagers' main concern is, therefore, with local events. Villages are very homogeneous places. Not only do villagers share the same set of values, but they have spent their whole lives together and know the intimate details of each others' past—both the good and the bad.[18] Although most villagers are content to continue with their traditional life style, population growth and changing economic conditions are making it harder and harder to do so (see Chapter 16).

In the industrialized nations, traditional village life is largely a thing of the past. Of course, many people still live on farms and in small towns, but their numbers have decreased sharply over the last two centuries. Moreover, the character of rural life has changed. People who live in open country and small towns are no longer as isolated as they once were. Universal education instills a similar cultural outlook in people regardless of where they live and brings rural residents into the cultural mainstream by giving them the ability to read books and newspapers. The spread of telephones, radio, television, and modern transportation has also increased the integration of rural areas into a unified national fabric. Farm families no longer raise their own vegetables, butcher their own hogs, milk their own cows, or cut their own wood for lumber and fuel. They buy their beans, pork, and milk at the supermarket and order building materials and fuel oil from local distributors. Gone are the days when spare time meant sitting around the stove telling tales, mending clothes, or repairing tools. Today's rural families watch television or go to the movies, just as families in the cities and suburbs do.

Another major factor in the transformation of rural life is the sharp decine of farming as an occupation. Traditionally, the vast majority of people who lived in the country were farmers. But as nations industrialize, agricultural technology improves and fewer and fewer people are needed on the farm (see Figure 15.1).[19] People born in rural areas are therefore continuing to migrate to cities in search of opportunity, as they have for centuries. In the last two decades, however, the number of people migrating from the cities to the rural areas and small towns has greatly increased. Between 1970 and 1988 the percentage of the population living in cities of over half a million people decreased, while the percentage of those living in communities of from 10,000 to 50,000 people went up.[20] The reasons people are moving to small towns are probably much the same as the reasons they move to the suburbs: the lure of cheaper land, a slower-paced life style, and the desire to escape from urban problems.

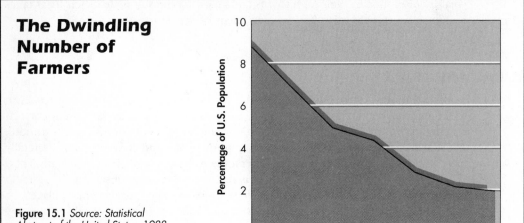

The Dwindling Number of Farmers

Figure 15.1 *Source: Statistical Abstract of the United States, 1988, p. 607; Statistical Abstract of the United States, 1991, p. 643.*

Despite all these changes, life on a farm or in a small town retains many special features. People know one another as people rather than as role players. The background of residents of rural communities tends to be more homogeneous than that of city dwellers, giving them a stronger feeling of group identity and a clearer sense of where they fit in as individuals. Deviant behavior is less common in rural areas than in urban ones; and though crime rates have been increasing faster in rural than in urban areas, they are still considerably lower. Living in a small town has its drawbacks, however. There is less deviance because everyone knows everyone else's business. The absence of anonymity reduces opportunities for many types of crime, but it also affects personal freedom, innovation, and individuality. Because individuals cannot get lost in the crowd, their neighbors often know the details of their personal lives, and small-town gossip can be malicious and spiteful. Rural communities lack much of the spice of city life because they are so small and homogeneous. Still, as we have seen, people in rural areas report being far more satisfied with their community than do those in the cities.[21]

PROBLEMS OF URBANIZATION

As the process of urbanization has transformed the way we live, it has brought a new range of problems. Many farms and rural areas were left to decay as people rushed to the cities; then the growth of the suburbs led to the decline of many inner-city neighborhoods. Because of population pressures, housing costs in desirable areas have skyrocketed and there is an ever-increasing demand on the transportation system.

Crisis on the Farm No one has been harder hit by the process of urbanization than the farmers. The percentage of farmers in the population has been declining for generations. In 1920, there were around 6.4 million farms in the United States. In 1950, the number had fallen to 5.4 million; in 1987 there were only a little over 2 million farms, and by the year 2000 that figure is expected to be closer to 1 million. But on top of the long-term decline, the 1980s saw an increase in farm foreclosures and bankruptcies of crisis proportions. In some years, as many as 1 out of 10 farms went out of business, and in the vast majority of the cases those were family farms, not big agribusiness corporations.[22] The early 1990s have seen some improvement in the farm economy, but the prospects for the small farmer remain bleak. One result of this trend has been the "graying" of the American farmer, as children born on the farm seek more promising careers in other lines of work. In just five years, between 1982 and 1987, the number of farmers under 25 dropped by 43 percent.[23]

There are several reasons for the crisis of the family farmer. Agriculture has always been a volatile business. Nature's unpredictability makes the price of farm goods bounce up and down more than virtually any other product. In the past, hard times meant that family farmers had to cut back and live off the food they produced themselves. But today, agriculture is run like any other business, and, good times or bad, the loans must be paid. Ironically, the farmers' most recent problems have their origins in the good times of the 1970s, which encouraged them to borrow too heavily to expand their production. During the 1980s, the price of farm products plummeted.

This abandoned farm in Amsterdam, New York, is one reflection of the continuing financial crisis of the family farmer.

The big corporate farms had the financial resources to weather the storm, but many family farmers did not. As a result, well-financed corporate farms were able to buy up prime land at bargain prices. About 5 percent of the farms now hold over half of all agricultural land. These powerful agribusiness enterprises also receive most of the government farm subsidies, even though such assistance was originally intended to help the family farmer. The farm economy of the early 1990s is much improved over the 1980s, but the next downturn is bound to force more family farmers out of business. The plain fact is that the family farm, which once was the backbone of American life, is hopelessly outmatched by the wealth and power of its huge corporate competitors.

While most rural people no longer work on the farm, the plight of the family farmer has still sent economic shock waves through many parts of the country already facing hard times. The mass migration to the cities and suburbs and the narrow economic base of many rural communities have left their residents with lower average income, poorer health care, and less education than their urban counterparts. Some rural towns have been flooded with new immigrants from the cities, while others have seen their population dwindle away. Although an influx of new residents requires many difficult adjustments, the towns with declining populations suffer the most. For one thing, a smaller population means higher taxes, because the cost of maintaining essential services must be carried by fewer people. Stores and businesses that depend on local trade go bankrupt, further reducing the tax base. As job opportunities dry up and education, health care, and other community services decline, even more people move out and the problems become more severe. Since it is usually the young adults who migrate to the cities, they leave a disproportionately large dependent population of children and elderly people, who must be supported by the productive workers who remain.

Decline of the Central City   The big cities used to be a dominant political and economic force in North America, but year by year the flight to the suburbs has eroded their power. Congestion, rising costs, crime, and pollution have driven out large segments of the middle class, leaving the inner cities with a disproportionate share of the poor, the minorities, and the new immigrants. Although our cities are still major centers of corporate and government activity, an increasing number of businesses have followed the middle class to the suburbs. The result has been a more or less permanent crisis in many big-city governments, as they struggle to repair their crumbling **infrastructure** (roads, sewers, water systems, and other basic necessities) and meet the growing needs of their poor and minority populations with a shrinking tax base. In the past, the big cities could always turn to the state or federal governments to get them through hard times. But the loss of the middle class has also meant the loss of political power. Since the early 1980s, the federal government has slashed the revenue-sharing funds that used to go to the cities, and more and more big-city mayors in search of financial aid face skeptical and unsympathetic state legislatures.

Some urban neighborhoods have managed to flourish despite these difficulties, but others have deteriorated into the kinds of festering slums seldom seen in the cities of Europe or Japan. The general decline in the demand for unskilled labor has combined with the economic disintegration of the inner city to produce pockets of intense poverty. Since 1975, the percentage of poor African Americans who live in *extreme* poverty has increased by about 50 percent.[24] And studies show that the people who live in the poverty-stricken urban ghettos are trapped by formidable economic barriers. For example, welfare mothers who are assigned subsidized housing in the inner cities are less likely to find a job or to earn a decent wage than those assigned housing in suburban areas (see Chapter 6).[25]

Almost inevitably, many of the residents of these poverty zones—especially the young men—turn to the illegal economy to find the opportunities otherwise denied them. Prostitution, gambling, and extortion all flourish, but in recent times it is the drug business that has been the most profitable. Big cities from coast to coast now have what police term "dead zones," ruled by street criminals and gang violence, where people from all over the region come to buy drugs on the streets and in the crack houses (fortified houses that are used to sell cocaine and other drugs). Life in these lawless neighborhoods can be a nightmare for many of the residents. But because such communities often include low-income housing projects and some of the least expensive private apartments, many people simply cannot afford to move out.[26]

Local Government Local governments are beset by a variety of problems, ranging from graft and corruption to wasteful duplication of services. Zoning changes, for example, have repeatedly been the focus of corruption scandals. Millions of dollars are often involved in an agency's decision to change the zoning of a piece of land. Developers and land speculators looking for a fast profit go to great lengths to convince officials to make the "right" decision. Officials are sometimes bribed with cash payments or given a percentage of a developer's profits. The result is likely to be a new suburban community that turns its real estate operators into millionaires but fails to meet the needs of local residents.[27]

Another product of urbanization is the creation of a confusing network of fragmented local governments and overlapping service districts. Metropolitan areas often have dozens of police chiefs, fire chiefs, and department heads when only a few would be sufficient. This overlap and duplication of services is expensive and inefficient.

Many town and city governments have surprisingly little control over their own affairs. For one thing, states often place tight legal restrictions on their freedom to act, particularly with respect to the types and amounts of taxes that can be levied on their citizens. Local governments also rely on federal grants that specify how the money is to be spent. The economies of many cities are heavily dependent on a few large corporate employers. When these firms make demands on local government, elected officials often have little choice but to comply or face the financial devastation that would result from a corporate decision to move to another area. And even when local officials do oppose corporate plans, the businesses are often able to use their influence on the state or federal level to overpower local opposition.

Housing The stunning increase in the cost of buying a private home has been a major contributor to the growing division between the haves and the have-nots in our society (see Chapter 2). Those who already own a home have received windfall profits, but first-time home buyers are often shut out of the market. The cost of an average home

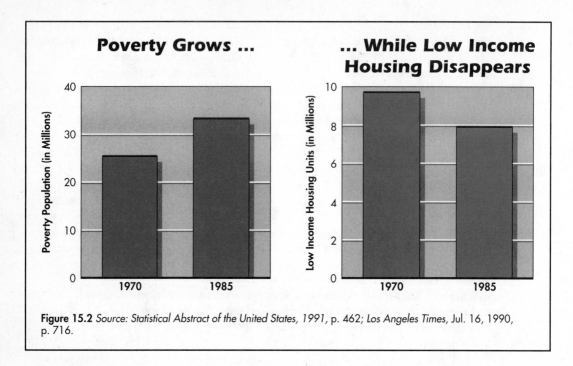

Figure 15.2 *Source: Statistical Abstract of the United States, 1991, p. 462; Los Angeles Times, Jul. 16, 1990, p. 716.*

more than doubled in the last decade (see Figure 15.2). As a result, the average buyer was older and more likely to need two incomes to make the payments.[28]

But these problems pale in comparison with the critical shortage of low-cost housing for those without comfortable middle-class incomes. Since 1978 more than two million units of low-cost housing have been abandoned or converted into more expensive housing. Thus, while the number of poor people has been growing, the supply of affordable housing has been shrinking.[29] As a result, rents for the least expensive apartments are rising much faster than the income of the tenants.[30] The average poor family now spends about 65 percent of its income on housing—more than double the maximum amount the Department of Housing and Urban Development says they should have to spend.[31] An increasing number of people are being forced to move in with relatives and friends or are living in converted garages, old cars and vans, tents, or on the streets. Estimates of the number of homeless people in the United States vary widely (see Chapter 6), but virtually everyone agrees that their numbers have soared in the last decade.

What happened to the supply of low-cost housing? One problem is known as **gentrification**: the refurbishing of old, low-cost neighborhoods to accommodate more wealthy people. One good example of this is the area known as Capitol Hill in Washington, D.C. In the 1960s it was occupied by poor and working-class blacks. But because of its close proximity to downtown employment centers, young artists, architects, and students began purchasing homes in the neighborhood and fixing them up. These first immigrants were soon followed by upper-income professionals and government workers. Over 90 percent of the newcomers were whites, and over 90 percent had college educations. The former residents had to move on to search for other accommodations from the city's shrinking supply of affordable housing.[32]

A second cause of this shortage can be laid directly at the government's doorstep. For one thing, the efforts of local community redevelopment agencies have tended to have much the same impact as private gentrification: old neighborhoods are renovated, and the poor are moved out to make way for the affluent. Perhaps more important, the federal government has also turned its back on the housing needs of the poor. In the last decade, federal appropriations for subsidized housing were cut by 75 percent, and the Tax Reform Act of 1986 eliminated the tax breaks designed to encourage private investment in rental properties.[33]

Inefficient Transportation   It is often said that Americans have a love affair with the car. Even kings in their carriages did not know the speed, comfort, or convenience of the automobile that an average wage earner can now afford. But this romantic picture hardly fits the realities of American life, where pollution fouls the air and over 45,000 people die in traffic accidents every year.[34] Traffic congestion is growing so bad in some urban areas that it often approaches **gridlock**, a situation in which traffic simply stops moving and no one gets anywhere. Local, state, and national governments spend

The automobile provides one of the fastest and most convenient forms of transportation, but we have too much of a good thing. In urban areas around the world, traffic clogs city streets, exhaust pollutes the air, and engines consume huge amounts of fuel.

billions of dollars a year in a losing battle to build roads faster than new cars clog them up. Still, four out of five commuters go to work by car, and most of those vehicles carry only a single passenger.[35] Our dependence on the automobile imposes a severe hardship on many of the more than one out of ten households that do not own one,[36] making it difficult for the poor to get to work and the elderly to their doctor's office.

Why do we depend on such an inefficient system of transportation? Part of the answer is simply that we like cars. But there is another reason as well: the automobile, tire, and petroleum industries decided that there was more money to be made from the automobile, and they intentionally set out to impede the growth of public transportation. In Los Angeles, for example, General Motors and Standard Oil organized a corporation that acquired a controlling interest in the Pacific Electric Railway, which operated what was then the world's largest system of electric trolleys. The quiet and efficient trolleys were then replaced by polluting diesel-powered buses. The new owners gave up the special rights-of-way enjoyed by the trolleys and pulled up the tracks. After these "improvements" passenger mileage on the trolleys plummeted, and Los Angeles is now one of the most automobile-dependent big cities in the world.[37]

Ethnic Segregation   Most large cities have a number of "ethnic villages": areas populated mostly by members of a particular ethnic group. Whether such a residential pattern is desirable or not is open to debate. As was noted in Chapter 7, pluralists hold that such communities provide support for new immigrants and a place where their children and grandchildren can go to renew ties with their cultural roots. New immigrants often find jobs working for other members of their own group, and access to this supply of cheap labor provides an opportunity for other immigrants to move up the social ladder.[38] But the advocates of integration argue that the isolation of immigrants and minorities in ethnic communities actually cuts them off from many economic opportunities and makes them easy victims of exploitation, by members either of their own group or of another. They point out that such segregated communities encourage the separate ethnic identities that divide us against each other and have created so much hatred and conflict through the years.

But whatever they think about the value of separate ethnic neighborhoods, both pluralists and integrationists agree that no one should be forced to live in them. Yet that is exactly the position in which many black and other nonwhite minorities find themselves. The laws explicitly requiring racial segregation have all been overturned, but racial minorities are still excluded from many neighborhoods by the hostility and prejudice of the residents, and by the landlords and rental agents who cater to it. Although sociologists use different ways of measuring segregation, it appears that about three out of four blacks in American cities live in segregated neighborhoods.[39] Analysis of data collected by Karl and Alma Taeuber shows a slow decrease in the level of segregation in American cities over the years.[40] Logan and Molotch, on the other hand, found that segregation has been increasing in the suburbs,[41] but other research indicates that they are still less segregated than the cities.[42] If this pattern of forced segregation is to be broken, the federal government will have to take much more vigorous action than it has since the 1970s.

Urban Problems in the Third World   The population explosion has prevented rural de-population from developing in Third World nations, as it has in some industrialized ones. But with this one exception, the Third World has been experiencing the same kinds of problems just discussed. Because Third World countries have more than double the population growth rate of the industrialized nations and only a fraction of their wealth, urban problems often take on staggering proportions. Moreover, the process of urbanization is occurring much faster in the Third World than it ever did in the West, as we noted earlier.[43]

The impact of this runaway urbanization can be most easily seen by comparing individual cities. In 1950 the population of Mexico City was less than one-fourth of the New York City area's 12 million people. In the next 25 years, Mexico City's growth rate was five times New York's, though in 1975 New York City was still larger, with 17 million people to Mexico City's 11 million. But by the year 2000, Mexico City is expected to have over 26 million residents, making it the world's largest city, while New York will probably have about 15.5 million people. Mexico City's rapid growth is typical of most other large Third World cities as well. By the turn of the century, São Paulo, Brazil, will be almost as large, with a population of 24 million, and there will be *two* cities in India larger than New York, with a third quickly closing in.[44]

Shantytowns, like this one, are common in cities around the world.

How are such impoverished cities to build enough new housing to accommodate all these people? Sadly, the answer is that they probably cannot. Most of the people will either crowd into existing housing (most of it already crowded and dilapidated) or become urban squatters, building small shacks from whatever materials they can beg, borrow, or steal. Almost half the residents of Mexico City now live in slums and shantytowns, as do 55 percent of the residents of Manila in the Philippines, and 67 percent of the residents of Calcutta, India.[45] These shantytowns are more than just overcrowded: they lack the basic services necessary for a decent life. The streets are unpaved, there is little fire or police protection, clean water is scarce, and proper sewage facilities are nonexistent. As a result, health conditions are deplorable, death rates are high, and epidemic disease is common. Because urban squatters have no legal rights to the land they live on, they are in constant danger of losing their homes. If the government decides it needs the land for some new public-works project or that the squatters are an eyesore or a source of political unrest, they can simply be moved out. Nonetheless, in one sense the residents of these shantytowns are the lucky ones, for most Third World cities have a substantial number of "pavement people" who sleep in the streets, without any permanent home. For example, Calcutta, one of the world's most troubled cities, has between 330,000 and 1 million of these homeless people.[46]

Of course, all the residents of Third World cities do not live in such deplorable conditions. The Westernized elite typically live in conditions of luxury that would make most middle-class Americans envious. And even the common people often find the city a far more rewarding place to live than rural villages. One survey of migrants who had been living in Mexico City for four years found that 80 percent of those interviewed were satisfied with their decision to move.[47] After all, millions of people wouldn't migrate to Third World cities every year if they didn't think that their life would be better there. The urban problems of Third World nations must therefore be seen in the context of the crowding, unemployment, and hunger of the rural areas (see Chapter 14).

RESPONDING TO PROBLEMS OF URBANIZATION

Despite the complexity of the problems brought on by the process of urbanization, there is no shortage of proposals for solving them. Some are wildly utopian and others too narrow to be worthwhile. But all have one thing in common: their successful implementation will require two scarce commodities, money and the political will to get the job done.

Governmental Reorganization Many proposals for solving metropolitan political and financial problems in the industrialized nations call for governmental reorganization. This means, generally, the creation of larger governmental units. For example, some planners suggest that cities be abolished and that county or even regional governments take their place. Others propose that only some functions of government be regionalized by creating larger school, water, sewage, airport, and pollution control districts. Such regional governmental units could provide services more economically and would spread the tax burden more evenly over inner cities, suburbs, and rural areas. Some urban planners believe that these governmental units would eventually encourage a sense of regional cooperation and identity. A person would no longer be loyal to Boston or San Francisco; instead, he or she would identify with New England or the Bay Area.

Annexing suburbs or otherwise merging two or more governments appears to be the easiest form of reorganization. In the nineteenth century, important mergers took place in New York City, Philadelphia, Boston, and New Orleans. But there seems to be increasing resistance to mergers and annexations. Voters in suburban areas are seldom willing to link their futures with nearby cities. They moved to their homes to avoid the problems of the big cities and see in proposed mergers only higher taxes and loss of autonomy.

Urban Renewal The first **urban renewal** programs in the United States were begun during the Great Depression to improve housing and provide employment for construction workers. To this day urban renewal usually means housing renewal, although a renewal of business and other economic activities is also desperately needed in many urban neighborhoods. From the beginning, urban renewal projects were plagued with problems. The original idea was simple: government agencies were to buy up decaying central-city areas, demolish the buildings, and sell the land to private developers, who would build apartments for people with low and moderate incomes. But the developers were not required to build inexpensive housing. Most built office buildings, factories, and luxury apartments, which bring in higher profits. The poor were forced to move from substandard homes in one area to substandard homes in another area. This caused many black leaders to say that urban renewal was just another term for "Negro removal."

The federal government also tried a smorgasbord of programs including building its own low-income housing and guaranteeing mortgages so that low-income people could afford to buy a home. One of the most popular programs provided subsidized loans for developers to build or substantially rehabilitate rental units for qualified low-income tenants. The developer then rents the apartment to low-income families below the going rate, and the government makes up the difference with a cash payment. Many such agreements allowed the developer to pay off the loan after 20 years and then sell the building or divert it to some other use. According to a report from the National Housing Preservation Task Force, the United States will lose as many as 1.5 million units of such low-income housing by 1995.[48]

In the 1980s the federal government began moving away from such specific programs to deal with housing problems and instead came to rely on general "block grants" and "revenue sharing," to be spent as the community sees fit. The idea that local leaders know more about the needs of their own community makes a great deal of sense, but such programs ignore the political reality that poor people have little influence over the decisions of their local government. According to research by Kenneth K. Wong and Paul E. Peterson, the block-grant program has resulted in a smaller—not a larger—proportion of federal money actually going to help the poor.[49]

The history of government programs to improve housing in the United States has been one of misplaced priorities. Most federal assistance has gone to the wealthy and

DEBATE

Should We Limit Suburban Growth?

YES Greedy developers have ruined one scenic area after another, replacing trees and grass with asphalt and tract houses. The destruction of animal habitat has already led to the extinction of numerous species, and more are soon to follow. The ever-growing number of automobiles required by the suburban explosion is choking our skies with smog, burning up our reserves of petroleum, and maiming or killing hundreds of thousands of people in traffic accidents every year. If we don't change our course, we will soon face a crisis that will threaten the very survival of our society.

Those who spread this suburban blight claim that any new restrictions would be a violation of their civil rights, but all that has to be done is shift the costs of suburban developments from the public to the entrepreneurs who get rich from them. Runaway suburban growth would no longer be a problem if developers were forced to pay all the costs of the roads, schools, hospitals, police stations, and other facilities needed to serve these new communities, and were required to pay for pollution reduction systems to offset the smog created by the additional automobile traffic.

Developers always claim that anything that cuts their income will cause an economic disaster. But new homes will still be needed to accommodate a growing population; they will simply be built in existing urban areas where developers have a harder time making such exorbitant profits. Despite what the real estate investors say, increasing the density of existing urban areas is clearly the best way to meet our housing needs because it costs less, saves transportation and energy costs, and protects our fragile environment. If we stop the subsidies for the developers and make them pay for the

NO The growth of the suburbs was not the result of some plot between the developers and the politicians. The suburbs have grown because people want to live there. Numerous public opinion polls have shown that people who live in the suburbs are far happier with their communities than those who live in big cities. Proposals to restrict suburban growth violate civil liberties because they trap people in crowded cities and prevent them from living where they choose.

But aside from that, the half-baked plans to cut off suburban growth would have a devastating economic impact. For one thing, such drastic restrictions would probably cost hundreds of thousands of well-paying jobs in the construction industry and produce a chain reaction with devastating economic consequences. Retail stores and service workers who depend on customers who work in the construction industry would go broke, and local governments would be forced to increase taxes to make up for the decline in their revenues. As usual, the effects of this antigrowth policy would hit average workers far more severely than the wealthy and powerful. As the supply of new suburban housing ran out, prices in the suburbs would go through the ceiling, and eventually no one but the wealthy would be able to afford the private homes that are so much a part of the American dream. Supporters of such limits on growth suffer from a "drawbridge" mentality: they move to pleasant suburbs and want to pull up the drawbridge so that no one else can follow them.

There is no denying that some suburbs have serious problems with traffic congestion and air pollution. But the best solution to such difficulties is not some radical damage they do, the problem of suburban sprawl will take care of itself.

program to strangle suburban growth but a concerted effort to build more mass transit, less polluting cars, and more superhighways.

---

the middle class in the form of low-interest home loans and tax exemptions for home mortgage payments, while programs to help the poor have consistently been short-changed. To deal with the growing need for low-income housing, these priorities must be reversed. For example, if some or all of the tax exemption for home mortgages were repealed, billions of dollars would be freed to provide housing for the poor.

The proposals for reducing poverty discussed in Chapter 6 would obviously go a long way toward improving poor inner-city communities as well. Another idea, popular among conservatives, is to make such communities into **enterprise zones** that offer special tax breaks and other incentives to encourage businesses to locate there. Although several states have already created such enterprise zones, their effectiveness has yet to be determined. Critics charge that they simply move businesses from one part of the city to another and do little to cure the underlying economic problems. But a real test of this approach will probably require exemptions from federal as well as state taxes in order to provide large enough rewards to get a significant number of businesses to move into run-down inner-city neighborhoods.

Controlling Urban Growth   The need for more low-income housing has been recognized for generations, but the helter-skelter growth of our cities has created other serious problems that have only recently won public attention. The destruction of the natural environment, endless urban sprawl, traffic congestion, air pollution, and a feeling that our overall quality of life is declining have led us to question the old assumption that more growth means more prosperity and a better society. An increasing number of people are calling for tighter government controls to regulate growth and ensure that we protect the environment, expand public transportation, and conserve our natural resources. The logical approach is to redirect urban development away from the sprawling automobile-based suburbs and increase the population density of existing cities and towns. This high-density strategy has many advantages over the current policies that allow the proliferation of new suburban housing tracts. Not only does it protect virgin land from the developers' bulldozers, but higher-density housing is less expensive to build, more energy-efficient, and much more compatible with effective public transportation. Another important way to save energy and alleviate transportation headaches is to zone cities and suburbs so that residential areas are near the offices and factories where most people work.

The primary obstacle to the implementation of such proposals is economic. Developers stand to make far more money building whole new housing tracts on empty land than they would remodeling existing buildings, tearing down and replacing dilapidated structures, and building on small vacant lots in existing urban areas. Pitched battles between developers and local homeowners who want to restrict growth have already broken out in small towns and suburbs across the United States. But money buys influence, and studies show that developers usually win in the end.[50] A successful effort to redirect urban growth will therefore probably require federal assistance. One approach, for example, would be to provide tax breaks for higher-density structures, near existing urban services, that were balanced by increased taxes on low-density suburban developments.

Improving Third World Cities   As serious as they are, the plight of the cities in the industrialized nations looks almost trivial when compared with the urban problems of the Third World. It is easy to make a list of the steps that must be taken to improve the cities of the Third World: millions of new dwellings must be constructed, transportation must be improved, vast networks of sewage and water lines must be built, makeshift buildings and shacks need to be improved or replaced, and, of course, jobs must be created for an exploding population. It is far more difficult to list realistic ways to achieve these goals. But in one way or another they all depend on improving the economic foundation of Third World nations. (See Chapter 14 for a discussion of the different proposals for promoting economic development in the poor countries.)

Another obvious response is to slow down the unprecedented speed of Third World urbanization to allow time for the needed improvements to be made. Some experts propose strict government controls that directly limit the size of the cities. Planners in the People's Republic of China, for example, set a quota for the number of people allowed to move to the cities, and no other immigration is permitted. But most urban experts recommend a more positive approach that discourages migration to the cities by making rural areas more attractive. Effective programs to bring electricity, running water, modern sanitation, and health care facilities to the rural villages of the Third World could help alleviate some of the pressure on the cities as well. Another essential requirement is for economic development programs that create jobs in rural areas so that fewer villagers will have to move to the cities to search for work.

But even if all these measures were put into effect, they are unlikely to be successful without another critical step—bringing the population explosion under control. Lowering birthrates will obviously work to slow down both urban and rural growth. And equally important, it will allow impoverished countries to get off the treadmill that requires their economy to grow 2 or 3 percent a year just to stay even with population growth. (See Chapter 16 for a discussion of population control programs.)

SOCIOLOGICAL PERSPECTIVES ON URBANIZATION

The Functionalist Perspective   Most functionalists believe that the rapid urbanization of North America has disrupted family life as well as economic, educational, political, and religious institutions. The fact that bonds of affection have weakened and people have become more isolated is taken to be a symptom of more general social disorganization. When masses of people left rural villages to settle in cities, the villages became disorganized and unable to meet the needs of those who remained. Likewise, the cities were not prepared to assimilate the migrants and to provide them with a sense of mutual identity that would encourage loyalty and contentment. The old cultural patterns that were functional for village living were abandoned, but new integrating patterns did not arise. As a consequence, rates of crime, suicide, and mental illness grew, as did other symptoms of social disorganization. But before a new balance could be established, another shift in population—the flight to the suburbs—threw the social system back into chaos.

Functionalists see similar problems developing in the Third World, even though the process of urbanization has taken a somewhat different course than in the industrialized nations. In Western countries, industrialization and urbanization developed at the same time, but in the Third World, the cities started growing before there had been much industrialization. Some experts have therefore concluded that the Third World is "overurbanized" because the population of the cities has grown too large for the economic system to support. The difficulty with such claims is that the rural population of the Third World is also growing at a rapid pace. Generally, there is even less economic opportunity in the countryside than there is in the cities. Thus, the urban disorganization must be seen in the context of the economic disorganization that affects all aspects of life in Third World nations.

Functionalists argue that we must slow the pace of social change and allow metropolitan areas to adjust to these new conditions. Of particular importance is the need to reduce the rapid rate of urbanization in the Third World before the cities collapse under their crushing burdens. This goal can be achieved either by placing restrictions on immigration to the cities or by launching large-scale development programs that create new economic opportunities in rural areas. For the developed countries, functionalists tend to favor centralization of metropolitan government rather than decentralization, believing that centralized administration might get metropolitan communities running smoothly again. Indeed, it is possible that such reorganization could bring order to highly disorganized areas such as urban and rural slums. In a properly functioning metropolitan system, the people in each area would develop a new sense of community, identifying with one another and with the larger metropolitan community.

The Conflict Perspective   From the conflict perspective, the problems of urbanization are seen as the result of struggles between competing interest groups. When rural landowners were a dominant political force in North America, they did all they could to maintain their power, using it to obtain special economic benefits. For example, in the 1930s they persuaded the federal government to build farm-to-market roads, provide electricity for farms, and pay farmers more than the free-market price for their crops. But urbanization resulted in a shift of power to the cities, where industrialists took advantage of cheap labor provided by those who could no longer make a living on the farm. Because these powerful groups placed profits ahead of social welfare, our rural communities began to deteriorate. These small towns were exploited and then abandoned, the way people abandon worn-out cars.

As wealthy and influential people moved from the cities to the suburbs, another shift in power took place. The cities were filled with ever-increasing numbers of the poor, the weak, and the powerless. Meanwhile, well-to-do suburbanites began to dominate the political scene, using their power to gain advantages for themselves.

The federal government responded by favoring suburbs with freeways and express-ways, low-interest loans for single-family houses, and other benefits that diverted funds away from projects to help the inner-city residents who were left behind.

The struggle for power takes a different form in the Third World, but its effects are just as profound. Conflict theorists point out that the ruling class in most Third World nations (especially in those countries with large investments by foreigners) are much more Western and more urban in their outlook than the masses of the poor. As a result, they tend to support programs that will help generate the money they need to buy foreign luxury goods and maintain a Western standard of living. Peasants are often driven from their land to make room for large corporate farms, whose products are then sold on the world market. Government tax policies frequently place a heavy burden on rural villagers in order to pay for grandiose industrialization pro-grams and the prices paid to peasants for their crops are often kept artificially low in order to prevent political unrest among the urban masses. The few well-paying jobs that are created by the new industries spur unrealistic dreams of urban affluence among poor villagers. The effect of all this has been a staggering wave of immigration to the cities that Third World nations have found impossible to handle.

Conflict theorists are convinced that the solution to urban problems lies in political organization and action. People in city slums and poor rural areas must band together and demand fairer treatment. Such a movement should not be directed at isolated problems such as poor housing or crime but rather should attack inequality in every social sphere. This kind of movement is particularly important in Third World nations, where conflict theorists often see the overthrow of the old ruling elites and the expulsion of the foreign multinationals that support them as the only hope for real improvement.

Social Psychological Perspectives Centuries ago Thomas Jefferson warned that city life could corrupt the virtue and undermine the political liberty of the American people. As already noted, the original urban sociologists expressed similar attitudes around the turn of this century. To Simmel and Wirth, the impersonality and the hectic pace of urban life were clearly harmful to most city dwellers. But the next generation of sociologists, who were more likely to have been raised in the urban areas themselves, often rejected such conclusions as the mere product of small-town bias.

Yet despite the claims made in defense of urban life, it is hard to avoid the con-clusion that small-town living, with its sense of community and identity, has some important psychological advantages over the cold impersonality of the city. There-fore, social psychologists often propose programs to bring some of the benefits of the small town back into urban life. For example, they often recommend the decen-tralization of the city into smaller units, each with its own government and commer-cial and recreational centers, so that genuine neighborhoods can develop. These so-cial psychologists also note that some urban areas have already produced such neighborhoods. Some ethnic neighborhoods in North American cities, for instance, are as tightly knit as any rural village, and some suburbs are characterized by a strong sense of neighborliness and mutual identification. Nonetheless, those are the excep-tions and not the rule. The breakdown of community is probably worst in the inner-city slums, which also have the highest rates of alcoholism, mental disorder, and drug addiction. Social psychologists therefore advocate special programs aimed specifically at those neighborhoods that seek to bring people together to attack their common problems.

SUMMARY

The shift from rural to urban living has profoundly altered the lives of millions of people. Traditionally, most families lived on farms in rural areas, but industrialization spurred the rapid growth of cities. In the past few decades there has been a new shift of population, this time toward the suburbs.

Pioneering sociologists such as Georg Simmel and Louis Wirth argued that city life creates certain characteristics in urban residents, including impersonal social relationships, a blasé attitude toward life, a materialistic outlook, and a feeling of indifference toward others. More recently, Herbert Gans argued that this picture exaggerates the negative aspects of city life and is true only for some types of city dwellers.

The availability of government-backed loans, a growing system of highways, and the prosperity following World War II made it possible for many people to move to the suburbs. Although the stereotype of suburbia pictures miles of well-kept houses populated by young, middle-class, white professionals on the way up, there is actually a great deal of diversity in the suburbs. An increasing number of suburbs are business and industrial centers. As suburbs have aged, they have come to resemble the cities near them. They are no longer islands in a sea of urban problems, and the suburban way of life is coming to resemble the urban way of life.

Rural towns and villages have been deeply affected by urbanization and the decline in their population. With the growth of mass transportation and communication, rural life itself has become increasingly "urban." Yet life on a farm or in a small town retains its distinctive characteristics, including closer personal relationships, a sense of identity and belonging, a homogeneous culture, and intolerance of deviant behavior.

The process of urbanization has contributed to a crisis on the farm that is making it increasingly difficult for middle-sized family farmers to survive. The economic and political decline of many big cities in North America has left them with growing inner-city slums that have high rates of poverty and crime. The growth of the suburbs has left us with an inefficient and environmentally destructive system of transportation, and has created a financial predicament for many local governments. The lack of low-cost housing is a growing national problem that is aggravated by segregation and housing discrimination against blacks and other minorities. But as bad as all these problems are, conditions are far worse in the poverty-stricken and rapidly expanding cities of the Third World.

There are many proposals for dealing with the problems created by urbanization. Some urban planners recommend that local governments be reorganized into larger and more efficient units. So far, urban renewal programs have not been successful in producing adequate housing for the poor, and much greater efforts are needed to create low-cost housing and improve economic conditions in our inner cities. Environmentalists recommend tighter controls on suburban growth and policies that encourage greater urban density rather than suburban sprawl. Perhaps most important, programs of economic development and population control are needed to help Third World cities with their heavy burdens.

According to functionalists, rapid urbanization has disrupted our basic social institutions: economics, education, family, government, and religion. The rates of crime, suicide, and mental illness have grown as the disorganization brought about by rapid urbanization has increased. Conflict theorists see the problems of urbanization as resulting from the competition between interest groups. Each group exercises power for its own benefit and not for the general welfare. Social psychologists are most concerned with the effects of urbanization on the psychological well-being of the millions of city dwellers. They recommend decentralizing metropolitan areas into small units so that people will have the opportunity to live in genuine communities and neighborhoods.

KEY TERMS

gentrification   The renovation of older low-cost neighborhoods to accommodate more wealthy residents.

infrastructure   The underlying physical framework of society—roads, sewers, buildings, and the like.

megalopolis   An area in which several large cities are fused together.

suburb   The part of an urban area that lies outside the central city.

urbanization   The movement of people from rural areas to cities.

urban renewal   A program intended to upgrade decaying city neighborhoods.

FURTHER READINGS

William Julius Wilson, "Studying Inner-City Social Dislocations: The Challenge of Public Agenda Research," *American Sociological Review* 56 (Feb. 1991): 1–14. An insightful look at the causes of inner-city problems.

John Palen, *The Urban World*, 3rd ed. (New York: McGraw-Hill, 1987). A good general text on urban sociology.

John R. Logan and Harvey L. Molotch, *Urban Fortunes: The Political Economy of Place* (Berkeley: University of California Press, 1987). An analysis of the growth of cities and suburbs from a conflict perspective.

William H. Whyte, *City: Rediscovering the Center* (New York: Doubleday, 1988). One of the best-known urban sociologists explores city life and some ways to improve it.

Louis Wirth, "Urbanism as a Way of Life," *American Journal of Sociology* 44 (1938): 1–14. Perhaps the single most influential essay on the nature of urban life.

chapter 16

Population

- What is the cause of the population explosion?
- How does runaway population growth affect our way of life?
- Can food production keep up with population growth?
- How can population growth be controlled?

The world's population is exploding. The number of men, women, and children is now over 5 billion—twice as many people as there were only 40 years ago. If the current rate of growth continues, the world's population will double again in the next 40 years.[1] Many scientists doubt that the earth can support such growth. They note that half of the world's people already have an inadequate diet and that 14 to 18 million people starve to death every year.[2] But these current problems seem minor compared with the disaster that many see on the horizon.

The dangers of runaway population growth can be viewed in historical perspective by looking at the world population in units of 1 billion people. It took all of human history until 1800 for the world's population to reach 1 billion. But the next unit of 1 billion was added in only 130 years (1800–1930), the unit after that in 30 years (1930–1960), and the next in 15 years (1960–1975). The last billion people were added in only 12 years (1975–1987).[3] (See Figure 16.1.)

If this trend continues, the world will soon be adding a billion people a year, and eventually every month. Obviously, the earth will not be able to sustain such an enormous population. And indeed, United Nations statisticians now expect the world's population to stabilize sometime in the next two centuries, but estimates vary widely as to when that will be and at what population. The earliest possible date would be around 2075, at which time there would be about 10.2 billion people in the world. But the experts believe that zero population growth is more likely to be achieved sometime in the twenty-second century at a population of over 11.5 billion people.[4] The crucial task facing the human race is to ensure that the population explosion is curbed by a rational program of population control and not by massive famines or devastating wars.

The long-range forecasts are ominous, but the population crisis is not a thing of the future. It is here now. Next year the world must house, clothe, and feed about 90 million more people. To make matters worse, the 250,000 who will be added in the next 24 hours will not be evenly distributed throughout the world.[5] Most will be

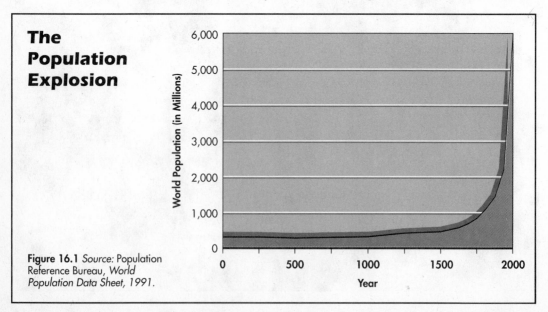

The Population Explosion

Figure 16.1 *Source:* Population Reference Bureau, *World Population Data Sheet, 1991.*

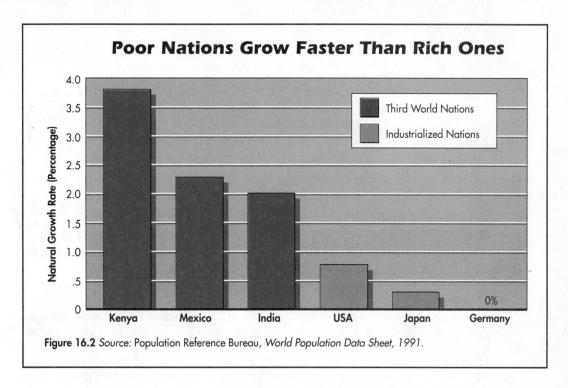

Figure 16.2 *Source:* Population Reference Bureau, *World Population Data Sheet, 1991.*

born in the underdeveloped nations of Africa, Latin America, and Asia—countries that are too poor to provide for the populations they already have (see Figure 16.2).

Although these nations may seem alike to Western eyes, there are important differences in their population problems. The most immediate crisis is in the overcrowded nations of Asia (including Bangladesh, India, Pakistan, Indonesia, and China), which already contain over half the world's people. The current growth rate in Asia is 1.8 percent per year, much higher than the rates of the industrialized nations of Europe (0.2 percent) or North America (0.8 percent) but generally lower than those of poor nations in other parts of the world. Although current population densities are lower in Africa and Latin America than in Asia, their growth rates are higher: 3.0 percent in Africa and 2.1 percent in Latin America.[6] But these continent-wide generalizations cover up many important differences between nations. The Philippines, for example, has a growth rate of 2.6 percent a year, which is much higher than the average in Asia as a whole. At that rate, its population of 62 million will double in only 27 years. In 60 years, if its growth rate does not go down, the Philippines will have a population as large as the United States today, but with less than one-thirtieth of the land area.[7]

WHY THE EXPLOSIVE GROWTH?

If the population explosion is to be brought under control, it must be understood. And that task falls largely to the scientific discipline known as **demography**, which studies the causes and effects of the changes in human population. Demographers must be mathematicians as well, for they study such things as the rates of births and deaths, the flow of migration, and the age and sex distribution of a population.

Growth Rates A nation's rate of population growth is obviously affected by the number of people who move into or out of the country. But the world's population is not affected by immigration and emigration: it is determined by birthrates and death rates alone. The **birthrate** is the number of babies born in a year divided by the total population. The **death rate** is the number of people who die divided by the total population. For convenience, the numbers refer to 1,000 members of the population rather than to the total. For example, in 1989 the population of the United States totaled 247 million. In that year 3,977,000 births and 3,155,000 deaths occurred, for a birthrate of 16 per 1,000 and a death rate of 8.7 per 1,000. The **growth rate** is determined by subtracting the death rate from the birthrate and then adjusting the figures to account for migration. Thus, for every 1,000 Americans in 1989, there were 7.3 more births than deaths, and immigration added another 2.7 people, making the total growth rate 1.0 percent.[8]

However, these are only crude rates. They are called "crude" by demographers because they do not take the sex and age composition of the population into account. National populations usually consist roughly of half men and half women, but age composition varies from time to time. Therefore, the age composition of a population

On the average, women in industrialized nations have only about half as many children as those in Third World nations.

must be examined to determine whether its growth rate is unusually high or low. The percentage of the population below the age of 15 is much higher in poor countries (36 percent) than in industrialized ones (21 percent). Because the girls in this age group are normally too young to have children, the crude birthrate actually underestimates the differences in fertility between women in the rich and poor countries. To measure this more accurately, demographers calculate the **total fertility rate**, which is an estimate of the number of children a woman is likely to have in her lifetime. The average woman in an industrialized country is now projected to have about 1.9 children, whereas a woman in a poor country can be expected to have 3.9 children. The replacement rate—the number of children each woman must have to keep the population from growing or shrinking—is between 2.1 and 2.5 children, depending on the death rate. Therefore, if the total fertility rate does not change, the population in the industrialized countries could be expected to decline slowly, while the population of the poor countries continues its rapid growth.[9] However, migration from the poor countries is likely to keep the population of most industrialized nations from actually shrinking.

Many people believe that increasing birthrates are the cause of the population explosion, but, overall, birthrates have in fact declined. The real cause is the decrease in death rates resulting from the rise in the average life span. Throughout most of human history, the average life expectancy seldom exceeded 30 years. Under such conditions, a woman must have 4 children for 2 to survive to adulthood and have children of their own. As we have seen, this is just about how many children Third World women are having today,[10] but the life expectancy in these countries is now about 60 years, and the result is an exploding population.

The origins of the population crisis, thus, are to be found in the remarkable decline in death rates that began in Western Europe in the second half of the eighteenth century and later spread throughout most of the world. In the early years of the population explosion, the European nations led the world in population growth. However, birthrates began decreasing in most of the industrialized nations in the latter part of the nineteenth century, thus reducing their rates of population growth. In the poor agricultural nations birthrates did not begin to decrease until much more recently, and they have not gone down nearly as rapidly as their death rates. As a result, the patterns of world population growth have been reversed, and the poor nations are now growing much faster than the rich ones. In 1991 the growth rate in Third World nations was more than four times higher than in the industrialized nations.[11]

The Demographic Transition Explaining these trends in world population has been one of the central tasks of modern demography. The most popular explanation is known as the theory of **demographic transition**. According to this theory, populations go through three stages. In the first stage, characteristic of all traditional societies, both birth and death rates are high and population growth is moderate. In the second stage, the process of industrialization begins, and technological improvements bring a sharp decline in death rates. However, birthrates decline more slowly, and there is a population explosion. Finally, in the last stage birthrates drop down far enough to balance death rates, and population stabilizes.

Why does industrialization bring down death rates? For one thing, industrial technology increases the food supply, thereby reducing the number of deaths from starvation. Industrialization also prolongs life by giving people pure water and better diets, clothing, housing, and sanitation. Insecticides prevent epidemics spread by insects and thus increase life spans even more. As was noted in Chapter 8, improvements in medical technology also contributed to declining death rates. Vaccinations have brought numerous contagious diseases under control, and the discovery of antibiotics produced a cure for such killers as syphilis and pneumonia.

Industrialization eventually brings down birthrates because it produces economic changes that affect family size. Children in agricultural societies make an important contribution to farm labor and usually support their parents when they grow old. In contrast, children in industrial societies are economic liabilities rather than assets. They make little economic contribution to the family, and they consume considerably more resources than their counterparts in agricultural societies. Changes in traditional gender roles are another factor in the lowering of birthrates. Bearing and rearing children is no longer a woman's primary occupation.

The invention of more efficient methods of birth control, such as the contraceptive pill and the IUD (intrauterine device) and improvements in abortion and sterilization techniques have also led to declining birthrates. Modern technology has made it easier for couples to have the number of children they want and no more, but we should not overestimate its impact. As Charles F. Westoff has pointed out, some of the lowest birthrates in many European countries occurred during the Great Depression of the 1930s, before the invention of the pill and the IUD, and before the legalization of abortion.[12] Thus, it appears that social change was a more important factor in bringing down birthrates than the mere availability of contraceptive technology.

The theory of demographic transition has clear implications for the future of world population. According to the theory, the Third World nations with rapidly growing populations are in the second phase of the demographic transition. Once these countries become industrialized, their birthrates will come down and their population problems will be over. But critics point out that the demographic transition is really a theory explaining the changes in population during the industrialization of the Western countries, and that the situation in the Third World is quite different than the theory implies. There is little doubt that industrialization was the direct cause of the decrease in the birthrates and death rates in the Western nations (and in Japan as well). But the decline of the death rates in the Third World have not been caused by industrialization but by the importation of foreign technology and know-how. Since the population explosion in the Third World started before the process of industrialization, it will probably take a much longer period of time before industrialization progresses far enough to bring the birth and death rates back into balance naturally (if indeed that ever happens).[13]

THE IMPACT OF POPULATION GROWTH

As we have seen, environmental limitations make it impossible for the human population to keep growing at its present pace forever. The question is not *whether* the growth rate should decrease but, rather, *how* it will decrease. Only two remedies are possible: decreasing births or increasing deaths.

One of the first people to recognize the dangers of unrestricted population growth was an English minister, Thomas Malthus. His famous book, *Essay on the Principle of Population*, raised a storm of controversy when it was published in 1798.[14] Malthus argued that the human population naturally increases much more rapidly than its food supply. Food supplies increase arithmetically (1, 2, 3, 4, 5, etc.), but uncontrolled populations increase geometrically (1, 2, 4, 8, 16, etc.). The doubling effect occurs because two parents can produce four children; each of the four children can marry and produce four more children; and so on. Eventually, Malthus said, a population that keeps doubling in this way is doomed to outrun its food supply. He believed that only death-dealing disasters—famine, pestilence, and war—kept the human population within its environmental limits.

This gloomy theory was not popular in Malthus's time, when most Europeans believed in the inevitability of progress and the bright future of the human race. And it does seem that Malthus underestimated the world's capacity to produce food for its people. But most of the recent improvements in farming techniques require more energy than before. And many contemporary demographers fear that as the world's supply of fossil fuel is used up, Malthus will be proven right after all.

The Third World Runaway population growth contributes to a host of Third World problems, from mass poverty to the environmental crisis. But none of these is more overwhelming than the lack of enough food. Of course, famines were a common event long before the population explosion. But modern technology has enabled the industrialized nations with slow growth rates to banish this ancient scourge, while millions still starve in the overpopulated nations of the Third World.

Since the end of World War II, food production has, nonetheless, more than kept pace with population growth. Between 1950 and 1986, world food production increased almost 30 percent per person, and as a result some significant improvements were possible in the diet of the world's people.[15] Although per capita food consumption went up in the Third World, most of the benefits went to the people of the industrialized nations, who were already well fed. Moreover, the increases that did occur in the Third World have not been evenly distributed. In many countries the poor continue to starve, while the rich grow fat. And although several Asian nations have been successful in improving their agricultural production, some other parts of the world have not. Since 1980 per capita food production has been decreasing 0.8 percent a year in Africa and 0.2 percent a year in the Middle East.[16] There have been nine major famines in the Third World since 1960, which have cost well over 12 million lives.[17]

Even though most people are able to get enough food to survive, from 10 to 20 percent of the world's people suffer from chronic hunger or malnutrition.[18] A poor diet during the childhood years delays physical maturity, produces dwarfism, impairs brain development, and reduces intelligence, even if the children affected receive an adequate diet later. The undernourished adult is apathetic, listless, and unable to work as long or as hard as the well-fed adult. Diseases caused directly by dietary deficiency, such as beriberi, rickets, and marasmus, are common in poor nations. Malnutrition also lowers resistance to disease, so the undernourished are likely to have a number of other health problems. The danger of epidemics is always high in overpopulated

Rapid population growth contributes to hunger and overcrowding in the Third World.

and underfed areas.[19] Moreover, research shows that the damage of malnutrition is passed on from one generation to the next. The babies born to malnourished mothers are weaker and in poorer health than the babies of well-fed mothers.[20]

Aside from the lack of proper nutrition, explosive population growth creates a host of other problems for Third World nations. One of the most difficult is the pressure it places on traditional village life style. Because tiny plots of family land can support only so many people, many young men and women are forced to migrate to the cities. The flood of unskilled and uneducated immigrants from the countryside is creating serious urban problems throughout the Third World. A substantial percentage of people in the major cities of the Third World already live in slums and in shantytowns built by squatters on land they do not own. These homes often lack running water, sewers, and electricity, and the rapid urbanization projected for the next decade can only make matters worse.

The people in this photograph live in the streets. Like millions of other people in the Third World, they have no permanent home, not even a crowded shack.

Poverty is another problem intensified by the population explosion. Because the population of the poor nations is growing more than twice as fast as the population of the rich ones, the percentage of the world's people who live in poverty is increasing every year. Moreover, rapid population growth in the Third World makes it far more difficult to improve the living conditions of the average person. More people inevitably means more congestion, more crowding, and more damage to the environment. At the present rate of population growth, the economies of most Third World nations must grow more than 2 percent a year just to keep their standard of living from falling. Egypt provides a good example of the way population growth can negate economic development. More than three decades ago, the Egyptian government, hoping to increase usable farmland and reduce poverty, began construction of a giant dam on the Nile River near the city of Aswan. The completed dam boosted Egypt's arable land by over 12 percent, but by the time it was finished, Egypt's population had risen more than 70 percent.[21] The dam's economic benefits were swallowed up by population growth before the project was ever completed.

The age composition of their populations places an additional burden on most Third World nations. In a rapidly expanding population there are so many children that working-age adults make up a bare majority of the total population. For example, Africa is growing much faster than North America, and as a result only 52 percent of all Africans are in their most productive years (15 to 64), compared with 66 percent of all North Americans.[22] And because a smaller percentage of working-age adults actually have jobs in Africa, every 100 workers must support about 92 dependents, whereas 100 workers in the industrialized countries support only 50 people. Yet these problems are just the beginning. As today's children grow up, they must find jobs, and about 45 percent of the workers in Third World countries are already unemployed or underemployed.[23] According to the projections from the U.S. Bureau of the Census, the number of working-age people in the world will increase by 500 million in the next decade.[24]

The Industrialized Nations   Population growth creates similar problems for agricultural and industrialized nations. The difference is in scale. The growth rates of industrialized countries are lower, but at the current pace their population will still double every 137 years.[25] If the growth rate of the United States remains unchanged for the next 200 years, its population will be almost 1.5 billion people. Most demographers expect these growth rates to decrease, but until zero population growth is achieved, population growth will continue to have profound effects on the quality of life in industrialized countries.

Although the industrialized nations clearly have enough money to provide food, shelter, and clothing for an expanding population, many are concerned that they will not actually do so. One of the main stumbling blocks is that birthrates are highest among the poorest people, who are least able to support their children. The other principal source of population growth—immigration from the underdeveloped countries—also tends to swell the ranks of the poor. The current pattern of population growth in the industrial nations therefore aggravates the problem of poverty and increases the level of social inequality. The kinds of antipoverty programs discussed in Chapter 6 could go a long way toward resolving these conditions, but it remains to be seen if the political will can be found to carry out such projects.

Another important issue concerns the serious shortages of energy and essential raw materials expected in the near future. This question will be discussed in Chapter 17. Here we merely note that the growing population of industrialized nations is a major contributor to the problem. One American baby will use more resources in its lifetime than 30 Asian babies. Thus, even the relatively slow population growth of the industrialized nations places great burdens on the environment and on available natural resources. If the population of the industrialized nations continues to grow and demand for consumer goods is not curtailed, there may be no energy or raw materials left for the poor nations when they try to industrialize.

The effects of population growth on the overall quality of life in the industrialized nations are more difficult to measure. No dollar value can be placed on the loss of a beautiful lake or forest. Yet the cost of destroying nature so that more humans may live in comfort is certainly very high, and it is a cost that must be borne by all the generations to come. When the territories of birds, mammals, and reptiles are invaded and they become extinct, we are all poorer. Destruction of this kind is nothing new, but population growth has greatly accelerated the process. Scientists estimate that 500,000 to 1 million species will soon face extinction at the hands of the ever-growing numbers of humans on this planet.[26] As the population of the industrialized nations increases, there are other effects as well. The cities grow larger, the traffic gets worse, and the amount of noise, air pollution, and toxic waste inevitably increases.

RESPONDING TO POPULATION PROBLEMS

Some observers argue that there is no population crisis at all and that the dire warnings about the future are the cries of alarmists and doomsayers. But an increasing number of demographers, politicians, and informed citizens have come to agree that the world indeed faces a grave population emergency. And this awareness is itself a response to the problem. It is the first step that must be taken toward an effective solution. The next two steps before us are clear: work to feed the hungry people already on the planet, and take stronger action to reduce population growth.

Feeding the Hungry   Scientists in laboratories around the world are working hard to invent new methods for growing more food. The greatest single advance in recent decades was the creation of new strains of wheat and rice that yield much more food per acre. A "green revolution" occurred in places where these "miracle" seeds were planted. This new technique has been one of the main reasons that world food production has kept ahead of population growth in the last 30 years.[27] But the green revolution is not a cure-all for the problem of world hunger. The new strains of wheat and rice require more fertilizer, insecticides, and irrigation if they are to produce higher yields, and many poor farmers simply cannot afford such things. Moreover, all three depend on petroleum, which was in short supply several times in the last two decades. Research also shows that increasing inputs of water, fertilizer, and pesticides produce diminishing returns: in the first few years the new crops produce dramatically improved yields, but as time goes on, the productivity levels off. Finally, the green revolution has encouraged the trend toward larger farms and that has often had devastating effects on peasants who have been forced off their traditional lands.[28]

The American way of improving agricultural production relies heavily on mechanization, but this approach is not appropriate for most poor countries with severe population problems. Few of the world's farmers can afford even the least expensive tractors. When the price of such machines is subsidized by the government or some other agency, they still cannot be operated economically on the small plots of land owned by most peasant farmers. It is often suggested that small farms be consolidated so they can be worked with such labor-saving equipment. Even if a program of this sort were politically feasible, it would create a staggering unemployment problem. It is hard to imagine anything that makes less sense for Third World countries with runaway population growth than spending their precious reserves on labor-saving machinery. Furthermore, a greater dependance on sophisticated mechanized equipment will only exhaust the planet's supply of petroleum that much faster, and make the poor nations that much more dependent on the rich ones.

The late English economist E. F. Schumacher advocated an ingenious compromise. He proposed that poor nations use **intermediate technology**: machines that are less sophisticated than the gas-guzzling marvels of the industrialized nations but more effective than the traditional reliance on human and animal power.[29] What the world needs, Schumacher said, is simple machines that can be manufactured in poor nations at low cost and are suitable for small-scale farming. Schumacher himself helped design a small gasoline-powered plowing machine that is more efficient than a horse or an ox but much less costly than a tractor.

Another way to get farmers to grow more food is to reorganize the agricultural economy. One of the most important steps is **land reform**: taking land away from rich landlords and redistributing it among the peasants who actually do the work. Land-reform programs in Mexico and Taiwan have shown that people work harder and produce more when they own their own land and receive the benefits of their own labor. A different version of this approach has also proven effective in the communist nations. Officials have found that agricultural production is far higher from plots of land in which the farmers are allowed to sell their own crops and keep the profits, than from land in collective farms that provide few incentives for farmers to increase production.[30] A serious problem in some poor nations, especially in Africa, is that their governments intentionally hold down the price of agricultural products, to keep down the cost of food for urban workers. The result is that farmers often lose money on their crops, and production decreases. A better approach is to encourage farm prices to rise and subsidize the food budgets of the urban poor from taxes on the local elite.

Some propose feeding the world's hungry by merely cultivating more land. But almost all the good land is already in use. The remainder would require large amounts of oil and other energy to produce even low yields. Some arid soil could be put into production with new irrigation projects, and perhaps new hydroelectric power would come as a bonus. However, the history of Egypt's Aswan Dam and other big development projects casts doubt on the notion that this approach can meet the growing demand for food. The proposal that tropical jungles be cleared for farming is even less realistic. Jungle land is not farmland. Brazil's attempts to farm the Amazon valley have shown that rain-forest land has few plant nutrients and that tropical rains quickly wash away artificial fertilizers.[31]

As land runs out, humanity must turn to the sea. Fish and other seafoods now contribute almost a quarter of all the animal protein consumed by humans.[32] But in recent years, the world's total catch of fish has been growing far more slowly than the human population.[33] The lakes and oceans can support only a limited number of fish, and some species are already near extinction. Nevertheless, experts believe that the total catch of fish could be expanded by concentrating on smaller and less appetizing species of fish, and through more careful management and control of the fishing industry. Several Asian countries, including China, South Korea, and Japan, raise fish specifically for human consumption, and "fish farming" is bound to increase as the human population grows. But future efforts to get more food from the sea will have to focus on plants as well as animals. Various forms of edible algae and seaweed are already being harvested in Asia, but if marine plants are to make a major contribution to the human food supply, they too will have to be farmed. Several experimental sea farms are now in operation, but it will be some time before this technology is economically feasible for large-scale use.

Finally, a different way to get more food for the hungry is to waste less. It has been estimated that people in the wealthy nations throw away one pound of food for every three that are finally eaten.[34] Poor nations also waste a great deal of food, but for different reasons: insects and rats eat up food in storage, and slow and inefficient methods of distribution allow more food to rot before it finds its way to the dinner tables of hungry people. Another way to increase food supplies without increasing food production is to get more people to eat a vegetarian diet. Eight to ten kilograms of grain must be fed to a cow to produce one kilogram of meat, and it is far more efficient, and often more healthful, simply to eat the grain and other vegetable products ourselves.[35]

Controlling Population Growth Gaining control over the world's explosive population growth is the most urgent task before the human race today. If we fail, we will surely have to face our ancient enemies—famine, pestilence, and war—on a new and unprecedented scale. At present the industrialized nations are much closer than their Third World neighbors to achieving population control. The population of the industrialized nations is growing at about 0.5 percent a year, which is less than one-quarter the rate for poor nations. The following discussion will therefore focus on the Third World. However, the proposals and programs designed for the poor nations can be modified to fit the industrialized nations as the need arises.

Some political leaders see a large population as a national asset and have used government programs to encourage population growth. As far back as the thirteenth century, a number of European nations established tax benefits for parents. Hitler's Germany enacted a variety of measures aimed at increasing its population, as have several communist countries. Romania's communist dictator Nicolae Ceausescu created a program designed to increase his country's population by one-third. He forbade abortion and birth control and created a so-called baby police to give monthly tests to female workers to guard against any illegal termination of pregnancy. In late 1990, shortly after Ceausescu's overthrow, there were 200,000 abandoned children in state care in Romania's orphanages.[36] Fortunately, such efforts are the exception, not the rule. The harsh realities of unchecked population growth are forcing one nation after another to adopt population control programs.

Many political leaders who are interested in controlling population focus their efforts on industrialization, believing that attitudes toward the family and reproduction will change as the economy develops. As we have already shown, industrialization does bring about a demographic transition—a change in basic birthrates and death rates that ultimately results in slower overall growth. Many leaders insist that the population problem will take care of itself if we wait for this "natural" process to occur in the agricultural nations. Such expectations are, however, ill founded. The fact that industrialization has occurred in a few poor countries hardly means that it will occur in all of them. But even if all the poor nations of the world were somehow to industrialize, the demographic transition could not possibly occur quickly enough to limit the world's population to a manageable size.

Industrialization is not, however, the only economic influence on population control. The key variable may be the maintenance of a minimum standard of living for the poor. As Jon Bennett put it: "High birth rates are primarily related to economic uncertainty. In nearly every country where malnutrition has been reduced and child death rates have decreased, birth rates have also dropped dramatically."[37]

Most population control programs try to encourage people to limit the size of their families voluntarily. The assumption is that the birthrate will decrease if couples have only the number of children they desire. To help families achieve that goal, information and birth control devices are usually given to the poor without charge. Such programs are called **family planning**, but the real objective is to cut the birthrate. Some countries support their family-planning programs with publicity stressing the desirability of small families and the dangers of overpopulation. In India, for example, the symbol of population control—a red triangle with the smiling faces of two parents and two children—can be seen in every village.

Such programs help reduce the number of unwanted children, but by themselves they have failed to achieve the kind of reduction in birthrates that the world needs to stabilize its population. Many Third World family-planning programs have been poorly organized and underfunded. There is a more basic problem, however: publicity campaigns and speeches simply cannot change deeply rooted attitudes favoring large families. The most successful family-planning programs have therefore been in countries like South Korea and Taiwan, which have also been undergoing rapid industrialization.[38]

The traditional attitude in most cultures is that more children means a stronger family. In the past, big families have always been essential to the prosperity of the

Voluntary family-planning programs are common all over the world. But such programs have little chance of success unless traditional attitudes about the value of a large family are changed.

peasants, and often to their very survival. The belief in the value of having many children is often reinforced by religious and political doctrines as well. For one reason or another, it is considered moral to "be fruitful and multiply." Buddhism and Hinduism are silent on the issue of birth control, although there is an implication that humans should not deliberately interfere with the eternal process of reincarnation. Islam is generally opposed to birth control, but there is a wide range of interpretations of religious doctrine on this question. Jews and Protestants today generally accept the practice of birth control, but their faiths were not always so favorable. Roman Catholicism is one of the world's religions that is most strongly opposed to birth control. In 1968, Pope Paul reaffirmed church doctrine by ruling that all forms of artificial contraception block the normal "transmission of life" in marriages and thereby violate the "creative intention of God." According to Catholic doctrine, only two methods of birth control are permitted: total abstinence from sexual relations or periodic abstinence during a woman's most fertile period (that is, the rhythm method). However, both methods have proven unreliable, since they demand a higher level of self-control than most people appear to possess.[39]

One of the most effective ways to stimulate new attitudes about the ideal family size is to promote changes in traditional gender roles. Women in Third World countries often live a very restricted life under the domination and control of their husband and other relatives. They have few roads to status or social rewards other than bearing and rearing a large family. One of the best ways to reduce this pressure is, as John R. Weeks put it, to change "the sex roles taught to boys and girls, giving equal treatment to the sexes in the educational and occupational spheres. If a woman's adulthood and femininity are expressed in other ways besides childbearing, then the pressures lessen to bear children as a means of forcing social recognition."[40] The power of women's labor can also provide a big boost to industrialization, thus making an indirect contribution to lower birthrates as well. Equal opportunities and equal status for women are revolutionary ideas in many Third World countries. But the success of that revolution would go a long way toward solving the problems of poverty and overpopulation.

Because of the weaknesses in family-planning programs, some nations are now using programs that provide specific incentives for parents to limit the size of their families: bonuses for couples with few children and penalties for those with many children. Some countries have even proposed mandatory restrictions, which require all families to limit the number of children they have (see the Debate in this chapter).

Of all the large Third World nations, the People's Republic of China has made the greatest progress in reducing its birthrate (see Figure 16.3). China's powerful and highly centralized government has urged its people to abstain from premarital sex, to delay marriage and childbearing, and to use birth control and abortion. China also has a strong incentive program designed to encourage each family to have no more than one child. Couples who agree to this limit are given a "single-child certificate," which entitles them to such benefits as priority in housing, better wages, a special pension, and preference in school admissions. Couples who have too many children are often fined and required to pay for all the maternity, medical, and educational costs their children may incur. As a result of this program, China's birthrate has shown

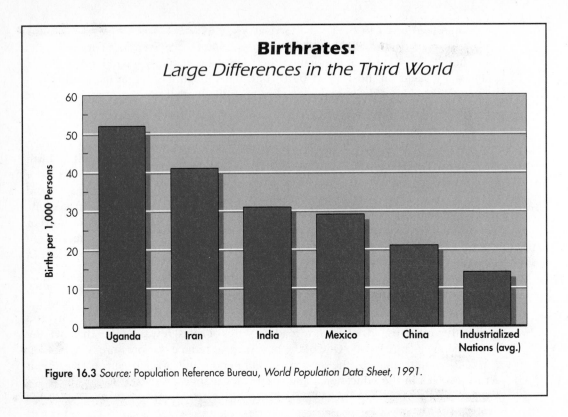

Birthrates:

Large Differences in the Third World

Figure 16.3 *Source:* Population Reference Bureau, *World Population Data Sheet, 1991.*

a significant decline. Although an increase in the number of women in their prime childbearing years (due to a "baby boom" in the 1960s) has kept up the total number of babies born each year, China's current growth rate is still only about 1.4 percent—an extremely low figure for a poor agricultural nation.[41] It is clear that China is now firmly committed to an all-out effort to stabilize the size of its population. Not only is that good news for the future of China, it is good news for the entire world, for one of every five people in the world lives in China.

These gains have not been made without considerable social cost, however. The government pressure for population control in China's highly centralized society has been so great that the one-child limitation has become virtually mandatory for some Chinese. This policy has placed a particularly great strain on rural villagers. Chinese peasants have traditionally put a high value on having sons, who live with the extended family throughout their lives. Daughters, on the other hand, are expected to move in with their husband's family and are therefore considered more of a burden than an asset. The result has been a startling increase in female infanticide as the new population limitation measures have been put into effect. The Chinese government does, however, recognize the problem and has in some cases relaxed its rigid rules for rural families whose first child is a girl.[42]

D E B A T E

Are Mandatory Limits on Family Size Needed to Control the Population Explosion?

Family-planning programs are now common around the world, and several nations also offer various incentives to encourage families to have fewer children. But some people feel such efforts do not go far enough, and they call on the governments of the poor, over-populated nations to set strict legal limits on the number of children a family is allowed to have.

YES The population explosion is the greatest problem facing humanity today. If forceful and effective action is not taken to reduce growth rates, it soon will be too late to head off international disaster. Near-starvation diets are already common in some countries, and unchecked population growth will certainly lead to a massive international famine, disrupting the political and economic balance of the entire planet. Battles among the hungry nations for control of scarce food reserves would be likely, and it is doubtful that the industrialized world could avoid the spreading conflict. Because some of the poorest nations already have nuclear weapons and others are developing the capacity to build them, it is conceivable that the population explosion could lead to a nuclear holocaust.

In the face of such dreadful prospects, it is clear that population growth must be controlled. Mandatory limits on family size are repugnant, but there may be no other choice. Most voluntary programs have failed and unless a new approach is found, strict limits may be the only solution to this menacing problem. Legal restrictions on family size would violate some of our traditional rights, but it is far better to give up a little freedom than to face the international disaster that otherwise seems certain.

NO The world's population problem is not as serious as the alarmists claim. Many overpopulated nations are already reducing their growth rates. The claim that population growth will result in international disaster is wild speculation without scientific support. It would be foolish to invoke measures as drastic as mandatory population controls because of such fears. The world's food supply has always kept up with population growth, and it will continue to do so.

Limits on the number of children that parents could legally conceive violate basic human freedoms. How could we send a person to prison for becoming a parent? Government has neither the right nor the wisdom to tell us how many children we may have. Trampling on individual rights may occasionally solve a problem, but democratic solutions are best in the long run.

If population problems became as serious as the doomsayers predict, parents would limit the size of their families voluntarily. Indeed, voluntary programs are already proving effective in a number of nations. Mandatory controls are therefore an unnecessary violation of our basic rights and should not be invoked.

The population-control program in the People's Republic of China has been more successful than in any other large Third World nation.

SOCIOLOGICAL PERSPECTIVES ON POPULATION

Only a few centuries ago, the main population problem was not how to reduce its growth but how to encourage it. Plagues and disasters sometimes brought sharp declines in population, and at times people must have thought the very survival of humanity to be in doubt. As we have seen, improvements in technology and changes in social organization sent death rates plunging and created the problem of over-population. But most people were slow to recognize this fundamental change and continued in their old ways. Social scientists, including sociologists, were the first to recognize these new realities and to urge government leaders to take action. Although there is now a specialized discipline devoted to the study of population, a great many demographers are trained as sociologists as well, and the major sociological perspectives provide important insights into the population problem.

The Functionalist Perspective Functionalists argue that population expansion may perform several important functions. Because greater size often means greater strength, a large population offers more security during natural disasters and a stronger defense against foreign aggressors. Many economists believe that economic growth is essential to the prosperity of an industrial society and that an increasing population promotes economic growth by providing labor and creating new markets for consumer goods.

Population growth may also be dysfunctional, however. Although all the services an expanding population requires, such as the construction of more houses, the cultivation of more land, and the manufacture of more clothing, may stimulate the economy, these activities lead to an increase in the consumption of dwindling natural resources. Moreover, the intense competition for jobs among the growing number of young adults and the resulting unemployment foster alienation and even despair. Overcrowding contributes to urban decay, the spread of disease, and a general decline in the standard of living.

When the world's population was low and there was no shortage of natural resources, the functions of population growth far outweighed its dysfunctions. Now the same social forces that promoted population growth in the past when it was desirable produce hunger, poverty, and social instability. For this reason, functionalists say, the population problem will be solved only when dysfunctional attitudes, values, and institutions that promote excessive birthrates are changed. Given time, the social system will reach a new balance. The critical question is whether this balance will come about as a result of famine, wars, or other disasters, or from well-organized programs to change traditional attitudes toward childbearing.

The Conflict Perspective   The conflict perspective sees the population crisis in the Third World as a direct result of European colonialism and the growth of world economy that is divided between rich industrialized nations and poor agricultural ones. In the nineteenth century, when technological advances were producing a sharp decline in death rates in Western Europe, the process of industrialization was creating economic incentives that were eventually to bring the birthrate down as well. Conflict theorists note that these same technological developments also began lowering the death rate in the Third World, but the Europeans prevented their colonies from industrializing. As a result, the economic system continued to reward those with large families, and the population of the Third World exploded. Daniel Chirot cites the role of the British in India as a classic example of this process:

> Along with maintaining a colonial class structure, the British also prevented the imposition of protective tariffs which would have helped Indian industry compete against the more advanced British industries. . . . By the time India had escaped from British colonial rule, . . . the country's overpopulation problem was quite severe, and world technology still more advanced and capital intensive than in the early 1900s [thus making it still harder for India to industrialize].[43]

Conflict theory also provides important insights into the forces that oppose population control. Official opposition to contraception and abortion is viewed as a reflection of a conflict between the interests of the masses and those of leaders and ruling elites. Overpopulation is harmful to most people, but an expanding population is an economic and political asset to the ruling class. A large national population means greater international power. Population growth among a society's lower classes also helps the elite by keeping wages down and providing a large pool of laborers. Unionization and strikes are less likely when jobs are scarce and there are many unemployed workers waiting to replace those who protest poor working conditions.

In the long run, religious groups that prevent their followers from practicing birth control are likely to have more members than those that allow contraception.

Perhaps the most significant contribution of the conflict perspective is its analysis of the causes of malnutrition and hunger. Conflict theorists point out that the current "food shortage" is really a problem of distribution, not production. The world currently produces more than enough food to provide an adequate diet for all people. Starvation and malnutrition result from the unequal distribution of the food that is produced. The rich industrialized countries have only a quarter of the world's people, but they consume more than half its food.[44] While millions of people starve to death every year in poor countries, many people in wealthy countries are suffering from obesity. Moreover, the same system of unequal distribution is found within nations. The ruling elite in even the poorest countries eat well, while some of the poor people in rich countries such as the United States and Canada are malnourished.

The obvious solution to this problem is to redistribute the world's food so that everyone is adequately fed. But there are enormous political and economic barriers to any international programs for redistributing the world's food supplies. Most of the surplus food is in the wealthy industrialized nations, and most of the hungry are too poor to pay for it. Even if the wealthy nations could be persuaded to give away a substantial proportion of their surplus food, which is doubtful, redistribution might drive many marginal Third World farmers out of business and create even more poverty and deprivation. On a national level, however, the outlook for an effective program of redistribution is much brighter. In fact, such countries as Sweden and Norway already guarantee a good diet to their poor by means of welfare programs, and the Chinese government carefully controls, and when necessary rations, its limited food supplies to ensure that they are distributed fairly.

Social Psychological Perspectives Biosocial theorists see human evolution as the root of the population problem. Because the most fertile individuals pass more genes on to the next generation, humans developed a high level of fertility. Throughout most of human history, this process promoted the survival of the species. But although overpopulation is now a serious threat to human survival, the evolutionary process continues to favor high fertility. Many biosocial theorists see the development of more effective artificial means of birth control as the best solution to the population problem because such an approach directly attacks the biological processes that they consider the root of the problem.

Other social psychologists point out, however, that learned attitudes and beliefs must change before birth control measures can be effective. Peasant farmers in traditional societies have a fatalistic attitude toward life. The idea of planning a family, let alone a world population, is alien to them. Fertility continues to be seen as a sign of virility and competence. The "real man" is one who has fathered many sons, and the "real woman" is one who has borne and reared them. Even in industrialized nations childless couples are sometimes pitied, and the inability to bear children may be reason enough for a husband to divorce his wife.

Effective population control requires that these attitudes be changed. But social psychologists have demonstrated that attitudinal changes do not occur in a vacuum; rather, they interact with shifting economic, social, and political conditions. Mere propaganda and personal appeals are not enough; they must be accompanied by concrete economic and social improvements. For example, a sound social security plan can do much to convince people that a large family is not necessary for support in their old age. Similarly, women who are provided with alternatives to the roles of wife and mother will soon learn that caring for a large family is not the only important activity in life.

SUMMARY

The world's population is growing at a rapid rate. Demographers agree that the reason for the population explosion is that high birthrates have been maintained while death rates have been cut dramatically. According to the theory of demographic transition, this process is caused by industrialization. Industrialization raises the average life span by increasing food production and improving public-health conditions. In the early stages of industrialization, birthrates remain high and there is a population explosion. But eventually, economic changes make children more of a financial liability than an asset, and birthrates come down. Thus, this theory implies that industrialization will soon lower the birthrates in the Third World, where the population growth is now the highest. But critics point out that unlike the rich countries, the decline in death rates in the Third World was not caused by industrialization but by the importation of foreign technology and know-how. Industrialization therefore seems far less likely to solve the current population problems of the poor nations.

Thomas Malthus was among the first to point out the dangers of unrestricted population growth. He argued that the human population naturally multiplies much faster than its food supply. So far, Malthus has been wrong because food supplies have kept up with or exceeded population growth. But many demographers feel that there is a limit to the number of people the world can support and that Malthus will eventually be proven right.

The runaway population growth of recent years has caused problems throughout the world. Poor agricultural nations with high growth rates are exhausting their land and other natural resources. Millions of people starve to death every year, and many of the world's people are underfed. Increasing numbers of people in Third World nations are migrating to cities, where unemployment is high and social integration is low, thus making political upheaval more likely. And industrialized nations must spend enormous sums to provide for their increasing populations, thus aggravating the world's shortage of essential raw materials and severely damaging the environment.

There are two general ways to deal with the population explosion: increasing the amount of food and lowering birthrates. Proposals for expanding the world's food supply include enhancing the productivity of agriculture, increasing the sea's food production, and wasting less of the food that we do produce. In order to lower birthrates, the governments of many countries have established family-planning programs. Such programs encourage the use of birth control, on the assumption that the birthrate will decline if couples have only the number of children that they desire. Because these programs have failed to reduce birthrates enough, some nations have introduced incentive programs that give bonuses to families with few children and penalize those with many. Another approach is to provide more economic and social opportunities for women, so that they will have a real alternative to the role of mother and child rearer.

Many sociologists of all theoretical persuasions agree that the traditional attitudes toward reproduction and family life may threaten human survival. Functionalists note that as death rates have dropped, attitudes encouraging fertility have become dysfunctional. Conflict theorists point out that the food shortage is caused by a distribution system that gives too much food to the wealthy and too little to the poor. Social psychologists have shown that the attitudes promoting high birthrates are learned and can therefore be changed.

KEY TERMS

demographic transition The changes in the birthrates and death rates that occur during the process of industrialization.

demography The scientific discipline that studies human population.

family planning A program that seeks to control population by assisting husbands and wives to have only the number of children they desire.

intermediate technology Technology that is less complicated and expensive than that typically used in the industrialized nations but more efficient than animal power and other traditional technologies.

land reform The redistribution of land from wealthy landlords to peasant farmers.

FURTHER READINGS

Thomas Malthus, *An Essay on the Principle of Population* (London: Reeves & Turner, 1872). The classic essay that started the modern study of demography.

Jon Bennett, *The Hunger Machine: The Politics of Food* (Cambridge, England: Polity Press, 1987). A dramatic account of the way the modern world economy produces Third World hunger.

John R. Weeks, *Population: An Introduction to Concepts and Issues*, 3rd ed. (Belmont, Calif.: Wadsworth, 1986). A good general text covering the population problem.

E. F. Schumacher, *Small Is Beautiful: Economics As If People Mattered* (New York: Harper & Row, 1974). A brilliant critique of the human and environmental irrationality of the current economic system.

William Alonso, ed., *Population in an Interacting World* (Cambridge, Mass.: Harvard University Press, 1987). A good reader on current population issues and problems.

chapter 17

The Environment

- How have we damaged our environment?
- Are we running out of natural resources?
- What are the causes of the environmental crisis?
- How can we clean up the environment and conserve our resources?

For centuries we have seen our environment as a boundless storehouse of wealth. Nature was to be conquered, tamed, and used in any way we saw fit. Until recently only a few people realized how fragile and limited our world really is. Now the damage done by exploitive technologies and the enormous growth of the human population are forcing this realization on us all. One by one the natural resources on which we have come to depend are dwindling away. And as they are used up, their by-products are fouling our land, air, and water and disrupting the delicate web of life on which our very existence depends.

ECOLOGY

Western culture views us as special creatures, separate and apart from our environment. Humans are seen not as animals but as superior beings destined to rule over the planet and its lesser creatures. There is, however, no scientific evidence to support such beliefs. The science of **ecology**—the study of the interrelations among plants, animals, and their environment—shows us that humans are but one part of a complex network of living things. No human could live more than a few seconds if separated from the sheltered terrestrial environment with just the right proportions of water, oxygen, heat, and the other essential components that support human life. These components, like our food, are entirely dependent on plants and the other animals of the earth. We could not even digest our food properly without microorganisms that live inside our bodies.

Life on this planet exists in only a thin surface layer of soil and water, and the air immediately surrounding it. This life zone, known as the **biosphere**, is a mere 14 kilometers (9 miles) thick. Within the biosphere there are many **ecosystems**: self-sufficient communities of organisms living in an interdependent relationship with one another and with their environment. Each ecosystem has its own natural balance, both internally and with other self-sufficient ecosystems, and human interference may set off a chain reaction with deadly consequences.

All ecosystems require energy, and virtually all energy comes from the sun. Green plants convert solar energy into food through a process known as **photosynthesis**. In addition to carbohydrates (food), photosynthesis produces the oxygen required for respiration in both plants and animals. Respiration, in turn, produces carbon dioxide, which is used in photosynthesis. Thus, like other aspects of an ecosystem, photosynthesis is part of a cycle that continually reuses the same basic elements. All that is needed from outside is the energy that comes from the sun.

Because animals cannot make direct use of the sun's energy for food production, all of our food ultimately comes from plants. The food produced by green plants usually goes through many transformations in what is known as a **food chain** before it decomposes enough for natural recycling. For example, a simple food chain may start with the grass and other green foliage eaten by a deer. The deer is then eaten by a wolf, and when the wolf dies, its decomposed body provides nutrients so that more grass can grow. Of course, most food chains are much more complex than this, involving many intricate relationships between plants and animals.

THE HUMAN IMPACT

Early hunting and gathering people interfered very little with the ecosystems in which they lived. Their tools were limited, and muscle power was the main source of energy. As technology became more sophisticated and new sources of energy were tapped, the human impact on the environment grew ever larger. With the invention of agriculture, we attempted to replace the delicate complexity of the natural environment with a narrow range of plants and animals that were best suited to supporting human life. The surplus food produced by agriculture made the development of cities possible. And with the cities came a host of new threats to the earth's ecological balance. Forests were cut down, rivers rechanneled, and tons of human waste dumped into the water and plowed into the soil. Some organisms were exterminated; others multiplied more rapidly than ever before. Humans soon became the single greatest force in changing the ecological balance of the planet. But this process did not stop there. Industrialization, with its countless new machines and technologies, once again intensified the human role in shaping the course of environmental change. Time and again the human impact on the environment has produced unexpected, unpleasant, and even dangerous consequences.

Air Pollution Few of us give a second thought to the invisible and seemingly inexhaustible ocean of air in which we live. But consider the fact that a person can live for weeks without food and for days without water, but can survive for only a few minutes without air. We have been able to take our atmosphere for granted because rain and other processes naturally cleanse and renew it. But we are now dumping more pollutants into the air than can be removed by these natural processes. Air pollution is worst in the big cities, but because the ocean of air connects all parts of our planet together, it is rapidly becoming a global problem. Smog has already been detected at the North Pole and the lead content of the northern ice caps has increased substantially.[1]

The single greatest source of air pollution in North America is transportation. Coal, oil, and natural gas used for heating and for generating electricity are also major contributors. Additional tons of pollutants are spewed into the air by paper mills, steel mills, oil refineries, smelters, and chemical plants. Even trash burning is a substantial cause of air pollution.[2]

The amount and kinds of pollutants in the air vary greatly from one area to another. The most common pollutants are carbon monoxide, hydrocarbons, oxides of sulfur, oxides of nitrogen, ozone, and tiny particles of soot, ashes, and other industrial by-products. The amounts of these pollutants vary in different industrial regions. Thus, areas that depend on oil for power have different pollution problems from those that use coal.

No matter which chemicals are involved, valleys and closed air basins are more likely to have air pollution than plains and mountains, where the air can circulate freely. Air quality can become especially bad when a layer of warmer air moves over a layer of cooler air and seals in pollutants that would ordinarily rise into the upper atmosphere. This condition, known as **temperature inversion**, is temporary, but while it lasts, it may create an intense bout of air pollution. Local winds also affect the distribution of pollutants, carrying them from one area to another. Finally, climate has an important effect on the kinds of pollutants that are present in different areas. For instance, sunlight acts on oxygen, hydrocarbons, and nitrogen oxides to produce new compounds collectively known as **photochemical smog**.

Air pollution is not merely a minor irritant that burns our eyes and clouds the skies. It is a major health hazard, contributing to many chronic diseases and killing a substantial number of people each year. Air pollution is believed to contribute to the deaths of at least 53,000 Americans every year, and has been linked to such serious respiratory diseases as bronchitis, emphysema, and lung cancer. It is also a known contributor to several other types of cancer and to heart disease as well.[3]

The effects of individual pollutants on health are, however, difficult to determine because the various chemicals we release into the air combine to produce entirely new substances. Further, all people living in a particular area are not necessarily exposed to the same amount of pollution. An executive who drives an air-conditioned car from her home to an air-conditioned office is exposed to less pollution than a traffic officer who breathes smog all day long. Some people even expose themselves to pollution intentionally—for instance, by smoking cigarettes.

The damaging effects of air pollution are not limited to humans. Although there has been little research in this area, it appears that domesticated animals living in polluted areas suffer much the same problems as humans. It has been shown that air pollution has harmful effects on trees, shrubs, and flowers. The orange groves of California and the truck farms of New Jersey, for instance, both suffer from smog damage.

In many areas, chemicals from coal-burning power plants and other industrial sources combine with water in the atmosphere to produce acid rain. Not only do these rains harm plant life and eat away exposed metal surfaces and buildings made of limestone or marble; they decrease the fertility of some soils and destroy the life in streams and rivers. Acid rain has killed all the fish in hundreds of lakes in the United States, Canada, and northern Europe. Many scientists also believe that acid rain is a major contributor to the decline in forest lands in industrialized nations, but there are several other possible causes as well.[4] The control of acid rain poses a difficult international dilemma, because the pollution created in one country often rains down on another. For example, more than half the acid deposited in Canada by air pollution comes from the United States.[5]

Air pollution is also creating some disturbing changes in the upper atmosphere and the thin ozone layer that protects us from the ultraviolet rays of the sun. Scientists have known for years that a group of chemicals, the chlorofluorocarbons (CFCs), used in air conditioners, refrigerators, and Styrofoam containers, decompose ozone. But many refused to take the threat to the upper atmosphere seriously until a giant hole in the ozone layer was discovered over Antarctica. Although the hole develops only during the spring months, it has been getting larger every year.[6] And as scientists began to investigate conditions in the upper atmosphere more closely, they were soon shocked to discover how rapidly the ozone layer has been thinning out in the rest of the world as well. Between 4 and 5 percent of the ozone layer over North America, for example, has apparently been lost just since 1978. As a result of these

Photochemical smog has made the air in many cities unhealthy, while the breakdown of the ozone layer in the upper atmosphere is increasing the risks of contracting skin cancer from exposure to the sun.

new findings, the Environmental Protection Agency now predicts an additional 200,000 deaths from skin cancer over the next 50 years. The first international response to this crisis occurred in Montreal in 1987, when 24 major nations met and agreed to cut their CFC production in half by the turn of the century. And as the full scope of the threat became apparent, they met again in 1990 and tightened the restrictions. This time the industrialized nations agreed to stop all CFC production by the year 2000 and to provide financial assistance to the poorer nations so they could stop their production by 2010.[7]

But of all the hazards of air pollution, perhaps the greatest potential threat is known as the **greenhouse effect**. The buildup of gases from the burning of various fuels and other human activities is changing the composition of the atmosphere. These gases are holding in more of the energy that comes to earth from the sun and are thereby raising the temperature of the air, just like the greenhouse of an orchid grower. The biggest problem is with carbon dioxide, but methane and other gases also play a role. Worldwide, the air we breathe now contains about 25 percent more carbon dioxide than it did just a century ago.

The greenhouse effect is expected to raise the average temperature of the earth from 3 to 8 degrees Fahrenheit over the next 50 years. Although that may not seem like much of a difference, the consequences could be devastating. For one thing, the increases will not be spread evenly over the planet. Some areas will have much greater increases, while a few places may actually experience cooler weather. But more important, the changing temperatures will also change the pattern of rainfall, which could turn the American Midwest and other major agricultural areas into dust bowls. Moreover, as the temperature rises, the water in the oceans will expand and some of the polar icecaps will melt. The result will be a higher sea level and the flooding of many low-lying coastal areas.[8] But in sharp contrast to the response to ozone depletion, the world community has done little except talk about the dangers of global warming. It is far easier to ban CFCs than to kick our dependence on petroleum, coal, and the other fossil fuels that create so much of the problem.

Water Pollution Over two-thirds of the world's surface is covered by water. It is continually evaporating, forming clouds, and raining back to the earth in a cycle that provides a seemingly endless supply of clean water. Perhaps it is blind faith in the enormous reserves of water and the natural purification system that has led people to dump so much garbage into lakes, rivers, and oceans. For a time the earth's water resources could tolerate such an onslaught. But with the population explosion and the increased dumping of industrial wastes, marine animals and plants began to die in large numbers.

Organic wastes are important water pollutants. In small quantities, they are quickly broken down by waterborne bacteria, but if too much organic material is dumped into the water, the bacteria use up available oxygen as they decompose the waste. Fish and other complex organisms suffocate, and a barren body of water is left. Human waste is a major contributor to the problem. The sewage from New York City alone produces 5 million cubic yards of sludge a year, which is dumped into the ocean and now covers over 15 square miles of ocean bottom.[9] However, the wastes from animal feedlots, oil refining, food processing, textile and paper manufacturing, and other industries are actually a bigger source of pollution.

Chemical fertilizers have much the same effect as organic wastes and cause similar damage. When rains wash nitrogen fertilizers into rivers and lakes, they stimulate the growth of huge "blooms" of algae. When these blooms die, they decay, using up oxygen in the same way that other organic pollution does.[10]

Our rivers, lakes, and oceans are also polluted by a host of poisons and dangerous chemicals that include everything from industrial solvents to pesticides. Not only do these substances kill wildlife and threaten our drinking water, but many of them become more concentrated as they move up the food chain. When fish eat plants exposed to such substances as arsenic, mercury, and pesticides like DDT, the pollutants build up in their tissues. When these fish are eaten by larger fish, the toxins become still more concentrated, and so on. Because most of the seafood we eat comes from the top of the food chain, it is likely to have the highest levels of contamination. Moreover, no part of the world, however remote, is immune from the problem. The

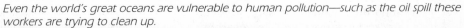

Even the world's great oceans are vulnerable to human pollution—such as the oil spill these workers are trying to clean up.

19th-Century Social Problems

State Chemist Daniels has furnished an analysis of Ashland's drinking water and says that it is contaminated with sewage.... The typhoid fever epidemic from which Ashland is suffering is now directly attributed to the water supply. Efforts will be made by the Attorney General to have the water company's franchise annulled.

April 9, 1894

These selections, which appear throughout the text, are from the *Badger State Banner*, a newspaper published in Black River Falls, Wisconsin.

Inuit people, who live in what many mistakenly believe to be the pristine wilderness of northern Canada, eat large amounts of seal meat, fish, and other local game. Their diet exceeds the Canadian government's maximum limit for PCBs (a family of dangerous organic chemicals) 10 to 20 percent of the time, and the milk of Inuit mothers contains five times more PCBs than the milk of mothers who live in southern Canada.[11]

To many people, the most important water is that coming out of the tap in their home. Water once commonly carried such dread diseases as cholera and typhoid, but modern water treatment has eliminated that risk. Now our drinking water is being threatened in another way: chemical contamination. Dangerous industrial chemicals are seeping into the water supplies of many towns and cities, and the underground water in many agricultural areas now contains a host of different pesticides. Water from wells in Battle Creek, Michigan, was found to contain vinyl chloride and benzene, among other dangerous chemicals. The unusually high rate of certain types of cancers among residents of New Orleans is believed to be linked to carcinogens in its water supply.[12] A four-year study of women who live around California's famous Silicon Valley (a national center for the computer industry) showed that those who drank tap water had significantly more miscarriages than those who drank bottled water.[13]

The Environmental Protection Agency estimates that only about 1 to 2 percent of usable groundwater reserves in the United States are polluted, but that figure greatly underestimates the situation. For one thing, the water near heavily populated urban areas is most likely to be contaminated, and that, of course, is also the water we will probably drink. Furthermore, the federal government commonly tests for only 38 of the more than 700 chemicals that are found in drinking water and has failed to establish a comprehensive program to test the nation's underground water supplies.[14]

The Deteriorating Land   Poor Third World nations, faced with overpopulation and short-ages of food and housing, have often looked at the environment as a problem that only the rich can afford to worry about. But many of these poor nations are now beginning to realize that they are caught in the grip of an even greater environmental crisis than the one faced by their industrialized neighbors. The world's forests are shrinking at an alarming rate, while the desert wastelands grow, and most of these changes are occurring in the Third World nations (see Figure 17.1). Every year, the world loses 12 million hectares of tropical forest—an area about the size of England.[15] At this rate there will be virtually no tropical forest left in 30 to 40 years, and if the rain forests are destroyed, over a million unique species of plants and animals will die with them. **Desertification**—the transformation of productive land into desert—is a slower process. But it is estimated that 20 million square kilometers, an area twice the size of Canada, is at risk of turning into desert.[16]

Natural forces such as the periodic droughts that have recurred throughout history are not the principal cause of this crisis. Most of the damage is being done by human beings. Deforestation is caused by logging to get lumber and fuel, and the intentional destruction of the forests to make room for the farms and cities demanded by a growing human population. Desertification results from overgrazing by livestock, poor irrigation techniques that poison the soil with salts and alkalis, and the desperate attempts to farm land that is not suited for agriculture.

Although conditions are worse in the Third World, the industrialized nations have serious problems of their own. Reforestation has allowed the industrialized nations to keep some of their temperate forests from shrinking,[17] but air pollution still poses a serious threat. Germany, for example, reports that over half its forests are damaged

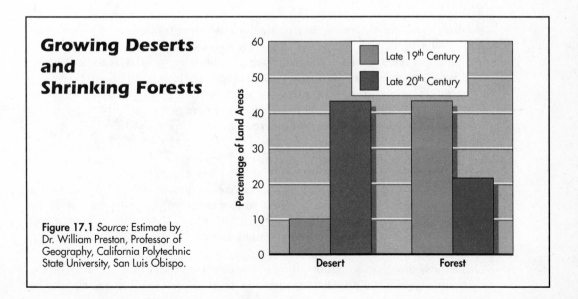

Growing Deserts and Shrinking Forests

Figure 17.1 *Source:* Estimate by Dr. William Preston, Professor of Geography, California Polytechnic State University, San Luis Obispo.

Logged-out forests, such as the one shown in this photograph, have become an increasingly common sight as a growing human population places more demands on limited environmental resources.

or dying.[18] The heavily mechanized techniques used by agribusiness do serious long-term damage to the soil, and North America is now facing a serious erosion problem. The impact of years of environmentally damaging plowing methods is adding up; and wind breaks, terraces, and antierosion ditches built during the 1930s are being torn out to make it easier to operate today's huge farming machines. The loss of topsoil from Iowa farms now averages almost 10 tons per acre per year.[19]

Another heavy burden on our beleaguered land is the huge quantities of solid waste produced by industry. Each year the United States generates about a ton of trash and garbage for every man, woman, and child in the country.[20] Some of this refuse is burned, thus adding to air pollution, but most of it is buried in landfills and dumps. This creates two problems. One is that an increasing number of ravines, gullies, valleys, and sloughs are being covered as the trash mounts up. Another comes from the disposal of plastic and other synthetic materials, which, unlike organic material, never decompose. Americans dump about 100 million tires and 38 billion bottles and jars each year.

As if these problems were not enough, new threats to the land are looming on the horizon. Just when the population explosion demands that more and more land be used for agriculture, the shortage of energy and raw materials is leading us to use more environmentally destructive methods to obtain them. For instance, there are enormous reserves of coal in North America, and much of the fuel lies close to the surface. This makes it cheaper to extract, but the strip-mining technique that is normally used creates severe environmental damage. Strip mines are long, shallow valleys gouged out of the earth. After the coal has been removed, the dislocated earth is dumped back into the hole. But unless the topsoil is carefully replaced (an expensive and time-consuming process), the land will not be fertile again for centuries, if ever.[21]

The growth of cities poses yet another threat to the ecological balance of our land. Great portions of the landmass of our planet are being covered by expanding cities and suburbs. These vast metropolitan areas are beginning to threaten the existence of the wilderness that harbors so many different species of plants and animals. Many ecosystems have already been destroyed by urban sprawl, and the outlook for the future is not bright. If population growth continues at its present rate, only the most remote mountains and deserts will remain unspoiled.

Chemicals and Radiation   The human race is dosing itself with thousands of chemicals. The air we breathe and practically everything we eat or drink contains synthetic substances. Although many of these chemicals seem harmless enough, the plain fact is that we know almost nothing about most of their long-term effects. Recent history is full of examples of supposedly harmless food additives, drugs, and industrial wastes that were found to be serious health hazards. A study by the National Academy of Sciences concluded that only 20 percent of the almost 710,000 chemicals in commercial use had been thoroughly tested, and a third had never been tested at all.[22]

Still, the toxic wastes that have been identified are a daunting problem. Each year the United States alone produces about 292 million tons of toxic wastes. A single day's waste is enough to fill the New Orleans Superdome four times.[23] The Environmental Protection Agency estimates that 90 percent of this waste is disposed of improperly. The EPA has already identified 25,000 toxic-waste sites in need of a cleanup, and the General Accounting Office estimates that a thorough inventory would uncover at least another 350,000 sites.[24] Many people have already been burned or poisoned by these toxic wastes, and the contamination of drinking water with dangerous chemicals threatens to become one of the most serious public health problems of the next decade.

The Environmental Protection Agency has, however, done little to meet the toxic-waste crisis. In 1980, Congress created a billion-dollar "superfund" to help clean up dangerous waste dumps. But more than a decade later, only 70 sites had been cleaned up even though tens of thousands of sites needed to be restored. Critics have charged, moreover, that the little work that was done was not done well. The EPA's approach to cleaning up most unsafe dumps is simply to move the dangerous chemicals to a different dump, which in some cases is no safer than the original site. The government has repeatedly been accused of dragging its feet on toxic-waste cleanups and, more generally, of supporting the interests of industrial polluters instead of the interests of the American public.[25]

Radiation pollution frightens people even more than toxic chemicals, probably because we know so little about it. Small doses of radiation have no immediate effects. Moderate doses cause vomiting, fatigue, loss of appetite, and diarrhea. Death is practically certain for people exposed to high doses. However, no one knows much about the long-term effects of low and moderate doses of radiation. Studies of the survivors of the nuclear bombings of Hiroshima and Nagasaki show a high incidence of leukemia and other cancers, but it is not known exactly how much exposure is needed to produce cancer. There is ample proof that radiation causes genetic mutations, but again there is little information about how dangerous specific doses of radiation actually are.

The ultimate environmental disaster—nuclear war—will be discussed in the next chapter. But there is also growing alarm about the spread of radiation from the use of nuclear reactors as a source of power and in the production of nuclear weapons. At present, such reactors contribute little to the overall levels of radiation in the world. But environmentalists fear that nuclear pollution will increase if the nuclear industry expands. One major concern is the danger of a nuclear accident. There is little chance of a reactor erupting in a nuclear explosion, but if the cooling system of such a plant should fail, the tremendous heat of the nuclear reaction would melt the concrete and steel surrounding it, thus releasing enough radiation to wipe out an entire city. Nuclear power plants have elaborate safeguards against such **meltdowns**, and advocates of nuclear power argue that the probability of such an accident occurring is very low. But the 1979 accident at the Three Mile Island reactor in Pennsylvania and the 1986 disaster at the Chernobyl reactor in the former Soviet Union have convinced many people that serious accidents are far more likely than the public has been led to believe. Although the official death toll from the Chernobyl accident is still only 32 people, it is now clear that figure was part of the government's effort to cover up the real extent of the damage. The head of the scientific team in charge of the evacuation zone around the remains of the plant recently estimated that there have already been 7,000 to 10,000 deaths (mainly among the cleanup crew), and the long-term effects of massive radiation exposure are mounting year by year. The rate of leukemia in Kiev, the nearest large city, is four times higher than normal, and the incidence of radiation-induced cancers is not expected to peak for another decade. Moreover, the economic losses have been staggering—an estimated $358 billion—including the permanent relocation of 200,000 people (leaving another 4 million people still living on contaminated ground) and the destruction of 20 percent of the farmland of the entire republic of Byelorussia.[26]

Even in the unlikely event that no major accidents occur, the radioactive wastes generated by nuclear plants are deadly pollutants, and we still have no effective way to handle them. The main problem is that these wastes remain dangerous for so long that scientists cannot agree on a safe disposal technique. For example, the EPA requires that spent fuel rods from nuclear plants be stored safely for 10,000 years. There are currently almost 50,000 of these old fuel rods stored temporarily at U.S. nuclear plants, but the federal government has yet to open a permanent disposal site. And even the temporary storage of nuclear wastes has proven to be inadequate. About 530,000 gallons of highly radioactive liquids have already leaked out of U.S. nuclear weapons plants. Although the public was never informed, there have apparently been over 14,000 leaks of radioactive waste from the Savannah River weapons plant alone. It is becoming clear that the cloak of national security has been used to cover up horrible safety conditions that would never have been allowed at civilian facilities.

Moreover, old nuclear power plants, whether civilian or military, are also a radiation hazard. Whatever techniques are ultimately developed to decommission such plants, the process is bound to be slow and costly.[27]

Another serious hazard in the use of nuclear energy is crime. Security is tight in nuclear power plants, but the more this energy source is used, the more shipments of radioactive materials there will be and the easier it will be for a terrorist group to steal them. Although it is difficult to turn low-grade nuclear fuels into bombs, there is still great danger. The explosion of a conventional bomb placed next to some radioactive materials could spread a deadly radioactive cloud big enough to poison a large area. A further problem might also spring from the development of breeder reactors that turn uranium 235, which is not usable as nuclear fuel, into plutonium, which is. Unlike other nuclear fuels, the plutonium produced by breeder reactors can be made directly into nuclear weapons. Thus, large-scale use of these reactors would create a distinct possibility that terrorists and the nations that support them might seize some plutonium and hold entire cities for ransom or even destroy them with atomic explosions.

DWINDLING RESOURCES

Photographs of the earth taken from space have done much to further the cause of conservation. One look at a picture of that tiny blue-green globe hanging in the vast emptiness of space shows us how limited our world and its resources really are. Through most of human history we have been acting as though the world were a rich mine to be exploited. We are just beginning to realize that there are only limited amounts of oil, coal, and uranium. When the supply is used up, there will be no more.

The United States, with less than 5 percent of the world's people, uses a quarter of all the energy consumed each year. All the industrialized nations combined hold only 25 percent of the world's people, but they use 85 to 90 percent of its resources (see Figure 17.2).[28] There is a growing feeling in Third World nations that the industrialized countries are using up the world's resources so rapidly that there will soon be nothing left for them. There is much talk about industrializing the poor nations so that they can stabilize their population growth and bring their level of living up to Western standards. But with current technology, the world's supply of oil and minerals cannot possibly support all the world's people in the style to which the wealthy nations have become accustomed.

Energy Modern industrial society would be impossible without massive supplies of energy. If enough energy is available, most raw materials—iron, copper, aluminum—can be recycled. But most of our energy currently comes from sources that are not renewable: once the supply is used up, it is gone forever. The fossil fuels (oil, coal, and natural gas) are **nonrenewable**: they took millions of years to form from organic materials deposited in the earth and cannot be replaced. Fortunately, other sources of energy are **renewable**. We can grow more wood and organic materials to burn in our fireplaces, and the supply of solar energy constantly renews itself, whether we use it or not.

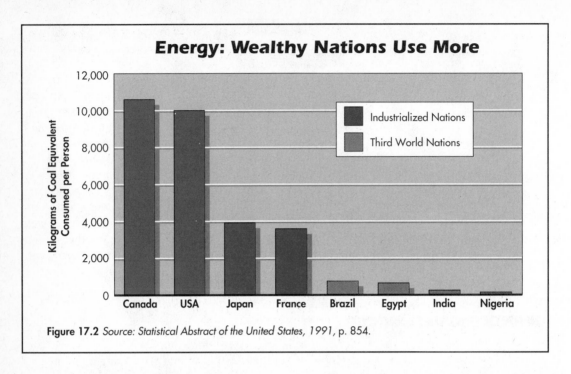

Figure 17.2 Source: Statistical Abstract of the United States, 1991, p. 854.

Worldwide consumption of nonrenewable energy resources has grown at a staggering pace. As recently as the nineteenth century, the vast majority of the world's energy came from renewable sources. Particularly important were human and animal labor and the burning of wood and dung. But the industrialized world's appetite for energy grew so rapidly that it could not be satisfied by these traditional sources. By the beginning of the twentieth century, coal was the world's principal source of energy, and oil was just coming into use. Now the world gets over half its energy from oil and natural gas, and a quarter from coal.[29] North Americans are particularly heavy users of fossil fuels and consume more total energy than people in other nations.

Until 1973, oil was plentiful and cheap. The price had been steadily declining for years,[30] and few people gave any thought to the possibility that we would ever run out of petroleum. But in 1973 the modern world was shaken by its first great energy crisis. War broke out in the Middle East, and the Arab oil producers tried to stop all shipments to nations that they believed to be supporters of their enemy, Israel. At the same time, the oil-producing countries quadrupled the price of oil. Although the oil boycott was soon ended, oil prices continued to rise. Energy consumption in the industrialized world fell the following year, but soon started to rise again. A second major petroleum shortage occurred in 1979, after the Iranian revolution disrupted that country's oil production. A "panic" soon followed, causing long lines and frustrated customers at gas pumps around the world. This second gas crisis seems to have been more effective than the first one in driving home the point that the energy supplies so essential to the industrialized nations are dependent on a fragile international web of political and economic relations. But as the prices of petroleum products have dropped, that important lesson seems to be fading from memory.

No one knows how much longer the world's supply of oil will last. Experts disagree widely about how much oil remains to be discovered and the rate at which we are likely to consume it. If we continue to use petroleum at the present rate and no new reserves are discovered, the world's supply will last only about 30 years.[31] But even if we eventually uncover three times today's proven reserves—and many experts believe this to be possible—most of the world's supply of oil will still be used up in another 100 years.[32] Moreover, the world's population is now growing at about 1.7 percent a year,[33] and a considerable effort will therefore be needed to keep consumption from increasing. Heavy oils from tar sands and oil shale could provide some additional reserves, but they will be costly and environmentally damaging to develop. And no matter what steps we take, it is clear that we are quickly approaching the day when there will be no more oil at affordable prices.

The world's reserves of coal are much greater than its reserves of oil and natural gas. Most experts believe that there is enough coal in the ground to meet the world's energy needs for several hundred years.[34] As with petroleum, however, the actual amount of coal available for human consumption is a matter of economics. The size of the world's usable coal reserves depends on the cost of mining them and the amount of energy we must use to dig them up. Finally, we should remember that coal, like oil, is fossilized organic matter. No matter how much we pay for it, no matter how much energy we use to mine it, and no matter how much land we destroy in the process, someday the supply will be exhausted.

Some people believe that nuclear power plants will be able to supply more of the world's energy as oil and coal are burned up. Nevertheless, it is highly unlikely that nuclear reactors, at least in their present form, can replace the energy now obtained from fossil fuels. For one thing, it takes enormous amounts of energy and labor to build a nuclear power plant, so a substantial portion of the energy produced by the plant merely replaces the energy consumed by its construction. With staggering increases in the cost of building new nuclear plants and doubts about their safety in the wake of the Chernobyl disaster, nuclear power seems to have reached a dead end in the United States. Plans for over 100 plants have been canceled, and no new plants have been ordered since 1978.[35]

For the poorest third of the human population, the real energy crisis is the shortage of wood to burn. Over two billion people in the world still rely on wood as their primary source of energy. More than half of them are unable to gather or buy enough to meet their needs, and the supply of wood is dwindling every year. For many poor families, it now costs as much to heat their supper bowl as to fill it. About half of all the wood cut every year is used for fuel, and that has been a major contributor to the acute problem of global deforestation.[36]

There are, fortunately, other sources of renewable energy that can yield greater energy. **Hydroelectric power**, generated by turbines turned by flowing water, is clean and efficient. New hydroelectric power stations appear every year, but the cost of transporting electricity limits the use of hydroelectric power. Currently, about 30 percent of North America's electricity bill pays for the production of power; the other 70 percent is for transporting the power from the generators to the consumers. However, recent breakthroughs in superconductivity may someday allow us to slash these costs by sharply reducing the amount of electricity lost from the wires during transmission. Geothermal energy—the heat of the earth's inner core—can be used to generate electricity and steam and is thus a possible substitute for fossil fuels. At present, however, this energy can be harnessed only in places with very special geological conditions. **Solar energy** is just beginning to make a contribution to our energy supplies. The sun bathes the earth with an enormous amount of energy every day, and if that energy can be efficiently used, a clean substitute for coal, oil, and wood will be at hand.

Minerals Although humans were using the earth's mineral wealth long before they used petroleum, it does not appear that there will be a mineral crisis any time in the near future. Modern industry depends on about 80 basic minerals. About three-fourths of them are either abundant enough to meet all our needs or can be easily replaced. There are about 18 minerals that present more of a challenge. The known reserves of zinc will last only about 40 years at the current rate of consumption, lead about 48 years, and copper 65 years.[37] Although the known reserves are likely to increase, no one can say by how much. It is clear, however, that as high-grade deposits of these materials are used up, we will be forced to turn to deposits of ever lower quality, which are difficult to collect and refine.

The seas and oceans contain many minerals both in the water and on the bottom. If it were economically feasible to mine these resources, they would greatly boost the world's supplies of raw materials. Currently, it costs more to mine many of these minerals than they are worth, but technological advances are rapidly reducing the cost. As a result, bitter political battles have been fought over the control of undersea mineral resources. After nine years of negotiations, a United Nations conference finally agreed on a Law of the Sea Treaty in 1982. But several major powers, including the United States, Great Britain, and West Germany, refused to sign it because of provisions that they believed were too generous to Third World nations unlikely to develop their own technology to exploit the mineral resources on the ocean floor.[38]

Unlike energy, most minerals can be recycled. A significant portion of the copper, lead, gold, silver, and aluminum being used today has been recycled at least once. Recycling of most other raw materials is not profitable at present prices. As world stores are emptied, prices will rise and recycling will look better and better, because it both conserves mineral resources and saves energy. An added benefit is that recycling can also reduce the production of solid wastes that are now choking our dumps and landfills. One problem, however, is that some industrial metals stay in use so long that only small amounts are available for recycling.

ORIGINS OF THE ENVIRONMENTAL CRISIS

Many ecologists and demographers predict that an ecological disaster is on the way, most likely in the form of a devastating famine in the Third World. Although everyone is not so pessimistic, there is no disagreement about the fact that we have been destroying the very ecosystems that sustain us. Such irrational behavior is not easy to explain. Its complex causes have roots stretching far back into history. Ironically, the same characteristics that have made humans such a successful species—high intelligence and an enormous ability to manipulate the environment—have also contributed to the development of the technology and cultural orientation that are now threatening life on earth.

Exploitive Technology   More and more people are coming to realize that the magnificent technological advances that have made life so much more comfortable have a dark side as well. As we have seen, agricultural technology has brought havoc to the biosphere; industrial technology is polluting the environment; and military technology has for the first time in history given humanity the means to destroy itself. And even if we do not destroy ourselves directly with nuclear bombs, we may do it indirectly by disrupting ecosystems, food chains, and the whole life-supporting system.

But condemning technology as though it were separate from the humans who use it is both pointless and misleading. Every group of humans, from prehistoric times to the present, has used some form of technology to meet its needs for food, clothing, and shelter. Only a few of those technologies, however, have caused serious damage to the environment. The real culprit is **exploitive technology**, designed to produce the greatest immediate rewards without regard to the long-term consequences to the environment or the quality of human life.

This problem is nothing new. Although the earliest hunting and gathering peoples did little damage to their environment, the human race has been using exploitive technologies for thousands of years. Historians now believe that many of the great agricultural societies of the past collapsed because unsound farming techniques led to an environmental crisis and a sharp reduction in food supplies. But the overall environmental damage done by industrial societies is far worse. For one thing, their technology is much more powerful and sophisticated, and, for another, they support many more people. Moreover, these people demand a much higher standard of living than people had in the past, and that requires more intensive exploitation of the environment. Industrialization also brings about a qualitative change in the kind of technology we use. From nuclear radiation to the destruction of the ozone layer in the upper atmosphere, the cornucopia of modern science has produced problems undreamed of by our ancestors.

Unregulated Growth   The average person in the industrialized nations has a higher standard of living and is using more nonrenewable resources than ever before in human history. At the same time, the people of the Third World nations are struggling to feed millions of new mouths every year. The environmental effects of such growth are obvious. The more people there are and the more resources each of them uses, the faster they will pollute the environment and deplete the world's reserves of raw materials.

The damage caused by reckless growth is easily seen, but our traditional belief in economic expansion and progress has blinded many people to the problem. Governments around the world pursue policies concerned more with the quantity of possessions than with the quality of life, and not a single nation officially opposes economic growth. Fifty years ago the same thing could have been said about population

DEBATE

Are We Headed for an Environmental Disaster?

Throughout history we have always faced environmental challenges. But the unprecedented size of today's population and the ever-growing power of its technology have led some observers to predict an environmental crisis in the years ahead that will have devastating effects around the world.

YES Predicting the future is always a risky business. But there are so many signs warning of an environmental crisis that the only question is when, not if, it will occur. Never before in the history of this planet has a single species had such a devastating impact on so many other organisms. Humankind is driving thousands of species of plants and animals into extinction every year. We are replacing complex and diversified ecosystems with simple, artificial systems such as farms and urban neighborhoods. And it is a basic ecological law that the narrower the ecosystem, the more fragile it will be.

There are two main forces driving us toward disaster—overpopulation and pollution. The world is now choking with over five billion people, but at the current rate of growth, there will be over *a trillion* people on earth in just three centuries. Of course, the world can't support that many individuals, and one of two things has to happen. Either we reduce our birthrates or increase our death rates. But all the talk and all the birth control programs have failed to stop the runaway population growth. Without a truly effective program of population control, only devastating plagues and famines can keep population growth in check.

As if the staggering increases in the size of the human population weren't bad enough, the average person is producing more and more pollution every year. Toxic chemicals and radioactive wastes are piling up in hundreds of thousands of sites around the world. Our rivers, lakes, and oceans are

NO Environmental problems are nothing new. And compared with the overwhelming difficulties our ancestors faced, we are actually far better off. Human history is a record of plagues, droughts, floods, and famines, which were all caused, in one way or another, by environmental forces. Life was precarious, and the slightest environmental disturbance could prove fatal. In contrast, today's environmental concerns are more a matter of esthetics than survival. Certainly trash dumps are unsightly, and unspoiled woodlands are more attractive than housing tracts, but such eyesores aren't much of a price to pay for our current standard of living.

Of course, some of the damage to the environment does create health hazards, but they are minor ones compared with the problems of the past. Otherwise, why would the average life span be going up year after year? In fact, the steady increase in human population that worries the environmentalists so much is actually proof that the human race is prospering. If things were really as bad as some scientists claim, the population should be declining, as it has in many other historical eras.

The alarmists who predict some kind of environmental disaster are basing their conclusions on emotion, not logic. They find a problem that is getting worse and then make wild predictions based on the assumption that it will never improve. Actually, most environmental problems are self-limiting. If a particular kind of pollution starts to cause a real threat, that very fact becoming toxic cesspools, and the fish they used to support are dying off or taking in so many pollutants that they are dangerous to eat. The ozone layer is breaking down, and the smoke from all the fuels we burn is clouding the air, poisoning our bodies, and transforming the weather in unpredictable ways. Year by year, the lush forests are shrinking while the deserts grow. How much more evidence do we need? Unless we voluntarily make a radical transformation in our attitudes and in our way of life, a devastating environmental crisis will soon force us to do so.

motivates people to do something about it. The more serious an environmental problem becomes, the harder we work to fix it. It is true that we face serious environmental issues today, but our difficulties can and will be resolved. In fact, the amazing technological progress of the last century has given us more power to shape our environment and tackle its problems than ever before. Far from an environmental collapse, the future holds the promise of unprecedented prosperity.

growth. In the past quarter-century, however, the harsh realities of the population explosion have forced numerous political leaders to change their minds and introduce population control measures. The same realities are now starting to eat away at the cherished belief in the value of economic growth at any cost.

One of the first widely publicized attacks on the values of growth came from a report published by a group known as the Club of Rome in 1972.[39] Working under the Club's direction, a team of scientists from the Massachusetts Institute of Technology constructed a computerized "world model." By programming the computer with different sets of figures, scientists derived a variety of predictions about the future of the world. All the projections led to the same conclusion—namely, that if humanity is to survive, it must abandon the age-old idea that growth is necessarily a good thing.

Numerous scientists have come to accept the idea that unless we change our attitudes and behavior, the world is headed for an ecological disaster. As a group they are known as **neo-Malthusians**, after the famous demographer Thomas Robert Malthus (see Chapter 16). But businesspeople and industrialists, as well as average workers, are usually skeptical about such gloomy predictions and reluctant to abandon the ideal of growth that has been profitable for so long. The scientists who hold this perspective are known as **cornucopians**, and they argue that by the time our resources are gone, we will have found new resources and new technologies to keep the economy growing.[40] It is impossible to prove or disprove either set of claims. But it appears extremely unwise to continue using up our resources at the present rate, thus gambling our future on possible technological advances that may never occur.

Culture Rapid population growth and increasing use of exploitive technologies are the direct causes of the environmental crisis. But underlying them both are culturally based attitudes toward nature and humanity's place in it. As was already noted, one fundamental characteristic of Western culture is the idea that humans are superior to the natural world they inhabit. According to the Book of Genesis, humans were made in the image of God, who told them, "Be fruitful, and multiply, and replenish the earth and subdue it; and have dominion over the fish of the sea, and over the birds of the sky, and over every living thing that moves upon the earth." Western culture tends to see nature as a wilderness to be conquered and subdued by human effort. The art, literature, and folktales of the West repeatedly show people in heroic struggles against the forces of nature.

The attitudes of most tribal peoples are quite different. In tribal cultures human beings are seen as part of nature. They are expected to live in harmony with their environment, not to subdue or conquer it. American Indians, Australian aborigines, and many other peoples see all of nature as sacred: the rocks, the trees, the mountains, the animals. To them, the Europeans' assault on the environment is not merely unwise; it is sacrilege: the desecration of a holy place.

The attitude that nature is something to be subdued and exploited has been overlaid with newer beliefs in progress and materialism. The people of many ancient civilizations believed that the past contained some lost utopia, and they looked to the past for guidance in making important decisions. But a radically different idea took hold in seventeenth-century Europe. In this new perspective the golden era lies in the future, when scientific progress will banish poverty, ignorance, disease, and perhaps even death itself. Thus, the faster technological development and economic growth take place, the sooner the new utopia will appear. But such optimism about the future has been hard to sustain in a century that has seen the two most devastating wars in human history, the development and use of nuclear weapons, and the extermination of countless species of plants and animals. Many people, however, still see little choice but to continue down the perilous path of "progress."

Although our faith in progress may be shaken, our materialism seems stronger than ever. Day after day we are bombarded with advertising that tells us that we are what we own. A woman is judged by her clothes and jewelry, and a man by the car he drives. A society that sees the road to happiness in wealth and the accumulation of material possessions is hardly likely to value the environment over the economic rewards its destruction may bring.

It is easy to see how these attitudes have led to our current crisis. We have mastered some living things but destroyed others. We have transformed the natural world in our quest for wealth and progress, but we have not conquered it. Sooner or later we will inevitably pay the price for abusing the web of life on which we all depend.

RESPONDING TO ENVIRONMENTAL PROBLEMS

Pollution, energy consumption, and economic growth are interdependent problems. Effective programs for dealing with one of them often aggravate the others. For example, devices that clean automobile exhaust and reduce air pollution also decrease fuel economy, thereby using up our limited oil reserves more rapidly. Exploiting new reserves of fossil fuel worsens environmental pollution, as land, animals, and scenery are sacrificed for strip mines and oil wells, and the wastes produced by the fuel are dumped into the environment. But ignoring the need for more energy retards the economy, thereby contributing to unemployment and possibly reducing food production. There is a way out of this trap, however. In a word, it is sacrifice. The fact is that there is no way to clean up the environment and conserve natural resources without changing the life style of people in the industrialized nations. The challenge is that of motivating people to make the necessary changes now, before a worldwide disaster forces much more difficult adjustments upon us.

Political Action   In North America, it was the observance of Earth Day on April 22, 1970, that first brought the environmental crisis to public attention. As a result of the unprecedented media attention this event received, membership in environmental organizations skyrocketed. The pressure from these groups and the publicity created by a seemingly endless string of environmental disasters helped win the passage of new legislation aimed at protecting North America's air, land, and water. Many hope that the 1992 Earth Summit in Rio de Janeiro, which brought together political leaders and environmental activists from around the world, will help start a new era of international cooperation and environmental concern. But many formidable obstacles stand in the way. From the smallest decisions over local land use to overriding global concerns about the greenhouse effect and the depletion of the ozone layer, environmentalists face powerful foes who reap huge profits from their environmentally destructive activities. And those profits in turn provide the opponents of environmental protection with enormous financial resources to make campaign contributions, hire lobbyists, fund scientific research, purchase advertising, and pay for hundreds of other things that the defenders of the environment simply cannot afford. Moreover, environmentally destructive patterns of behavior are already deeply ingrained in modern society, and will require a great effort to change.

There are, however, grounds for optimism in the fact that the world's people are becoming increasingly aware of the current crisis and the ways in which their prosperity and even their survival depend on the environment. For example, pollster Louis Harris concluded in 1987 that the American public has consistently shown a "deep worry, and concern about the ecological state of the country."[41] When asked if factories should be required to install the best possible antipollution systems even if it costs jobs, two-thirds of Americans polled said yes. And more than 80 percent felt that a factory that has been shown to produce dangerous pollution should be required to install antipollution devices, even if it means that the owners will lose money, that the workers will lose jobs, or that the whole factory will have to be shut down.[42] A 1992 poll by the Gallup International Institute found much the same attitudes around the world. The majority of people in 16 of the 22 nations studied (including such poor countries as Mexico, Brazil, and India) said they would be willing to pay higher prices for what they buy in order to protect the environment.[43]

If we are to preserve the natural environment for ourselves and the generations to come, two important steps must first be taken. First, a stronger educational campaign must be launched to spread awareness of the environmental crisis. Second, people from around the world must join together and get involved in the political and social actions necessary to bring about meaningful change.

Conserving Resources   There is no doubt that our existing resources can be used far more efficiently. Just as the necessities of life are used by one organism after another in various ecological cycles, so human society could reuse many of its essential raw materials over and over. To take a simple example, garbage could be used as fuel to run mills to make recycled paper, the wastes from which could also be burned as fuel. Similarly, it is possible that community water districts will someday become closed systems, meaning that the water would be used again and again, never being discharged into an ocean or river. Some factories already have such closed systems. It is possible to envision larger closed systems designed so that no industrial material would ever be discarded as either waste or pollution.

Energy conservation can also stretch our natural resources. North Americans waste so much energy that significant amounts of oil, gas, and coal could be saved without lowering our standard of living. Sweden has a higher standard of living than Canada but uses less than half as much energy per person.[44] Insulating homes, driving smaller cars at slower speeds, riding trains and buses instead of driving cars, recycling the heat used in factories, and restricting the manufacture of energy-wasting gadgets are obvious ways of eliminating waste. In addition to developing new technologies that are more energy efficient, we must find ways of persuading people to use the conservation measures that are already available.

Better Technology   Conservation will stretch our energy supplies, but new sources of energy will be needed eventually. We have already mentioned proposals for more nuclear, hydroelectric, and geothermal power stations. Some scientists are now proposing the development of power plants equipped with nuclear reactors using fusion (the merging of atoms) rather than fission (the splitting of atoms). However, nuclear fusion generates temperatures comparable to those of the sun, and no one knows whether it is possible to control such a powerful force or how safe such a source of power would be.

A growing number of scientists and concerned citizens are coming to see solar power as the best answer to the world's energy problems. Solar power units use the endless supply of energy from the sun, are nonpolluting, and pose no threat of radiation or explosion. Solar energy is already being used on a small scale to heat water, homes, and offices. Most experts are confident that an efficient technology for storing and using the sun's energy can be developed. Considerable effort is being made to find cheap methods of turning sunlight directly into electricity through the use of what are known as photovoltaic cells. Other promising approaches use specially prepared ponds of water to trap solar energy or mirrors to concentrate it on a single location where it can be used to generate electrical power. There are also many indirect forms of solar energy that can be tapped for human purposes. Power generated by wind, ocean tides, rivers, and dams all depend on the sun, and they all offer environmentally sound alternatives to our current dependence on burning fossil fuels. Such technology is an imitation of nature, since nearly all the energy in natural ecosystems ultimately comes from the sun.[45]

Limiting Growth   Technological solutions are attractive, but it is doubtful that they alone can resolve the environmental crisis. Any effective response to the environmental crisis must include some form of population control. If the world's population keeps on doubling every 40 or 45 years, there is bound to be more pollution and an ever-increasing drain on natural resources. Restrictions on unplanned economic growth

These New York apartments use solar power to heat their water. Because solar energy is clean and virtually limitless, it is one of the brightest prospects for our energy future.

will be needed as well. It seems inescapable that the wrong kind of economic growth means faster depletion of resources and more pollution.

It is often argued that industrial growth is necessary to create new jobs for a growing population, but those who make this argument tend to ignore many other possible solutions. These include creating service jobs or working fewer hours a week in order to distribute the existing jobs among more people. Advocates of a decentralized solar technology point out that installing and maintaining solar collectors in millions of homes and offices would create far more jobs than the highly centralized technology based on burning fossil fuels that we now use. The argument that economic growth is necessary to eliminate poverty and create a more egalitarian society is also misleading. Despite decades of rapid economic growth, the industrialized nations continue to show enormous inequalities of wealth and power. The most egalitarian societies are those that depend on simple hunting and gathering technologies. This does not mean that the answer to the environmental crisis is for everyone to return to hunting and gathering; the world's current population is far too large even to consider such an idea. But it does seem likely that the world would be more peaceful and more secure if the people of the industrialized nations learned to accept a more leisurely life style and a lower standard of living, while encouraging economic growth in the Third World.

SOCIOLOGICAL PERSPECTIVES ON THE ENVIRONMENT

Pollution of the air and water, degradation of the land, and wasteful use of oil and other natural resources seem to be topics for engineers, biologists, and geologists to ponder. But environmental issues are also sociological issues. Sociologists take the broad view, repeatedly pointing out that social institutions are organized systems similar to the ecosystems of nature; that one must understand interacting physical, biological, economic, political, and psychological conditions if one is to understand collective human behavior; and that purposive human actions have unanticipated consequences. In short, sociologists try to teach people to understand that few human problems are as simple as they seem. The origins of the environmental crisis are not to be found in a few polluting industries but in the basic social organization and cultural outlook of the modern world.

The Functionalist Perspective   Functionalists see today's environmental problems as latent dysfunctions of industrialization. Most of the technological advances that help society perform its basic functions easily and efficiently have had negative side effects as well. The manufacturing, distributing, and consuming processes that make increases in our standard of living possible also produce undesirable by-products: pollution and resource depletion. Thus, the economic changes that helped create modern industrial society also threw the environment out of balance and created our current problems.

To many functionalists, the answer to our environmental problems is simple: the dysfunctions of the industrial economy must be reduced through more efficient pollution control and through new technological improvements that will produce more energy and utilize new raw materials. Thus, the environmental crisis is best solved by refining and improving our present way of doing things, not by making basic changes in our social and economic system. Most functionalists are therefore cornucopians: they believe that the solution to the problems of modern technology is more and better technology.

However, other functionalists disagree, arguing that the present industrial economy is inherently unstable because it depends on steady growth to maintain economic prosperity, yet is using up the resources that are necessary for that growth. To this way of thinking, minor reforms cannot solve our environmental problems. Basic changes must be made because many of the central values of our social system have become dysfunctional. At one time, ideas about conquering nature and the importance of constantly increasing our personal wealth inspired the effort necessary for survival. Now, such attitudes threaten human existence because they ignore the long-term effects of the relentless pursuit of wealth by billions of people. The economic system is thus dysfunctional because it wastes resources and pollutes the environment in order to produce more than is necessary for the health and well-being of the people. To these functionalists, a solution to the environmental crisis will require major changes in our system of values and a reorganization of society.

The Conflict Perspective   Conflict theorists see exploitation of the environment as just one more result of social exploitation. More specifically, conflict theorists hold that the economic structure of capitalist nations not only depends on the exploitation of the poor by the rich but also on an ever-increasing exploitation of the natural environment. Private businesses must win the competitive struggle for profits if they are to survive, and that places enormous pressure on them to use exploitive technologies to gain quick profits regardless of the environmental costs. Conflict theorists argue that if a firm carried out more responsible policies, it would be driven out of business by less ethical competitors. One solution is obviously for the government to make firms pay for the environmental damage they cause. But conflict theorists point out that the giant corporate polluters are so powerful that they have been able to block the kind of effective environmental programs that are clearly in the interests of the vast majority of the people.

This same pattern of exploitation occurs internationally. According to conflict theorists, the wealthy industrialized nations are using their power to loot the poor nations of their irreplaceable nature resources, thus making the rich nations richer and the poor nations poorer. Now that the less developed nations are finally trying to industrialize, they find that the cheap energy and raw materials that helped develop the wealthy nations are gone (see Figure 17.2).

Conflict theorists insist that to solve the environmental crisis, we must create a new kind of world system based on equality and respect for the dignity of all humans. To stop the exploitation and destruction of our natural environment, we must reverse our priorities and put the welfare of humanity first and profits second. The competitive materialistic orientation that has produced such stunning economic achievements has also degraded us by making material possessions the measure of a person's worth. As long as this orientation, and the economic system that fostered it, continues, conflict theorists argue that we will continue to brutalize both the environment and ourselves.

Social Psychological Perspectives   Clearly, learned attitudes and values are at the root of the environmental crisis. The belief in progress, in materialism, and in our superiority to the natural world are all an important part of the problem. But social psychologists point out that more fundamental patterns of thought are also involved. Most of us evaluate the world in individualistic terms, doing what seems most likely to bring us what we want. Such an approach works fine for one or two isolated individuals, but when a large group all follow the individualistic road to happiness at the same time, the result is likely to be chaos and confusion. Environmental resources are often held in common for use by many people, and it is in the individualistic interest of each to use as much of these resources as possible before someone else does. In a phenomenon often known as the "tragedy of the commons," this individualistic pursuit of self-interest leads to the complete destruction of the resource and long-term harm to everyone.[46]

Such attitudes are learned. According to social psychologists, if we are to deal effectively with our environmental problems, these attitudes must be unlearned by an entire generation. As they are unlearned, new attitudes will take their place. Citizens of the twenty-first century must learn what tribal people have always known:

that our survival as individuals depends on our concern for the interests of the community; that nature is to be regarded with respect and reverence; and that a life style that attempts to achieve harmony with nature is more satisfying than one that attempts to conquer it.

SUMMARY

As exploitive technologies have grown, the by-products of industrialization have fouled the land, air, and water, thus disrupting the delicate web of life on which human existence depends. The science of ecology—the study of the interrelationships between plants, animals, and their environment—has shown that humans are but one part of a complex network of living things.

Humans have had a tremendous impact on natural ecosystems and are now the principal source of change in the biosphere. This interference has produced unintended effects that are harmful to humanity. Air pollution, for example, is a severe health hazard and is causing harmful changes in the world's weather and atmospheric conditions. Despite the world's enormous reserves of water, water pollution both above and below ground is becoming a serious concern. Organic wastes from human sewage and industry are water pollutants, as are the chemical fertilizers and pesticides used extensively in modern farming. Poisonous chemicals such as mercury and arsenic build up in the tissues of one marine animal after another, eventually reaching the humans at the top of the food chain.

Overgrazing, logging, urban sprawl, faulty irrigation, strip mining, and poor farming techniques have combined to deface the land. Over the years, forests have steadily shrunk as deserts, wastelands, and cities have grown. Further, the chemicals used in business and industry are being dumped on the land, in the water, and in the air. Although radiation pollution is not a major problem now, there is growing concern that nuclear reactors will foul the environment with cancer-causing waste.

The modern industrial economy is rapidly using up the world's irreplaceable natural resources. Many scientists estimate that the world's supply of oil and natural gas will be depleted in less than a century. Coal is more abundant, but even our coal reserves can supply the world's energy needs for only a limited period of time. Increasing emphasis is being placed on nuclear power, but the uranium that fuels nuclear reactors is another scarce natural substance that is not renewable, and there are growing doubts about the safety and high costs of nuclear power.

The complex causes of the environmental crisis have roots stretching far back in human history. Technology has become highly exploitive, using large amounts of energy and natural resources and producing a large volume of pollution in the process. The growth of the total human population and economic growth in the industrialized nations severely aggravate the problem. Underlying these conditions are three basic cultural attitudes: the belief in progress, the belief in materialism, and the idea that nature is something for humans to subdue and exploit.

The current concern about environmental problems first developed in the 1970s. The environmental movement met with some success, but government programs have often been stymied by powerful corporate polluters, and stiffer laws and more rigorous enforcement are needed. Many programs for using existing resources more efficiently have also been proposed. Among them are recycling and education about how to avoid waste. Although conservation will stretch energy supplies, new sources of energy will eventually be needed. Many scientists believe that solar energy offers the brightest hope for the future. Other proposals for solving this social problem ask for population controls, and still others call for restrictions on economic growth.

Because social institutions resemble the ecosystems of nature, it is logical that sociologists should show concern for the interaction between human systems and environmental systems. Functionalists see environmental problems as latent dysfunctions of the industrial revolution, because the attitudes that inspired the explosion of economic growth are no longer functional. Conflict theorists see exploitation of the environment as part of a continuing struggle between the rich and the poor. They note that profits have been given a higher priority than human welfare, and they call for a reversal of these priorities. Social psychologists have identified the attitudes and patterns of thought that underlie the environmental crisis. Such attitudes are learned, and if we are to deal effectively with our environmental problems, these attitudes must be unlearned by an entire generation of citizens.

KEY TERMS

biosphere   The life-containing region of the earth; from roughly 200 feet below sea level to about 10,000 feet above it.

cornucopian   Someone who believes that scientific progress will allow continued economic expansion and prosperity despite population growth and the depletion of natural resources.

ecology   The study of the interrelationships among plants, animals, and their environment.

ecosystem   A self-sufficient community of living organisms.

exploitive technology   Technology designed to produce immediate rewards, without regard to its long-term consequences.

greenhouse effect   The increase in the world's temperature caused by atmospheric changes.

neo-Malthusian   Someone who believes we are heading for a crisis resulting from overpopulation, resource depletion, and environmental destruction.

FURTHER READINGS

Lester R. Brown, ed., *The State of the World* (New York: Norton, published yearly). An excellent collection of articles examining current environmental issues that is revised yearly.

G. Tyler Miller, *Living in the Environment: An Introduction to Environmental Science*, 5th ed. (Belmont, Calif.: Wadsworth, 1988). A good general text covering environmental issues.

Norman Myers, ed., *GAIA: An Atlas of Planet Management* (Garden City, N.Y.: Anchor Books, 1984). A fascinating book that combines charts, graphs, maps, and pictures to explore our environmental problems.

Susanna Hecht and Alexander Cockburn, *The Fate of the Forests: Developers, Destroyers, and Defenders of the Amazon* (New York: Verso, 1989). A look at the forces that will determine the fate of the world's largest rain forest.

Michael R. Edelstein, *Contaminated Communities: The Social and Psychological Impact of Residential Toxic Exposure* (Boulder, Colo.: Westview Press, 1988). An examination of the human impact of the exposure to toxic chemicals.

chapter 18

Warfare and International Conflict

- What are the differences between international wars and revolutions?
- What are the consequences of war?
- What are the causes of war?
- How does terrorism differ from conventional warfare?
- How can international conflict be prevented?

The mushroom cloud that loomed over Hiroshima on August 6, 1945, irrevocably changed the course of human history. Until that day, warfare was commonly considered an unavoidable evil like droughts, famines, and plagues. But the dawn of the nuclear age has forced the world to change its attitude. The means for our own destruction are at hand, and the realization is spreading that future international conflicts must be controlled if the human race is to survive.

Yet despite the harsh realities of the nuclear age, it is far from certain that we will change our ways in time to head off a global catastrophe. The world's leaders always deny that they have any aggressive intentions toward their neighbors. But they all maintain national military forces and all claim the right to use those forces when the interests of their nation require it. Year after year new conflicts break out, while many of the old ones remain unresolved; and the world appears to be a simmering caldron of conflict and hatreds.

THE NATURE OF WAR

Although warfare goes back to the earliest recorded history, it is difficult to define precisely. Part of the problem is that the difference between war and peace is a matter of degree. Everyone will agree that World War II deserves to be called a war and that a typical murder does not. But what about an ethnic riot in which two groups throw rocks and insults at each other? What if they throw hand grenades and bullets? To qualify as a war, such incidents must be organized, violent, and last over a reasonably long period of time. Thus, **war** may be defined as a protracted military conflict between two or more organized groups. This definition still does not tell us, however, exactly how long or how violent these conflicts must be to qualify as a war. Wars are classified in many different ways, but for sociological understanding, a simple division between **international wars** and **revolutionary wars** is most useful. The former are armed conflicts between governments of two or more sovereign nations. The latter are armed conflicts between an official government and one or more groups of national rebels.

THE ESCALATION
OF MILITARY VIOLENCE

Throughout human history, war has been the rule and peace the exception. Melvin Small and J. David Singer's study of warfare from 1816 to 1980 found only 20 years in which there were no international wars in progress.[1] This century alone has seen two "world" wars and dozens of lesser conflicts. Even in the most peaceful times, the next war is seldom far away. There are so many international and national tensions, and the traditions of warfare are so deeply entrenched, that the world is likely to show this pattern of almost constant warfare for years to come.

Although history records a seemingly endless series of wars, the nature of those conflicts has changed significantly over the years. Traditionally, wars were limited. They usually aimed to achieve fairly narrow objectives, such as seizing part of a neighboring ruler's territory. A small group of military men, who were ordinarily from wealthy and privileged backgrounds, did most of the fighting. In fact, these professional soldiers actually had far more in common with the enemies they fought than with the average men and women who watched from the sidelines. The behavior of soldiers in battle was often regulated by a code of gallantry, and those who did not conform ran the risk of losing honor in the eyes of their comrades.

Modern warfare, starting with Napoleon (Emperor of France, 1805–1815), has been marked by a steady escalation of violence. Modern warfare is often total war— an all-out national effort to kill or subdue enemy civilians and soldiers alike. Today's armies are no longer made up solely of professional soldiers and privileged elites; most soldiers are now average citizens, often drafted against their will. Civilians now have a key role in the military effort: manufacturing ball bearings, producing oil, growing food. In modern warfare, victorious nations are those with the greatest productive capacity. It follows that civilians contributing to such production are prime military targets. The tremendous range and destructiveness of modern weapons have moved most civilians into the combat zone.

Over the years we have invented more and more efficient ways of killing our enemies at longer distances. The spear was replaced by the bow and arrow, which became the crossbow. The musket developed into the cannon, the rifle, and the machine gun. In World War I (1914–1918) the cannon and rifle were fused into the long rifle, a huge gun that enabled the Germans to shell Paris from a distance of 75 miles. The hand grenade of World War I became the bomb of World War II, dropped from high-flying airplanes a thousand miles from their base. The TNT bomb gave way

The frightening power of modern military technology has made it possible to wreak destruction in any part of the world at a moment's notice.

to the atom bomb, and the bomber was replaced with the guided missile.[2] Now a military force can wreak destruction virtually anywhere in the world at any time.

Some people consider this tremendous destructive power an instrument of peace. At a minimum, it makes total war less appealing, since even the victors in a nuclear war are likely to suffer terrible devastation. Although modern nations are organized for total war, the wars that have occurred since the development of nuclear weapons have been confined to limited areas, as in Korea, Southeast Asia, and the Middle East. It appears that fear of a nuclear war has headed off global conflict. Nevertheless, the possibility remains that such limitations will be broken. All-out nuclear war remains a constant threat to human survival.

One of the main reasons that this threat remains so strong is **nuclear proliferation**: the spread of nuclear weapons to more and more nations around the world. At the dawn of the nuclear age, only the United States had these frightening weapons. But the Soviet Union, Britain, and France soon developed their own atomic bombs. Then, for a few years, nuclear weapons were exclusively in the hands of the major industrial powers. But in the 1960s China developed its own atomic bomb, and it was soon followed by its neighbor to the south, India, which admits having tested a nuclear bomb but denies having produced any more. However, Western experts believe that India now has between 12 and 20 nuclear weapons. It also seems certain that Israel has a large stockpile of nuclear weapons (probably over 100), since an Israeli nuclear technician, Mordechai Vanunu, published photographs of the inside of the Israeli nuclear weapons plant. Although the Israeli government still denies that it possesses nuclear weapons, Vanunu was subsequently kidnapped by Israeli agents and sentenced to 18 years in prison.[3] Although the evidence is less conclusive, it appears that one of Israel's Muslim enemies, Pakistan, has nuclear capability and that South Africa may have as many as 20 nuclear devices.[4]

It is becoming increasingly clear that the "peaceful" nuclear power plants and technical know-how that the United States, Canada, and other Western powers have sold to nations around the world have made it far easier for these nations to make nuclear bombs. And as more nations develop their own nuclear weapons, it seems almost inevitable that someone, somewhere, will use them.

THE CONSEQUENCES OF WAR

Human history is filled with the carnage of war. Small and Singer concluded that there have been an average of 7.9 international and 6.4 revolutionary wars every decade for the last 165 years.[5] And these wars have reaped a staggering toll in human lives. In the last two centuries, wars have killed over 150 million people.[6] The battles of World War II alone are believed to have cost about 15 million lives, and when civilian casualties are added in, the total comes to almost 48 million deaths.[7] But the dead are not the only victims. Every war leaves a human legacy of the maimed and crippled, widows, grieving parents, and orphans.

Economically, the price tag for even a small war is astronomical. Property worth hundreds of millions of dollars has often been destroyed in a single day. Military technology has made it possible to transform a thriving community into a pile of rubble in a matter of seconds. But even if there were no loss of property, the costs of war are still enormous. Businesses fail; production of consumer goods slows down or stops; fields go unplanted and crops unharvested for want of labor. Many nations have plunged from affluence to starvation during a single war.

Even in times of peace, we pay a price for war. World expenditures for arms were over a *trillion dollars* in 1988 (see Figure 18.1). Of this amount, about 16 percent was spent by underdeveloped nations that often have trouble just feeding their people.[8] These figures are so large that they are difficult to grasp. There are a number of ways to put them in perspective. We could, for example, build 12,000 high schools for the cost of a single aircraft carrier. The cost of developing one new bomber would pay the yearly salaries of one-quarter of a million teachers to staff those schools, and the cost of building just 14 jet bombers would provide free lunches for 14 million students. Yet as huge as these military costs seem to us, they are an even heavier burden to the poor countries, where money spent on human needs goes much further. The cost of one tank, a relatively low-priced piece of military hardware in the industrialized world, could buy 1,000 classrooms in a Third World nation. And some experts believe that we could eradicate malaria with the money the world spends on the military in just 12 hours.[9]

Some economists argue that the enormous outlays for military spending are beneficial because they create jobs and stimulate the economy. This might be true. But if it is true, it also follows that much greater benefits would be reaped if the money were spent on goods and services that are economically useful. A nation is no better off economically with a thousand nuclear missiles than it is with one, but a nation is much better off with a thousand hydroelectric power plants than with only one. The two developed countries with the healthiest and fastest-growing economies, Germany and Japan, both have small armed forces and low military budgets.[10]

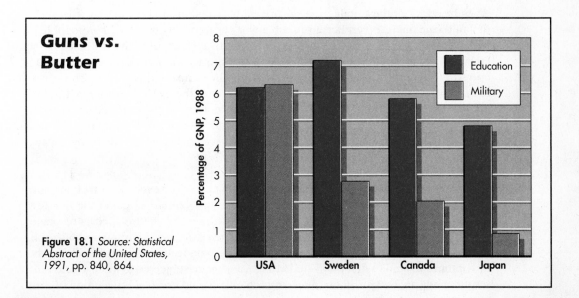

Guns vs. Butter

Percentage of GNP, 1988

Education
Military

USA   Sweden   Canada   Japan

Figure 18.1 *Source: Statistical Abstract of the United States, 1991, pp. 840, 864.*

These cows belonged to a dairy farm destroyed by burning oil wells intentionally set afire during the war in the Persian Gulf. The fires illustrated the environmental havoc modern warfare can create.

As heavy as all these military costs are, they are minuscule compared with those of a full-scale nuclear war. Because such a war has never occurred, it is impossible to be sure what would actually happen. But scientists have been able to make some educated guesses. The best source of data are the two atomic explosions that occurred in populated areas: the U.S. attacks on Hiroshima and Nagasaki. Those two bombs killed 110,000 people in the first seconds after the blast, and another 100,000 people died within a year. Tens of thousands more were severely injured, and people are still dying from the long-term effects of radiation poisoning. Despite this horrible toll, the bombs dropped on those two cities were small and primitive by today's standards. There are about *53,000* nuclear warheads in the hands of the world's governments today, and some of them are over *4,000 times* more powerful than the bombs dropped on Japan.[11] Scientists estimate that a nuclear exchange involving only about one-third of those weapons would kill over one billion people in the first few hours. As clouds of radiation spread throughout the globe, entire species of plants and animals would die, along with 50 to 75 percent of the world's human population.

Grim as this scenario is, many scientists are coming to believe that it still may be too optimistic. Studies first published in 1983 and since subjected to intense scientific scrutiny indicate that an all-out nuclear exchange would create a huge cloud of dust and smoke that would cover the globe. Estimates based on studies of much smaller clouds released by volcanic eruptions suggest that some 96 percent of the sunlight normally reaching the Northern Hemisphere would be blocked out. The result would be a **nuclear winter** in which the average temperature, even in warm areas, would drop below freezing for several months. The lack of sunlight and plummeting temperatures would have a devastating effect on the plants and animals that produce our food, perhaps changing the ecological system of the earth in an irreversible way.[12]

The threat of an all-out nuclear war is a nightmare that has haunted humanity for almost half a century. But many feel that more limited military conflicts can still have beneficial effects. The most obvious is the overthrow of oppressive and unjust governments. For example, both Germany and Japan developed stable democratic states after their totalitarian regimes were destroyed in World War II. Although some argue that even the most ruthless dictatorship can be changed by nonviolent resistance, most people doubt that such tactics would have been successful against the bloodthirsty tyrants that fill the pages of the history books. Warfare can also promote the solidarity of a nation or some of the groups within it. And it has often been a stimulant to scientific and technological progress.[13]

There are, nonetheless, many other ways of acquiring the benefits of war without paying its staggering costs. Technology has, as we have seen, brought great increases in the costs of war and reduced its benefits. Since it is quite possible that no human beings would survive an all-out nuclear conflict, the ancient practice of warfare can only be seen as a menacing social problem of the greatest magnitude for the modern world.

TERRORISM

Although politicians and journalists talk with great authority about the problem of terrorism, the concept is usually vaguely defined and its application charged with political bias. Even social scientists have had little success in agreeing on a definition. One review of the literature found over 100 different definitions, often with substantial differences in the kinds of acts they included.[14] Most students of terrorism would agree that it must involve violence used for political ends. But as it stands, such a definition is far too broad, for it would include everything from total war to everyday police work. Many proposals have been made to narrow the definition down, but there is no agreement about which one is best. Perhaps one of the problems is that terrorism is used primarily as an emotional label to brand political acts we dislike, so that scientific definitions are largely beside the point. Those groups we support are "freedom fighters" and those we oppose are "terrorists." From a sociological perspective, it would probably be better to dispose of the concept of terrorism altogether and simply consider such acts as one more form of political violence, but the term seems to have become too popular in the media and the political arena to ignore.

Despite the vagueness of its definition, it is possible to distinguish two general types of terrorism. The best known is **revolutionary terrorism**. It is used by groups trying to bring about major political changes in a particular country. Some such groups believe that random terrorist attacks will create such chaos that the government they oppose will fall, or at least will meet their demands. Terrorists often try to goad a

Although acts of revolutionary terrorism, like this hijacking of a TWA plane to Beirut, receive the most publicity, repressive terrorism that governments direct against their own people actually cause far more deaths and injuries.

government into taking such extreme measures to combat them that it will lose popular support. Underground groups also hope that their acts of violence will make the public more aware of their cause, enabling them to recruit more members and build stronger popular support. Some of today's more sophisticated terrorists openly cultivate reporters and other representatives of the media by granting special interviews, releasing prepared statements for the press, and holding open press conferences. Some terrorists even time their attacks to avoid other newsworthy events that might compete for media attention.[15] Revolutionary terrorists often secretly receive the help of established governments that support their goals and objectives.

Repressive terrorism is the opposite of revolutionary terrorism, in that its goal is to protect an existing political order. Although revolutionary terrorists receive most of the publicity, repressive terrorism is probably a far greater threat. Governments all over the world—from South Africa to the People's Republic of China—use violence to terrorize their political opponents and maintain their grip on power. Time after time, the opponents of Third World leaders disappear and are never seen again. Torture and imprisonment without just cause are also common tools of repressive terrorists. The most extreme example since the end of World War II occurred in the small country of Cambodia (now known as Kampuchea), where about two million of its citizens were killed in less than four years.[16] Although the scale of the violence in Cambodia was unusual, repressive terrorism is a fact of political life in most of the nations of the world today.

Many experts fear that revolutionary terrorists might someday build or steal nuclear weapons. No one has ever used nuclear terrorism, but it remains a disturbing possibility. For a group that has a supply of the right fuel, a nuclear bomb is relatively simple to build. With such a weapon, a band of revolutionary terrorists would gain enormous power. Nuclear weapons are less suited to repressive terrorism. Still, a government controlled by a small and unpopular minority, such as South Africa's, might conceivably use such weapons against its own population. In the modern world, nuclear weapons are the ultimate source of terror.

THE CAUSES OF WARFARE

Many people believe that warfare is part of human nature. The same "aggressive instinct" that is said to make us violent is also said to lead inevitably to war. However, there is a great deal of evidence that this is not the case. Most important is the fact that the people of some cultures have never gone to war. As Marvin Harris, a noted anthropologist, put it:

> Although humans may have aggressive tendencies, there is no reason that such tendencies cannot be suppressed, controlled or expressed in ways other than by armed combat. . . . There is no instinct for war. War is found only to the extent that it is advantageous for some of the combatants.[17]

Another common approach seeks to find the causes of a particular war in the specific acts that set it off and the leaders who make the key decisions. It may be argued, for example, that if Hitler had not been born, World War II would never have happened. Since it is impossible to rerun history, there is no way of proving or disproving such claims. But it does appear that individual decisions have made the difference between war and peace in some cases. During the Cuban missile crisis of 1962, for example, the world seemed to be teetering on the brink of a nuclear war. The leaders of the United States and the Soviet Union made decisions that averted war, but one leader could well have plunged the world into a holocaust. Even so, this approach explains only the superficial causes of warfare. Certain social conditions must be present before war is possible. If the United States and the Soviet Union had not had enormous military machines and the willingness to fight, no conflict could have taken place, no matter what the decisions of their leaders.

Revolutionary Warfare   Revolutions are romantic. They have given us some of the most dramatic episodes in human history. The revolutionary theme—a small group of freedom-loving patriots fighting against overwhelming odds—has captured the imagination of countless writers and artists. Even American cowboy stories show plain and simple folk in heroic struggles against land barons and railroad tycoons. Several theories help make sense of revolutions—but these theories are far from perfect. All the conditions that are said to cause revolutions are sometimes present in societies in which no revolutionary conflict takes place, and revolutions sometimes take place in societies that lack the important characteristics mentioned by the theorists. The unique cultural traditions of individual societies play an important part in revolutionary struggles, as does the influence of individual leaders.

Exploitation and Oppression One of the earliest and most influential theories of revolution was formulated by Karl Marx and Friedrich Engels.[18] They believed that the injustices of capitalism would produce a worldwide revolution. As the workers in capitalist nations sank deeper and deeper into poverty and personal alienation, they would eventually come to realize that they were being exploited by the owners of the factories in which they worked. The workers would then band together, overthrow their oppressors in a violent revolution, and create a classless utopia with liberty and justice for all.

The Marxist theory of revolution is almost a century and a half old, and the revolutionary movement it predicted has not occurred. The revolutions fought in the name of Marxism in China, Russia, Cuba, and elsewhere did not happen the way Marx's theory predicted and did not produce anything like the communist utopia he described. Nevertheless, many Marxists and non-Marxists alike still believe that exploitation and oppression of the lower classes may eventually produce revolutionary action. Less accepted is Marx's idea that such a revolution will necessarily destroy capitalism and create a new, utopian economic system.

Relative Deprivation Considerable research since Marx's time suggests that it is relative poverty, not absolute poverty, that sparks revolutions. According to **relative-deprivation theory**, revolutions are caused by differences between what people have and what they think they should have.

James C. Davies, one of the leading exponents of this theory, presented some interesting data on several major revolutions.[19] He concluded that "revolutions are most likely to occur when a prolonged period of objective economic and social development is followed by a short period of sharp reversal."[20] In other words, the people were actually better off at the start of the revolutions he studied than they had been in previous decades. Apparently, improvement in social conditions creates an expectation of even greater progress. If a sharp downturn occurs and the people are unwilling to reduce either their standard of living or their expectations, they rise up against the government.

Institutions and Resources Psychologically oriented approaches such as relative-deprivation theory hold, in effect, that misery breeds revolt. More recent theorists have argued that to understand why people rise up against their government, we also need to look at the imbalances in the social institutions of their society. Samuel P. Huntington, for example, asserts that the changes created as a country modernizes its economy throw its institutions out of equilibrium. As people become more educated, their desire to become involved in politics increases faster than traditional political institutions can accommodate, and the result may be a revolution.[21]

Charles Tilly responded to Huntington's theory by pointing out that the discontent caused by such institutional imbalances is unlikely to lead to a revolt as long as the discontented remain disorganized and lacking in resources. Arguing that conflict is a normal part of politics, Tilly felt that political violence is likely to occur only when dissatisfied groups are able to mobilize enough resources to mount a significant challenge to the existing government.[22]

Failure of the Government Studies of the world's great revolutions show that the people who ran the governments that were overthrown had been doing a very poor job of it. Crane Brinton's study of American, British, French, and Russian revolutions concluded, for example, that the old ruling class in all these societies was "divided and inept."[23] The authorities seemed to make the wrong decisions and then overreact or underreact to the beginnings of revolutionary ferment. Brinton also showed that these prerevolutionary governments were teetering on the verge of bankruptcy, although the economies of their societies were reasonably sound.[24]

Theda Skocpol, among other current theorists, emphasizes the fact that governments do not always reflect the interests of the social elite of their society.[25] Often, the government and its top officials have special interests of their own that conflict with those of elite groups. For example, governments often become enmeshed in the game of international power politics, and the cost of the wars it creates may threaten the welfare of substantial segments of the elite. When this occurs, the likelihood of an armed revolt is greatly increased, especially when elite groups have sufficient resources to mount a credible challenge to government forces.

Partitions and Divisions Virtually all sociologists who have studied the subject agree that class conflict precedes many revolutions. Before a revolution, the various social classes come to view one another as hostile economic competitors. The English and French revolutions, for example, were fueled by the revolt of the merchants and traders against the feudal aristocracy.

Another major source of revolutionary conflict involves geographic and ethnic differences. Regional differences were, for example, a major factor in the American Civil War. History is also full of examples of revolts by an ethnic group in one part of a nation against its central government. When a rebellious group wins control of an entire region, these conflicts are similar to international war. Generally, if the rebels are successful, the nation is divided into two or more new countries. Sometimes, however, the rebellious group takes over the entire nation and reverses its relationship with the old dominant group.

International Warfare The causes of revolutionary and international wars are usually quite different, but in some cases the internal conditions conducive to a revolutionary uprising may also contribute to an international war. For example, political leaders who are having trouble at home sometimes stir up an international conflict in an attempt to divert the people's attention from domestic problems. It is said that "nothing makes friends like a common enemy," and such a strategy sometimes reunites a nation. But in the long run the internal problems reemerge, often aggravated by the strains of the international conflict.

Militarism There are two faces of **militarism** which both contribute to international wars. The first is glorification of war. International warfare is obviously more likely when a society sees it as a heroic show of strength or when young people see it as a path to personal fame and fortune. Such attitudes are still common in the nuclear age, but they seem to be on the decline. The growth of complex military technology has taken the glory out of person-to-person combat, and the fear of nuclear annihilation has quieted the cheers of civilians.

The second face of militarism is the demand for enormous "defensive" forces. With an apparent decline in justifications of war for its own sake, there seems to have been an increase in national desires to deter and ward off aggressors. These desires are reflected in enormous military budgets and constant preparation for war. Nations that devote major parts of their economies to military purposes now claim that they are doing so merely for defensive purposes. But the line between aggression and defense is fuzzy, as is indicated by the United States' "defense" of itself by moving into Vietnam or by the Soviet Union's "defense" of itself by moving into Afghanistan. The idea that the strength and integrity of a nation depend on military superiority over its competitors often leads a country to a frantic effort to build up its military forces faster than its enemies. Such an arms race usually increases rather than decreases a nation's sense of insecurity and has often led to major international conflicts.[26]

Nationalism and Ideology Like patriotism, **nationalism** is a sense of identification with and devotion to one's nation. In the past, growing nationalism discouraged local wars by unifying petty feudal kingdoms into larger and more stable national units. In the

Nationalism was an important part of the motivation for Nazi Germany's attempt to conquer Europe in World War II.

19th-Century Social Problems

The crushing of Admiral Cevera's fleet [at Santiago] has had a beneficial effect on the lumber market. . . . A large number of Eastern buyers are negotiating some large purchases at Marinette. Hayes and Company bought 2,000,000 feet of good lumber from Marinette growers.

July 21, 1898

These selections, which appear throughout the text, are from the *Badger State Banner*, a newspaper published in Black River Falls, Wisconsin.

modern world, however, unthinking nationalism all too often produces the opposite result.[27] Many wars have been fought over some petty incident that was interpreted as an affront to "national honor." Rational settlements based on fair compromise are difficult when nationalistic feelings are involved. After all, what wise politician would dare compromise his or her nation's honor? Nationalism is also a critical part of the motivation for **imperialism** (the creation or expansion of an empire). As Quincy Wright pointed out in his classic study of war, some wars arise "because of the tendency of a people affected by nationalism . . . to acquire an attitude of superiority to some or all other peoples, to seek to extend its cultural characteristics throughout the world, and to ignore the claims of other states and of the world community."[28]

Nationalism is not, however, the only kind of ideology that can stimulate violent confrontations. Sometimes the conflict between secular political ideologies such as Marxism and capitalism has led to full-scale war, but religion has more often played this role. From the European Crusades to the conflicts in the Middle East in our time, the belief that one must protect and expand one's faith by force of arms has sent millions of people off to war.

Economic Gain Most wars are fought for profit. One nation may attack another in an attempt to capture valuable natural resources, desirable land, or cheap labor. Sometimes an entire nation reaps economic advantages from its conquests, but more often only a small segment of a society benefits from a war. Some people stand to gain from an outbreak of almost any sort of war—for example, high-ranking military officers and those who supply the arms and materials necessary to keep a war going. Other interest groups may profit from a war if it helps secure beneficial resources; exporters profit from the conquest of a new seaport, while farmers gain by winning access to valuable land or water. Although its political leaders gave various justifications, it is clear that Iraq's invasion of Kuwait in 1990 was prompted by the desire to gain a better port on the Persian Gulf and to seize Kuwait's rich oil fields. Similarly, the American-led invasion that freed Kuwait was justified on many idealistic grounds, but it was primarily motivated by the desire to protect the industrialized world's supply of low-cost petroleum.

It appears, however, that modern warfare has made it difficult for any nation as a whole to profit from an international war. As Kurt Finsterbusch and H. C. Greisman put it:

> Not only have the costs of wars increased greatly because of the vastly improved technology of devastation and the practice of total warfare, the benefits have also declined decidedly. Wars no longer gain booty, spoils or tribute; and they infrequently gain economic concessions.[29]

International Political Organization In many ways, the most basic cause of international war is the way in which the world is politically organized. Our planet is divided into hundreds of sovereign states, most of which have their own military forces and a belief in their right to use them to protect or advance their national interests. With so many different governments and so many different armies, it is no surprise that international wars are frequent. Indeed, the threat of war is often just one more chip in the pokerlike political bargaining between nations. In the famous phrase of the nineteenth-century military strategist Karl von Clausewitz, "War is nothing but a continuation of political intercourse, with a mixture of other means."[30]

But despite appearances to the contrary, the nations of the world do not act like a pack of gunslingers in the Old West. There is a delicate and long-standing balance of power among the nations in the world system. Although it is often claimed that peace is most likely when there is rough equality among the groups of nations competing for power, A. F. K. Organski and Jacek Kugler found just the opposite to be true.[31] According to their research, peace is most likely when one power is clearly dominant and the others are afraid to challenge it, as was the case when Britain dominated the world system in the nineteenth century. Major wars break out when a new nation grows stronger than the old leader and upsets the balance.

PREVENTING WAR AND INTERNATIONAL CONFLICT

People have long dreamed of creating a world without war. Like other idealistic visions, this one may never come true. It may be that war cannot be altogether eliminated. But it is not too idealistic to believe that international conflict can be reduced in both frequency and scope. Ironically, this optimism is partially justified by the destructive power of military technology. Pacifists who would have been dismissed as head-in-the-clouds dreamers in the past are now given serious attention. Practically every educated person in the world recognizes the incredible destruction that a nuclear war would produce, and political leaders all over the world are trying to ensure that it will never happen.

Deterrence Most military and political leaders assert that the best way to prevent another devastating world war is through **deterrence**. The idea is that our side (whichever one that is) must be so strong that its adversaries will be afraid to attack it. Thus, it is argued that building up a vast military machine actually promotes peace because it improves a nation's capacity to deter potential enemies. In the nuclear age this strategy has become known by a very appropriate acronym: *MAD*, short for *mutual assured destruction*. To guarantee mutual assured destruction, both sides must not only be able to deliver enough nuclear weapons to devastate their opponent but be able to do it even after their opponent has launched a surprise attack and destroyed a good portion of their military forces.

As a strategy to prevent war, deterrence has serious weaknesses. It assumes that important political decisions are made in a cool, rational way. But in fact, nationalistic or religious fervor have often whipped nations into an emotional frenzy and led to an unrealistic belief in their invulnerability to the attacks of foreign enemies. Technology is also a destabilizing factor in the system of deterrence. Innovations in defensive techniques threaten to weaken one side's deterrent threat and touch off a new conflict. Moreover, the massive military forces both sides must keep in constant readiness greatly increase the chances of an accidental war. And even if an armed conflict never breaks out, the constant preparations for war required by the deterrence strategy are extremely expensive. All things considered, it seems obvious that a system of mutual deterrence cannot be counted on to maintain international peace. It is a desperate arrangement among enemies based on fear, not cooperation. Yet trying to maintain a strong deterrent threat seems to be the only thing that many world governments are doing to keep the peace.

Arms Control and Disarmament The advocates of arms control argue that attempting to achieve peace by building up the means to make war is ridiculous. They recommend a balanced reduction in weapons or, ideally, total disarmament and the elimination of all means for making war. But even proposals for relatively minor arms reductions often meet strong opposition. The most obvious obstacle is the lack of trust between competing nations, and the fear that the other side will cheat and hide a secret cache of weapons. But there is also an underlying economic and political issue that diplomats seldom openly admit to: the opposition of what President and career army officer Dwight D. Eisenhower called the "military-industrial complex" (the armed forces and the civilian industries that supply their needs; see Chapter 3).

Arms control agreements are most likely to be reached when the actual threat of war is lowest. In the decades following the end of World War II, when the cold war between the United States and the Soviet Union was at its peak and there was a serious danger of nuclear conflict, only a few minor treaties were signed. But as the communists fell from power and the Soviet Union broke apart, several important agreements were finally reached. Thus, arms control treaties may not head off an impending conflict between enemy states, but they can play an important role in helping those nations to stop seeing each other as enemies.

There is, moreover, another kind of arms control that is desperately needed: the control of the international trade in military equipment. Between $20 and $30 billion in armaments are exported every year and these figures actually underestimate the true size of the arms trade, since they do not include the sale of the equipment and technology that underdeveloped nations purchase in order to manufacture their own weapons.[32] Four of the top five arms importers are Third World nations, and three of those are in the Middle East—one of the world's most unstable regions. An international agreement among the industrialized nations to stop the sale of sophisticated arms and the means to produce them would have several important benefits. First and foremost, it would limit the proliferation of nuclear weapons. After the end of the Persian Gulf War in early 1991, the western powers discovered that Saddam Hussein's totalitarian regime in Iraq was much closer to producing its own nuclear weapons than anyone had previously believed. If the international community does not ban the sale of nuclear technology and equipment, the next time the world may not be as lucky as it was with Iraq. A second major benefit of curbing arms equipment exports would be economic. The cost of high-tech weaponry is a major financial drain on many poor countries, and a ban on its sale would free them from the fear that they need to buy such weapons before their neighbors do. Finally, while such an export ban is unlikely to stop new wars from breaking out in the Third World, it could reduce their scope and intensity.

Social Justice   As was pointed out earlier, feelings of resentment among exploited groups are a major factor in uprisings, rebellions, and revolutions. Although it is possible to reduce such resentment without reducing inequality, the best way to prevent revolutionary violence is to change the conditions of inequality that cause the resentment. This seems to be a rather obvious principle, but it is seldom followed, largely because most elites—whether national or international—are either unable or unwilling to use it. Some are unaware that their special status is unjust; others simply don't care. They are indifferent to the need for compromise until it is too late. A stable government depends on **legitimation**: the consent of the governed based on their belief that the governors are just and fair. The more quickly a government moves to rectify just grievances, the more peaceful and secure it will be.

As the world develops into a more tightly knit economic and political community, the causes of international war will increasingly come to resemble the cause of revolutionary wars. The vast inequalities in wealth between the north and south are creating a festering sense of resentment and hostility in the Third World. Citizens of the industrialized countries are beginning to realize that something must be done to improve the standard of living of the world's impoverished masses. Handouts of food and other essential supplies can help stave off immediate disasters, but they are obviously not a long-term solution. Chapter 14 discusses some proposals to help promote the economic growth of the Third World. But whichever approach is used, it is clear that the hunger and desperation of the peoples of the Third World fuel a political instability that is as much a threat to the wealthy nations as to the poor ones.

Encouraging Global Cooperation   In addition to improving the poverty-stricken economies of the Third World, there are many other steps that must be taken to build the foundations for a more peaceful world. Cultural exchanges and direct networks of international communication help promote global understanding. Programs designed to encourage economic cooperation among nations could also build stronger bonds of mutual support and understanding.

Another necessary ingredient in the formula for world peace is international guidance and control. Just as national governments use their power and authority to settle disputes among their citizens, so a world organization could limit conflicts among

Many international organizations, such as the United Nations, are working to promote global cooperation.

nations. Two components are needed in any serious effort to create international controls to prevent war. First is the formulation and acceptance of a body of international law. Like criminal law, international statutes must state what kinds of actions constitute international aggression and then specify punishments for each. The second requirement is an international organization to enforce the law. There must be an arrangement whereby an international body (a "court") decides whether an accused nation has broken the law and punishes the violator.

A framework for international law already exists. The United Nations—and the League of Nations before it—have already created a considerable body of legal codes. The Universal Declaration of Human Rights, for example, is an international equivalent of the Bill of Rights in the Constitution of the United States, and it clearly prohibits the repressive terrorism practiced by so many countries around the world. International law also explicitly forbids aggression by one country against another. Although some of these statutes are vague, they are no less specific than the statutes outlawing murder or manslaughter. As in criminal law, international legal principles and traditions will develop only with experience.[33]

A more fundamental stumbling block to international control over warfare is the difficulty in establishing an organization to enforce international law. Again, the basics

D E B A T E

Is World Government the Way to Eliminate International Warfare?

The United Nations has been an active participant in world politics since it was created at the end of World War II, but it can take action only when it wins consent of all the most influential nations. Some observers, therefore, advocate the creation of a world government with the independent power to stop international aggression and keep the peace.

YES   As long as sovereign nations control their own military forces, there will always be wars. World government is the only solution to this ancient problem. Such a government could curb international wars by limiting each nation's military strength and forcing nations to settle their differences in accordance with international law.

Although it would certainly be difficult to create a world government, critics who say that it cannot be done are wrong. The United Nations has already laid the foundation for world unification. World government would be weak and ineffective at first, but if it were well managed, its strength and unity would grow. There is no basis for the fear that such a government would violate national sovereignty and subject small countries to the domination of large ones. The new government would be a federation of independent states very much like the United States or Canada. Each nation would be permitted to keep some armed forces and to control its domestic affairs. The international government would concern itself only with the economic and political relations between countries in order to promote the common good of all people. Just as the unification of the small feudal states of Europe provided great economic and social benefits for their people, world government would provide similar benefits for the entire human race.

NO   Dreamers and idealists have talked about the need for a world government for centuries, but such an idea is as unrealistic today as it was a hundred years ago. History shows that governments rarely surrender their sovereignty voluntarily. Only the gun and the sword can meld small states into larger ones. The idea that this quarreling planet could be unified peacefully without an international holocaust is hopelessly naive. Can you imagine trying to get the Iranians, Chinese, and Americans to agree on a common government? Getting the whole world to go along would clearly be impossible.

But even if world government were possible, it would be a mistake. No matter how decentralized and limited such a government might be in the beginning, it would inevitably grow larger and more powerful. Because the people of the democratic nations are vastly outnumbered by those who have been raised under totalitarian regimes, a world government would eventually reflect the political traditions of the totalitarian majority. The dictatorial superstate that could be expected to emerge would be vastly more powerful than today's totalitarian regimes, for it would not be hampered by pressure from other, hostile states. Its overwhelming power would leave its opponents no place to hide. Clearly, world government is both an impractical and dangerous idea.

are already in place. The problem is to obtain the consent of the governed. Most nations refuse to give up any of their authority to a global organization because they do not believe in international law. The United Nations has been effective only when its most powerful members were able to agree on a course of action. When they disagree, it becomes obvious that the United Nations has no power of its own. And, unfortunately, there are many good reasons for such disagreements. The resolution of international grievances is such a delicate process that there are bound to be injustices.

Despite these problems, there are signs of hope. The development of advanced technology and changes in the world economy have made nations more dependent on one another than ever before. No modern society can survive entirely on its own resources, and international trade and commerce can help build bonds between nations. For example, William K. Domke found that the more deeply involved a country is in foreign trade, the less likely it is to go to war.[34] As the nations of the world become more and more interdependent, the demand for greater international law and order is likely to grow.

THE PROSPECTS FOR PEACE

Almost everyone seems to have an idea about how to solve the world's political problems, but what are the prospects that the planet really will be more peaceful in the years ahead? To explore this difficult question, we must understand the background of the current world order. Until relatively recently, there was no common world system, because the traditional methods of transportation and communication were simply too slow and inefficient. People from one part of the globe often did not even know of the existence of other civilizations. But the coming of the industrial revolution changed all that, and, in the nineteenth century, Great Britain became the first global power. Britain not only had a far-flung network of colonies that it ruled directly, it exercised unequaled financial and political muscle around the world. As Britain's power waned, the twentieth century saw a struggle for control that produced the two bloodiest conflicts in human history. After the second of the two world wars, Germany and Japan were in ruins, and the United States assumed Britain's position as the world's dominant power. But the United States still had strong opposition from the Soviet Union and the other communist countries. For the next four decades, the communist and capitalist nations were locked in a bitter nuclear standoff. During this cold war, the two sides struggled for control of the poor nations that were finally throwing off the colonial domination of the European powers. But the two superpowers nonetheless managed to avoid the direct military confrontation they knew would destroy them both. (See Chapter 14 for more details on colonialism.)

With the crumbling of Soviet power, the era of the cold war has finally come to an end, and the world now stands at a historic crossroads. Many paths lead to the future, and no one is sure which one we will take. In the most optimistic scenario, the end of the cold war produces a general reduction in political tensions, and the nations of the world accept the obvious fact that international cooperation is in all of their long-term interests. The United Nations and the principles of international law gain increasing support. The wealthy nations recognize that they must help the

Third World in order to prevent a global disaster that would devastate rich and poor alike. The pessimistic scenario, on the other hand, sees a continuation of the short-term nationalistic thinking that has so often prevailed in international relations. The United States goes it alone and is financially and morally drained by its intervention in one Third World crisis after another. The lands formerly ruled by the Soviet Union disintegrate into political chaos and ethnic bloodshed. Their stockpiles of nuclear weapons fall into the control of hostile regional governments, and nuclear weapons and technology are secretly sold to any country that can pay the price. Overpopulation and a deteriorating economy lead an increasing number of Third World nations to turn to militaristic dictators who arm themselves with nuclear weapons, and the inevitable result is a global holocaust. Of course, the world is most likely to follow a course between those two extremes, but it is clear that we face both unique opportunities and unprecedented dangers in the years ahead.

SOCIOLOGICAL PERSPECTIVES ON WARFARE AND INTERNATIONAL CONFLICT

In political science more time and attention are given to warfare than to almost any other single subject. This is not true of sociology or of social science in general. Research on war and military matters is a minor specialty within the sociological discipline. For this reason, the three principal sociological perspectives are not as sharply defined with reference to warfare as they are with reference to, say, crime or poverty. In recent years, however, a great deal of attention has been paid to the economic development of the Third World and to other problems of the world system, and warfare itself is gaining increasing sociological attention.

The Functionalist Perspective Functionalist theory sees international conflict and warfare as an inevitable result of the world's political disorganization. From time immemorial, humanity has been creating political structures that are conducive to warfare. When there are so many large and small countries with so numerous conflicting interests, disagreements are bound to occur. The international organizations set up to handle these disputes simply cannot do the job.

Because of this high degree of international disorganization, war is actually functional: it is the only effective method for settling major international disputes. Warfare also provides short-term psychological and political benefits to individual nations and may function to keep a weak, divided society together for a time. For these reasons, we denounce warfare but nevertheless organize ourselves to retain it. It follows that the best solutions to the problem of international war are those that try to reorganize the world's political system. The primary need is for a program to replace our patchwork of international relations with a genuine world order.

To functionalists, revolutionary warfare arises from a different kind of disorganization. When national systems do not work smoothly and become increasingly dysfunctional, revolution is one possible result. For example, a society might exclude capable people from positions of power and distribute its wealth so unequally that citizens become bitter and resentful. Political organization also becomes dysfunctional when it champions established ways of doing things while the citizens' attitudes, values, and opinions are changing. Such rigidity is sometimes softened by revolution. Functionalists therefore believe that the best way to head off revolutionary conflict is to implement the kinds of gradual reforms already described in the chapters on economics, government, poverty, and ethnic minorities.

The Conflict Perspective Conflict theorists ordinarily do not separate economics and politics. Instead, they speak of "political economy." To them, the world system is not disorganized; it is organized for economic and political exploitation. The powerful capitalist nations buy cheap raw materials and labor from the Third World and in return sell high-cost services and manufactured goods. The result is a steady flow of wealth from the Third World to the industrialized countries, and ever-deepening poverty and desperation among the disadvantaged of the world. In this view, revolutionary wars usually result from the effort of the downtrodden people of a Third World country to throw off the yoke of the rich nations and to topple the local elites who are in league with them.

On the international level, conflict theorists see a vicious struggle for worldwide dominance and the economic rewards it brings. As long as one power or group of allied powers is strong enough to intimidate the rest of the world, we enjoy relative peace. But sooner or later, challengers will arise to question the existing international order. Sometimes they can be accommodated peacefully, but bloody global conflicts, such as the ones in World War I and World War II, are the more common result.

According to the conflict perspective, the best way to eliminate warfare and international conflict is to eliminate oppression, both international and national. Some conflict theorists advocate a system of deterrence, but one in which economic goods and the military power to protect them are distributed equally. Others call for radical economic changes that would make all government unnecessary; in this utopian state, both governments and the wars that they fight would vanish. But conflict theorists are not necessarily against war, at least in the short run. Their position is that conflict is basic to all human societies, and some recommend that collective violence be used to undo economic injustices that are maintained by military power. The ultimate aim of conflict theorists is, nonetheless, a peaceful world with full equality among all peoples.

Social Psychological Perspectives Social psychologists have identified both individual and cultural characteristics that are conducive to warfare. The individual traits, as we have seen, are associated with an assumed instinctual aggressiveness. The cultural traits are clearly learned. Each culture champions a certain "ideal personality," and people are then encouraged in both subtle and open ways to develop personality traits consistent with this ideal. For example, people growing up in cultures that place great importance on honor and pride are likely to encourage warlike national policies, as are people growing up in cultures that emphasize competition and individual aggressiveness. Cultures in which people learn to put a high value on humility and cooperation are much more likely to be peaceful in both national and international affairs.

One's sense of nationalism or internationalism is also learned, as is the ethnocentric belief that one's own culture and social institutions are superior to others. Some people learn to identify so strongly with their country that any international setback is seen as a personal threat. Such people are not likely to encourage a peaceful foreign policy. Even Western religions put emphasis on conquering evil in an aggressive way. War allows people to identify enemies as evil and then win honor, glory, and a sense of righteousness by conquering them.[35]

In the long run, social psychologists say, the only sure way to reduce the frequency of warfare is to emphasize cultural characteristics that favor the peaceful resolution of differences. Rather than glorifying victory over evil, it would be more useful to applaud the rational compromise that heads off deadly conflict. The ideals of nonviolence must be substituted for the glorification of violence that is so common in the mass media and in our everyday lives.

SUMMARY

War can be defined as protracted military conflict between two or more organized groups. Wars can be classified on the basis of the groups involved as international (between independent nations) or revolutionary (between groups within a nation).

Through the years, warfare has been more the rule than the exception. The cost of such warfare has been enormous. Hundreds of millions of people have been killed or injured in wars. Economically, the cost of war is staggering. But the greatest potential cost is the devastation of nuclear war.

Since the nineteenth century there has been a steady escalation of the scale of violence in revolutionary and international conflicts. Although some claim that wars produce economic benefits by increasing the demand for armaments and other products, in the vast majority of cases modern wars have had devastating economic and social consequences. In fact, some scientists even doubt the ability of the human race to survive an all-out nuclear war.

Terrorism involves attacks on civilians to gain political ends and is often used in situations that stop just short of full-scale war. The two main types are revolutionary terrorism, aimed at changing an existing government, and repressive terrorism, aimed to protect it.

The causes of revolutionary and international wars overlap but are nevertheless distinct. There are many theories about the causes of revolutionary wars. One says that they stem from exploitation and oppression of subordinate groups by a society's ruling elite. Another asserts that relative deprivation stimulates the discontent essential to a revolution. Other theories hold that revolutions occur when imbalance exists in the institutions of a society, when dissatisfied groups are able to mobilize sufficient resources to challenge the existing government, or when the government weakens and loses its political support. A final theory notes that class conflict, geographic divisions, and ethnic segregation all contribute to revolutionary conflict.

Militarism and the buildup of armaments are a major cause of international war. Ethnocentrism, when expressed in nationalism or dogmatic religious ideologies, may also encourage the conquest of other people. Plain greed cannot be ignored either: some wars are fought more for profit than for anything else. But underlying all international wars is the nature of the world's political organization. The large number of heavily armed independent states, each determined to advance its own interests, makes warfare almost inevitable.

Despite its obvious weaknesses, the most common proposal for preventing war is to urge nations to become so strong that they can deter any possible aggression by their neighbors. A second approach advocates some form of arms control or total disarmament. A third set of proposals calls for social justice and the economic development of the poor nations. If inequality were greatly reduced, the chief motivation for revolution would disappear and international tensions would relax. Finally, many leaders propose that military aggression be eliminated by the development of world government, including world law, world courts, and world law enforcement.

Functionalists see warfare and international conflicts as inevitable results of the way the world is politically organized into large numbers of competing nations. National systems do not function smoothly either, and revolution is evidence of this fact. Conflict theorists hold that the world system is far from disorganized. It is organized for economic exploitation of the weak by the strong. Conflict theorists favor a system in which economic goods and the military power to protect them are distributed equally. Social psychologists have identified personal and cultural traits that are conducive to warfare. In the long run, they say, the only sure way to prevent wars is to emphasize nonviolent cultural traits that favor the peaceful resolution of differences.

KEY TERMS

deterrence The attempt by a nation to prevent war by maintaining such a strong military force that other states will be afraid to attack it.

international war A protracted military conflict between two or more nations.

militarism The glorification of war and combat, or an economic system that is dependent on military spending.

nationalism A form of ethnocentrism based on a sense of identification with and devotion to one's nation.

nuclear proliferation The spread of nuclear weapons to an ever-larger number of countries.

repressive terrorism Acts of violence against civilians, intended to protect the existing political order of a nation.

revolutionary terrorism Acts of violence against civilians, intended to bring about major political changes in a nation.

revolutionary war A protracted military conflict between a national government and one or more groups of rebels.

FURTHER READINGS

David P. Barash, *Introduction to Peace Studies* (Belmont, Calif.: Wadsworth, 1991). A comprehensive text that looks at the ways to maintain peace as well as the wars that disrupt it.

Jonathan R. White, *Terrorism: An Introduction* (Pacific Grove, Calif.: Brooks/Cole, 1991). One of the numerous textbooks on the subject of terrorism that have been published in the past few years.

Jack A. Goldstone, ed., *Revolutions: Theoretical, Comparative, and Historical Studies* (San Diego: Harcourt Brace Jovanovich, 1986). A fine collection of articles about revolutions that provides useful historical and sociological perspectives.

James F. Dunnigan and William Martel, *How to Stop a War: The Lessons of Two Hundred Years of War and Peace* (New York: Doubleday, 1987). An interesting attempt to promote peace through the understanding of past wars.

Karl von Clausewitz, *On War*, trans. O. J. Matthkijs Jolles (Washington, D.C.: Infantry Journal Press, 1950). A classic work on warfare written by a Prussian general.

GLOSSARY

absolute approach Defining poverty by dividing the poor from the nonpoor on the basis of an objective standard (e.g., income).

absolute deprivation Lack of one or more of the necessities of life.

acquired immune deficiency syndrome (AIDS) A fatal disease that attacks the body's defenses against illness.

activity theory A theory of aging that holds that older people are happiest when they continue to be actively involved in social life.

addiction The intense craving for a drug that develops after a period of physical dependence stemming from heavy use.

adolescence The age grade of persons who have reached puberty but have not been given full status as adults.

adulthood The age grade of persons who are considered to have reached full social and physical maturity.

affirmative action A program designed to make up for past discrimination by giving special assistance to members of the groups that were discriminated against.

age composition The percentage of a population in each age category.

age grade People of similar age, such as children, adolescents, and adults.

aging A set of biological and social changes that develop in all people throughout life, but at different rates.

alcoholic A person whose work or social life is disrupted by drinking.

androgynous Having both the characteristics traditionally ascribed to males and to females.

assault An attack on a person with the intention of hurting or killing the victim.

assimilation A process by which a person takes on a new culture.

authoritarian personality A personality that is rigid and inflexible, has a very low tolerance for uncertainty, and readily accepts orders from above.

aversion therapy A form of behavioral therapy that uses punishment to discourage a particular behavior.

bail A sum of money put up as security to be forfeited if a person accused of committing a crime does not show up for trial.

balance of power The condition in which the military strength of the world's strongest nations or groups of nations is roughly equal.

behavioral theory A theory explaining human actions in terms of observable behavior.

behavioral therapy Modification of the specific behavior that is causing a patient's problems.

bilingualism The policy of giving two languages equal legal status.

biosocial theory A theory that explains social behavior by reference to biological traits.

biosphere The life-containing region of the earth extending from about 200 feet below sea level to about 10,000 feet above it.

birthrate The number of babies born in a year divided by the total population.

bisexual A person willing to have sexual relations with individuals of either sex.

blended family   A family in which at least one of the marital partners brings in children from a previous relationship.

blockbusting   A practice of realtors in which residents of a neighborhood into which a minority family has moved are convinced that property values in the neighborhood will fall; the residents sell cheaply to the realtors, who resell the property to minority families at a higher price.

blue-collar worker   Someone employed in a job requiring manual labor.

bourgeoisie   The class of people who, according to Marx, own capital and capital-producing property.

bureaucracy   A form of social organization characterized by division of labor, a hierarchy of authority, a set of formal rules, impersonal enforcement of rules, and job security.

business cycle   The ups and downs that characterize the economies of all capitalist nations.

capitalism   An economic system characterized by private property, the exchange of commodities and capital, and a free market for goods and labor.

case study   A detailed examination of specific individuals, groups, or situations.

chemotherapy   The use of drugs to treat certain mental and physical disorders.

childhood   The earliest age grade, lasting from birth to the onset of puberty.

child molestation   A sexual act between an adult and a child.

class conflict   The disagreements and strife that develop between different social classes because of their different social, economic, and political interests.

classical conditioning   Learning that occurs without the active participation of the subject.

client-centered therapy   Psychotherapy in which the patient chooses the topic and sets the pace and direction of the therapy session, while the therapist provides encouragement and support (also called nondirective therapy).

colonialism   A system in which one nation extends its political and economic control over other nations or other peoples and treats them as dependent colonies.

commune   A small self-supporting community voluntarily joined by individuals committed to living together in a family-like environment.

compensatory education program   A special program whose goal is to help disadvantaged students reach educational levels comparable to those achieved by more privileged students.

conflict perspective   A sociological viewpoint that sees conflicts between different groups as a basic social process and holds that the principal source of social problems is exploitation and oppression of one group by another.

conglomerate   A large firm that owns businesses in many areas of production and distribution.

control theory   A criminological thesis holding that people commit crimes when social norms and other social forces no longer control them.

conventional war   A war in which two or more armies meet directly without guerrilla tactics or nuclear weapons.

core   The wealthy industrialized nations that dominate the world system.

cornucopian   Someone who believes that scientific progress will allow continued economic growth and prosperity despite population growth and the depletion of natural resources.

corporate interest groups   Groups of corporations that are controlled by the same financial interests.

corporate technostructure   The group of technically skilled corporate managers who, according to Galbraith, make the important decisions.

crime Violation of a criminal law.

crime-control model A model of criminal justice that favors speedy arrest and punishment of anyone who commits a crime.

cultural imperialism The attempt by one social group to impose its values, beliefs, and standards of behavior on another group or groups.

cultural lag The delay between technological change and a culture's adaptation to it.

culture The way of life of the people in a certain geographic area, particularly their ideas, beliefs, values, patterns of thought, and symbols.

culture of poverty A self-perpetuating subculture among some (but not all) poor people that traps them in poverty.

cyclical unemployment Unemployment resulting from changes in the business cycle, which in turn cause changes in the demand for labor.

death rate The number of people who die in a year divided by the total population.

decriminalization The proposal that penalties for possession and use of a drug be abolished even if sales of the drug remain illegal.

de facto segregation Segregation of minority groups that results from existing social conditions (such as housing patterns) but is not legally required.

deinstitutionalization The movement to reduce the number of patients treated in mental hospitals.

de jure segregation Segregation of minority groups that is required by law.

demographic transition Changes in basic birthrates and death rates occurring during the process of industrialization.

demography A scientific discipline dealing with the distribution, density, and vital statistics of populations.

depressant A drug that slows the responses of the central nervous system, reduces coordination, and decreases mental alertness.

desertification The transformation of productive land into desert.

deterrence The strategy of preventing war by maintaining so strong a military force that other nations will be afraid to attack.

deviant An individual who violates a social norm.

deviant subculture A set of perspectives, attitudes, and values that support criminal or other norm-violating activity.

differential association A theory holding that people become criminals because they are exposed to more behavior patterns that are favorable to a certain kind of crime than are opposed to it.

disarmament Elimination of armed forces and weaponry, usually by means of a treaty.

discrimination The practice of treating some people as second-class citizens because of their minority status.

disengagement theory A theory of aging that holds that older people are best off when they slowly disengage from social activities as they age.

displacement of goals The shifting of organizational goals away from the organization's original purpose, as when an employee does something that interferes with the achievement of the organization's goals in order to protect his or her job.

diversion program A program whose goal is to keep juveniles out of the courts.

domination   A national system in which one (ethnic) group holds power and other groups are subordinate to it.

double bind   A situation in which a parent gives a child two conflicting messages at the same time.

double standard   A code of behavior that gives men greater sexual freedom than women.

dual-earner family   A family in which both wife and husband are employed.

due-process model   A model of criminal justice that places more emphasis on protecting human rights and dignity than on punishing criminals.

dysfunction   An action of an institution that interferes with the carrying out of essential social tasks.

ecology   The study of the interrelationships among plants, animals, and their environments.

ecosystem   A self-sufficient community of organisms living in an interdependent releationship with each other and their environment.

ego   According to Freud, the individual's conscious, reality-oriented experience.

electroconvulsive therapy   The use of electric shocks to treat mental disorders.

elitist   One who believes that nations are ruled by a small elite class.

ethnic group   A group whose members share a sense of togetherness and the conviction that they form a distinct group or "people."

ethnocentrism   The tendency to view the norms and values of one's own culture as absolute and to use them as a standard against which to measure those of other cultures.

exclusion   Income received from certain sources (e.g., municipal bonds) that is not counted for tax purposes.

experiment   A research method in which the behavior of individuals or groups is studied under controlled conditions, usually in a laboratory setting.

exploitive technology   Technology designed to produce immediate profits without regard to long-term consequences.

extended family   Members of two or more related nuclear families living together in the same place.

extinction   Modification of a behavior by removing the reinforcement (reward) for that behavior.

extramarital affair   A sexual relationship of a married person with someone other than his or her spouse.

family   A group of people related by marriage, ancestry, or adoption who live together in a common household.

family planning   A population control program whose objective is voluntary reduction of the birthrate.

federal system   A system of government in which national affairs are handled by a central government and local affairs are left to semiindependent local governments.

federation   A system of government in which each city, county, or state operates independently on some issues but fuses other activities with those of allied governments.

fee-for-service compensation   A form of payment in which a physician is paid a fixed fee for each service rendered.

felony A serious offense, usually punishable by death or by confinement in a central prison.

folkway A custom whose violators are not strongly condemned.

food chain The set of transformations beginning with production of food by green plants and ending with decomposition of the bodies of animals.

forcible rape Sexual intercourse forced on someone against his or her will.

fraud The acquisition of money or property through the use of deception or false pretenses.

free school A school in which teachers encourage pupils to set their own educational goals and tempo.

frustration-aggression theory A theory holding that frustration produces aggression.

function The contribution of each part of society to the maintenance of a balanced order.

functionalist perspective A sociological theory viewing society as a delicate balance of parts and holding that social problems arise when societies become disorganized.

fundamental education Education that concentrates on the teaching of reading, writing, and arithmetic.

gender inequality The differences in the economic, social, and political conditions of females and males.

gender role A social role assigned on the basis of biological sex.

gender socialization The process by which a person learns the behaviors and attitudes that are expected of the female or male gender.

general deterrence Punishment of criminals in order to frighten others so much that they will not violate the law.

generalized other A person's system of values and standards that, according to Mead, reflect the expectations of people in general.

gentrification The renovation of older low-cost neighborhoods in the central cities to accommodate more wealthy residents.

geothermal energy The heat of the earth's inner core.

grade inflation The assignment of higher student grades than were formerly given for the same quality of work.

great-man theory of history The theory holding that individual decision makers determine the course of history.

greenhouse effect The trapping of heat in the atmosphere by manmade gases.

gridlock Extreme traffic congestion that virtually stops all traffic in an area.

group A set of individuals with organized and recurrent relationships with one another.

group marriage A family that includes three or more adults as the marriage partners.

group therapy A procedure in which each member of a group is encouraged to reveal his or her problems and experiences to the group, which discusses and examines them.

growth rate The birthrate minus the death rate.

guerrilla war A war conducted by small bands of rebels using hit-and-run tactics.

health A state of physical and mental well-being.

health maintenance organization An organization in which a group of medical personnel offer a range of medical services to subscribers who pay a fixed monthly fee.

hegemonic power The dominant nation in the world system.

heterosexual   One whose preference is for sexual relations with persons of the opposite sex.

hidden curriculum   The concepts that students must learn in order to succeed in school that are not part of the formal curriculum, such as obedience to authority.

high-tech industry   An industry, such as computers, that is based on rapidly changing and sophisticated technology.

holistic medicine   A medical approach that focuses on the overall health of the patient and not on individual symptoms.

homicide   The killing of a human being.

homosexual   One whose preference is for sexual relations with persons of the same sex.

id   The instinctual drives, particularly sex, that, according to Freud, motivate all human behavior.

identity crisis   The personal crisis, typical of adolescence, in which a person tries to define who he or she is and how he or she fits into society.

imperialism   The creation or expansion of an empire.

incapacitation   The prevention of crime by imprisoning criminals so that they cannot commit more crimes against the public.

incest taboo   The prohibition of sexual relations between close relatives, e.g., parents and their children.

income   The amount of money a person makes in a given year.

industrial espionage   The hiring of investigators to gain information about one's business competitors, for instance by "bugging" their offices and telephones.

inflation   An increase in the overall prices consumers must pay for the goods they buy.

infrastructure   The basic physical necessities of modern society, e.g., roads, power plants, and sewers.

institution   A relatively stable pattern of thought and behavior centered on the performance of an important social task.

institutional discrimination   Discrimination against minority groups that is practiced by economic, educational, and political organizations rather than by individuals.

institutional racism   Prejudice and discrimination against a particular race that are built into a society's economic, educational, and political institutions.

integration   A national system in which ethnic backgrounds are ignored and all individuals are treated alike.

interactionist theory   A theory that explains behavior in terms of each individual's social relationships.

interlocking directorate   The situation that exists when some of the same individuals sit on the boards of directors of competing firms, or when directors of competing firms sit together on the board of directors of a firm in a different industry.

intermediate technology   Machines that are less complicated than expensive energy-intensive machines but more efficient than human and animal power.

international war   Prolonged armed conflict between the governments of two or more nations.

iron law of oligarchy   The tendency for any large organization to be ruled, according to Michels, by a few powerful people.

juvenile delinquency   Behavior by minors (usually defined as individuals below the age of 18) that is in violation of the criminal law or the special standards set for juveniles.

labeling theory   A theory holding that branding a person as a criminal often encourages rather than discourages criminal behavior.

land reform   The redistribution of land from rich landlords to peasant farmers.

latent dysfunction   A hidden dysfunction performed by a social institution or agency.

latent function   A hidden function performed by a social institution or agency.

legalization   The proposal that the use and sale of a drug be made legal, with government regulation.

legitimation   Consent of the governed based on a belief that those who govern have the right to do so.

lesbian   A female homosexual.

life cycle   The regular progression of persons through the age grades of their society as they grow older.

limited war   A war whose goals are restricted to a set of specific objectives and in which a rather small group of military personnel do the fighting.

lobbying   The activities of special-interest groups aimed at convincing lawmakers to pass the kind of legislation that they desire.

lower class   The social class at the bottom of the social hierarchy, composed of people whose incomes are below the poverty line.

machismo   Tough, aggressive masculinity.

macro theory   A sociological theory that is concerned with the behavior of large groups and entire societies.

magnet schools   Schools with special enriched programs designed to attract students from all ethnic groups, thus encouraging integration.

maintenance program   A program that supplies addicts or habitual users with a drug, while denying it to the public at large.

manic depression   A mental disorder characterized by extreme swings in mood.

manslaughter   The unlawful killing of another person without malice.

market control   Domination of a market by a few giant firms.

medicaid   A U.S. program designed to help the poor, the blind, and the disabled pay for medical care.

medicare   A U.S. program that pays for medical care of people over 65 years old.

megalopolis   An area in which several large cities are fused together.

meltdown   An accident in which the cooling system of a nuclear power plant fails, allowing the heat of the nuclear reaction to melt the core, thus releasing huge amounts of radiation.

melting-pot theory   The belief that U.S. society acts as a sort of crucible in which people from around the world are blended together to form a new and distinctive culture.

membership group   A group in which an individual is a member, whether willingly or not.

mental disorder   A mental condition that makes it difficult or impossible for a person to cope with everyday life.

metropolitan statistical area (MSA)   The U.S. Department of Census term for a central city and the surrounding suburbs that depend on it.

micro theory   A sociological theory that is concerned with the behavior of individuals and small groups.

middle class   The social class composed of professionals, managers, and most bureaucrats and white-collar workers.

mid-life crisis   The crisis faced by middle-aged persons in which they must accept the passing of their youth and the limitations on their earlier aspirations.

militarism   (a) Glorification of war and combat; (b) Strong belief in "defense" combined with huge military expenditures.

misdemeanor   A minor offense, usually punishable by confinement in a local jail or by payment of a fine.

modernization   The process by which a nation moves from a traditional agricultural society to an industrialized state.

monogamy   The practice of being married to only one person at a time.

monopoly   The situation existing when a single corporation has gained complete control of a market.

mood disorder   A mental disorder involving severe disturbances in affect and emotion.

mores   Customs whose violators are punished or otherwise strongly condemned.

murder   The unlawful killing of a human being with malice aforethought.

nationalism   A form of ethnocentrism based on a sense of identification with and devotion to one's nation.

neo-Malthusian   Someone who believes that we are quickly approaching a crisis because of overpopulation, resource depletion, and environmental destruction.

neurosis   A personal problem, not as severe as psychosis, accompanied by anxiety and chronically inappropriate responses to everyday situations.

nonrenewable resource   A resource for which there is a fixed supply that cannot be replenished.

norm   A social rule telling us what behavior is acceptable in a certain situation and what is not.

nuclear family   A married couple and their children.

nuclear proliferation   The spread of nuclear weapons to an ever-larger number of countries.

nuclear war   Any war employing nuclear weapons.

nuclear winter   The sharp decline in average temperatures produced by the dense clouds that would cover the earth after a major nuclear war.

occupational crime   A crime committed in the course of the offender's occupation but without the support or encouragement of his or her employer.

old age   The last age grade, usually considered to start around age 65.

oligopoly   The situation existing when an industry is dominated by a few large companies.

open marriage   A marriage in which the partners are committed to their own and each other's growth and which allows the widest possible range of outside contacts.

operant conditioning   Conditioned learning that requires the active participation of the subject.

opiate   Any of a group of natural and synthetic drugs with pain-relieving properties, including opium, codeine, morphine, heroin, meperidine, and methadone.

organic disorder   A mental disorder that has a clear-cut physical cause, such as brain damage.

organizational crime   A crime committed by someone acting on behalf of a larger organization, often his or her employer.

overeducation   Training more people for occupations than there are jobs available in those occupations.

paranoid disorder   A mental disorder in which the person suffers from overpowering, irrational fears.

parole   Release of a criminal from prison after part of his or her sentence has been served.

participant observation   A research method in which the researcher participates in the activities of the group under study.

patriarchal society   A society dominated by males.

personal interview   A research method that asks people about their activities and attitudes.

personality   The relatively stable characteristics and traits that distinguish one person from another.

personality theory   A theory holding that social behavior is determined by differences in personality.

photochemical smog   A group of noxious compounds produced by the action of sunlight on oxygen, hydrocarbons, and nitrogen oxides.

photosynthesis   The process by which green plants convert solar energy to food.

plea bargaining   A process by which a defense attorney and a prosecutor agree to let the defendant plead guilty in return for a reduction in the charge or other considerations.

pluralism   A national system in which several ethnic groups maintain a high level of independence and equality.

pluralist   One who believes that political decisions are made by changing coalitions of political forces.

political party   An organized group whose goals are to get its members elected to political office and to influence the decisions of those who already hold office.

political socialization   The process by which people learn their political values and perspectives.

polygyny   The practice of being married to more than one wife at a time.

pornography   A form of entertainment judged to be obscene.

poverty   (a) The state of having an income below some specified level; (b) The state of having significantly less income and wealth than the average person in the society of which one is a member.

power   The ability to force other people to do something whether they want to or not.

power elite   A group of wealthy and powerful persons who, according to Mills, pursue their own interests at the expense of the average citizen.

prejudice   Antipathy, either felt or expressed, based on a faulty and inflexible generalization and directed toward a group as a whole or toward an individual because he or she is a member of that group.

preliminary hearing   A hearing at which a judge decides whether the evidence against an accused person is sufficient to justify further legal proceedings.

premarital intercourse Sexual intercourse before marriage.

preventive medicine The theory or practice of staying healthy by maintaining good health habits.

price fixing Collusion by several companies to cut competition and set uniformly high prices.

price leader A firm whose prices are used as a guide by other firms in its industry.

probation Suspension of the sentence of a person who has been convicted but not yet imprisoned, on condition of continued good behavior and regular reporting to a probation officer.

proletariat The working class in an industrial society.

proportional representation An electoral system in which offices are won on the basis of the proportion of the vote each party receives, and not on a winner-take-all basis.

prostitution The practice of selling the services of oneself or another person for purposes of intercourse or other sexual activities.

psychedelic A drug that produces hallucinations and other significant alterations in the user's consciousness.

psychoanalysis Long-term therapy designed to uncover the repressed memories, motives, and conflicts assumed to be at the root of the patient's psychological problems.

psychosis A mental disorder in which a person has lost contact with reality and may suffer hallucinations, delusions, and the like.

psychotherapy Any program for helping a patient understand and then overcome the causes of his or her personality problems.

pushouts Children who leave their family home because they are no longer wanted there.

race People who are thought to have a common set of physical characteristics but who may or may not share a sense of unity and identity.

racism Stereotyping, prejudice, and discrimination based on race.

reference group A group with whose values and standards an individual identifies and of which he or she would like to be a member.

rehabilitation The process of changing a person's criminal behavior by nonpunitive methods.

reinforcement The reward or punishment received by an individual for a particular behavior.

relative approach Dividing the poor from the nonpoor on the basis of the wealth and income of the average person.

relative deprivation The situation in which persons have considerably less income, wealth, or prestige than they believe they deserve.

relative-deprivation theory A theory holding that revolutions are caused by differences between what people have and what they think they should have.

renewable resource A resource that is renewed through natural processes.

repressive terrorism Terrorism intended to protect the existing political order in a nation.

retribution The idea that the goal of the criminal-justice process should be to make criminals suffer for their crimes.

revolutionary terrorism Terrorism intended to bring about major political changes in a nation.

revolutionary war Armed conflict between an official government and one or more groups of rebels.

rite of passage A ritual that marks the transition from one state of life to another, especially from childhood to adulthood.

robbery   The unlawful taking of another person's property by force or threat of force.

role   A set of expectations and behaviors associated with a social position.

role conflict   The feelings experienced by people when two or more of their social roles place conflicting demands on them.

romantic love   The powerful attraction that is expected to form the basis of marriage in most Western societies.

runaways   Children who move away from their homes without parental consent.

sample   A cross section of subjects selected for study as representative of a larger population.

scapegoat   A person or group that is unjustly blamed for the problems of others.

schizophrenia   A mental disorder involving extreme disorganization in personality, thought patterns, and speech.

sedative-hypnotic   A drug that depresses the central nervous system.

self-concept   The image one has of who and what one is.

semi-periphery   The partially industrialized nations that have characteristics of both the core and the periphery.

sexism   Stereotyping, prejudice, and discrimination based on gender.

sexual harassment   Unwanted sexual comments, gestures, or physical advances.

sexual stereotyping   The portrayal of all females or males as having similar fixed traits.

sexually transmitted disease   A disease passed from one person to another during a sex act.

single-parent family   A family in which only one parent lives with one or more children.

smokestack industries   Those older industries, such as automobiles and steel, that produce heavy machinery and goods.

social behaviorism   A more sophisticated version of behaviorism that gives more emphasis to the social aspects of human behavior.

social class   A category of people with similar shares of the things that are valued in a society, particularly life chances, such as the opportunity to get a good education.

social disorganization   The condition that exists when an institution is poorly organized and fails to perform its social functions.

socialization   The process by which individuals learn the ways of thinking and behaving of their culture.

social movement   A social group organized to bring about or resist certain social changes.

social problem   (a) A condition that a significant number of people believe to be a problem; (b) A condition in which there is a sizable difference between the ideals of a society and its actual achievements.

social psychological theories   Micro theories dealing with the effects of individuals and groups on each other.

social security   A government-administered old-age pension program whose formal title is Old Age and Survivors' Insurance.

social structure   The organized patterns of human behavior in a society.

society   A group of people in the same geographic area who share common institutions and traditions.

sociology   The study of social relations, organization, and change.

sociopathic personality   An antisocial person with a complex of personality characteristics including impulsiveness, immaturity, and a lack of concern for other people.

solar energy   The energy supplied by the sun.

special-interest group   People who have a stake in a specific area of public policy.

specific deterrence   Punishment of criminals in order to change their ways.

status   (a) A social position made up of rights and obligations; (b) Prestige inherited from one's family or derived from occupation and life style.

status offense   A juvenile offense that does not violate the criminal law.

statutory rape   Sexual intercourse with someone below the legally defined age of consent (usually 16 or 18).

stereotype   The portrayal of all the members of a particular group as having similar fixed, usually unfavorable, traits.

stimulant   A drug that arouses the central nervous system, increases the metabolic rate, and reduces drowsiness.

strain theory   A theory holding that crime is caused by the strain produced when societies tell people that wealth is available to all but nevertheless restrict access to the means for achieving wealth.

structural unemployment   Unemployment resulting from long-term changes in the economy, such as technological changes.

subculture   A culture that exists within a larger culture and is influenced by it but has its own unique ideas and beliefs.

substance abuse disorder   A category of mental disorder applied to people who use excessive amounts of alcohol or other drugs.

suburb   A district, usually residential, located on or near the outskirts of a city; often a separately incorporated city or town.

suicide   The taking of one's own life.

superconductivity   The ability of special materials to conduct electricity with very little loss of power.

superego   According to Freud, the individual's conscience or sense of morality.

surrogate mothering   One woman bearing a child for another.

survey   A research method that asks people about their attitudes and activities, either in personal interviews or by means of questionnaires.

symbol   (a) A word or set of words; (b) Something that stands for or represents something else (e.g., an object used to represent something abstract).

systematic desensitization   A form of behavioral therapy in which the patient is gradually exposed to a feared stimulus so that the fear is slowly overcome.

temperature inversion   A condition in which a layer of warm air moves over a layer of cool air, sealing in pollutants that would otherwise rise into the upper atmosphere.

terrorism   Attacks against civilians to achieve political ends.

Third World   The poor agricultural nations of the world.

tolerance   (a) The immunity to the effects of a drug that builds up after repeated use; (b) The practice of ignoring behavior patterns that are personally objectionable.

total fertility rate   The number of children a woman in a particular group is likely to have in her lifetime.

total institution   A prison, mental hospital, monastery, or similar place where like-situated individuals lead an enclosed, formally administered round of life.

total war   A war whose goal is unconditional surrender of an enemy nation and in which both military personnel and ordinary citizens participate.

underclass   The lowest social strata made up of the long-term poor who are excluded from the mainstream of society.

underemployment   The problem suffered by workers who want full-time work but can find only part-time or temporary work.

unemployment   The problem suffered by workers who want a job but are unable to find one.

upper class   The social class at the top of the social hierarchy composed of the very wealthy, who often hold top positions of corporate power.

urbanization   The movement of people from rural areas to cities.

urban renewal   A program, usually financed by the government, intended to upgrade decaying city areas.

value conflict   A clash in the attitudes and beliefs held by different social groups.

victimization survey   A survey in which people are asked in personal interviews to report whether they have been the victims of various kinds of criminal offenses.

victimless crime   A crime in which the harm, if any, is not suffered by anyone except the offender.

violence   Behavior intended to cause bodily pain or injury to another; may be legitimate or illegitimate.

voucher system   An educational system in which the government gives students vouchers that may be used to pay for education at any school they or their parents choose.

wage-price spiral   A repetitive inflationary circle in which prices are raised to cover the costs of higher wages, and wages are then raised to cover the increased cost of living.

war   Protracted military conflict between two or more organized groups.

wealth   A person's total economic worth (e.g., real estate, stocks, cash).

white-collar crime   Crime committed by people of respectability and high social status in the course of their occupations.

white-collar workers   Persons employed in nonmanual labor, such as business managers or office workers.

withdrawal   The sickness that a habitual drug user experiences when the drug is discontinued after a period of steady use.

workfare   A government program for welfare mothers that provides job training and placement.

working class   The social class made up of blue-collar and lower-level service workers.

world economy   The international system of economic relationships in which all countries participate.

world system   The system of economic and political relationships that links the nations of the world together.

youth culture   The distinctive subculture created by adolescents in industrial society.

REFERENCES

CHAPTER 1 SOCIOLOGY AND SOCIAL PROBLEMS

1. See Robert K. Merton, "The Sociology of Social Problems," in Robert K. Merton and Robert Nisbet, eds., *Contemporary Social Problems*, 4th ed. (New York: Harcourt Brace Jovanovich, 1976).
2. Herbert Blumer, "Social Problems as Collective Behavior," *Social Problems* 18 (1971): 298–306; Malcolm Spector and John I. Kitsuse, "Social Problems: A Reformation," *Social Problems* 21 (1973): 145–159.
3. See Robert H. Lauer, "Defining Social Problems: Public Opinion and Textbook Practice," *Social Problems* 24 (1976): 122–130.
4. See Howard S. Becker, *Outsiders* (New York: Free Press, 1963).
5. Karl Marx, *Capital: A Critique of Political Economy* (New York: Random House, 1906).
6. Max Weber, *From Max Weber: Essays in Sociology*, ed. and trans. Hans H. Gerth and C. Wright Mills (New York: Oxford University Press, 1946).
7. See Harold R. Kerbo, *Social Stratification and Inequality: Class Conflict in Historical and Comparative Perspective*, 2nd ed. (New York: McGraw-Hill, 1991).
8. Émile Durkheim, *The Elementary Forms of Religious Life* (New York: Free Press, 1965; originally published 1912); Robert K. Merton, *Social Theory and Social Structure*, rev. ed. (New York: Free Press, 1957); Talcott Parsons, *The Social System* (New York: Free Press, 1964).
9. See Marx, *Capital*; Max Weber, *The Theory of Social and Economic Organization* (Glencoe, Ill.: Free Press, 1947); Randall Collins, *Conflict Sociology* (New York: Academic Press, 1979).
10. Karl Marx and Friedrich Engels, *The Communist Manifesto*, ed. Samuel Beer (New York: Appleton Century Crofts, 1955).
11. Edward C. Wilson, *Sociobiology: The New Synthesis* (Cambridge, Mass.: Belknap Press, 1975).
12. Sigmund Freud, *The Psychopathology of Everyday Life* (New York: Norton, 1971).
13. B. F. Skinner, *About Behaviorism* (New York: Knopf, 1974).
14. George Herbert Mead, *Mind, Self, and Society* (Chicago: University of Chicago Press, 1934).
15. See, for example, Herbert Blumer, *Symbolic Interactionism: Perspective and Method* (Englewood Cliffs, N.J.: Prentice-Hall, 1969), and Tamotsu Shibutani, *Society and Personality* (Englewood Cliffs, N.J.: Prentice-Hall, 1961).

CHAPTER 2 PROBLEMS OF THE ECONOMY

1. *World Population Data Sheet* (Washington, D.C.: Population Reference Bureau, 1991).
2. Adam Smith, *An Inquiry into the Nature and Causes of the Wealth of Nations* (New York: Random House, 1937 [originally pub. 1776]).
3. Ibid., p. 128.
4. Senate Committee on Government Affairs, *Voting Rights in Major Corporations* (Washington, D.C.: Government Printing Office, 1978).
5. New York Stock Exchange, *Fact Book* (New York: New York Stock Exchange, 1986).
6. Harold R. Kerbo, *Social Stratification and Inequality: Class Conflict in Historical and Comparative Perspective*, 2nd ed. (New York: McGraw-Hill, 1991), p. 207.

7. See Beth Mintz and Michael Schwartz, *The Power Structure of American Business* (Chicago: University of Chicago Press, 1985).

8. David R. James and Michael Soref, "Profit Constraints on Managerial Autonomy: Managerial Theory and the Unmaking of the Corporate President," *American Sociological Review* 46 (Feb. 1981): 1–18.

9. John A. Byrne, "The Flap over Executive Pay," *Business Week*, May 6, 1991, pp. 90–112.

10. C. Wright Mills, *The Power Elite* (New York: Oxford University Press, 1956), p. 141.

11. Jonathan Schell, "Capital Is No Respecter of Ideologies," *Los Angeles Times*, Jun. 17, 1991, p. B5.

12. Robert B. Reich, "The REAL Economy," *Atlantic*, Feb. 1991, pp. 35–52.

13. Wayne D. Thompson, *Canada 1986* (Washington, D.C.: Stryker Post, 1986), p. 106.

14. Stanley Meiser, "Canada Cools Efforts to Nationalize in Face of Tension with U.S.," *Los Angeles Times*, Nov. 29, 1982, sec. 4, p. 1; Statistics Canada, *Canada's International Position* (Ottawa: Queen's Printer, 1982).

15. Jonathan Peterson, "Weak Dollar, Deficits Put U.S. on Sale," *Los Angeles Times*, Feb. 24, 1988, sec. 1, p. 13.

16. Volker Bornschier and Christopher Chase-Dunn, *Transnational Corporations and Development* (New York: Praeger, 1985).

17. Kitty Calavita and Henry N. Pontell, " 'Other People's Money' Revisited: Collective Embezzlement in the Savings and Loan and Insurance Industries," *Social Problems* 38 (Feb. 1991): 94–111.

18. James William Coleman, *The Criminal Elite: The Sociology of White Collar Crime*, 2nd ed. (New York: St. Martin's Press, 1989).

19. For a review of this and other studies on the frequency of price fixing, see Coleman, *The Criminal Elite*, p. 28.

20. John Kenneth Galbraith, *The New Industrial State* (New York Library/Signet, 1967), pp. 304–305.

21. Morton Mintz and Jerry S. Cohen, *America, Inc.* (New York: Dial, 1971), p. 70.

22. *Forbes*, Jul. 1987, p. 116.

23. U.S. Bureau of the Census, *Statistical Abstract of the United States, 1991* (Washington, D.C.: U.S. Government Printing Office, 1991), pp. 395, 397.

24. Reich, "The REAL Economy."

25. U.S. Bureau of the Census, *Statistical Abstract 1991*, p. 390.

26. Waiter Russel Mead, "Why the Roller Coaster Only Goes One Way: Down," *Los Angeles Times*; Apr. 15, 1991, p. M1.

27. Bob Baker, "U.S. Jobless Figures Fail to Add 'Hidden Unemployed,' " *Los Angeles Times*, Apr. 11, 1991, pp. A1, A29.

28. Lee May, "No Frills Jobs: More Work for Less," *Los Angeles Times*, Jun. 19, 1988, sec. 1, pp. 1, 13.

29. David J. Charrington, *The Work Ethic* (New York: AMACON, 1980).

30. Bob Baker, "Assembly Line Stress in Offices," *Los Angeles Times*, Jun. 13, 1991, pp. A1, A28–29.

31. Coleman, *The Criminal Elite*, pp. 6–8: Lawrence White, *Human Debris: The Injured Worker in America* (New York: Putnam, 1983), pp. 15–23.

32. Coleman, *The Criminal Elite*, pp. 31–41.

33. Theodore Caplow, *American Social Trends* (San Diego: Harcourt Brace Jovanovich, 1991), p. 88.

34. Bob Baker, "Unions Try Bilingual Recruiting," *Los Angeles Times*, Mar. 25, 1991, pp. A1, A22–23.

35. Caplow, *American Social Trends*, p. 90.

36. Bob Baker, "Emotional Issue Unresolved in N.Y. News Case," *Los Angeles Times*, Mar. 13, 1991, p. D2.
37. Mead, "Why the Roller Coaster Only Goes One Way."
38. Stanley Meisler and Sam Fulwood III, "Economic Gap Bodes Ill for U.S.," *Los Angeles Times*, Jul. 15, 1990, p. A23; Susan Dentzer, "The Vanishing Dream," *U.S. News & World Report*, Apr. 22, 1991, pp. 39–43.
39. U.S. Bureau of the Census, *Statistical Abstract 1991*, pp. 316, 317.
40. Edmondson, "Remaking a Living."
41. Susan Moffat, "Record Number of Bankruptcies in 1991 Forecast," *Los Angeles Times*, Sep. 5, 1991, pp. D1, D4.
42. Elliot Currie and Jerome H. Skolnick, *America's Problems* (Glenville, Ill.: Scott, Foresman, 1988), pp. 399–400.
43. Reich, "The REAL Economy."
44. Jonathan Weber, "U.S. Urged to Spend More on High-Tech R&D," *Los Angeles Times*, Mar. 21, 1991, p. D3.
45. Reich, "The REAL Economy."
46. U.S. Bureau of the Census, *Statistical Abstract 1991*, p. 449.
47. Harris, *Inside America*, p. 17.
48. Ibid., p. 8.
49. Michael Kinsley, "Yes, the Rich Got Richer Under Reagan's Regime: The Poor Fared as Usual," *Los Angeles Times*, Apr. 11, 1988, sec. 2, p. 7.
50. Caplow, *American Social Trends*, p. 134.
51. M. Harvey Brenner, *Estimating the Cost of National Economic Policy*, U.S. Congress, Joint Economic Committee, 1976.

CHAPTER 3 PROBLEMS OF GOVERNMENT

1. U.S. Bureau of the Census, *Statistical Abstract of the United States, 1991* (Washington, D.C.: U.S. Government Printing Office, 1991), pp. 280, 433.
2. U.S. Bureau of the Census, *Statistical Abstract 1991*, pp. 400–401.
3. Theodore Caplow, *American Social Trends* (San Diego: Harcourt Brace Jovanovich, 1991), p. 92.
4. Max Weber, *From Max Weber: Essays in Sociology*, trans. Hans H. Gerth and C. Wright Mills (New York: Oxford University Press, 1946), pp. 196–244.
5. Max Weber, *The Theory of Social and Economic Organization*, trans. A. M. Henderson and Talcott Parsons (New York: Free Press, 1947), p. 337.
6. See Francis Rourke, *Bureaucracy, Politics and Public Policy*, 3rd ed. (Boston: Little, Brown, 1984).
7. See Kenneth Janda, Jeffrey M. Berry, and Jerry Goldman, *The Challenge of Democracy* (Boston: Houghton Mifflin, 1987), pp. 427–457.
8. Caplow, *American Social Trends*, p. 113.
9. U.S. Bureau of the Census, *Statistical Abstract 1991*, p. 268.
10. Caplow, *American Social Trends*, p. 114.
11. Senator David L. Boren, "A Way Off the Merry-Go-Round," *Los Angeles Times*, Mar. 24, 1991, p. M5.
12. Sara Fritz and Dwight Morris, "Political Money by the Bundle," *Los Angeles Times*, Jul. 30, 1990, pp. A1, A14–15.
13. Robert W. Stewart and Tracy Wood, "Political Giving: Corporate Contributions Buy Access," *Los Angeles Times*, Oct. 26, 1986, sec. 1, pp. 1, 3, 36.

14. Maura Dolar, "Friendly Lawmakers Get Chemical Industry Help," *Los Angeles Times*, Oct. 26, 1987, sec. 1, pp. 1, 26, 27; Thomas Byrne Edsall, "The Return of Inequality," *Atlantic*, Jun. 1988, pp. 86–94.

15. C. Wright Mills, "The Structure of Power in American Society," in *Power, Politics and People: The Collected Papers of C. Wright Mills* (New York: Ballantine Books, 1963), p. 288.

16. See, for example, Thomas R. Dye, *Who's Running America: The Conservative Years* (Englewood Cliffs: Prentice-Hall, 1986); Leonard Silk and Mark Silk, *The American Establishment* (New York: Basic Books, 1980).

17. David Riesman, *The Lonely Crowd* (New York: Doubleday, 1953).

18. Arnold M. Rose, *The Power Structure: Political Process in American Society* (New York: Oxford University Press, 1967), p. 6.

19. G. William Dumhoff, *The Higher Circles: The Governing Class in America* (New York: Random House, 1970), p. 309.

20. U.S. Bureau of the Census, *Statistical Abstract 1991*, p. 344.

21. Ralph Vartabedian and John Broder, "Legacy of Failure in Defense," *Los Angeles Times*, Jan. 1, 1991, pp. A1, A14.

22. U.S. Bureau of the Census, *Statistical Abstract 1991*, pp. 316–317.

23. David R. Simon and D. Stanley Eitzen, *Elite Deviance*, 2nd ed. (Boston: Allyn & Bacon, 1986), p. 138.

24. Vartabedian and Broder, "Legacy of Failure in Defense."

25. James William Coleman, *The Criminal Elite: The Sociology of White Collar Crime*, 2nd ed. (New York: St. Martin's Press, 1989), pp. 55–72.

26. Ibid.

27. Brian Glick, *War at Home: Covert Action Against U.S. Activists and What We Can Do About It* (Boston: South End Press, 1989).

28. Associated Press, "Most Polygraph Use by Employers Banned," *San Luis Obispo Telegram-Tribune*, Oct. 22, 1988, p. D1.

29. Marcia Staimer, "Do Workers Have Private Lives?" *USA Today*, May 13, 1991, pp. 1A–2A.

30. Ted Gest, "Who Is Watching You?" *U.S. News & World Report*, Jul. 12, 1982, pp. 34–37.

31. Associated Press, "Government Created 6.8 Million Secrets in 1990, Not Counting War," *San Luis Obispo Telegram-Tribune*, Apr. 3, 1991, p. A7.

32. Harold R. Kerbo, *Social Stratification and Inequality: Class Conflict in Historical and Comparative Perspective*, 2nd ed. (New York: McGraw-Hill, 1991), pp. 167–169.

33. Harry Bernstein, "U.S. Is Poor Model for Social Services," *Los Angeles Times*, Jun. 11, 1991, p. D3.

34. Robert B. Reich, "The Budget Debacle," *Los Angeles Times,* Oct. 7, 1990, pp. M1, M8.

35. Robert B. Reich, "The REAL Economy," *Atlantic*, Feb. 1991, pp. 35–52.

36. Nancy Gibbs, "Keep the Bums In," *Time*, Nov. 19, 1991, pp. 32–42.

37. Caplow, *American Social Trends*, p. 114.

38. Tamar Jacoby, "Going After Dissidents," *Newsweek*, Feb. 8, 1988, p. 29.

39. W. Adorno, E. Frenkel-Brunswick, D. J. Devinson, and P. N. Sandord, *The Authoritarian Personality* (New York: Harper & Row, 1950).

CHAPTER 4 PROBLEMS OF EDUCATION

1. Quoted in Mavis Hiltunen Biesanz and John Biesanz, *Introduction to Sociology*, 2nd ed. (Englewood Cliffs, N.J.: Prentice-Hall, 1973), p. 616.

2. U.S. Bureau of the Census, *Statistical Abstract of the United States, 1991* (Washington, D.C.: U.S. Government Printing Office, 1991), p. 138.

3. Ibid., pp. 143, 167.

4. Robert James Parelius and Ann Parker Parelius, *The Sociology of Education*, 2nd ed. (Englewood Cliffs, N.J.: Prentice-Hall, 1987), p. 265.

5. See S. Leonard Syme and Lisa F. Berkman, "Social Class, Susceptibility and Sickness," in Howard D. Schwartz, ed., *Dominant Issues in Medical Sociology*, 2nd ed. (New York: Random House, 1987), pp. 643–649.

6. Parelius and Parelius, *The Sociology of Education*, pp. 280–282.

7. U.S. Bureau of the Census, *Statistical Abstract 1991*, p. 149.

8. Bob Secter, "Gaps Between Rich, Poor Schools Ignite Legal Fights," *Los Angeles Times*, Nov. 26, 1990, pp. A1, A20.

9. Ginny Carroll, "Who Foots the Bill?" *Newsweek*, Special Edition on Education, Fall–Winter 1990, pp. 81–85.

10. James S. Coleman et al., *Equality of Educational Opportunity* (Washington, D.C.: U.S. Government Printing Office, 1966); Christopher Jencks et al., *Inequality: A Reassessment of the Effects of Family and Schooling in America* (New York: Harper & Row, 1972); Harvey A. Averch et al., *How Effective Is Schooling: A Critical Synthesis and Review of Research Findings* (Englewood Cliffs, N.J.: Prentice-Hall, 1974); Samuel Bowles and Herbert Gintis, *Schooling in Capitalist America* (New York: Basic Books, 1976).

11. Carroll, "Who Foots the Bill?"

12. Michael W. LaMorte and Jeffrey D. Williams, "Court Decisions and School Finance Reform," *Educational Administration Quarterly* 21 (Spring 1985): 59–89.

13. U.S. Bureau of the Census, *Statistical Abstract 1991*, p. 133.

14. See Parelius and Parelius, *The Sociology of Education*, pp. 293–296.

15. Robert Rosenthal and Lenore Jacobson, *Pygmalion in the Classroom* (New York: Harper & Row, 1969).

16. See Roy Nash, *Teacher Expectations and Pupil Learning* (London: Routledge and Kegan Paul, 1976); Parelius and Parelius, *The Sociology of Education*, pp. 293–296.

17. D. G. Harvey and G. T. Slatin, "The Relationship Between a Child's SES and Teacher Expectations," *Social Forces* 54 (1975): 140–159.

18. See Jeannie Oakes, *Multiplying Inequalities* (Santa Monica, Calif.: Rand Corporation, 1990).

19. Karl Alexander, Martha Cook, and Edward L. Dill, "Curriculum Tracking and Educational Stratification," *American Sociological Review* 43 (1978): 47–66.

20. Elaine Woo, "Judge Tells L.A. Schools, NAACP to Settle Lawsuit," *Los Angeles Times*, Jun. 21, 1988, sec. 1, pp. 1, 16.

21. Coleman et al., *Equality of Educational Opportunity*.

22. Rita E. Mahard and Robert L. Crain, "Research on Minority Achievement in Desegregated Schools," in Christine H. Rossell and Willis D. Hawley, eds., *The Consequences of School Desegregation* (Philadelphia: Temple University Press, 1983), pp. 103–125.

23. Janet Eyler, Valerie J. Cook, and Leslie E. Ward, "Resegregation: Segregation Within Desegregated Schools," in Rossell and Hawley, *The Consequences of School Desegregation*, pp. 126–162.

24. U.S. Bureau of the Census, *Statistical Abstract 1991*, p. 139.

25. Christopher Jencks, "Is the American Underclass Growing?" in Christopher Jencks and Paul E. Peterson, eds., *The Urban Underclass* (Washington, D.C.: Brookings Institution, 1991), pp. 28–100.

26. Thomas Byrne Edsall, "Race," *Atlantic*, May 1991, pp. 53–85.

27. U.S. Bureau of the Census, *Statistical Abstract 1991*, p. 139; Jencks, "Is the American Underclass Growing?"

28. Joan Newman and Graeme Newman, "Crime and Punishment in the Schooling Process: A Historical Analysis," in Keith Baker and Robert J. Rubel, eds., *Violence and Crime in the Schools* (Lexington, Mass.: Lexington Books, 1980), p. 14.

29. Stanley Meisler, "Reading the Signs of a Crisis," *Los Angeles Times*, May 11, 1990, pp. A1, A18–19.

30. National Commission on Excellence in Education, *A Nation at Risk: The Imperative for Educational Reform* (Washington, D.C.: U.S. Government Printing Office, 1983).

31. Jerry Adler, "Creating Problems," *Newsweek*, Special Edition on Education, Fall–Winter 1990, pp. 16–22.

32. Robert J. Samuelson, "Why School Reform Fails," *Newsweek*, May 27, 1991, pp. 62, 68.

33. Larry Gordon, "Verbal SAT Scores Slip Again in 1990," *Los Angeles Times*, Aug. 28, 1990, p. A17.

34. Nina Darnton, "A Mother's Touch," *Newsweek*, Special Edition on Education, Fall–Winter 1990, pp. 60–61.

35. Parelius and Parelius, *The Sociology of Education*, pp. 334–335.

36. David G. Savage, "U.S. School Aid: Looking for Results," *Los Angeles Times*, Apr. 11, 1985, sec. 1, p. 1.

37. For an exception to this rule, see John R. Berrueta-Clement et al., *Changed Lives: The Effects of the Perry Preschool Program on Youths Through Age 19* (Ypsilanti, Mich.: High/Scope, 1984).

38. Steven Waldman, "The Stingy Politics of Head Start," *Newsweek*, special edition on education, Fall–Winter 1990, pp. 78–79.

39. Harry Bernstein, "How Teachers' Unions Hope to Improve the Schools," *Los Angeles Times*, Mar. 6, 1990, p. D3.

40. Michael Rutter, *15,000 Hours: Secondary Schools and Their Effect on Children* (Cambridge, Mass.: Harvard University Press, 1979).

41. James S. Coleman, Thomas Hoffer, and Sally Kilgore, *High School Achievement: Public, Catholic and Private Schools* (New York: Basic Books, 1982), p. 178.

42. Michael J. Barrett, "The Case for More School Days," *Atlantic*, Nov. 1990, pp. 78–106.

43. Tom Morganthau, "The Future Is Now," *Newsweek*, special edition on education, Fall–Winter 1990, pp. 72–76.

44. Jean Merl, "Failed 'System for Choice' Serves as Lesson to Schools," *Los Angeles Times*, Mar. 12, 1991, pp. A1, A22–23.

45. A. S. Neill, *Summerhill: A Radical Approach to Child Rearing* (New York: Hart, 1960).

46. Ronald E. Kotzsch, "Waldorf Schools: Education for Head, Hands, and Heart," *Utne Reader*, Sep.–Oct. 1990, pp. 84–90.

47. Jonathan H. Mark and Barry Anderson, "Teacher Survival Rates: A Current Look," *American Journal of Educational Research* 15 (1978): 379–383.

48. Tom Hayden, "Running Short of Good Teachers," *Los Angeles Times*, Jun. 24, 1983, sec. 2, p. 5.

CHAPTER 5   PROBLEMS OF THE FAMILY

1. George P. Murdock, "World Ethnographic Sample," *American Anthropologist* 59 (1957): 664–687.

2. Mark Hunter, *The Changing Family: Comparative Perspectives*, 2nd ed. (New York: Macmillan, 1988), pp. 532–535.

3. For an analysis of the preindustrial family, see Randall Collins, *Sociology of Marriage and the Family: Gender, Love, and Property*, 2nd ed. (Chicago: Nelson-Hall, 1988), pp. 87–149.

4. See Hunter, *The Changing Family*, pp. 28–80.

5. "Size of Average American Household Continues to Decline," *San Luis Obispo Telegram-Tribune*, May 15, 1985, p. A8; U.S. Bureau of the Census, *Statistical Abstract of the United States, 1991* (Washington, D.C.: U.S. Government Printing Office, 1991), p. 49.

6. U.S. Bureau of the Census, *Statistical Abstract 1991*, p. 43.

7. Ibid., p. 51.

8. Louis Harris, *Inside America* (New York: Vintage Books, 1987), p. 87.

9. James C. Coleman, *Intimate Relationships, Marriage, and Family* (Indianapolis: Bobbs-Merrill, 1984), p. 335.

10. U.S. Bureau of the Census, *Statistical Abstract 1991,* pp. 390–391.

11. Harris, *Inside America*, p. 87.

12. Joseph Veroff, Elizabeth Douvan, and Richard A. Kulka, *The Inner American: A Self-Portrait for 1957 to 1976* (New York: Basic Books, 1981).

13. Harris, *Inside America*, p. 87.

14. See Ralph Linton, "The Natural History of the Family," in Ruth N. Ashen, ed., *The Family: Its Function and Destiny* (New York: Harper & Row, 1959); Louis Wirth, "Urbanism as a Way of Life," *American Journal of Sociology* 44 (1938): 1–24; Talcott Parsons, "The Kinship System of the Contemporary United States," *American Anthropologist* 45 (1943): 22–38.

15. For a good analysis of this debate, see Arlene S. Skolnick, *The Intimate Environment: Exploring Marriage and the Family* (Boston: Little, Brown, 1987), pp. 135–142.

16. Claude S. Fischer, "The Dispersion of Kinship Ties in Modern Society: Contemporary Data and Historical Speculation," *Journal of Family History* 7 (Winter): 353–375.

17. U.S. Bureau of the Census, *Statistical Abstract 1991*, pp. 62, 838.

18. Ibid., p. 86.

19. Collins, *Sociology of Marriage and the Family*, pp. 360–361.

20. U.S. Bureau of the Census, *Statistical Abstract 1991*, p. 43.

21. Collins, *Sociology of Marriage and the Family*, pp. 357–358.

22. Judith S. Wallerstein and Joan Kelley, *Surviving the Breakup: How Children and Parents Cope with Divorce* (New York: Basic Books, 1980).

23. J. Ross Eshleman, *The Family: An Introduction*, 5th ed. (Boston: Allyn & Bacon, 1988), pp. 611–615.

24. Thomas H. Maugh II, "Study Disputes Divorce as Cause of Child's Problems," *Los Angeles Times*, Jun. 7, 1991, pp. A1, A39.

25. James L. Peterson and Nicholas Zill, "Marital Disruption, Parent-Child Relationships and Behavior Problems in Children," *Journal of Marriage and the Family* 48 (May 1986): 295–301.

26. Quoted in Maugh, "Study Disputes Divorce as Cause of Child's Problems."

27. U.S. Bureau of the Census, *Statistical Abstract 1991*, p. 67.

28. William Julius Wilson, *The Truly Disadvantaged: The Inner City, the Underclass, and Public Policy* (Chicago: University of Chicago Press, 1987).

29. Theodore Caplow, *American Social Trends* (San Diego: Harcourt Brace Jovanovich, 1991), pp. 161–162.

30. U.S. Bureau of the Census, *Statistical Abstract 1991*, pp. 66–67.

31. William J. Goode, "Family Disorganization," in Robert K. Merton and Robert Nisbet, eds., *Contemporary Social Problems*, 4th ed. (New York: Harcourt Brace Jovanovich, 1976), p. 519.

32. U.S. Bureau of the Census, *Statistical Abstract 1991*, p. 67.

33. Zack Nauth, "Poverty Up 53 Percent Among Children, New Study Finds," *Los Angeles Times*, May 23, 1985, p. 5.

34. Mildred Daley Pagelow, *Family Violence* (New York: Praeger, 1984), pp. 67–68.

35. Murray A. Straus, Richard J. Gelles, and Suzanne K. Steinmetz, *Behind Closed Doors: Violence in the American Family* (New York: Doubleday, 1980), pp. 37–60, 148.

36. Ibid., pp. 190–197.

37. Jan E. Stets and Murray A. Straus, "Gender Differences in Reporting Marital Violence and

Its Medical and Psychological Consequences,'' in Murray A. Straus and Richard J. Gelles, eds., *Physical Violence in American Families* (New Brunswick, N.J.: Transactions Publishers, 1990), pp. 151–166.

38. See Eshleman, *The Family*, pp. 573–577; for a dissenting view, see Pagelow, *Family Violence*, pp. 223–257.

39. Letty Pogrebin, *Family Politics* (New York: McGraw-Hill, 1985), p. 101.

40. Straus, Gelles, and Steinmetz, *Behind Closed Doors*, pp. 190–197.

41. Samuel X. Radbill, ''A History of Child Abuse and Infanticide,'' in Ray E. Helfer and C. Henry Kempe, eds., *The Battered Child*, 2nd ed. (Chicago: University of Chicago Press, 1974).

42. Murray A. Straus and Richard J. Gelles, ''Societal Change and Change in Family Violence from 1975 to 1985 as Revealed by Two National Surveys,'' *Journal of Marriage and the Family* 48 (Aug. 1986): 465–479.

43. David G. Gil, *Violence Against Children: Physical Child Abuse in the United States* (Cambridge, Mass.: Harvard University Press, 1970), pp. 98–99; ''Violence Against Children,'' *Journal of Marriage and the Family* 33 (1971): 644–648.

44. Harris, *Inside America*, pp. 130–131.

45. U.S. Bureau of the Census, *Statistical Abstract 1991*, p. 53.

46. U.S. Bureau of the Census, *Statistical Abstract 1991*, p. 375.

47. Robert Greenstein, ''Universal and Targeted Approaches to Relieving Poverty,'' in Christopher Jencks and Paul E. Peterson, eds., *The Urban Underclass* (Washington, D.C.: Brookings Institution, 1991), pp. 437–459; Nancy Gibbs, ''Shameful Bequests to the Next Generation,'' *Time*, Oct. 8, 1990, pp. 42–46; Scripps Howard News Service, ''Study: Hunger Hits 1 in 4 American Kids,'' *San Luis Obispo Telegram-Tribune*, Mar. 26, 1991, p. C5.

48. L. Edward Wells and Joseph H. Rankin, ''Families and Delinquency: A Meta-analysis of the Impact of Broken Homes,'' *Social Problems* 38 (Feb. 1991): 71–93.

49. Larry J. Siegel and Joseph J. Senna, *Juvenile Delinquency: Theory, Practice, and Law*, 3rd ed. (St. Paul, Minn.: West, 1988), p. 246.

50. Thomas C. Taveggia and Ellen M. Thomas, ''Latchkey Children,'' *Pacific Sociological Review* 17 (1974): 27–34.

51. Harris, *Inside America*, p. 96.

52. Ibid., p. 95.

53. Coleman, *Intimate Relationships*, p. 441.

54. Myron Brenton, *The Runaways* (New York: Penguin, 1978), pp. 28–32.

55. Joan Smith, ''Transforming Households: Working-Class Women and Economic Crisis,'' *Social Problems* 5 (Dec. 1987): 416–436.

56. Harris, *Inside America*, p. 19.

57. Janice Peskin, ''Measuring Household Production for the GNP,'' *Family Economics Review* (Summer 1982): 10.

58. Harris, *Inside America*, pp. 39–40.

59. U.S. Bureau of the Census, *Statistical Abstract 1991*, p. 87.

60. See Caplow, *American Social Trends*, pp. 55–56.

61. M. D. Newcomb and R. R. Bentler, ''Cohabitation Before Marriage,'' *Journal of Marriage and the Family* 41 (Feb. 1980): 597–602.

62. J. Jacques and K. J. Chason, ''Cohabitation: Its Impact on Marital Success,'' *Family Coordinator* 28 (Jan. 1979): 35–39.

63. William Masters and Virginia Johnson, *Human Sexual Inadequacy* (Boston: Little, Brown, 1970).

64. Harris, *Inside America*, p. 99.

65. Gibbs, ''Shameful Bequests to the Next Generation.''

66. Alison Clarke-Stewart, *Daycare* (Cambridge, Mass.: Harvard University Press, 1982).

67. Bob Sipchen, "Who Should Be Raising the Kids?" *Los Angeles Times*, Feb. 8, 1990, pp. E1, E5.
68. Jesus Sanchez, "No Major Burden Seen in Family-Leave Laws," *Los Angeles Times*, May 23, 1991, pp. D1, D3.
69. Robin Abcarian, "How Other Countries Compare," *Los Angeles Times*, May 13, 1991, p. E2.
70. See, for example, George P. Murdock, *Social Structure* (New York: Free Press, 1949); William J. Goode, *The Family* (Englewood Cliffs, N.J.: Prentice-Hall, 1946); Kingsley Davis, *Human Society* (New York: Macmillan, 1949).

CHAPTER 6   THE POOR

1. U.S. Bureau of the Census, *Statistical Abstract of the United States, 1991* (Washington, D.C.: U.S. Government Printing Office, 1991), p. 462.
2. Ibid., p. 455.
3. John A. Byrne, "The Flap over Executive Pay," *Business Week*, May 6, 1991, pp. 90–112; Stanley Meisler and Sam Fulwood III, "Economic Gap Bodes Ill for U.S.," *Los Angeles Times*, Jul. 15, 1990, pp. A1, A22–23.
4. Harold R. Kerbo, *Social Stratification and Inequality: Class Conflict in Historical and Comparative Perspective*, 2nd ed. (New York: McGraw-Hill, 1991), p. 40.
5. Paul Glastris, "The New Way to Get Rich," *U.S. News & World Report*, May 7, 1990, pp. 26–36.
6. See Kerbo, *Social Stratification and Inequality*, pp. 38–40.
7. Byrne, "The Flap over Executive Pay."
8. U.S. Bureau of the Census, *Statistical Abstract 1991*, pp. 834, 835.
9. Michael Kinsley, "Yes, the Rich Got Richer Under Reagan's Regime: The Poor Fared as Usual," *Los Angeles Times*, Apr. 11, 1988, sec. 2, p. 7.
10. Byrne, "The Flap over Executive Pay."
11. Meisler and Fulwood, "Economic Gap Bodes Ill for U.S."
12. U.S. Bureau of the Census, *Statistical Abstract 1991*, p. 467.
13. William Julius Wilson, "Studying Inner-City Social Dislocations: The Challenge of Public Agenda Research," *American Sociological Review* 56 (Feb. 1991): 1–14.
14. U.S. Bureau of the Census, *Statistical Abstract 1991*, p. 51.
15. Ibid., p. 463.
16. Ibid.
17. Ibid.
18. Ibid., p. 38.
19. Paul E. Peterson, "The Urban Underclass and the Poverty Paradox," in Christopher Jencks and Paul E. Peterson, eds., *The Urban Underclass* (Washington, D.C.: Brookings Institution, 1991), pp. 3–27.
20. Ibid.
21. Christopher Jencks, "Is the American Underclass Growing?" in Jencks and Peterson, *The Urban Underclass*, pp. 28–100.
22. Wilson, "Studying Inner-City Social Dislocations."
23. Associated Press, "Count of Homeless Useless, Official Says," *Los Angeles Times*, May 10, 1991, p. A27.
24. Mitchel Levitas, "Homeless in America," *New York Times Magazine*, Jun. 10, 1990, pp. 44–45, 82–91.

25. James D. Wright, "The Mentally Ill Homeless: What Is Myth and What Is Fact?" *Social Problems* 35 (Apr. 1988): 182-191.

26. David A. Snow, Susan G. Baker, Leon Anderson, and Michael Martin, "The Myth of Mental Illness Among the Homeless," *Social Problems* 33 (Jun. 1986): 407-423.

27. Levitas, "Homeless in America."

28. Ibid.; Marta Elliott and Lauren J. Krivo, "Structural Determinants of Homelessness in the United States," *Social Problems* 38 (Feb. 1991): 113-131.

29. Wilson, "Studying Inner-City Social Dislocations"; Jencks, "Is the American Underclass Growing?"

30. Kerbo, *Social Stratification and Inequality*, p. 313.

31. Wilson, "Studying Inner-City Social Dislocations"; Ken Auletta, *The Underclass* (New York: Vintage Books, 1983), p. 27.

32. Wilson, "Studying Inner-City Social Dislocations."

33. Herbert J. Gans, "Deconstructing the Underclass: The Term's Danger as a Planning Concept," *Journal of the American Planning Association* 56 (Summer 1990), p. 271.

34. William Julius Wilson, *The Truly Disadvantaged: The Inner City, the Underclass, and Public Policy* (Chicago: University of Chicago Press, 1987), pp. 6-8.

35. Wilson, "Studying Inner-City Social Dislocations."

36. Robert Lewis, "Poverty Traps More Workers," *San Francisco Examiner*, Apr. 15, 1990, p. A8.

37. Janice C. Simpson, "What $152 a Week Buys," *Time*, Sep. 10, 1990, pp. 64-66.

38. Joe R. Feagin, *Subordinating the Poor: Welfare and American Beliefs* (Englewood Cliffs, N.J.: Prentice-Hall, 1975) pp. 91-92.

39. See Kerbo, *Social Stratification and Inequality*, pp. 314-317.

40. Frances Fox Piven and Richard A. Cloward, *Regulating the Poor: The Functions of Public Welfare* (New York: Vintage Books, 1971); Michael Betz, "Riots and Welfare: Are They Related?" *Social Problems* 21 (1974): 345-355; Larry Isaac and William Kelly, "Racial Insurgency, the State and Welfare Expansion," *American Sociological Review* 45 (1980): 1348-1386.

41. Piven and Cloward, *Regulating the Poor*, pp. 61-62.

42. Ibid., pp. 184-185.

43. Daniel Patrick Moynihan, *The Politics of a Guaranteed Income: The Nixon Administration and the Family Assistance Plan* (New York: Random House, 1973).

44. Bob Drogin, "True Victims of Poverty: The Children," *Los Angeles Times*, Jul. 30, 1985, pp. 1, 10-11; Kevin Roderick, "Case History of a 20-Year War on Poverty," *Los Angeles Times*, Jul. 31, 1985, pp. 1, 8-9.

45. Robert Greenstein, "Universal and Targeted Approaches to Relieving Poverty," in Jencks and Peterson, *The Urban Underclass*, pp. 437-459.

46. Jencks, "Is the American Underclass Growing?" p. 59.

47. Kerbo, *Social Stratification and Inequality*, pp. 330-337.

48. Levitas, "Homeless in America."

49. Greenstein, "Universal and Targeted Approaches to Relieving Poverty," p. 441.

50. Jencks, "Is the American Underclass Growing?" p. 41.

51. James E. Rosenbaum and Susan J. Popkin, "Employment and Earnings of Low-Income Blacks Who Move to Middle-Class Suburbs," in Jencks and Peterson, *The Urban Underclass*, pp. 342-356.

52. Meisler and Fulwood, "Economic Gap Bodes Ill for U.S."

53. See Paul Jacobs, "Keeping the Poor Poor," in Jerome Skolnick and Elliott Currie, eds., *Crisis in American Institutions*, 5th ed. (Boston: Little, Brown, 1988), pp. 134-140.

54. Oscar Lewis, *La Vida* (New York: Random House, 1965), pp. xlii-lii.

55. Ibid.
56. Charles A. Valentine, *Culture and Poverty: Critique and Counter-Proposals* (Chicago: University of Chicago Press, 1968).
57. Herbert J. Gans, "The Uses of Poverty: The Poor Pay All," *Social Policy* 2 (1971): 21–23.
58. Richard B. Freeman, "Employment and Earnings of Disadvantaged Young Men in a Labor Shortage Economy," in Jencks and Peterson, *The Urban Underclass*, pp. 103–121.
59. David Whitman, "The Key to Welfare Reform," *Atlantic*, Jun. 1987, p. 25.
60. Kingsley Davis and Wilbert E. Moore, "Some Principles of Stratification," *American Sociological Review* 10 (1945): 242–249.

CHAPTER 7   THE ETHNIC MINORITIES

1. Richard T. Schaefer, *Racial and Ethnic Groups*, 3rd ed. (Glenview, Ill.: Scott-Foresman, 1988), pp. 9–10.
2. See ibid., pp. 473–478.
3. Ibid., p. 56.
4. Schaefer, *Racial and Ethnic Groups*, pp. 176–177.
5. Nancy Oestreich Lurie, "The American Indian: Historical Background," in Norman Yetman and C. Hoy Steel, eds., *Minority and Majority: The Dynamics of Racial and Ethnic Relations*, 4th ed. (Boston: Allyn & Bacon, 1985).
6. Schaefer, *Racial and Ethnic Groups*, p. 177.
7. Lurie, "The American Indian," p. 179.
8. Peter H. Schuck, "Coming Together," *Los Angeles Times*, May 5, 1991, pp. M1, M6; Felicity Barringer, "Census Shows Profound Change in Racial Makeup of the Nation," *New York Times*, Mar. 11, 1991, pp. A1, A12.
9. U.S. Bureau of the Census, *Statistical Abstract of the United States, 1991* (Washington, D.C.: U.S. Government Printing Office, 1991), pp. 38–40.
10. Joseph H. Cash, "Indian Education: A Bright Path or Another Deal End?" in Editors of the Winston Press, *Viewpoints: Red and Yellow, Black and Brown* (Groveland Terrace, Minn.: Winston Press, 1972), p. 14.
11. U.S. Bureau of the Census, *Statistical Abstract 1991*, pp. 38, 40, 460.
12. Ibid., pp. 38, 40.
13. U.S. Bureau of the Census, *Statistical Abstract 1988*, p. 429.
14. Jim Schachter, "Unequal Opportunity: Minorities Find That Roadblocks to the Executive Suite Are Still in Place," *Los Angeles Times*, Apr. 17, 1988, sec. 4, p. 1.
15. Quoted in Charles E. Reasons and Jack E. Kuykendall, eds., *Race, Crime and Justice* (Pacific Palisades, Calif.: Goodyear, 1972).
16. David G. Savage, "1 in 4 Young Blacks in Jail or in Court Control, Study Says," *Los Angeles Times*, Feb. 27, 1990, pp. A1, A16.
17. Barringer, "Census Shows Profound Change in Racial Makeup of the Nation"; S. Dale McLemore, *Racial and Ethnic Relations in America*, 3rd ed. (Allyn & Bacon: Boston, 1991), pp. 375–425.
18. Richard T. Schaefer, *Sociology* (New York: McGraw-Hill, 1989), p. 253.
19. Anthony Wilson-Smith and Glen Allen, "Legacies of Mistrust," *Maclean's*, Sep. 10, 1990, pp. 26–27.
20. McLemore, *Racial and Ethnic Relations in America*.
21. Richard D. Alba, "The Twilight of Ethnicity Among Americans of European Ancestry: The Case of Italians," in Richard D. Alba, ed., *Ethnicity and Race in the U.S.A.* (Englewood Cliffs, N.J.: Prentice-Hall, 1988), pp. 134–158.

22. Stanley Lieberson and Mary C. Waters, *From Many Strands* (New York: Russell Sage Foundation, 1988).

23. Andrew M. Greeley, *Religious Change in America* (Cambridge, Mass.: Harvard University Press, 1989).

24. Barringer, "Census Shows Profound Change in Racial Makeup of the Nation."

25. Thomas Byrne Edsall, "Race," *Atlantic*, May 1991, pp. 53–85.

26. William Julius Wilson, "Studying Inner-City Social Dislocations: The Challenge of Public Agenda Research," *American Sociological Review* 56 (Feb. 1991): 1–14.

27. Oswald Johnson, "Bulk of Americans Living Longer But Blacks Are Not," *Los Angeles Times*, Apr. 9, 1991, pp. A1, A16.

28. Ron Harris, "NAACP Seeks Solutions to Crisis of Black Males," *Los Angeles Times*, Jul. 10, 1990, pp. A1, A25; Edsals, "Race."

29. Wilson, "Studying Inner-City Social Dislocations."

30. Theodore Caplow, *American Social Trends* (San Diego: Harcourt Brace Jovanovich, 1991), pp.191–193.

31. Barringer, "Census Shows Profound Change in Racial Makeup of the Nation."

32. Richard T. Schaefer, *Racial and Ethnic Groups* (Glenview, Ill.: Scott, Foresman, 1990), pp. 346–372.

33. Gordon W. Allport, *The Nature of Prejudice* (New York, Doubleday, 1956), p. 10.

34. Robert K. Merton, "Discrimination and the American Creed," in Robert M. MacIver, ed., *Discrimination and National Welfare* (New York: Harper & Row, 1949).

35. T. W. Adorno, E. Frenkel-Brunswik, D. J. Devinson, and R. N. Sandord, *The Authoritarian Personality* (New York: Harper & Row, 1950).

36. See Judith Andre, "Stereotypes: Conceptual and Normative Considerations," in Paula S. Rothenberg, ed., *Racism and Sexism: An Integrated Study* (New York: St. Martin's Press, 1988), pp. 257–262.

37. William Julius Wilson, *The Declining Significance of Race: Blacks and Changing American Institutions* (Chicago: University of Chicago Press, 1978).

38. Louis Harris, *Inside America* (New York: Vintage, 1987), pp. 188–192.

39. U.S. Bureau of the Census, *Statistical Abstract 1991*, p. 454.

40. Stephanie Chavez, "Anti-Semitic Incidents Reported Rising," *Los Angeles Times*, Feb. 2, 1992, pp. A3, A38; *Los Angeles Times* Special Report, "Understanding the Riots: The Path to Fury," *Los Angeles Times*, May 11, 1992, p. T12.

41. Robert Conot, "Watts: Out of the Fire," *Los Angeles Times,* Aug. 5, 1990, pp. M1, M8.

42. Lee May, "Activists React to Affirmative Action Losses," *Los Angeles Times,* Nov. 18, 1990, pp. A1, A26, A27.

CHAPTER 8 HEALTH AND ILLNESS

1. Quoted in Paul I. Ahmed and Aliza Kolker, "The Role of Indigenous Medicine in WHO's Definition of Health," in Paul I. Ahmed and George V. Coelhi, eds., *Toward a New Definition of Health* (New York: Plenum, 1979), p. 113.

2. John B. McKinlay and Sonja M. McKinlay, "Medical Measures and the Decline of Mortality," in Howard D. Schwartz, ed., *Dominant Issues in Medical Sociology*, 2nd ed. (New York: Random House, 1987), pp. 691–702.

3. See William L. Haskell, "Overview: Health Benefits of Exercise," in Joseph D. Matarazzo et al., eds., *Behavioral Health: A Handbook of Health Enhancement and Disease Prevention* (New York: Wiley, 1984), pp. 409–423; James F. Fixx, *The Complete Book of Running* (New York: Random House, 1977), p. 51.

4. See D. M. Hegsted, "What Is a Healthful Diet?" in Matarazzo et al., *Behavioral Health*, pp. 552–574.

5. Otto Schaefer, "Pre- and Post-Natal Growth Acceleration and Increase in Sugar Consumption in Canadian Eskimos," *Canadian Medical Association Journal* 103 (1970): 1059–1060.

6. Associated Press, "Koop: Tobacco Like Heroin, Cocaine," *San Luis Obispo Telegram-Tribune*, May 16, 1988, p. A1; Oakley Ray, *Drugs, Society and Human Behavior*, 3rd ed. (St. Louis: Mosby, 1983), pp. 183–205; U.S. Department of Health and Human Services, *Smoking and Health: A Report of the Surgeon General* (Washington, D.C.: U.S. Government Printing Office, 1979).

7. Associated Press, "EPA Official Tries to Bury Smoking Report," *San Luis Obispo Telegram-Tribune*, May 30, 1991, p. B8.

8. Sidney Cobb and Robert M. Rose, "Hypertension, Peptic Ulcer, and Diabetes in Air Traffic Controllers," *Journal of the American Medical Association* 224 (1973): 489–492.

9. *New York Times*, Apr. 3, 1983.

10. Marlene Cimons, "Car Fumes Linked to High Medical Costs," *Los Angeles Times*, Jan. 20, 1990, p. A18.

11. Susan Okie, "Some Cancer Rates Rising Rapidly, Study Finds," *Los Angeles Times*, Aug. 24, 1990.

12. James William Coleman, *The Criminal Elite: The Sociology of White Collar Crime*, 2nd ed. (New York: St. Martin's Press, 1989), pp. 1–2, 35–36.

13. U.S. Department of Labor, *Interim Report to Congress on Occupational Diseases* (Washington, D.C.: U.S. Government Printing Office, Jun. 1980), pp. 1–2; Patrick Derr et al., "Worker-Public Protection: The Double Standard," *Environment*, Sep. 1981.

14. John H. Dingle, "Ills of Man," in *Life and Death and Medicine* (San Francisco: Freeman, 1973), p. 53.

15. Irene Wielawski, "Measles Epidemic a Sign of Health Care System's Ills," *Los Angeles Times*, Jul. 25, 1990, pp. A1, A13.

16. Howard Haitt, *America's Health in the Balance: Choice or Chance?* (New York: Harper & Row, 1987), p. 121.

17. Steven Findlay, "AIDS: The Second Decade," *U.S. News & World Report*, Jun. 17, 1991, pp. 20–23.

18. Ibid.; Gina Kolata, "AIDS Epidemic May Be on Decline in U.S.," *Santa Barbara News Press*, Jun. 22, 1991, p. A15; Marlene Cimons, "AIDS Cases Up 29% for U.S. Women," *Los Angeles Times*, Nov. 30, 1990, pp. A1, A40.

19. Robert Steinbrook, "Speaking of: AIDS," *Los Angeles Times*, Jun. 25, 1991, p. H8; Haitt, *America's Health in the Balance*, p. 121.

20. U.S. Department of the Census, *Statistical Abstract 1991*, pp. 834–835. Colin McCord and Harold P. Freeman, "Excess Mortality in Harlem," *New England Journal of Medicine*, 322 (1990): 173–177; "Forgotten Americans," *American Health*, special report, Nov. 1990, pp. 41–42; Leonard Syme and Lisa Berkman, "Social Class, Susceptibility, and Sickness," in Schwartz, *Dominant Issues in Medical Sociology*, pp. 643–699; U.S. Department of Health and Human Services, *Health: United States, 1986* (Washington, D.C.: U.S. Government Printing Office, 1986), p. 20.

21. Syme and Berkman, "Social Class, Susceptibility, and Sickness," p. 644.

22. Robert C. Carson, James N. Butcher, and James C. Coleman, *Abnormal Psychology and Modern Life*, 8th ed. (Glenview, Ill.: Scott, Foresman, 1988), p. 4.

23. U.S. Department of the Census, *Statistical Abstract 1991*, p. 110.

24. Carson, Butcher, and Coleman, *Abnormal Psychology and Modern Life*, pp. 28–43.

25. Thomas Szasz, *The Myth of Mental Illness* (New York: Harper & Row, 1974).

26. Robert E. L. Faris and H. Warren Dunham, *Mental Disorders in Urban Areas* (Chicago: University of Chicago Press, 1939).

27. August B. Hollingshead and Frederick C. Redlich, *Social Class and Mental Illness: A Community Study* (New York: Wiley, 1958).

28. Leo Strole, T. S. Langer, S. T. Michael, M. K. Opler, and T. A. L. Rennie, *Mental Health in the Metropolis: The Midtown Manhattan Study* (New York: McGraw-Hill, 1962).

29. Bruce P. Dohrenwend and Barbara Snell Dohrenwend, *Social Status and Psychological Disorder: A Causal Inquiry* (New York: Wiley, 1969), p. 165.

30. Joseph W. Eaton and Robert J. Weil, *Culture and Mental Disorder* (New York: Free Press, 1955).

31. Eleanor Leacock, "Three Variables in the Occurrence of Mental Illness," in Alexander Leighton, John Clausen, and Robert Wilson, eds., *Explorations in Social Psychiatry* (New York: Basic Books, 1957), pp. 308–340.

32. Carson, Butcher, and Coleman, *Abnormal Psychology and Modern Life*, p. 369.

33. Franz Kallmann and B. Roth, "Genetic Aspects of Preadolescent Schizophrenia," *American Journal of Psychiatry* 112 (1956): 599–606.

34. A. Hoffer and W. Polin, "Schizophrenia in the NAS-NRC Panel of 15,909 Twin Pairs," *Archives of General Psychiatry* 23 (1970): 469–477.

35. Seymour S. Kety, "The Biological Roots of Schizophrenia," *Harvard Magazine* 78 (1976): 20–26.

36. Alfie Kohn, "Getting a Grip on Schizophrenia," *Los Angeles Times*, Jun. 25, 1990, p. B2.

37. Carson, Butcher, and Coleman, *Abnormal Psychology and Modern Life*, pp. 115–124.

38. Gregory Bateson, Don D. Jackson, Jay Haley, and John Weakland, "Toward a Theory of Schizophrenia," *Behavioral Science* 1 (1956): 251–264.

39. David Mechanic, *Mental Health and Social Policy* (Englewood Cliffs, N.J.: Prentice-Hall, 1969), p. 39.

40. See Thomas J. Scheff, *Being Mentally Ill: A Sociological Theory* (Chicago: Aldine-Atherton, 1966), pp. 55–101.

41. Bruce Link, "Mental Patient Status, Work, and Income: An Examination of the Effects of Psychological Labeling," *American Sociological Review* 47 (Apr. 1982): 202–215.

42. Robert Rosenblatt, "U.S. Medical Spending Soars 11% During 1989," *Los Angeles Times*, Dec. 21, 1990, p. A4; "The Crisis in Health Insurance," *Consumer Reports* 55 (Sep. 1990): 608–617.

43. U.S. Department of the Census, *Statistical Abstract 1991*, p. 103.

44. Helaine Olen, "Doctor Supply Grows Faster Than Patients," *Los Angeles Times*, Jul. 3, 1991, p. A5.

45. Ibid.; Howard D. Schwartz, "Irrationality as a Feature of Health Care in the United States," in Schwartz, ed., *Dominant Issues in Medical Sociology*, p. 478.

46. Robert Steinbrook, "Medicine's Appeal to Internists Fades," *Los Angeles Times*, Jan. 1, 1991, p. A3.

47. Robert Steinbrook, "Thousands of Surgeries Called Unnecessary," *Los Angeles Times*, Nov. 13, 1987, sec. 1, pp. 1, 30.

48. "Rate High on Unneeded Surgeries," *Los Angeles Times*, Oct. 29, 1990, p. B3.

49. U.S. Department of the Census, *Statistical Abstract 1991*, p. 395.

50. Schwartz, "Irrationality as a Feature of Health Care in the United States," p. 477.

51. K. Steel, P. M. Gertman, C. Crescsenzi, and J. Anderson, "Iatrogenic Illness on a General Medical Service at a University Hospital," *New England Journal of Medicine* 304 (1981): 638–642; Darrel Montero and Judith McDowell, *Social Problems* (New York: Macmillan, 1986), p. 112.

52. Coleman, *The Criminal Elite*, p. 155.

53. Daniel S. Greenberg, "Lawyers' Pay Would Cure Nursing Shortage," *Los Angeles Times*, Jun. 12, 1988, sec. 5, p. 5.

54. R. V. Pattison and A. M. Katz, "Investor-Owned and Not for Profit Hospitals," *New England Journal of Medicine* 309 (1983): 353-374.

55. Peter Downs, "Your Money or Your Life," *Progressive* 51 (Jan. 1987): 24-28.

56. Erving Goffman, *Asylums: Essays on the Social Situation of Mental Patients and Other Inmates* (New York: Doubleday, 1961).

57. Anastasia Toufexis, "From Asylum to Anarchy," *Time*, Oct. 22, 1990, pp. 58-59.

58. Tom Morganthau, "Abandoned," *Newsweek*, Jan. 6, 1986, pp. 14-19.

59. Rosenblatt, "U.S. Medical Spending Soars 11% During 1989"; Sam Fulwood III and Stanley Meisler, "High Medical Costs Add to Ills of Poor Medical System," *Los Angeles Times*, Jul. 17, 1990, pp. A1, A14-15; Janny Scott, "The *Times* Poll: Many Believe They Can't Afford Good Health Care," *Los Angeles Times*, Feb. 5, 1990, pp. A1, A23.

60. "The Crisis in Health Insurance"; Associated Press, "Health Insurers' Efficiency Is Questioned," *Los Angeles Times*, Oct. 19, 1990, p. D6.

61. "The Crisis in Health Insurance"; Wanda Coyle, "Diagnosis: U.S. Health Care System Is Critically Ill," *San Luis Obispo Telegram-Tribune*, Jul. 18, 1990, pp. A1, 12.

62. "The Crisis in Health Insurance."

63. Irene Wielawski, "State Panel Gives Medi-Cal a Poor Bill of Health," *Los Angeles Times*, Nov. 15, 1990, pp. A3, A29.

64. Associated Press, "Nursing Homes Impoverish Elderly," *San Luis Obispo Telegram-Tribune*, Nov. 9, 1987.

65. Mary Lake Polan, "Medical Researchers, Heal Thyselves of Gender Bias," *Los Angeles Times*, Feb. 24, 1991, p. M1.

66. U.S. Department of the Census, *Statistical Abstract 1991*, p. 92.

67. Rosenblatt, "U.S. Medical Spending Soars 11% During 1989"; "The Crisis in Health Insurance."

68. See Coleman, *The Criminal Elite*, pp. 112-118.

69. Theodore Caplow, *American Social Trends* (San Diego: Harcourt Brace Jovanovich, 1991), p. 164.

70. Richard Merrit and Mona J. Rowe, "AIDS 2000: Where the Fight Will Be Fought," in John Stimson, Ardyth Stimson, and Vincent N. Parrillo, *Social Problems: Contemporary Readings*, 2nd ed. (Itasca, Ill.: Peacock, 1991), pp. 329-430.

71. Caroline Kaufmann, "Rights and the Provision of Health Care: A Comparison of Canada, Great Britain, and the United States," in Schwartz, *Dominant Issues in Medical Sociology*, pp. 491-508; Harry Nelson, "Crisis Grips Health Care in Britain," *Los Angeles Times*, Mar. 7, 1988, sec. 1, pp. 1, 8; Alan Maynard, *Health Care in the European Community* (Pittsburgh: University of Pittsburgh Press, 1975).

72. "The Crisis in Health Insurance."

73. Ibid.; Mary Williams Walsh, "Socialized Medicine Cuts Canada's Costs—and Care," *Los Angeles Times*, Apr. 9, 1990, pp. A1, A12.

74. U.S. National Center for Health Statistics, *Health: United States, 1986* (Washington, D.C.: U.S. Government Printing Office, 1987), p. 94.

75. Ernest Conine, "Canada's Sensible Approach," *Los Angeles Times*, Mar. 26, 1990, p. B1; Walsh, "Socialized Medicine Cuts Canada's Costs—and Care."

76. Roxane Arnold, "Medicine's Best Only Delayed the Inevitable," *Los Angeles Times*, Apr. 7, 1985, sec. 1, pp. 24, 26.

77. Daniel P. Reid, *The Tao of Health, Sex and Longevity* (New York: Simon & Schuster, 1989), p. 233.

78. Caplow, *American Social Trends*, p. 167.

79. Howard D. Schwartz, Peggy L. DeWolf, and James K. Skipper, "Gender, Professionalization, and Occupational Anomie: The Case of Nursing," in Schwartz, *Dominant Issues in Medical Sociology*, pp. 559–569.
80. "The Crisis in Health Insurance."
81. Paul Starr, *The Social Transformation of American Medicine* (New York: Basic Books, 1982).

CHAPTER 9   THE OLD AND THE YOUNG

1. See Vern L. Bullough, "Age at Menarche: A Misunderstanding," *Science* 213 (1981): 365–366.
2. P. B. Baltes and S. L. Willis, "Enhancement of Intellectual Functioning in Old Age: Penn State's Adult Development and Enrichment Program," in F. I. M. Craik and S. E. Trehrib, eds., *Aging and Cognitive Process* (New York: Plenum, 1982).
3. Melinda Beck, "Trading Places," *Newsweek*, Jul. 16, 1990, pp. 48–54.
4. See Daniel J. Levison, *The Season of a Man's Life* (New York: Knopf, 1978).
5. U.S. Bureau of the Census, *Statistical Abstract of the United States, 1991* (Washington, D.C.: U.S. Government Printing Office, 1991), p. 462; Nancy Gibbs, "Shameful Bequests to the Next Generation," *Time*, Oct. 8, 1990, pp. 42–46.
6. Gibbs, "Shameful Bequests to the Next Generation."
7. Ron Harris, "Youth Isn't Kid Stuff These Days," *Los Angeles Times*, May 12, 1991, pp. A1, A20.
8. Ibid.; Barbara Kantrowitz, "Children Lost in the Quagmire," *Newsweek*, May 13, 1991, p. 64.
9. Richard Zoglin, "Is TV Ruining Our Children?" *Time*, Oct. 15, 1990, p. 75.
10. Elizabeth Douvan, "The Age of Narcissism, 1963–1982," in Joseph M. Hawes and N. Ray Hiner, eds., *American Childhood: A Research Guide and Historical Handbook* (Westport, Conn.: Greenwood Press, 1985), pp. 587–617.
11. Erik H. Erikson, *Childhood and Society*, rev. ed. (New York: Norton, 1964).
12. Hans Sebald, *Adolescence: A Social Psychological Analysis* (Englewood Cliffs, N.J.: Prentice-Hall, 1984).
13. Harris, "Youth Isn't Kid Stuff These Days."
14. Anastasia Toufexis, "Struggling for Sanity," *Time*, Oct. 8, 1990, pp. 47–48.
15. Marlene Cimons, "Study Shows a Million Teen Suicide Attempts," *Los Angeles Times*, Sep. 20, 1991, pp. A1, A26.
16. Harris, "Youth Isn't Kid Stuff These Days."
17. U.S. Bureau of the Census, *Statistical Abstract 1991*, pp. 402, 463.
18. Ibid., p. 13.
19. E. Kaye Fulton and Nancy Wood, "A Reasonable Limit," *Maclean's*, Dec. 17, 1990, pp. 20–21.
20. Arthur N. Schwartz, Cherie L. Snyder, and James A. Peterson, *Aging and Life*, 2nd ed. (New York: Holt, Rinehart & Winston, 1984), pp. 37–38.
21. Fred Cottrell, *Aging and the Aged* (Dubuque, Iowa: Brown, 1974), p. 19.
22. U.S. Bureau of the Census, *Statistical Abstract 1991*, p. 463.
23. Theodore Caplow, *American Social Trends* (San Diego: Harcourt Brace Jovanovich, 1991), pp. 141–142.
24. Beth B. Hess and Elizabeth Markson, eds., *Growing Old in America*, 3rd ed. (New Brunswick, N.J.: Transaction Books, 1985), p. 14.
25. U.S. Bureau of the Census, *Statistical Abstract 1991*, p. 363.

26. Hess and Markson, *Growing Old in America*, p. 8.
27. See Walter R. Cunningham and John W. Brookbank, *Gerontology* (New York: Harper & Row, 1988), pp. 228–245; Robert C. Atchley, *The Sociology of Retirement* (Cambridge, Mass.: Schenkman, 1976), pp. 87–108; Herman J. Loether, *Problems of Aging: Sociological and Social Psychological Perspectives*, 2nd ed. (Encino, Calif.: Dickensen, 1975), p. 86.
28. Gibbs, "Shameful Bequests to the Next Generation."
29. Fulton and Wood, "A Reasonable Limit."
30. See Jon Hendricks and C. David Hendricks, *Aging in Mass Society: Myths and Realities*, 2nd ed. (Cambridge, Mass.: Winthrop, 1981), pp. 14–18.

CHAPTER 10   WOMEN AND MEN

1. See, for example, Ann Ferguson, "Androgyny as an Ideal for Human Development," in Paula S. Rothenberg, ed., *Racism and Sexism: An Integrated Study* (New York: St. Martin's Press, 1988), pp. 362–371.
2. Sandra L. Bem, "Androgyny and Gender Schema Theory," in T. B. Sonderegger, ed., *Nebraska Symposium on Motivation: Psychology of Gender* (Lincoln: University of Nebraska Press, 1985).
3. Jane B. Lancaster and Chet S. Lancaster, "The Watershed: Changes in Parental Investment and Family Formation Strategies in the Course of Human Evolution," in Jane B. Lancaster et al., eds., *Parenting Across the Lifespan* (New York: Aldine de Gruyter, 1988), p. 191.
4. See Hilary M. Lips, *Sex and Gender* (Mountain View, Calif.: Mayfield, 1988), pp. 1–26.
5. Ibid., pp. 105–109.
6. Bruce Svare and Craig H. Kinsley, "Hormones and Sex-Related Behavior," in Kathryn Kelley, ed., *Females, Males and Sexuality: Theories and Research* (Albany: State University of New York Press, 1987), pp. 13–58.
7. Laurel Richardson, *The Dynamics of Sex and Gender: A Sociological Perspective* (New York: Harper & Row, 1988), p. 145.
8. Richard Borsay Lee, *The !Kung San: Men, Women and Work in a Foraging Society* (Cambridge, England: Cambridge University Press, 1979); Margaret Mead, *Sex and Temperament in Three Primitive Societies* (New York: Mentor Books, 1935); James A. Doyle, *The Male Experience* (Dubuque, Iowa: Brown, 1983), pp. 82–85.
9. Margaret L. Anderson, *Thinking About Women: Sociological Perspectives on Sex and Gender*, 2nd ed. (New York: Macmillan, 1988), pp. 49–52; John Money and A. A. Ehrhardt, *Man, Woman, Boy and Girl: The Differentiation and Dimorphism of Gender Identity from Conception to Maturity* (Baltimore: Johns Hopkins University Press, 1972).
10. Ernestine Friedl, *Women and Men: An Anthropologist's View* (New York: Holt, Rinehart & Winston, 1975).
11. See, for example, Eleanor Leacock, "Women's Status in Egalitarian Society: Implications for Social Evolution," *Current Anthropology* 19 (Jun. 1978): 247–255.
12. Richardson, *Dynamics of Sex and Gender*, pp. 155–156.
13. Anderson, *Thinking About Women*, pp. 82–83.
14. See Richardson, *Dynamics of Sex and Gender*, pp. 16–34; Simone de Beauvoir, *The Second Sex* (New York: Knopf, 1957).
15. Ruth E. Hartley, "Sex-Role Pressures and the Socialization of the Male Child," in Deborah S. David and Robert Brannon, eds., *The Forty-nine Percent Majority: The Male Sex Role* (Reading, Mass.: Addison-Wesley, 1976), p. 236.
16. Leslie Brody, "Gender Difference in Emotional Development: A Review of Theory and Research," *Journal of Personality* 53 (1985): 102–149.
17. Richardson, *Dynamics of Sex and Gender*, pp. 56–59.

18. Myra Sadker, David Sadker, and Susan S. Klein, "Abolishing Misconceptions About Sex Equity in Education," *Theory into Practice* 25 (Autumn 1986): 220.

19. Beverly A. Stitt, *Building Gender Fairness in Schools* (Carbondale: Southern Illinois University Press, 1988), pp. 29-32.

20. John Ernest, "Mathematics and Sex," *American Mathematical Monthly* 83 (1976): 595-614.

21. Alison Kelly, *Changing Schools and Changing Society: Some Reflections on the Girls in Sciences and Technology Project* (New York: Open University, 1984).

22. J. H. Feldstein and S. Feldstein, "Sex Differences on Televised Toy Commercials," *Sex Roles* 8 (1982): 581-587.

23. F. E. Barcus, *Commercial Children's Television on Weekends and Weekday Afternoons* (Newtonville, Mass.: Action for Children's Television, 1982).

24. N. S. Feldman and E. Brown, "Male Versus Female Differences in Control Strategies: What Children Learn from Saturday Morning Television" (paper presented at the Eastern Psychological Association, Baltimore, April 1984).

25. See Richardson, *Dynamics of Sex and Gender*, pp. 69-82.

26. U.S. Bureau of the Census, *Statistical Abstract of the United States, 1991* (Washington, D.C.: U.S. Government Printing Office, 1991), pp. 161, 167.

27. Ann P. Parelius, "Mathematics and Science Majors: Gender Differences in Selection and Persistence," in Laura Kramer, ed., *The Sociology of Gender* (New York: St. Martin's Press, 1991), pp. 140-160.

28. U.S. Bureau of the Census, *Statistical Abstract 1991*, pp. 386, 387.

29. Janice Castro, "Get Set: Here They Come!" *Time*, special issue, "Women: The Road Ahead" (Fall 1990), pp. 50-52.

30. Brenda Dalglish, "Having It All," *Maclean's*, Sep. 3, 1990, pp. 32-35; Francine D. Blau and Marianne A. Ferber, *The Economics of Women, Men, and Work* (Englewood Cliffs, N.J.: Prentice-Hall, 1986), pp. 310-311.

31. Amy Saltzman, "Trouble at the Top," *U.S. News & World Report*, Jun. 17, 1991, pp. 40-48.

32. Sara E. Rix, ed., *The American Woman 1987-88: A Report in Depth* (New York: Norton, 1987).

33. Monica Roman, "Women Beware: An MBA Doesn't Mean Equal Pay," *Business Week*, Oct. 29, 1990, p. 57.

34. *Time*, "Women: The Road Ahead," p. 26.

35. Nancy Gibbs, "The Dreams of Youth," *Time*, "Women: The Road Ahead," pp. 10-14.

36. See Barbara R. Bergmann, *The Economic Emergence of Women* (New York: Basic Books, 1986), pp. 119-145; Blau and Ferber, *The Economics of Women, Men, and Work*.

37. U.S. Bureau of the Census, *Statistical Abstract 1991*, pp. 395-397.

38. Saltzman, "Trouble at the Top."

39. Dalglish, "Having It All."

40. Ann M. Morrison, "Up Against a Glass Ceiling," *Los Angeles Times*, Aug. 23, 1987, sec. 1, p. 3.

41. Blau and Ferber, *The Economics of Women, Men, and Work*, pp. 152-181.

42. Castro, "Get Set: Here They Come!"

43. Margaret Carlson, "It's Our Turn," *Time*, "Women: The Road Ahead," pp. 16-18.

44. Pippa Norris, "The Political Position of Women in Elites," in Kramer, *The Sociology of Gender*, pp. 354-367.

45. Richardson, *Dynamics of Sex and Gender*, pp. 162-163.

46. Theodore Caplow, *American Social Trends* (San Diego: Harcourt Brace Jovanovich, 1991), pp. 153-154.

47. Carol McGraw, "Employers, Workers Act to Fight Job Harassment," *Los Angeles Times*, Oct. 21, 1990, pp. A1, A30.

48. Lloyd D. Elgart and Lillian Schanfield, "Sexual Harassment of Students," *Thought & Action* 7 (Spring 1991): 21–42.

49. Gibbs, "The Dreams of Youth."

50. U.S. Bureau of the Census, *Statistical Abstract 1991*, p. 86.

51. Andrew Kimbrell, "A Time for Men to Pull Together," *Utne Reader*, May–Jun. 1991, pp. 66–74.

52. Warren Farrell, "Men as Success Objects," *Utne Reader*, May–Jun. 1991, pp. 81–84.

53. See Josephine Donovan, *Feminist Theory* (New York: Ungar, 1985); Anderson, *Thinking About Women*, pp. 287–361.

CHAPTER 11 SEXUAL BEHAVIOR

1. Clellan S. Ford and Frank A. Beach, *Patterns of Sexual Behavior* (New York: Ace Books, 1951), p. 14.

2. William H. Davenport, "Sex in Cross-Cultural Perspective," in Frank A. Beach, ed., *Human Sexuality in Four Perspectives* (Baltimore: Johns Hopkins University Press, 1977), p. 124.

3. Ian Robertson, *Sociology*, 3rd ed. (New York: Worth, 1987), pp. 227–229.

4. Davenport, "Sex in Cross-Cultural Perspective," pp. 122–124.

5. Ibid., p. 125.

6. Conrad Phillip Kottak, *Cultural Anthropology*, 4th ed. (New York: Random House, 1987), pp. 152–153. For a more detailed description of the homosexual tribes of New Guinea, see V. van Baal, *Dema: Description and Analysis of Marid Anim Culture* (Hague: M. Nijhoff, 1966).

7. Quoted in Robertson, *Sociology*, p. 230.

8. Alfred C. Kinsey, Wardell B. Pomeroy, and Clyde E. Martin, *Sexual Behavior in the Human Male* (Philadelphia: Saunders, 1948); Alfred C. Kinsey, Wardell B. Pomeroy, Clyde E. Martin, and Paul H. Gebhard, *Sexual Behavior in the Human Female* (Philadelphia: Saunders, 1953).

9. Morton Hunt, *Sexual Behavior in the 1970s* (New York: Dell, 1974), pp. 147–149.

10. Marlene Cimons, "Study Says More Young Women Have Sex," *Los Angeles Times*, Jan. 5, 1991, p. A2.

11. June M. Reinisch, *The Kinsey Institute New Report on Sex* (New York: St. Martin's Press, 1990), p. 6.

12. Reinisch, *The Kinsey Institute New Report on Sex*, p. 7; Thomas H. Maugh II, "Sex American Style: Trend to the Traditional," *Los Angeles Times*, Feb. 19, 1990, pp. A1, A22; Scripps News Service, "Sexual Revolution: Most of America Missed It," *San Luis Obispo Telegram-Tribune*, Feb. 19, 1990, p. A1.

13. Reinisch, *The Kinsey Institute New Report on Sex*, p. 132.

14. James Leslie McCary and Stephen P. McCary, *McCary's Human Sexuality* (Belmont, Calif.: Wadsworth, 1982), pp. 367–369, 382–389.

15. Ibid., pp. 446–450.

16. Ibid., p. 431.

17. Maugh, "Sex American Style"; Scripps News Service, "Sexual Revolution."

18. Evelyn Hooker, "The Adjustment of the Male Overt Homosexual," *Journal of Projective Techniques* 21 (1957): 18–31, and "Male Homosexuality and the Rorschach," *Journal of Projective Techniques* 22 (1958): 33–54.

19. Reinisch, *The Kinsey Institute New Report on Sex*, pp. 139–141.

20. See Philip Feldman, "The Homosexual Preference," in Kevin Howells, ed., *The Psychology of Sexual Diversity* (Oxford, England: Basil Blackwell, 1984), pp. 20–22.

21. Hilary M. Lips, *Sex and Gender* (Mountain View, Calif.: Mayfield, 1988), pp. 114–115; Feldman, "The Homosexual Preference," pp. 22–24.

22. Feldman, "The Homosexual Preference," pp. 24–28; A. P. Bell, M. S. Weinberg, and S. K. Hammersmith, *Sexual Preference* (Bloomington: Indiana University Press, 1981).

23. Richard Green, *The "Sissy Boy Syndrome" and the Development of Homosexuality* (New Haven: Yale University Press, 1987).

24. See Ronald L. Akers, *Deviant Behavior: A Social Learning Approach*, 3rd ed. (Belmont, Calif.: Wadsworth, 1985), pp. 192–203.

25. McCary and McCary, *Human Sexuality*, pp. 446–450; Reinisch, *The Kinsey Institute New Report on Sex*, pp. 139–140; Maugh, "Sex American Style"; Scripps News Service, "Sexual Revolution."

26. Marlene Cimons, "AIDS: 'It's Changed Us Forever,'" *Los Angeles Times*, May 31, 1991, pp. A1, A19–20.

27. Marshall B. Clinard, *The Sociology of Deviant Behavior*, 4th ed. (New York: Holt, Rinehart & Winston, 1974), pp. 545–546.

28. Gerald R. Adams and Thomas Gullotta, *Adolescent Life Experiences* (Monterey, Calif.: Brooks/Cole, 1983), pp. 330–335.

29. Cimons, "Study Says More Young Women Have Sex"; Maugh, "Sex American Style"; Scripps News Service, "Sexual Revolution."

30. Calculated from U.S. Bureau of the Census, *Statistical Abstract of the United States, 1991* (Washington, D.C.: U.S. Government Printing Office, 1991), pp. 13, 67.

31. Claudia Wallis, "Children Having Children," *Time*, Dec. 9, 1985, pp. 78–90.

32. Frank F. Furstenberg, *Unplanned Parenthood: The Consequences of Teenage Childbearing* (New York: Free Press, 1976), pp. 57–58.

33. Robert Steinbrook, "Speaking of: AIDS," *Los Angeles Times*, Jun. 25, 1991, p. H8.

34. Robert Steinbrook, "AIDS Costs Will Nearly Double by 1994," *Los Angeles Times*, Jun. 20, 1991, p. A6.

35. Steven Findlay, "AIDS: The Second Decade," *U.S. News & World Report*, Jun. 17, 1991, pp. 20–23.

36. Ibid.

37. McCary and McCary, *Human Sexuality*, p. 413.

38. A. C. Jaffe, "Child Molestation," *Medical Aspects of Human Sexuality*, Apr. 1976, pp. 73, 93.

39. Charles H. McCaghy, "Child Molesting," *Sexual Behavior*, Aug. 1971, pp. 16–24.

40. Sue Titus Reid, *Crime and Criminology*, 4th ed. (New York: Holt, Rinehart & Winston, 1985), p. 260.

41. James Patterson and Peter Kim, *The Day America Told the Truth* (New York: Prentice-Hall, 1991), p. 7.

42. Alex Thio, *Deviant Behavior*, 3rd ed. (New York: Harper & Row, 1988), pp. 157–160; McCary and McCary, *Human Sexuality*, pp. 412–414.

43. See Reid, *Crime and Criminology*, pp. 261–263.

44. Hunt, *Sexual Behavior in the 1970s*, p. 145; McCary and McCary, *Human Sexuality*, p. 431.

45. David F. Luckenbill, "Deviant Career Mobility: The Case of Male Prostitutes," *Social Problems* 33 (Apr. 1986): 283–296.

46. *Report of the President's Commission on Obscenity and Pornography* (New York: Bantam Books, 1970), p. 49.

47. Aric Press, "The War Against Pornography," *Newsweek*, Mar. 18, 1985, pp. 58–66.
48. W. Cody Wilson, "Facts Versus Fears: Why Should We Worry About Pornography?" *Annals of the American Academy of Political Science* 397 (1971): 105–117.
49. Ibid., p. 113; Clinard, *Sociology of Deviant Behavior*, p. 534; David G. Savage, "Violence Against Women," *Los Angeles Times*, Jun. 1, 1985, sec. 2, pp. 1, 6; Press, "The War Against Pornography."
50. See Frank E. Hagan, *Introduction to Criminology* (Chicago: Nelson-Hall, 1986), p. 247.
51. Edward Donnerstein and L. Berkowitz, "Victim Reactions in Aggressive Erotic Films as a Factor in Violence Against Women," *Journal of Personality and Social Psychology* 41 (1981): 710–724.
52. Edward Donnerstein, Daniel Linz, and Steven Penrod, *The Question of Pornography: Research Findings and Policy Implications* (New York: Free Press, 1987), pp. 172–179.
53. Press, "The War Against Pornography."
54. Savage, "Violence Against Women."
55. Elizabeth Mehren, "New Study Claims TV Fails to Balance Sex, Responsibility," *Los Angeles Times*, Jan. 27, 1988, sec. 4, pp. 1, 12.
56. Sharon Bernstein, "Condoms: Television's Dirty Little Secret," *Los Angeles Times*, Oct. 19, 1990, pp. F1, F24–25.
57. Tom Gorman, "Sex Classes: A Changing Direction," *Los Angeles Times*, Jul. 19, 1985, pp. 1, 19; Wallis, "Children Having Children."
58. Kingsley Davis, "The Sociology of Prostitution," *American Sociological Review* 2 (1937): 744–755.
59. Donald Symons, *The Evolution of Human Sexuality* (New York: Oxford University Press, 1979).

CHAPTER 12 DRUG USE

1. U.S. Bureau of the Census, *Statistical Abstract of the United States, 1991* (Washington, D.C.: U.S. Government Printing Office, 1991), p. 754.
2. Ibid., p. 122.
3. Richard G. Schlaadt and Peter T. Shannon, *Drugs*, 3rd ed. (Englewood Cliffs, N.J.: Prentice-Hall, 1990), p. 35; Associated Press, "Cocaine Use in Five-Year Drop, Report Claims," *San Luis Obispo Telegram-Tribune*, Dec. 19, 1990, p. A2; Marlene Cimons, "Illicit Drug Use Falls to 47.9% for Young Adults," *Los Angeles Times*, Jan. 25, 1991, p. A4; U.S. Bureau of the Census, *Statistical Abstract 1991*, p. 121; Amy Stevens, "Student Drug Use Falls, But Alcohol Abuse Is Unchanged, Survey Finds," *Los Angeles Times*, Jun. 15, 1988, Pt. A, pp. 1, 22.
4. Schlaadt and Shannon, *Drugs*, p. 45.
5. U.S. Bureau of the Census, *Statistical Abstract 1991*, p. 121.
6. See Craig MacAndrew and Robert B. Edgerton, *Drunken Comportment: A Social Explanation* (Chicago: Aldine-Atherton, 1966).
7. Schlaadt and Shannon, *Drugs*, p. 175.
8. Jack H. Mendelson and Nancy K. Mello, *Alcohol Use and Abuse in America* (Boston: Little, Brown, 1985), p. 225.
9. Timothy J. Flanagan and Kathleen Maguire, eds., *Sourcebook of Criminal Justice Statistics, 1989*, U.S. Department of Justice, Bureau of Justice Statistics (Washington, D.C.: U.S. Government Printing Office, 1990), p. 319; Louis Harris, *Inside America* (New York: Vintage, 1987), pp. 60–61.

10. Schlaadt and Shannon, *Drugs*, p. 185.
11. Ibid., p. 181.
12. Flanagan and Maguire, *Sourcebook of Criminal Justice Statistics, 1989*, p. 320.
13. *Potsdam College News*, "National Study Indicates Decrease in Drinking, Drunken Driving Among College Students," Mar. 3, 1988.
14. U.S. Bureau of the Census, *Statistical Abstract 1991*, p. 122.
15. Ibid.
16. *Potsdam College News*, "National Study Indicates Decrease in Drinking."
17. Oakley Ray, *Drugs, Society, and Human Behavior*, 3rd ed. (St. Louis: Mosby, 1983), p. 174.
18. U.S. Bureau of the Census, *Statistical Abstract 1991*, pp. 121, 122; Schlaadt and Shannon, *Drugs*, p. 117.
19. Ray, *Drugs, Society, and Human Behavior*, pp. 199–202.
20. Quoted in Matt Clark, "Slow-Motion Suicide," *Newsweek*, Jan. 22, 1979, pp. 83–84; see also U.S. Department of Health and Human Services, *Smoking and Health: A Report of the Surgeon General* (Washington, D.C.: U.S. Government Printing Office, 1979).
21. Associated Press, "Koop: Tobacco Like Heroin, Cocaine," *San Luis Obispo Telegram-Tribune*, May 16, 1988, p. A1.
22. Schlaadt and Shannon, *Drugs*, pp. 116–150.
23. Associated Press, "EPA Official Tries to Bury Smoking Report," *San Luis Obispo Telegram-Tribune*, May 30, 1991, p. B8.
24. Jeff Bingaman, "Tobacco Has Dead Aim on Latinos," *Los Angeles Times*, Feb. 11, 1990, p. M5.
25. Ibid.; Donna K. H. Walters, "Cigarettes: Makers Aim at Special Niches to Boost Sales," *Los Angeles Times*, Sep. 15, 1985, sec. 5, p. A3; Associated Press, "EPA Official Tries to Bury Smoking Report."
26. Flanagan and Maguire, *Sourcebook of Criminal Justice Statistics, 1989*, p. 315.
27. Ibid.; U.S. Bureau of the Census, *Statistical Abstract 1991*, p. 121.
28. Janny Scott, "Pot Takes a Hit in New Study of Health Dangers," *Los Angeles Times*, Feb. 11, 1988, sec. 1, pp. 3, 36.
29. Howard S. Becker, *Outsiders* (New York: Free Press, 1963), pp. 41–58.
30. Schlaadt and Shannon, *Drugs*, pp. 258–259.
31. Gina Kolata, "AIDS Epidemic May Be on Decline in U.S.," *Santa Barbara News Press*, Jun. 22, 1991, p. A15; Schlaadt and Shannon, *Drugs*, p. 215.
32. Flanagan and Maguire, *Sourcebook of Criminal Justice Statistics, 1989*, p. 314.
33. Ray, *Drugs, Society, and Human Behavior*, pp. 342–359; James William Coleman, "The Myth of Addiction," *Journal of Drug Issues* 6 (1976): 135–141.
34. Schlaadt and Shannon, *Drugs*, pp. 238–243; Ray, *Drugs, Society, and Human Behavior*, pp. 336–337.
35. Harry Nelson, "LSD Still on Some Minds," *Los Angeles Times*, Mar. 25, 1991, p. B3; Schlaadt and Shannon, *Drugs*, p. 240.
36. Ray, *Drugs, Society, and Human Behavior*, pp. 314–319.
37. Schlaadt and Shannon, *Drugs*, p. 154; Ray, *Drugs, Society and Human Behavior*, pp. 311–314.
38. Schlaadt and Shannon, *Drugs*, pp. 155–163.
39. Schlaadt and Shannon, *Drugs*, pp. 82–87.
40. Ibid., pp. 91–100.
41. Associated Press, "Cocaine Use in Five-Year Drop"; Flanagan and Maguire, *Sourcebook of Criminal Justice Statistics, 1989*, p. 314; Cimons, "Illicit Drug Use Falls to 47.9% for Young Adults."

42. Schlaadt and Shannon, *Drugs*, pp. 39–44.

43. Marlene Cimons, "Youth Steroid Use Believed Rising," *Los Angeles Times*, Sep. 8, 1990, p. A2.

44. Sidney Cohen, *The Alcoholism Problems: Selected Issues* (New York: Haworth Press, 1983), p. 86; D. W. Goodwin, "Genetics of Alcoholism," in R. W. Pickens and L. L. Heston, eds., *Psychiatric Factors in Drug Abuse* (New York: Grune & Stratton, 1979).

45. E. M. Jellinek, *The Disease of Alcoholism* (Highland Park, N.J.: Hillhouse Press, 1960).

46. Kathleen Whalen Fitzgerald, *Alcoholism: The Genetic Inheritance* (New York: Doubleday, 1985), pp. 1–21.

47. Alfred R. Lindesmith, *Addiction and Opiates* (Chicago: Aldine-Atherton, 1968), pp. 64–67.

48. G. E. Barnes, "The Alcoholic Personality: A Reanalysis of the Literature," *Journal of Studies on Alcohol* 40 (1979): 622.

49. Ray, *Drugs, Society and Human Behavior*, p. 160.

50. Isador Chein, Donald Gerard, Robert Lee, and Eva Rosenfeld, *The Road to H* (New York: Basic Books, 1964).

51. George Vaillant, *The Natural History of Alcoholism* (Cambridge, Mass.: Harvard University Press, 1983).

52. James William Coleman, "The Dynamics of Narcotic Abstinence: An Interactionist Theory," *Sociological Quarterly* 19 (1978): 555–564; Coleman, "The Myth of Addiction."

53. D. F. Musto, "The History of Legislative Control over Opium, Cocaine, and Their Derivatives," in Ronald Hamowy, ed., *Dealing with Drugs: Consequences of Government Control* (San Francisco: Pacific Research Institutes for Public Policy, 1987), pp. 37–71.

54. Coleman, "The Myth of Addiction."

55. See Randy E. Marnett, "Curing the Drug-Law Addiction: The Harmful Side Effects of Legal Prohibition," in Hamowy, *Dealing with Drugs*, pp. 73–102.

56. Ray, *Drugs, Society and Human Behavior*, pp. 314–319, 334–335, 377–380.

57. Richard H. Blum, Eva Blum, and E. Garfield, *Drug Education: Results and Recommendations* (Lexington, Mass.: Heath, 1976).

58. Janny Scott, "Debate Resurrected over Risks of Casual Drug Use," *Los Angeles Times*, Aug. 10, 1988, sec. 1, pp. 1, 20.

59. See Marshall B. Clinard, *The Sociology of Deviant Behavior*, 4th ed. (New York: Holt, Rinehart & Winston, 1974), pp. 412–419; Erich Goode, *Drugs and American Society* (New York: Knopf, 1972), pp. 147–148.

60. Roger Meyer, *Guide to Drug Rehabilitation* (Boston: Beacon Press, 1972), pp. 61–63.

61. David Gelman, "Clean and Sober—and Agnostic," *Newsweek*, Jul. 8, 1991, pp. 62–63.

62. See Rita Vokman and Donald R. Cressey, "Differential Association and the Rehabilitation of Drug Addicts," *American Journal of Sociology* 69 (1963): 129–142.

63. Meyer, *Guide to Drug Rehabilitation*, p. 72; Ray, *Drugs, Society, and Human Behavior*, pp. 360–362.

64. Thomas Szasz, *Ceremonial Chemistry: The Ritual Persecution of Drugs, Addicts, and Pushers*, rev. ed. (Holmes Beach, Fla.: Learning Publications, 1985).

65. Katherine M. Jamieson and Timothy J. Flanagan, eds., *Sourcebook of Criminal Justice Statistics, 1986*, U.S. Department of Justice, Bureau of Justice Statistics (Washington, D.C.: U.S. Government Printing Office, 1987), p. 65.

66. Ibid., p. 134.

67. For a discussion of maintenance programs see Ray, *Drugs, Society and Human Behavior*, pp. 362–366.

68. Rone Tempest, "Drugs: Dutch Gain with a Tolerant Tack," *Los Angeles Times*, Sep. 22, 1989, pp. A1, A10–11.

CHAPTER 13   CRIME AND VIOLENCE

1. U.S. Department of Justice, *Criminal Victimization 1989* (Washington, D.C.: U.S. Government Printing Office, Oct. 1990).
2. Timothy J. Flanagan and Kathleen Maguire, eds., *Sourcebook of Criminal Justice Statistics 1990* (Washington, D.C.: U.S. Government Printing Office, 1991), p. 185; Nora Underwood, "High Anxieties," *Maclean's*, Jan. 1, 1991, pp. 30–31.
3. Flanagan and Maguire, *Sourcebook of Criminal Justice Statistics 1990*, p. 184.
4. Ibid., p. 418.
5. Marvin E. Wolfgang, *Patterns in Criminal Homicide* (Philadelphia: University of Pennsylvania Press, 1958).
6. Flanagan and Maguire, *Sourcebook of Criminal Justice Statistics 1990*, p. 387.
7. U.S. Department of Justice, *Criminal Victimization 1989*.
8. Flanagan and Maguire, *Sourcebook of Criminal Justice Statistics 1990*, p. 618.
9. U.S. Department of Justice, *Violent Crime in the United States* (Washington, D.C.: U.S. Government Printing Office, Mar. 1991); Flanagan and Maguire, *Sourcebook of Criminal Justice Statistics 1990*.
10. Flanagan and Maguire, *Sourcebook of Criminal Justice Statistics 1990*, p. 265.
11. Ibid., p. 271.
12. See Sue Titus Reid, *Crime and Criminology*, 5th ed. (New York: Holt, Rinehart & Winston, 1988), pp. 234–235.
13. Quoted in Timothy Beneke, "Male Rape: Four Men Talk About Rape," *Mother Jones*, Jul. 1983, pp. 13–22.
14. Flanagan and Maguire, *Sourcebook of Criminal Justice Statistics 1990*, p. 261.
15. Ibid., pp. 262, 264, 266.
16. Ibid., p. 269.
17. Calculated from data in Robert J. Bursik, "Property Crime," in Joseph F. Sheley, *Criminology: A Contemporary Handbook* (Belmont, Calif.: Wadsworth, 1991), pp. 160–173, and Piers Beirne and James Messerschmidt, *Criminology* (San Diego: Harcourt Brace Jovanovich, 1991), pp. 97, 106.
18. Beirne and Messerschmidt, *Criminology*, p. 116.
19. Ibid., pp. 204–238.
20. See Donald R. Cressey, *Theft of the Nation: The Structure and Operations of Organized Crime in America* (New York: Harper & Row, 1969).
21. James William Coleman, *The Criminal Elite: The Sociology of White Collar Crime*, 2nd ed. (New York: St. Martin's Press, 1989), pp. 6–8.
22. Flanagan and Maguire, *Sourcebook of Criminal Justice Statistics 1990*, p. 384.
23. Kitty Calavita and Henry N. Pontell, " 'Other People's Money' Revisited: Collective Embezzlement in the Savings and Loan and Insurance Industries," *Social Problems* 38 (Feb. 1991): 94–112.
24. Coleman, *The Criminal Elite*, pp. 6, 55–72.
25. Edwin H. Sutherland, *White Collar Crime* (New York: Dryden, 1949), p. 9.
26. See Coleman, *The Criminal Elite*, pp. 153–198.
27. Marshall B. Clinard and Peter C. Yeager, *Corporate Crime* (New York: Free Press, 1980), pp. 122–125.
28. Anthony M. Platt, *The Child Savers: The Invention of Delinquency* (Chicago: University of Chicago Press, 1969).
29. Anthony R. Harris, "Race, Class and Crime," in Sheley, *Criminology*, pp. 94–119.
30. L. Edward Wells and Joseph H. Rankin, "Families and Delinquency: A Meta-analysis of the Impact of Broken Homes," *Social Problems* 38 (Feb. 1991): 71–93.
31. Flanagan and Maguire, *Sourcebook of Criminal Justice Statistics 1990*, p. 353.

32. U.S. Department of Justice, *Criminal Victimization 1989.*

33. U.S. Bureau of Justice Statistics, *Prisoners in 1989* (Washington, D.C.: U.S. Government Printing Office, May 1990); Flanagan and Maguire, *Sourcebook of Criminal Justice Statistics 1990*, p. 422.

34. Darrell Steffensmeier and Emilie Allan, "Gender, Age and Crime," in Sheley, *Criminology*, pp. 66–93.

35. Ibid.

36. Flanagan and Maguire, *Sourcebook of Criminal Justice Statistics 1990*, p. 414.

37. Ibid., p. 424.

38. Charles R. Tittle, Wayne J. Villemez, and Douglas A. Smith, "The Myth of Social Class and Criminality," *American Sociological Review* 43 (1978): 643–656.

39. Delbert Elliott and Suzanne Ageton, "Reconciling Race and Class Differences in Self-Reported and Official Estimates of Delinquency," *American Sociological Review* 45 (1980): 95–110; Delbert Elliott and David Huizinga, "Social Class and Delinquent Behavior in a National Youth Panel: 1976–1980," *Criminology* 21 (1983): 149–177.

40. U.S. Department of Justice, *Criminal Victimization 1989.*

41. Harris, "Race, Class and Crime."

42. U.S. Bureau of Justice Statistics, *International Crime Rates* (Washington, D.C.: U.S. Government Printing Office, May 1988).

43. Martin Daly and Margo Wilson, *Homicide* (New York: Aldine de Gruyter, 1988).

44. Barry Hutchings and Sarnoff A. Mednick, "Criminality in Adoptees and Their Adoptive and Biological Parents: A Pilot Study," in S. A. Mednick and K. O. Christiansen, eds., *Biosocial Bases of Criminal Behavior* (New York: Gardner Press, 1977); for a follow-up study with a different population, see Sarnoff A. Mednick, William Gabrielli, and Barry Hutchings, "Genetic Influences in Criminal Behavior: Evidence from an Adoption Cohort," in Katherine S. Van Dusen and Sarnoff Mednick, eds., *Prospective Studies of Crime and Delinquency* (Boston: Kluver-Nijhoff, 1983), pp. 39–57.

45. Janet Katz and William J. Chambliss, "Biology and Crime" in Sheley, *Criminology*, pp. 244–271.

46. James Q. Wilson and Richard Herrnstein, *Crime and Human Behavior* (New York: Simon & Schuster, 1985).

47. Edwin H. Sutherland and Donald R. Cressey, *Criminology*, 10th ed. (New York: Lippincott, 1978), pp. 158–191.

48. Karl Schuessler and Donald R. Cressey, "Personality Characteristics of Criminals," *American Journal of Sociology* 55 (1950): 476–484; Gordon Waldo and Simon Dinitz, "Personality Attributes of the Criminal: An Analysis of Research Studies 1950–1965," *Journal of Research in Crime and Delinquency* 4 (1967): 185–201; David Tennenbaum, "Research Studies of Personality and Criminality," *Journal of Criminal Justice* 5 (1977): 1–19.

49. Sutherland and Cressey, *Criminology*, pp. 77–98.

50. Murray A. Straus, Richard J. Gelles, and Suzanne K. Steinmetz, *Behind Closed Doors: Violence in the American Family* (New York: Doubleday, 1981), p. 101.

51. See, for example, Reid, *Crime and Criminology*, pp. 240–246; David G. Gil, *Violence Against Children: Physical Child Abuse in the United States* (Cambridge, Mass.: Harvard University Press, 1970), pp. 113–114.

52. Murray A. Straus, "Discipline and Deviance: Physical Punishment of Children and Violence and Other Crimes in Adulthood," *Social Problems* 38 (May 1991): 133–152; Joan McCord, "Parental Aggressiveness and Physical Punishment in Long-Term Perspective," in Gerald T. Hotaling, David Finkelhor, John T. Kirkpatrick, and Murray A. Straus, eds., *Family Abuse and Its Consequences* (Newbury Park, Calif.: Sage, 1988), pp. 91–98.

53. National Commission on the Causes and Prevention of Violence, *The Challenge of Crime in a Free Society* (Washington, D.C.: U.S. Government Printing Office, 1976).

54. Straus, Gelles, and Steinmetz, *Behind Closed Doors*, p. 121.

55. See Walter Reckless, "A New Theory of Delinquency and Crime," *Federal Probation* 25 (1961): 42-46; Travis Hirschi, *Causes of Delinquency* (Berkeley: University of California Press, 1969); James Q. Wilson, *Thinking About Crime* (New York: Random House, 1975); Marvin Krohn, "Control and Deterrence Theories," in Sheley, *Criminology*, pp. 294-313.

56. Robert K. Merton, "Social Structure and Anomie," *American Sociological Review* 3 (1938): 672-682.

57. Walter B. Miller, "Lower Class Culture as a Generating Milieu of Gang Delinquency," *Journal of Social Issues* 14 (1958): 5-19.

58. Émile Durkheim, *Suicide* (New York: The Free Press, 1966).

59. See Gary Cavender, "Alternative Theory: Labeling and Critical Perspectives," in Sheley, *Criminology*, pp. 315-332.

60. Herbert L. Packer, *The Limits of Criminal Sanction* (Palo Alto, Calif.: Stanford University Press, 1968).

61. Bureau of Justice Statistics, *Report to the Nation on Crime and Justice: The Data* (Washington, D.C.: U.S. Government Printing Office, 1983), p. 47; Eric J. Scott, *Calls for Service: Citizen Demand and Initial Police Response*, National Institute of Justice (Washington, D.C.: U.S. Government Printing Office, Jul. 1981), p. 26.

62. Barbara Boland, Wayne Logan, Ronald Sones, and William Martin, *The Prosecution of Felony Arrests, 1982*, Bureau of Justice Statistics (Washington, D.C.: U.S. Government Printing Office, May 1988), p. 7.

63. See, for example, Allen J. Beck, *Recidivism of Prisoners Released in 1983*, U.S. Bureau of Justice Statistics (Washington, D.C.: U.S. Government Printing Office, Apr. 1989); John Wallerstedt, *Returning to Prison*, U.S. Bureau of Justice Statistics (Washington, D.C.: U.S. Government Printing Office, 1984).

64. U.S. Bureau of Justice Statistics, *Prisoners in 1989*.

65. Ronald J. Ostrow, "U.S. Imprisons Black Men at 4 Times S. Africa's Rate," *Los Angeles Times*, Jan. 5, 1991, pp. A1, A24.

66. Ibid.

67. Joan Petersilia, *Probation and Felony Offenders*, National Institute of Justice (Washington, D.C.: U.S. Government Printing Office, 1985).

68. U.S. Department of Justice, *Violent Crime in the United States*, p. 11; Chris Wood, "Violent Land," *Maclean's*, Jun. 10, 1991, pp. 12-13.

69. Flanagan and Maguire, *Sourcebook of Criminal Justice Statistics 1990*, pp. 174-176.

70. National Institute of Mental Health, *Television and Behavior*, vol. 1. *Summary Report* (Washington, D.C.: U.S. Government Printing Office, 1982); Surgeon General's Scientific Advisory Committee on Television and Social Behavior, *Television and Growing Up: The Impact of Televised Violence* (Washington, D.C.: U.S. Government Printing Office, 1972); George A. Comstock and Eli Rubenstein, eds., *Television and Social Behavior*, vols. 1-5 (Washington, D.C.: U.S. Government Printing Office, 1972).

71. Jeffrey H. Goldstein, *Aggression and Crimes of Violence*, 2nd ed. (New York: Oxford University Press, 1986), p. 39.

CHAPTER 14   THE GLOBAL DIVIDE

1. See Daniel W. Rossides, *Social Stratification: The American Class System in Comparative Perspective* (Englewood Cliffs, N.J.: Prentice Hall, 1990), pp. 496-521.

2. Harold R. Kerbo, *Social Stratification and Inequality*, 2nd ed. (New York: McGraw-Hill, 1991), pp. 494-523.

3. Population Reference Bureau, *World Population Data Sheet, 1991* (Washington, D.C.: Population Reference Bureau, 1991).

4. Population Reference Bureau, *World Population Data Sheet, 1991.*

5. United Nations, *Statistical Yearbook, 1987* (New York: United Nations, 1990), pp. 200–209.

6. United Nations, *Statistical Yearbook, 1987*, p. 410.

7. G. Tyler Miller, *Living in the Environment*, 5th ed. (Belmont, Calif.: Wadsworth, 1988), p. 245; Jon Bennett, *The Hunger Machine: The Politics of Food* (Cambridge, England: Polity Press, 1987), p. 12.

8. United Nations, *Statistical Yearbook, 1987*, pp. 252–254.

9. Population Reference Bureau, *World Population Data Sheet, 1991.*

10. Kerbo, *Social Stratification and Inequality*, p. 494.

11. Gerhard Lenski, Jean Lenski, and Patrick Nolan, *Human Societies*, 6th ed. (New York: McGraw-Hill, 1991), pp. 394–395.

12. One of the best discussions of international stratification patterns is found in Daniel Chirot, *Social Change in the Modern Era* (San Diego: Harcourt Brace Jovanovich, 1986).

13. See Gerhard Lenski, *Power and Privilege* (New York: McGraw-Hill, 1966).

14. For a comprehensive history of the development of the Third World, see L. S. Stavrianos, *Global Rift: The Third World Comes of Age* (New York: Morrow, 1981).

15. See, for example, Talcott Parsons, *Societies: Evolutionary and Comparative Perspectives* (Englewood Cliffs, N.J.: Prentice Hall, 1966); Wilbert Moore, *Social Change*, 2nd ed. (Englewood Cliffs, N.J.: Prentice Hall, 1974).

16. Walter W. Rostow, *The Stages of Economic Growth* (New York: Cambridge University Press, 1960).

17. See Walter W. Rostow, *The World Economy: History and Prospect* (Austin: University of Texas Press, 1980).

18. For a contemporary discussion of these issues from a Weberian perspective, see Daniel Chirot, "The Rise of the West," *American Sociological Review* 50 (1985): 181–195.

19. Andre Gunder Frank, *Capitalism and Underdevelopment in Latin America* (New York: Monthly Review Press, 1967).

20. See, for example, Wallerstein's three-volume historical work entitled *The Modern World-System* (New York: Academic Press, 1974, 1980, 1988).

21. For an excellent summary of world system theory and an analysis of its strengths and weaknesses, see Thomas Richard Shannon, *An Introduction to the World-System Perspective* (Boulder, Colo.: Westview Press, 1989).

22. William R. Long, "Poles' Debt Relief Plans Stir Envy Among Latins," *Los Angeles Times*, May 28, 1991, p. H4.

23. Richard Boudreaux, "After the 'Lost Decade,' a Strong Latin Spirit," *Los Angeles Times*, Aug. 6, 1991, pp. H1, H5.

24. U.S. Bureau of the Census, *Statistical Abstract of the United States, 1991* (Washington, D.C.: U.S. Government Printing Office, 1991), pp. 431, 803.

25. Ibid., p. 863.

26. See James William Coleman, *The Criminal Elite: The Sociology of White Collar Crime* (New York: St. Martin's Press, 1989), pp. 67–72.

27. On the control of foreign policy by elite groups, see G. William Domhoff, *The Power Elite and the State* (New York: Aldine de Gruyter, 1990).

28. Population Reference Bureau, *World Population Data Sheet, 1991.*

29. See Population Reference Bureau, *World Population Data Sheet, 1991* for a description of each nation's official view of its current rate of population growth.

30. See Volker Bornschier and Christopher Chase-Dunn, *Transnational Corporations and Underdevelopment* (New York: Praeger, 1985).

31. See Chirot, *Social Change in the Modern Era*.

CHAPTER 15 URBANIZATION

1. Population Reference Bureau, *World Population Data Sheet, 1991* (Washington, D.C.: Population Reference Bureau, 1991).

2. Rafael M. Salas, "Cities Without Limits," *Unesco Courier*, Jan. 1987, pp. 10–13, 16–17.

3. Harvey M. Choldin, *Cities and Suburbs: An Introduction to Urban Sociology* (New York: McGraw-Hill, 1985), pp. 73–74.

4. Ibid., pp. 143–144.

5. Salas, "Cities Without Limits."

6. See Claude S. Fischer, *The Urban Experience*, 2nd ed. (New York: Harcourt Brace Jovanovich, 1984).

7. Choldin, *Cities and Suburbs*, pp. 303–304.

8. Georg Simmel, "The Metropolis and Mental Life," in Kurt Wolf, ed. and trans., *The Sociology of Georg Simmel* (New York: Free Press, 1950). This article was originally published in 1903.

9. Louis Wirth, "Urbanism as a Way of Life," *American Journal of Sociology* 44 (1938): 1–14.

10. Herbert J. Gans, "Urbanism and Suburbanism: Ways of Life," in Arnold M. Rose, ed., *Human Behavior and Social Processes: An Interactionist Approach* (Boston: Houghton Mifflin, 1962), pp. 625–648.

11. Ivan Light, *Cities in World Perspective* (New York: Macmillan, 1983), pp. 214–215; Fischer, *The Urban Experience*, p. 209.

12. Light, *Cities in World Perspective*, pp. 208–215.

13. Choldin, *Cities and Suburbs*, pp. 363–366.

14. Ibid., pp. 366–367.

15. Ibid., p. 264.

16. John R. Logan and Harvey L. Molotch, *Urban Fortunes: The Political Economy of Place* (Berkeley: University of California Press, 1987), p. 194.

17. Ibid., p. 198.

18. Choldin, *Cities and Suburbs*, pp. 478–479.

19. U.S. Bureau of the Census, *Statistical Abstract of the United States, 1991* (Washington, D.C.: U.S. Government Printing Office, 1991), pp. 23, 644.

20. Ibid., p. 34.

21. Choldin, *Cities and Suburbs*, pp. 303–304.

22. Bob Secter and Tracy Shryer, "Farming's Exodus of the Young," *Los Angeles Times*, Jul. 23, 1991, pp. A1, A10–11.

23. Ibid.

24. William Julius Wilson, "Studying Inner-City Social Dislocations: The Challenge of Public Agenda Research," *American Sociological Review* 56 (Feb. 1991): 1–14.

25. James E. Rosenbaum and Susan J. Popkin, "Employment and Earnings of Low-Income Blacks Who Move to Middle-Class Suburbs," in Christopher Jencks and Paul E. Peterson, eds., *The Urban Underclass* (Washington, D.C.: Brookings Institution, 1991), pp. 342–356.

26. Thomas Moore, "Dead Zones," *U.S. News & World Report*, Apr. 19, 1989, pp. 20–32.

27. See Logan and Molotch, *Urban Fortunes*, pp. 195–199.

28. Theodore Caplow, *American Social Trends* (San Diego: Harcourt Brace Jovanovich, 1991), p. 134.
29. Sam Fulwood III and Stanley Meisler, "Poor Feeling the Pinch as Low-Rent Housing Shrinks," *Los Angeles Times*, Jul. 16, 1990, pp. A1, A16-17; Michael Dear, "Our 'Third World' of Housing Have-Nots Need Action," *Los Angeles Times*, Feb. 8, 1988, sec. 2, p. 7.
30. Marta Elliott and Lauren J. Krivo, "Structural Determinants of Homelessness in the United States," *Social Problems* 38 (Feb. 1991): 113-131.
31. Fulwood and Meisler, "Poor Feeling the Pinch as Low-Rent Housing Shrinks."
32. Choldin, *Cities and Suburbs*, pp. 333-334.
33. Mitchel Levitas, "Homeless in America," *New York Times Magazine*, Jun. 19, 1990, pp. 82-91; W. John Moore, "Lost in America: Low-Rent Housing," *Los Angeles Times*, Jun. 12, 1988, sec. 5, p. 2.
34. U.S. Bureau of the Census, *Statistical Abstract 1991*, p. 85.
35. Light, *Cities in World Perspective*, p. 209.
36. U.S. Bureau of the Census, *Statistical Abstract 1991*, p. 729.
37. Bradford Curie Snell, "American Ground Transport," in Jerome H. Skolnick and Elliott Currie, eds., *Crisis in American Institutions*, 7th ed. (Glenview, Ill.: Scott, Foresman, 1988), pp. 321-344; Light, *Cities in World Perspective*, pp. 210-211.
38. Logan and Molotch, *Urban Fortunes*, pp. 124-126.
39. Calculated by Richard A. Shaffer from data in Choldin, *Cities and Suburbs*, pp. 247-249.
40. Choldin, *Cities and Suburbs*, p. 246.
41. Logan and Molotch, *Urban Fortunes*, p. 194.
42. Douglas S. Massey and Nancy A. Denton, "Suburbanization and Segregation in U.S. Metropolitan Areas," *American Journal of Sociology* 94 (Nov. 1988): 592-626.
43. Population Reference Bureau, *World Population Data Sheet, 1991*; John Palen, *The Urban World* (New York: McGraw-Hill, 1981), p. 336.
44. Salas, "Cities Without Limit."
45. Ibid.
46. Palen, *The Urban World*, p. 406.
47. Choldin, *Cities and Suburbs*, p. 485.
48. Moore, "Lost in America: Low-Rent Housing."
49. Kenneth K. Wong and Paul E. Peterson, "Urban Response to Federal Program Flexibility: Politics of Community Development Block Grants," *Urban Affairs Quarterly* 21 (Mar. 1986): 293-309.
50. Logan and Molotch, *Urban Fortunes*, pp. 159-162.

CHAPTER 16   POPULATION

1. Population Reference Bureau, *World Population Data Sheet, 1991* (Washington, D.C.: Population Reference Bureau, 1991).
2. Jon Bennett, *The Hunger Machine: The Politics of Food* (Cambridge, England: Polity Press, 1987), p. 12.
3. Population Reference Bureau, *World Population Data Sheet, 1991.*
4. United Nations Population Fund, *The State of the World Population, 1991* (New York: United Nations, 1991).
5. Calculated from U.S. Bureau of the Census, *Statistical Abstract of the United States, 1991* (Washington, D.C.: U.S. Government Printing Office, 1991), p. 830.
6. Population Reference Bureau, *World Population Data Sheet, 1991.*
7. Calculated from Population Reference Bureau, *World Population Data Sheet, 1991.*

8. U.S. Bureau of the Census, *Statistical Abstract of the United States, 1991* (Washington, D.C.: U.S. Government Printing Office, 1991), p. 14.
9. Population Reference Bureau, *World Population Data Sheet, 1991.*
10. John R. Weeks, *Population: An Introduction to Concepts and Issues*, 3rd ed. (Belmont, Calif.: Wadsworth, 1986), p. 55.
11. Population Reference Bureau, *World Population Data Sheet, 1991.*
12. Charles F. Westoff, "Populations of the Developed Countries," *Scientific American* 231 (1974): 114.
13. For an analysis of the theory of demographic transition, see Weeks, *Population*, pp. 39–48.
14. Thomas Robert Malthus, *Essay on the Principle of Population* (Baltimore: Penguin, 1971). The work was first published in 1798.
15. Calculated from Bennett, *The Hunger Machine*, p. 32; U.S. Bureau of the Census, *Statistical Abstract 1991*, p. 856.
16. U.S. Bureau of the Census, *Statistical Abstract 1991*, p. 856.
17. Lester R. Brown, "Putting Food on the World's Table," in Robert M. Jackson, ed., *Global Issues 88/89* (Guilford, Conn: Dushkin, 1988), pp. 87–97.
18. Bennett, *The Hunger Machine*, p. 12; G. Tyler Miller, *Living in the Environment*, 5th ed. (Belmont, Calif.: Wadsworth, 1988), p. 245.
19. See Miller, *Living in the Environment*, pp. 242–245.
20. Robert N. Ross, "The Hidden Malice of Malnutrition," in Jackson, *Global Issues 88/89*, pp. 98–101.
21. Kingsley Davis, "The World's Population Crisis," in Robert K. Merton and Robert Nisbet, eds., *Contemporary Social Problems*, 4th ed. (New York: Harcourt Brace Jovanovich, 1976), p. 274.
22. Population Reference Bureau, *World Population Data Sheet, 1991.*
23. Norman Myers, ed., *GAIA: An Atlas of Planet Management* (Garden City, N.Y.: Anchor, 1984), pp. 182–183.
24. U.S. Bureau of the Census, *Statistical Abstract 1991*, p. 833.
25. Population Reference Bureau, *World Population Data Sheet, 1991.*
26. Miller, *Living in the Environment*, pp. 295–296.
27. Ibid., p. 247.
28. Ibid., pp. 247–249; Bennett, *The Hunger Machine*, pp. 23–27.
29. E. F. Schumacher, *Small Is Beautiful: Economics As If People Mattered* (New York: Harper & Row, 1974), pp. 171–190.
30. Weeks, *Population*, p. 385.
31. Ibid., pp. 381–383.
32. Miller, *Living in the Environment*, pp. 253–254.
33. Miller, *Living in the Environment*, p. 252.
34. Weeks, *Population*, pp. 385–386.
35. Bennett, *The Hunger Machine*, p. 37.
36. Carol Williams, "The Unwanted Children: Casualties Left by a Tyrant," *Los Angeles Times*, Dec. 10, 1990, pp. A1, A16–17.
37. Bennett, *The Hunger Machine*, p. 22.
38. See Weeks, *Population*, pp. 417–423.
39. Charles B. Nam and Susan Gustavus Philliber, *Population: A Basic Orientation*, 2nd ed. (Englewood Cliffs, N.J.: Prentice-Hall, 1984), pp. 298–301.
40. Weeks, *Population*, p. 423.
41. Population Reference Bureau, *World Population Data Sheet, 1991.*

42. David Holley, "China Orders New Drive to Prevent Unapproved Births," *Los Angeles Times*, Feb. 16, 1988, sec. 1, pp. 1, 19.

43. Daniel Chirot, *Social Change in the Modern Era* (San Diego: Harcourt Brace Jovanovich, 1986), p. 177.

44. Bennett, *The Hunger Machine*, p. 34.

CHAPTER 17   THE ENVIRONMENT

1. Andrew Goudie, *The Human Impact on the Natural Environment*, 2nd ed. (Cambridge, Mass.: MIT Press, 1986), pp. 276–277; Norman Myers, ed., *GAIA: An Atlas of Planet Management* (Garden City, N.Y.: Anchor, 1984), p. 118.

2. U.S. Bureau of the Census, *Statistical Abstract of the United States, 1991* (Washington, D.C.: U.S. Government Printing Office, 1991), p. 209.

3. G. Tyler Miller, *Living in the Environment: An Introduction to Environmental Science*, 5th ed. (Belmont, Calif.: Wadsworth, 1988), p. 432.

4. Jon R. Luoma, "Forests Are Dying: But Is Acid Rain Really to Blame?" *Audubon*, Mar. 1987.

5. Miller, *Living in the Environment*, p. 432.

6. Ibid., pp. 438–440.

7. Sharon Begley, "A Bigger Hole in the Ozone," *Newsweek*, Apr. 15, 1991, p. 64.

8. Miller, *Living in the Environment*, p. 441; Thomas H. Maugh II, "Thinning Ice Pack May Be Result of Greenhouse Effect," *Los Angeles Times*, Jul. 2, 1990, p. B3; Sharon Begley, "The Endless Summer?" *Newsweek*, Jul. 11, 1988, pp. 18–20.

9. R. F. Damann, *Environmental Conservation*, 5th ed. (New York: Wiley, 1984), p. 402.

10. Miller, *Living in the Environment*, pp. 458–459.

11. Goudie, *The Human Impact on the Natural Environment*, pp. 178–179; Mary Williams Walsh, "In Arctic, a Toxic Surprise," *Los Angeles Times*, Jun. 18, 1991, pp. A1, A9.

12. John Carey, "Is It Safe to Drink?" *National Wildlife*, Feb.–Mar. 1984, pp. 19–21.

13. *Sacramento Bee*, May 25, 1988, p. A5.

14. Miller, *Living in the Environment*, p. 474.

15. Myers, *GAIA*, p. 42.

16. Damann, *Environmental Conservation*, p. 179.

17. Myers, *GAIA*, p. 42.

18. "The State of the World: An Interview with Lester Brown," *Technology Review*, Jul. 1988, pp. 51–58.

19. Tom Morgenthau, "The Disappearing Land," *Newsweek*, Aug. 23, 1982, pp. 24–26.

20. U.S. Bureau of the Census, *Statistical Abstract 1988*, p. 193.

21. See Branley Allan Branson, "Is There Life After Strip Mining?" *Natural History* 95 (Aug. 1986): 30–36.

22. Miller, *Living in the Environment*, pp. 499–500.

23. Ibid., p. 499.

24. Jeffrey Heil and James Van Blarcom, "Superfund: The Search for Consistency," in John Allen, ed., *Environment 88/89* (Guilford, Conn.: Dushkin, 1988), pp. 107–111.

25. Miller, *Living in the Environment*, p. 499; Joel Havemann, "Europe Has Toxic Troubles," *Los Angeles Times*, May 28, 1991, pp. H1, H4.

26. Scripps News Service, "Tragedy of Chernobyl Keeps on Building in Byelorussia," *San Luis Obispo Telegram-Tribune*, Mar. 27, 1991, p. D1; Associated Press, "Mystery Ailments Plague Chernobyl," *San Luis Obispo Telegram-Tribune*, Apr. 22, 1991, pp. A1, A12; Michael Parks, "Chernobyl," *Los Angeles Times*, Apr. 23, 1991, pp. H1, H6; Scripps News

Service, "Chernobyl Worse Than Earlier Feared," *San Luis Obispo Telegram-Tribune*, Apr. 28, 1991, p. A1.

27. Miller, *Living in the Environment*, pp. 375–378.
28. U.S. Bureau of the Census, *Statistical Abstract 1991*, p. 574.
29. Miller, *Living in the Environment*, pp. 338–339.
30. U.S. Bureau of the Census, *Statistical Abstract 1988*, p. 542.
31. Myers, *GAIA*, pp. 112–113.
32. See Miller, *Living in the Environment*, pp. 343–345.
33. Population Reference Bureau, *World Population Data Sheet, 1991* (Washington, D.C.: Population Reference Bureau, 1991).
34. Ibid., p. 354; Myers, *GAIA*, p. 113.
35. Christopher Flavin, "Reforming the Electric Power Industry," in Lester R. Brown et al., *State of the World, 1986* (New York: Norton, 1986), p. 100.
36. Miller, *Living in the Environment*, pp. 409–411; Myers, *GAIA*, pp. 114–115.
37. Myers, *GAIA*, pp. 110–111.
38. Ibid., pp. 96–97.
39. Donella Meadows, Dennis L. Meadows, Jorgen Randers, and William W. Behrens, *The Limits of Growth* (New York: Universe Books, 1972); Donella Meadows et al., *Groping in the Dark: The First Decade of Global Modeling* (New York: Wiley, 1982).
40. For a discussion of the differences between the neo-Malthusians and the cornucopians, see Miller, *Living in the Environment*, pp. 17–19.
41. Louis Harris, *Inside America* (New York: Vintage, 1987), p. 245.
42. Ibid., pp. 248–249.
43. Associated Press, "Most Would Pay Higher Prices to Save Environment, Poll Finds," *Los Angeles Times,* Jun. 8, 1992, p. A11.
44. U.S. Bureau of the Census, *Statistical Abstract 1991*, p. 854.
45. See Miller, *Living in the Environment*, pp. 387–408.
46. See Garrett Hardin, "The Tragedy of the Commons," *Science* 162 (1968): 1243–1248.

CHAPTER 18 WARFARE AND INTERNATIONAL CONFLICT

1. Melvin Small and J. David Singer, *Resort to Arms: International and Civil Wars, 1816–1980* (Beverly Hills, Calif.: Sage, 1982), p. 293.
2. See Rudi Volti, *Society and Technological Change* (New York: St. Martin's Press, 1988), pp. 171–201.
3. Frank Barnaby, "The Nuclear Arsenal in the Middle East," *Technology Review*, May–Jun. 1987.
4. David P. Barash, *Introduction to Peace Studies* (Belmont, Calif.: Wadsworth, 1991), pp. 126–127; Rod Norland, "The Bombs in the Basement, *Newsweek*, Jul. 11, 1988, pp. 42–45.
5. Small and Singer, *Resort to Arms*, pp. 293–294.
6. James F. Dunnigan and William Martel, *How to Stop a War: The Lessons of Two Hundred Years of War and Peace* (New York: Doubleday, 1987), p. 81.
7. Dunnigan and Martel, *How to Stop a War*, p. 239; Small and Singer, *Resort to Arms*, p. 91.
8. U.S. Bureau of the Census, *Statistical Abstract of the United States, 1991* (Washington, D.C.: U.S. Government Printing Office, 1991), p. 339.
9. Rex de Silva, "Developing the Third World," *World Press Review*, May 1980, p. 48.
10. U.S. Bureau of the Census, *Statistical Abstract 1991*, pp. 864–865.

11. G. Tyler Miller, *Living in the Environment: An Introduction to Environmental Science*, 5th ed. (Belmont, Calif.: Wadsworth, 1988), p. 128.
12. Ibid., p. 129; Barash, *Introduction to Peace Studies*, pp. 107–113.
13. See Quincy Wright, *A Study of War*, abridged by L. L. Wright (Chicago: University of Chicago Press, 1964), p. 85.
14. Peter C. Sederberg, *Terrorist Myths: Illusion, Rhetoric, and Reality* (Englewood Cliffs, N.J.: Prentice-Hall, 1989), pp. 22–43.
15. See Harold J. Vetter and Gary R. Perlstein, *Perspectives on Terrorism* (Pacific Grove, Calif.: Brooks/Cole, 1991), pp. 87–104.
16. Dunnigan and Martel, *How to Stop a War*, p. 247.
17. Marvin Harris, *Culture, People, Nature*, 5th ed. (New York: Harper & Row, 1988), p. 364.
18. Karl Marx and Friedrich Engels, *The Communist Manifesto* (Englewood Cliffs, N.J.: Prentice-Hall, 1955). This pamphlet was originally published in 1848.
19. James C. Davies, "Toward a Theory of Revolution," *American Sociological Review* 27 (1962): 5–19; James C. Davies, "The J-Curve of Rising and Declining Satisfactions as a Cause of Some Great Revolutions and a Contained Rebellion," in Hugh Davis Graham and Ted Robert Gurr, eds., *Violence in America: Histories and Comparative Perspectives* (New York: Holt, Rinehart and Winston, 1958), pp. 547–576.
20. Davies, "Toward a Theory of Revolution," p. 5.
21. Samuel P. Huntington, *Political Order in Changing Societies* (New Haven: Yale University Press, 1968).
22. Charles Tilly, *From Mobilization to Revolution* (Reading, Mass.: Addison-Wesley, 1978).
23. Crane Brinton, *The Anatomy of Revolution* (New York: Random House, 1965), p. 51.
24. Ibid., pp. 28–39.
25. Theda Skocpol, *States and Social Revolution* (Cambridge, England: Cambridge University Press, 1978).
26. See Ronald J. Glossop, *Confronting War* (Jefferson, N.C.: MacFarland, 1987), pp. 66–68.
27. Ibid., pp. 58–65.
28. Wright, *A Study of War*, pp. 213–214.
29. Kurt Finsterbusch and H. C. Greisman, "The Unprofitability of Warfare in the Twentieth Century," *Social Problems* 22 (Feb. 1975): 451.
30. Karl von Clausewitz, *On War*, trans. O. J. Matthkijs Jolles (Washington, D.C.: Infantry Journal Press, 1950), p. 16.
31. A. F. K. Organski and Jacek Kugler, *The War Ledger* (Chicago: University of Chicago Press, 1980).
32. William Tuohy, "A World Armed and in Conflict," *Los Angeles Times*, Jul. 12, 1991, p. A5.
33. See Raymond J. Michalowski and Ronald Kramer, "The Space Between the Laws: The Problem of Corporate Crime in a Transnational Context," *Social Problems* 34 (Feb. 1987): 34–53.
34. William K. Domke, *War and the Changing Global System* (New Haven: Yale University Press, 1988).
35. Walter H. Capps, "The Vietnam War and American Values," *Center Magazine*, Jul.–Aug. 1978, pp. 17–26.

ACKNOWLEDGMENTS

Chapter 1: 1, Weisbrot, Stock, Boston; *4*, © Dion Ogust, The Image Works; *7*, © 1991, Ulrike Welsch; *13*, © Mercado, The Picture Cube; *21*, © Carey, The Image Works.

Part One: *29*, © Alper, Stock, Boston.

Chapter 2: 31, © Rowan, The Image Works; *35*, Franken, Stock, Boston; *37*, Menzel, Stock, Boston; *40*, Dietz, Stock, Boston; *44*, UPI/Bettman.

Chapter 3: 59, © Carey, The Image Works; *62*, © Rabeuf, The Image Works; *70*, Menzel, Stock, Boston; *72*, © Ogust, The Image Works; *80*, © Gardner, The Image Works.

Chapter 4: 83, Forsyth, Monkmeyer Press Photo; *84*, Crews, Stock, Boston; *92*, AP/Wide World; *99*, © Crews, The Image Works; *103*, © Daemmrich, The Image Works.

Chapter 5: 109, © Siluk, The Image Works; *111*, Daemmrich, The Image Works; *116*, © Scherr, Jeroboam; *123*, Barnes, Southern Light; *129*, © Crews, Stock, Boston.

Part Two: *137*, © Glassman, The Image Works.

Chapter 6: 139, © Glassman, The Image Works; *141 (left)*, © Skytta, Jeroboam; *141 (right)*, © Herwig, The Picture Cube; *147*, Player, NYT Pictures; *154*, © 1973, Gardner, The Image Works; *159*, © 1983, Kroll, Taurus.

Chapter 7: 165, © 1992, Urike Welsch; *171*, EKM-Nepenthe; *175*, Reuters/ Bettman; *176*, © Boretz, The Image Works; *181*, © Spratt, The Image Works; *186*, UPI/Bettmann Newsphotos.

Chapter 8: 195, © Daemmrich, The Image Works; *201*, © Davidson, The Image Works; *204*, © The Washington Post 1978/Johnston, Woodfin Camp; *218*, Grant, The Picture Cube; *223*, © Kalman, The Image Works.

Chapter 9: 231, © Crews, Stock, Boston; *237*, © 1990, Ulrike Welsch; *242*, © Davidson, The Image Works; *246*, Campione, Taurus; *248*, © Hine, The Picture Cube.

Chapter 10: 253, © Antman, The Image Works; *255*, © Daemmrich, The Image Works; *257*, Chostak, Anthro-Photo; *260 (left)*, © Takatsuno, The Picture Cube; *260 (right)*, Brilliant, The Picture Cube; *267*, Conklin, Monkmeyer Press; *269*, UPI/Bettmann Newsphotos.

Part Three: *277*, © Gantier, The Image Works.

Chapter 11: 279, © Carey, The Image Works; *284*, UPI/Bettmann Newsphotos; *287*, Grant, The Picture Cube; *289*, Brown, The Picture Cube; *294 (left)*, Maher, The Picture Cube; *294 (right)*, © 1979, Roth, The Picture Cube.

Chapter 12: 303, © Levy, Photo Researchers; *314*, © Litteu, Stock, Boston; *318*, © Vintoniv, Stock, Boston; *320*, Hayman, Stock, Boston; *322*, © Delevingne, Stock, Boston.

Chapter 13: 332, Cassidy, The Picture Cube; *338*, Reuters/ Bettmann; *343*, © Shaefer, PhotoEdit; *349*, © Richards, PhotoEdit; *352*, Franken, Stock, Boston.

Part Four: *363*, Caputo, Stock, Boston.

Chapter 14: 365, © Ulrike Welsch; *368*, © Welsch, PhotoEdit; *370*, © Ulrike Welsch; *371*, © Rutledge, The Picture Cube; *374*, Reuters/Bettmann; *381*, © Ulrike Welsch; *383*, Reuters/Bettmann.

Chapter 15: 390, Gardner, The Image Works; *392*, © Holland, Stock, Boston; *397*, © Wojnarowicz, The Image Works; *401*, Franken, Stock, Boston: *403*, © 1992, Ulrike Welsch.

Chapter 16: 413, © Antman, The Image Works; *420*, Reuters/Bettmann; *421*, Laffont, Sygma; *426*, Botts, Nancy Palmer; *430*, © 1979 Kroll, Taurus.

Chapter 17: 435, © Mendoza, The Picture Cube; *439 (top)*, Eckert, Jr., Stock, Boston; *439 (bottom)*, © Alper, Stock, Boston; *441*, © Sully, The Image Works; *444*, © 1979, Gardner, Stock, Boston; *457*, © Antman, The Image Works.

Chapter 18: 463, UPI/Bettmann; *465*, Wojnarowicz, The Image Works; *468*, Menzel, Stock, Boston; *470*, Nogues, Sygma; *474*, UPI/Bettmann Newsphotos; *479*, United Nations.

AUTHOR INDEX

SUBJECT INDEX

Note: Page numbers in *italics* indicate glossary words.